WILDFLOWERS

of

TENNESSEE

the

OHIO VALLEY

and the

SOUTHERN APPALACHIANS

COMPILED AND EDITED BY

Dennis Horn and Tavia Cathcart

TECHNICAL EDITOR

Thomas E. Hemmerly

PHOTO EDITORS

David Duhl and Dennis Horn

TECHNICAL EDITING AND OTHER CONTRIBUTIONS BY

Mary P. Priestley	Milo Pyne
Claude Bailey	Bart G. Jones
Todd Crabtree	Kevin Fitch

THE OFFICIAL FIELD GUIDE OF THE TENNESSEE NATIVE PLANT SOCIETY

Lone Pine Publishing

The Distributor: Lone Pine Publishing
1808 B Street NW, Suite 140
Auburn, WA, USA 98001
Website: www.lonepinepublishing.com

National Library of Canada Cataloguing in Publication
Horn, Dennis, 1935–
   Wildflowers of Tennessee, the Ohio Valley, and the Southern Appalachians: the official field guide of the Tennessee Native Plant Society / compiled and edited by Dennis Horn and Tavia Cathcart; technical editor: Thomas E. Hemmerly; photo editors: David Duhl and Dennis Horn.

   Includes bibliographical references and index.
   ISBN-13: 978-1-55105-428-5
   ISBN-10: 1-55105-428-0

   1. Wild flowers—Tennessee—Identification. 2. Wild flowers—Ohio River Valley—Identification. 3. Wild flowers—Appalachian Mountains—identification. I. Cathcart, Tavia, 1963– II. Hemmerly, Thomas E. (Thomas Ellsworth), 1932– III. Duhl, David IV. Tennessee Native Plant Society. V. Title.

QK115.H64 2005   582.13'09768   C2005-901907-7

Editorial Director: Nancy Foulds
Project Editor: Nicholle Carrière
Editorial: Nicholle Carrière, Dawn Loewen, Linda Kershaw, Genevieve Boyer, Gary Whyte, Rachelle Delaney
Illustrations Coordinator: Carol Woo
Production Manager: Gene Longson
Book Design, Layout & Production: Heather Markham, Elliott Engley
Cover Design: Gerry Dotto
Cover Photo: Golden St. Johnswort, by Betty Hyche
Maps: Elliot Engley
Scanning & Digital Film: Elite Lithographers Co.

All photos have been reproduced with the kind permission of the photographers.

Illustrations for family keys to genera from *An Illustrated Flora of the Northern United States and Canada*, 2nd ed., by N.L. Britton and A. Brown. 3 vols. Charles Scribner's Sons: New York, 1913.

Glossary illustrations and text excerpts (glossary and family keys to genera) from *Guide to the Vascular Plants of the Blue Ridge* by B. Eugene Wofford. Copyright 1989 by the University of Georgia Press. Reprinted by permission of the University of Georgia Press.

This field guide does not advocate the picking or digging of wildflowers. Wild plants should never be removed from their natural habitats and most would not survive transplantation because their habitat conditions cannot be duplicated.

Disclaimer: This guide is not meant to be a "how-to" reference for using plants. We do not recommend experimentation by readers, and we caution that many plants, including some traditional medicines, may be poisonous or otherwise harmful. Self-medication with herbs is unwise, and wild plant foods should be used with caution and only with expert advice.

PC: P1

TABLE OF CONTENTS

Region Map

The primary coverage area for the wildflowers in this book encompasses a 16-state region that includes Tennessee, the entire Ohio Valley, all of the central and southern Appalachians, the Piedmont, the mid-Mississippi Valley, and the Ozarks.

Over 1250 species in 90 families are described in detail.

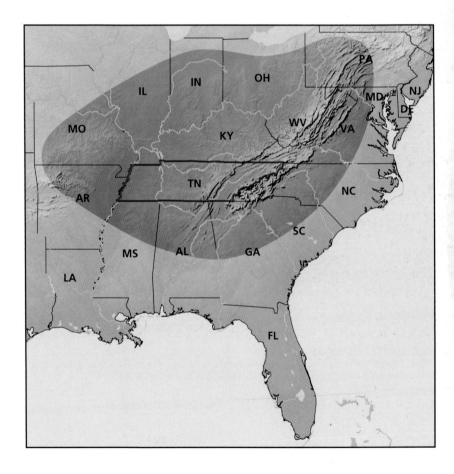

Acknowledgments

DEDICATION

To the late James I. ("Bus") Jones of Chattanooga who promoted the original idea for a book on the wildflowers of Tennessee. Bus was the president of the American Association of Field Botanists, an avid wildflower enthusiast, and an active member of the Tennessee Native Plant Society.

To the many people who protect and care for open spaces throughout Tennessee where our rare and beautiful wildflowers flourish.

THE TENNESSEE NATIVE PLANT SOCIETY
For membership and other information contact:
Tennessee Native Plant Society
P. O. BOX 159274
Nashville, TN 37215
www.tnps.org

The idea of producing a comprehensive field guide to the wildflowers of Tennessee was conceived by this organization 14 years ago. TNPS gratefully acknowledges the dedication and support of its members and other volunteers as we have seen this project to fruition.

2003–2004 Officers and Directors

President: Karl Heinzman, Norris
Vice-President: Dennis Horn, Tullahoma
Secretary: Bart G. Jones, Memphis
Treasurer: Kay Jones, Hampshire
Past President: Jane Norris, Nashville
Directors:
Bertha Chrietzberg, Murfreesboro
Todd Crabtree, Smyrna
Al Good, Signal Mountain
Nita R. Heilman, Clarksville
Mary P. Priestley, Sewanee
Susan Sweetser, Powell
Ex-Officios:
Tavia Cathcart, Franklin
Ashley Crownover, Nashville

David Duhl, Nashville
Michelle Haines, Gallatin
Thomas E. Hemmerly, Murfreesboro
David Lincicome, Hermitage
Rita Venable, Franklin
Past Presidents:
Jane Norris 1999–2002
Kay Jones 1996–1998
Milo Pyne 1996
Mary Martin Schaffner 1991–1995
John Churchill 1989–1990
Scott Gunn 1986–1988
Thomas S. Patrick 1984–1985
A. Murray Evans (co-founder) 1981–1983
Rob Farmer (co-founder) 1978–1980

WRITER ACKNOWLEDGMENTS

The TNPS sincerely appreciates the contributions of the following people whose text and plant description writing talents were instrumental in the successful compilation of the book.

Introduction
Tavia Cathcart, Franklin; **Dennis Horn**, Tullahoma; **Betty McNeely**, Murfreesboro; **Mary P. Priestley**, Sewanee

Plant Description Writers
Dennis Horn, Chairman, Tullahoma; **Andrea Shea Bishop**, Nashville; **Tavia Cathcart**, Franklin; **Edward W. Chester**, Clarksville; **Bertha Chrietzberg**, Murfreesboro; **Edward E.C. Clebsch**, Greenback; **Richard K. Clements**, Chattanooga; **Maureen Cunningham**, Oak Ridge; **Hal R. DeSelm**, Knoxville; **Kurt Emmanuele**, Chattanooga; **A. Murray Evans**, Knoxville; **Nita R. Heilman**, Clarksville; **Thomas E. Hemmerly**, Murfreesboro; **Otto R. Hirsch**, Nashville; **Duane Houck**, Ooltewah; **Ronald L. Jones**, Richmond, KY; **Linda Mann**, Lenoir City; **Landon McKinney**, Erlanger, KY; **Joyce Merritt**, Chattanooga; **Sally Mirick**, Knoxville; **Zack E. Murrell**, Boone, NC; **Shirley Nicholson**, Knoxville; **Thomas S. Patrick**, Monticello, GA; **Larry Pounds**, Oak Ridge; **Mary P. Priestley**, Sewanee; **Milo Pyne**, Durham, NC; **Scott Ranger**, Marietta, GA; **Gene Van Horn**, Chattanooga; **Miriam Weinstein**, Nashville; **Herb White**, Liberty; **Chuck Wilson**, Hixson; **Larry Wilson**, Memphis

Notes
Tavia Cathcart, Chairman, Franklin; **Thomas E. Hemmerly**, Murfreesboro; **Dennis Horn**, Tullahoma; **Mary P. Priestley**, Sewanee

COMMITTEE ACKNOWLEDGMENTS
The TNPS gratefully acknowledges the committee members responsible for the many tasks accomplished during the completion and publication of the book.

Book Committee
Tavia Cathcart, Chairman, Franklin; **David Duhl**, Nashville; **Karl Heinzman**, Norris; **Thomas E. Hemmerly**, Murfreesboro; **Dennis Horn**, Tullahoma; **Kay Jones**, Hampshire; **Jane Norris**, Nashville; **Mary P. Priestley**, Sewanee

Botanical Keys Committee
Milo Pyne, Chairman, Durham, NC; **Todd Crabtree**, Smyrna; **Bart G. Jones**, Memphis; **Mary P. Priestley**, Sewanee

Plant Selection Committee
Dennis Horn, Chairman, Tullahoma; **Andrea Shea Bishop**, Nashville; **Tavia Cathcart**, Franklin; **James I. Jones**, Chattanooga; **Milo Pyne**, Durham, NC; **Paul Somers**, Ashburnham, MA; **Larry Wilson**, Memphis

Finance Committee
Mary P. Priestley, Chairman, Sewanee; **Andrea Shea Bishop**, Nashville; **Dennis Horn**, Tullahoma; **Kay Jones**, Hampshire; **Jane Norris**, Nashville

Technical Editing Committee
Thomas E. Hemmerly, Chairman, Murfreesboro; **Claude Bailey**, Hendersonville; **Tavia Cathcart**, Franklin; **Todd Crabtree**, Smyrna; **Kevin Fitch**, Hillsboro; **Dennis Horn**, Tullahoma; **Bart G. Jones**, Memphis

Technical Review Committee
Dennis Horn, Chairman, Tullahoma; **Claude Bailey**, Hendersonville; **Tavia Cathcart**, Franklin; **Edward W. Chester**, Clarksville; **Edward E.C. Clebsch**, Greenback; **Hal R. DeSelm**, Knoxville; **Dwayne Estes**, Knoxville; **Chris A. Fleming**, Nashville; **Thomas E. Hemmerly**, Murfreesboro; **Duane Houck**, Ooltewah; **Bart G. Jones**, Memphis; **Edgar B. Lickey**, Knoxville; **Mary P. Priestley**, Sewanee; **Joey Shaw**, Knoxville; **Alan Sweetser**, Powell; **B. Eugene Wofford**, Knoxville

Lone Pine Publishing
We extend our heartfelt appreciation to our fine editor, Nicholle Carrière, for her untiring patience and direction, supreme organizational talents, and sense of humor. Also to Dawn Loewen, Nancy Foulds, Ken Davis, Gerry Dotto, Elliott Engley, Heather Markham, Genevieve Boyer, Gary Whyte, Carol Woo, Linda Kershaw, and the rest of the highly skilled and motivated staff at Lone Pine Publishing. A special thank you goes to the president, Shane Kennedy, whose vision and commitment to the natural world were indispensable to this project. We are grateful for his confidence and support, as well as his continued friendship.

PHOTOGRAPHER ACKNOWLEDGMENTS
The TNPS thanks the following photographers whose images appear in this book:
Thomas G. Barnes, Lexington, KY; **Barry J. Brown**, Crossville; **Bill M. Campbell**, MD, Oak Ridge; **Edward W. Chester**, Clarksville; **Richard Connors**, Nashville; **W. Michael Dennis**, Winter Park, FL; **Dick Doub**, Andersonville; **Jerry Drown**, Gatlinburg; **David Duhl**, Nashville; **Douglas H. Ehleben**, DDS, McMinnville; **Kurt Emmanuele**, Chattanooga; **Janie Cooper Finch**, Algood; **Susan Finger**, Tullahoma; **Garth Fraser**, Decatur, AL; **Al Good**, Signal Mountain; **Ann Goodpasture**, Brentwood; **Calysta Haglage**, Nashville; **Alan S. Heilman**, Knoxville; **Nita R. Heilman**, Clarksville; **Thomas E. Hemmerly**, Murfreesboro; **Darel G. Hess**, Antioch; **Ann Hut Hill**, Knoxville; **Otto R. Hirsch**, Nashville; **Ed Honicker**, Franklin; **Dennis Horn**, Tullahoma; **Becky Hughes**, Russell Springs, KY; **Betty Hyche**, Fairview; **Alice Jensen**, Shelbyville; **James I. 'Bus' Jones**, Chattanooga; **David Kocher**, Oak Ridge; **James W. Lea**, Murfreesboro; **Terry Livingston**, Franklin; **Carol Nourse**, Athens, GA; **Hugh Nourse**, Athens, GA; **John Oates**, Nashville; **Luis C. Prieto, Jr.**, Memphis; **Milo Pyne**, Durham, NC; **William F. Rainey, Jr.**, Columbia; **Margret Rhinehart**, Spencer; **Dorothy Richardson**, Bartlett; **James Richardson**, Bartlett; **Mary Martin Schaffner**, Nashville; **Edward Schell**, Johnson City; **Stanley Sims**, Nashville; **Paul Somers**, Ashburnham, MA; **Sherman (Dick) Sooy**, Stockbridge, MI; **B. Wayne Swilley**, Goodlettsville; **Robert Vantrease**, Nashville; **Kathy Wallace**, Hendersonville; **Miriam Weinstein**, Nashville; **B. Eugene Wofford**, Knoxville; **Norval Ziegler**, Oak Ridge

DONOR ACKNOWLEDGMENTS

The TNPS appreciates the generosity of the following donors and sponsors, whose financial support was instrumental to the completion of this project.

Lady's Slipper: $5000 & above
Benwood Foundation
Tennessee Department of
    Environment and
    Conservation**
Woods-Greer Foundation

Trillium: $1000 to $4999
Robert Brown
Hamico, Inc.
Horticultural Association
    of TN
Olan Mills

Crested Iris: $500 to $999
Bowater-Calhoun Woodlands
Alynne Massey
The Nature Conservancy
Edward and Shirley
    Nicholson
Margret Rhinehart
Myrtle Seno
Westvaco Corporation

Fire Pink: $200 to $499
American Rhododendron
    Society, TN Valley Chapter
Bertha Chrietzberg
Bradley Currey
Colenda Emory
A. Murray Evans
Nita Heilman
J.M. Huber Corporation
Kennedy Foundation
Lichterman Nature Center
Carl Nordman
William and Lynn Patten
Elizabeth S. Porter
William and Mary Priestley
Elsie Quarterman
Helen Rodgers
Susan Stahl
Allen and Susan Sweetser
Tennessee Wildflower Society
George and Harriet Waller

Passionflower: $100 to $199
Tavia Cathcart
Friends of South Cumberland
    State Recreation Area
Adele Hampton
Katrina R. Hayes
Annie Heilman
Jean and Karl Heinzman
Edward and Shirley Honicker
Duane Houck
Patsy Huffman
William Manier III
Robert W. Meyer
Monteagle Sunday School
    Assembly
John Noel and Melinda
    Welton
Charles and Gerry Nokes
Mrs. Reinhold Nordsieck
Wendell Norman
Raymond and Jane Norris
Northern Rim Herbal Society
Dr. and Mrs. John Oates
Kenneth and Marjorie
    Raines
Flournoy S. Rogers
Harold Scott
William and Mary Sullivan
Tennessee Aquarium
Josephine Von Nieda
Emily Wright

Black-Eyed Susan: up through $99
Ronald Arildsen
Rodgers and Marion Beasley
Sid A. Berry II
Susan Brock
Charles & Marion Burger
Lamar Field
Susan Finger
Flower Lovers Circle
Grace Foster
Pamela Foster
Calysta Haglage

Bill and Cherrie Hall
Otto Hirsch
Louise Jackson
Bart G. Jones
Miriam Keener
Knoxville Garden Club
James W. Lea
Phyllis Morris
Eileen Neiler
Donald Newton
Kim Sadler
Carol D. Shelton
Tommie Slayden
Carol Thomas
Tennessee Federation of
    Garden Clubs
Kenneth S. Warren
Richard Wiser
Mary K. Myers
Grace Paine
Paris Garden Club
Kathleen Robinson
Nancy Scott
Carol D. Shelton
Radford Smith
Wanda Thomas
Julia Ann Walker
Wildflower Society of Sumner
    County
Flora Yando

LOANS
Trillium: $1000 to $4999
Perennial Plant Society of
    Middle Tennessee

Fire Pink: $200 to $499
Moore and Moore Garden
    Center
Tennessee Federation of
    Garden Clubs, District II

** This project was funded, in part, under an agreement with the Tennessee Department of Environment and Conservation. The TNPS greatly appreciates this financial support. This book was one part of the Flora 2001 Project, approved by the Tennessee State Legislature, to commemorate the 100th anniversary of Dr. Augustin Gattinger's *Flora of Tennessee and Philosophy of Botany*, published in 1901.

Lizard's Tail
p. 45

Fragrant Water Lily
p. 49

White Baneberry
p. 53

Wood Anemone
p. 54

WHITE

Black Cohosh
p. 56

Virgin's Bower
p. 57

Prairie Larkspur
p. 59

Tassel Rue
p. 65

WHITE

Twinleaf
p. 67

Mayapple
p. 67

Bloodroot
p. 68

Dutchman's Breeches
p. 70

WHITE

Star Chickweed
p. 81

Canada Violet
p. 96

Garlic Mustard
p. 109

Mountain Sweet
Pepperbush p. 123

WHITE

Spotted Wintergreen
p. 125

Wintergreen
p. 126

Dog Hobble
p. 127

Galax
p. 132

WHITE

Shooting Star
p. 133

Wild Stonecrop
p. 137

Ashy Hydrangea
p. 140

Kidneyleaf Grass-of-
Parnassus p. 142

WHITE

Early Saxifrage
p. 144

Foamflower
p. 144

Goatsbeard
p. 147

Wild Strawberry
p. 148

WHITE

American Ipecac
p. 150

Multiflora Rose
p. 154

White Clover
p. 181

Enchanter's Nightshade
p. 184

WHITE

Bastard Toadflax
p. 192

Flowering Spurge
p. 195

New Jersey Tea
p. 197

Dwarf Ginseng
p. 207

WHITE

Queen Anne's Lace
p. 212

Cowbane
p. 216

Hedge Bindweed
p. 236

Basil Bee Balm
p. 264

WHITE

Clammy Hedge Hyssop
p. 284

Mecardonia
p. 286

Moth Mullein
p. 291

Pale-Spiked Lobelia
p. 302

WHITE

Virginia Buttonweed
p. 304

Cleavers
p. 304

Partridgeberry
p. 308

Common Elderberry
p. 310

WHITE

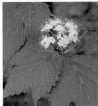

Mapleleaf Viburnum
p. 312

Beaked Corn Salad
p. 313

Yarrow
p. 320

White Snakeroot
p. 321

WHITE

Hyssopleaf
Thoroughwort p. 344

Wild Quinine
p. 366

White-Flowered Leafcup
p. 367

Narrowleaf White-
Topped Aster p. 375

WHITE

White Crownbeard
p. 385

Broadleaf Arrowhead
p. 388

Mud Plantain
p. 404

Colicroot
p. 408

WHITE

Fairy Wand
p. 411

Speckled Wood Lily
p. 412

American Lily-of-the-
Valley p. 412

Canada Mayflower
p. 419

WHITE

Solomon's Plume
p. 422

Featherbells
p. 423

Bent Trillium
p. 427

Turkeybeard
p. 436

WHITE

Carolina Spider Lily
p. 437

Spanish Bayonet
p. 438

Monkey-Face Orchid
p. 461

Oval Ladies' Tresses
p. 466

WHITE

Woolly Croton
p. 193

Rattlesnake Master
p. 214

Plantainleaf Pussytoes
p. 322

American Bur Reed
p. 402

NEARLY WHITE (BROWNISH, GREENISH)

Fly Poison
p. 410

Bur Cucumber
p. 106

Buttonbush
p. 303

Pale Indian Plantain
p. 329

NEARLY WHITE (YELLOWISH)

Silverrod
p. 378

False Garlic
p. 420

Rue Anemone
p. 64

Virginia Spring Beauty
p. 75

NEARLY WHITE (YELLOWISH) **NEARLY WHITE (PINKISH)**

Bouncing Bet
p. 78

Cutleaf Toothwort
p. 114

Purple Rocket
p. 118

Trailing Arbutus
p. 125

NEARLY WHITE (PINKISH)

Mountain Laurel
p. 126

Indian Pipe
p. 128

Great Rhododendron
p. 131

Wood Vetch
p. 181

NEARLY WHITE (PINKISH)

Slender Gaura
p. 186

Allegheny Spurge
p. 192

Carolina Cranesbill
p. 204

Fogfruit
p. 253

NEARLY WHITE (PINKISH)

Cutleaf Water
Horehound p. 262

Guyandotte Beauty
p. 274

White Turtlehead
p. 282

Venus' Pride
p. 305

NEARLY WHITE (PINKISH)

Teasel
p. 314

Leafy Elephant's Foot
p. 340

Marsh Fleabane
p. 367

Wild Garlic
p. 408

NEARLY WHITE (PINKISH)

Pennywort
p. 222

Wild Comfrey
p. 247

Turnsole
p. 248

One-Flowered Cancer
Root p. 294

NEARLY WHITE (PALE LAVENDER)

Tennessee Glade Cress
p. 118

Tennessee Milk Vetch
p. 163

Japanese Honeysuckle
p. 309

Western Daisy
p. 327

YELLOW AND WHITE

Oxeye Daisy
p. 331

Tall Flat-Topped White
Aster p. 338

Common Fleabane
p. 341

Goldenclub
p. 391

YELLOW AND WHITE

Swamp Rose Mallow
p. 91

Goat's Rue
p. 178

Mountain Wood Sorrel
p. 202

White Milkweed
p. 230

PINK/PURPLE AND WHITE

Jimsonweed
p. 233

American Water Willow
p. 295

Showy Orchis
p. 453

Yellow Pond Lily
p. 49

PINK/PURPLE AND WHITE   **YELLOW**

Hispid Buttercup
p. 62

Celandine Poppy
p. 69

Golden St. Johnswort
p. 86

Reclining St. Andrew's
Cross p. 89

YELLOW

Halberdleaf Yellow Violet
p. 98

Field Mustard
p. 111

Fringed Loosestrife
p. 134

Common Cinquefoil
p. 152

YELLOW

Partridge Pea
p. 166

Pencil Flower
p. 178

Low Hop Clover
p. 179

Seedbox
p. 186

YELLOW

Creeping Water Primrose
p. 187

Sundrops
p. 188

Common Yellow Flax
p. 197

Illinois Wood Sorrel
p. 201

YELLOW

Hairyjoint Meadow
Parsnip p. 217

Virginia Ground Cherry
p. 234

Hoary Puccoon
p. 249

Northern Horse Balm
p. 258

YELLOW

Southern Fernleaf False
Foxglove p. 281

Butter-and-Eggs
p. 285

Common Mullein
p. 291

Ozark Tickseed
Sunflower p. 328

YELLOW

Whorled Coreopsis
p. 336

Lanceleaf Gumweed
p. 348

Autumn Sneezeweed
p. 349

Maximilian's Sunflower
p. 352

YELLOW

Prairie Golden Aster
p. 356

Hairy Hawkweed
p. 358

Oppositeleaf Dwarf
Dandelion p. 360

Gray-Headed
Coneflower p. 369

YELLOW

Black-Eyed Susan
p. 370

Butterweed
p. 374

Cup Plant
p. 376

Yellow Leafcup
p. 378

YELLOW

Giant Goldenrod
p. 380

Yellow Goatsbeard
p. 383

Coltsfoot
p. 384

Twisted Yellow-Eyed Grass
p. 393

YELLOW

Beaked Trout Lily
p. 415

Yellow Trillium
p. 429

Large-Flowered Bellwort
p. 434

Wild Oats
p. 435

YELLOW

Yellow Stargrass
p. 437

Large Yellow Lady's
Slipper p. 452

Prickly Pear
p. 73

Pinesap
p. 128

YELLOW   **YELLOW/ORANGE**

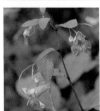
Spotted Touch-Me-Not
p. 205

Cross Vine
p. 296

Common Daylily
p. 415

Yellow Fringed Orchid
p. 458

YELLOW/ORANGE

Flame Azalea
p. 129

Trumpet Creeper
p. 297

Michigan Lily
p. 417

Wood Lily
p. 418

ORANGE

Blackberry Lily
p. 440

Wild Columbine
p. 55

Indian Pink
p. 220

Small Red Morning Glory
p. 237

ORANGE **YELLOW AND RED**

Fire Pink
p. 80

Crimson Bee Balm
p. 264

Indian Paintbrush
p. 282

Cardinal Flower
p. 300

RED

Trumpet Honeysuckle
p. 310

Southern Red Trillium
p. 432

Scarlet Smartweed
p. 82

Mountain Azalea
p. 130

RED **PINK**

Carolina Rose
p. 153

Crown Vetch
p. 167

Hairy Milk Pea
p. 171

Sensitive Brier
p. 174

PINK

Showy Evening Primrose
p. 190

Drumheads
p. 198

Curtiss' Milkwort
p. 198

Rose Pink
p. 223

PINK

Obedient Plant
p. 266

American Germander
p. 274

Field Thistle
p. 333

Purple Coneflower
p. 339

PINK

Hollow Joe-Pye Weed
p. 343

Catesby's Trillium
p. 425

Pink Lady's Slipper
p. 450

Rose Pogonia
p. 464

PINK

Wild Bleeding Heart
p. 71

Deptford Pink
p. 77

Catawba Rhododendron
p. 130

Steeplebush
p. 157

MAGENTA

Gattinger's Prairie Clover
p. 169

Everlasting Pea
p. 171

Red Clover
p. 180

Virginia Meadow Beauty
p. 191

MAGENTA

Gaywings
p. 200

Wild Geranium
p. 204

Swamp Milkweed
p. 227

Smooth Phlox
p. 241

MAGENTA

Rose Vervain
p. 252

Henbit
p. 261

Smooth Purple Gerardia
p. 279

Dense Blazing Star
p. 364

MAGENTA

Southern Blazing Star
p. 365

Grass Pink
p. 448

Upland Spreading
Pogonia p. 449

Purple Fringeless Orchid
p. 463

MAGENTA

Round-Lobed Hepatica
p. 60

Passionflower
p. 105

Hog Peanut
p. 161

Spurred Butterfly Pea
p. 165

LAVENDER

Violet Wood Sorrel
p. 203

Apple-of-Peru
p. 233

Horse Nettle
p. 235

Wild Blue Phlox
p. 241

LAVENDER

Miami Mist
p. 247

Narrowleaf Vervain
p. 254

Downy Wood Mint
p. 257

Wild Bergamot
p. 265

LAVENDER

| Lyreleaf Sage p. 269 | Blue Toadflax p. 285 | Sharpwing Monkey Flower p. 287 | Longsepal Beardtongue p. 289 |

LAVENDER

| Dwarf Larkspur p. 58 | Birdfoot Violet p. 100 | Purple Phacelia p. 245 | Ground Ivy p. 260 |

PURPLE/VIOLET

| Heal All p. 267 | Hairy Skullcap p. 270 | Hairy Ruellia p. 295 | Downy Lobelia p. 301 |

PURPLE/VIOLET

| New England Aster p. 325 | Virginia Spiderwort p. 395 | Pickerelweed p. 404 | Dwarf Crested Iris p. 441 |

PURPLE/VIOLET

| Monkshood p. 53 | Common Blue Violet p. 103 | Blue False Indigo p. 164 | Soapwort Gentian p. 221 |

BLUE

Eastern Blue Star
p. 224

Periwinkle
p. 225

Ivyleaf Morning Glory
p. 238

Greek Valerian
p. 243

BLUE

Virginia Bluebell
p. 250

Common Speedwell
p. 292

Tall Bellflower
p. 298

Southern Harebell
p. 298

BLUE

Venus' Looking Glass
p. 302

Creeping Bluet
p. 307

Bachelor's Button
p. 330

Chicory
p. 332

BLUE

Florida Blue Lettuce
p. 362

Virginia Dayflower
p. 394

Wild Hyacinth
p. 410

Eastern Blue-Eyed Grass
p. 445

BLUE

Blue Cohosh
p. 66

Wood Nettle
p. 71

Common Ragweed
p. 321

Jack-in-the-Pulpit
p. 390

GREEN/TAN/BROWN/MAROON

False Nutsedge
p. 398

River Oats
p. 400

Indian Cucumber Root
p. 419

Smooth Solomon's Seal
p. 421

GREEN/TAN/BROWN/MAROON

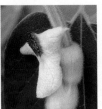

Huger's Carrion Flower
p. 439

Large Whorled Pogonia
p. 455

Woolly Dutchman's Pipe
p. 46

Little Brown Jug
p. 47

GREEN/TAN/BROWN/MAROON

Squaw Root
p. 293

Soft Rush
p. 396

Common Cattail
p. 403

Crested Coralroot
p. 454

GREEN/TAN/BROWN/MAROON

Sweet Shrub
p. 45

Wild Ginger
p. 47

Leather Vasevine
p. 57

Groundnut
p. 161

GREEN/TAN/BROWN/MAROON

Roundhead Bush Clover
p. 172

Wood Betony
p. 288

Sweet Betsy
p. 426

Lilyleaf Twayblade
p. 456

GREEN/TAN/BROWN/MAROON

Introduction

Old hawthorn and ragworts on Roan Mountain

EDWARD SCHELL

About This Guide

The plants in this guide can be found across Tennessee in various ecosystems: from lush and moist forests to windswept and exposed ridges over 6000 feet in elevation, and from dense swamp forests to the sunny floor of a cedar glade, to rocky slopes and grassy meadows. Outside of tropical rainforests, these ecosystems are considered some of the most biologically diverse in the world. Tennessee boasts over 2800 species of vascular plants, including wildflowers, ferns, and woody plants.

The broader area covered in this book is based on regional ecosystems rather than state boundaries. It includes the central and southern Appalachian Mountains, the Ozarks, the Piedmont, and the Ohio, Tennessee, and mid-Mississippi River Valleys. Please refer to the map on page 5 to view the regions covered in this field guide.

In addition to providing excellent general coverage of the wildflowers of Tennessee and the surrounding region, this book gives particular attention to several key elements of the Tennessee flora. For example, all 13 species of milkweeds (*Asclepias*), all 17 species of trilliums (*Trillium*), and most of the 50 members of the Orchid Family (Orchidaceae) that occur in Tennessee are included. Also described are many unique cedar glade endemics (plants that are restricted to a particular habitat) from the Central Basin, as well as coastal and prairie elements from the Eastern Highland Rim that occur as extensions of their primary ranges.

The Wildflowers of Tennessee, the Ohio Valley, and the Southern Appalachians is the most complete, comprehensive, and informative book covering the flora of this region to date. With nearly 800 full-color photographs and descriptions of over 1250 species and varieties, we believe all levels of wildflower enthusiasts will find this book beneficial, informative, and a worthwhile companion in the field or on a wildflower walk.

Owing to space limitations, the ferns and all but a few examples of grasses and sedges have been excluded. None of the trees and only the showiest shrubs are included. A few plants with inconspicuous flowers also have been excluded.

For regular updates on Tennessee plants and to view more photographs, information, and an online atlas, please visit the University of Tennessee Herbarium website at http://tenn.bio.utk.edu/.

How to Use This Guide

As with all living things, plants are organized into a system of classification: related species are grouped into genera, related genera into families, and so forth. Plants in the same family have similar floral characteristics that help in plant identification.

In this book, plant families are arranged phylogenetically; that is, the plant families considered by botanists to be more primitive are presented first, followed by those that have more derived or specialized characteristics. Genera within each family and species within each genus are arranged alphabetically. The order followed is that of Dr. Arthur Cronquist's *Manual of Vascular Plants of the Northeastern United States and Adjacent Canada*, (New York Botanical Garden, 1991). This field guide includes 90 plant families, divided into 26 groups of related families.

EDWARD SCHELL

Autumn on Little Pigeon River in the Great Smoky Mountains National Park

The families included in each group, along with their scientific names, can be found in the Table of Contents.

There are several methods for using this book to find a particular plant:
1) If you know the common or scientific name of a plant, look in the Index to locate a description of the species.
2) Many readers may find the quickest way to identify an unfamiliar plant is to turn to the Color Key beginning on page 9. This easy-to-use pictorial guide presents photographs of 300 flowers that represent various plant families, organized by

flower color along with a corresponding page reference.

3) Taxonomic keys to the genera are given for 12 of the more complex families. Some readers may know to which family a plant belongs but not its genus or species. In this case, a key may be useful. The keys, along with a short family description and line drawings of representative family members, are located before the first account for each of these families. Use the key to determine the genus, then turn to the page(s) indicated to find the species.

Families with keys are:

Buttercup (Ranunculaceae), p. 51
Mustard (Brassicaceae), p. 107
Heath (Ericaceae), p. 124
Saxifrage (Saxifragaceae), p. 138
Rose (Rosaceae), p. 145
Bean or Pea (Fabaceae), p. 158
Carrot or Parsley (Apiaceae), p. 208
Mint (Lamiaceae), p. 255
Figwort (Scrophulariaceae), p. 277
Aster or Sunflower (Asteraceae), p. 315
Lily (Liliaceae), p. 405
Orchid (Orchidaceae), p. 446

4) If none of the above methods work for you, enjoy turning the pages of the book to find your mystery plant! Although this is not always the quickest identification method, it can be fun and is another way to become more familiar with plant relationships, the layout of this book, and the plants of our region. Note that not all the wildflowers of Tennessee are included in this book. For the identification of some plants, you may need to consult a botanical manual. Several are listed in the reference list on page 479.

About the Plant Descriptions

The plant photographs themselves serve as a primary tool for identification. Each photograph is accompanied by a description to further aid in plant identification and to add other useful and interesting information. Many related species are also described.

While an attempt has been made to keep the descriptions as non-technical as possible, the use of some botanical terms cannot be avoided. A complete glossary of the technical terms used can be found on page 469. Included in the glossary are illustrations that show leaf arrangement, leaf types and characteristics, inflorescence types, and flower types, parts, and characteristics.

Descriptions include the following:

Common Name(s): Each species account begins with one or more recognized common names. Common names are not standardized. Some plants have one or more well-established common names that are used throughout their range, while others have names that vary from location to location. Often, the same common name is used for different plants in other locations! The names in the header bar at the beginning of each description are those that seem most appropriate for the wildflowers of Tennessee. Other common names are listed in the **Notes** section (see below).

Scientific Name: Each plant has a botanical name, also called a scientific name, which is recognized anywhere in the world. Botanical names consist of two Latin (or Latinized) or Greek words: the first is the genus name, followed by the epithet (informally called the "species name" throughout this book). The scientific name is *italicized* and displayed after the common name. Sometimes, even scientific names are changed, as earlier published names are discovered or the plant is reclassified. In these cases, the previously used name is listed at the end of the **Where Found** section.

If the plant is *not native* to Tennessee, an asterisk (*) is placed after the species name. The scientific names used in this book generally follow the *Atlas of Tennessee Vascular Plants*, Vols. 1 and 2, The Center for Field Biology at Austin Peay State University, 1993 and 1997; and the online Database of Tennessee Vascular Plants at the University of Tennessee Herbarium website, http://tenn.bio.utk.edu/vascular/vascular.html.

General: This section describes the type of plant (annual, perennial, vine, shrub), its height, and other important general features.

Leaves: Leaf arrangement, type (simple or compound), shape, size, and other characteristics are described in this part of the account.

Flowers: Included in this section is a description of the inflorescence type, flower, color, size, and any unusual characteristics. The flowering period of each plant is given at the end of this section. For example, "April–June" indicates that the plant flowers from April through June and generally indicates the flowering times throughout its range, not just in Tennessee. Flowering times may vary considerably from year to year, based on rainfall and overall weather conditions. Elevation, habitat, and latitude also affect flowering time. It is not uncommon for plants in the Smoky Mountains at lower elevations to flower three weeks ahead of those that grow near the mountaintops. Also, flowering usually occurs earlier in the southern part of the range than in the northern.

Fruits: This section gives the fruit type (capsule, berry, achene, etc.), size, shape, and color.

Where Found: If a plant is not native to Tennessee, then the origin is listed at the beginning of this section. Next, the type of setting where the plant grows (its habitat) is described, followed by the broader range where it is found, such as "from VA to GA." (Please note that standard two-letter postal

codes have been applied.) Next, the Tennessee distribution is listed, such as "Middle TN," with particular counties listed when the plant extends beyond its normal range or is rare. References to West TN, Middle TN, and East TN indicate the three grand divisions of Tennessee, as indicated on the map on page 29.

The frequency of occurrence within Tennessee is also given for each plant. The categories are defined according to the number of documented reports found within the 95 counties in Tennessee, as shown in the table below.

If the plant has recently been assigned a different scientific name, the synonym, a previously used scientific name, is given at the end of this section.

Similar Species: One or more closely related plants may be included in this section. Unique characteristics are **bolded** to help the reader distinguish the similar species from the primary plant shown in the photograph.

Notes: This section is meant to paint a picture of a plant as a member of the ecosystem and perhaps reveal its unique "personality." Information may include the meaning or origin of the scientific name, and a list of additional common names of the plant. The more commonly used names are **bolded**. This section may also contain information about a plant's edibility and medicinal and other uses, as applicable. Also, any folkloric, historical, or mythological references may be included for the reader's general interest.

Frequency of Occurrence	% of TN Counties	Number of TN counties
Common	50% or greater	48 or more
Frequent	31–49%	30–47
Occasional	11–30%	11–29
Infrequent	6–10%	6–10
Rare	5% or less	5 or fewer

Grand Divisions of Tennessee

Throughout the **Where Found** sections in this book are references to West TN, Middle TN, and East TN (see map on next page). These are known as the three grand divisions of Tennessee, signified by the three stars in the Tennessee state flag, indicating their contrasting geographical divisions.

West Tennessee is bordered by two rivers—on the west by the Mississippi River, and on the east by the north-flowing Tennessee River—and contains rich river-bottom land. The metropolitan city of Memphis is located in West Tennessee.

The Tennessee River is also the western boundary of **Middle Tennessee**. As defined here, Middle Tennessee is bordered on the east by the Central and Eastern time zone line that extends along the western borders of Hamilton, Rhea, Roane, Morgan, and Scott counties, near the eastern edge of the Cumberland Plateau. This region is known for its rolling hills. Historically, the area has been used for livestock and dairy farming, and is home to many fine horse farms. The state capital, Nashville, is located in Middle Tennessee.

The time zone line also serves as the western edge of **East Tennessee**, which is bounded on the east by the North Carolina border. This grand division is known for the high mountains along the eastern boundary, as well as its many forested ridges and pastoral valleys. Knoxville and Chattanooga are found in East Tennessee.

Physiographic Provinces and Sub-Provinces

If you were to look out from Clingman's Dome, the highest peak on the Tennessee–North Carolina border, the undulating Appalachian Mountains would seem like a vast, neverending tapestry in subtle shades of green and blue. Beyond view, almost 400 miles to the west, lies the western border of the state, defined by the meandering reaches of the Mississippi River.

Tennessee cuts across five main geographic regions, known as physiographic provinces, characterized by particular geologic, topographic, and edaphic (soil) conditions. From east to west, they are the Blue Ridge, Ridge and Valley, Cumberland Plateau, Interior Low Plateau, and the Coastal Plain. Some of these are further divided into sub-provinces.

This complex physiography is the foundation for the state's diverse vegetation, a rich natural heritage of over 2800 species of wildflowers, ferns, and woody plants. The physiographic provinces and sub-provinces are illustrated in the map on the next page.

Blue Ridge

The Blue Ridge province of the southern Appalachian Mountains, also referred to as the Unaka Mountains in Tennessee, anchors the eastern end of Tennessee and forms a natural boundary with North Carolina. Clingman's Dome straddles this boundary, and at 6642 feet above sea level, it is the highest point in the state and the second highest in the eastern U.S.

More than 500 million years ago, geologic forces caused the landmasses that are now North America and Africa to collide, pushing older and deeper rock layers up and over younger ones to create the Appalachian Mountains, which stretch from Alabama to

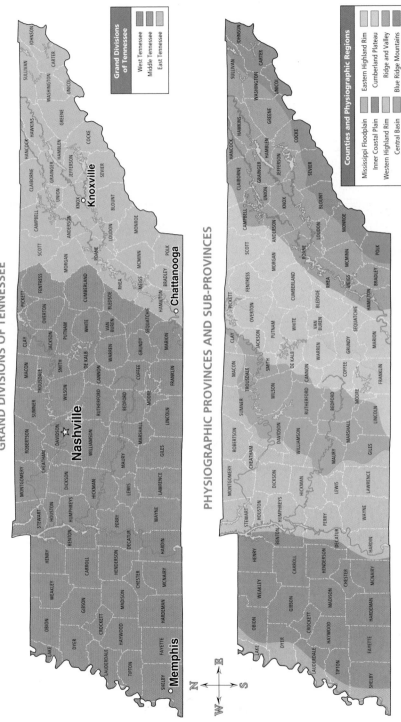

GRAND DIVISIONS OF TENNESSEE

Grand Divisions of Tennessee
- West Tennessee
- Middle Tennessee
- East Tennessee

PHYSIOGRAPHIC PROVINCES AND SUB-PROVINCES

Counties and Physiographic Regions
- Mississippi Floodplain
- Inner Coastal Plain
- Western Highland Rim
- Central Basin
- Eastern Highland Rim
- Cumberland Plateau
- Ridge and Valley
- Blue Ridge Mountains

EDWARD SCHELL

Roan Mountain with rhododendrons, Blue Ridge (Unaka) Mountains

Newfoundland, Canada. Evidence of this overthrusting can be seen today in places such as Cades Cove in the Great Smoky Mountains National Park. There, the relatively young limestone rock is exposed, whereas elsewhere in the Appalachians, it is buried beneath these ancient mountains.

The southern Appalachian Mountains, which include the Blue Ridge, are the most botanically diverse in the Appalachian chain. Records show that this region supports more than 400 species of mosses, 130 species of trees, and over 2500 species of flowering plants, many of which cannot be found anywhere else in the world.

Specifically, the Blue Ridge of Tennessee contains about 1650 species of plants. This province includes 516,000 acres of the Great Smoky Mountains National Park, which botanically is the richest of any national park in the contiguous United States. Factors contributing to the large number of species are ample rainfall, a mild climate, and a significant variation in elevation. The change in altitude that a hiker experiences when ascending the mountain from Gatlinburg to nearby Clingman's Dome is similar to the change in latitude when traveling from Gatlinburg to Canada. Botanically, the hiker and the traveler would pass through a number of similar plant communities.

The upper elevations of Clingman's Dome, like other peaks of the Smoky Mountains, are at the southern limit of the spruce-fir forest range. Upper-elevation plant communities include treeless grassy and shrub "balds," and beech gaps consisting of nearly pure beech stands within the spruce-fir forest.

Below the spruce-fir forest, northern hardwood forests of beech and yellow birch can be found. Hemlock forests, oak-hickory forests, or open oak-pine stands, depending upon local environmental factors, are found farther down the mountain slopes and on ridge tops.

Broader valleys and "coves" are occupied by the richest plant communities—cove hardwood forests containing buckeye, basswood, sugar maple, black walnut, and tulip-poplar trees. The largest tracts of old-growth forest in the eastern United States are located in Tennessee's Appalachian Mountains. In the springtime, wildflower fanciers flock to the Smoky Mountains to experience the remarkably abundant and diverse flora.

The Blue Ridge Mountains, the Cumberland Plateau and, to some extent, the Ridge and Valley of East Tennessee, have been referred to as the "Noah's Ark" of the flora of eastern North America. The glaciers that covered much of the continent during the most recent ice age forced northern species of plants to migrate southward ahead of the ice sheets. The glaciers never reached Tennessee, and when they retreated northward about 10,000 years ago, many northern species, known as "relicts," remained. They can be found today on the higher slopes of the Blue Ridge and in isolated pockets of the Cumberland Plateau and the Ridge and Valley where cool microclimates have allowed their survival. These relicts have been joined by southern species, resulting in a profusion of plant species.

Ridge and Valley
The Ridge and Valley province, part of the Great Valley that extends northeast from Alabama through Virginia and beyond, is a 45-mile-wide strip of land bounded on the east by the Blue Ridge Mountains and on the west by the Cumberland Plateau. It is characterized by many rows of northeast-southwest trending ridges and low-lying valleys that range from an elevation of over 3000 feet at Bays Mountain in the north to 640 feet near Chattanooga in the south. The many valleys form a complex system of streams and rivers that converge to form the main stream of the Tennessee River.

This distinctive topography, somewhat resembling the pleats of an accordion, was formed from numerous folds and faults in the bedrock created by the same continental collision that formed the Appalachian Mountains. One hundred and fifty million years of weathering and erosion of the rocks of the Great Valley have resulted in a sculpted landscape: a series of relatively erosion-resistant ridges and knobs separated by valleys composed of softer, more easily eroded rock, which developed into streambeds and waterways.

Several types of deciduous forests covered this area when humans first arrived thousands of years ago. Most of these forests have since been logged, some many times. Forests dominated by oak and hickory can still be found. A few moist, well-drained coves and north- and east-facing slopes harbor mixed hardwood forest (mesophytic) communities that boast a rich diversity of herbaceous plants. The Oak Ridge National Laboratory manages a 34,000-acre reservation in the Ridge and Valley that protects over 1100 plant species, including 21 state-listed rare plants. There, a number of natural openings, referred to as glades and barrens, are found in places where the soil is extremely shallow. These small but ecologically significant areas often harbor rare and unusual plants, some of which are endemic and limited to these unique habitats.

Cumberland Plateau
Rising abruptly 1000 feet from the Ridge and Valley to the east, the 50-mile-wide Cumberland Plateau is composed of relatively flat sedimentary rocks that were buried at great depth until the last few tens of millions of years. The plateau is approximately 1700 to 2000 feet above sea level, with the exception of the Cumberland Mountain section in the northeastern part, which reaches 3500 feet in elevation. Recognizable by the small "mountains" stacked on top of the Cumberland Plateau, the Cumberland Mountain section is distinctive. The bulk of the plateau contains rolling hills dissected by numerous deep gorges.

EDWARD SCHELL

Angel Falls Overlook on Big South Fork, Cumberland Plateau

There is some folding and faulting on the plateau, but not to the same degree as seen in the Blue Ridge and the Ridge and Valley. The clearest example, the Sequatchie Valley, is an eroded upward fold (anticline) or cleft that divides the southern half of the plateau in a northeast-southwest direction. The Sequatchie Valley is geologically significant because it is considered one of the longest and straightest clefts in the world.

The flat to rolling plateau surface is underlaid with sandstone, creating dry, exposed hills and poorly drained, acidic watercourses. In contrast, the gorges dissecting the plateau have bedrock underlying the more mesic slopes and ravines made of calcium-rich limestone. The upland and slope habitats, with their different substrates and topographic features, harbor distinct plant communities.

The typical upland plateau habitats are dominated by oak-hickory forests, though plant communities ranging from red maple–blackgum seepage bogs to pine communities on dry ridges and cliff edges can be found. Both wetland and cliff environments provide habitats for a number of unusual plants. Relict plant species, though not common, may be found in cool ravines, gorges, and sinkholes throughout the plateau. Many of the lower slopes of the plateau exhibit karst topography, where the limestone has collapsed or dissolved into underlying caverns to form caves or sinkholes.

In many places along the escarpment where erosion has breached the sandstone cap, steep and deep ravines have formed. Several of these sites are state-protected natural areas, including places such as Fall Creek Falls, Savage Gulf, and Fiery Gizzard. At 256 feet, Fall Creek Falls is the highest waterfall in the United States east of the Rocky Mountains. Savage Gulf contains the only large tract (between 1500 and 2000 acres) of old-growth mixed mesophytic forest in Tennessee.

Interior Low Plateau

Included in this physiographic province are the Highland Rim and the Central Basin. From the Cumberland Plateau, elevations drop sharply on the west to the Highland Rim, an upland plain that surrounds the Nashville or Central Basin.

The Highland Rim resembles a doughnut completely encircling the Central Basin, which appears as a depressed bull's-eye on a topographic map of Middle Tennessee. The Highland Rim rises above the Central Basin, averaging 1000 feet above sea level in the east to 650 feet in the west.

The Eastern and Western Highland Rims sometimes are considered to be two separate sub-provinces, because in Tennessee, they are mostly separated by the Central Basin. The rocks of both regions formed underwater between 600 and 325 million years ago. The entire rim is underlaid by limestone and shale, and similar to the lower slopes of the Cumberland Plateau, areas of karst topography are present.

Eastern Highland Rim

Early explorers and travelers in Tennessee ascribed the name "barrens" to grass-dominated openings in the forest of the Eastern Highland Rim that were apparently unsuitable for cultivation. The barrens are now recognized for their remarkable number of rare plants. All barrens appear to be successional; that is, the vegetational composition is in transition. Only naturally occurring fires and human intervention have kept areas like May Prairie, a relict tall-grass prairie on the Eastern Highland Rim, intact. May Prairie is extraordinary because of disjunct plant populations that are isolated from their primary geographical ranges in the midwestern prairies and the Atlantic and Gulf Coastal Plain.

Another interesting habitat in this region is the upland swamp. Many of these swamps, such as Mingo Swamp, Goose Pond, and Sinking Pond, are associated with sinkholes or karst features. As with many wetland habitats, upland swamps were more common in the past than now. They contain unique assemblages of plants, often including rare or endangered species.

DENNIS HORN

Machine Falls at Short Springs State Natural Area, Eastern Highland Rim

Central Basin

The Central Basin was originally a high dome in the center of the Highland Rim, which fractured and eroded around 40 million years ago to form the present sunken basin. Today, the Central Basin is from 300 to 500 feet lower than the Highland Rim. The oldest rocks at the center of the basin are about 500 million years old.

Much of the basin exhibits karst terrain—caves and sinkholes are common. The most distinctive plant communities of this sub-province are the limestone cedar glades, natural openings in cedar-deciduous forests that have limestone bedrock at or near the surface. The rock is bare or covered with thin soil and populated by herbaceous plants, especially grasses. Tending toward wet conditions in winter and spring and drought conditions in summer and fall, cedar glades are known for their remarkable number of endemic plants.

Western Highland Rim

This sub-province extends west from the Central Basin to the sand hills of the Coastal Plain, a few miles west of the Tennessee River. Some consider the corridor of the north-flowing Tennessee River to be a separate sub-province, but here it is treated as an extension of the Western Rim. This region is more dissected by rivers and small tributaries than the Eastern Rim. The soils

on top of the rim generally are not well suited for cultivation.

In addition to the Tennessee River, several other rivers, including the Cumberland, the Duck, and the Buffalo, have cut into the Rim, as they flow generally northwestward. The slopes and steep ravines along these streams and their tributaries harbor a number of unusual floral elements. Many rare plants are found around springy seeps near the source of these tributaries. The uplands immediately west of the Tennessee River contain unique limestone and shale formations with several small barrens that support an abundance of rare plants and fossils.

Cedar Glade with Tennessee Coneflower, Central Basin

KURT EMMANUELE

Coastal Plain

In West Tennessee, the Coastal Plain province is the area mostly between the Tennessee River and the Mississippi River. It is divided into two sub-provinces, the Inner Coastal Plain and the Mississippi Floodplain.

Inner Coastal Plain

The Inner Coastal Plain forms part of the Mississippi Embayment, an area that was most recently submerged 75 million years ago under an extension of the Gulf of Mexico. This inland sea retreated about 40 million years ago, at which time both the western portion of the Tennessee River and the Mississippi River came into being. This sub-province encompasses two distinct areas: the sand hills just west of the Western Valley of the Tennessee River and the loess-capped, broad, flat plain that extends westward to the Chickasaw Bluffs along the Mississippi River. Following the retreat of the glaciers 10,000 years ago, tens of feet of windborne soil (loess) were deposited along the western portion of the Inner Coastal Plain, particularly in the Chickasaw Bluffs area.

Although largely under cultivation today, much of the Inner Coastal Plain was once covered with bottomland forest, broken up by intermittent prairies and savannas, occasional remnants of which are visible today. Oak and hickory trees dominate both the dry upland and moist forest slopes east of the Chickasaw Bluffs, in company with maples, sweetgum, and American Holly. Swamps and bottomlands provide habitat for bald-cypress trees and other wetland species.

Loess-capped bluffs, rising 100 feet above the alluvial plain of the Mississippi River, extend from Kentucky to Louisiana. The four Chickasaw Bluffs of West Tennessee are populated by forests and wildflowers that are more similar to the cove hardwood forests of the Smoky Mountains and the Cumberland Plateau than to the forests of the Mississippi Embayment.

EDWARD SCHELL

Reelfoot Lake with bald-cypress trees, Mississippi Floodplain

Mississippi Floodplain

As a snowflake melts on Clingman's Dome in the Smoky Mountains, it combines with other runoff water that makes its way to the Tennessee River. It is bound for the Mississippi River, flowing through all the physiographic provinces of the state.

Aerial views of the Mississippi reveal a serpentine river and a multitude of oxbow lakes, evidence that the channel has migrated many times. The Mississippi Floodplain comprises the alluvial plain subject to flooding along the Mississippi River and, in Tennessee, averages less than eight miles wide.

Windborne soil and recent sediments from the floodwaters of the Mississippi River fill the flood plain. The area is a vast complex of bottomland hardwood forest, dominated by sweetgum, blackgum, and white ash, and swamp forest, by bald-cypress and water tupelo.

Active faults underlie the floodplain, as evidenced by the well-known series of massive earthquakes that occurred along the New Madrid Fault during the winter of 1811–12, temporarily reversing the flow of the Mississippi River and creating Reelfoot Lake. This, the largest natural lake in the state, has a complex aquatic plant community dominated by bald-cypress trees.

***

Tennessee's five distinct physiographic provinces and their sub-provinces provide numerous diverse habitats for plants. From the evergreen forests that cap the ancient

mountains of the Blue Ridge to the bald-cypress swamps that track the shifting course of the Mississippi River, the state encompasses a wide variety of plant communities, populated by an abundance of wildflowers.

Native Americans in Tennessee

The name Tennessee is believed to be from *Tanasi*, a name given by the Cherokee people to a village located on the Little Tennessee River and subsequently used for the region encompassing the river. Before the Europeans arrived, the various Native American peoples who lived in Tennessee and the broader southeastern region mostly lived in harmony with the land and its offerings.

According to studies of artifacts recovered in Russell Cave, Alabama, early humans entered the Southeast 10,000 years ago, or earlier, in pursuit of the massive mastodon, the saber-toothed tiger, and the giant beaver. Then, in approximately 6000 to 5000 BCE, a new era began. Although long hunting trips still took place and some native peoples still moved in seasonal cycles to hunt and gather resources, people began to roam less and settle in villages, an example of which is the Eva Site, a prehistoric Native American encampment in Benton County, in West Tennessee. Besides hunting, they fished and gathered wild foods like roots, nuts, and berries.

After villages were established, people in Tennessee began cultivating wild and "domesticated" native plants, around 4000 years ago. Several thousand years later, when maize (corn) and other non-native plants such as pumpkin and beans were brought from Mexico and South America, agriculture gained importance. Maize was cultivated as a primary crop and could be stored and adapted to multiple uses—from vegetable to bread to nutritious beverage—and village life was transformed. Religion, arts, and the development of skills and crafts, medicine, and clothing became essential elements of the culture.

The first white man known to have come to Tennessee was the Spanish explorer Hernando de Soto in 1540. Later written accounts from the 1700s tell us that European immigrants found vast tracts of forested land, interspersed with prairie-like openings and barrens, abundant and untapped underground resources, and wild and free-flowing waterways. At this time, Tennessee was inhabited by several different Native American groups. From west to east, it is thought that the most dominant peoples were the Chickasaw (also known as Chikasah), the Yuchi, and the Cherokee.

The Chickasaw claimed western Tennessee, while the Cherokee lived on the upper portions of the Tennessee River and proclaimed the eastern part of the state as hunting territory. Around 1700, the Yuchi, who were considered part of the Creek people, and other small tribes, were driven from the central areas to the south. About this time, the Chickasaws and Cherokees joined to force the Shawnees out of the north-central region into an area north of the Ohio River. In fact, in 1715 and again in 1745, the Chickasaws and Cherokees cooperated to expel bands of Shawnees from the rich hunting lands on the site that is now Nashville. Thereafter, Middle Tennessee was used primarily as a hunting ground, causing territorial disputes between the Chickasaw and Cherokee peoples, but inhabited by neither. Both tribes maintained their claims to much of Tennessee into the 1800s, at which time the Native American peoples were displaced by European settlers, and the traditional way of life for the Native Americans would never be the same again.

Ethnobotany

Ethnobotany is the study of the relationship between people and plants. Native Americans developed an intimate knowledge of plants and their uses, which dates back to early times (at least 10,000 years ago) and was passed down through generations as traditional knowledge, as well as newer uses that resulted from plant introductions by European settlers.

Plants were used by Native Americans for medicine, food, fibers, dyes, contraceptives, cleaning agents, containers, fertilizers, fuels, incense and fragrance, insecticides, jewelry, lubricants, musical instruments, preservatives, smoking material and snuff, tools, toys, and weapons. When applicable, the **Notes** section of a wildflower description in this book highlights some of the relationships and uses of plants by Native Americans and early settlers in the hope that readers may gain an appreciation of how all our lives are influenced by plants.

Ethnobotany is a science that may hold the keys for important discoveries in the future. The diminishing rain forests may harbor plants that will help us conquer diseases, and undiscovered or as yet unstudied plants may provide solutions for expanding energy and food resources for our planet's escalating population.

Plants Used as Medicine

According to the World Health Organization (WHO), 25 percent of modern medicines are derived from plants that were first used traditionally. WHO also states that in some developing countries (in Africa, for example), roughly 80 percent of the people rely on traditional medicine for their primary health care needs. Plants continue to yield important pharmacological breakthroughs, while providing an arena for continued exploration and experimentation.

Plants are useful as medicines in part owing to the evolution of secondary chemicals, which they produce to enhance their survival. For example, willows (*Salix*) produce salicylic acid, a water-soluble plant poison that washes off the leaves to the ground below and inhibits the growth of competing plants. This salicylic acid is the same substance from which aspirin was first derived and is an active ingredient in many "sports creams" for relieving muscle pain. In search of new medicines, ethnobotanists recognize that the difference between a poison, a medicine, and a narcotic may only be an adjustment in dosage or in preparation. Some plant substances taken in large doses can be fatal, while smaller doses may prove medicinal. An instance of this is Monkshood (*Aconitum*), which traditionally has been used to treat acute respiratory and throat infections and as an anesthetic. This plant is also regarded as being highly poisonous.

When reading about a traditional use of a plant, a reader may ask, "Does it work?" The effectiveness of many of these herbal medicines has been supported, both by their continued usage over hundreds of years and by firsthand accounts from individuals, their families, and communities. Even so, disagreements still exist over whether or not certain plants are as effective as once thought. Many plants that have been used as medicine overlap as a source of food (please see the next section). Plants in the Rose Family (Rosaceae) produce apples (*Malus*); almonds, cherries, peaches (all *Prunus*); and pears (*Pyrus*). Yet they also produce toxic

substances, found in the leaves, bark, and fruits of many species, which have been used medicinally.

Information on the traditional medicinal uses of plants has been provided in this book only as a point of interest or topic for further discussion or research. Because of the fragile status of many of the plants, we encourage you to enjoy viewing them **without picking or disturbing them in any way.**

Plants Used as Food

For thousands of years, Native Americans have used plants to add flavor, essential nutrients, and minerals to their meals. The main meat of the meal was from fish, birds, deer, raccoons, opossums, and other game. It has been estimated that 60 percent of the food supply of southeastern Native Americans came from plant foods.

EDWARD SCHELL

April in Tennessee with redbuds and dogwoods

In no way should this book be viewed as a "how-to" reference for using plants as medicine, nor do we advocate using plants in the manner described. We DO NOT recommend experimentation by readers and caution that many of the plants described in this book can be harmful or poisonous.

By 2500 years ago, cultivation of native plants for food had become important, but beginning about 1000 years ago, corn, beans, and squash became staple foods for many Native Americans in our region. Bernard Romans, in *A Concise Natural History of East and West Florida*, published in 1775, noted that the Creeks prepared corn in at least 42 different ways. Although there were many kinds of corn, the dent, flint, and sweet varieties were the most common. Corn was boiled, roasted, parched, baked, dried and ground into flour, used in bread, combined with water to make an unfermented drink, and eaten alone or in combination with other foods.

Other plants that were commonly used in meals include fruits, such as persimmons (*Diospyros*), strawberries (*Fragaria*), blueberries and huckleberries (both *Vaccinium*), crab apples (*Malus*), and wild grapes (*Vitis*); green vegetables, which were mostly shoots and leaves; root vegetables, from bulbs, tubers, rhizomes, and corms; seasonings and flavorings, collected from seeds and leaves; and salt substitutes that were made from the ashes of herbs. Nutritious seeds, which are high in protein, carbohydrates, fat, and essential amino acids, were an essential element of the Native American diet, as well. Sunflower seeds were collected, as well as seeds from grasses, pond lilies, and other plants. Nuts from various trees were also important, primarily pecans and hickories (both *Carya*), walnuts (*Juglans*), chestnuts (*Castanea*), and hazelnuts (*Corylus*).

In Virginia and the Carolinas and as far south as northern Georgia, the Cherokee made maple sugar and syrup by tapping sugar maple trees (*Acer saccharum*). These products were an important source of barter for goods that could not otherwise be obtained in the Cherokee region.

Today, some families in the South still make use of traditional plants. For example, Pokeweed (*Phytolacca americana*), also called Poke Salad, is harvested for the young shoots and leaves, which are edible when cooked as greens. This ongoing usage relates to documented stories of Native Americans and their rich knowledge and understanding of plants.

Plants Used as Fibers and Dyes

Native Americans used plants to weave baskets, mats and even cloth, and plant fibers were tightly spun into rope, thread, and fishing line, among other practical uses. One of the more commonly used fiber plants is Common Cattail (*Typha latifolia*), with almost every part of the plant being useful: fibers were woven into containers, such as baskets for carrying water, the fuzzy down was used as stuffing for mattresses and making diapers, and the yellow pollen was used as flour for eating! Some of the other plants found in this book that were used for their fibers are Common Sunflower (*Helianthus annuus*), Indian Hemp (*Apocynum cannabinum*), Rattlesnake Master (*Eryngium yuccifolium*), Stinging Nettle (*Urtica dioica*), and Swamp Milkweed (*Asclepias incarnata*).

WARNING!
Use extreme care when looking for edible plants, because poisonous plants may look similar to and grow alongside those that are edible. This book does not advocate that readers harvest plants for eating at any time. There are numerous issues regarding harvesting—plant identification, permission for collecting, the possibility of poisoning, bacterial infections and pathogenic microorganisms, proper washing, and preparation. Also, plant conservation is a major concern in this time of increased human population and diminished natural habitats.

Some plants contain substances that make useful dyes, such as Bloodroot (*Sanguinaria canadensis*), from which a red dye can be made. Dyes are most often obtained from the petals of the flowers, but as in the case of Bloodroot, dye is made from the rhizomes. Dyes are also prepared from the fruit and bark. Some plants that have been used as dyes by Native Americans are Garden Coreopsis (*Coreopsis tinctoria*), Goldenseal (*Hydrastis canadensis*), Gray-Headed Cone-flower (*Ratibida pinnata*), Hoary Puccoon (*Lithospermum canescens*), Marsh Marigold (*Caltha palustris*), Prairie Larkspur (*Delphinium virescens*), and White Baneberry (*Actaea pachypoda*).

Field Botany in Tennessee

The diverse flora of Tennessee has attracted botanists for more than two centuries. The state's ancient mountains, bald-cypress swamps, limestone glades, and grassy prairies have offered naturalists and other scientists a wealth of plants to discover, collect, catalog, and otherwise study.

English-born nurseryman John Fraser (1750–1811) was the first explorer-naturalist of note to visit Tennessee. He was followed by a host of others, including French botanist André Michaux (1746–1802) and his son François (1770–1855); botanist and scholar Thomas Nuttall (1786–1859), who later joined the faculty at Harvard; and the eccentric Constantine Samuel Rafinesque (1783–1840), who taught at Transylvania University in Lexington, Kentucky. Asa Gray (1810–88), who dominated American botany during the late 19th century, collected plants in Tennessee, as did Florida physician A.W. Chapman (1809–99), the foremost voice in Southern botany at the time.

German-born physician Augustin Gattinger (1825–1903) was the first Tennessee botanist of national stature. He emigrated from Germany to the United States in 1849 and settled in East Tennessee, where he practiced medicine. During the Civil War, he moved to Nashville, where he later served as Tennessee's State Librarian. Gattinger wrote the first books devoted specifically to the plant life of Tennessee, most notably *The Flora of Tennessee and a Philosophy of Botany*, published in 1901. He corresponded with eminent botanists of the day and was the source of many Tennessee plants listed in Chapman's *Southern Flora*. In 1890, the University of Tennessee acquired Gattinger's extensive plant collection as the nucleus of their growing herbarium. The University's Department of Botany was becoming the center of taxonomic and floristic studies in the state.

A.J. "Jack" Sharp (1904–97) taught botany at the University of Tennessee for 45 years. He spearheaded the rebuilding of the UT herbarium after it was destroyed by fire in 1934. Sharp, assisted by Edward E.C. Clebsch and other faculty, took numerous collection trips throughout the state to find specimens to replace and augment those that had been lost in the fire. On one of those trips, in July 1947, they discovered May Prairie in Coffee County, the largest and best relict prairie remaining in the state.

Jesse Shaver (1888–1961), professor of biology at George Peabody College for Teachers in Nashville, was also an influential botanist. In 1953, Shaver published *Ferns of Tennessee*. As an editor of the *Journal of the Tennessee Academy of Science* for 25 years, he made this publication a repository of much of the botanical work being done in the state.

In the late 1940s, Elsie Quarterman, professor of biology at Vanderbilt University, and her students began comprehensive studies of the cedar glade communities of Middle Tennessee. Also at Vanderbilt, Robert Kral expanded the Vanderbilt herbarium to house over 300,000 specimens. (That collection has since been relocated to the Botanical Research Institute of Texas.)

Currently, Tennessee is seeing a resurgence of interest in field botany. In 1993 and 1997, Kral co-authored, with Edward W. Chester of Austin Peay State University and B. Eugene Wofford, Hal R. DeSelm, and A. Murray Evans of the University of Tennessee, the

KURT EMMANUELE

Roan Mountain Highlands

two-volume *Atlas of Tennessee Vascular Plants*. In addition, Austin Peay operates a center for field biology, while a center for cedar glade studies has recently been established at Middle Tennessee State University. Since 1997, an All-Taxa Biodiversity Inventory has been ongoing in the Great Smoky Mountains National Park, with a similar survey now underway in the Tennessee state parks.

The Tennessee Native Plant Society

In 1978, A. Murray Evans of the University of Tennessee and Robert Farmer of the Tennessee Valley Authority co-founded the Tennessee Native Plant Society (TNPS). They asked people to send $1 in exchange for a charter membership. The promotion was successful, and in less than two months, 400 people from across the state had joined. Members of TNPS include professional and amateur botanists, as well as many others who simply enjoy wildflowers.

The society offers its members frequent field trips to botanically interesting sites. The quarterly newsletter contains plant-related information about the field trips and articles of interest to the membership. The annual meeting is always held in a picturesque locale in the state where members can take advantage of presentations and field trips.

A Brief History of This Project

This adventure began in 1991, when James I. ("Bus") Jones spearheaded the idea of producing a field guide to the wildflowers of Tennessee. In producing this book, almost 100 dedicated volunteers, most from the Tennessee Native Plant Society, have given generously of their time and expertise—hundreds of miles of trails have been hiked in search of the "perfect" photograph of a wildflower, untold cases of poison ivy, spider bites, bee stings, blisters, and sunburns were endured, and five presidents of TNPS have served seven terms. Remarkable timing brought together TNPS and Lone Pine Publishing, and generous donors enthusiastically supported the project with their contributions. This book represents a monumental 14-year achievement by passionate wildflower enthusiasts from Tennessee and beyond.

Plant Conservation

The Tennessee Native Plant Society actively supports the protection and enhancement of wild plant communities, the places where the wildflowers in this book are found.

The official purposes of TNPS are to assist in the exchange of information and encourage fellowship among Tennessee's botanists, both amateur and professional; to promote public education about Tennessee flora and wild plants; to provide, through publication of a newsletter or journal, a formal means of documenting information on Tennessee flora and of informing the public about wild plants; and to promote the protection and enhancement of Tennessee's wild plant communities.

For more information about TNPS and to become a member, please visit http://www.tnps.org or write TNPS, P.O. Box 159274, Nashville, TN 37215.

Clearly, many species of plants and animals have met their match in humans, because extinction rates are at an all-time high. Habitat destruction is the primary cause of species endangerment and extinction. Also, exotic species are outcompeting native plants, introducing parasites and pathogens, and disrupting the balance of ecosystems. Furthermore, we are loving our plants to death—ironically, **interest in the use of native plants for gardening and ethnobotany has led to the unethical collection of plants from the wild, which can damage or even obliterate local populations.**

Habitat Destruction

In order to survive, wild plants need wild places. Our natural areas are the repositories for the plants and animals that represent the diversity of life on Earth, but these are shrinking rapidly. Residential, agricultural, and

EDWARD SCHELL

Fall Creek Falls from the gorge below, Cumberland Plateau

commercial development are crowding out natural communities. Deforestation is occurring in some parts of Tennessee and the surrounding region at an historic and frightening pace. Human beings and our activities, particularly urbanization and deforestation, have caused habitat devastation and degradation to occur at an unprecedented rate. We must preserve our natural communities if we expect our diverse flora to survive.

Exotic Pest Plants

Native species are those plants and animals that have been a part of a specific geographic area for a long time. Exotic species, on the other hand, are those that evolved elsewhere and have been introduced into new environments by way of human activity, either purposefully or accidentally. Approximately 550 non-native plants have been introduced since European settlement and now comprise nearly 20 percent of Tennessee's flora.

Exotic plant species vary in their impact on natural communities. The most famous example in the Southeast is Kudzu (*Pueraria lobata*), a vine native to Japan that was introduced in 1876 at the U.S. Centennial Exposition in Philadelphia. Subsequently, it was widely distributed by the U.S. Department of Agriculture (USDA) to prevent soil erosion. Some people call it the "Mile-a-Minute Vine" and "The Vine that Ate the South," but actually, there are pest plants much more destructive and aggressive than Kudzu.

Discretion should be used when choosing plants for landscaping and gardening to protect neighboring natural areas from exotic species. For more information, please visit the Tennessee Exotic Pest Plant Council's website at http://www.tneppc.org/. A list of the major culprits, as well as an online pest plant management manual is posted.

Plant Collecting

Wild plants never should be removed from their natural habitats for personal or commercial purposes unless they are being rescued from destruction by development. Today, with the current popularity of gardening with native plants, there are many reputable nurseries that propagate these plants. Gardeners and those who use plants for medicinal or edible purposes are encouraged to look for these nurseries and ask about the sources of their native plant stock. If a plant will survive in the garden, a nurseryman is propagating it. **Ask for plants labeled "nursery propagated" to ensure that a plant was not dug from the wild.**

Appreciate and Preserve

TNPS advocates enjoying—indeed, celebrating—wildflowers in their natural habitats. The Society shares Augustin Gattinger's love for Tennessee's splendid diversity of plants, which is evident in his timeless advice to readers of his *Flora of Tennessee and a Philosophy of Botany*, in which he states, "For truth, my honored Tennessee friends, go and see, and learn to appreciate and to preserve such great ornaments of your native land."

Sweet Shrub, Carolina Allspice
Calycanthus floridus var. *floridus*

GENERAL: Highly variable **deciduous shrub**, 3–10 ft. tall. **LEAVES:** Aromatic, opposite, oval, pointed at both ends, 2–6 in. long, often with a **soft fuzz beneath**. **FLOWERS:** Perfect, **maroon or brownish**, cup-shaped, 1–3 in. wide, radially symmetric, **many sepals and petals** (that appear similar), also many stamens and pistils; solitary on short branches; **crushed petals have an aroma of strawberry**, cantaloupe or fermenting grapes. April–May. **FRUITS:** Indehiscent with numerous achenes enclosed. **WHERE FOUND:** Streambanks, hillsides, and moist woods. In the eastern U.S., from NY and OH, south to the Gulf Coastal Plain. In TN, primarily from the Eastern Highland Rim eastward, also found sporadically westward. Occasional.

JERRY DROWN

NOTES: The genus name *Calycanthus* comes from the Greek words *calyx*, an easy reference to "calyx," the outer envelope of the flower formed by sepals, and *anthus*, meaning "flower." • The name **Carolina Allspice** refers to the **smell of the crushed leaves**. This plant is also known as Eastern Sweetshrub and Strawberry Shrub for the fragrance of the flowers. • A tea made from the roots and bark was used by the Cherokee as a diuretic for kidney and urinary complaints and as eye drops to treat worsening vision.

Lizard's Tail • *Saururus cernuus*

GENERAL: Erect, branched, leafy perennial herb, 2–4 ft. tall, with **jointed stems**. **LEAVES:** Alternate, asymmetrically heart-shaped, 2.5–6.0 in. long and ½ as wide; on long, basally sheathing petioles. **FLOWERS:** Perfect; sepals and petals absent; filaments, 6–8, are **white** and much longer than pistils; borne in a dense terminal **spike**, 2.5–6.0 in. long, **nodding at the tip like a "tail."** May–August. **FRUITS:** Nearly round, strongly wrinkled capsules, about 0.1 in. wide. **WHERE FOUND:** Forms **large colonies** along the edges of swamps and shallow water throughout the eastern U.S. In TN, more common in the western region. Common.

NOTES: This plant can be used in gardens or to stabilize banks. It survives in sun or shade and has a **pleasant fragrance**. • This species is also called Water-Dragon and Breastweed, which refers to its use by Native Americans as a root poultice on infected breasts, wounds, and inflammations. It has been studied for its chemical and pharmacological properties; several of its compounds have a sedative effect.

NITA R. HEILMAN

Pipe Vine, Dutchman's Pipe
Aristolochia macrophylla

GENERAL: Woody perennial, high-climbing, **twining vine** to 65 ft. long. **LEAVES:** Alternate, **heart-shaped**, 4–10 in. wide, smooth to slightly hairy beneath. **FLOWERS:** Typically **purplish green**, about 1.6 in. long, strongly bent and **pipe-shaped**; pipe "face" is about 1 in. wide, with 3 equal lobes and **purple-brown mouth**; borne on long stalks from the leaf axils. April–June. **FRUITS:** Cylindric, 6-sided capsules, 3 in. long. **WHERE FOUND:** Rich woods in the Appalachian Mountains from southern PA to northern GA. In TN, from the Eastern Highland Rim eastward, also Giles County. Occasional. *A. durior.*

NOTES: The genus name *Aristolochia* is derived from a Greek phrase meaning "assist in childbirth" referring to the medicinal use of some plants in this genus. The genus name more specifically reveals that the plant contains **aristolochic acid**, an antiseptic and antitumor compound. The species name *macrophylla* means "large leaf," referring to the noticeably large leaves of this plant. • The unusual flowers of Pipe Vine attract and trap small flies or midges. The following day, the flower stops producing the scent that attracted the flies and releases pollen onto them. Only then does the flower release the flies so the pollen may be transported to another flower. • The larvae of Pipevine Swallowtail butterflies feed on the leaves of Pipe Vine. • Surprisingly, some Virginia farmers consider this picturesque plant a weed.

DENNIS HORN

Woolly Dutchman's Pipe
Aristolochia tomentosa

GENERAL: Woody perennial, twining, downy **vine** to 80 ft. long. **LEAVES:** Alternate, **heart-shaped** to nearly round, 4–6 in. wide, **softly hairy underneath**. **FLOWERS:** Yellowish (sometimes greenish); about 1.6 in. long; **covered with matted, woolly hairs**; strongly bent and **pipe-shaped**; pipe "face" is about 1 in. wide, with **3 equal lobes** and **purple-brown mouth**; borne on long stalks from the leaf axils. April–May. **FRUITS:** Cylindric, 6-sided capsules, 1–3 in. long. **WHERE FOUND:** Wet woods and streambanks from southern IN to KS, southward. In TN, mostly in the western 2/3 of the state. Occasional. **SIMILAR SPECIES:** VIRGINIA SNAKEROOT (**A. serpentaria**) is an erect herb, 8–24 in. tall; with **arrow-shaped leaves**; small, pipe-shaped flowers on stalks from the lowest leaf nodes; pipe face has **3 unequal lobes**. Rich upland woods throughout the eastern U.S. and TN. Frequent. May–June.

NOTES: The species name *tomentosa* means "densely woolly with matted hairs," referring to the hairs on the flowers. • The larvae of the Spiny Gulf Fritillary butterfly store toxins from eating **Woolly Dutchman's Pipe** in their bodies to protect them from predators. • Traditionally, a weak tea made from small amounts of the root was used to treat fevers, stomach ailments, and snakebite, and was gargled for sore throats, among other medicinal uses.

MARY MARTIN SCHAFFNER

Wild Ginger • *Asarum canadense*

GENERAL: Early spring perennial herb, **stemless**, with a pair of leaves on long, downy stalks arising from an elongated rhizome; **rhizomes have the taste and smell of true ginger. LEAVES:** Opposite, simple, downy, heart-shaped, 3–5 in. wide; leaves disappear completely in winter. **FLOWERS:** Solitary, on a 1–2 in. peduncle emerging from the fork at the base of the leaf stalks; **petals absent; flower is a maroon, urn-shaped calyx**, about 1 in. long, with 3 long, spreading to reflexed, pointed lobes; flowers commonly lie on the ground beneath leaf litter. April–May. **FRUITS:** Small, 6-celled capsules. **WHERE FOUND:** Rich woods from New Brunswick, Ontario, and MN, south to northern GA and AL. Throughout TN. Common.

NOTES: As the flowers of this plant lie on the ground, they are **pollinated by crawling and flying insects,** such as ants, beetles, and flies. • The rhizomes were collected by Native Americans and used to **flavor meat and fish dishes** and to make a tea for relieving many ailments, including indigestion, coughs, heart conditions, cramps, fevers, colds, and sore throats.

KURT EMMANUELE

Little Brown Jug

Hexastylis arifolia var. *ruthii*

GENERAL: Small, **stemless** perennial herb, with leaves arising from a short rhizome. **LEAVES:** Smooth, shiny, mottled, evergreen, mostly **arrow-shaped**, 2–6 in. long, on long stalks; usually one new leaf is added each year. **FLOWERS:** One to several, on stalks about 1 in. long arising from the rhizome; **petals absent;** flower is a **brown, jug-shaped calyx** about 1 in. long, constricted at the top, with 3 small, **erect lobes.** March–May. **FRUITS:** Fleshy capsules. **WHERE FOUND:** Rich woods in most of the southeastern U.S. In TN, from the Eastern Highland Rim eastward. Frequent. *Asarum arifolium.* **SIMILAR SPECIES: VARIABLELEAF HEARTLEAF (*H. heterophylla*)** has smooth, roundish, **evergreen leaves** with **heart-shaped bases;** flower is a brown calyx about 0.5 in. long, constricted at the top, with 3 small, **spreading lobes greater than 0.2 in. long.** Rich woods in the southern Appalachian Mountains. In TN, in Roane, Claiborne, Hawkins, Sullivan, Carter, Unicoi, Washington, Greene, and Cocke counties. Infrequent. April–June. **VIRGINIA HEARTLEAF (*H. virginica*)** is similar to Variableleaf Heartleaf, but the 3 small, **spreading calyx lobes are less than 0.16 in. long.** Moist or dry woods in the southern Appalachian Mountains. In TN, in Johnson, Scott, and Unicoi counties. Rare. April–May.

JERRY DROWN

NOTES: The genus name *Hexastylis* comes from the Greek words *hexa* and *stylis*, and refers to the six styles. • **Little Brown Jug** is the most widespread species in this genus. Its flowers are often hidden in leaf litter on the ground.

Shuttleworth's Ginger
Hexastylis shuttleworthii

GENERAL: Small, **stemless** perennial herb with several basal leaves arising from a somewhat elongated rhizome. **LEAVES:** Smooth, evergreen, heart-shaped, 2–4 in. long, often with a light green or white netting along the veins, on long stalks; usually 1 new leaf is added each year. **FLOWERS:** One to several, on stalks about 1 in. long arising from the rootstock; **petals absent**; flower is a **brown, jug-shaped calyx**, to **1.6 in. long**, wide at the bottom and narrower at the top, with 3 large, **spreading lobes** mottled with purple. April–June.
FRUITS: Fleshy capsules. **WHERE FOUND:** Rich woods in highlands of the southeastern U.S. In TN, in Franklin, Hamilton, Polk, McMinn, Monroe, Blount, Morgan, and Greene counties. Infrequent.
SIMILAR SPECIES: SOUTHERN HEARTLEAF (*H. contracta*) has a **brown calyx, 1 in. long**, encircled by a second constricted band. Rich woods in the uplands of KY, TN, and NC. In TN, in the Cumberland Plateau region. Infrequent. May–July.

NOTES: You may have to get on your hands and knees to see the flowers of **Shuttleworth's Ginger** because they lie prostrate on the ground. However, the flowers are large compared to other gingers.

HUGH NOURSE

Water Chinquapin, American
Lotus • *Nelumbo lutea*

GENERAL: Aquatic perennial, rising up to 3 ft. above the water surface. **LEAVES:** Often 24 in. across, round, peltate, at the water surface or emergent. **FLOWERS:** Solitary, **yellow, showy, to 10 in. wide**; borne above the leaves on long stalks. July–September. **FRUITS:** Numerous acorn-like **nuts**, 0.4 in. thick, loosely embedded in the 4-inch-wide receptacle, **rattle when mature. WHERE FOUND:** Ponds, lakes, and sloughs with mud bottoms. Irregular across the eastern U.S. Thinly scattered across TN. Occasional. **SIMILAR SPECIES:** SACRED LOTUS (*N. nucifera**) has **pink** flowers and is rarely seen in the wild, but has been reported from Montgomery County in TN. Introduced from eastern Asia and likely escaped.

NOTES: Water Chinquapin often **carpets the surface of a shallow pond or lake**, where it provides an excellent habitat and food source for aquatic wildlife. • Native Americans would boil the starchy rhizomes repeatedly to remove their acrid taste before eating them. The seeds and young leaves are edible as well. • The dried seedpods are borne erect until they mature, when they bend over and resemble a shower-head. They are often used in dried flower arrangements. • The stamens of **Sacred Lotus** flowers are reportedly used in Indochina for flavoring black tea.

DENNIS HORN

Yellow Pond Lily, Spatterdock
Nuphar luteum ssp. *macrophyllum*

GENERAL: Aquatic perennial herb, developing from a large submerged rhizome. **LEAVES:** Floating or erect, 4–12 in. long, broadly elliptic with a heart-shaped notch at the base. **FLOWERS: Cup-shaped, yellow,** 1.25–2.0 in. wide; borne at or slightly above the water surface. May–September. **FRUITS:** Broadly egg-shaped, leathery berries, about 0.6 in. long; many small seeds. **WHERE FOUND:** Ponds, lakes, and sloughs from southern ME to WI, south to FL and TX. More prevalent in West TN, scattered in Middle and East TN. Occasional. ***N. advena.***

NOTES: The **flowers** of this species are **small in size compared to the foliage** and to other water lilies, always seeming not yet ready to open, even when they are in full flower. • Even though the rhizomes are difficult to harvest, they have been used as food for many years. They are best gathered in winter, which involves digging in mud, usually many feet below the water surface. The rhizomes must be boiled repeatedly and peeled before being eaten.

TERRY LIVINGSTONE

Fragrant Water Lily
Nymphaea odorata

GENERAL: Aquatic perennial herb, flowering from large rhizomes. **LEAVES: Floating,** peltate, 4–12 in. across, nearly round with a slight heart-shaped flare at the notch, shiny on top and often purplish red underneath. **FLOWERS:** Solitary, **white, fragrant,** 3–6 in. across, 4 sepals, numerous petals and yellow stamens; borne at or above the water surface. July–August. **FRUITS:** Berry-like, about 1 in. in diameter, surrounded by remnant petals. **WHERE FOUND:** Ponds, lakes, and sloughs. More common on the Coastal Plain, but found throughout the eastern U.S. and southeastern Canada. In TN, in Lake, Obion, Stewart, Lewis, Davidson, Putnam, and Sevier counties. Infrequent.

CAROL NOURSE

NOTES: The genus *Nymphaea* is named after the nymphs of Greek mythology, who were reputed to live in streams and ponds, the natural habitat of water lilies. • Water lilies are considered primitive flowering plants; to date, the oldest fossil record of angiosperm pollen, dating from 140 million years ago, is from a water lily. • The **leaves** are of particular interest—the **underside is made up of a series of ribs and air pockets that help the large leaves to float,** and the stomates (air holes) are on the top of the leaves. • Native Americans are reputed to have popped water lily seeds like popcorn and ground the dried rhizomes into flour.

W. MICHAEL DENNIS

Water Shield · *Brasenia schreberi*

GENERAL: Aquatic perennial with submerged stems to 6 ft. long, **covered with a slippery gelatinous material. LEAVES:** Alternate, floating, long-petioled, oval blades, 2–4 in. long; **undersurfaces of** leaves and underwater parts are heavily **coated with a mucilaginous, jelly-like substance. FLOWERS:** Solitary, sepals and petals are 3–4 each, mostly alike, **dull purple;** flowers are axillary, emergent on stout stalks several inches long. June–July. **FRUITS:** Small, indehiscent, leathery, and nut-like; 1–2 seeds. **WHERE FOUND:** Not common, but may be locally abundant in ponds and quiet waters throughout the eastern U.S. Mostly in Middle and West TN. Occasional. **SIMILAR SPECIES:** FANWORT (*Cabomba caroliniana*) has dissected, submerged leaves and floating peltate **leaves without the jelly-like material; white petals** have a yellow base. Found in similar habitat from NJ to OH and MO, south to FL and TX. In West TN, in Lake, Obion, and Weakley counties. Rare. May–June.

NOTES: Water Shield is also known as Deerfood, Egg Bonnet, Frogleaf, and Water Jelly.
• A characteristic that distinguishes Water Shield from water lilies is the small, oval leaves without a slit or notch. • Water Shield was well known by Native Americans: the leaves and roots are edible, and it was used as an herbal remedy for pulmonary complaints and dysentery. The roots are eaten worldwide, and the small, round seeds are an important food source for wildlife.

Buttercup Family (Ranunculaceae)

The Buttercup Family, also known as the Crowfoot Family, contains mostly annual or perennial herbs, shrubs, and woody vines (*Clematis*) found primarily in cooler temperate regions, and especially in the Northern Hemisphere. Many species are valuable as ornamentals, especially anemone, clematis, columbine, delphinium, hellebore, and peony. Several members of the family are important medicinally, containing compounds for treating a wide variety of ailments from headaches, fever, halitosis, and snakebites to preventing the plague. Several species are very poisonous and can be lethal. Historically, the juice of *Aconitum* species was used on the tips of arrows for killing wolves.

1a. Flowers bilaterally symmetric **2**
   2a. Upper sepal hooded; petals 2 . . . . **Aconitum**
   2b. Upper sepal spurred; petals 2 or 4 . . . . **3**
      3a. Petals 2, united; carpel 1; introduced . . . . **Consolida**
      3b. Petals 4, distinct; carpels 2 or more; native . . . . **Delphinium**
1b. Flowers radially symmetric **4**
   4a. Petals distinctly spurred . . . . **Aquilegia**
   4b. Petals either not spurred or absent **5**
      5a. Low shrubs, wood yellow . . . . **Xanthorhiza**
      5b. Herbs **6**
         6a. Sepals or petals yellow **7**
            7a. Petals present, with a nectar gland at the base;
                fruit an achene . . . . **Ranunculus**
            7b. Petals absent, sepals showy; fruit a follicle . . . . **Caltha**
         6b. Sepals or petals (if present) not yellow, either white
           or variously colored **8**
            8a. Vines; leaves all opposite; mature styles plumose and several times longer
                than achene body . . . . **Clematis**
            8b. Not vines; at least some leaves alternate, whorled, or basal (involucral leaves
                occasionally opposite or whorled); mature styles not plumose **9**
               9a. Leaves all basal, 3-lobed, often purple beneath . . . . **Hepatica**
               9b. Stem leaves present, variously compound or simple,
                  typically green **10**
                  10a. Perianth (if present) small and inconspicuous (less than 0.3 in. long),
                     often early deciduous; stamens often showy **11**
                     11a. Leaves simple or palmately lobed **12**

Actaea
p. 53

Anemone
p. 54

Aquilegia
p. 55

12a. Flowers solitary; fruit a berry . . . . ***Hydrastis***

12b. Flowers numerous; fruit a dehiscent,
1-seeded utricle . . . . ***Trautvetteria***

11b. Leaves 1–3-ternately compound **13**

13a. Flowers in branched panicles, often unisexual; leaflets
entire or 3–5-lobed toward the tip . . . . ***Thalictrum***

13b. Flowers in simple or 2–4-branched racemes; leaflets coarsely
toothed **14**

14a. Racemes elongate, 6 in. long or more;
fruit a follicle . . . . ***Cimicifuga***

14b. Racemes short, less than 2 in. long;
fruit a white berry . . . . ***Actaea***

10b. Perianth showy (0.3 in. or more long), present at flowering **15**

15a. Leaves ternately compound, leaflets
usually 3-lobed toward the tip **16**

16a. Fruit a follicle, ovules 2 or more, leaves distinctly lobed;
plants patch-forming . . . . ***Enemion***

16b. Fruit an achene, ovule 1, leaves only notched;
plants distinct individuals . . . . ***Thalictrum***

15b. Leaves palmately divided, often appearing compound,
coarsely toothed . . . . ***Anemone***

Keener, C.S. 1975a. Studies in the Ranunculaceae of the southeastern United States. I. *Anemone* L. Castanea 40:36–44.

1975b. Studies in the Ranunculaceae of the southeastern United States. III. *Clematis* L. Sida 6:33–47.

1976a. Studies in the Ranunculaceae of the southeastern United States. II. *Thalictrum* L. Rhodora 78:457–472.

1976b. Studies in the Ranunculaceae of the southeastern United States. IV. Genera with zygomorphic flowers. Castanea 41:12–20.

1976c. Studies in the Ranunculaceae of the southeastern United States. V. *Ranunculus* L. Sida 6:266–283.

1977. Studies in the Ranunculaceae of the southeastern United States. VI. Miscellaneous genera. Sida 7:1–12.

1981. The status of *Thalictrum hepaticum* Greene (Ranunculaceae). Castanea 46:43–49.

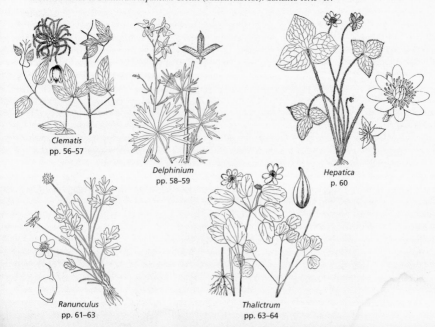

Clematis
pp. 56–57

Delphinium
pp. 58–59

Hepatica
p. 60

Ranunculus
pp. 61–63

Thalictrum
pp. 63–64

Monkshood · *Aconitum uncinatum*

GENERAL: Perennial with stems to 5 ft. tall; stems are often weak and recline on other plants. **LEAVES:** Alternate, petioled, about 4 in. long, deeply 3–5-parted into toothed segments. **FLOWERS: Irregular, blue**, about 0.75 in. tall; **upper sepal shaped as a "hood"**; borne in small, loose clusters of a few flowers, terminal on the stem and arising from leaf axils. August–October. **FRUITS:** Ellipsoid, beaked follicles, about 0.4 in. long; several seeds. **WHERE FOUND:** Rich woods from southern PA to northern GA, west to IN and AL. In TN, from the Eastern Highland Rim eastward, also Davidson, Hickman, and Lewis counties. Occasional. **SIMILAR SPECIES: WOLFSBANE (A. reclinatum)** has hairs on the stems between the **whitish flowers**. Rich mountain woods from VA and WV, south to GA. In TN, in Carter County. Rare. June–September.

NOTES: The species name *uncinatum* means "hooked," referring to the shape of the flower, and lending other names, such as Thor's Hat and Helmetflower. • **Monkshood** is pollinated mainly by bumblebees, which are among the few insects strong enough to enter the hood. • All *Aconitum* species are considered **poisonous**; they contain the alkaloid **aconitine**, once used by Native Americans as an arrow poison. A doctor once wrote (c. 1863) that aconitine is "useful as an external anesthetic in frontal neuralgia, local pains, etc. No remedy, save chloroform, equals it when applied locally for relief of pain."

DENNIS HORN

White Baneberry, Doll's Eyes
Actaea pachypoda

GENERAL: Aromatic perennial herb to 3 ft. tall. **LEAVES:** Large, 2–3-compound, long-petioled; largest leaves may have more than 20 lobed and sharply toothed leaflets, 2–3 in. long. **FLOWERS: Small, white**, 4–10 narrow petals, each 0.1–0.2 in. long; flowers are grouped in a compact raceme at the end of the stalk. April–May. **FRUITS:** Round, **white, many-seeded berries**, 0.3–0.4 in. across, with a **single dark dot at the tip**; on **thick, red pedicels**, 0.5–1.0 in. long. **WHERE FOUND:** Rich woods throughout the U.S. and Canada, including TN. Common. *A. alba*.

NOTES: The name **White Baneberry** warns against eating the berries, which are **poisonous**. The other common name, **Doll's Eyes**, comes from the resemblance of the fruit to the porcelain eyes once used in dolls. When crushed and mixed with alum, the berries produce a black dye. • **All parts of this species contain a cardiac glycoside**, a powerful heart stimulant.

HUGH NOURSE

Wood Anemone
Anemone quinquefolia

GENERAL: Perennial herb to 8 in. tall. **LEAVES:** Basal leaves are 3-parted (but often appear 5-parted); stem leaves beneath the flower are similarly shaped, but smaller. **FLOWERS:** Solitary, about 1 in. wide, **petals absent**; usually 5 **white, petal-like sepals**, often reddish beneath. March–May. **FRUITS:** Separate achenes in a fruiting head less than 0.5 in. long. **WHERE FOUND:** Rich woods in most of the southeastern U.S. In TN, from the Eastern Highland Rim eastward, also Lawrence and Wayne counties. Frequent.

NOTES: Anemones take their name from the Greek god of the winds, Anemos. Anemones are sometimes called windflowers. According to Greek mythology, the god of the west wind, Zephyr, loved the beautiful nymph, Anemone. When his jealous wife, Flora, turned Anemone into a flower, Zephyr abandoned the nymph. She was wooed by Boeeas, the god of the north wind, to whose words she would open in the early spring. • **If you find a Wood Anemone during the evening, night, or on a cloudy day, its flower will be closed.** This behavior helps protect the delicate reproductive structures when pollinators are not hovering around.

Thimbleweed • *Anemone virginiana*

GENERAL: **Hairy** perennial herb to 3 ft. tall, from a short rhizome. **LEAVES:** Basal and upper leaves similar, whorled, to 3 in. long, lobed, with the lateral lobes deeply incised; **stem leaves petioled. FLOWERS:** Solitary on long stalks, **petals absent**; 5 **petal-like, whitish sepals** are very hairy beneath; larger flowers may be more than 1 in. across. May–July. **FRUITS:** Cylindric fruiting heads, to 1.2 in. tall, which **resemble thimbles. WHERE FOUND:** Rich woods throughout the eastern U.S. and TN. Common. **SIMILAR SPECIES:** CAROLINA ANEMONE (*A. caroliniana*), to 16 in. tall, usually has long-stalked basal leaves and 2–3 **sessile leaves located halfway up the stem**, all 3-lobed and deeply incised into narrow segments; single flower, solitary at the end of the stem, has 5 **bluish to white sepals**; fruiting head is cylindric, about 0.8 in. tall, of separate fruits. From SD to IN and NC, south to GA and TX. In TN, in the cedar glades of Bedford, Davidson, Rutherford, and Wilson counties. Rare. April–May.

NOTES: Thimbleweed is also called **Tall Anemone.** • Varieties of this plant have been used by Native Americans to treat diarrhea and whooping cough, and as a stimulant, a love potion, a remedy for tuberculosis, and for protection against witchcraft. • **Many *Anemone* species have only one type of underground stem.** Some species, such as Thimbleweed, have both **rhizomes and caudices.** In this case, the aerial shoots arise from the apex of the caudex attached to the rhizome.

Wild Columbine · *Aquilegia canadensis*

DENNIS HORN

GENERAL: Perennial herb, 1–4 ft. tall. **LEAVES:** Stem and basal leaves mostly 3-lobed, the lobes incised and with rounded tips. **FLOWERS:** Nodding, to 1.6 in. long; 5 **yellow petals with red spurs** that contain the nectar; 5 red sepals; **numerous yellow stamens form a column** projecting well beyond the petals; completely yellow or salmon flowers are rarely found. March–May. **FRUITS:** 5-parted follicles that appear capsular. **WHERE FOUND:** Usually dry woods, limestone bluffs, and limestone glades, but tolerates moisture. Throughout the eastern U.S. In TN, from the Western Highland Rim eastward. Frequent.

NOTES: This plant's common name, **columbine**, means "dove" or "pigeon," and the genus name, *Aquilegia*, means "eagle," both referring to the resemblance of the nectaries (spurs) to talons. • Insects whose probosces are too short to reach the nectar the conventional way bite holes in the nectaries. This species, **the only native columbine** of eastern North America, is **pollinated by hummingbirds.** • Native Americans used the crushed seeds of this plant to treat headaches and control lice, and treated digestive problems with a tea made from the roots. • Traditionally, the gift of columbine, unlike most other flowers, was not a gift of love. To a man, it meant bad luck, and to a woman it was an insult.

Marsh Marigold
Caltha palustris

GENERAL: Perennial herb to 24 in. tall with **hollow stems**. **LEAVES:** Basal leaves have long stalks and glossy, rounded blades to 6 in. across; stem leaves are greatly reduced in size. **FLOWERS:** To 1.5 in. across, **petals absent**; 5–9 shiny, **bright yellow sepals**; **numerous stamens.** April–June. **FRUITS:** Follicles with **red, lustrous seeds.** **WHERE FOUND:** Marshes and other wet areas. A plant primarily of the northeastern states, its range extends south to TN in the mountains, including Carter, Greene, and Johnson counties. Rare.

DENNIS HORN

NOTES: Although this species is not a true marigold (which is a member of the Aster Family), the genus name *Caltha* does mean "marigold"; *palustris* refers to its swampy habitat. • This plant is called by a great many names, including Bull's Eyes, Cowslips, Horse Blob, and Soldier's Buttons. The names Capers and Water Fennel indicate its edibility. The flowers preserved in salted vinegar "are a good substitute for capers." • Ojibwas and other Native Americans used this plant to treat a variety of ailments, including snakebites and coughs. However **contact with skin can cause blistering.** • The flowers can be used to dye yarn.

JERRY DROWN

Black Cohosh · *Cimicifuga racemosa*

GENERAL: Perennial herb with **flower stems to 8 ft. tall**. **LEAVES:** Both basal and alternate on the stem, 2–3-ternately compound, with broad, sharp-pointed, coarsely toothed leaflets, 2–4 in. long, the terminal leaflet generally 3-lobed. **FLOWERS:** About 0.5 in. wide; **petals absent; numerous showy, white stamens**; flowers have an **unpleasant odor**; borne in crowded racemes to 12 in. long on vertical stalks; each flower has **1 ovary** (rarely 2), **about 0.25 in. long**, not on a distinct stalk. May–July. **FRUITS:** Many-seeded, ellipsoid follicles. **WHERE FOUND:** Rich woods. A northeastern species extending south into the eastern ²/₃ of TN. Frequent. *Actaea racemosa.* **SIMILAR SPECIES:** AMERICAN BUGBANE (**C. americana**) grows to 5 ft. tall; each flower has **3–8 stalked ovaries**. Rich woods from PA to NC. In East TN. Infrequent. July–September. *Actaea americana.* APPALACHIAN BUGBANE (**C. rubifolia**) has **1–2 ovaries, each over 0.5 in. long**, per flower. Rich woods from southwestern VA to NC and TN, also western KY and southern IL. In TN, in the Ridge and Valley and Western Highland Rim. Rare. September. *Actaea rubifolia.*

NOTES: The genus name *Cimicifuga* means "bugbane" (*cimex* means "bug" and *fuga* means "flight"), in reference to these plants' insect repellant qualities. • **Black Cohosh** is also known as Black Snakeroot and Rattlesnakeroot for its use in treating snakebites. • Black Cohosh, a popular herb in Europe and the U.S., is commonly used to alleviate menopausal systems and pains during labor and after childbirth. Traditionally, it has also been used to treat rheumatism, arthritis, asthma, and hysteria, and as a gargle for sore throats. • **Bumblebees release the pollen by sonic vibrations**. • Three *Cimicifuga* species are found in TN.

MILO PYNE

Blue Jasmine, Swamp Leatherflower
Clematis crispa

GENERAL: Climbing or weakly ascending **herbaceous vine**, 6–10 ft. long, with smooth, multiple-angled stems. **LEAVES:** Opposite, smooth, pinnately compound with usually 3–5 leaflets of variable shape, occasionally lobed, 1–3 in. long. **FLOWERS:** Solitary, terminal, petals absent; 4 fleshy, urn-shaped sepals, 1–2 in. long, **purplish blue**, tips reflexed, with **wavy or crisped margins**; numerous styles, 1 in. long when mature, with short ascending hairs. April–August. **FRUITS:** Achenes with **silky or smooth "tails."** **WHERE FOUND:** Wet woods, thickets, bottomlands, and swamps from PA to MO, southward. Coastal Plain counties of West TN. Infrequent.

NOTES: The species name *crispa* means "finely waved" or "closely curled," lending another name, **Curly Clematis**, for this plant's wavy flower margins. It is also known as Marsh Clematis for its preferred habitat. • Several *Clematis* species were reputedly eaten as vegetables in Europe and Asia and were pickled in vinegar. • The *Clematis* genus includes perennial vines, usually herbaceous with opposite leaves. The flowers lack true petals and instead have 4 showy sepals. The flowers are followed by clusters of plume-like fruits. There are 8 species in TN.

Leather Vasevine · *Clematis viorna*

GENERAL: Climbing perennial **vine** to 18 ft. long, hairy at the leaf nodes. **LEAVES:** Pinnately compound with 3–9 leaflets, lanceolate to ovate, 1–3 in. long, entire or sometimes lobed, veins not prominent. **FLOWERS:** Petals absent; sepals are thick and firm, thinly hairy on the back, quite hairy on the margins, and form a **leathery red (to pink or purple), urn-shaped calyx to 1 in. long**; styles are hairy throughout. May–July. **FRUITS:** A round cluster of achenes with **long, feathery, curved tails.**

WHERE FOUND: Wet woods throughout most of the central South, mainly away from the Coastal Plain. In the eastern ²/₃ of TN. Frequent. **SIMILAR SPECIES:** LEATHERFLOWER (*C. pitcheri*), also called **BLUEBILL**, has climbing stems and similar leaves with 3–5 leaflets; **purplish sepals to 1 in. long**; style of mature **fruit** has short hairs near the seed, **no hairs toward the tip**. From IN and NE, south to AR and NM. In TN, only in Montgomery County. Rare. June–August. **PALE LEATHERFLOWER** (*C. versicolor*) usually has 4 pairs of leaflets that are glaucous on the back; **purple sepals less than 1 in. long**, with **long hairs on the style** of mature fruit. Dry woods from KY to MO, south to AL and TX. Mostly Middle and East TN. Frequent. June–July.

NOTES: The genus name *Clematis* means "vine"; *viorna* is derived from *vias ornas*, which means "road ornament," referring to the habit of **Leather Vasevine** of adorning roadsides. • **Plants in this genus contain a substance that can cause immediate welts,** and for this reason were used in the Middle Ages by beggars to attract sympathy and donations.

Virgin's Bower, Devil's Darning Needles · *Clematis virginiana*

GENERAL: Climbing herbaceous perennial **vine** to 10 ft. long, with angled stems. **LEAVES:** Opposite, long-stalked, each normally with **3 toothed, ovate leaflets,** 1–4 in. long. **FLOWERS:** Numerous, showy, about 1 in. across, petals absent; **4 white or whitish, petal-like sepals,** spreading widely; **anthers less than 0.06 in. long**; mature styles have long hairs. July–September. **FRUITS:** Hairy achenes, each with a **long, silky, curved tail. WHERE FOUND:** Wet woods and along streams, commonly seen on fences and at the edges of woods. From ND to TX, eastward. Throughout TN.

Common. **SIMILAR SPECIES:** SATIN CURLS (*C. catesbyana*) has leaves divided into **5 leaflets** or that are biternate. In the southern U.S., west to KS. In Middle TN. Occasional. July–August. *C. micrantha.* **YAM-LEAF CLEMATIS** (*C. terniflora**) is introduced from Japan; leaves usually have **5 leaflets that are not toothed**; **white** flowers are about 1 in. wide, with **anthers longer than 0.06 in**. May be seen scrambling on other vegetation or over fences almost anywhere in open areas in the eastern U.S. and in Middle and East TN. Occasional. July–September.

NOTES: When Charles Darwin studied **Virgin's Bower**, he discovered that each new leaf stalk revolves as it grows, completing a full circle every 5 or 6 hours until it finds an object to climb (called thigmotropism). • Although Virgin's Bower can cause **severe skin irritation**, it has been used in liniments to treat skin sores and itching. • Virgin's Bower and **Yam-Leaf Clematis** can be easily confused. A quick method of determining the species is to **study the leaves**— Virgin's Bower's are toothed and the leaves of Yam-Leaf Clematis are smooth.

DENNIS HORN

Tall Larkspur · *Delphinium exaltatum*

GENERAL: Slender, smooth-stemmed perennial **to 6 ft. tall**. **LEAVES:** Alternate, pale beneath, divided into lanceolate segments 0.4–1.0 in. wide; each segment has 1–4 coarse, sharp lobes above the middle. **FLOWERS:** Blue or purple, bilaterally symmetric, about 0.8 in. tall with a **spur** about 0.5 in. long; borne in a loose, terminal raceme over 1 ft. tall. July–September. **FRUITS:** Beaked follicles with several seeds. **WHERE FOUND:** Barrens from PA to NC, west to southern MO. In TN, in Anderson, Hamilton, Knox, and Roane counties. Rare.

NOTES: The species name *exaltatum* refers to the elevated height of this plant. • Flowers of *Delphinium* are irregular with a single, long spur projecting backward, numerous stamens, and usually 3 ovaries (occasionally 5). • All *Delphinium* species are **toxic** and contain alkaloids, such as delphineidine, delphinine, and ajacine. Ingestion of any leaves or seeds may cause **nervous symptoms or even death.** Plants in this genus are sometimes called locoweeds, staggerweeds, and cow poisons. All 3 species found in TN are **poisonous** when ingested. In the western states, larkspurs often kill livestock.

JERRY DROWN

Dwarf Larkspur · *Delphinium tricorne*

GENERAL: Perennial herb **to 24 in. tall**. **LEAVES:** Few, mostly basal, 1–5 in. wide, deeply divided into several narrow oblong-linear segments. **FLOWERS:** Blue, white, or bicolored, 1.0–1.5 in. long, **bilaterally symmetric, spurred**; 3 ovaries are spreading; borne in a loose terminal raceme. March–May. **FRUITS:** 3-beaked follicles; shiny, black, 3-angled seeds. **WHERE FOUND:** Damp to dry woods and barrens, preferring calcareous soil. Widespread in the eastern U.S. and eastern ⅔ of TN, with small local populations. Common.

NOTES: *Delphinium* comes from Greek and means "dolphin," referring to the shape of the spurred flower when budding; the species name *tricorne* means "three-horned," for the 3-pointed fruit. • This species is also called Spring Larkspur. • When admiring this plant, you may hear a buzzing noise coming from the flower, probably a pollinator maneuvering inside the tube, most likely a hard-working bumblebee. It is also pollinated by butterflies and moths. • The Hopi Indians extracted a blue dye from larkspur flowers. Later settlers did the same, but mixed the dye with a fixative to make blue ink. • **All *Delphinium* species are poisonous.**

Prairie Larkspur · *Delphinium virescens*

GENERAL: Perennial herb, 18–48 in. tall; **stem is finely and densely hairy**, often glandular. **LEAVES:** Basal or alternate below the middle of the stem, deeply dissected into numerous linear segments, 0.1–0.2 in. wide. **FLOWERS: Whitish to light blue, bilaterally symmetric, spurred**; about 30 flowers on a spike to 10 in. long. May–July. **FRUITS:** Beaked follicles; wingless seeds are covered with scales. **WHERE FOUND:** Barrens and plains, occasionally dry woods and cedar glades. A prairie species extending eastward from the Great Plains into TN, where it is found in the cedar glades and barrens of Middle TN, as well as the barrens of Hamilton and Meigs counties. Occasional. ***D. carolinianum* ssp. *calciphilum*.** **SIMILAR SPECIES:** ROCKET LARKSPUR (***Consolida ajacis****), formerly in the genus *Delphinium*, is an introduced **annual**, to 4 ft. tall, which often escapes from cultivation; leaves are highly dissected into thread-like segments; flowers vary in color from **blue to pink or white**. Found mostly in Middle TN. Occasional. June–September. ***Consolida ambigua, D. ajacis, D. ambiguum*.**

DENNIS HORN

NOTES: Prairie Larkspur is one of the taller prairie wildflowers. • The seeds of Prairie Larkspur were used by some Native American tribes in ceremonial rattles. The juices or seeds of many *Delphinium* species were also used as insecticides, internal parasiticides, and to control lice and ticks. The flowers were used to make green or orange dyes. • Though many western *Delphinium* species are poisonous to livestock, this species seems to be fairly innocuous.

False Rue Anemone
Enemion biternatum

GENERAL: Perennial to 12 in. tall with fibrous, yellowish roots that have tuberous thickenings. **LEAVES:** Basal, long-petioled, divided 2–3 times, often with 9 leaflets, about 1 in. long; upper leaves are smaller, broadly obovate, with 3 deep, round-tipped lobes. **FLOWERS:** One to few flowers, each to 0.75 in.

DICK SOOY

wide; **petals absent; 5 white, showy sepals**, numerous stamens. March–May. **FRUITS:** Beaked follicles, usually clustered in a head. **WHERE FOUND:** Rich woods, floodplains, and limestone bluffs, especially near watercourses. In most of the eastern U.S. In Middle TN, also in Lauderdale and Loudon counties. Occasional. ***Isopyrum biternatum*.**

NOTES: This plant superficially resembles **Rue Anemone** (p. 64). However, **False Rue Anemone** is a more robust plant with **5 white sepals**, deeply lobed leaves, and few-seeded follicles, whereas Rue Anemone has leaves with rounded teeth, flowers with **5–10 sepals**, and the fruits are achenes.

JERRY DROWN

Sharp-Lobed Hepatica
Hepatica acutiloba

GENERAL: Stemless perennial herb to 6 in. tall.
LEAVES: Basal only, on hairy stalks; leaves 1–3 in. wide, wider than long, **3-lobed with pointed tips**, lobes extend to well past the middle of the leaf; older leaves last through winter. **FLOWERS:** About 1 in. wide, petals absent; 5–12 petal-like sepals may be **white, pink, lavender, purple, or blue**; numerous stamens and ovaries; flowers are borne singly on long, hairy stalks and subtended by 3 green bracts with pointed tips. February–April. **FRUITS:** Single-seeded achenes. **WHERE FOUND:** Rich upland woods, commonly on basic soils. In most of the eastern U.S. and Canada. In TN, from the Western Highland Rim eastward, also Haywood County. Common.

NOTES: The genus name *Hepatica* means "of the liver" and *acutiloba* means "sharp tips," referring to the leaf shape. • This plant is also known as **Liverwort** and **Liverleaf**. • Conforming to the "Doctrine of Signatures" (the belief that whatever a plant looked like, it could cure), *Hepatica* species have been used traditionally for the treatment of liver ailments. In fact, this plant was used by the Greeks, who called it *hepar*, meaning "liver," to treat cowardice, freckles, and indigestion, which were thought to be symptoms of liver dysfunction.

DAVID KOCHER

Round-Lobed Hepatica
Hepatica americana

GENERAL: Stemless perennial herb to 6 in. tall.
LEAVES: Basal only, on hairy stalks; leaves 1–3 in. wide, wider than long; **3-lobed with rounded tips**, lobes extend to near the middle of the leaf; older leaves persist through winter. **FLOWERS:** About 1 in. wide, petals absent; 5–12 petal-like sepals, usually **white to pale lavender**; numerous stamens and ovaries; flowers are borne singly on long, hairy stalks and subtended by 3 green bracts with rounded tips. February–April. **FRUITS:** Single-seeded achenes. **WHERE FOUND:** Rich upland woods, commonly on acidic soils. In most of the U.S. and Canada. In TN, from the Western Highland Rim eastward. Frequent.

NOTES: *Hepatica* species are pollinated and the seeds dispersed by insects. In spring, bees and flies are the main pollinators; later in the season, ants disperse the seeds. • The Chippewa placed hepatica roots near their animal traps in the belief that this would help capture prey.

Goldenseal
Hydrastis canadensis

DICK SOOY

GENERAL: Perennial herb, about 12 in. tall, from a **knotty, yellow rhizome**. **LEAVES:** Single basal leaf and 2 more leaves near the top of the stem, 5–7 in. wide, palmately veined and deeply lobed; **leaves appear wrinkled** during flowering, completing growth after flowering. **FLOWERS:** Solitary, 0.5 in. wide, on a hairy stalk; petals absent; 3 **greenish white sepals** drop early, leaving numerous **white stamens** as a primary visual attractant for pollinators. April–May. **FRUITS:** Dark red berries, 1–2 seeded, borne in a cluster. **WHERE FOUND:** Rich woods. Widespread across most of the northeastern U.S. and TN. Found in many counties in TN, but populations are declining because the rhizomes are collected for medicinal purposes. Frequent.

NOTES: The genus name *Hydrastis* is from the Greek *hydro*, meaning "water," and refers to the preferred moist habitats where the plant is found, and possibly to the medicinal compounds derived by infusing the root in cold water. • This plant is used in teas or tinctures as **an antibiotic, antiseptic, and immune-system stimulant**. In 1918, the U.S. Department of Agriculture estimated that between 200,000 and 300,000 pounds of the drug produced from the root were used annually. • Other common names, such as Indian-Dye, Orange-Root, Turmeric, and Yellow-Puccoon, refer to the yellow dye that can be produced from the juice of this plant.

Kidneyleaf Buttercup • *Ranunculus abortivus*

GENERAL: Annual to 24 in. tall with a **mostly smooth, vertically ridged stem** and branches. **LEAVES:** Basal leaves are long-stalked, sometimes partially lobed and with scalloped margins, normally **kidney-shaped**, 0.6–1.6 in. wide; alternate stem leaves, uppermost leaves mostly sessile and divided into 3–5 narrow lobes. **FLOWERS: Yellow**, about 0.25 in. wide, **petals shorter than sepals**. March–June. **FRUITS:** Swollen achenes clustered in a head that resembles a berry cone. **WHERE FOUND:** Meadows, woods, and lawns. Widespread in the eastern U.S., eastern Canada and across TN. Common. **SIMILAR SPECIES:** SMALL-FLOWERED BUTTERCUP or ROCK BUTTERCUP (*R. micranthus*) has **hairy** young stems and leaves. Rich woods, usually on calcareous soils. Northeastern U.S. and Plains States. Middle TN. Occasional. April–May.

NOTES: Kidneyleaf Buttercup is also called **Small-Flowered Crowfoot**. • An interesting characteristic of Kidneyleaf Buttercup is its different types of leaves. The basal and lower leaves are spade- or kidney-shaped, with some occasional lobes. Farther up the stalk, the leaves are split into well-defined lobes.

DENNIS HORN

• Plants in the *Ranunculus* genus usually have 5 petals, 5 (or fewer) sepals, numerous yellow stamens, and many greenish, single-seeded ovaries. Most species have bright, shiny, waxy, yellow petals. About 30 species are known from the Southeast (23 in TN), some quite variable.

DENNIS HORN

Early Buttercup · *Ranunculus fascicularis*

GENERAL: Perennial herb to 12 in. tall with **appressed-hairy stems** and often tuberous roots. **LEAVES:** Mostly basal, longer than wide, divided into toothed segments, the terminal segment stalked; the 1–3 stem leaves are smaller and less divided. **FLOWERS:** Less than 0.75 in. across, 5 **glossy, yellow, ovate petals, spreading sepals**. April–May. **FRUITS:** Achenes, each with a straight, slender beak. **WHERE FOUND:** Open areas, dry woods. Widespread in the eastern U.S. and TN. Frequent. **SIMILAR SPECIES:** WATER-PLANTAIN SPEARWORT (**R. ambigens**) is a hollow-stemmed perennial **lacking basal leaves**; stem leaves are narrow, alternate, undivided, normally 3–5 in. long, and slightly toothed; flowers are 0.5–0.75 in. across with 5 glossy, yellow, **narrow petals**. Marshes. In the eastern U.S. Thinly spread across TN. Infrequent. April–August. BULBOUS BUTTERCUP (**R. bulbosus***) is a hairy perennial to 24 in. tall; base of erect stem resembles a bulb; leaves are deeply divided into 3 parts, these normally again divided; flowers are 1 in. wide with 5 glossy, yellow, **obovate petals** and **reflexed sepals**. Introduced from Europe. Fields and pastures. Eastern ⅔ of TN. Occasional. April–June.

NOTES: Early Buttercup is also called **Prairie Buttercup**. • The genus name *Ranunculus* is Latin for "little frog," in reference to the moist and marshy habitats preferred by the majority of plants in this genus; *fascicularis* comes from the appearance of the leaves, which are "clustered or grouped together in bundles." • Early Buttercup produces more pollen than nectar, and thus attracts pollen-eating bees, flies, and beetles that feed on the pollen but do not generally pollinate the plant.

DENNIS HORN

Hispid Buttercup · *Ranunculus hispidus* var. *hispidus*

GENERAL: Tufted perennial herb, 12–36 in. tall; **stems are very hairy** in the basal portion. **LEAVES:** Basal and alternate on the stem, 2–4 in. wide, on long, hairy stalks; leaves are partially or completely divided into 3 parts, segments are lobed or toothed. **FLOWERS:** Bright yellow, about 1 in. across, 5 petals, **spreading sepals**. March–June. **FRUITS:** Smooth, rounded achenes. **WHERE FOUND:** Dry upland woods, but occasionally in moist situations. Widespread in the eastern U.S. and eastern ⅔ of TN. Common. **SIMILAR SPECIES:** HAIRY BUTTERCUP (**R. sardous***) is an **erect, hairy-stemmed annual** to 2 ft. tall; leaves are mostly basal and 3-parted, each leaflet deeply cleft; flowers are about 0.75 in. across with 5 glossy, yellow petals and **reflexed sepals**; **achenes have knobby sides**. Introduced from Europe. Moist fields. Most of the eastern U.S. Widespread across TN. Frequent. April–July. SWAMP BUTTERCUP (**R. hispidus** var. **nitidus**) has **smooth, weak, and reclining stems**; lower leaves are divided into broad-lobed leaflets; yellow flowers are about 1 in. across. Wet woods and meadows. From NY to MN, south to FL and TX. In TN, from the Western Highland Rim eastward, also Lauderdale County. Occasional. April–June. **R. septentrionalis**.

NOTES: "Hispid" and the species name *hispidus* both mean "bristly," in reference to the hairy stems. **Hispid Buttercup** is also called **Bristly Buttercup**. • The fruits provide a food source for ducks and other waterfowl. • In spring, the introduced **Hairy Buttercup** may be found invading lawns and parks and can become a **troublesome weed** when established. • **Swamp Buttercup** is also known as Creeping Buttercup because it often spreads by rooting where its stems touch the ground.

Hooked Buttercup · *Ranunculus recurvatus*

GENERAL: Highly variable perennial to 24 in. tall, with hairy stems. **LEAVES:** Mostly basal and lower stem, 3–5 in. long, deeply 3-cleft, the segments broad and toothed with stiff hairs above and below. **FLOWERS:** Light yellow, 5 petals, **0.15–0.25 in. long**, are shorter than or equal to sepals; strongly hooked styles. April–June. **FRUITS:** Achenes, each with a strongly curved beak (style). **WHERE FOUND:** Rich, moist woods. Widespread in the eastern U.S. and across TN. Common. **SIMILAR SPECIES:** LOW SPEARWORT (**R. pusillus**) has small, **ovate basal leaves**, progressively narrower upward; tiny, yellow **petals less than 0.1 in. long**. Ditches and shallow water from NY to MO, southward. Widespread across TN. Frequent. May–June. **STICKSEED BUTTERCUP (R. parviflorus*)** has leaves that are palmately 3–5 lobed; yellow **petals are less than 0.15 in. long**; achenes have hooked spines. Introduced from Europe. In lawns and waste places in the eastern U.S. and throughout TN. Frequent. April–July.

NOTES: The species name *recurvatus* means "curved backward," referring to the hooked styles on the fruit. • The shallow blossoms of buttercups are perfect for beetles and bees. • Buttercups are also known as **crowfoots**, for their divided leaves. • **All are poisonous when fresh.** However, the poison is volatile and loses its potency over time, so dry hay laced with buttercups is not toxic.

OTTO R. HIRSCH

Early Meadow Rue
Thalictrum dioicum

GENERAL: Perennial herb to 24 in. tall; **plants are either male or female** (dioecious). **LEAVES:** Alternate, long-petioled, ternately divided 2x into 9 rounded and toothed leaflets, 0.5–2.0 in. wide, with 5 lobes toward the outer margin. **FLOWERS:** Petals absent; **male and female flowers on separate plants**; male plants have **dangling stamens** with **yellow or yellowish anthers**; female plants have small, **greenish (sometimes purple)** flowers. March–April (flowers before other meadow rues). **FRUITS:** Strongly ribbed achenes. **WHERE FOUND:** Moist woods in much of the eastern U.S. In the eastern ⅔ of TN, also Obion County in West TN. Frequent.

CAROL & HUGH NOURSE

NOTES: The genus name *Thalictrum* is Greek and describes a plant with divided leaves; *dioicum* means "two houses" referring to the fact that the male and female parts grow on separate plants. • The *Thalictrum* genus consists of perennials with 4 or 5 sepals and no petals. The color is provided by the stamens, except in **Rue Anemone** (p. 64). The flowers are often unisexual, with numerous stamens or single-seeded, flat ovaries. All species in this genus have ternately divided leaves that are divided a second time. Seven species occur in TN.

Skunk Meadow Rue · *Thalictrum revolutum*

GENERAL: Stout perennial to 5 ft. tall with a greenish or reddish purple, glaucous, slightly hairy stem; foliage has a pungent aroma when crushed. **LEAVES:** Alternate, compound, upper leaves sessile, lower leaves on petioles; variably divided, **margins rolled backward** (revolute); leaflets, 0.5–1.5 in. wide, have 3 rounded teeth; pale green or whitish lower leaflet surface is covered with waxy glands visible with a 10x lens. **FLOWERS:** Male and female flowers, **petals absent**; male flowers have 4–5 **light green sepals** and drooping, **greenish white stamens**; female flowers are **bur-like and greenish**; borne in panicles to 2 ft. long. May–July. **FRUITS:** Achenes, often minutely glandular-hairy. **WHERE FOUND:** Moist or dry woods, meadows, and barrens throughout the eastern U.S. In the eastern ⅔ of TN, also Shelby County. Frequent. **SIMILAR SPECIES:** TALL MEADOW RUE (*T. pubescens*) has flower stamens in showy, white plumes that do not droop. From eastern Canada southward. In TN, primarily from the Cumberland Plateau eastward. Occasional. June–August.

NOTES: The name **Skunk Meadow Rue** comes from the **skunk-like aroma** emitted when the foliage is crushed. This plant is also called **Waxy Meadow Rue** for the waxy appearance of the lower leaf surfaces. • Members of some Native American tribes are said to have surreptitiously placed *Thalictrum* seeds in the food of quarreling couples to help end their disagreements. • The flowers are wind-pollinated, so are rarely visited by insects.

Rue Anemone
Thalictrum thalictroides

GENERAL: Perennial herb under 10 in. tall with tuberous roots. **LEAVES:** Basal leaves divided into 9 toothed, rounded leaflets; upper leaves in a whorl, each divided into 3 leaflets, 0.5–1.0 in. wide, tips of leaflets usually have 3 shallow lobes. **FLOWERS:** Usually 0.5–1.0 in. across, petals absent, 5–10 **showy, white to pinkish petal-like sepals**; borne on stalks originating from a single point; double flowers are often seen. March–May. **FRUITS:** Achenes, each tipped by a persistent stigma. **WHERE FOUND:** Woods. Widespread across eastern U.S. and TN. Common. *Anemonella thalictroides*. **SIMILAR SPECIES:** CLIFF MEADOW RUE (*T. clavatum*) is a hairless perennial to 2 ft. tall; sparsely flowered inflorescence; flowers have **broad, white stamens**; fruits are curved upward. In moist woods and on **wet cliffs** in the southern Appalachian Mountains. From MD, south to AL and GA, and in the eastern half of TN. Occasional. May–July.

NOTES: The tuberous roots of **Rue Anemone** are considered edible, although they may also contain toxic substances. Native Americans are reputed to have used this plant to treat diarrhea and vomiting. • For **Cliff Meadow Rue**, the species name *clavatum* comes from *clav*, meaning "club," in reference to the dilated filaments of the stamens.

Tassel Rue, False Bugbane
Trautvetteria caroliniensis

GENERAL: Stout, branched, perennial herb, 2–4 ft. tall, from rhizomes, roots often clustered. **LEAVES:** Basal leaves long-petioled, to 12 in. wide; alternate stem leaves mostly sessile and much smaller; all leaves palmately and deeply divided into 3–11 lobes, irregularly toothed or incised. **FLOWERS:** White, 0.5–0.8 in. wide; petals are absent and sepals fall early, so the white color comes from the many stamens; borne in a **corymb-like inflorescence** that extends well above the foliage, terminating the stem and branches. June–July. **FRUITS:** Single-seeded, thin-walled utricles. **WHERE FOUND:** Moist mountain woods from PA and KY, south to GA; also prairies from southern IN to western IL. In TN, from the Eastern Highland Rim eastward, also Davidson and Cheatham counties in Middle TN. Occasional.

NOTES: This plant is also called **Carolina Bugbane** and **Carolina Tassel Rue**. The genus name commemorates Ernest R. von Trautvetter (1809–89), a Russian botanist; the species name *caroliniensis* indicates that this plant was first found in the Carolinas. • Another variety of Tassel Rue, *Trautvetteria caroliniensis* var. *occidentalis*, may be found in the western regions of Canada and the U.S. • All tassel rues are considered **poisonous**.

KURT EMMANUELE

Shrub Yellowroot
Xanthorhiza simplicissima

GENERAL: Low **shrub** to 24 in. tall; grows in colonies; **roots and inside of the stems are yellow. LEAVES:** Alternate, pinnately compound with sharply toothed leaflets, the leaves clustered toward the top of the stem. **FLOWERS:** Petals absent; tiny flowers have 5 **maroon to yellowish green sepals**; borne in several **narrow, drooping racemes** to 5 in. long. April–June. **FRUITS:** Follicles with 1–2 seeds. **WHERE FOUND:** Shaded streambanks in most of the southeastern U.S. In TN, from the Cumberland Plateau eastward, also Chester, Hardin, Henderson, and Lewis counties. Occasional.

NOTES: The genus name *Xanthorhiza* means "yellow root"; *simplicissima* indicates that the plant is unbranched. • Traditionally, the roots of **Shrub Yellowroot** were used to make a tea to treat a variety of ailments. It is now known that the plant contains **berberine**, which has many physiological effects on humans.

OTTO R. HIRSCH

Blue Cohosh
Caulophyllum thalictroides

GENERAL: Erect, gray-green, smooth perennial herb, 12–36 in. tall. **LEAVES:** Single, large, sessile, 3-ternately compound leaf above the middle of the stem; 1 (rarely 2) smaller, but similar compound leaf just below the inflorescence; oval leaflets, 1–3 in. long, are irregularly lobed above the middle. **FLOWERS: Yellow-green to purple-green**, about 0.5 in. wide, petals absent, 6 **petal-like sepals**; 1–3 terminal, panicle-like flower clusters (rarely a branch with more leaves and flowers). April–May. **FRUITS:** Dark blue, **poisonous** berry-like seeds. **WHERE FOUND:** Rich woodlands. Mostly a northeastern species that extends south to northern GA and northern AL. In the eastern ²/₃ of TN. Frequent. **SIMILAR SPECIES: GIANT BLUE COHOSH (C. giganteum)** has **larger, fewer, consistently purple flowers; flowers 2 weeks earlier.** Rich woods of the northeastern U.S., south to TN and NC. In TN, in Cannon, Overton, and Sumner counties in Middle TN, and Greene, Sullivan, Washington, and Unicoi counties in East TN. Infrequent. April–May.

NOTES: The genus name *Caulophyllum* is from the Greek *kaulon*, "a stem," and *phyllon*, "a leaf." The stem of **Blue Cohosh** acts as a stalk for the large compound leaf. • Other names for this plant include Blueberry Root, Blue Ginseng, and Lion's Foot. • The names Papoose Root and Squaw Root were given to Blue Cohosh because Native Americans used the roots of this plant to make a tea for facilitating childbirth and to aid in menstruation. The Cherokee would "hold root ooze in the mouth for toothache" and rub the leaves on poison oak rash. In the late 1800s, this plant was also used as a sedative and an antispasmodic, as well as to treat hysteria, rheumatism, and bronchitis.

Umbrella Leaf • *Diphylleia cymosa*

GENERAL: Smooth perennial herb, 12–36 in. tall, arising from a thick rhizome. **LEAVES:** Usually 2, **peltate**, 12–24 in. across, cleft and radially lobed, the lobes pointed and toothed; nonflowering plants have only 1 leaf. **FLOWERS: White**, 0.6 in. wide, 6 petals, sepals, and stamens; petals are ovate-elliptic with round tips; sepals fall early; flowers resemble those of **Mayapple** (p. 67), but are much smaller; borne in a single cluster to 4 in. wide, **extending above the leaves**. May–June. **FRUITS:** Round, **dark blue**, fleshy berries, to 0.5 in. wide; conspicuous late in the growing season. **WHERE FOUND:** Rich woods in moist coves and seepage slopes of the Blue Ridge Mountains from VA to GA. In TN, only in extreme eastern counties. Occasional.

NOTES: The genus name *Diphylleia* is from the Greek *dis*, meaning "double," and *phyllon*, for "leaf," referring to the leaves having 2 deep lobes; *cymosa* describes the inflorescence, which is usually a cyme. • This plant is also commonly known as **American Umbrella Leaf**. • A tea made from the roots was used by the Cherokee to induce sweating. • In order to see this plant, visit Great Smoky Mountains National Park or other Blue Ridge areas in May or June, when it is in flower. It is likely to be found near small streams and seepages at altitudes of 3200–5200 ft.

Twinleaf · *Jeffersonia diphylla*

GENERAL: Smooth, herbaceous perennial herb, 8–20 in. tall, arising from a rhizome. **LEAVES:** Basal, on stalks 6 in. tall (taller after flowering), divided into **2 kidney-shaped leaflets**, each 1.5 in. wide, becoming much wider after flowering; leaves persist throughout summer. **FLOWERS:** Solitary, showy, **8 white petals**, each about 0.75 in. long, 4 white sepals that shed early, 8 stamens, 1 pistil; borne on leafless stalks extending above the leaves. March–April. **FRUITS:** Pear-shaped capsules about 0.8 in. tall, **opening by a lid at the top**. **WHERE FOUND:**

DICK SOOY

Rich, moist woods, especially on limestone soils, throughout most of the eastern U.S. In TN, from the Western Highland Rim eastward. Frequent.

NOTES: Other common names for this species include Ground Squirrel Pea, Helmet Pod, Rheumatism Root, and Yellow Root. • This plant was named in honor of **Thomas Jefferson** (1743–1826) by early American botanist William Bartram, who said, "In the various departments of this science, but especially in botany and zoology, the information of this gentleman is equaled by that of few persons in the United States." Jefferson, who later served as president of the United States from 1801–09, was an honored plantsman and patron of botany with a devoted interest in horticulture and farming. • This is the only species of *Jeffersonia* in North America; one other is found in eastern Asia.

Mayapple, Mandrake · *Podophyllum peltatum*

GENERAL: Perennial herb to 18 in. tall from a creeping rhizome; usually occurs in **large colonies**. **LEAVES:** Umbrella-like, 8–15 in. across, radially divided into 5–9 segments; flowering plants have a forked stem with 1 leaf on each branch; juvenile and nonflowering plants have 1 leaf on an unforked stem. **FLOWERS:** Solitary, **nodding, white**, waxy, about 1.5 in. wide, **6–9 petals**, numerous stamens, 6 sepals that fall early; on a short stalk arising from the fork of the stem. April–May. **FRUITS:** Yellow, fleshy, many-seeded berry about the size of a small lemon. **WHERE FOUND:** Moist woods and meadows throughout the eastern U.S. and TN. Common.

NOTES: The genus name *Podophyllum* means "foot leaf" and is derived from another name, *Anapodophyllum*, meaning "duck foot leaf," in reference to the shape of the leaves. • Other common names for this species include **Maypop**, Devil's Apple, Duck's Foot, and Hog Apple. • Although the ripe fruit can be used to make jelly and preserves, the leaves and rootstocks are **poisonous**. • Long used for medicinal purposes, this plant is now a source of extracted compounds used in the treatment of venereal warts. Etoposide, which is prepared from the roots, has been used to treat small-cell carcinoma.

JERRY DROWN

Orange Poppy, Blind Eyes • *Papaver dubium**

GENERAL: Sparingly branched, stiff-haired, **annual** herb to 24 in. tall. **LEAVES:** Alternate, 2–4 in. long, pinnately divided, the lobes merely toothed to deeply incised. **FLOWERS:** Petals (usually 4), to 1.6 in. long, are **red to pink or red-orange** with **1 dark basal spot**, and purple anthers; long-stalked flower terminates the stem and branches. May–August. **FRUITS:** Capsules that open by small valves. **WHERE FOUND:** Introduced from Europe. Waste places. Naturalized from NY and SC, west to KS and OK. Thinly scattered in Middle and East TN. Occasional. **SIMILAR SPECIES:** WHITE PRICKLY POPPY (***Argemone albiflora****) has **white flowers** to 3 in. wide, normally with **6 overlapping petals**. Introduced and escaped into open, dry, disturbed sites. Throughout the southeastern U.S. In TN, in Jackson County. Rare. May–August.

NOTES: The genus name *Papaver* and the common name "poppy" derive from the Latin *papaver*, which may derive from the Sumerian *pa pa*, referring to the popping noise made when the seeds are chewed. • Some prickly poppies are called wild hollyhocks. • The seeds of Mexican Prickly Poppy (*Argemone mexicana*) are used for their oil, which has been used in paints and to manufacture soap.

DENNIS HORN

Bloodroot • *Sanguinaria canadensis*

GENERAL: Early spring flowering perennial to 6 in. tall, consisting of a single leaf and flower stalk, each arising separately from a horizontal, underground rhizome. **LEAVES:** Single, pale green, 3–9-lobed, round, **embracing the flower scape**; leaf expands after flowering and may become 8 in. wide. **FLOWERS:** Showy, **solitary**, 1–2 in. across, 8–16 **white petals with 4 petals** slightly longer than the others; the 2 sepals are rarely seen as they drop early. March–April. **FRUITS:** Capsules with 2 valves that open by splitting from bottom to top. **WHERE FOUND:** Rich woods from Canada, southward to AL and FL. Widespread in TN. Common.

NOTES: *Sanguinaria* is from the Latin *sanguis*, meaning "blood," referring to the rhizome, which oozes an **orange-red juice** (or sap) when cut. Native Americans used the juice as body paint, lending the name, Indian Paint. The root juice has been used to make a yellow-orange fabric dye, known as Puccoon, another name for the plant. • The flowers are delicate and easily destroyed by wind. • The **rhizomes contain the alkaloid sanguinarine**, an antibacterial, antifungal, and anti-inflammatory ingredient that is used in toothpastes and mouthwashes to help reduce dental plaque and gingivitis. Research indicates that sanguinarine may also offer protection against skin cancer. However, the FDA considers Bloodroot unsafe even in small doses, as the plant can be **toxic**. • This is the only species in the *Sanguinaria* genus.

DENNIS HORN

Celandine Poppy · *Stylophorum diphyllum*

GENERAL: Showy perennial herb, 12–20 in. tall when in flower. **LEAVES:** Several basal leaves, 6–10 in. long, as well as a pair of smaller stem leaves; all leaves are long-stalked, deeply pinnately lobed, smooth, and pale beneath. **FLOWERS:** Deep yellow, 1.5–2.0 in. wide, **4 petals**, numerous stamens; solitary or in small clusters at the top of the stem. March–May. **FRUITS:** Ovoid, hairy capsules. **WHERE FOUND:** Rich damp woods. Mainly a plant of the northeastern U.S., extending south into TN, where it is found from the Western Highland Rim eastward. Frequent.

NOTES: The genus name *Stylophorum* is from the Greek words *stylos*, "a column," and *phoreo*, "to bear," referring to the columnar style of this plant. The yellow flowers give this plant another common name, **Yellow Wood Poppy.** • A tincture made from this poppy was used to heal skin outbreaks and hemorrhoids. • This plant is considered **poisonous.**

KURT EMMANUELE

Yellow Corydalis, Harlequin
Corydalis flavula

GENERAL: Small, green or glaucous **annual** to 12 in. tall, erect or later reclining. **LEAVES:** Alternate, compound, lower leaves finely dissected on long stalks, reduced in size upward. **FLOWERS: Pale yellow**, less than 0.5 in. long; **upper petal has a toothed crest** and the corolla a short spur, so the flower looks as if it is simply "balanced" on the stalk. April–May. **FRUITS:** Capsules with 2 valves. **WHERE FOUND:** In moist soil throughout most of the northeastern U.S. and TN. Frequent. **SIMILAR SPECIES: PALE CORYDALIS (C. sempervirens)** has **pink flowers.** Dry or rocky woods. A northern species extending south in the mountains to GA. In TN, from the Cumberland Plateau eastward, in Fentress, Bledsoe, Monroe, Sevier, Unicoi, and Carter counties. Infrequent. May–September.

DENNIS HORN

NOTES: **Yellow Corydalis** is also known as Yellow Harlequin and Yellow Fumewort. • The astringent roots of Yellow Corydalis traditionally have been used to stop bleeding and to treat irregular menses, pain, and problems of the stomach. Native Americans placed the roots on smoldering coals and inhaled the smoke "to clear the head." However, this plant is considered **toxic** even in low doses. • The **Bleeding Heart Family** includes delicate woodland plants with finely segmented and divided leaves. All have flowers with 2 sepals, 4 petals, and 6 stamens. Some botanists group them with the Poppy Family because of certain similarities. Three genera and 6 species are found in TN.

KURT EMMANUELE

Squirrel Corn · *Dicentra canadensis*

GENERAL: Perennial herb to 12 in. tall, from a cluster of **yellow corms**. **LEAVES:** Basal, long-stalked, 2–6 in. long and wide, compound and finely divided, somewhat bluish green and usually covered with a whitish bloom, typically 1 per flowering stem. **FLOWERS:** Pinkish white, 0.6–0.8 in. long, drooping, **noticeably fragrant**; borne in a raceme on a nearly vertical stalk that extends well above the leaves; flowers are similar to those of **Dutchman's Breeches** (see below), but have **spurs that are more rounded, appearing somewhat heart-shaped**. April–May. **FRUITS:** Capsules with black, shiny seeds. **WHERE FOUND:** Rich woods. A mostly northeastern U.S. and Canada species extending south to TN, where it is thinly scattered in the eastern half of the state. Occasional.

NOTES: The common name **Squirrel Corn** comes from the shape of the underground stems, which have little **yellow bulblets (corms) that resemble grains of corn.** Other names include Turkey Corn, Ladies and Gentlemen, Lyre Flower, and Colicweed. The Onondaga called this species Ghost Corn, believing that it was "food for spirits." • In the past, this plant was used as a tonic and to treat syphilis.

DAVID KOCHER

Dutchman's Breeches
Dicentra cucullaria

GENERAL: Perennial herb, to 12 in. tall, from a cluster of small, **pink corms**. **LEAVES:** Basal, long-stalked, 2–4 in. long and wide, somewhat yellowish green, compound and finely divided; typically 2 per flowering stem. **FLOWERS:** White, hanging, **not fragrant**, 0.6–0.8 in. long, 4 petals, the outer 2 with **long, divergent spurs**; in a raceme on an arching stalk that usually extends well above the leaves. April–May. **FRUITS:** Capsules with black, shiny seeds. **WHERE FOUND:** Rich woods from Québec to ND, southward into northeastern OK, AR, northern GA, and central NC. In TN, from the Western Highland Rim eastward. Occasional.

NOTES: The genus name *Dicentra* is Greek for "twice-spurred," referring to the shape of the flowers. This plant gets its common name from the flowers, which resemble the baggy pants worn by "Dutchmen" hanging upside down on an arching clothesline. • This species was used by some Native Americans as a love charm. It is told that if the root was nibbled by a man, his breath would attract a woman, even against her will. • Medicinally, a poultice was made from the leaves to calm skin flare-ups, and the plant has also been used to treat paralysis and tremors.

Wild Bleeding Heart · *Dicentra eximia*

GENERAL: Perennial herb to 20 in. tall, from a short, scaly rhizome. **LEAVES:** On long petioles and much divided, giving the bluish-green foliage a very delicate appearance, though the leaves are **less finely cut** than those of **Dutchman's Breeches** (p. 70) or **Squirrel Corn** (p. 70). **FLOWERS: Deep pink,** 0.7–1.0 in. long, **heart-shaped** with **short, rounded spurs.** April–September. **FRUITS:** Capsules with black, shiny seeds. **WHERE FOUND:** On rocky banks or ledges, especially shale, in the Appalachian Mountains from TN to NY. In TN, in Polk, Blount, Sevier, Unicoi, Carter, Johnson, and Union counties. Infrequent. **SIMILAR SPECIES: ALLEGHENY VINE (Adlumia fungosa),** also called **CLIMBING FUMITORY,** is a **biennial climbing vine** with 3-lobed leaflets; flowers are similar but paler. In the northeastern U.S., south in the mountains to TN. Infrequent. June–September.

DAVID KOCHER

NOTES: Wild Bleeding Heart is so named because of the dark pink color of the blossoms and their resemblance to small hearts hanging from the stem. It is also known as **Eastern Bleeding Heart** and **Turkey Corn.** This plant, a cousin to the Opium Poppy (*Papaver somniferum*), has also been called Staggerweed owing to its intoxicating effects on browsing cattle. • **Garden Bleeding Heart (D. spectabilis*),** introduced from Asia, has larger, deep pink, heart-shaped flowers, and is often cultivated in the southeastern U.S.

NETTLE FAMILY • NETTLES, PINKS, & RELATIVES

Wood Nettle · *Laportea canadensis*

GENERAL: Rhizomatous, fibrous-rooted perennial to 3 ft. tall. **LEAVES:** Alternate, 2.5–8.0 in. long, broadly ovate, serrate, long-stalked; **stems and leaves have stinging hairs. FLOWERS:** Greenish, 0.2 in. across, **petals absent;** male flowers in cymes from the lower leaf axils, 5 distinct sepals, 5 stamens; female flowers in loose, widely spreading, branched cymes from the upper axils, 4 sepals. June–August. **FRUITS:** Oblique achenes.

THOMAS G. BARNES

WHERE FOUND: Damp, rich woods throughout the eastern U.S. and TN. Frequent. **SIMILAR SPECIES: STINGING NETTLE (Urtica dioica)** grows to 6 ft. tall; **opposite leaves and stinging hairs.** Waste places. A widespread weed, but in TN, found only in Cocke, Greene, Montgomery, and Shelby counties. Rare. May–September. **FALSE NETTLE (Boehmeria cylindrica)** has long-stalked, **opposite leaves without stinging hairs;** compact clusters of tiny greenish flowers in upward-arching spikes. Moist soil of low woodlands and streams throughout the eastern U.S. and TN. Common. June–August. **CLEARWEED (Pilea pumila)** is an annual with opposite leaves and a smooth, translucent stem; greenish flowers in short, drooping clusters. Moist, rich woods throughout the eastern U.S. and TN. Frequent. July–October.

NOTES: The leaves and young shoots of *Laportea*, *Urtica*, and *Boehmeria* contain many beneficial minerals and vitamins and make fine-tasting boiled greens. • **Stinging Nettle** has been used in Europe for over 2000 years to aid in pregnancy, alleviate menopausal symptoms, strengthen bones, ease depression, and enhance sexual performance. • All *Urtica* and *Laportea* species have flowers without petals and **downy hairs containing formic acid.** If the plant touches bare skin, it will cause **a painful stinging sensation** that may last from hours to days.

Pokeweed
Phytolacca americana

GENERAL: Tall, smooth, **stout, branched perennial herb, 6–10 ft. tall. LEAVES:** Alternate, 3.5–12 in. long, smooth, lanceolate to elliptic-lanceolate, entire and acute, on petioles 0.5–2.0 in. long. **FLOWERS:** About 0.25 in. wide, petals absent, 5 **greenish white sepals**, 1 superior ovary, 5–30 stamens; borne in racemes 2–8 in. long, opposite the leaves, sometimes erect in flowering, but nodding in fruit. May–September. **Fruits: Dark purple, nearly round berries,** about 0.4 in. across. **WHERE FOUND:** Open, usually disturbed sites throughout the eastern U.S. and all of TN. Common.

NOTES: The genus name *Phytolacca* is from the Greek *phyton*, meaning "plant," and *lacca*, meaning "crimson lake," referring to the plant's **red juice.** • This plant is commonly called **Poke** and **Poke Sallet** (Sallet is local slang for salad). Early pioneers used the juice of the purple berries for ink, which led to this plant being called Inkweed. • Another name, Indian Greens, refers to the edibility of the young shoots and leafy tips, which must be boiled in at least two changes of water. Pokeweed is well known in the south as a tasty cooked green. However, the **berries, seeds, roots, and mature stems and leaves are very poisonous.**

Wild Four-O'Clock
*Mirabilis nyctaginea**

GENERAL: Smooth, erect, branching perennial herb, to 5 ft. tall, with nearly square stems. **LEAVES:** Opposite, smooth, to 4 in. long, on short petioles, **heart-shaped** with entire margins and pointed tips. **FLOWERS:** About 0.5 in. wide, petals absent, **pink-red, 5-lobed calyx**; borne in terminal clusters with up to **5 flowers attached to a shallow, veiny, green cup** (involucre). May–October. **FRUITS:** Achene-like, hairy, about 0.2 in. long, more or less cylindric with 5 ribs. **WHERE FOUND:** Disturbed dry soil, prairies, and roadsides. In the Plains States, east to WI and AL; now established as a weed to the East Coast. In TN, sporadically scattered from the Eastern Highland Rim westward. Occasional. **SIMILAR SPECIES:** WHITE FOUR-O'CLOCK **(M. albida)**, also called **PALE UMBRELLAWORT**, has whitish stems, **narrow leaves**, and pink flowers. Dry prairies, sandhills, and barrens from SC to KS, southward. In TN, in Wilson and Rutherford counties. Rare. July–October. GARDEN FOUR-O'CLOCK **(M. jalapa)**, also known as **MARVEL OF PERU**, sometimes escapes from cultivation; **showy, white, pink, red, or yellow flowers**, each with a funnel-shaped calyx up to 1.5 in. long and 2.0 in. wide, which opens in late afternoon. June–October.

NOTES: The family name Nyctaginaceae is Greek for *nuktos*, which means "by night," referring to the flowers that primarily open in the evening or night. • **Wild Four-O'Clock** is also called Heartleaf Four-O'Clock, Snotweed, and Umbrellawort. • Native Americans used the roots to treat wounds, sprains, and burns.

Prickly Pear
Opuntia humifusa

GENERAL: Erect or decumbent perennial with **fleshy, flattened, jointed, green stems**; each "pad" is 2–4 in. by 4–6 in. and dotted with clusters of fine spines and a few single long spines; the small **spines (glochids) can become embedded in the skin** if touched. **LEAVES:** Small, scale-like, quickly deciduous. **FLOWERS:** Large, brilliant yellow, numerous petals and sepals in several rows; numerous stamens; borne singly on an inferior, swollen ovary that is 1–2 in. long. May–June. **FRUITS:** Red-purple, fleshy, 1–2 in. long, with tiny, hair-like spines; edible. **WHERE FOUND:** On rock outcrops, gravelly soils, sand dunes, and cedar glades throughout the eastern U.S. and across TN. Occasional.

NITA R. HEILMAN

NOTES: Other names for this plant include Barberry, **Devil's Tongue**, and Old Man's Hand. It is also called Indian Fig because of the **edible fruits**. • The young, tender pads can be peeled and cooked like green beans, while the pulp of the pads can be used to make candy and syrup. • The broken-off joints are sometimes used by Eastern Woodrats to protect their nests. • This species is **the only native cactus of TN.**

Lamb's Quarters • *Chenopodium album*＊

GENERAL: Erect annual to 6 ft. tall, often branched. **LEAVES:** Alternate, rhombic, 1.5–2 times as long as broad, almost always **toothed**; leaf surface covered with **white, mealy powder**, especially when young. **FLOWERS:** Minute, greenish; borne in dense paniculate spikes or cymes from the axils of upper leaves. August–October. **FRUITS:** Small, indehiscent utricles; 1 black, lenticular seed; **seed covering is difficult to dislodge. WHERE FOUND:** Introduced from Europe. Waste places, barnyards, and cultivated fields. Scattered throughout the U.S. and TN. Occasional. **SIMILAR SPECIES:** MEXICAN TEA (*C. ambrosioides*＊), also called WORMSEED, has **leaves with resinous glands or hairs**. Introduced from tropical America. Throughout the U.S. and TN. Frequent. August–October. WOODLAND GOOSEFOOT (*C. standleyanum*) is native and has lanceolate **leaves with few or no teeth; seed covering is easily removed**. Dry, open woods. Widespread in eastern North America and thinly scattered in the eastern ⅔ of TN. Infrequent. July–October.

NOTES: Young stems and leaves of **Lamb's Quarters** are delicious in salads or as boiled greens. • However, the **leaves of Mexican Tea should not be eaten.** The aromatic oil in the glands of Mexican Tea and other *Chenopodium* species **smells like turpentine**, is very **toxic**, and has been known to cause vertigo through casual contact. • Nine *Chenopodium* species occur in TN.

DENNIS HORN

Alligator Weed
*Alternanthera philoxeroides**

GENERAL: Invasive perennial with stems to several feet long, forming **extensive mats in shallow water** and on mud; stems root at each node, and a stem section with 1 intact node may form a new colony. **LEAVES:** Opposite, linear-elliptic, 2–3 in. long. **FLOWERS:** White, clover-like flower heads, 0.6 in. wide; on long stalks from leaf axils or at the ends of stems. May–October. **FRUITS:** Fruits and seeds are not produced at this latitude. **WHERE FOUND:** Introduced from South America. Occurs in most of the southeastern coastal states. First reported from TN in the 1970s, now documented from at least 14 counties. Large local populations, mostly in shallow water along the Tennessee River and its tributaries, but apparently spreading. Occasional.

NOTES: Alligator Weed is considered a **noxious aquatic weed.** • The **Amaranth Family** is a large family with 800 species, which are primarily tropical. Familiar representatives are Pigweed and Tumbleweed (*Amaranthus*), Globe Amaranth (*Gomphrena*), and Cockscomb (*Celosia*). Five genera and 13 species are recorded in TN.

Spiny Amaranth, Thorny Pigweed
*Amaranthus spinosus**

GENERAL: Smooth, reddish-stemmed annual, mostly erect, to 3 ft. tall, widely branching, bearing a pair of **sharp spines** at most nodes. **LEAVES:** Alternate, ovate, entire, 1–3 in. long, tapering at the base to a long leaf stalk. **FLOWERS:** Minute, tawny flowers without petals occur in numerous terminal and axillary spikes, 2–5 in. long. May–October. **FRUITS:** Thin-walled utricle containing 1 black seed. **WHERE FOUND:** Introduced from tropical America. Barnyards and waste places from NY to MO, southward. Widely scattered across TN. Occasional. **SIMILAR SPECIES:** REDROOT PIGWEED (**A. retroflexus**), also called GREEN AMARANTH, has a greenish, downy stem to 5 ft. tall, **without sharp spines; greenish flower spikes;** the common name refers to the reddish root. Introduced from tropical America; now naturalized throughout most of the U.S. as a common garden weed. Recorded from only 4 counties in TN, but likely more common. July–October. TALL WATER-HEMP (*A. tuberculatus*) is a **smooth, green-stemmed annual**, 3–8 ft. tall, normally erect and unbranched; narrowly ovate leaves; **greenish flower spikes.** A native weed of damp ground, often found in cultivated crops. In the eastern U.S. and the western ½ of TN. Infrequent. July–October. *A. ambigens, Acnida altissima*.

NOTES: The Greek word *amarantos* means "unfading," and indicates the lasting quality of some of the flowers in this genus; *spinosus* means "spiny," referring to the spines at the nodes. • **Spiny Amaranth** is edible and is best picked when young. • **Redroot Pigweed** has many other names, including Borax, because the leaves contain saponin and were once used to wash clothes. Another common name, Lighthouses, refers to this plant's ability to grow quickly so that it towers above crops in the field.

Carolina Spring Beauty
Claytonia caroliniana

GENERAL: Early spring perennial to 6 in. tall, arising from a corm. **LEAVES:** Single pair of stem leaves, petioled, each leaf 1–4 in. long and 0.4–1.2 in. wide, lanceolate-ovate blade is clearly distinguished from the petiole. **FLOWERS:** Showy, white or pinkish, 5 petals, 0.4–0.6 in. long, **pink-veined**; borne in a loose raceme of 2–18 flowers. March–May. **FRUITS:** Ovoid capsules with 6 seeds. **WHERE FOUND:** Mesic forests. A northern species extending south to TN and GA in the uplands and mountains. In TN, in the eastern ½ of the state. Occasional.

NOTES: Other names for this plant are Rose Elf, Good Morning Spring, and Wide-Leaved Spring Beauty. • The genus name is in honor of John Clayton (1686–1773), who botanized Virginia for 51 years. He corresponded with many of the great botanists of that time, including Linnaeus, Gronovius, and John Bartram, as well as Thomas Jefferson and Benjamin Franklin. He was later called the greatest botanist in America by Peter Collinson (whose namesake is the genus *Collinsonia*).

DENNIS HORN

Virginia Spring Beauty • *Claytonia virginica*

JERRY DROWN

GENERAL: Early spring perennial herb, 3–9 in. tall, arising from a corm. **LEAVES:** Usually a single pair of stem leaves, petioled, seldom less than 3 in. long, more than 8 times as long as wide; **narrow leaf blade gradually merges into an unclearly defined petiole**; long basal leaves are sometimes present. **FLOWERS:** Showy, white or pinkish, 5 petals, 0.4–0.6 in. long, **pink-veined**; borne in a loose raceme of 4–13 flowers. February–April. **FRUITS:** Ovoid capsules with 6 seeds. **WHERE FOUND:** Mesic forests, lawns, roadsides. In most of the eastern U.S. and Canada. Throughout TN. Common.

NOTES: This plant is one of the earliest to flower in spring, and it is enjoyed not only by humans, but the flowers are eaten by deer, elk, and sheep. • Other common names include Fairy Spuds, Good Morning Spring, Grass Flower, and Mayflower. More commonly, it is known as Wild Potato because the corms can be collected like potatoes, boiled for 10–15 minutes, and eaten. Raw, they have the sharp flavor of radishes. Fernald and Kinsey wrote in *Plants of Eastern North America* (1943), "The roundish, irregular roots when boiled in salted water, are palatable and nutritious, having the flavor of chestnuts." • A popular plant, it has been recorded as being visited by as many as 71 different species of insect pollinators.

Limestone Fameflower
Talinum calcaricum

GENERAL: Low perennial, 4–9 in. tall, with 1–3 stems from an enlarged base. **LEAVES:** Succulent, 0.5–1.5 in. long, **linear, circular in cross-section**; in a cluster near the base of the stem. **FLOWERS:** Pink to rose red, 0.5 in. wide, 5 petals, **25–45 stamens**; borne in a branched, bracteate cyme of 2–20 flowers. May–September. **FRUITS:** Capsules with minutely roughened seeds. **WHERE FOUND:** Thin soils of less disturbed **limestone cedar glades** in KY, TN, and AL. In the Central Basin of Middle TN. Infrequent. **SIMILAR SPECIES: MENGES' FAMEFLOWER** (*T. mengesii*) has **50–80 stamens**. In TN, in Rhea County. Rare. May–September. **APPALACHIAN FAMEFLOWER** (*T. teretifolium*), also called **QUILL FAMEFLOWER**, has flowers with **15–20 stamens**. Both species are found on open **sandstone outcrops** of the southeastern U.S. and on the Cumberland Plateau in TN. Infrequent. June–August.

PAUL SOMERS

NOTES: The species name *calcaricum* refers to this plant's usual habitat of limestone areas. • Fameflowers are also called **rock pinks**, and are able to survive in thin, rocky, dry soil by storing water in their thick, succulent leaves. • The brightly colored *Talinum* flowers are short-lived, only opening in bright sunlight for a few hours, usually in mid-afternoon.

Corn Cockle · *Agrostemma githago**

GENERAL: Annual to 3 ft. tall, stem thinly hairy. **LEAVES:** Opposite, entire, linear to lanceolate, to 5 in. long and 0.4 in. wide. **FLOWERS:** Solitary, 5 **rose to reddish, oblanceolate petals**, 0.8–1.2 in. long; **calyx tube**, 0.5–0.7 in. long, with **lanceolate-linear lobes**, 0.8–1.6 in. long, **usually longer than petals**; borne at the ends of the branches on stalks to 8 in. long. July–September. **FRUITS:** Capsules splitting into 4–5 valves. **WHERE FOUND:** Introduced from Europe; now established as a weed in fields and waste places across most of the eastern U.S. Thinly scattered in TN. Occasional.

NOTES: The genus name *Agrostemma* is Latin for "field chaplet," perhaps referring to the tiny seeds. • Other common names include Cockle, Corn Campion, Corn Pink, Crown of the Field, and Woolly Pink. • The **seeds are toxic** and when opened, may release **poisonous saponins**. • The **Pink Family** has over 2000 species in the northern temperate regions, including weeds, attractive wildflowers, and ornamentals of commercial value such as carnations and baby's breath. Members of this family can be identified by their swollen stem nodes and undivided leaves that are opposite or sometimes whorled. TN species have white, pink, or red flowers with 4–5 petals that are often deeply notched or "pinked." Fifteen genera and 45 species are found in TN.

OTTO R. HIRSCH

Glade Sandwort · *Arenaria patula*

GENERAL: Small, bushy, **smooth annual**, 4–10 in. tall, highly branched at the base. **LEAVES:** Opposite, numerous, **needle-like**, to 0.8 in. long. **FLOWERS:** Numerous, **white, about 0.5 in. wide, 5 notched petals**; 5 sepals are narrowly lanceolate and slightly shorter than petals. April–June. **FRUITS:** Capsules splitting along 3 primary valves. **WHERE FOUND:** Limestone cedar glades, shallow sandy soil, and dry limestone cliffs from OH to MN, south to VA, AL and TX. In TN, in Middle and East TN. Frequent. *Minuartia patula*. **SIMILAR SPECIES:** MOUNTAIN SAND-WORT (**A. groenlandica**) has lower leaves that **often form thick mats** from which stems grow 2–5 in. tall. Rock crevices. A northern species extending south to GA and TN in the mountains. In TN, in Carter County. Rare. May–September. THYME-LEAF SANDWORT (**A. serpyllifolia***) is a **softly hairy**, wiry annual to 12 in. tall; **oval leaves** to 0.3 in. long; **white flowers about 0.25 in. wide**. Dry sandy fields and roadsides. Throughout most of the U.S. and Middle and East TN. Frequent. April–July.

PAUL SOMERS

NOTES: The genus name *Arenaria* is Latin, from *arena*, meaning "sand," in reference to the fact that most species of these herbs prefer sandy areas; *patula* means "spreading," referring to the low-growing and spreading habits of these plants. • **Glade Sandwort** is easily over-looked because of its small size and thin stems. This plant is very short-lived, but the dead stems can be found year round. • Throughout the world, there are more than 150 *Arenaria* species.

Deptford Pink · *Dianthus armeria**

GENERAL: Slender, stiff-stemmed **annual or biennial** to 24 in. tall. **LEAVES:** Opposite, 5–10 pairs of **narrow**, hairy stem leaves, to 3 in. long. **FLOWERS:** **Rose pink dotted with white**, about 0.5 in. wide; calyx is hairy, 0.5–0.8 in. long, with narrow lobes; borne in a dense cyme of 3–9 flowers often surpassed by slender, erect bracts. May–August. **FRUITS:** Capsules split-ting along 4 valves; capsules are as long as calyx. **WHERE FOUND:** Intro-duced from Deptford, England. Dry fields, roadsides, and waste places throughout the eastern U.S., southern Canada, and TN. Com-mon. **SIMILAR SPECIES:** SWEET WILLIAM (**D. barbatus***) is a **perennial** that sometimes escapes from gardens to roadsides and fields; **wider leaves**; **whitish to red petals**, to 0.4 in. long, are finely toothed around the summit. Becoming widespread in the U.S. Thinly scattered across TN. June–August.

JERRY DROWN

NOTES: *Dianthus* is from the Greek words *dios*, "divine," and *anthos*, "flower." • Pinks first came to Britain in the 16th century. Remarkably, at the time, pink was not a specific color, so almost certainly the color was named after flowers of the Pink Family. • The *Dianthus* genus includes carnations and several introduced species that are widely naturalized.

DENNIS HORN

Bouncing Bet, Soapwort
*Saponaria officinalis**

GENERAL: Smooth, **colonial perennial herb,** 12–24 in. tall, spreading by rhizomes. **LEAVES:** Opposite, smooth, ovate to lanceolate, 2–4 in. long and ½ as wide. **FLOWERS: Pink to white,** about 1 in. wide, 5 **slightly notched petals** are spreading to reflexed; inflorescence is a dense cluster of flowers at the top of the thick-jointed stem. June–September. **FRUITS:** Capsules with veiny seeds. **WHERE FOUND:** Introduced from Europe. Waste places, fields, and along roadsides and railroad beds throughout the U.S. and most of TN. Large, showy clumps of flowering plants are common. Frequent.

NOTES: *Saponaria* is from the Latin *sapo,* for "soap," referring to the **soapy lather** that forms when the leaves and roots are crushed and mixed with water. • Other names for this plant include Scourweed, Bouncing Bess, Chimney Pink, Crowsoap, Ragged Sailor, and Latherwort. • A poultice can be made and applied on poison ivy rash, acne, boils, eczema, and psoriasis. Native Americans used the poultice for boils and spleen pain. • Plants of the *Saponaria* genus contain saponins, which are **poisonous.**

DENNIS HORN

Wild Pink, Pennsylvania Catchfly
Silene caroliniana ssp. *pensylvanica*

GENERAL: Taprooted perennial with slender, **simple stems** to 12 in. tall, usually glandular-hairy. **LEAVES:** Oblanceolate, to 5 in. long, basal leaves petioled but the 2–3 pairs of opposite stem leaves usually sessile. **FLOWERS: Pink, tubular,** 5 wedge-shaped petals to 0.6 in. long, the margins entire or slightly notched; in a short, dense inflorescence with 5–13 flowers. April–May. **FRUITS:** Capsules containing inflated seeds with tubercles. **WHERE FOUND:** Sandy, dry, and open woodlands. From NH to eastern OH, south to NC and TN, in the mountains. Rare. **SIMILAR SPECIES:** FORKING CATCHFLY (*S. dichotoma**) is a **hairy annual** with a **forked upper stem;** sessile flowers borne on a one-sided, raceme-like inflorescence. Introduced, escaped, and found in waste places throughout the U.S. In TN, in Union and Carter counties. Rare. June–September.

NOTES: The "pink" in the name of many plants in the Pink Family is not a reference to the flower color; rather it refers to the notched petals that bear a resemblance to the ragged or serrated pattern caused by cutting material with **pinking shears.**

White Campion, Evening Lychnis
*Silene latifolia**

GENERAL: Short-lived, usually downy perennial herb, 12–24 in. tall. **LEAVES:** Several pairs of ovate leaves to 4 in. long. **FLOWERS:** White, 5 petals, 0.8–1.6 in. long, cut deeply into 2 lobes; 5 styles; **male and female flowers occur on different plants;** male calyx to 0.8 in. long and 10-nerved; female calyx to 1.2 in. long, 20-nerved, becoming much inflated; inflorescence usually much branched; **fragrant flowers open in the evening** to attract moths as pollinators. June–September. **FRUITS:** Capsules splitting into 10 teeth; gray seeds. **WHERE FOUND:** Introduced from Europe. Waste places. Naturalized throughout much of North America, including Middle and East TN. Occasional. **Lychnis alba, S. pratensis.**

NOTES: The *Silene* genus includes many plants that are called pinks, campions, or lychnis. Although **White Campion** is a *Silene*, it was formerly placed in the genus *Lychnis*. Many *Silene* species are called pinks because they are in the Pink Family, but true pinks are in the *Dianthus* genus.

JERRY DROWN

Roundleaf Catchfly · *Silene rotundifolia*

GENERAL: Taprooted perennial to 28 in. tall, weak stems, freely branched, thinly glandular-hairy. **LEAVES:** Opposite, 5–8 pairs of stem leaves are mostly sessile, broadly lanceolate to nearly round, to 4 in. long and 3 in. wide. **FLOWERS:** Crimson to red, tubular, 1.0–1.5 in. across, 5 **petals deeply notched into 2 narrow segments,** the tips turned abruptly outward; in an **open inflorescence with few flowers.** June–July. **FRUITS:** Capsules splitting along 6 teeth. **WHERE FOUND:** Shaded sandstone cliffs from OH to WV, south to GA and AL. In TN, in the Cumberland Plateau region. Occasional. **SIMILAR SPECIES:** SLEEPY CATCHFLY (**S. antirrhina**) is a branched **annual** to 3 ft. tall, often sparsely hairy below; basal leaves to 2.5 in. long, mostly spatulate; stem leaves smaller; **numerous small white or pink flowers** with 2-lobed petals equaling or barely exceeding the 0.4-inch-long calyx. Waste places in most of the U.S. Throughout TN. Frequent. April–July.

NOTES: Many *Silene* species are commonly referred to as **catchflies** because small crawling insects **get caught in a sticky secretion** that coats the flower tubes, hairy stems, and leaves, keeping the insects from reaching the flowers. This is the plant's method of facilitating cross-pollination while reserving its pollen for airborne insects. Unlike the insect-trapping and -eating sundews, the insects that get caught on a *Silene* can free themselves and continue on their way.

KURT EMMANUELE

JERRY DROWN

Starry Campion · *Silene stellata*

GENERAL: Perennial to 4 ft. tall with sparsely hairy stems. **LEAVES:** Lanceolate to ovate stem leaves, 2–4 in. long, in **whorls of 4**. **FLOWERS:** Star-shaped, white, about 0.75 in. wide, 5 fringed petals are woolly at the base, petal blades have 8–12 segments; **inflated, bellshaped calyx**; borne in loosely branched terminal clusters. July–September. **FRUITS:** Capsules splitting into 6 teeth. **WHERE FOUND:** Dry woods and clearings, from MA to MN, south to GA and TX. Throughout TN. Common. **SIMILAR SPECIES:** ROUGHLEAF CAMPION (**S. ovata**) is taller, to 6 ft.; ovate to broadly lanceolate **leaves are usually opposite**; deeply dissected **petals usually have 8 segments and are not woolly at the base.** Rich woods, from VA to KY, south to GA, AL, and AR. Thinly scattered across TN. Infrequent. August–September.

NOTES: The species name *stellata* is derived from the Greek word *stella*, meaning "starry," and refers to the shape of the flower. • Other common names for **Starry Campion** are Widow's Frill, King's Cure-All, and Thurman's Snakeroot. • Asa Gray (1810–88), a preeminent botanist, wrote that he was told that the plant was an antidote to the bite of the rattlesnake and copperhead. The story goes that its use was indicated by markings on the root beneath the bark, where the likeness to the skin of a rattlesnake was seen.

KURT EMMANUELE

Fire Pink · *Silene virginica*

GENERAL: Perennial herb, 12–30 in. tall, with downy and sticky stems. **LEAVES:** Basal leaves form a rosette and are stalked, oblanceolate to spatulate, to 4 in. long; stem leaves are opposite, sessile, and narrow, 2–6 in. long or longer. **FLOWERS:** Richly scarlet red, 1–2 in. wide, 5 narrow, notched petals; cream-colored stamens protrude from the center; sticky calyx; open inflorescence with several flowers growing on thin stalks from the axils of the upper leaves. April–June. **FRUITS:** Ellipsoid capsules, 0.5–0.75 in. long, splitting into 6 teeth. **WHERE FOUND:** Open woods and rocky slopes from NJ to MN, south to GA, AL, AR, and OK. Throughout TN. Common. **SIMILAR SPECIES:** ROYAL CATCHFLY (**S. regia**), 2–4 ft. tall, has red petals that are usually entire, sometimes slightly notched. Prairies from MO to OH, southward. In TN, only in Knox County. Rare. June–August.

NOTES: The splash of brilliant red in spring makes **Fire Pink** and **Royal Catchfly** two of our most popular and conspicuous wildflowers. The scarlet flowers with narrow tubes are favorite nectar plants of **hummingbirds.** • Historical reports tell that Fire Pink has been used as a worm-expellent (vermifuge).

Bladder Campion · *Silene vulgaris**

GENERAL: Perennial herb, 8–18 in. tall (or taller), usually **smooth and glaucous**. **LEAVES:** Stem leaves are opposite, lanceolate to oblanceolate, often clasping, to 3 in. long. **FLOWERS:** White, 0.5–0.75 in. wide, 5 deeply notched petals; smooth, **inflated calyx sac is veined and papery**, about 0.5 in. long, and looks like a balloon or small melon. June–August. **FRUITS:** Capsules splitting into 6 teeth. **WHERE FOUND:** Introduced from Europe into fields, waste places, and roadsides. Naturalized throughout most of temperate North America. In TN, in Montgomery, Davidson, Cannon, Polk, Jefferson, and Carter counties. Infrequent. *S. cucubalus*.

NOTES: This plant is also called Bird's Eggs, Bull Rattle, Cowbell, Devil's Rattlebox, Snappers, and Spattling Poppy. The name Spattling Poppy refers to the "spattle," now known as "spittle," which is the frothy secretion deposited on plants by nymphs of the **Spittlebug**. At the time, the name was given to this plant because the spittle "more aboundeth in the bosomes of the leaves of these plants than in any other." • Medicinal folklore tells of the leaves being used to heal skin eruptions.

Star Chickweed, Giant Chickweed · *Stellaria pubera*

GENERAL: Erect but weak-stemmed perennial to 16 in. tall, thinly spreading and hairy. **LEAVES:** Stem leaves are bright green, opposite, mostly lanceolate, to 3.5 in. long. **FLOWERS:** White, star-like, to 0.5 in. wide, **5 petals so deeply notched that they appear as 10; sepals are obtuse to acute and shorter than petals**; numerous flowers occur in a leafy, open, terminal cyme. April–May. **FRUITS:** Capsules, shorter than sepals. **WHERE FOUND:** Rich woods and shaded bluffs, from NY to IL, south to northern FL and LA. Throughout TN. Common. **SIMILAR SPECIES: TENNESSEE CHICKWEED (*S. corei*) has acuminate sepals, equal to or exceeding the petals**. Rich woods and seeps in the northeastern U.S., south to AL. Scattered throughout Middle and East TN. Occasional. April–June. **COMMON CHICKWEED (*S. media**)** is a cosmopolitan weed introduced from Europe; **white flowers to 0.25 in. wide** bloom most of the year. Forms dense mats in lawns and waste places throughout the U.S. and TN. Common. March–November.

NOTES: The genus name *Stellaria* means "star," referring to the shape of the flower; *pubera* means "hairy," for the stem. • **Star Chickweed** is very similar to the introduced **Common Chickweed**, but can be distinguished from its invasive relative by the large size of its flowers. • Common Chickweed is considered a delicacy in parts of Europe. The young, tender leaves should be harvested in spring before flowering for use in salads; they are a source of vitamins A and C.

DENNIS HORN

Harper's Umbrella Plant
Eriogonum harperi

GENERAL: Taprooted perennial, 3–6 ft. tall, **branched above with long, soft, spreading hairs.** **LEAVES:** Numerous, alternate, 4–6 in. long, hairy beneath, smooth above, sessile, lanceolate or lance-elliptic. **FLOWERS:** Softly hairy with **tiny, white tepals** that are **yellowish inside;** borne in panicles to 15 in. tall and 10 in. wide. June–August. **FRUITS:** Triangular achenes. **WHERE FOUND:** Limestone glades and cliff edges in TN, and AL. In Middle TN, mostly on cliffs of the Caney Fork River in DeKalb, Smith, Wilson, and Putnam counties. Rare. ***E. longifolium*** var. ***harperi.***

NOTES: The genus name *Eriogonum* is from the Greek words *erion,* "wool," and *gonu,* "joint," referring to the downy and knotty stem. There are about 200 *Eriogonum* species, also called **buckwheats,** in North America. Many are very similar in appearance and require a magnifying glass for identification. Species in this genus have hairy, densely matted leaves that retain moisture by keeping drying winds away from the surface of the leaves.

J. & D. RICHARDSON

Scarlet Smartweed
Polygonum amphibium

GENERAL: Aquatic or terrestrial, rhizomatous perennial, **usually forming large colonies;** terrestrial form grows to 6 ft. tall, while the aquatic form has floating branches. **LEAVES:** Alternate, the **base of the leaf forming a short sheath (ocrea) around the stem,** with the sheath usually flared and with (or without) bristles; terrestrial form has hairy, lanceolate leaves, 5–8 in. long, tapering to the tip; aquatic form has smooth, elliptic leaves more rounded to the tip. **FLOWERS:** 5 bluntly rounded, **pink or red tepals,** about 0.2 in. long; borne in a stout, **dense raceme,** 1–6 in. tall and to 0.8 in. wide, usually singly, but may be in pairs, at the tips of major branches. June–August. **FRUITS:** Dark, shiny, doubly convex achenes to 0.2 in. long. **WHERE FOUND:** Low, wet places throughout most of the U.S. Thinly scattered across TN. Occasional. *P. coccineum.*

NOTES: Smartweed gets its name from the sharp taste of the foliage. • There are 22 *Polygonum* species in TN, both native and introduced, including knotweeds, climbing buckwheats, and smartweeds. • Some *Polygonum* species may cause dermatitis with prolonged exposure to the skin or photosensitivity when ingested.

Mild Water-Pepper · *Polygonum hydropiperoides*

DENNIS HORN

GENERAL: Erect perennial herb to 3 ft. tall, from a rhizome; **sheaths at stem joints have a fringe of slender, appressed bristles** up to 0.35 in. long. **LEAVES:** Alternate, narrow, less than 0.5 in. wide, 3–4 times longer than wide, tapering to a long point. **FLOWERS:** Tiny **white or pink flowers without dotted glands; borne in erect spikes**; flowers generally sparse with gaps between clusters. May–frost. **FRUITS:** Dark, shiny achenes, about 0.1 in. long and almost as wide, sharply 3-angled. **WHERE FOUND:** Wet soils, shores, and shallow water in most of the eastern U.S. Throughout TN, but not common in the Central Basin or the Blue Ridge Mountains. Common. **SIMILAR SPECIES:** COMMON SMARTWEED or WATER-PEPPER (*P. hydropiper**) is a smooth, reddish-stemmed annual; stem with **joint sheath bristles short or lacking; greenish white flowers with dotted glands,** on **spikes nodding at the tip.** Introduced from Europe. Damp soil and shallow water throughout most of the U.S. Thinly scattered across TN. Occasional. June–frost.

NOTES: Another common name for **Mild Water-Pepper** is **False Water-Pepper**, indicating the slight peppery taste of the young leaves and shoots, which is caused by an acrid essential oil. This plant should be eaten only in moderation. • Mild Water-Pepper has been used to make a yellow dye for wool, cotton, and linen. • **Common Smartweed** has leaves that are very peppery tasting.

Pennsylvania Smartweed
Polygonum pensylvanicum

JERRY DROWN

GENERAL: Erect, branching annual to 4 ft. tall; stems have **reddish joints without fringes;** upper stem has numerous hair-like glands. **LEAVES:** Alternate, lanceolate, up to 5 in. long, smooth, shiny, long-pointed tip, tapering to the base. **FLOWERS: Rose pink or rarely white;** in rather tight, erect cylindric racemes, 1–2 in. long and 0.5 in. wide. May–October. **FRUITS:** Lens-shaped achenes, 0.15 in. across, dark brown, shiny, sides flat or concave. **WHERE FOUND:** Damp soils, roadsides, and waste places throughout most of the eastern U.S. and TN. Common. **SIMILAR SPECIES:** LONG-BRISTLED SMARTWEED (*P. caespitosum**) is a spreading, mostly smooth, annual to 3 ft. tall; stems have **sheaths at the joints with bristles up to 0.4 in. long;** lanceolate leaves are thin, dark green, to 3 in. long; **deep reddish pink flowers** on one or more erect terminal spikes only 0.2 in. wide; shiny, black, **3-angled achenes.** Along roadsides, on waste ground, and in wet places. Naturalized from Southeast Asia, now widespread east of the Mississippi River and throughout TN. Frequent. June–October.

NOTES: Various Native American tribes used a leaf infusion of **Pennsylvania Smartweed** to treat diarrhea and related gastrointestinal problems. The leaves were rubbed on children's thumbs to discourage thumb sucking.

HUGH NOURSE

Virginia Knotweed, Jumpseed
Polygonum virginianum

GENERAL: Erect rhizomatous perennial to 3 ft. tall.
LEAVES: Alternate, lanceolate to ovate, to 6 in. long, tapered to the tip, on short stalks to 1 in long; base of the leaf stalk forms a short sheath (ocrea) around the stem, with the sheath both hairy and fringed above.
FLOWERS: 4 greenish white (to pinkish) tepals about 0.1 in. long, with the base of each flower or its stalk in a sheath; ocrea are well separated below, becoming nearly overlapping above, and 1–3-flowered; borne in very slender, terminal racemes to 24 in. long. July–October. **FRUITS:** Lenticular achenes, each with a **persistent style forming a triggering mechanism for seed dispersal. WHERE FOUND:** Moist woods and low, wet areas throughout the eastern U.S. and TN. Common. *Tovara virginiana.*

NOTES: When pressure is applied to the style tips of the mature fruit (achenes), the seeds "jump" from the plant, thus its common name, **Jumpseed.**
• Many plants in this genus, also called knotweeds, have medicinal value, and the young shoots and leaves of most are edible. A few are cultivated as vegetables in Asia.

NITA R. HEILMAN

Sheep Sorrel · *Rumex acetosella**

GENERAL: Dioecious, introduced, perennial **weed to 18 in. tall. LEAVES:** Alternate, to 2 in. long, petioled; long, elliptic to oblong central lobe with 2 small basal lobes (ears) at right angles to the middle one. **FLOWERS:** Tiny, to 0.06 in. long, **yellowish or reddish;** borne in clusters; inflorescence may occupy 1/2 the stem. April–August. **FRUITS:** 6 narrow sepals adhere to each achene, which is about 0.12 in. long, shiny, and brown. **WHERE FOUND:** Introduced from Eurasia. On acid soils over most of North America. In fields and pastures throughout TN. Common. **SIMILAR SPECIES: BITTER DOCK (*R. obtusifolius**)** is a perennial **to 3 ft. tall, not dioecious;** large leaves, 6–10 in. long, oval, sometimes heart-shaped at the base but not lobed; minute flowers; achenes, about 0.12 in. long, have 3 wings with spiny teeth. Introduced from Europe. Moist waste ground throughout the U.S., Canada, and TN. Frequent. May–June.

NOTES: The leaves of all *Rumex* species are edible. However, it is best to harvest the leaves when they are very young, as they rapidly become bitter and astringent with age. The leaves contain high quantities of vitamins A, B1, B2, and C, as well as iron, chlorophyll, tannin, and oxalic acid. • In people with sensitive or allergy-prone skin, **Sheep Sorrel** has been known to cause dermatitis. • There are 8 *Rumex* species in TN.

Curly Dock, Sour Dock · *Rumex crispus**

GENERAL: Smooth, robust, taprooted perennial to 4 ft. tall, unbranched below the inflorescence. **LEAVES:** Alternate, 6–10 in. long, 1–3 in. wide, with **strongly wavy margins**. **FLOWERS:** Many large, wand-like branches of **inconspicuous greenish flowers** at the top of the stem; flower calyx has 3 narrow outer sepals and 3 inner sepals that expand in fruit. March–May. **FRUITS:** 3-winged achenes, about 0.2 in. long, with smooth margins. **WHERE FOUND:** Introduced from Europe. A weed in fields and waste places throughout the U.S., southern Canada, and TN. Frequent. **SIMILAR SPECIES:** The following 2 species have **flat leaves without wavy margins**. Both are native. **SWAMP DOCK (*R. verticillatus*)**, also called **WATER DOCK**, has **pedicels 2–5 times as long as the fruit**. In swamps, stream margins, and standing water throughout the eastern U.S., West TN, and thinly scattered eastward. Occasional. April–May. **PALE DOCK (*R. altissimus*)** has lighter green leaves, only 3–6 in. long and more numerous; **pedicels are about the same length as the fruit**. Wet alluvial soil, east of the Rocky Mountains. West and Middle TN. Occasional. April–June.

DENNIS HORN

NOTES: The leaves and seeds of **Curly Dock** are **edible**, and the roots are known to contain tannin and minerals, especially iron. • Traditionally, Curly Dock was eaten or prepared as a tea to treat coughs, fever, scurvy, tumors, and cancer. The crushed root was used as a poultice for wounds and skin irritations.

ST. JOHNSWORT FAMILY • ST. JOHNSWORTS, MALLOWS, & SUNDEWS

St. Peterswort · *Hypericum crux-andreae*

GENERAL: Erect, branched, **woody shrub** to 40 in. tall. **LEAVES:** Opposite, elliptic-oblong, 0.6–1.4 in. long, rounded at the tip, slightly clasping at the base. **FLOWERS:** Yellow, **4 broad petals** about 0.7 in. long, 4 sepals (2 outer broadly round-ovate, 2 inner narrowly lanceolate), numerous stamens. July–August. **FRUITS:** Capsules extending just beyond the persistent calyx. **WHERE FOUND:** Pine barrens and sandy areas from southern NY to eastern OK, south. In TN, in the Eastern Highland Rim and Cumberland Plateau, also Lawrence, Lewis, Dickson, Hamilton, and Polk counties. Occasional. *H. stans*, *Ascyrum stans*.

NOTES: *Crux* in the species name, *crux-andreae*, means "cross," the symbol formed by the petals of this plant. • There are 24 *Hypericum* species, also called St. Johnsworts, listed for TN. The genus is characterized by entire, paired leaves and pale to bright yellow flowers. • Some plants in this genus are edible in small quantities, and have a variety of medicinal uses. *Hypericum* species contain large amounts of tannin, various glycosides, and the essential oil catechol. Native Americans used these plants in a tea that was used to treat tuberculosis and other ailments.

DENNIS HORN

KURT EMMANUELE

Coppery St. Johnswort
Hypericum denticulatum

GENERAL: Erect perennial to 28 in. tall, with a **4-angled stem** branched above. **LEAVES:** Opposite, elliptic to nearly round, to 0.8 in. long, often erect or ascending. **FLOWERS:** Resemble pinwheels; 5 **coppery yellow** petals, 0.4 in. long, asymmetric; 50–80 stamens. July–September. **FRUITS:** Capsules to 0.25 in. long. **WHERE FOUND:** Pine barrens, sandy shores, and wet areas from MD to southern IL, southward. In TN, mostly from the Highland Rim and Cumberland Plateau. Frequent. **SIMILAR SPECIES: CREEPING ST. JOHNSWORT** (*H. adpressum*) is an erect, somewhat woody, **mostly unbranched** perennial to 3 ft. tall, with a leafy stem; leaves mostly narrowly elliptic, to 2.5 in. long and 0.4 in. wide, margins revolute; terminal inflorescence has many yellow flowers, the petals to 0.33 in. long. Marshes from MA to GA and TN. In TN, in Coffee, Warren, and Marion counties. Rare. July–August.

NOTES: The genus name *Hypericum* comes from the Greek *hypo*, meaning "almost," and *ereike*, meaning "heather," in reference to characteristics shared between heathers and St. Johnsworts. • **Coppery St. Johnswort** is easily separated from other *Hypericum* species by its square stem and coppery yellow flowers.

BETTY HYCHE

Golden St. Johnswort
Hypericum frondosum

GENERAL: Branched, **woody shrub** to 4 ft. tall. **LEAVES:** Opposite, narrowly oblong to elliptic to ovate-lanceolate, 1.2–2.5 in. long and 0.4–0.6 in. wide. **FLOWERS:** Showy, 5 wide, **yellow petals** about 1 in. long, numerous stamens; 1–3 flowers with **broad green bracts at the ends of branches**, giving them a **leafy appearance**. May–July. **FRUITS:** Cone-shaped capsules, about 0.6 in. long; numerous small, black seeds. **WHERE FOUND:** Cedar glades and rocky areas in the east-central U.S. Scattered in Middle TN. Frequent. **SIMILAR SPECIES: NAKED ST. JOHNSWORT** (*H. nudiflorum*) is a branching shrub to 7 ft. tall; linear to narrowly elliptic leaves; numerous flowers in open cymes; minute bracteal leaves and **small petals**, 0.4 in. long, give **inflorescence a naked appearance**. Wet areas in most of the southeastern U.S. In TN, in the Cumberland Plateau, also Carter and Humphreys counties. Infrequent. June–August. **SHRUBBY ST. JOHNSWORT** (*H. prolificum*) is a shrub to 7 ft. tall, **twigs sharply 2-edged**; narrow, petioled leaves; **small petals**, 0.4 in. long; usually 3–7 flowers in each cyme. Diverse habitats from wet lowlands to dry cliffs from the northeastern U.S., south to GA and LA. Mostly in the eastern ⅔ of TN. Frequent. July–September.

NOTES: The name **St. Johnswort** comes from the festival day of St. John the Baptist on June 24, when the days are long and the bright flowers begin to open, thereby embodying "the power of light over darkness," as an ancient couplet suggests. During the Dark Ages, priests used St. Johnswort in exorcisms and to protect against evil spirits and sickness.

Pineweed, Orangegrass
Hypericum gentianoides

GENERAL: Erect **annual** to 12 in. tall, repeatedly branched into numerous **wiry, thread-like branches. LEAVES:** Scale-like, to 0.1 in. long, appressed to the stem. **FLOWERS:** Yellow, 5-petaled, about 0.3 in. across, nearly sessile, mostly solitary at the nodes. June–September. **FRUITS:** Slender, **dark red, cone-shaped capsules,** about 0.25 in. long. **WHERE FOUND:** Sterile, sandy soil throughout most of the eastern U.S. In TN, from the Western Highland Rim eastward. Frequent. **SIMILAR SPECIES:** NITS-AND-LICE (*H. drummondii*) is taller, to 24 in., with less branching; numerous, linear leaves to 0.6 in. long; larger flowers, to 0.4 in. wide; **egg-shaped fruits.** Dry soil from MD and OH to southeastern KS, southward. Widely distributed across TN. Occasional. July–September.

NOTES: Other names for **Pineweed** are Ground Pine and Poverty Grass. Another name, Knitweed, comes from the resemblance of the branches to knitting needles. • John Bartram (1699–1777), an 18th-century American botanist, reported that this plant was "of excellent virtue" as an ointment for bruises and strains. • **Nits-and-Lice** gets its name from the tiny, scale-like leaves that resemble nits, the eggs of lice.

Clasping-Leaf St. Johnswort • *Hypericum gymnanthum*

GENERAL: Erect annual or perennial, 8–24 in. tall, simple or **sparingly branched. LEAVES:** Opposite, simple, **triangular-lanceolate,** 0.6–1.2 in. long, **5–7-nerved;** base rounded to nearly cordate, sessile or clasping. **FLOWERS:** Orangy yellow, about 0.25 in. wide, 5 petals; 5 **lanceolate sepals,** broadest near the base, slightly longer than petals; borne in open, few-flowered cymes extending above the foliage. June–September. **FRUITS:** Cone-shaped capsules, 0.1–0.2 in. long. **WHERE FOUND:** Moist soil. A mostly Atlantic and Gulf Coastal Plain species. In TN, in Coffee, Franklin, Hickman, Lawrence, and Van Buren counties. Rare. **SIMILAR SPECIES:** DWARF ST. JOHNSWORT (*H. mutilum*) is **highly branched,** with **ovate, blunt-tipped leaves;** oblong sepals are **blunt-tipped,** broadest near the middle; inflorescence of many-flowered cymes. Moist areas throughout the eastern U.S., eastern Canada, and TN. Common. July–September. **CANADA ST. JOHNSWORT** (*H. canadense*) has **1–3-nerved, linear leaves.** Wet soil. Eastern U.S. In TN, in the Cumberland Plateau region. Infrequent. July–September.

NOTES: Clasping-Leaf St. Johnswort is also called **Least St. Johnswort.** Its leaves sometimes turn a rose orange or copper color. • Small orange-yellow flowers with 12 or fewer stamens and broad, ovate leaves are characteristics of **Dwarf St. Johnswort.**

Common St. Johnswort · *Hypericum perforatum* *

GENERAL: Leafy, branched perennial herb to 32 in. tall.
LEAVES: Opposite, sessile, linear-oblong, 0.8–1.6 in. long, with **translucent dots** that look like holes or "windows." **FLOWERS:** Yellow, 5 petals to 0.4 in. long are **black-dotted near the margin**, numerous stamens; numerous flowers borne in a compound cyme. June–September. **FRUITS:** Cone-shaped capsules, about 0.2 in. long; brownish, cylindric seeds, 0.04–0.05 in. long, with rows of pits. **WHERE FOUND:** Introduced from Europe. Fields, meadows, and roadsides throughout the U.S. and southern Canada. In TN, in the eastern ²⁄₃ of the state, also Henry, Hardin, and McNairy counties in West TN. Frequent. **SIMILAR SPECIES:** MOUNTAIN ST. JOHNSWORT (*H. graveolens*) is an erect perennial to 24 in. tall, **mostly unbranched**; ovate, **black-spotted leaves**, about 1 in. wide, sessile or clasping; **aromatic**, yellow flowers have 5 petals, 0.4–0.7 in. long, often black-lined or black-dotted; inflorescence few-flowered cymes at the ends of branches. Balds and wet seeps at high elevations (5500–6600 ft.) in the mountains of NC and TN. In TN, in Carter, Johnson, Sevier, and Unicoi counties. Rare. July.

OTTO R. HRISCH

NOTES: In herbal medicine, **Common St. Johnswort** has been used widely to treat mild to moderate forms of **depression and nervous disorders**. Almost 20 clinical trials have confirmed its effectiveness and safety. Traditionally, the fresh flowers steeped in tea or olive oil were applied as a treatment for skin wounds, sores, cuts, and bruises. However, the compound **hypericin may cause skin burns** on sensitive skin when exposed to light.

Spotted St. Johnswort · *Hypericum punctatum*

GENERAL: Erect perennial to 40 in. tall, with a few branches below the inflorescence. Leaves, stems, sepals, and petals are heavily black-dotted. **LEAVES:** Opposite, oblong-elliptic to oblong-ovate, blunt-tipped and sometimes notched, 1.2–2.6 in. long and to 0.7 in. wide. **FLOWERS:** Bright yellow, 5 petals, about 0.25 in. long, **spotted or streaked with black on the undersides**; inflorescence terminal on the stem and branches, small and crowded with short-stalked flowers. June–August. **FRUITS:** Capsules about 0.25 in. long. **WHERE FOUND:** Wet or dry areas throughout the eastern U.S. and TN. Common. **SIMILAR SPECIES:** FALSE SPOTTED ST. JOHNSWORT (*H. pseudomaculatum*) has lanceolate to lanceolate-ovate leaves; **petals over 0.3 in. long**. Wet or dry areas from IL to OK, southward. In TN, in counties near the Tennessee River. Infrequent. June–August. BLUE RIDGE ST. JOHNSWORT (*H. mitchellianum*) is a sparingly branched perennial to 36 in. tall; **sessile leaves, somewhat clasping**, ovate-oblong, to 2.5 in. long and ½ as wide; few flowers in small, crowded cymes; **yellow petals to 0.5 in. long, scarcely black-dotted**; sepals to 0.4 in. long, marked with black lines. Moist slopes at high elevations from southwestern VA to NC and TN. Rare. July.

JERRY DROWN

NOTES: Spotted St. Johnswort is often confused with **Common St. Johnswort** (see above), but Spotted St. Johnswort has smaller, paler yellow flowers with black spots or streaks on the underside of the petals, not on the margins; the leaves are larger and more elliptic and have diffuse black spots, not translucent ones.

Round-Fruited St. Johnswort
Hypericum sphaerocarpum

GENERAL: Erect perennial to 30 in. tall; **woody stems** are clustered and often rhizomatous. **LEAVES:** Opposite, linear-oblong to narrowly elliptic, tapering to the base, 1.2–2.8 in. long and 0.2–0.6 in. wide, often with **evident lateral veins**. **FLOWERS:** Yellow, 5 petals, 0.2–0.35 in. long, **45–85 stamens**; sepals 0.1–0.2 in. long, lanceolate to ovate, **uniform** or nearly so; numerous flowers in an often compact, much-branched inflorescence. June–August. **FRUITS:** Depressed-globular or round (ovoid) capsules, about 0.25 in. long, with a slender beak; large, very rough-pitted seeds. **WHERE FOUND:** Cedar glades and barrens from OH to IA, south to AL and AR. In Middle TN, also Benton, McNairy, Rhea, and Knox counties. Occasional. **SIMILAR SPECIES: STRAGGLING ST. JOHNSWORT (H. dolabriforme)** is less erect, sometimes spreading, with narrower, shorter **leaves**, 0.8–1.6 in. long, **without evident lateral veins**; petals more than 0.35 in. long; **120–200 stamens; sepals are very unequal**, the outer pair 0.28–0.5 in. long, the others much smaller; inflorescence is compact with few flowers. Barrens from southern IN and KY to GA. In TN, in the Central Basin, Sequatchie Valley, and Ridge and Valley. Occasional. June–August.

NOTES: The species name *sphaerocarpum* means "with round fruits." **Round-Fruited St. Johnswort** is also called Roundseed St. Johnswort. Studies have shown that it is visited by both short- and long-tongued bees, which eat the pollen. • Several *Hypericum* species have flowers that last less than one day, opening in the morning and wilting rapidly in full sun.

Reclining St. Andrew's Cross
Hypericum stragulum

GENERAL: Perennial **decumbent shrub** to 10 in. tall with numerous prostrate branches **forming a mat or mound** and short, erect flowering stems. **LEAVES:** Opposite, linear to oblanceolate, about 1 in. long, narrowed to the base, rounded at the tip. **FLOWERS:** Yellow, 4 **narrow, pointed petals** to 0.5 in. long **in an elongated "X,"** numerous stamens, 4 sepals (2 outer broadly rounded, 2 inner much smaller). July–August. **FRUITS:** Cone-shaped capsules to 0.3 in. long. **WHERE FOUND:** Dry or moist areas from NY to northern GA, west to eastern OK. Throughout TN. Common. **H. hypericoides ssp. muticaule. SIMILAR SPECIES: ST. ANDREW'S CROSS (H. hypericoides)** is an **erect, woody shrub** to 4 ft. tall, with a **single main stem**, freely branched above; leaves typically broadest near the middle; 4 yellow petals are narrowly oblong-linear to oblong-elliptic. Dry or moist areas from NJ to OK, southward. Throughout TN. Frequent. June–August. *Ascyrum hypericoides*.

NOTES: The root of **St. Andrew's Cross** was chewed by Native Americans for snakebites and was made into a tea to treat fevers and toothaches. Tea made from the leaves was used to treat skin problems as well as bladder and kidney ailments. • Like **Common St. Johnswort**, in laboratory experiments, St. Andrew's Cross has shown some potential for working against HIV-infected cells.

DENNIS HORN

DENNIS HORN

DENNIS HORN

Greater Marsh St. Johnswort
Triadenum walteri

General: Erect perennial herb with stems to 40 in. tall. **Leaves:** Opposite, lanceolate-elliptic to oblong or oblong-lanceolate, to 5 in. long and 1.2 in. wide, **tapering to a short petiole**, dotted with **translucent glands**, dark-dotted beneath. **Flowers:** Pinkish, about 0.5 in. across, 5 petals, 5 blunt-tipped, greenish sepals; borne in a terminal cyme or in the leaf axils. July–September. **Fruits:** Ellipsoid capsules, about 0.4 in. long, frequently rounded at the tip. **Where Found:** Swamps and marshes. A mostly Coastal Plain species found from MD to TX, occasionally inland to southern MO and southern IN. The western ⅔ of TN, also Knox and Polk counties in East TN. Occasional. **Similar Species:** VIRGINIA MARSH ST. JOHNSWORT (*T. virginicum*) is shorter, to 24 in. tall, with purple-tinged stems and leaves; **smaller, sessile leaves** to 2.4 in. long, heart-shaped at the base, embracing the stem; cylindric fruits. Swamps and marshes from Nova Scotia to MS, inland to IL. In TN, from the Eastern Highland Rim, eastward. Infrequent. July–August. LESSER MARSH ST. JOHNSWORT (*T. tubulosum*) has leaves **without translucent glands; greenish white flowers**. Wooded swamps from VA to TX, inland to southern MO. Thinly scattered across TN. Infrequent. July–September.

Notes: There are 4 species of *Triadenum* known in TN. The genus is characterized by entire, paired leaves and pinkish to greenish, 5-petaled flowers that open in the afternoon and close the next morning.

MILO PYNE

Halberdleaf Rose Mallow
Hibiscus laevis

General: Smooth perennial herb to 5 ft. tall. **Leaves:** Alternate, toothed, smooth, **heart-shaped or hastate (halberd-shaped)** with basal lobes at right angles. **Flowers:** Pale pink with a **darker, reddish center**, 5 petals, 2–3 in. long; **numerous stamens** surround the style, united at the base but free at the tips, forming a **showy**, tube-like structure that protrudes from the flower center; flowers are clustered at the ends of the stem. July–September. **Fruits:** Roundish capsules, 1 in. long, with an abruptly pointed tip; seeds are densely covered with reddish brown hairs. **Where Found:** Alluvial marshes and riverbanks. Widespread in the eastern U.S. and TN (mostly West TN). Occasional. *H. militaris*.

Notes: *Hibiscus* species have large, showy flowers, with the corolla twisted in bud, and **numerous stamens united in a tube around the style.** Leaves are alternate, and the margins have teeth or lobes. There are 4 species of *Hibiscus* in TN. • The **Mallow Family** is mostly tropical, with several economically important genera, such as Upland Cotton (*Gossypium hirsutum*) and Okra (*Hibiscus esculentus*). All species have 5 petals that are distinct. There are 8 genera and 17 species in the Mallow Family listed for TN.

Swamp Rose Mallow · *Hibiscus moscheutos*

JAMES W. LEA

GENERAL: Robust perennial herb, 4–7 ft. tall, with hairy stems. **LEAVES:** Alternate, ovate to elliptic-lanceolate, 4–8 in. long, heart-shaped to obtuse at the base, lower leaves often with 2 shallow lateral lobes; **downy-white beneath**, soft to the touch. **FLOWERS:** White to pink with a crimson center, 5 petals, 2–3 in. long; calyx and bractlets with star-shaped hairs; flowers are clustered on stout stalks at the stem tip. June–September. **FRUITS:** Smooth capsules, about 1.5 in. long, usually tipped with a short beak; dark brown seeds are smooth, but appear rough. **WHERE FOUND:** Swamp edges, meadows, and brackish marshes. Widespread in the eastern U.S and TN. Frequent. **SIMILAR SPECIES:** ROSE-OF-SHARON (*H. syriacus**) is a commonly **cultivated shrub** that sometimes escapes to woodland borders. Smaller flowers in a variety of colors including white, rose, and lavender with a dark red center. Occasional in the wild. June–September.

NOTES: Swamp Rose Mallow is also known as Crimson-Eyed Rose Mallow, Breast Root, Mallow Rose, Muskplant, and Wild Cotton. • The leaves and roots of Swamp Rose Mallow, like those of many *Hisbiscus* species, are very **slimy** (mucilaginous) and have been used as a soothing and softening agent for treating gastrointestinal disorders, as well as lung and urinary ailments.

Flower-of-an-Hour · *Hibiscus trionum**

GENERAL: Annual to 24 in. tall, with several hairy stems arising from a taproot; stems also have thick mats of hairs in 2 lines from the base of one leaf to the next leaf below. **LEAVES:** Alternate, long-stalked, 1–3 in. long, deeply 3-parted, the segments oblong to obovate and coarsely lobed or toothed. **FLOWERS:** 5 petals are **pale yellow**, to 1.6 in. long, with a pale purple band running up the side and a large, **red-purple base**; short, narrow bractlets surround the beautifully nerved, downy, 5-angled, inflated calyx; flowers only open for a few hours. July–September. **FRUITS:** Minutely hairy capsules, about 0.5 in. long; black, flattened seeds. **WHERE FOUND:** Introduced from Europe. Fields, roadsides, and waste places throughout the eastern U.S. In TN, in Henry, Knox, Grainger, Hawkins, and Greene counties. Rare. **SIMILAR SPECIES:** CAROLINA MALLOW (*Modiola caroliniana**), also called BRISTLY MALLOW, has leaves that are palmately divided into 6–7 lobes; smaller flowers have brilliant **orange-red petals with a blackish-purple base**. Introduced from the tropics. Low ground, lawns, and pastures throughout the southeastern U.S. In TN, in Knox and Shelby counties. Rare. March–June.

NITA R. HEILMAN

NOTES: The most commonly known *Hibiscus* is Rose of China (*H. rosa-sinensis*), the magnificent shrub that grows in tropical areas. There is a story that the women of Tahiti and other Pacific islands wore the flowers as a symbol of freedom from marriage or commitment to another person. In some areas it is also called **Shoe-Back Plant**, because the large petals were used to put polish on shoes.

Common Mallow, Cheeses · *Malva neglecta**

GENERAL: Small, creeping, **weedy annual or biennial** to 3 ft. tall, generally branched from the base; stems have branched (star-like) hairs. **LEAVES:** Alternate, 1–2 in. wide, rounded with a heart-shaped base, 5–7 shallow lobes to nearly unlobed, hairy on both sides; long, hairy petioles. **FLOWERS:** Pale pink or white, 0.5–0.6 in. wide, 5 notched **petals are 2x as long as sepals**; grow from leaf axils. April–October. **FRUITS:** Flattened ring of carpels, separating into about 15 indehiscent, single-seeded chambers. **WHERE FOUND:** Introduced from Eurasia; now established as a weed in waste places throughout temperate North America. In TN, in several counties, mostly near the KY border. Occasional. **SIMILAR SPECIES:** DWARF MALLOW (**M. rotundifolia***) has flowers that are ¹/₂ as large; **petals are slightly longer than sepals**; ring of carpels with about 10 single-seeded chambers. Introduced from Europe, now widely scattered in the U.S. In Davidson and Rutherford counties in Middle TN. May–September. **M. pusilla**.

NOTES: The name **Cheeses** refers to this plant's flat, rounded fruits and its general edibility. Most *Malva* species are edible in some manner. Young shoots, leaves, and roots are edible raw, while more mature leaves are slimy (mucilaginous) and can be used in soups. The leaves contain vitamins A, B1, B2, and C, as well as minerals. If eaten in large quantities, they can **produce a laxative effect.**

High Mallow
*Malva sylvestris**

GENERAL: Erect **biennial**, 1–3 ft. tall, freely branched; stems generally have long, unbranched hairs. **LEAVES:** Alternate, rounded, crinkly, 2–6 in. across with 5–7 **shallow lobes**, the margins toothed, upper surface without hairs; petioles 2–6 in. long. **FLOWERS:** Pink-purple with dark red **radial veins**, 1.0–1.5 in. across, 5 notched petals much longer than sepals; flowers on pedicels 2–4 in. long spring from the leaf axils. May–July. **FRUITS:** Ring of about 10 carpels, smooth, but with raised veins on the back. **WHERE FOUND:** Introduced from Eurasia. Escaped from cultivation and found occasionally over most of the U.S. Thinly scattered in Middle and East TN. Infrequent. **SIMILAR SPECIES:** MUSK MALLOW (**M. moschata***) is a perennial herb; **upper stem leaves deeply divided** into 3–7 segments, these again divided; **white or pink flowers** about 1.5 in. across, the 5 petals shallowly notched. Introduced from Europe. Escaped from cultivation to roadsides and waste places in the northeastern and northwestern U.S. Rare in TN, found only in Johnson County. May–August.

NOTES: Other common names for **High Mallow** include Cheesecake, Country Mallow, Malice, Maul, Pancake Plant, and Round Dock. • High Mallow has been reported to be "good for the belly" and the seed mixed with wine "doth assuage the griefs about the bladder."

Coastal Plain Sida
Sida elliottii

GENERAL: Branching perennial herb to 3 ft. tall; stems have dense, short hairs. **LEAVES:** Alternate, linear to linear-oblong, 0.8–2.4 in. long, short-petioled to sessile, sharply toothed to almost entire. **FLOWERS:** Bright, almost **translucent yellow**; 5 rounded to slightly notched petals about 0.6 in. long; occur singly in the leaf axils on stalks 0.2–1.0 in. long. June–August. **FRUITS:** Commonly 10 carpels, each tipped with **2 erect beaks** covered with soft, short hairs. **WHERE FOUND:** Dry to moist sandy soils in fields and barrens of the southeastern U.S. In TN, in Decatur, Davidson, Rutherford, Hamilton, and Meigs counties. Rare. **SIMILAR SPECIES:** CUBAN JUTE (**S. rhombifolia***) has **flowers only ¹/₂ as large**; carpels have only 1 beak. Introduced from the tropics. Roadsides and waste places in the southern U.S. Thinly scattered across TN. Infrequent. June–October.

PAUL SOMERS

NOTES: Coastal Plain Sida is named for its discoverer, American botanist Stephen Elliott (1771–1830). • *Sida* species have no bractlets at the base of the calyx, and the calyx surrounds 10 pistil chambers that separate at maturity, each with a single hanging seed. There are 4 species in TN.

Prickly Mallow
Sida spinosa*

GENERAL: Softly hairy, **weedy annual** to 3 ft. tall, with a taproot and fibrous root system. **LEAVES:** Alternate, **ovate to oblong-lanceolate**, 1–2 in. long, toothed, base rounded to heart-shaped, slender petioles more than 1 in. long; a small tubercle (hardened, sharp stipule) at the base of the lower leaves gives this plant its name. **FLOWERS:** Pale yellow, to 0.5 in. wide, 5 petals; borne singly in leaf axils, but sometimes appearing as 2 because of the short, flower-bearing branches. July–October. **FRUITS:** 5 carpels, each tipped with 2 hairy beaks. **WHERE FOUND:** Introduced from the tropics. Waste places and open ground. Widespread in the eastern U.S. and TN. Frequent. **SIMILAR SPECIES:** VIRGINIA MALLOW (**S. hermaphrodita**) is a perennial herb to 6 ft. tall; broad, **deeply lobed leaves**; **white flowers**. Northeastern U.S. In East TN, in Claiborne, Cocke, and Washington counties. Rare. June–August.

DENNIS HORN

NOTES: Prickly Mallow is also known as Prickly Fanpetals, Prickly Sida, and Teaweed. • In the southern states, it is considered **a troublesome weed**, especially in fields of peanuts, cotton, and soybeans. • In India and Sri Lanka, Prickly Mallow is known as Nagabala and is used medicinally to treat gonorrhea and mild cases of debility and fever.

Dwarf Sundew
Drosera brevifolia

GENERAL: Small, **insect-eating perennial** herb to 3 in. tall. **LEAVES:** Prostrate basal, pale green to reddish leaves form a small rosette, about 1 in. across; blades are wedge-shaped at the base and rounded at the end; petioles are smooth and dilated; **sticky, reddish, gland-tipped hairs on the leaves trap tiny insects**; leaves die back after the plant flowers. **FLOWERS: Rose or white**, 5 obovate petals about 0.25 in. long; **glandular-hairy flower scape** rises from the center of the rosette to 3 in. tall, bearing 1–8 small flowers. May. **FRUITS:** Capsules, usually 3-valved; black seeds. **WHERE FOUND:** Sandy, bare soil in the southeastern U.S. In TN, in Coffee, Franklin, Lewis, and Warren counties. Rare. **SIMILAR SPECIES: PINK SUNDEW** (*D. capillaris*) has **pink flowers** and a **smooth scape**; prostrate leaf rosette persists throughout the year; capsules, usually 3-valved, contain brown seeds. Low, wet areas in the southeastern U.S. In TN, in Cumberland, Bledsoe, McNairy, and Van Buren counties. Rare. May–August.

NOTES: The genus name *Drosera* comes from the Greek *droseras*, which means "dewy" or "glistening in the sun." • Sundews are **carnivorous** plants. Small insects are caught by the shining, mucilaginous droplets that are produced at the tips of slender red hairs on the basal leaf rosette. Insects are attracted by both the red color and the sweet, sticky secretions. When an insect touches a leaf, the leaf rolls the hairs toward the victim, firmly trapping it. Flowers are open for approximately 2 hours in the middle of the day and ordinarily only in full sun.

Spatulate-Leaf Sundew
Drosera intermedia

GENERAL: Insect-eating perennial herb, to 4 in. tall. **LEAVES:** Pale green to reddish, in a basal rosette and also at intervals on the scape, to 2.5 in. long, short, **spoon-shaped blades**, long, narrow petioles; numerous **reddish, sticky, gland-tipped hairs on the leaves trap small insects**. **FLOWERS: White**, about 0.25 in. wide; 5 obovate petals; scape, to 4 in. tall, rises from the rosette center bearing 1 to several small flowers. May–June. **FRUITS:** Capsule, usually 3-valved; reddish brown seeds. **WHERE FOUND:** Wet, open places in the eastern U.S. In TN, in the Cumberland Plateau and Eastern Highland Rim. Infrequent. **SIMILAR SPECIES: ROUNDLEAF SUNDEW** (*D. rotundifolia*) has **flat petioles; leaf blades are nearly round**; capsules, usually 3-valved, contain light brown, shiny seeds. Bogs and swamps in Canada and the northern and southeastern U.S. In TN, in Carter, Fentress, Johnson, and Sevier counties. Rare. July–September.

NOTES: Roundleaf Sundew contains plumbagin, which can be used in small doses to stimulate the immune system. Fresh leaves have been used to treat lung ailments, were used in Europe in the preparation of cheeses and junkets, and were applied to corns and warts. • Sundews are pollinated by mosquitoes, midges, and gnats. Those insects that do not escape are captured by the sticky leaves to provide nourishment for the plant.

Low Frostweed
Helianthemum propinquum

GENERAL: Erect perennial to 12 in. tall with **scattered stems** from a creeping rhizome; branching hairs on stem and leaves. **LEAVES:** Alternate, linear-spatulate, to 1.5 in. long, tapering to a narrow base. **FLOWERS: Yellow**, about 1 in. wide, 5 petals; **2–6 flowers in a terminal cyme**; some flowers remain closed and are self-pollinating. May–July. **FRUITS:** Ovoid capsules. **WHERE FOUND:** Dry, open areas. A northeastern U.S. species with disjunct populations in TN in Coffee, Cumberland, Monroe, and Van Buren counties. Rare. **SIMILAR SPECIES: CANADA FROSTWEED (*H. canadense*)** has **clustered stems** arising from the erect, woody base; **flowers usually solitary**; fruits are capsules with 3 sharp angles. Dry, sandy soil. A northeastern species extending south to TN and GA. In TN, in Blount and Sevier counties. Rare. May–July.

KURT EMMANUELE

NOTES: The genus name *Helianthemum* is from the Greek *helios*, "the sun," and *anthemon*, "a flower," which combined mean "sunflower." The flowers of these plants open only in full sunlight. • Frostweeds are so called because, in winter, **ribbons of ice emerge from the stem**. Water in the stem freezes and is forced out of the stem through cracks in the husk, forming "**frost flowers**."

Green Violet · *Hybanthus concolor*

GENERAL: Perennial, somewhat coarse and hairy, up to 3 ft. tall, from a crown of fibrous roots. **LEAVES:** Alternate, 3–6 in. long, broadly elliptic to ovate-oblong with an abruptly acuminate tip; leaves taper to a narrow stalk, 0.4–0.8 in. long. **FLOWERS:** About 0.2 in. long, sepals and petals are both **greenish white; on drooping stalks from the leaf axils.** April–June. **FRUITS:** Shallowly lobed, oblong, 3-valved capsules, 0.6–0.8 in. long. **WHERE FOUND:** Rich woodlands, usually on neutral soils, throughout the eastern U.S. In Middle and East TN, also Obion and Shelby counties in West TN. Common.

NOTES: While it does not resemble typical violets, examination of this species' flowers will reveal similarities. This species is the only representative of the *Hybanthus* genus in TN. • The **Violet Family** contains about 16 genera and 800 species worldwide. There are around 80 violet species in the U.S., with 23 species and 3 varieties occurring in TN.

HUGH & CAROL NOURSE

Sweet White Violet · *Viola blanda*

GENERAL: Stemless perennial herb, about 4 in. tall, from slender rhizomes, later developing runners (stolons). **LEAVES:** All basal, dark green with a satiny sheen, heart-shaped, on long stalks. **FLOWERS:** White, mildly fragrant, petals more than 0.4 in. long, upper 2 petals often bent backward, lower 3 petals usually purple-veined near the base; borne on separate, long stalks extending just above the leaves; self-pollinating flowers that do not open develop later on reclining stalks, 1–3 in. long; both flower and leaf stalks are tinged with red. April–May. **FRUITS:** Capsules, about 0.25 in. long; dark brown seeds. **WHERE FOUND:** Rich woodlands in the northeastern U.S. and the eastern ½ of TN. Occasional. **SIMILAR SPECIES: NORTHERN WHITE VIOLET (*V. macloskeyi* ssp. *pallens*) has petals less than 0.4 in. long.** Rich, wet places in the northeastern U.S., south in the mountains to GA. In TN, in the Blue Ridge Mountains. Rare. April–July.

NITA R. HEILMAN

NOTES: Traditionally, the Cherokee people used the **Sweet White Violet** as a vegetable. The leaves and stems, mixed with other greens, were parboiled, rinsed, and fried in fat seasoned with salt. • *Viola* species have either above-ground stems (caulescent), with leaves and flowers on the same stalk (stemmed), or below-ground stems in the form of rhizomes (acaulescent), with leaves and flowers on separate stalks (stemless). Most produce both 5-petaled flowers (2 upper and 3 lower petals) and other fertile flowers that produce seed without opening (cleistogamous).

Canada Violet
Viola canadensis

GENERAL: Perennial herb with leafy stems to 16 in. tall, creeping stolons, and short, thick rhizomes. **LEAVES:** Basal leaves, 2–4 in. long, narrowly to broadly heart-shaped, on long stalks; alternate stem leaves are similar and numerous, with entire, narrowly lanceolate stipules. **FLOWERS:** White with a yellow center, 5 petals are purple-veined near the base and slightly purple-

GARTH FRASER

tinged on the back side; flowers are terminal, on long stalks from the leaf axils; **self-pollinating flowers not produced.** April–July. **FRUITS:** Ellipsoid to globose capsules. **WHERE FOUND:** Mesic woodlands from Newfoundland to AK, south to AL, AR, and AZ. Eastern ½ of TN. Frequent.

NOTES: In the 19th century, enormous quantities of violets were grown for perfume until the chemical formula for the scent was discovered in 1893 by German scientists, and it was thereafter replicated in laboratories. • In herbal medicine, Native Americans used the roots of this plant to treat pain in the bladder region, and the roots and leaves were used to induce vomiting and as a poultice for cuts and skin irritations.

Dog Violet · *Viola conspersa*

JERRY DROWN

GENERAL: Perennial herb with numerous smooth, **leafy stems to 8 in. tall,** in clusters from a rhizome which is sometimes branched. **LEAVES:** Basal, kidney-shaped, rounded or blunt, on long stalks; stem leaves are alternate, also long-stalked, but are heart-shaped, to 1.6 in. long, with broadly lanceolate **stipules that are fringed** toward the top of the plant. **FLOWERS:** Usually **pale violet,** sometimes white, 5 petals with dark veining, 2 lateral petals bearded, bottom petal about 0.2 in. long; style slightly hairy; **spur less than 0.3 in. long**; numerous, from leaf axils on long stalks that extend above the leaves; in summer, self-pollinated flowers that do not open (cleistogamous) grow from the same axils that bore the spring flowers. April–June. **FRUITS:** Ellipsoid capsules; light brown seeds. **WHERE FOUND:** Mesic woodlands. A mostly northeastern species extending southward in the uplands to TN and AL. Eastern ½ of TN. Occasional.

NOTES: The species name *conspersa* is Latin for "scattered" or "sprinkled," in reference to the dots on the lower leaf surface. • Contrary to popular belief, the flowers of most violets are not fragrant, except for **Sweet White Violet** (p. 96), Sweet Violet (*V. odorata**), and a few others. Violets rely on visual beauty rather than scent to attract pollinators. • In traditional medicine, an infusion of the **Dog Violet** plant was used to treat heart trouble.

Marsh Blue Violet
Viola cucullata

PAUL SOMERS

GENERAL: Smooth, **stemless,** perennial herb, 6–8 in. tall. **LEAVES:** All basal, heart-shaped, 2–4 in. long, on long stalks. **FLOWERS: Blue-violet to white,** 5 petals usually have **dark-veined "eye zone"** at the center, 2 lateral petals densely bearded; borne on tall, very erect stalks that usually **extend well above the leaves**; also self-pollinated flowers that do not open on long, erect stalks. April–June. **FRUITS:** Ovoid-cylindric capsules; seeds almost black. **WHERE FOUND:** Rich, wet places. In most of the eastern U.S., from TN and GA northward. Throughout TN. Common.

NOTES: The **flowers of all violet species are edible** and can be added uncooked as a nutritious and pleasing decorative element to salads and desserts. The leaves of several species of violets are cooked as greens in Asia, and were often used as thickening agents in soups and sauces. • This plant has been used medicinally by the Cherokee people for many uses. A poultice of the leaves was used to treat headaches, a sweetened infusion was used to treat coughs, and an infusion was taken as a spring tonic to lighten the mood. • Although many violet species have been used traditionally in herbal medicine and are edible, they contain saponins, which may be **toxic** when eaten or taken in larger doses.

Glade Violet
Viola egglestonii

GENERAL: Smooth, **stemless**, perennial herb, 4–6 in. tall. **LEAVES:** All basal, **divided into 3–5 segments** which may be 2–3 cleft, usually toothed at the tip, with a few long, narrow teeth below. **FLOWERS: Blue-violet with whitish center**, 5 petals, each about 0.4 in. long, lower 3 petals bearded; borne on long stalks; also self-pollinated flowers that do not open, on underground stalks until ripe, then aboveground and erect. March–May. **FRUITS:** Ellipsoidal capsules; brown seeds. **WHERE FOUND:** Limestone barrens and cedar glades, from southern IN, south to northern AL, and northwestern GA. In TN, in the Central Basin, also Hamilton and Meigs counties. Occasional. *V. septemloba* **ssp.** *egglestoni*.

NOTES: Another common name for this plant is **Eggleston's Violet**, as indicated by the species name, *egglestonii*. It is closely related to and often considered a variety of **Wood Violet** (p. 99). • Violets have been mentioned in theatrical performances ranging from William Shakespeare's *Hamlet, King John, Twelfth Night, Midsummer Night's Dream,* and *Cymbeline,* as well as Lerner and Loewe's *My Fair Lady.* • Violets are frequently grown as ornamentals and often escape from cultivation.

Halberdleaf Yellow Violet • *Viola hastata*

GENERAL: Perennial herb, stems to 10 in. tall, from a long, branching rhizome. **LEAVES:** Alternate, usually 2–4, generally long, **triangular-shaped, flared at the base, upper leaf surfaces often mottled with silvery blotches**; on short stalks from the upper portion of the stem, occasionally 1 leaf on a long stalk from the base of the stem. **FLOWERS: Bright yellow**, 5 petals; borne on slender erect stalks that extend just above the leaves. April–May. **FRUITS:** Ellipsoid capsules; light brown seeds. **WHERE FOUND:** Mesic woodlands from PA and OH to SC, northern GA, and eastern TN. In TN, from the Eastern Highland Rim eastward. Occasional.

NOTES: The arrowhead leaves of this violet are said to somewhat resemble the halberd, a type of battle-ax that was used in the 15th and 16th centuries. • In folklore, the violet is a symbol of simplicity and modesty, and in William Shakespeare's writings, it represented humility and loyalty paired with love. • Compounds in some violet species can destroy skin tissue and have been used to treat skin cancer, but this has not been validated by scientific research.

Lanceleaf Violet · *Viola lanceolata*

GENERAL: Smooth, stoloniferous, **stemless** perennial herb, 4–6 in. tall, from slender rhizomes. **LEAVES:** Basal, erect, narrowly lanceolate and tapering at the base, to 4 in. long and generally **more than 3 times as long as wide**; leaf stalks usually reddish. **FLOWERS:** Solitary, **white, 5 beardless petals**, lower 3 petals have brownish purple veins near the base; borne on long, reddish stalks; also self-pollinated flowers that do not open, on erect stalks. April–June. **FRUITS:** Ellipsoid, green capsules; dark brown seeds. **WHERE FOUND:** Wet places in most of the eastern U.S. In TN, widely scattered from the Western Highland Rim eastward, in Montgomery, Robertson, Overton, Fentress, Scott, Morgan, Sevier, Warren, Coffee, and Franklin counties. Infrequent.

NOTES: The species name *lanceolata* is a reference to the narrow, lance-shaped leaves. This plant is also called **Strapleaf Violet**, another reference to the leaves. • Historically, violets were used for cosmetic purposes: women would blend the flowers in goat's milk and apply it to their faces to improve their complexions.

NITA R. HEILMAN

Wood Violet · *Viola palmata*

GENERAL: Hairy, **stemless** perennial herb, 4–6 in. tall. **LEAVES:** All basal, on long stalks, **palmately 3–11-lobed** with the segments variously toothed or cleft and generally hairy, but the earliest leaves may be merely ovate. **FLOWERS:** Variable from **blue-violet, streaked violet and white, to solid white**, up to 1 in. across, 5 petals; borne on long stalks; also self-pollinated flowers that do not open, on reclining stalks. April–May. **FRUITS:** Ovoid, purple-brown mottled capsules; brown seeds. **WHERE FOUND:** Woodlands and glades throughout most of the eastern U.S. and TN. Common. *V. triloba*.

NOTES: The species name *palmata* refers to the palm-like appearance of some of the leaves. • The flowers of some violets can be made into candy, jam, jelly, preserves, and syrup. They can even be made into an acceptable sweet wine. In herbal medicine, used as a tea, violets are said to cure headaches.

THOMAS G. BARNES

JERRY DROWN

Birdfoot Violet · *Viola pedata*

GENERAL: Smooth, **stemless** perennial herb, 4–6 in. tall.
LEAVES: All basal, long-stalked, 3-parted lateral segments are 3–5 cleft, making the leaf appear to be more or less divided into 9–15 lanceolate, spatulate, or **linear segments** that sometimes are 2–4-toothed at the tip.
FLOWERS: To 1.2 in. across, 5 smooth, **beardless petals may be uniformly of one color, blue-violet to white, or bicolored** (upper 2 petals dark purple, lower 3 lavender), other color variations exist; conspicuous, large, **orange stamens** extend well outside petals; flowers are borne on long stalks that extend above leaves; **self-pollinating flowers not produced.** April–June. **FRUITS:** Green capsules; light brown, shiny seeds. **WHERE FOUND:** Open, often sandy places, from ME to MN, south to northern FL and eastern TX. In the eastern ⅔ of TN, also Hardin, McNairy, and Carroll counties. Frequent.

NOTES: This plant's common name refers to the finely cut leaves with narrow segments, said to resemble a bird's foot. • The large, flat-faced flowers with prominent, orange stamens make this plant a perennial favorite. • The large flowers of **Birdfoot Violet** distinguish it from all of the other violets in TN. • The Cherokee people would soak the seeds of corn in an infusion made from the roots of this plant to repel insects.

OTTO R. HIRSCH

Primrose-Leaved Violet
Viola primulifolia

GENERAL: Stemless perennial herb, 4–6 in. tall, developing runners (stolons) after flowering. **LEAVES:** All basal, elliptic to ovate-oblong, **less than 3x as long as wide**, rounded to truncate, blade tissue tapers down petioles, giving a broadly winged appearance. **FLOWERS:** White, 5 petals, **3 lower petals have brownish purple veins** near the base, 2 lateral petals slightly bearded or beardless; borne on long stalks, usually surpassing the leaves; also self-pollinated flowers that do not open, on short stalks. April–June. **FRUITS:** Green, ellipsoid capsules; reddish brown seeds. **WHERE FOUND:** Wet places. In most of the eastern U.S. In TN, from the Eastern Highland Rim eastward, also Lawrence, Hardin, McNairy, Benton, Carroll, and Henry counties. Occasional.

NOTES: The species name *primulifolia* indicates that this plant has somewhat similar foliage to species of primrose (*Primula*). • Some violets, usually those with flowers held higher than the leaves, such as **Primrose-Leaved Violet**, have an explosive seed-dispersal device. As the capsule dries, the walls fold in on themselves, eventually expelling the seeds under pressure and propelling them into the air.

Yellow Woodland Violet · *Viola pubescens*

RICHARD CONNORS

GENERAL: Softly hairy, **stemmed**, perennial herb, 4–18 in. tall. **LEAVES:** Alternate, on long stalks, narrowly to broadly ovate, 2–4 in. long, several arising from the stem and one to several from the stem base. **FLOWERS:** 5 **bright yellow petals have brownish purple veins** near the base, **lateral petals bearded**, lower petal with a short spur; borne on smooth or downy stalks that rise a little above the leaves; also self-pollinated flowers that do not open, on short, axillary stalks. April–May. **FRUITS:** Ovoid, smooth, or sometimes woolly capsules; brown seeds. **WHERE FOUND:** Rich mesic woodlands in most of the eastern U.S. Throughout TN. Common. *V. pensylvanica*, *V. eriocarpa*.

NOTES: The flowers and leaves of violets are very high in vitamins A and C. Pound for pound, violet blossoms are said to contain more vitamin C than oranges. • Some violet seeds have growths called "oil-bodies" on the outer surface. The seeds are carried away from the plant by ants, which then eat the "oil-bodies." • The Iroquois people traditionally used a decoction of **Yellow Woodland Violet** to treat indigestion.

Field Pansy · *Viola rafinesquii*

DENNIS HORN

GENERAL: **Smooth annual** herb to 16 in. tall, often branched from the base, with leafy stems. **LEAVES:** Alternate, on short stalks, spatulate, about 1 in. long; **very large, leafy, lobed stipules** at the base. **FLOWERS:** Blue to bluish white to cream-colored, 0.3–0.4 in. across, on long stalks, 5 petals, **sepals about ¹/₂ as long as petals**; also self-pollinated, closed flowers on short stalks. March–April. **FRUITS:** Oblong-ellipsoid capsules; light brown seeds. **WHERE FOUND:** Waste places throughout most of the eastern U.S. and TN. Common. **SIMILAR SPECIES:** EUROPEAN FIELD PANSY (*V. arvensis**) is a more robust species; stems have reflexed hairs on the edges; **pale yellow to ivory flowers**; broadly lanceolate **sepals longer than petals**; globose fruits with brown seeds. Introduced. Cultivated fields and roadsides. In TN, in Knox, Lawrence, Maury, Sumner, Williamson, and Wilson counties. Infrequent. April–September.

NOTES: Over 120 varieties of violets are cultivated as ornamentals and are economically important in the florist's trade. • The popular evergreen **Garden Pansy** is *Viola* x *wittrockiana*, a hybrid with many variations.

Long-Spurred Violet
Viola rostrata

GENERAL: Smooth-stemmed perennial herb to 10 in. tall. **LEAVES:** Alternate, long-stalked, more or less ovate with a heart-shaped base, 1–2 in. long, arising from the stem and stem base; **stipules lanceolate and fringed. FLOWERS: Blue-violet, 5 beardless petals,** lower petal with noticeably elongated, aft-extending, **narrow spur usually 0.6–0.8 in. long;** on long stalks rising well above the leaves, terminal or from leaf axils; also self-pollinated, closed flowers produced in upper leaf axils. April–June. **FRUITS:** Smooth, ovoid, 3-chambered capsules; light brown seeds. **WHERE FOUND:** Rich, moist lower slopes and ravines. Extended range from ME and southeastern Canada to WI, south to GA and AL. In TN, from the Western Highland Rim eastward. Frequent. **SIMILAR SPECIES: WALTER'S VIOLET (*V. walteri*)** is a **smaller, hairy, more prostrate plant; round leaves;** purplish, ovoid-globose fruits with brown seeds. Rich woodlands from southern OH to VA, south to FL and TX. In TN, in Bedford, Blount, Cumberland, Hamilton, Jefferson, Sevier, and White counties. Infrequent. April–June.

NOTES: The species name *rostrata* means "beaked," referring to the long-spurred, lower petal of **Long-Spurred Violet.** • Holes in the spurs are often caused by bumblebees that bite through them to retrieve the nectar.

OTTO R. HIRSCH

Roundleaf Yellow Violet
Viola rotundifolia

GENERAL: Stemless perennial herb, 2–4 in. tall, from a long, wiry rhizome that appears jagged because of persistent bases of old leaves. **LEAVES:** Basal, long-stalked, **broadly ovate or rounded,** about 1 in. long at flowering and almost as wide, becoming 2x as large by mid-summer. **FLOWERS: Bright yellow,** 5 petals, 3 lower petals brown-veined at the base, **2 lateral petals bearded;** on short, stout stalks; also self-pollinated flowers that do not open, dotted with purple, on stalks that are bent downward. March–April. **FRUITS:** Ovoid capsules; seeds almost white or pale brown. **WHERE FOUND:** Rich mesic woodlands. A northeastern species extending south to SC and GA in the mountains. In TN, from the Cumberland Plateau eastward. Occasional.

NOTES: The species name *rotundifolia* means "round leaves," referring to the characteristic glossy leaf on this plant. • This species is easily identified as it is the only yellow violet in eastern North America with **leaves and flowers on separate stalks.**

DAVID KOCHER

Arrowleaf Violet · *Viola sagittata*

GENERAL: Stemless perennial herb, 3–6 in. tall. **LEAVES:** Basal, 2–4 in. long, oblong-lanceolate to narrowly triangular, often **sagittate or hastate**, incised or toothed at the truncate base; on erect stalks usually longer than the blades; leaves in late summer often triangular. **FLOWERS:** Blue-violet, 0.8–1.0 in. across, 5 petals, **lower petals bearded** and usually prominently dark-veined at the base; borne on long stalks; also self-pollinated flowers that do not open, on erect stalks. April–June. **FRUITS:** Ovoid capsules; brown seeds. **WHERE FOUND:** Usually dry, open woods, clearings, and fields throughout most of the eastern U.S. In TN, from the Western Highland Rim eastward, also Henry and Obion counties. Frequent. **SIMILAR SPECIES: SOUTHERN WOOD VIOLET (*V. hirsutula*)** has **cordate-ovate to kidney-shaped leaves, silvery-hairy above, purplish and smooth below**; bright purple flowers; also self-pollinated fruits that do not open on short reclining stalks; ovoid, purplish fruits with pale brown seeds. Woodlands. A more southeastern species extending north into TN and KY. In TN, from the Western Highland Rim eastward. Frequent. April–June.

NOTES: **Arrowleaf Violet** can be identified by its narrow, elongate leaf with projecting lobes at the base. • The **Southern Wood Violet** was first described by Ezra Brainerd (1844–1924), president of Middlebury College in Vermont. • A preparation of Arrowleaf Violet was used by the Iroquois people to detect if a person had been bewitched.

Common Blue Violet · *Viola sororia* var. *sororia*

GENERAL: Smooth, **stemless** perennial herb, 4–6 in. tall, from a stout horizontal rhizome. **LEAVES:** Basal, more or less ovate or **broadly heart-shaped**, 2–4 in. long and wide, often hairy, on long stalks. **FLOWERS:** Blue-violet to white with a whitish center, to 1.2 in. across, 5 petals, **lateral petals bearded**; also self-pollinated flowers that do not open, on horizontal stalks. April–June. **FRUITS:** Ellipsoid or cylindric capsules, commonly purplish; dark brown seeds. **WHERE FOUND:** Woodlands, thickets, and wasteground throughout most of the U.S. and TN. Common. *V. papilionacea*. **SIMILAR SPECIES: CONFEDERATE VIOLET (*V. priceana*)** is a grayish white color form of **Common Blue Violet** with violet veins forming a blue "eye." **MISSOURI VIOLET (*V. sororia* var. *missouriensis*)** differs by its **more triangular-shaped leaves, paler flowers**, and preference for alluvial woodlands; broadly ellipsoid fruits have fine brown dots and bright buff seeds. From IN to NE, south to TN and TX. Throughout TN. Occasional. April–June.

NOTES: The violet, generally considered to be the **Common Blue Violet**, is the state flower of Illinois, Rhode Island, and Wisconsin. Curiously, although a 1913 resolution of the New Jersey Legislature designated the Common Blue Violet (also called the **Common Meadow Violet**) as the NJ state flower, it officially wasn't enacted until 1971. • Violets are known to contain salicylic acid (aspirin is acetylsalicylic acid) and large amounts of some vitamins.

Pale Violet, Cream Violet · *Viola striata*

GENERAL: Smooth, clustered perennial herb, 4–12 in. tall, with **leafy stems** from a short rhizome. **LEAVES:** Both stem and basal leaves are long-stalked, more or less ovate to heart-shaped, 1–3 in. long; **prominent leafy stipules** are deeply cut to toothed. **FLOWERS: Cream-colored or ivory**, petals usually have prominent **brown-purple veins** near the base, **lateral petals strongly bearded**, lower petals with a blunt, thick spur to 0.16 in. long; flowers are plentiful, on stalks extending well above the leaves; closed, self-pollinated flowers are produced in the upper leaf axils. April–June. **FRUITS:** Smooth, ovoid capsules; seeds pale brown. **WHERE FOUND:** Open or wooded alluvial places with an occasional weedy tendency. From MA to southern WI, south to GA and AR. In TN, from the Western Highland Rim eastward. Frequent.

NOTES: The species name *striata* means "striped," referring to the purple veins on the petals. • Violets can be invasive in garden settings owing in part to their advanced method of reproducing. With many species, spring flowers are large and showy to attract pollinators, while summer flowers never open and grow close to the ground. These are self-pollinated, ensuring a dependable seed production. Insects pollinate the flowers that open, but are not necessary for the survival of the species.

Three-Parted Yellow Violet
Viola tripartita var. *tripartita*

GENERAL: Perennial herb, 4–10 in. tall, stem smooth to downy. **LEAVES:** 2–4 alternate leaves, 1–3 in. long, at the top of the stem; **each leaf has 3 narrow segments and truncate or wedge-shaped base. FLOWERS:** 5 petals, **bright yellow with brown-purple lines** near the base, upper 2 petals purplish on the back, lower 3 bearded; also self-pollinated flowers that do not open on short stalks in the upper leaf axils. April–May. **FRUITS:** Stoutly ellipsoid capsules; pale seeds. **WHERE FOUND:** Rich woods from PA and OH, south to GA and MS. In TN, found in Cumberland, Franklin, Marion, and Hamilton counties. Rare. **SIMILAR SPECIES:** WEDGE-LEAVED YELLOW VIOLET (*Viola tripartita* var. *glaberrima*) has **leaves that are rhombic, not parted.** Scattered across Middle and East TN. Occasional. April–May.

NOTES: Elizabethans called violets "heart's-ease" and associated them with innocent love, which is appropriate because the violet flowers, in addition to producing seeds as other plants do, also produce seeds prolifically by unopened self-pollinating flowers.

Passionflower, Maypops, Passion Vine · *Passiflora incarnata*

DAVID DUHL

GENERAL: Climbing or trailing vine, stems slightly hairy, 10–30 ft. long. **LEAVES:** Alternate, 3–5 in. long and wide, **deeply 3-lobed**, sparsely hairy beneath, truncate or rounded to the base with a long petiole; lobes are ovate, finely toothed, narrowed at the base, tips acute; **petiole has a pair of nectar-producing glands** near the leaf blade. **FLOWERS:** Solitary, from the leaf axils, nearly 3 in. wide; 5 whitish petals and 5 sepals provide a backdrop for a **strikingly beautiful corona**, consisting of numerous thread-like, radial fringes that form **circular bands of purple and white**; 5 prominent pale yellowish anthers form a circle below the 3 arching styles and enlarged stigmas. June–September. **FRUITS:** Edible, ellipsoid, many-seeded, green or yellowish, lemon-sized berries, about 2 in. long; seeds have fleshy outer covering. **WHERE FOUND:** Fields, thickets, roadsides, and open woodlands in most of the eastern U.S. Widespread in TN. Common.

NOTES: This plant is also known as **Apricot Vine**. Its large, showy flower is often frequented by butterflies in search of nectar and is a host plant for the Gulf Fritillary and Variegated Fritillary butterflies. • Medicinal use of this herb began in the late 19th century in the U.S. It was especially used to treat anxiety resulting from mental worry or overwork. • **Passionflower** is the official state wildflower of TN.

Yellow Passionflower
Passiflora lutea

KURT EMMANUELE

GENERAL: Climbing or trailing vine, 3–10 ft. long, stem soft-hairy when young. **LEAVES:** Alternate, 1–4 in. wide, much broader than long, **shallowly 3-lobed**, heart-shaped at the base; lobes are rounded, without teeth, with a small point at the tip; **petioles glandless. FLOWERS:** Greenish yellow, 1.0–1.5 in. wide, 5 slender, greenish white petals, 5 greenish sepals, **corona of thread-like, greenish yellow segments**; 5 pale yellowish anthers and 3 long, green styles with enlarged stigmas that arch downward. June–September. **FRUITS:** Globose-ovoid, dark purple berries, about 0.5 in. across. **WHERE FOUND:** Edges of woods and thickets from PA, south to FL and AL. Widespread in TN. Common.

NOTES: Passionflowers were named by scholar-priests who accompanied the Spanish Conquistadors. The unusual form of the flowers reminded them of the Crucifixion and the Passion of Christ. The 3 styles and stigmas in the center represented nails, the 5 stamens beneath them were Christ's wounds, the fringe was the crown of thorns, and the 10 petals and sepals behind the fringe were the apostles except for Judas and Peter. Biblically, "passion" means "suffering."

DENNIS HORN

Bur Cucumber · *Sicyos angulatus*

GENERAL: Annual (usually) **vine**, with **branched tendrils** opposite the leaves, climbing to 10 ft. or more; stems have sticky hairs. **LEAVES:** Alternate, broad, with 5 shallow, pointed lobes and a heart-shaped base. **FLOWERS: Greenish white** with 5-lobed corollas; male (staminate) flowers about 0.4 in. across, in long-stalked racemes; female (pistillate) flowers in smaller clusters from a short stalk. July–September. **FRUITS:** Oval, single-seeded pepos, about 0.6 in. long, are dry, dehiscent, and covered with bristles; in tight, spherical clusters. **WHERE FOUND:** Riverbanks and damp ground throughout the eastern U.S. Widely scattered across TN. Frequent. **SIMILAR SPECIES: CREEPING CUCUMBER (*Melothria pendula*)** is a smooth, slender vine, 3–6 ft. long, with **unbranched tendrils**; bell-shaped, **yellow flowers** are 5-lobed; female flowers solitary, about 0.25 in. across; male flowers even smaller, in a cluster; smooth, greenish black, oval berries contain up to 20 white seeds. Woods, roadsides, and fields throughout the southeastern U.S. Thinly scattered across TN. Occasional. June–September.

NOTES: Bur Cucumber also is known as **Oneseeded Bur Cucumber** for its unique fruit. • Several species in this genus are also called **Nimble Kate**, indicating the quickness and dexterity with which they climb. • The barbed bristles of Bur Cucumber fruit adhere to the fur of animals, which unknowingly help to spread the seeds. • There are 5 species of the **Gourd Family** represented in TN, each in a different genus. This is the only species of *Sicyos* in the U.S. (others occur in Australia and Polynesia).

Mustard Family (Brassicaceae)

The Mustard Family is represented by 32 genera and 78 species in TN. Members are characterized by having 4 sepals, 4 petals, and 6 stamens (the 2 outer ones shorter than the 4 inner ones). Petals are alternate to the sepals and usually narrow at the base, but enlarged and spreading at the tip. Together, the 4 petals are in the shape of a cross, which is the basis for the other name of this family, Cruciferae. The Mustard Family has considerable economic importance because many of its members are food crops, including broccoli, brussels sprouts, cabbage, cauliflower, kale, kohlrabi, mustard greens, radish, rutabaga, turnip, and watercress, as well as condiments, such as mustard and horseradish. Along with these beneficial plants are ornamentals, such as candytuft (*Iberis*), rock cress (*Arabis*), and wallflowers (*Erysimum*).

1a. Petals yellow, yellow-orange, or absent 2
  2a. Plants hairy with stellate or forked hairs . . . .***Erysimum***
  2b. Plants smooth or with simple unbranched hairs 3
    3a. Fruits about as long as wide . . . .***Lesquerella***
    3b. Fruits at least 3x as long as wide 4
      4a. Fruits distinctly flattened; leaves mostly basal . . . .***Leavenworthia***
      4b. Fruits rounded in cross-section or 4-angled, not flattened; stem leaves present 5
        5a. Stem leaves entire or shallowly lobed, sometimes clasping . . . .***Brassica***
        5b. Stem leaves prominently lobed to pinnatifid . . . .***Barbarea***
1b. Petals white, pink, or purple 6
  6a. Fruits short and broad, not more than 3x as long as wide 7
    7a. Plants aquatic . . . .***Armoracia***
    7b. Plants terrestrial 8
      8a. Fruits triangular, broadest at the tip . . . .***Capsella***
      8b. Fruits not triangular 9
        9a. Fruits slightly winged above, style partially filling the notch
          between the wings . . . .***Lepidium***
        9b. Fruits not winged, style evident 10
          10a. Fruits flattened . . . .***Draba***
          10b. Fruits not flattened . . . .***Lesquerella***
  6b. Fruit at least 4x as long as wide 11
    11a. Leaves simple, rarely lobed, margin entire or toothed, but not deeply divided . . .12

Barbarea
p. 110

Capsella
p. 111

Cardamine
pp. 112–13

12a. Petals purple . . . .*Hesperis*

12b. Petals white to pink **13**

   13a. Plants decumbent and stoloniferous at base . . . .*Cardamine*

   13b. Plants upright, not stoloniferous **14**

      14a. All leaves petiolate, blades rhombic, about as broad as long . . . . .*Alliaria*

      14b. All or at least upper leaves sessile, blades ovate to lanceolate **15**

         15a. Plant bulbous at the base; fruits rounded . . . .*Cardamine*

         15b. Plant not bulbous at the base; fruits flat or slightly rounded . . . . . .*Arabis*

11b. Leaves either ternate, palmately divided, or pinnatifid **16**

16a. Plants aquatic, rooting at the nodes . . . .*Nasturtium*

16b. Plants terrestrial, not rooting at the nodes **17**

   17a. Leaves palmate or ternately divided . . . .*Dentaria*

   17b. Leaves, at least the basal, pinnately divided or lobed **18**

      18a. Fruits distinctly flattened or constricted between seeds; leaves mostly basal . . . .**Leavenworthia**

      18b. Fruits rounded to slightly flattened; stem leaves present **19**

         19a. Leaf petioles rounded in cross-section . . . .*Cardamine*

         19b. Leaf petioles margined-winged . . . .*Iodanthus*

Dentaria
pp.113–15

Hesperis
p. 117

Draba
pp. 115–16

Leavenworthia
pp. 118–20

Lepidium
p. 120

Garlic Mustard
Alliaria petiolata*

DENNIS HORN

GENERAL: Mostly smooth, erect, sparsely **branched biennial** to 3 ft. tall. **LEAVES:** Alternate, mostly **triangular, coarsely toothed**, short-stalked, to 2.6 in. long and wide; **leaves have a garlic odor. FLOWERS: White, 4 petals** to 0.25 in. long are spatulate and gradually narrowed to a claw; in a raceme to 12 in. long, terminal or from the leaf axils. April–May. **FRUITS:** Narrow fruits (siliques), 1–2 in. long, curve upward and are 4-sided when dry. **WHERE FOUND:** Introduced from Europe. A weedy species of woodlands and gardens, found in most of the eastern U.S. Sparsely distributed across TN. Occasional.

NOTES: The genus name *Alliaria* is from the Latin *allium* and means "garlic," referring to the pungent odor of the plant. This plant is also called **Hedge Garlic.** • The edible leaves have the odor and taste of garlic and make a nice addition to salads. When cooked, the leaves lose their aroma but retain their bitterness, so are best eaten raw. Although the seeds are bitter, they can be used for seasoning.

Smooth Rock Cress
Arabis laevigata

GENERAL: Erect, smooth, gray-green biennial to 3 ft. tall, **sparsely branched above. LEAVES:** Stem leaves alternate, to 6 in. long, narrowly lanceolate, covered with a whitish bloom (glaucous), **clasping at the base**; basal rosette withers early. **FLOWERS:** Greenish white, 4 narrow petals to 0.25 in. long, 4 sepals, slightly shorter than petals. April–May. **FRUITS:** Narrow siliques to 4 in. long, flat and widely recurved-spreading; oblong, broadly winged seeds. **WHERE FOUND:** Rocky woods and slopes, from Québec to Ontario, south to GA and AR. Throughout TN. Common. **SIMILAR SPECIES:** SICKLEPOD (**A. canadensis**) has **green, sessile leaves** that are slightly hairy; siliques are more abruptly recurved. Woods. ME to MN, south to GA and TX. Mostly in Middle and East TN. Frequent. May–July. **LYRE-LEAF ROCK CRESS** (**A. lyrata**) is smaller, to 16 in. tall, with wiry **stems branching from the base.** Rocky or sandy habitat. Mostly a northern species occurring south to GA and TN in the mountains. Infrequent. May–July.

HUGH & CAROL NOURSE

NOTES: **Smooth Rock Cress** is commonly confused with **Sicklepod** because of its elongate, drooping seedpods. However, note that Sicklepod does not have clasping leaves and the overall color is not gray-green.

MILO PYNE

Lake Cress · *Armoracia lacustris*

GENERAL: **Aquatic perennial**, with submersed or prostrate stems, 12–36 in. long. **LEAVES:** Submersed leaves are pinnately dissected into numerous thread-like segments; leaves (if any) above the waterline are lanceolate to narrowly oblong, to 2.8 in. long, **toothed or dissected**. **FLOWERS:** White; 4 petals, to 0.33 in. long, are obovate and narrowed to the claw; inflorescence is a loose raceme, the flowers on short, spreading stalks. May–August. **FRUITS:** Inflated, egg-shaped siliques, about 0.25 in. long; fruit rarely matures. **WHERE FOUND:** Quiet water and muddy shores. From Québec to MN, south to FL and TX. In TN, in Lauderdale, Lake, Obion, Stewart, Montgomery, and Grundy counties. Infrequent. *A. aquatica.* **SIMILAR SPECIES:** HORSERADISH (*A. rusticana**) is an **erect-stemmed perennial** to 36 in. tall; **lower leaves oblong**, stalked, to 12 in. long, **resembling those of dock** (*Rumex* ssp.). Introduced from Europe. Often cultivated and escaped into damp soil. Rare in the wild, recorded from Stewart, Montgomery, and Robertson counties in TN. May–July.

NOTES: The genus name *Armoracia* has been used for horseradish by European botanists for centuries; *lacustris* means "pertaining to lakes." • The well-known condiment, horseradish, is made from the grated root of **Horseradish** mixed with vinegar, salt, and a little honey. The root contains a large quantity of vitamin C and various minerals; the leaves are edible raw or cooked, but can be bitter.

OTTO R. HIRSCH

Winter Cress, Yellow Rocket
*Barbarea vulgaris**

GENERAL: **Winter annual or biennial** to 36 in. tall; erect with dark, **smooth leaves and stems**. **LEAVES:** Basal leaves to 6 in. long with **1–4 pairs of small lateral lobes** and 1 larger terminal lobe; alternate stem leaves are similar, but progressively reduced toward the top and usually clasping. **FLOWERS:** Yellow, 4 petals to 0.4 in. long; borne in a crowded terminal raceme. April–June. **FRUITS:** Narrow seedpods (siliques) to 1.25 in. long, on short, slender stalks; beak is 0.07–0.12 in. long; seeds in 1 row in each chamber of the fruit. **WHERE FOUND:** Introduced from Eurasia. In fields, wet meadows, and waste places in most of the eastern U.S. In Middle and East TN, also Lake and McNairy counties. Frequent. **SIMILAR SPECIES:** EARLY WINTER CRESS (*B. verna**) has **more dissected basal leaves with 4–10 pairs of lateral lobes**; fruits to 2.5 in. long, on stalks as thick as the fruit. Introduced from Eurasia. Damp soil, fields, and roadsides in most of the U.S. and southern Canada. In Middle and East TN. Frequent. April–June.

NOTES: In early spring, when the leaves of **Winter Cress** appear, they are already too bitter to eat raw and must be boiled in a change of water. The small flower buds, which look and taste like broccoli, are edible after boiling. The leaves and buds contain vitamins A and C. • Although the flowers of Winter Cress are small, they have prominent UV patterns that aid in attracting insects such as bees.

Field Mustard, Turnip · *Brassica rapa**

GENERAL: Winter annual to 3 ft. tall; **smooth stem with a whitish bloom**. **LEAVES:** Lower leaves stalked and pinnately lobed, up to 12 in. long and 4 in. wide; **upper leaves unlobed**, toothed or entire, **clasping the stem**. **FLOWERS:** Yellow, to 0.4 in. wide, 4 petals; borne in a terminal cluster. March–June. **FRUITS:** Seedpods (siliques), 1–2 in. long, erect to ascending, **round in cross-section**; beak is 0.3–0.6 in. long; dark brown seeds. **WHERE FOUND:** Introduced from Europe. Fields and roadsides throughout the southeastern U.S. and TN. Frequent. ***B. campestris****. **SIMILAR SPECIES:** BLACK MUSTARD (***B. nigra****) has **stalked upper and lower leaves; seedpods are 4-angled in cross-section**, 0.4–0.8 in. long; beak is 0.1 in. long. Introduced from Europe. In TN, in Shelby, Lauderdale, Obion, and McNairy counties in West TN, and Davidson in Middle TN. Rare. May–August.

NOTES: The genus name *Brassica* is the Latin name for "cabbage," indicating the edibility of most plants in this genus. **Field Mustard** is the wild ancestor of the cultivated turnip. • The young shoots, leaves, flowering tops, and roots of **Black Mustard** can be eaten raw or cooked. The seeds are used in the yellow mustard put on hot dogs and are also used whole in Indian cuisine.

DENNIS HORN

Shepherd's Purse · *Capsella bursa-pastoris**

GENERAL: Winter annual to 24 in. tall; stem has a few ascending branches. **LEAVES:** Basal rosette of oblong, lobed leaves to 4 in. long; stem leaves are alternate, linear to lanceolate and much smaller. **FLOWERS:** Minute, white, **4 petals** about 0.1 in. long; borne in a raceme to 12 in. long; racemes have spreading fruit stalks. March–June. **FRUITS: Strongly flattened, triangular siliques** to 0.33 in. long, attached at the longest point; reddish brown, pitted seeds. **WHERE FOUND:** Introduced from Europe. Naturalized as a widely distributed weed throughout the eastern U.S. In TN, in lawns, fields, and waste places. Frequent.

NOTES: The genus name *Capsella* is Latin for "small box," referring to the shape of the fruit. • The young leaves of this plant are edible raw or cooked and provide an excellent wild salad in early spring. After the stem has appeared, the basal leaves become tougher and soon wither and disappear. The seeds can be used as a spice or seasoning. • Low-growing herbs such as **Shepherd's Purse** are favorite plants of the Checkered White butterfly for laying its eggs.

MILO PYNE

Purple Cress · *Cardamine douglassii*

GENERAL: Perennial to 16 in. tall from a knotty rhizome; **leaves and stems sparsely or densely covered with short hairs. LEAVES:** Basal leaves are **purplish beneath,** to 1.6 in. long, roundish with entire or wavy margins, petioles to 3.5 in. long; 3–4 alternate stem leaves are reduced, sessile, ovate, usually toothed. **FLOWER: Pink to pale violet,** 4 petals, each about 0.5 in. long, on stalks about 0.4 in. long; purple sepals become brown with age; borne in a terminal raceme. April–May. **FRUITS:** Siliques up to 0.8 in. long excluding the beak (0.12 in. long); brown seeds. **WHERE FOUND:** Rich, moist, wooded slopes, from NH to southern MN, south to VA, TN, and MO. In Middle TN, also Loudon, Knox, Claiborne, and Scott counties in East TN. Occasional.

NOTES: The genus name *Cardamine* is both Greek and Latin for "cress." • The leaves of this species are edible raw or cooked. When growing in the same area, this plant's peak flowering may occur 2–3 weeks earlier than **Spring Cress** (p. 113).

OTTO R. HIRSCH

DENNIS HORN

Hoary Bittercress
Cardamine hirsuta*

GENERAL: Erect, smooth-stemmed **winter annual,** 4–16 in. tall. **LEAVES:** Mostly basal, 1–3 in. long, in a prominent rosette, deeply pinnately lobed; **2–5 alternate stem leaves** are smaller and narrower than basal leaves; **petioles have a short fringe. FLOWERS: White,** 4 petals about 0.1 in. long; clustered at the top of the stem. March–April. **FRUITS:** Erect pods (siliques), 0.6–1 in. long, with a short beak, less than 0.05 in. long; light brown seeds. **WHERE FOUND:** Introduced from Europe. Naturalized in lawns and waste places from southern NY to IL, south to AL, and throughout TN. Common. **SIMILAR SPECIES: PENNSYLVANIA BITTERCRESS (C. pensylvanica)** is an annual or biennial to 24 in. tall; basal leaves mostly absent at flowering time; **5–10 stem leaves, 2–3 in. long, petioles not fringed.** Wet woods. Widespread over the entire U.S. and in TN. Frequent. April–June. **SMALL-FLOWERED BITTERCRESS (C. parviflora)** is an annual or biennial up to 16 in. tall and similar to Pennsylvania Bittercress, but the **stem leaves are only 1–2 in. long.** Dry sandy areas. Most of the eastern U.S. and all of TN. Frequent. April–June.

NOTES: The leaves of **Hoary Bittercress** are milder than those of other *Cardamine* species. They are edible raw or cooked and are commonly eaten in North America.

Spring Cress · *Cardamine rhomboidea*

GENERAL: Perennial, 8–24 in. tall, with 1 to few **smooth stems** from a stout rhizome. **LEAVES:** Simple, entire to dentate; basal leaves **green beneath**, roundish, to 1.6 in. long, on petioles to 3.5 in. long; 4–8 alternate stem leaves are reduced, narrowly oblong or ovate, the upper ones sessile. **FLOWERS:** White (rarely pink), on stalks about 0.4 in. long, 4 petals are about 0.5 in. long, green sepals fade to yellow after flowering; borne in a terminal raceme. April–June. **FRUITS:** Siliques, slightly over an inch long; beak is 0.25 in. long. **WHERE FOUND:** Moist woods near floodplains and shallow water from Québec to SD, south to FL and TX. Throughout TN. Common. ***C. bulbosa.***

NOTES: This species is also known as **Bulbous Bittercress.** · Tender plants have the flavor of horseradish and can be used in salads. The tuberous rhizome was used as a spice by Native Americans. · **Use caution: the roots are considered poisonous in large amounts.**

NITA R. HEILMAN

Crinkleroot, Broadleaf Toothwort · *Dentaria diphylla*

GENERAL: Perennial with stems 8–16 in. long, from a **long rhizome almost completely uniform in diameter. LEAVES:** Basal leaves **mostly evergreen**, with 3 broad, toothed, ovate, prominently veined segments to 4 in. long, petioles to 6 in. long; **2 stem leaves** on short stalks have 3 ovate leaflets, crenate to coarsely toothed, to 3 in. long and 1/2 as wide. **FLOWERS: Off-white**, frequently turning pinkish with age, 4 petals, 0.4–0.6 in. long; borne in terminal clusters. April–May. **FRUITS:** Siliques to 1.5 in. long with a short beak. **WHERE FOUND:** Rich wooded slopes and ravines from New Brunswick to MN, south to GA and AL. Middle and East TN. Common. ***Cardamine diphylla.***

JERRY DROWN

NOTES: The genus name *Dentaria* refers to the ivory-colored, tooth-like projections on the rhizome as well as the toothed margins of the leaves. The "Doctrine of Signatures" (the belief that a plant could be used to cure ailments of the body part it resembled) held that these plants would relieve toothaches. · Another common name, **Pepperroot**, refers to the peppery flavor of the rhizome. It can be diced and added to salads, providing a flavor similar to that of **Watercress** (p. 123).

DENNIS HORN

Slender Toothwort
Dentaria heterophylla

GENERAL: Perennial with stems from 8–16 in. long, from a **rhizome constricted at irregular intervals** into segments about 1.5 in. long. **LEAVES:** Basal leaves have long petioles and 3 broad, toothed, mostly obovate segments to 3 in. long; **2 stem leaves** have short stalks and 3 linear to narrowly oblong leaflets, entire or toothed, to 3 in. long. **FLOWERS:** White to light pink, 4 petals, 0.4–0.6 in. long; borne in a terminal cluster. March–May. **FRUITS:** Siliques to 1.5 in. long with a short beak. **WHERE FOUND:** Rich alluvial woods from NJ to IN, south to GA and MS. In Middle and East TN. Frequent. *Cardamine angustata*.

NOTES: The caterpillars (larvae) of West Virginia White butterflies subsist entirely on the leaves of toothworts (*Dentaria* ssp.), which shrivel and disappear by summer. Look for the chartreuse caterpillars with lighter yellow-green stripes on the sides and back in early to middle spring and you might catch a glimpse; otherwise, you'll have to wait another year to see them.

KURT EMMANUELE

Cutleaf Toothwort
Dentaria laciniata

GENERAL: Perennial with short-hairy stems 8–16 in. long, from a **rhizome constricted at irregular intervals** into sections about 0.75 in. long. **LEAVES:** Whorl of 3 stem leaves, each with 3 narrow, toothed segments, central segment may be so deeply divided that there appear to be 5 segments; similar **basal leaves usually not present at flowering**. **FLOWERS:** White (may vary from light pink to pale lavender), 4 petals, 0.5–0.8 in. long; borne in terminal clusters. March–May. **FRUITS:** Siliques to 1.5 in. long with a short beak. **WHERE FOUND:** Moist rich woods from ME to MN, south to FL, LA, and OK. Throughout TN. Common. *Cardamine concatenata*, *C. laciniata*.

NOTES: The rhizome and leaves of this plant are peppery tasting. The leaves can be eaten raw or cooked, like other mustard greens. The rhizomes can be grated and preserved in vinegar, like horseradish, and diced into salads. • Native Americans made a poultice from the root and used it to treat headaches.

Fineleaf Toothwort · *Dentaria multifida*

GENERAL: Smooth-stemmed perennial herb, 8–16 in. tall, from a **rhizome constricted at irregular intervals** into elongated segments. **LEAVES: 2 stem leaves finely divided** many times into narrow, linear, entire segments, 0.04–0.12 in. wide; similar **basal leaves usually present at flowering. FLOWERS:** White (may vary from light pink to pale lavender), 4 petals, 0.5–0.7 in. long; borne in terminal clusters. March–April. **FRUITS:** Siliques to 1.5 in. long with a short beak. **WHERE FOUND:** Rich alluvial woods from central OH and central IN, south to northern GA and northern AL. In Middle TN, also Hamilton, Polk, Union, and Claiborne counties in East TN. Occasional. *Cardamine multifida, C. dissecta.*

NOTES: The species name *multifida* means "many times divided," in reference to the shape of the leaves. • Falcate Orangetip butterflies use toothworts as host plants for their caterpillars, which eat the leaves. The caterpillars are green with bold, white side stripes and a yellow-orange stripe along the top of the back.

DENNIS HORN

Shortpod Whitlow Grass
Draba brachycarpa

GENERAL: Winter annual, 2–8 in. tall, with several branches from the base. **LEAVES:** Basal leaves are **elliptic or obovate**, to 0.8 in. long, petioled; basal rosette usually withers by time of fruiting; stem leaves are alternate, smaller, narrower, sessile, extending to the base of the inflorescence. **FLOWERS:** White or yellow, 4 petals to 0.12 in. long, slightly indented at the tip or may be absent; numerous flowers in terminal racemes. February–April. **FRUITS:** Smooth, ellipsoid siliques, **about 0.12 in. long. WHERE FOUND:** Roadsides, lawns, and fields from VA to KS, southward. Scattered throughout TN. Occasional. **SIMILAR SPECIES: WEDGELEAF WHITLOW GRASS (*D. cuneifolia*)** has obovate, hairy, coarsely toothed, **leaves with wedge-shaped bases;** few stem leaves, all near the base; white flowers with 4 petals about 0.2 in. long; **hairy fruits, 0.3–0.4 in. long.** Dry rocky soils and barrens from KY to KS, south to FL and CA. In TN, only in Decatur and Wayne counties. Rare. February–April.

DENNIS HORN

NOTES: In Old England, a "whitlow" was an inflammation located under or around a fingernail or toenail, for which the acidic juices of these plants were reputed to be a remedy, thus giving these plants their common names.

B. EUGENE WOFFORD

Rocktwist · *Draba ramosissima*

GENERAL: Low, highly branched **perennial herb, forming mats to 12 in. across,** with flowering stems to 18 in. tall. **LEAVES:** Alternate stem and basal rosette leaves are oblanceolate with a few sharp teeth and sessile; upper leaves somewhat clasping; basal leaves, 1–2 in. long, taper to a narrow base. **FLOWERS: White,** 4 petals, 0.25 in. long; borne in loose racemes. April–May. **FRUITS:** Short, hairy siliques, **spirally twisted,** 0.15–0.4 in. long. **WHERE FOUND:** Dry, calcareous rocky cliffs of mountainous portions of the southern Appalachian Mountains. Found sporadically in the eastern 1/2 of TN. Infrequent.

NOTES: The genus name *Draba* is from the Greek *drabe*, meaning "sharp or acrid," referring to the burned taste of the leaves; *ramosissima* means "much branched," in reference to the branching habit of this plant. The common name refers to the spirally twisted fruits and rocky habitat where it grows. It also is known as **Branched Whitlow Grass.**

Vernal Whitlow Grass
*Draba verna**

GENERAL: Winter annual, 2–8 in. tall. **LEAVES:** Crowded in a **basal rosette;** leaves are hairy, to 0.8 in. long, mostly spatulate to oblanceolate. **FLOWERS: White,** to 0.2 in. wide, **4 petals are cleft about halfway, appearing as 8;** inflorescence of loose racemes occurs on slender, wiry, branched scapes. February–April. **FRUITS:** Smooth, flattened, egg-shaped siliques to 0.4 in. long. **WHERE FOUND:** Introduced from Eurasia. Fields, lawns, and open, dry places. Naturalized across much of North America, including TN. Common. *Erophila verna.*

NOTES: The species name *verna* means "spring," in recognition of this plant's early blooming period. • Other common names include Nailwort, Shad-Blossom, Shad-Flower, and White Blow. • Although tiny and time-consuming to harvest, the leaves and flower heads are edible. In 1949, wildlife ecologist Aldo Leopold wrote of this plant, "Sand too poor and sun too weak for bigger, better blooms are good enough for Draba. After all it is no spring flower, but only a postscript to a hope...just a small creature that does a small job quickly and well."

DENNIS HORN

Western Wallflower
Erysimum capitatum

MARY MARTIN SCHAFFNER

GENERAL: Showy biennial herb to 3 ft. tall. **LEAVES:** Alternate, lanceolate, 1–5 in. long, slightly toothed to entire, hairy. **FLOWERS:** Orange to orange-yellow, to 0.8 in. across, 4 petals; in clusters at the top of the stem. May–July. **FRUITS:** Slender, linear seedpods (siliques) to 4 in. long, 4-angled and hairy. **WHERE FOUND:** Limestone bluffs, glades, and rocky open ground. Primarily a western species. In TN, recorded from Davidson, Smith, DeKalb, Putnam, Scott, and Roane counties. Infrequent. *E. asperum*. **SIMILAR SPECIES:** BUSHY WALLFLOWER (*E. repandum**) is a widely branched **annual to 16 in. tall**; **pale yellow flowers** to 0.4 in. across. Introduced from Europe. A weed found across the U.S. and in Middle TN. Occasional. May–July.

NOTES: Wallflowers are showy plants that are often in popular demand by gardeners. The name "wallflower" comes from the plant's habit of pushing its way through cracks in the rocks of old, dry walls. These plants can also be found adding color around rocky cliffs and outcroppings.

Dame's Rocket · *Hesperis matronalis**

DENNIS HORN

GENERAL: Erect **perennial herb to 40 in. tall**, usually branched at the top. **LEAVES:** Alternate, simple, lanceolate to deltoid-lanceolate, 2–6 in. long, faintly or sharply toothed, and hairy. **FLOWERS:** Conspicuous, **usually purple** but can vary to pink or white, to 0.8 in. wide, 4 petals; flowers are clustered at the top of the stem and branches. May–July. **FRUITS:** Linear siliques, to 4 in. long, somewhat constricted between the seeds, giving a "beaded" appearance. **WHERE FOUND:** Introduced from Europe. Cultivated for gardens and escaped; now considered a pest plant in most northern states as it invades natural areas. Along roads and fencerows and in open woods from southeastern Canada to MI and IA, south to KY and GA. Thinly scattered in Middle and East TN. Occasional.

NOTES: The genus name *Hesperis* is from the Greek *hesperos*, meaning "evening," because the flowers become fragrant in the evening; *matronalis* means "matronly," suggesting another common name, **Mother-of-the-Evening**. It is also called Damewort, Eveweed, and Night Rocket. • *Hesperis* species, called **rockets**, were cultivated in ancient Rome. They were brought to America as garden plants and have escaped into the wild. **Dame's Rocket** is a prolific self-seeder. • The leaves, flowers, and buds are edible and make a tasty addition to salads.

DENNIS HORN

Purple Rocket · *Iodanthus pinnatifidus*

GENERAL: Smooth perennial herb to 40 in. tall, unbranched below the inflorescence. **LEAVES:** Alternate; upper leaves simple, thin, elliptic to oblong, sharply toothed or entire; **lower leaves pinnatifid near the base**, sharply toothed, about 4 in. long, **clasping the stem. FLOWERS:** Pale violet to nearly white, 4 petals to 0.5 in. long, **club-shaped**, rounded at the tip, tapering to a narrow base; borne in a terminal raceme. May–June. **FRUITS:** Linear siliques to 1.6 in. long with many seeds. **WHERE FOUND:** Moist or wet alluvial woods from western PA to MN, south to TN and OK. Widespread throughout Middle TN, also found in Knox and Loudon counties in East TN, and Lake and Obion counties in West TN. Occasional.

NOTES: The genus name *Iodanthus* comes from the Greek *iodes*, meaning "violet-colored," and *anthus*, meaning "flower"; *pinnatifidus* means "cut in feather form" in reference to the shape of the lower leaves. • This is one of the more unusual members of the Mustard Family because it is native, nonweedy, has pale violet flowers, and does not resemble any other species in the family. • As these flowers become older, their color fades to white.

DENNIS HORN

Tennessee Glade Cress
Leavenworthia exigua var. *exigua*

GENERAL: Winter annual, about 4 in. tall. **LEAVES:** Flattened basal rosette, leaves 1–3 in. long, pinnately lobed, **terminal lobe prominent**, lateral lobes much smaller. **FLOWERS:** Solitary, **white** to light lavender, sometimes with a **light yellow center**, 4 petals to 0.4 in. long, tips with shallow notches; style is 0.04–0.12 in. long; borne on erect stalks from the center of the leaf rosette. March–April. **FRUITS:** Strongly flattened, non-fleshy siliques are obtuse, oblong, to 0.8 in. long and 0.2 in. wide. **WHERE FOUND:** Wet limestone glades and adjacent ditches from southern KY to northern AL and northwest GA. In TN, primarily in the Central Basin and the Western Highland Rim of Middle TN, also Decatur County in West TN. Occasional. **SIMILAR SPECIES:** The variety *L. exigua* var. *lutea* has **entirely yellow flowers**. Endemic to the cedar glades of Middle TN and northern AL. In TN, in Maury and Bedford counties. Rare.

NOTES: Tennessee Glade Cress is also called Pasture Glade Cress. • *Leavenworthia* species are smooth winter annuals reaching 6 in. tall. Seeds germinate in autumn, and the plants overwinter as a rosette. Mature leaves are all basal and pinnatifid. Early flowers occur on erect stalks originating at the center of the rosette, but later flowers occur in loose racemes on true stems. The flowers remain closed on cloudy days. Four species occur in TN, with 3 found primarily in the Central Basin.

Long-Styled Glade Cress
Leavenworthia stylosa

GENERAL: Winter annual, 3–4 in. tall. **LEAVES:** Basal rosette, leaves 1–4 in. long, pinnately lobed, lateral lobes much smaller than terminal lobe. **FLOWERS:** Solitary, **showy, fragrant, yellow, white, or lavender**, with yellow center, 4 petals, 0.4–0.6 in. long, are **deeply notched**; numerous flower stalks, to 3 in. long, emerge from the leaf rosette; style, to 0.3 in. long, persists as a prominent projection at the end of the fruit pod. March–May. **FRUITS:** Oblong to linear, **fleshy seedpods** (siliques), to 1.2 in. long and 0.2 in. wide; siliques sometimes slightly torulose (bead-like) and easily confused with **Beaded Glade Cress** (see below), but **seeds are winged. WHERE FOUND:** Wet limestone glades, ditches, and low fields. Endemic to Middle TN. Found in Sumner, Smith, Wilson, Davidson, Rutherford, and Bedford counties. Infrequent.

DENNIS HORN

NOTES: Both the common and species names refer to this plant's special characteristic—it has the **longest style** of all the *Leavenworthia* species. This plant also has the **largest flowers** in the genus, reaching 1 in. wide. The yellow color form seems to occur more frequently in the northern part of its range and the white form most frequently in the southern; all color forms can occur in any population.

Beaded Glade Cress
Leavenworthia torulosa

GENERAL: Winter annual, 2–6 in. tall. **LEAVES:** Basal rosette, leaves 1–4 in. long, pinnately lobed, terminal lobe much larger than lateral lobes. **FLOWERS: Usually white** to light lavender with yellow center, but rarely entirely yellow, 4 petals, 0.3–0.4 in. long, have tips with **shallow notches**; styles to 0.2 in. long. March–May. **FRUITS:** Linear, **strongly torulose** (bead-like) siliques, even when young, to 1.2 in. long and 0.16. in wide;

DENNIS HORN

resembles a smaller version of **Long-Styled Glade Cress** (see above), but **seeds are wingless. WHERE FOUND:** Wet limestone glades, adjacent wet ditches, low fields, and lawns in northern AL, northwestern GA, southern KY, and Middle and East TN. Occasional.

NOTES: This plant is also called **Necklace Glade Cress** because the seedpods outline the seeds within, thus resembling beads on a necklace. An early flowering plant, it begins to bloom in late winter and continues into late spring.

DIVISION OF NATURAL HERITAGE

Small Glade Cress
Leavenworthia uniflora

GENERAL: Smooth **winter annual**, 2–4 in. tall. **LEAVES:** Basal rosette; early leaves have 1 terminal, slightly toothed lobe; mature leaves, 1–3 in. long, are highly pinnately dissected, the **terminal lobe only slightly larger** than the adjacent pair. **FLOWERS:** White with yellowish center, 4 petals, to 0.3 in. long, have rounded tips without notches; style 0.06–0.12 in. long. February–May. **FRUITS:** Thick, **fleshy**, cylindric siliques to 1.2 in. long and 0.2 in. wide; **seeds are widely winged** and margined. **WHERE FOUND:** In limestone glades, old fields, wet areas, ditches, and barrens from southwestern OH to northwest GA and northwest AR. Middle and East TN. Occasional.

NOTES: This plant is also called **Michaux's Glade Cress**. Of the *Leavenworthia* species in TN, this plant has **the smallest flower with the earliest flowering**, beginning in late winter and continuing into mid-spring.

DENNIS HORN

Poor-Man's Pepper
Lepidium virginicum

GENERAL: Erect **annual or biennial**, 12–18 in. tall, bright green, generally smooth, branched from upper leaf axils. **LEAVES:** Basal leaves, 1–4 in. long, sharply toothed to pinnately lobed; stem leaves alternate, smaller, toothed or entire, narrowed at the base but **not clasping the stem. FLOWERS:** Tiny, white, entire, **4 petals are 2x the length of the sepals**; borne in numerous racemes to 4 in. long. April–September. **FRUITS:** Ellipsoid, flattened seed-pods (silicles), about 0.12 in. long, indented at the tip. **WHERE FOUND:** Dry or moist fields, roadsides, and gardens throughout the U.S. and TN. Common. **SIMILAR SPECIES:** PRAIRIE PEPPERGRASS (**L. densiflorum***) has **petals shorter than sepals** or absent. Introduced. Roadsides and waste ground throughout most of the U.S. Scattered throughout TN. Occasional. May–September. **L. neglectum**. FIELD PEPPERGRASS (**L. campestre***), also called **COW CRESS**, is a densely hairy annual or biennial to 18 in. tall; pale green; narrow, **clasping leaves**; white petals to 0.1 in. long. Native of Europe found in fields and waste places throughout the U.S. Middle and East TN. Frequent. May–September.

NOTES: Poor-Man's Pepper is also called American Pepperwort and Virginia Pepperweed. As indicated by its name, the seedpods and seeds of this plant can be used as a peppery season-ing for soups and salads, and the young shoots can be eaten raw in salads. The seeds are eaten by a variety of wildlife.

Duck River Bladderpod
Lesquerella densipila

GENERAL: Winter annual to 20 in. tall. **LEAVES:** Basal leaves 2–3 in. long, stalked, pinnately lobed; stem leaves alternate, 0.5–1.5 in. long, simple, toothed to lobed with **clasping bases. FLOWERS:** Yellow, about 0.6 in. wide, 4 petals; borne in racemes to 8 in. long. March–May. **FRUITS:** Silicles or fruit pods (bladders), **mostly rounded, usually smooth** but may be uniformly covered with short, simple or forked hairs. **WHERE FOUND:** Principally in the Duck River floodplain in soils that have been disturbed by agriculture or flooding. Endemic to Middle TN and adjacent northern AL. Recorded in Bedford, Cheatham, Davidson, Giles, Hickman, Marshall, Maury, Rutherford, and Williamson counties in Middle TN. Infrequent.

NOTES: The common name "bladderpod" refers to the inflated, rounded seedpods, a feature of *Lesquerella* species. These small herbaceous plants sometimes occur in limestone glades, but more often in disturbed floodplains or agricultural fields, where they can form large masses. Five species are found in TN, most listed as state rare plants. The bladderpods of the area were first described by Dr. Reed Rollins (1911–98), a botanist from Harvard University, who believed that they originated in the Southwest and evolved into several unique species in TN.

DIVISION OF NATURAL HERITAGE

Short's Bladderpod
Lesquerella globosa

GENERAL: Perennial to 20 in. tall; grayish green hairy stems radiate from the base and have a bushy appearance. **LEAVES:** Alternate, simple, to 1.2 in. long and 0.3 in. wide, **not clasping,** narrowly oblong to oblanceolate. **FLOWERS:** Yellow, about 0.6 in. wide, 4 petals; borne in racemes to 4 in. long, with as many as 50 flowers. April–May, but fruit may persist through June. **FRUITS:** Small, **globe-shaped,** hairy pods (silicles), about 0.1 in. wide (the smallest pod of all TN *Lesquerella* spp.); persistent **style is longer than the pod. WHERE FOUND:** Rocky limestone cliffs and river bluffs from Middle TN, north to southern IN. In TN, in Cheatham, Davidson, Maury, Montgomery, Smith, and Trousdale counties. Infrequent.

NOTES: The *Lesquerella* genus was named for 19th-century botanist, Leo Lesquereux, the foremost authority of the time on American plant fossils. The species name *globosa* means "round" or "spherical" in reference to the shape of the fruit.

DENNIS HORN

PAUL SOMERS

Nashville Mustard
Lesquerella lescurii

GENERAL: Winter annual to 20 in. tall; stems branched from the base and densely hairy. **LEAVES:** Basal leaves 1–3 in. long, pinnately lobed; smaller stem leaves alternate, simple, toothed to lobed with **clasping bases. FLOWERS:** Yellow, about 0.6 in. wide, 4 petals; borne in racemes to 8 in. long. March–May. **FRUITS:** Roundish pods (silicles), **strongly flattened** near the outer edge, bulging in the center, covered with a **mixture of longer, bulbous-based hairs and an understory of small, forked hairs. WHERE FOUND:** Wet limestone outcrops in fields, lawns, and roadsides. Endemic to southern KY, northern AL, and Middle TN, primarily the Central Basin. In TN, in Stewart, Montgomery, Sumner, Dickson, Cheatham, Davidson, Wilson, Smith, Williamson, and Rutherford counties. Infrequent.

NOTES: Prominent locations for this plant are along I-24 at Haywood Lane in south Nashville and at Old Hickory Boulevard north of Nashville, where it can be seen flowering from late March to early April.

Stones River Bladderpod
Lesquerella stonensis

GENERAL: Winter annual to about 12 in. tall, branched from the base, the stems grayish green and densely hairy. **LEAVES:** Basal leaves 1.0–2.5 in. long, pinnately lobed; stem leaves alternate, smaller, simple, narrowly oblong to ovate with shallow teeth and **clasping bases. FLOWERS:** White, about 0.6 in. wide, 4 petals, densely hairy style; borne in terminal racemes. February–April, but fruit can persist until mid-June. **FRUITS:** Roundish fruiting pods (silicles), slightly elongated, to 0.25 in. long and 0.16 in. wide, constricted slightly where the 2 halves join, **densely covered with stiff hairs. WHERE FOUND:** Disturbed floodplain fields of the East and West Forks of the Stones River, less common in nearby limestone glades. Endemic to Rutherford County of Middle TN. Rare. **SIMILAR SPECIES:** SPRING CREEK BLADDERPOD (**L. perforata**) also has white flowers, but the **pods are rhombic-shaped** with a mostly **smooth**, veiny, papery, indented surface. This federally endangered plant is found only along disturbed floodplains in Wilson and Rutherford counties in TN. Rare. March–April.

DENNIS HORN

NOTES: Bladderpod seeds contain an oil that is similar to castor oil, making bladderpods a potentially valuable commercial crop. Castor oil is widely used in fibers, paints, resins, lubricants, cosmetics, and hydraulic fluids in the U.S., and subsequently is imported at the rate of 70,000 tons per year. Since the 1980s, genes from a few bladderpod species from TN have been used in bladderpod breeding programs conducted by the U.S. Department of Agriculture.

Watercress
Nasturtium officinale *

JERRY DROWN

GENERAL: Smooth, submerged, or partly floating **aquatic perennial. LEAVES:** Alternate, dark green, 2–6 in. long, **pinnately compound,** the terminal lobe much larger and round. **FLOWERS:** White, about 0.2 in. wide, **petals are 2x as long as sepals;** borne in clusters at the tips of the stems. All summer. **FRUITS:** Linear, slender pods (siliques), to 1 in. long, with a short, persistent style. **WHERE FOUND:** Introduced from Eurasia. Cultivated as a salad plant and now widely established in clearwater streams and spring heads throughout the U.S. and southern Canada. In Middle and East TN. Frequent. ***Rorippa nasturtium-aquaticum.***

NOTES: The genus name *Nasturtium* is from the Latin word *nasus,* "nose," and *torqueo,* "twist," referring to the strong smell and taste of the plants in this genus. • The whole plant is edible, has a pleasant taste, is high in vitamin C, and is **prized for salads and fresh greens** wherever it grows. It also can be cooked in soups or as greens. Beware, however, of harvesting watercress from streams or ponds in or near pastures, as the plants may be contaminated by parasites from livestock.

Mountain Sweet Pepperbush · *Clethra acuminata*

THOMAS E. HEMMERLY

GENERAL: Deciduous shrub or small tree, 6–15 ft. tall; **cinnamon red bark** varies in appearance from smooth to peeling. **LEAVES:** Alternate, oval or oblong, 3–8 in. long, finely serrate margins, **acuminate tips,** rounded or tapering to the base. **FLOWERS:** White, 5 petals, about 0.3 in. long, are shorter than the 10 stamens and 1 pistil; hairy filaments; borne in solitary, woolly, **pendant, non-fragrant racemes** to 6 in. long with bracts longer than flowers. July–August. **FRUITS:** Hairy, 3-valved capsules with many seeds. **WHERE FOUND:** Rich moist woods in the Appalachian Mountains from PA to GA. In TN, in the northern Cumberland Plateau and the Blue Ridge Mountains. Occasional. **SIMILAR SPECIES: COASTAL SWEET PEPPERBUSH (C. alnifolia)** has smaller **leaves with acute tips;** flowers with smooth filaments are borne in **fragrant, erect racemes** with bracts shorter than flowers. Moist woods and swamps, mostly in coastal areas from ME to TX. In TN, known only from Coffee County. Rare. June–July.

NOTES: *Clethra* is the Greek name for "alder" and was given to this genus because the leaves resemble those of alder trees, which are in an unrelated genus, *Alnus.* The species name *acuminata* means "tapering to a long narrow point," also a reference to the leaves. • The flowers of **Mountain Sweet Pepperbush,** sometimes called **Cinnamonbark Clethra,** attract bees and butterflies; the seeds attract a variety of birds.

Heath Family (Ericaceae) includes Monotropaceae & Pyrolaceae

The Heath Family is widespread, mostly in temperate, subarctic, and subtropical regions, and includes shrubs, lianas, and small trees. Members of this family are mostly woody, often with showy flowers. The corolla and calyx are usually 5-parted with 5 or 10 stamens. The Heath Family includes azaleas, heathers, rhododendrons, and shrubs with delicious fruits such as cranberries, blueberries, and huckleberries. Sixteen genera and 42 species are found in TN, all native.

1a. Plants parasitic, lacking chlorophyll; leaves reduced to scales 2

  2a. Petals united; fruit a berry . . . . **Monotropsis**

  2b. Petals separate; fruit a capsule . . . . **Monotropa**

1b. Plants with chlorophyll; leaves not reduced to scales 3

  3a. Petals separate 4

    4a. Low shrubs . . . . **Leiophyllum**

    4b. Perennial herbs, with subterranean rhizomes . . . . **Chimaphila**

  3b. Petals fused or, if appearing separate, then the ovary inferior 5

    5a. Ovary superior (but appearing inferior in *Gaultheria*) 6

      6a. Corolla abruptly flared or bell-shaped, widest at the tip 7

        7a. Stems creeping; fruit berrylike . . . . **Epigaea**

        7b. Stems erect; fruit dry 8

          8a. Corolla radially symmetric; the anthers (in bud) held in
pockets of the corolla . . . . **Kalmia**

          8b. Corolla slightly bilaterally symmetric; anthers exserted, not held
in corolla pockets . . . . **Rhododendron**

      6b. Corolla tubular, ovoid, urn-shaped, usually constricted at the tip 9

        9a. Flowers solitary in leaf axils; lower leaf surface essentially smooth;
leaves with the odor of wintergreen; fruit a berry . . . . **Gaultheria**

        9b. Flowers in terminal or axillary racemes . . . . **Leucothoe**

    5b. Ovary inferior or appearing inferior in *Gaultheria* 10

    10a. Low, trailing shrub, leaves with the odor of wintergreen . . . . **Gaultheria**

    10b. Erect shrubs, without the odor of wintergreen . . . . **Vaccinium**

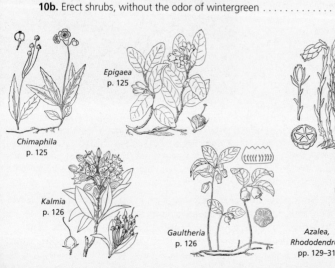

Epigaea
p. 125

Chimaphila
p. 125

Monotropa
p. 128

Kalmia
p. 126

Gaultheria
p. 126

*Azalea,
Rhododendron*
pp. 129–31

Spotted Wintergreen, Pipsissewa
Chimaphila maculata

JERRY DROWN

GENERAL: Short, erect perennial herb, 4–8 in. tall. **LEAVES:** 1–3 sets of alternate leaves that may appear opposite or whorled; **evergreen**, smooth, 1.5–2.0 in. long, tapering to a point, shallow teeth scattered along the margins, dark green with a **whitish stripe down the middle** and variegated along the veins. **FLOWERS:** Nodding, waxy, white or pinkish with a rounded green center, about 0.6 in. across, 5 distinct petals; borne in small clusters of 2–5 flowers at the top of the plant. June–July. **FRUITS:** Erect, 5-chambered capsules. **WHERE FOUND:** Dry, acidic woods and sandy soils. Throughout the eastern U.S. and TN, except for counties near the Mississippi River. Common.

NOTES: The genus name *Chimaphila* is from the Greek words *cheima*, for "winter," and *philo*, "to love," referring to the evergreen leaves that stay attractive through winter. • While most summer plants are found flowering in sunlit meadows, this species flowers in the shady woods. • The leaves can be chewed for refreshment. Until recently, the bittersweet taste of this useful plant made it an ingredient in commercial root beer. • The Native American name, **Pipsissewa**, comes from *pipsiskeweu*, which means "it breaks into small pieces," because this plant was used to treat kidney stones. • It is sometimes placed in the Shinleaf Family (Pyrolaceae).

Trailing Arbutus
Epigaea repens

DAVID KOCHER

GENERAL: Trailing evergreen **perennial** with brownish, hairy stems. **LEAVES:** Clustered, **elliptic, leathery,** 1–4 in. long, rounded or heart-shaped at the base. **FLOWERS:** Spicy, **pink-white**, about 0.5 in. wide, **5 corolla lobes flare abruptly from a short tube**; in clusters at the ends of small branches. March–May. **FRUITS:** Round berries with over 100 seeds. **WHERE FOUND:** Sandy, acid woods and rocky slopes. Extended range from Newfoundland to Saskatchewan, south to MS and FL. In TN, in the eastern ½ of the state, mostly in the Cumberland Plateau, the Ridge and Valley, and the Blue Ridge Mountains. Occasional.

NOTES: The genus name *Epigaea* is from the Greek *epi*, for "upon," and *gaia*, meaning "earth," in reference to this plant's habit of growing close to the ground. • Sometimes called **Mayflower**, this plant is prized in the northeastern U.S. for its showy displays. The fragrant flowers are sweet and are edible raw.

JERRY DROWN

Wintergreen, Teaberry, Checkerberry · *Gaultheria procumbens*

GENERAL: Evergreen shrub with short, erect stems to 4 in. tall, arising from creeping rhizomes. **LEAVES:** Only 3–4 alternate leaves crowded near the top of the stem; **dark green, thick, leathery,** shiny, 1–2 in. long, oval and slightly toothed; contain an aspirin-like compound; **young leaves have a wintergreen flavor. FLOWERS:** Solitary, **white,** waxy; barrel-shaped, **urn-like corolla** about 0.25 in. across and constricted at the tip, with 5 small, triangular lobes; flowers hang below the leaves. July. **FRUITS:** Mealy, fragrant, **bright red** berries with a **strong taste of wintergreen. WHERE FOUND:** Dry, acidic woods. A northeastern U.S. species extending southward in the uplands to TN, AL, and GA. The eastern 1/2 of TN. Occasional.

NOTES: The *Gaultheria* genus was named in honor of Jean Francois Gaulthier (1708–56), a physician from Québec, Canada. • This plant's many common names include Chickaberry, Deerberry, Drunkards, Eyeberry, Grouseberry, Ivory-Plums, Jersey-Tea, Kinnikinnik, Pollom, Spiceberry, and Youngsters, to name a few. • The red, aromatic berries are edible raw and taste like wintergreen. Native Americans reputedly ate the berries to "invigorate the stomach." • The name **Teaberry** refers to the leaves and berries, which were made into a tea that was used to treat asthma, restore strength, and promote lactation after childbirth. • This plant may be confused with young **Mountain Laurel** (see below), which has smooth leaves without shallow teeth and is **poisonous.**

KURT EMMANUELE

Mountain Laurel · *Kalmia latifolia*

GENERAL: Showy shrub to 10 ft. tall with **crooked, grooved branches;** forms dense thickets. **LEAVES:** Evergreen, shiny, to 4 in. long, oval-shaped (but widest beyond the middle), pointed at both ends. **FLOWERS:** Whitish pink, **cup-shaped,** about 0.75 in. wide; buds are strongly ribbed; 10 stamens form arching spokes that spring from depressions in the flower cup when mature; borne in **terminal clusters.** May–June. **FRUITS:** Erect capsules with glandular hairs; capsules split from top to bottom. **WHERE FOUND:** Dry, acidic soil and rocky woods. Upland areas of the eastern U.S. In TN, from the Western Highland Rim eastward. Common. **SIMILAR SPECIES:** CAROLINA SHEEP LAUREL (*K. carolina*) is much smaller (12–36 in. tall) with narrow leaves, mostly whorled, not shiny; lower leaves drooping; **deep pink flowers,** 0.5 in. across, **clusters not terminal;** new leaves appear at flowering time above flower clusters. Swamps, mountain bogs, and coastal areas from VA and TN to GA. Rare in TN, found only in Johnson County. May–June. *K. angustifolia* var. *carolina*.

NOTES: Mountain Laurel is also known as American Laurel, Broad-Leaved Kalmia, Calico Bush, and Wood Laurel. The names Poison Laurel and Sheepsbane signify that all parts of the plant, including honey made from the nectar, are **poisonous** if ingested. Other names, Spoon Hunt and Spoonwood, are in reference to Native Americans using the root for making small dishes, spoons, and other utensils. It was called **Ivy** by early pioneers in the Smoky Mountains.

Sand Myrtle, Mountain Myrtle · *Leiophyllum buxifolium*

GENERAL: Low, widely branched shrub to 12 in. tall. **LEAVES:** Alternate or sometimes opposite, **evergreen**, 0.5 in. long, oval to oblong, stiff, **leathery**, dark green, shiny. **FLOWERS:** Star-like, **white or pinkish**, 5 petals, 0.1–0.2 in. long, 10 spreading stamens tipped with **purple anthers** protruding from the small flowers; displayed in umbel-like clusters. May. **FRUITS:** Capsules, 3-parted, that split from top to bottom; reddish brown seeds. **WHERE FOUND:** Sandy barrens of NJ and coastal Carolinas, also scattered on exposed mountaintops and bluffs in the Blue Ridge and Smoky Mountains. In TN, in Carter, Greene, Sevier, and Blount counties. Rare.

DICK DOUB

NOTES: The genus name *Leiophyllum* means "smooth leaf," in reference to the glossy leaves. The genus includes only this single species. • Myrtle Point on Mount LeConte in the Great Smoky Mountains National Park was named for this plant. In the Smoky Mountains, it grows at elevations above 4000 ft. at the edges of rhododendrons in heath balds, known locally as "laurel slicks."

Dog Hobble
Leucothoe fontanesiana

GENERAL: Sprawling **shrub** to 5 ft. tall; forms **dense thickets along streams** in the mountains. **LEAVES:** Alternate, **evergreen, smooth, leathery**, 2–5 in. long, tapering to a narrow point. **FLOWERS:** White, **urn-shaped**, about 0.25 in. long; in **drooping clusters** that hang from the leaf axils. April–June. **FRUITS:** Capsules containing veiny, shiny seeds. **WHERE FOUND:** Acidic soils along mountain streams in the southern Appalachian Mountains. In TN, from the Cumberland Plateau eastward. Occasional. **SIMILAR SPECIES:** FETTERBUSH (**L. recurva**) is a more upright shrub with alternate **deciduous leaves**; white, urn-shaped flowers hang in elongated, **one-sided, curved clusters**. Dry ridges and rocky slopes in the Appalachian Mountains. In TN, in the northern Blue Ridge counties of East TN. Infrequent. April–June.

DOUGLAS H. EHLEBEN, DDS

NOTES: The *Leucothoe* genus was named after Leucothoe, a Persian princess who, according to legend, was one of the many loves of the god Apollo; *fontanesiana* honors René Desfontaines (1750–1833), a French botanist. • The name **Dog Hobble** suggests the difficulty early pioneers and their dogs encountered in traveling through nearly impenetrable thickets of this plant.

JERRY DROWN

Pinesap · *Monotropa hypopithys*

GENERAL: Saprophyte, 4–10 in. tall, **without chlorophyll**; yellowish red, soft-hairy stem; grows in clusters much like **Indian Pipe** (see below). **LEAVES:** Scales along the stem instead of leaves. **FLOWERS:** Nodding, **dull yellowish red, urn-shaped**, 0.3–0.6 in. long; 3–10 flowers arranged mostly on one side of the stem (Indian Pipe has a solitary nodding flower terminating the stem); remains colorful long after flowering while fruits are forming. May–September. **FRUITS:** Capsules that become erect upon maturity. **WHERE FOUND:** Acid pine or oak woods found in most of the U.S. and Canada. Scattered throughout TN. Occasional.

NOTES: The genus name *Monotropa* is from the Greek word *monos*, "one," and *tropos*, meaning "to turn," in reference to the flowers that are borne only on one side of the stem. • This plant is edible raw or cooked and contains an essential oil.

DENNIS HORN

Indian Pipe · *Monotropa uniflora*

GENERAL: One to several smooth, **translucent, waxy, white or pale pink** stems rise 3–9 in. tall from leaf litter, much like mushrooms after a warm rain. **LEAVES:** Stem bears a few scattered, pointed scales in place of leaves. **FLOWERS:** Solitary, nodding, urn-shaped, about 0.75 in. long, same color as the stem (pipe), 4–5 petals, 10 stamens; flower turns upright when in fruit and **becomes blackish with age.** June–September. **FRUITS:** Capsules that become erect upon maturity. **WHERE FOUND:** Rich, shady woods over much of the U.S. and Canada. Throughout TN. Frequent.

NOTES: Other common names for this species are Corpse Plant, Ice Plant, and Ghost Flower, referring to its white or translucent color and also because the plant turns black when picked. The color, or lack thereof, indicates that **this plant can live without chlorophyll**, and instead has a mutualistic relationship with small, wood-rotting fungi that free nutrients for the plant's use. After the flower has been fertilized, it turns a light shade of pink. • Native Americans collected the clear juice from the stem to use as eye medicine and to sharpen vision. • This genus is sometimes placed in the Indian Pipe Family (Monotropaceae).

Sweet Pinesap · *Monotropsis odorata*

GENERAL: Saprophyte, 2–4 in. tall with smooth, **dark brownish purple stems**; difficult to find in the dry leaf litter. **LEAVES:** Stems have many **light brown, overlapping scales** in place of leaves. **FLOWERS:** Numerous, **fragrant, purplish**, 0.3–0.4 in. long, barely extending beyond the brown scales at the end of the stem; petals are united into an **urn-shaped cup with 5 lobes** (the primary reason for placing this plant in a separate genus from **Indian Pipe** (p. 128) and **Pinesap** (p. 128), which have separate petals). February–April. **FRUITS:** Berries with brown seeds. **WHERE FOUND:** Usually in pine woods of the southern highlands, north to MD. In TN, in Grundy, Scott, Polk, Monroe, Blount, and Sevier counties. Infrequent.

NOTES: The species name *odorata* means "fragrant" and refers to the surprisingly fragrant flower. • **Sweet Pinesap** is a **saprophytic** plant that depends upon a mutualistic relationship with mycorrhizal fungi to obtain nutrinets. This species, like other pinesaps, lacks chlorophyll and therefore is not able to photosynthesize.

HUGH & CAROL NOURSE

Flame Azalea
Rhododendron calendulaceum

GENERAL: Much-branched **mountain shrub** to 10 ft. tall; not colonial; **flowers as leaves are opening or expanding.** **LEAVES:** Alternate, elliptic to obovate, about 3 in. long when fully mature and woolly-hairy beneath. **FLOWERS:** Brilliant yellow to deep orange (color is variable), 1.5–2.0 in. wide, slightly fragrant; upper lobe of flower is slightly wider than the other 4 lobes; 5 long, reddish, thread-like stamens and solitary pistil extend well beyond the flower tube. April–June. **FRUITS:** Hairy capsules, often with stalked glands; seeds taper at both ends. **WHERE FOUND:** Dry open woods, mostly in the Appalachian Mountains, from NY, south to GA and AL. In TN, mostly in the Blue Ridge Mountains. Occasional. **SIMILAR SPECIES:** CUMBERLAND AZALEA (*R. cumberlandense*) **bright red-orange flowers open after the leaves are fully open,** upper lobe is much wider and marked with a large orange spot. In mountain woods in the southern Appalachians, from WV to AL and GA. In TN, from the Cumberland Plateau eastward. Occasional. June.

DAVID KOCHER

NOTES: The genus name *Rhododendron* comes from the Greek *rhodon*, "a rose," and *dendron*, "a tree," referring to the showy flowers of these sometimes large plants; *calendulaceum* comes from the Latin *calendae*, for "marigold," indicating the often yellow color of the flowers. • **Flame Azalea** is a distinctive shrub of the Appalachian Mountains, and it is commonly cultivated as a spectacular ornamental. • The *Rhododendron* genus can be divided into **2 distinct groups**: deciduous azaleas and evergreen rhododendrons. Both groups have similar showy flowers. Eleven species are found in TN.

DENNIS HORN

Mountain Azalea, Piedmont Azalea
Rhododendron canescens

GENERAL: Shrub, 3–10 ft. tall, usually **not colonial**. **LEAVES:** Alternate, deciduous, elliptic, 2–4 in. long, mostly **felty-woolly underneath**. **FLOWERS:** White to deep pink, about 1.5 in. across, 5-lobed, **usually fragrant**; flower tube to 2x as long as lobes; stamens about 3 times the length of tube. April–May. **FRUITS:** Grayish-hairy capsules with no stalked glands. **WHERE FOUND:** Moist woods and swamps in the southeastern U.S. Throughout TN, except the high mountains. Frequent. **SIMILAR SPECIES:** PINXTER FLOWER (*R. periclymenoides*), also called **PINK AZALEA**, is **colonial; leaves mostly smooth beneath**; pink to white **flowers usually not fragrant**; flower tube about same length as lobes. Eastern U.S. Frequent across TN. April–May. **SWAMP AZALEA** (*R. viscosum*) is 3–6 ft. tall with **hairy twigs, leaves, and flowers**; flowers usually white; stamens extend beyond the floral tube less than the length of the tube. Eastern Seaboard and Gulf Coast states. Middle and East TN. Rare. June–July. **SMOOTH AZALEA** (*R. arborescens*) has **smooth leaves and twigs**; white flowers; showy, red stamens extend beyond the floral tube more than the tube length. From NY, south to GA and MS. Eastern ½ of TN, also Crockett and McNairy counties in West TN. Occasional. June–July.

NOTES: The name azalea is New Latin for "dry plant," indicating the preference of some plants for growing in dry soil. • The first rhododendron introduced to Britain in the 1670s was an Asian species, *R. ponticum*. The next rhododendrons to be introduced were from America, sent by the Quaker botanist, John Bartram, to Peter Collinson.

KURT EMMANUELE

Catawba Rhododendron
Rhododendron catawbiense

GENERAL: Woody shrub, 3–10 ft. tall, similar to **Great Rhododendron** (p. 131) but generally smaller. **LEAVES:** Alternate, smooth, **leathery, evergreen**, 2–6 in. long, elliptic-oblong, pale and **smooth beneath**; generally shorter and wider than Great Rhododendron leaves. **FLOWERS:** Showy, **rose pink to purple**, 5-lobed, to 2 in. across; in large clusters at the ends of the branches. May–June. **FRUITS:** Densely red-hairy capsules up to 0.75 in. long. **WHERE FOUND:** At higher elevations in the southern Appalachian Mountains. In TN, from the Cumberland Plateau eastward. Occasional. **SIMILAR SPECIES:** CAROLINA RHODODENDRON (*R. minus*) has **leaves with dense brown scales beneath** and **pale pink flowers**. Exposed ridges and rocky outcrops at higher elevations, also on stream bluffs. Southern Appalachian Mountains. In TN, in Monroe, Polk, Roane, Loudon, Blount, Sevier, Greene, Unicoi, Washington, and Carter counties in East TN. Infrequent. May–June.

NOTES: The species name *catawbiense* refers to the Catawba River, where this species was discovered in 1809 by John Fraser. • **Catawba Rhododendron**, commonly called **Mountain Rosebay Rhododendron**, provides a spectacular display in the natural gardens above 6000 ft. on Roan Mountain in northeastern TN during late June.

Great Rhododendron
Rhododendron maximum

GENERAL: Stout, **woody shrub**, 6–20 ft. tall; forms dense colonies; **largest of our rhododendrons**. **LEAVES:** Alternate, evergreen, 4–10 in. long and 1–3 in. wide, smooth above and fine-woolly beneath. **FLOWERS:** Showy, **white or pale pink**, 1.0–1.5 in. wide; corolla has 5 rounded lobes, with one lobe (usually the uppermost) having prominent **greenish yellow or orange spots within**; flower stalks are sticky; in rounded clusters at the ends of branches. June–July. **FRUITS:** Capsules up to 0.75 in. long; seeds taper at both ends. **WHERE FOUND:** Wet, acidic woods and along mountain streams from the northeastern U.S. and Canada, south in the uplands to GA and AL. In TN, from the Cumberland Plateau eastward, also Smith and Benton counties. Frequent.

TERRY LIVINGSTONE

NOTES: The nectar of many members of the Heath Family, including rhododendrons, contains **poisonous** andromedotoxin. Beekeepers must be very careful when deciding the location of their hives in spring. At various times, people have gotten sick from eating toxic honey. • Rhododendrons generally prefer **acidic soil**. • Early pioneers in the Smoky Mountains called rhododendrons **laurels**.

Deerberry · *Vaccinium stamineum*

GENERAL: Many-branched, **deciduous shrub**, 2–6 ft. tall; **older stems brownish gray**. **LEAVES:** Alternate, 2–4 in. long, highly variable, ovate to elliptic with acute or acuminate tips and short petioles, pale beneath. **FLOWERS:** Numerous, **white or pink**, open bell-shaped, 5-lobed, less than 0.25 in. long, protruding **yellow-orange stamens**; borne in racemes on branches with small, leafy bracts. May–July. **FRUITS:** Edible, greenish blue berries, 4–5 locules, many seeds; highly variable as to color and taste. **WHERE FOUND:** Dry woods of uplands, from ME to MO, southward. In most of TN, except the extreme western counties. Common. **SIMILAR SPECIES:** HIGHBUSH BLUEBERRY (*V. corymbosum*) is a crown-forming shrub, 3–8 ft. tall; **greenish white to pink, urn-shaped flowers**; dull blue or black **berries are juicy, edible**. In low woods or dry uplands from ME to IL and OK, southward. In TN, from the Eastern Highland Rim, eastward, less common west. Frequent. April–July. HILLSIDE BLUEBERRY (*V. pallidum*), also called LOWBUSH BLUEBERRY, is a low, colonial shrub to 2 ft. tall; **greenish twigs; greenish white, urn-shaped flowers**; glaucous, blue **berries are edible, tasty**. Dry upland woods from ME to MN, southward. Throughout Middle and East TN, absent in West TN. Common. April–June.

DENNIS HORN

NOTES: Deerberry is so named because the berries provide food for deer and other animals. • Identifying *Vaccinium* species can be confusing because hybridization between species is common. This genus includes blueberries, cranberries, and bilberries. Nine *Vaccinium* species occur in TN.

KURT EMMANUELE

Galax, Beetleweed · *Galax urceolata*

GENERAL: Rhizomatous, **stemless, evergreen perennial** with flowering stalks 18–24 in. tall. **LEAVES:** Basal, 2–6 in. wide, **circular to ovate**, heart-shaped at the base, toothed margins, long petioles. **FLOWERS:** White, 5 petals to 0.25 in. long, separate; calyx 0.12 in. long; numerous flowers in a **tall raceme or spike**. May–July. **FRUITS:** Tan capsules about 0.4 in. long. **WHERE FOUND:** Locally abundant, frequently **forming solid ground cover** in moist or dry woodlands on acidic soils. Found chiefly in the mountains from western MD to KY, south to GA and AL, and extending to the Coastal Plain of NC and southern VA. In TN, in Blue Ridge and adjacent counties in the Ridge and Valley. Occasional. **G. aphylla**.

NOTES: The name **Galax** comes from the Greek word *gala*, meaning "milk"; *urceolata* means "urn-shaped," referring to the shape of the flower buds. • Other common names for this plant include Coltsfoot, Galaxy, and Wandflower. Also, the names Carpenter's Leaf and Heal-All give an indication of its medicinal value. It was used in a poultice to heal cuts and wounds. • The leaves are important for greenery used in Christmas floral arrangements.

DENNIS HORN

Scarlet Pimpernel
*Anagallis arvensis**

GENERAL: Highly branched **annual** to 12 in. tall; erect or reclining, with a **nearly square stem**. **LEAVES:** Opposite, sessile, entire, elliptic to ovate, 0.4–0.8 in. long. **FLOWERS:** Orange-red (occasionally white or blue) corolla, to 0.4 in. wide, has **5 rounded, fringed lobes**; flowers are solitary in leaf axils, **on stalks longer than leaves**. June–August. **FRUITS:** Spherical capsules to 0.25 in. long; dark seeds. **WHERE FOUND:** Introduced from Europe and naturalized along roadsides, in fields, and in other waste places throughout most of North America. Thinly scattered across TN. Occasional. **SIMILAR SPECIES:** CHAFFWEED (**Centunculus minimus**) is sometimes placed in the *Anagallis* genus; smaller, **alternate leaves**; tiny, **white or pink, 4-lobed flowers are nearly sessile** in the leaf axils. Wet soil and sandy areas. Irregularly scattered across the eastern U.S. and TN. Occasional. April–September. **A. minima**.

NOTES: The species name *arvensis* means "cultivated fields," in reference to one of this plant's favorite places to grow. • **Scarlet Pimpernel** is also called Bird's Eye, Eyebright, Poison Chickweed, and Wink-a-Peep, among others. In England, it is called **Poor-Man's Weatherglass** since the flowers close as bad weather approaches.

Shooting Star · *Dodecatheon meadia*

JOHN OATES

GENERAL: Perennial spring herb to 24 in. tall, with showy flowers. **LEAVES:** Basal rosette, mostly oblanceolate, to 8 in. long, **reddish at the base.** **FLOWERS:** White, rarely pink or lavender; **5 swept-back petals** expose the 5 stamens and yellow anthers, which form a **pointed beak** (or "star trajectory"); borne in a cluster at the top of a naked stalk (scape) that may be 6–20 in. tall. April–June. **FRUITS:** Ellipsoid capsules, about 0.5 in. long; dark red seeds are variously flattened or angled. **WHERE FOUND:** Rich, moist, wooded slopes; also meadows, open woods, prairies, and limestone bluffs from MN to NY, south to FL and TX. In TN, from the Western Highland Rim eastward. Frequent.

NOTES: The genus name *Dodecatheon* means "twelve gods." In Greek mythology, the primrose was under the care of the 12 gods of Mount Olympus. The common name refers to the striking flower with a petal formation that resembles a star shooting across the sky. • Other common names include **Pride of Ohio**, as well as American Cowslip, Cyclamen, Lamb's Noses, Mosquito Bells, Indian Chief, and Rooster Heads. The shape of the flower conjures various images, such as a rooster head or the traditional feathered headdress worn by some Native Americans.

Featherfoil, Water Violet
Hottonia inflata

MILO PYNE

GENERAL: Unusual, **aquatic winter annual** with thick, **hollow, jointed stems** to 8 in. tall. **LEAVES:** Submersed leaves are pinnately divided into numerous, very narrow segments, **resembling pale green feathers**. **FLOWERS:** White, 5-lobed corolla is shorter than the calyx, which is 0.15–0.3 in. long, making the flowers appear too small for the inflated stem; 3–10 flowers in circles at the joints of the stem. May–August. **FRUITS:** Rounded capsules, about 0.1 in. long; reddish brown, wrinkled seeds. **WHERE FOUND:** Quiet, shallow pools, swamps, and ditches. Chiefly an Atlantic and Gulf Coastal Plain species that extends north in the Mississippi and Ohio River valleys. In TN, in Lake, Marion, Montgomery, Obion, and Stewart counties. Rare.

NOTES: The seeds of *Hottonia* species sprout in late summer and grow underwater during fall and winter. Then when conditions are right in spring (which is not often), the hollow, air-filled stems rise and flower. **Featherfoils** may bloom profusely one year and not reappear for several years.

Fringed Loosestrife
Lysimachia ciliata

GENERAL: Much-branched perennial to 4 ft. tall. **LEAVES:** Opposite, **broad**, 2–5 in. long, **hairy petioles appear fringed** (from which the common name is derived). **FLOWERS:** Yellow, 0.5–1.0 in. across, long-stemmed, facing outward or downward; **5 pointed corolla lobes have toothed edges.** June–August. **FRUITS:** Rounded capsules, about 0.25 in. long; dark brown seeds. **WHERE FOUND:** In moist or wet ground in shade or sun throughout most of the U.S. and TN. Frequent. **SIMILAR SPECIES:** APPALACHIAN LOOSESTRIFE (**L. tonsa**) has relatively **smooth petioles**. Southeastern U.S. In TN, from the Cumberland Plateau eastward. Occasional. June–August. LANCELEAF LOOSESTRIFE (**L. lanceolata**) has **narrow, sessile leaves** that taper at both ends. Moist or wet woods and barrens. Eastern U.S. Throughout TN. Frequent. June–August.

NOTES: A legend says that loosestrifes got their name when Lysimachus, a Sicilian king and the successor to Alexander the Great, was being chased by a bull, and in a desperate attempt to save himself, forced a sprig of loosestrife at the maddened animal. The bull was instantly calmed, or "loosened from its strife." Traditionally, the plant was placed between yoked animals to prevent them from fighting. • Loosestrife has also been used in herbal medicine for its tranquilizing effect, though no scientific evidence has been documented.

Whorled Loosestrife
Lysimachia quadrifolia

GENERAL: Erect perennial herb to 3 ft. tall; **stem is usually unbranched** and smooth to slightly hairy. **LEAVES:** Stem leaves are in **whorls of 3–7**, usually 4–5, from broadly to narrowly **lanceolate**, 2–4 in. long, hairy beneath, broadly spreading. **FLOWERS:** 5 nearly separate corolla lobes, each about 0.3 in. long, are **yellow** with dark lines and **reddish at the base**; flowers extend on spreading stalks, 2 in. long, from each leaf axil toward the middle of the plant. May–July. **FRUITS:** Rounded capsules, about 0.12 in. long; dark brown seeds. **WHERE FOUND:** Dry or moist soils, mostly in open woods, from ME to MN, south to AL. In TN, from the Western Highland Rim eastward. Frequent. **SIMILAR SPECIES:** MONEYWORT (**L. nummularia***) is a **trailing** perennial with small, **opposite, round, shining leaves**; yellow flowers extend on thin stalks from the leaf axils. A garden escape of European origin, now naturalized in moist ground of lawns and roadsides. Throughout the eastern U.S. and scattered across TN. Occasional. June–August.

NOTES: The genus name *Lysimachia* literally means "loosestrife": *lysis*, "to release from," and *mache*, "strife." The species name *quadrifolia* means "four leaves," a reference to the whorled stem leaves.

Swamp Candles · *Lysimachia terrestris*

NITA R. HEILMAN

GENERAL: Erect, smooth perennial, 18–36 in. tall, often branched, but usually with a single flowering raceme that terminates the stem. **LEAVES:** Opposite, narrowly lanceolate, 2–4 in. long. **FLOWERS:** About 0.5 in. wide, 5 narrowly elliptic, **yellow corolla lobes** are marked with dark lines and **red at the base**; on **short stalks** to 0.6 in. long; in an erect, many-flowered raceme to 12 in. long, with small, narrow bracts. May–July. **FRUITS:** Rounded capsules with dark brown seeds. **WHERE FOUND:** Swamps and open areas. Occurs more frequently in the northern U.S. and Canada, but extends south to GA and TN, where it is found in Coffee, Unicoi, and Johnson counties. Rare. **SIMILAR SPECIES:** TRAILING LOOSESTRIFE (**L. radicans**) is a **reclining plant** to 36 in. long; stem nodes are fringed with short hairs; **flowers on long stalks** from upper leaf axils. Wet woods and swamps from VA to MO, south to AL and TX. West TN. Infrequent. June–August.

NOTES: The species name *terrestris* means "of the ground." Linnaeus named this plant *terrestris*, thinking it was a terrestrial mistletoe. This plant produces axillary bulblets late in the season that fall to the ground, thus reproducing vegetatively. • **Swamp Candles**, as the name indicates, can often be found growing in swamps.

Starflower

Trientalis borealis

DENNIS HORN

GENERAL: Low, smooth, perennial herb with a simple erect stem, **4–8 in. tall**, from a slender rhizome. **LEAVES:** Single, **terminal whorl** of 5–9 simple, lanceolate, **veiny leaves**, 2–4 in. long, somewhat unequal in size; a few alternate scales along the stem below the leaves. **FLOWERS:** White, about 0.5 in. across; **flat, circular corolla**, normally with **7 pointed lobes**, giving a starlike appearance; 1–3 flowers extend above the leaves on slender, erect stalks, 1–2 in. long. May–July. **FRUITS:** Capsules, 5-valved, with several seeds. **WHERE FOUND:** Rich woods and bogs. Boreal forests of Canada and the northeastern U.S., south in the mountains to GA. In TN, only in Greene, Carter, and Sullivan counties in the northeast. Rare.

NOTES: The genus name *Trientalis* means "one-third of a foot in length"; *borealis* means "northern." Other names for this plant are Chickweed, Evergreen, and Maystar. Although it is also called Indian Potatoes for the small swellings at the base of the stem, these are **not considered edible**. • This plant is a small, dainty woodland flower, with its leaves withering and disappearing in autumn. Two other members of this genus are found on the West Coast.

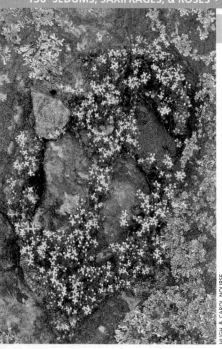

Elf Orpine · *Diamorpha smallii*

GENERAL: Clumped, low **winter annual** with **red stems**, branched at the base; 1.5–3.5 in. tall. **LEAVES:** Alternate, **reddish, succulent**, cylindric, sessile, to 0.25 in. long. **FLOWERS:** White, 4 petals to 0.12 in. long, 8 stamens; inflorescence is flat-topped, each stem with 3–12 flowers. April. **FRUITS:** A cluster of 4 dry capsules (follicles) that are erect, pointed, and united toward the base, splitting along 1 suture. **WHERE FOUND:** Plateau sandstone outcrops. Range from VA to AL and GA (on granite). In TN, in Cumberland, Franklin, Grundy, Hamilton, Marion, Putnam, and Rhea counties. Infrequent. *D. cymosa, Sedum smallii.*

NOTES: This plant's common name refers to its tiny size, though the species name honors American botanist John K. Small (1869–1938). • The Sedum Family name, Crassulaceae, comes from *crassus*, which means "thick," for the thick leaves of many species.

HUGH & CAROL NOURSE

KURT EMMANUELE

Widow's Cross, Glade Stonecrop · *Sedum pulchellum*

GENERAL: Low winter annual, 2–12 in. tall, usually branching at the base; **grows on exposed limestone. LEAVES:** Alternate, linear, **round in cross-section**, to 1.5 in. long. **FLOWERS:** Pink to white, usually **4 spreading petals**, 0.12–0.25 in. long, anthers often red; flowers are crowded on 3–7 short, divergent branches, each 1–3 in. long. April–May. **FRUITS:** Follicles, 0.2–0.3 in. long. **WHERE FOUND:** Limestone ledges, roadsides, and openings, from KY and GA, west to OK and TX. Characteristic plant of the cedar glades of Middle TN, but also occurs on cliffs; is currently spreading along TN roads in limestone gravel. Frequent. **SIMILAR SPECIES:** STRINGY STONECROP (*S. sarmentosum**) is a **perennial** with creeping stems that form mats; thick **leaves are flattened**, usually in whorls of 3; **yellow flowers**, mostly **5-petaled**, about 0.5 in. wide. Introduced from China, now escaped from cultivation in much of the eastern U.S. and scattered thinly across TN. Occasional. May–July.

NOTES: The name **Widow's Cross** comes from the shape of the 4-petaled flower. • Stonecrops generally prefer the arid climates of deserts, rocky shores, tundra, and other dry, open areas because their fleshy leaves store water. • The pores on the leaves conserve water by opening at night to admit carbon dioxide, which is needed for growing, and closing during the heat of the day to prevent water loss.

KURT EMMANUELE

Wild Stonecrop, Mountain Stonecrop · *Sedum ternatum*

GENERAL: Low, sprawling, forest perennial that grows on rocks, logs, or bare soil; flowering stems to 7 in. tall are topped by a branched inflorescence. **LEAVES:** Mostly in **whorls of 3**, generally flat, **usually spatulate**, to 0.75 in. long; leaves of the erect flowering stem are shorter, elliptic, and alternate; the low, larger, whorled leaves are present all year. **FLOWERS:** About 0.4 in. across, bracted, usually **4 white petals** and 4 sepals. April–May. **FRUITS:** Pointed, spreading follicles to 0.32 in. long. **WHERE FOUND:** Rich forests with moist soils all year. Range includes most of the eastern U.S. In TN, from the Western Highland Rim eastward, also Fayette County in West TN. Common. **SIMILAR SPECIES:** NEVIUS' STONECROP (*S. nevii*) has **alternate, linear leaves** on the flowering stems. On shale or limestone in TN, AL, and GA. In TN, only in Polk County in East TN. Rare. May–June.

NOTES: Many *Sedum* species are called Live Forevers because of their leaves' ability to stay fresh long after the plants are picked. • Several sedum species are cultivated as ornamentals, especially **Mossy Stonecrop** or **Wallpepper** (**S. acre***) and **Live Forever** (**S. telephium, including var. purpureum***), both originally from Eurasia. Some sedums, including **Roseroot** (**S. rosea**) and Live Forever, are edible. In these species, the leaves are edible raw and are tender and juicy, reported to have either a sour or acid taste.

Saxifrage Family (Saxifragaceae)

The Saxifrage Family is widespread and contains herbs and shrubs best adapted to temperate, cold, and often mountainous parts of the Northern Hemisphere. This family provides important ornamentals, including species in the genera *Astilbe, Heuchera, Hydrangea, Itea,* and *Saxifraga.* Many members of the Saxifrage Family are edible and can be used medicinally.

1a. Plants woody shrubs 2

  2a. Leaves alternate, 1.6 in. wide or less, flowers in racemes . . . . ***Itea***

  2b. Leaves opposite, more than 1.6 in. wide,
    flowers in dense terminal cymes . . . . ***Hydrangea***

1b. Plants herbaceous 3

  3a. Staminodia (false stamens) present;
    petals more than 0.4 in. long . . . . ***Parnassia***

  3b. Staminodia (false stamens) absent;
    petals less than 0.4 in. long **4**

    4a. Leaves ternately decompound; flowers unisexual . . . . ***Astilbe***

    4b. Leaves simple; flowers bisexual 5

      5a. Leaves basal and on the stem; petals pinnatifid or fringed . . . . ***Mitella***

      5b. Leaves chiefly basal; petals neither pinnatifid nor fringed **6**

        6a. Ovary 1-celled **7**

          7a. Stamens 10; inflorescence a raceme;
            carpels unequal at maturity . . . .*Tiarella*

          7b. Stamens 5; inflorescence a panicle;
            carpels equal at maturity . . . . ***Heuchera***

        6b. Ovary 2-celled . . . . ***Saxifraga***

Hydrangea
p. 140

Parnassia
p. 142

Saxifraga
pp. 143–44

Tiarella
p. 144

False Goatsbeard · *Astilbe biternata*

GENERAL: Coarse perennial herb, 3–6 ft. tall, with clustered stems arising from a short, stout rhizome; **upper stems glandular-hairy**. **LEAVES:** Both basal and alternate stem leaves, 2–3-ternately compound; leaflets ovate, tapering to a point, rounded or heart-shaped base, sharply toothed, **terminal leaflet usually 3-lobed**. **FLOWERS:** Tiny, **white or creamy**, perfect or unisexual, 5 petals, **2 pistils**, 10 stamens; borne in large panicles. May–July. **FRUITS:** Erect, lanceolate follicles, 0.15–0.20 in. long, splitting along 1 suture and converging at the tip; numerous seeds. **WHERE FOUND:** Rich wooded slopes in the southern Appalachian mountains from WV and VA, south to GA. Eastern 1/2 of TN. Frequent.

NOTES: The genus name *Astilbe* comes from the Greek words *a*, "without," and *stilbe*, "brightness," referring to the dullness of the leaves. • The **Saxifrage Family** includes plants with edible berries, including currents and gooseberries, as well as popular garden plants, hydrangeas, and saxifrages. • **Goatsbeard** (p. 147), of the Rose Family, is strikingly similar to **False Goatsbeard**, but has terminal leaflets that are usually not lobed and flowers with 3 or 4 pistils, whereas *Astilbe* species have 2 pistils per flower.

THOMAS E. HEMMERLY

Mapleleaf Alumroot · *Heuchera villosa*

GENERAL: Perennial herb, 12–36 in. tall, arising from rhizomes. **LEAVES:** Basal, 2–6 in. long and wide, palmately lobed with **5–7 sharp lobes**, resembling a maple leaf; leaf blade and long petioles are hairy. **FLOWERS:** Pink to white, 5 minute, linear petals; cup-shaped calyx, about 0.1 in. long, has long, white hairs on the outside; 5 long, extending stamens; borne in a panicle of numerous small flowers on a leafless, hairy stalk. June–September. **FRUITS:** Capsules with dark red seeds. **WHERE FOUND:** Moist, shaded ledges and cliffs. Occurs irregularly in the mountains from NY to GA, west to southern MO and AR. Throughout Middle and East TN. Common. **SIMILAR SPECIES:** COMMON ALUMROOT (*H. americana*) has leaves with blunt lobes. Rich woods. Throughout eastern U.S. and TN. Common. April–June. SMALL-FLOWERED ALUMROOT (*H. parviflora*) is shorter, **only to 18 in. tall**; soft, hairy, **roundish leaves**. Shaded rocks and ledges. From WV and GA, west to MO and AR. In TN, along the Cumberland Plateau. Occasional. July–September.

NOTES: The *Heuchera* genus was named in honor of Johann Heinrich von Heucher (1677–1747), professor of medicine at Wittenberg University, Germany. • **Mapleleaf Alumroot** is also commonly known as **Hairy Alumroot**. Native Americans made a powder from the dried root of Mapleleaf Alumroot and used it as an external remedy for sores, wounds, ulcers, and cancers. • **Common Alumroot** is sometimes called **American Sanicle**, and its root is a strong astringent.

JERRY DROWN

Ashy Hydrangea
Hydrangea cinerea

GENERAL: Spreading shrub to 6 ft. tall; **old stems have thin, light brown, peeling bark**, young are smooth or slightly hairy. **LEAVES:** Opposite, ovate, 2–7 in. long, fine-toothed margins, pointed tips, smooth above, **gray-hairy underneath**; petiole is about ⅓ as long as leaf blade. **FLOWERS:** In a terminal, round or **flat cluster**, 2–6 in. across, with small, **white**, 5-petaled central flowers; central flowers are fertile, developing into capsules; the few **sterile flowers along the outer edge are larger**, consisting of a 3–4-parted, showy calyx greater than 0.4 in. across. May–June. **FRUITS:** Capsules, consisting of a ribbed cup enclosing a compound ovary. **WHERE FOUND:** Rich woods and shady ledges. From IL, south to NC and GA, west to OK. Scattered across TN. Frequent. *H. arborescens* ssp. *discolor*. **SIMILAR SPECIES: WILD HYDRANGEA (*H. arborescens*)** has **leaves that are smooth and green beneath**; sterile flowers are less than 0.4 in. across. Eastern U.S. and throughout TN. Common. May–July. **SILVERLEAF HYDRANGEA (*H. radiata*)** has **leaves that are whitish-hairy beneath**; sterile flowers are numerous. In the mountains of TN, NC, SC, and GA. In East TN, in Polk, McMinn, Monroe, Blount, and Sevier counties. Rare. May–July. *H. arborescens* ssp. *radiata*.

NOTES: The species name *cinerea* is Latin for "ash-colored," from the gray down on the leaves of this shrub. **Ashy Hydrangea** is also called Seven Barks, for its tendency to peel, with each layer being a different color. • The roots of **Wild Hydrangea** are sometimes used for pipe stems, since they have a pleasant taste. In herbal medicine, this species has been used as a diuretic, purgative, and tonic. The Cherokee used it to great effect to treat calculous diseases, such as removing gravelly calcium deposits (stones) in the kidneys.

Oakleaf Hydrangea
Hydrangea quercifolia

GENERAL: Spreading shrub to 5 ft. tall, with multiple stems and **reddish, scaly bark**; young twigs are woolly and cobwebby, with long, tangled hairs. **LEAVES:** Opposite, 6–8 in. long, sharply 5–7-lobed, woolly-hairy beneath; **resemble the leaves of oak trees**. **FLOWERS:** Numerous tiny, fertile flowers and **many sterile, showy, white flowers** consisting of 4 large sepals that turn purple with age; in a **pyramid-shaped panicle** about 6 in. long. May–July. **FRUITS:** Capsules about 0.1 in. tall. **WHERE FOUND:** Bluffs, woods, and riverbanks from TN and NC, southward. In TN, found primarily in the southern counties along the MS and AL border. Occasional.

NOTES: The genus name *Hydrangea* comes from the Greek word *hydro*, meaning "water," and *angeion*, "a jar or vessel," in reference to the cup-shaped fruits; *quercifolia* means "leaves like *Quercus* or oak." • This species is used extensively in gardens. It enjoys moist, well-drained soil and can grow and flower in shady areas. • Many *Hydrangea* species have sterile-flowered forms that are important in horticulture.

Virginia Willow, Sweetspire • *Itea virginica*

GENERAL: Slender, deciduous shrub with **chambered pith,** 3–8 ft. tall; twigs hairy. **LEAVES:** Alternate, simple, smooth, 2–3 in. long, elliptic to oblong, narrowed abruptly to a pointed tip, margins finely toothed; **parallel, curved veins** similar to dogwoods (*Cornus* spp.); leaf stalks to 0.4 in. long. **FLOWERS:** Numerous, white, **fragrant**, 5 narrow petals, 0.2 in. long; borne in numerous hairy, arching, **narrow, terminal racemes**, 2–6 in. long. May–June. **FRUITS:** Woody, slender, 2-grooved capsules, 0.3 in. long; several smooth, shiny seeds. **WHERE FOUND:** Wet woods and swamps. Coastal Plain from NJ to TX, inland to OK and southern IN. Widespread across TN. Frequent.

DENNIS HORN

NOTES: The genus name *Itea* is the Greek word for "*willow.*" • This plant is also called **Tassel-White** and is often planted as an ornamental shrub for its long-lasting and spectacular fall color. Look for the smooth bark stem that is purplish red on the sun-exposed side and green on the opposite side. • The *Itea* genus is sometimes placed in the Gooseberry Family (Grossulariaceae) along with all the gooseberries of the *Ribes* genus. There is only one *Itea* species in North America, but 15 in Asia.

Bishop's Cap, Miterwort • *Mitella diphylla*

DAVID DUHL

GENERAL: Perennial herb, 10–18 in. high, with slender, unbranched stems arising from an underground rhizome. **LEAVES:** Long-petioled basal leaves, 2–3 in. long, 3–5-lobed, palmately veined, heart-shaped base; **single pair of sessile stem leaves. FLOWERS:** White, **5 deeply fringed petals** to 0.1 in. long; mostly cup-shaped calyx tube; borne in a raceme. April–June. **FRUITS:** Green capsules with 2 valves; black, shiny, smooth seeds. **WHERE FOUND:** Moist, rocky areas and mossy banks in rich woods. A more northern species extending south to GA and MS. In TN, from the Western Highland Rim eastward. Frequent.

NOTES: This plant is named **Bishop's Cap** for the shape of the **young seedpods, which resemble the tall, pointed hat** (miter) with two peaks that is **worn by bishops.** Other names for this plant are Crystal Flower, Fairy Cup, Fringe Cup, and Snowflake, referring to the tiny, delicate flowers, which are better appreciated when viewed with a 10x hand lens. It was also called Coolwort because the leaves were made into a tea that was used to treat fever, as well as Sanicle, after the famous healing herb. • *Mitella* species are native to both Asia and North America, lending support to the theory that these continents were once a single landmass.

Kidneyleaf Grass-of-Parnassus
Parnassia asarifolia

ED HONICKER

General: Smooth perennial herb, 8–16 in. tall. **Leaves:** **Kidney-shaped** basal leaves, 1–2 in. wide, almost as long, entire, on long stalks; each flowering stem has **1 sessile leaf**, similar but smaller, **near the middle of the stem.** **Flowers:** Solitary flower on each stem; 5 **white** petals, about 0.5 in. long, **prominently grayish-veined, narrow-stalked**; 5 stamens with anthers are separated by 5 shorter, sterile ones. September–October. **Fruits:** Capsules with 4 valves; numerous seeds. **Where Found:** Swamps and seepage slopes. From AR and eastern TX, east to VA and GA, chiefly in the mountains. In TN, from the Cumberland Plateau eastward. Occasional.

Notes: Though these plants do not resemble grass, the *Parnassia* genus was named by Dioscorides, a botanist of ancient Greece, after a grass-like plant that grew on the side of Mount Parnassus in Greece. This oddity comes from centuries of confusion over the translation of the word for "green plant." The species name *asarifolia* means "leaves resembling *Asarum* or Wild Ginger," and fortunately, this part of the name is appropriate. • The distinctive lines on the petals act as a guide to attract pollinators.

Largeleaf Grass-of-Parnassus
Parnassia grandifolia

HUGH & CAROL NOURSE

General: Smooth perennial herb, 8–16 in. tall. **Leaves:** Basal leaves **ovate**, 2–3 in. long, palmately veined, entire, on long stalks; single sessile leaf, similar but smaller, is attached midway on the flower stalk. **Flowers:** Solitary, **white**, about 1 in. wide, **5 petals, not stalked**, each petal has 5–9 **green veins**; 5 stamens with reddish anthers are separated by longer, pointed, sterile stamens. September–October.

Fruits: Capsules with 4 valves; numerous seeds; empty capsules may persist until the following spring. **Where Found:** Wet, rocky soils, especially on limestone. Throughout most of the southeastern U.S., chiefly in uplands and seepage areas. Thinly spread in TN from the Western Highland Rim eastward, in Lewis, Lawrence, Maury, Williamson, Dekalb, Anderson, Campbell, Claiborne, and Carter counties. Infrequent.

Notes: The species name *grandifolia* refers to this plant's large, basal leaves. • **Largeleaf Grass-of-Parnassus** is considered rare and threatened in some states and is similar to **Carolina Grass-of-Parnassus** (**P. caroliniana**) in its declining numbers. In the early 1900s, the abundance of Carolina Grass-of-Parnassus was noted by H.A. Rankin: "…hundreds of acres may be seen liberally dotted with its white stars…it finds its best development in the lower places, and here it often almost covers the ground." This is not the case today, with activities such as commercial and residential development causing the destruction of its habitat and leading to a diminished range.

Mountain Saxifrage
Saxifraga michauxii

GENERAL: Hairy perennial herb to 20 in. tall. **LEAVES:** Basal rosette, obovate to oblanceolate, to 6 in. long, **coarsely toothed. FLOWERS:** White, **irregular,** about 0.5 in. across, 2 narrow, spatulate petals and 3 wider, stalked petals that are spotted with yellow; borne in a **widely branched inflorescence.** June–August. **FRUITS:** Capsules with raised nerves; longitudinally striped seeds. **WHERE FOUND:** Moist rocks and seepage slopes. In the mountains from WV and KY, south to GA. In TN, at high elevations in the eastern mountains, also Scott, Fentress, and Pickett counties. Infrequent.

JERRY DROWN

NOTES: The name "saxifrage" comes from *saxum*, meaning "rock," and *frangere*, "to break," as these plants grow in rock crevices. Even though saxifrages are thought to have broken or split rocks, this was most likely caused by the action of freezing and melting water inside the cracks. • The species name honors André Michaux (1746–1802), a French botanist and early explorer of the Appalachian Mountains.

Mountain Lettuce, Brook Lettuce • *Saxifraga micranthidifolia*

GENERAL: Perennial to 32 in. tall, from a stout rhizome. **LEAVES:** Basal, to 8 in. long, **oblanceolate** to oblong, **sharply toothed,** gradually tapering to a winged petiole. **FLOWERS:** About 0.25 in. wide, 5 oval, **stalked petals,** white **with a yellow spot near the base;** inflorescence is branched above, forming a large, open panicle. April–June. **FRUITS:** Capsules, 0.25 in. long; longitudinally striped seeds. **WHERE FOUND:** Wet cliffs and mountain brooks, chiefly in the Blue Ridge Mountains from TN and NC to WV and eastern PA. In TN, in Polk, Monroe, Blount, Sevier, Cocke, Unicoi, Carter, and Johnson counties in East TN. Infrequent.

JERRY DROWN

NOTES: As the common names imply, early pioneers in the southern Appalachian Mountains collected leaves from this plant and used them in fresh green salads. A wilted salad was made by pouring hot bacon grease over the leaves and adding sugar and vinegar. • This plant is also called Deer Tongue.

DENNIS HORN

Early Saxifrage · *Saxifraga virginiensis*

GENERAL: Perennial herb with a hairy and sticky flowering stem to 16 in. tall. **LEAVES:** Basal rosette, essentially **ovate**, 1–3 in. long, **toothed**. **FLOWERS:** White, regular, 5 petals to 0.2 in. long, bell-shaped calyx tube, stamens are barely exserted; **carpels are joined to the floral cup** at the base of the flower. March–April. **FRUITS:** Capsules; seeds have a roughened surface. **WHERE FOUND:** Rocky, open woodlands, rock ledges, and streambanks. Range includes most of the eastern U.S. and southeastern Canada. Throughout most of TN, but concentrated in Middle TN. Frequent. **SIMILAR SPECIES:** CAREY'S SAXIFRAGE (**S. careyana**) flowers later; petals usually elliptic, to 0.15 in. long, occasionally with yellow spots near the base; **carpels are not joined to the floral cup**. Damp rocky areas. In the mountains of southern VA and NC, south to AL and GA. In TN, from the Cumberland Plateau eastward. Occasional. May–July.

NOTES: Early Saxifrage is also called Bread and Butter, Everlasting, Lungwort, Mayflower, St. Peter's Cabbage, and Sweet Wilson. It was commonly used to treat inflammations. • The hairs on the flowering stalk of Early Saxifrage are glandular and secrete a sticky substance that entraps insects trying to climb the stalk in search of nectar, thereby leaving the nectar for flying insects.

KURT EMMANUELE

Foamflower · *Tiarella cordifolia*

GENERAL: Erect perennial herb, 8–20 in. tall, from a rhizome. **LEAVES:** Basal, long-stalked, roughly heart-shaped, 2–4 in. long, **3–5-lobed, palmately veined, hairy. FLOWERS:** To 0.33 in. across, **5 white or pink-tinged petals**, 10 long stamens; borne in a **terminal raceme** to 6 in. long on a **leafless stalk**. April–June. **FRUITS:** 2-valved capsules with persistent styles; shiny, black, smooth seeds. **WHERE FOUND:** Rich woodlands throughout most of the eastern U.S. In TN, from the Western Highland Rim eastward. Frequent.

NOTES: The genus name *Tiarella* means "small crown" referring to the flowers; *cordifolia* means "heart-leaved." This plant was also called Coalwort, Coolwort, False Bitterwort, and Gem Fruit. • **Foamflower** has a high tannin content, which may explain its medicinal uses by Native Americans. In 1850, Susan Cooper wrote from New York "… the country people employ its broad, violet-shaped leaves for healing purposes. They lay them, freshly gathered, on scalds and burns, and, like all domestic recipes of the sort, they never fail, of course but 'work like a charm.'"

Additionally, the leaves were made into a tea to treat mouth sores and eye problems, and a root tea was used as a diuretic.

Rose Family (Rosaceae)

The Rose Family is characterized by 5-petaled flowers, many stamens, and a cup or receptacle at the base of each flower (called the hypanthium) and includes herbs, shrubs, and trees. Economically, this family is of great importance, especially in temperate and subtropical regions, providing fruits, such as almonds, apples, apricots, blackberries, cherries, nectarines, peaches, pears, plums, quinces, raspberries, and strawberries. Notable ornamentals include Cotoneaster, Flowering Quince, Hawthorn, Japanese Cherry, Mountain Ash, Ninebark, Rose, and Spiraea. There are 23 genera and 105 species listed for TN. This key covers mostly herbaceous members of the Rose Family.

1a. Shrubs **2**

  2a. Leaves simple **3**

    3a. Flowers purple, more than 0.8 in. wide; fruit an aggregate of small drupes . . . . .***Rubus***

    3b. Flowers white or pink, less than 0.8 in. wide; fruit a follicle **4**

      4a. Inflorescence a panicle or raceme . . . . ***Spiraea***

      4b. Inflorescence a corymb . . . . ***Physocarpus***

  2b. Leaves compound **12**

    5a. Ovaries concealed within the hypanthium and appearing inferior; stipules fused to the petiole ¹/₃ or more of their length . . . .***Rosa***

    5b. Ovaries distinctly superior; stipules and petiole not fused . . . . ***Rubus***

1b. Herbs (if woody at the base, then less than 20 in. tall) **6**

  6a. Leaves simple, sometimes deeply lobed . . . . ***Geum***

  6b. Leaves compound or deeply dissected **7**

    7a. Leaves palmately compound with 5 or more leaflets . . . .***Potentilla***

    7b. Leaves pinnately or ternately compound or dissected **8**

      8a. Leaves pinnate with more than 3 leaflets **9**

        9a. Petals absent; sepals 4, white . . . . ***Sanguisorba***

        9b. Petals present; sepals 5, green . . . . ***Geum***

      8b. Leaves ternately divided or compound **10**

        10a. Leaves 2–3-ternately compound; flowers unisexual . . . . ***Aruncus***

        10b. Leaves 1-ternately compound; flowers bisexual **11**

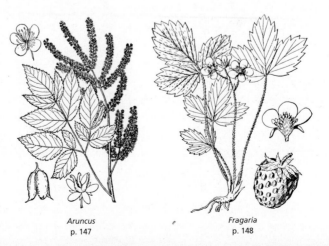

Aruncus
p. 147

Fragaria
p. 148

11a. Calyx lobes alternating with 5 similar bracts (epicalyx),
appearing as 10 sepals **12**

  12a. Epicalyx (outer calyx) 3–5-toothed at the tip . . . . ***Duchesnea***

  12b. Epicalyx (outer calyx) entire, petals white **13**

    13a. Leaflets with numerous teeth along the margin . . . . ***Fragaria***

    13b. Leaflets with 3–5 teeth at the tip . . . . . ***Potentilla (Sibbaldiopsis)***

11b. Calyx lobes 5; epicalyx (outer calyx) absent **14**

  14a. Pistils 2–6 . . . .**15**

    15a. Petals white . . . . ***Porteranthus***

    15b. Petals yellow . . . .***Waldsteinia***

  14b. Pistils more than 6 . . . .***Geum***

Robertson, K.R. 1974. The genera of Rosaceae in the southeastern United States. J. Arnold Arbor. 55:303–332, 344–401, 611–662.

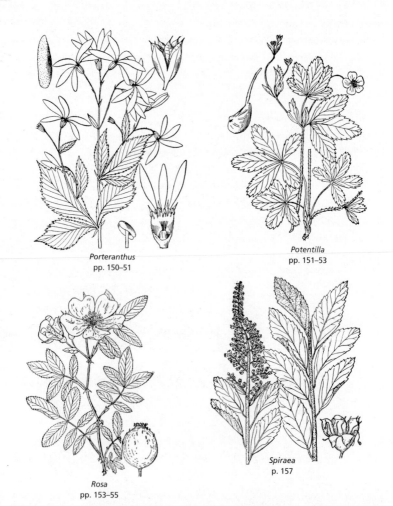

Porteranthus
pp. 150–51

Potentilla
pp. 151–53

Rosa
pp. 153–55

Spiraea
p. 157

Goatsbeard · *Aruncus dioicus*

GENERAL: Perennial with **smooth stems** arching to 5 ft. tall; spreads by rhizomes, creating dense clusters; plants are **dioecious**, meaning that male and female flowers are borne on separate plants. **LEAVES:** Alternate, compound, to 20 in. long; individual leaflets, 2–5 in. long, have double-toothed edges and resemble elm leaves, **terminal leaflet is unlobed**. **FLOWERS:** Male plants have **cream-colored spikes** of tiny, 5-petaled flowers with 15–20 stamens in clusters at the ends of the branches; **female plants have clusters of tiny, greenish white, 5-petaled flowers, each with 3 carpels**. May–June. **FRUITS:** Dry capsules consisting of 3 seed chambers per flower. **WHERE FOUND:** Rich slopes and moist, somewhat shaded, woodland borders throughout the eastern U.S. and West Coast states. In TN, from the Western Highland Rim eastward, also in Lauderdale and Tipton counties in West TN. Frequent.

JERRY DROWN

NOTES: This plant is also called Bride's Feathers and White Goatsbeard, and is commonly sold in nurseries. **Goatsbeard** creates a bold display when used in a woodland garden or shade border, and will spread by forming clumps. • Goatsbeard is often confused with **False Goatsbeard** (p. 139), of the Saxifrage Family, because of the similar arching plumes of flowers and shared habitats. However, False Goatsbeard has hairy stems, flowers with 10 stamens and 2 pistils per flower, and terminal leaflets that are usually 3-lobed.

Indian Strawberry
Duchesnea indica*

GENERAL: Trailing perennial herb **resembling Wild Strawberry** (p. 148) in general habit, but with yellow flowers. **LEAVES:** On long stalks, palmate with 3 toothed, elliptic leaflets, each 1–2 in. long. **FLOWERS:** Solitary, **yellow**, about 0.6 in. wide, 5 petals; **green bracts below the flower** usually have 3 teeth and are slightly longer than the sepals and petals; borne on stems arising from the leaf nodes. April–June. **FRUITS:** Bright red berries are strawberry-like, but

KURT EMMANUELE

tasteless. **WHERE FOUND:** Introduced from Asia. Lawns and damp waste ground. Widespread over much of the eastern U.S. and in TN. Occasional.

NOTES: The *Duchesnea* genus was named in honor of Antoine Duchesne (1747–1827), a French author and expert on strawberries; the species name *indica* was given to plants that originated in India, but was also given to those from the East Indies and as far away as China. • The fruit of this plant is deceptively similar to **Wild Strawberry**, (p. 148) but while edible, the taste is dry and not pleasing. This species also resembles **Barren Strawberry** (p. 157), but **Indian Strawberry** has runners and more pointed leaflets.

DAVID DUHL

Wild Strawberry · *Fragaria virginiana*

GENERAL: Low perennial, **spreading by runners (stolons)**, with **delicious fruit. LEAVES:** Palmate, on slender stalks, with 3 obovate, coarsely toothed leaflets, 1–4 in. long. **FLOWERS:** White, to 0.75 in. across, 5 petals; occur in flat clusters, on stalks separate from and **below the leaves.** April–May. **FRUITS:** Red, roundish strawberries dotted with achenes, which are the actual "fruit" of the plant; the strawberry itself is a false fruit, and is actually the enlarged receptacle of the flower; the strawberries are generally smaller than cultivated strawberries. **WHERE FOUND:** Roadsides, barrens, and woodland borders. Scattered throughout the U.S. and TN. Frequent. **SIMILAR SPECIES:** WOOD STRAWBERRY (*F. vesca*) has **smaller (0.5 in. wide), white flowers in clusters above the leaves**; seeds lie on the surface of the fleshy fruit, rather than in depressions. Rich woods in the northern U.S., south to TN in Blount County. Rare. May–June.

NOTES: Wild Strawberries are high in vitamins A, B, C, E, and K, as well as minerals. They can be made into pies and jams, and fermented into wine. • The cultivated strawberry that is sold in stores is an artificial hybrid between the Chilean form of *F. chiloensis* and Wild Strawberry. The luscious fruits are juicy, sweet, and aromatic, and the leaves and roots are also edible.

NITA R. HEILMAN

White Avens · *Geum canadense*

GENERAL: Perennial to 30 in. tall, with a mostly **smooth stem. LEAVES:** Alternate, lower stem leaves have 3 ovate, toothed leaflets, each 2–3 in. long, upper leaves usually simple. **FLOWERS:** Solitary, **white, about 0.5 in. wide**, 5 rounded **petals about equal in length to the sepals**; borne on long stalks from the upper leaf axils. May–July. **FRUITS:** Congregation of achenes in dry, bristly heads with **hook-like appendages. WHERE FOUND:** Streambanks and open woods in the eastern ⅔ of the U.S. and throughout TN. Common. **SIMILAR SPECIES:** SPRING AVENS (*G. vernum*) has cream or **yellow flowers only 0.25 in. across**, with petals and sepals about equal in length; fruit head on a stalk above the calyx; lower leaves variable, often with deeply cut lobes. Rich woods and borders. Found in most of the eastern and central U.S. In TN, from the Western Highland Rim eastward. Frequent. April–May. **PALE AVENS (G. virginianum)** has pale yellow to greenish flowers to 0.5 in. across, but with **petals shorter than sepals**; lower stem generally hairy. Woods and thickets. In the eastern U.S. and throughout TN. Frequent. June–July.

NOTES: Other common names for **White Avens** include Cramproot, Chocolate Root, and Throatroot in reference to the medicinal value of its roots. • The roots of many *Geum* species, such as **Prairie Smoke** (**G. ciliatum**), **Purple Avens** (**G. rivale**), Old Man's Whiskers (**G. triflorum**), and **Herb-Bennet** (**G. urbanum**), can be used in beverages and as a spice, added to food. • It has been said that the roots of White Avens, when added to ale, give it a pleasant flavor and prevent it from going sour.

Bent Avens
Geum geniculatum

GENERAL: Upright perennial herb, 20–30 in. tall, stems somewhat angled and hairy. **LEAVES:** Basal leaves have 3 large, terminal leaflets, 2–3 in. long and several pairs of small leaflets below; alternate stem leaves are trifoliolate or 3-lobed, with noticeable stipules. **FLOWERS:** Nodding, cup-shaped, yellowish, about 0.75 in. across, 5 spatulate petals up to 0.4 in. long; 5 hairy, greenish maroon sepals, acute-tipped, about the same length as petals; numerous stamens and pistils, **pistils longer than petals and sepals**; borne in loose terminal clusters. July–August. **FRUITS:** Achenes, 0.12 in. long, with a beak 0.3 in. long, both hairy; achenes occur in congregations. **WHERE FOUND:** Balds and wooded slopes at high elevations in the Blue Ridge Mountains of NC and TN. In TN, found only in Carter County on Roan Mountain on the NC–TN border. Rare. **SIMILAR SPECIES:** ROUGH AVENS (**G. laciniatum**) has somewhat similar foliage, but the **flowers are white** with narrow petals; **petals and pistils shorter than the triangular sepals**. Wet soils and meadows of the northeastern U.S., south in the mountains to AL. In TN, found only in Carter County in the Blue Ridge Mountains. Rare. May–July.

NOTES: Several *Geum* species are considered threatened or endangered in NC, TN, and NH. • In some of the woodland species of *Geum*, the seeds are uniquely designed with hooks to catch in the fur of animals or like sails to aid in wind dispersal.

B. EUGENE WOFFORD

Spreading Avens • *Geum radiatum*

GENERAL: Perennial herb to 24 in. tall. **LEAVES:** Compound basal leaves, 3–6 in. across, each with a large, **rounded, deeply toothed terminal leaflet**; alternate leaves on the flowering stems are usually simple and much smaller. **FLOWERS:** Solitary or few, showy, cup-shaped, **deep yellow, to 1.5 in. across**, 5 broad petals are notched at the rounded tip; terminal on the erect stems. June–July. **FRUITS:** Aggregate of achenes; achenes are 0.1 in. long, with a beak 0.4 in. long, achene body and base of beak hairy. **WHERE FOUND:** On exposed rocky outcrops at high elevations. Endemic to the border area of NC and TN. In TN, in Blount, Carter, and Sevier counties. Rare. **SIMILAR SPECIES:** YELLOW AVENS (**G. aleppicum**) has basal leaves with a **wedge-shaped, lobed terminal leaflet**; leaves on flowering stems similar, and not significantly reduced in size; bright yellow **flowers only 0.75 in. wide**. Swamps and wet meadows. A northern species, extending south in the mountains to GA. Only in Johnson County in East TN. Rare. June–July.

NOTES: Spreading Avens is also known as **Roan Mountain Avens** and **Appalachian Avens** for the specific habitats in which it grows. It is an **endangered species** and is restricted to only a few locations, including Roan Mountain in TN.

JERRY DROWN

THOMAS E. HEMMERLY

Ninebark
Physocarpus opulifolius

GENERAL: Loosely branched **deciduous shrub**, 4–10 ft. tall, with **bark that sheds** into numerous thin, papery layers; twigs without hairs. **LEAVES:** Alternate, simple, ovate, 2–3 in. long, mostly smooth, palmately 3-lobed (some leaves unlobed), margins round-toothed (crenate), paler beneath; leaf stalks to 1 in. long. **FLOWERS:** White, 0.3–0.4 in. wide, 5 rounded petals, 5 short, triangular sepals, numerous stamens, 3–5 pistils; arranged into compact umbel-like **corymbs, much like spi-** raea. May–July. **FRUITS:** Follicles, inflated, smooth, purplish, showy; hard, shiny seeds. **WHERE FOUND:** Streambanks and rocky bluffs from Canada, south to SC, AR, and CO. Widely spread across Middle and East TN. Frequent. **SIMILAR SPECIES:** ALABAMA SNOW-WREATH (*Neviusia alabamensis*) is another shrub in the Rose Family with similar habit, but is not closely related; deciduous with **biennial stems, like blackberries, but thornless**; flowers have numerous **showy, white stamens**; **petals absent**; 5–7 green sepals, toothed, persistent. Rich calcareous slopes from AR and TN, to MS, AL, and GA. First discovered in TN in 1981, and now known from Lincoln, Moore, and Rutherford counties in Middle TN. Rare throughout its range.

NOTES: The genus name *Physocarpus* is from the Greek *physa*, "a bladder," and *karpos*, "fruit," referring to the inflated follicles of this plant's fruit. • Native Americans used **Ninebark** to enhance fertility and treat gonorrhea, "female maladies," and tuberculosis. However, it is **potentially toxic** and must be taken in small quantities.

KURT EMMANUELE

American Ipecac, Indian Physic
Porteranthus stipulatus

GENERAL: Erect, many-branched perennial to 3 ft. tall. **LEAVES:** Alternate, divided into 3 lanceolate leaflets, 2–3 in. long; **2 large stipules** to 0.5 in. wide **make leaf look 5-parted**; both the leaflets and stipules are toothed; **lower leaves more dissected** or deeply cut than upper leaves. **FLOWERS:** White (sometimes pinkish), **5 narrow petals** are about 0.5 in. long and often slightly unequal in length. May–June. **FRUITS:** Capsules; wrinkled, 3-angled seeds. **WHERE FOUND:** Rich woods, often on calcareous soils. In most of the eastern U.S., except New England. Widespread in TN, except for the Mississippi River basin and much of East TN. Frequent. *Gillenia stipulata*.

NOTES: The genus *Porteranthus* was named in honor of Thomas Conrad Porter (1822–1901), a botanist from Pennsylvania. • This plant is also called Meadow Sweet and Western Dropwort.

• Medicinally, this plant was used primarily as an emetic (to cause vomiting), as a tonic for treating fever, and was even given to horses to increase appetite.

Bowman's Root
Porteranthus trifoliatus

JERRY DROWN

GENERAL: Branched perennial to 3 ft. tall, generally smooth. **LEAVES:** Alternate, divided into 3 narrow leaflets, 2–4 in. long, that taper at both ends; **upper and lower leaves similar** and finely toothed; **narrow stipules are not toothed and fall before flowering. FLOWERS:** White, 5 narrow petals about 0.75 in. long, somewhat unequal. May–June. **FRUITS:** Capsules; wrinkled, 3-angled seeds. **WHERE FOUND:** On rich but often acidic soils in most of the eastern U.S. In TN, from the Eastern Highland Rim eastward. Occasional. *Gillenia trifoliata*.

NOTES: The origin of the name, **Bowman's Root**, is obscure. Other common names for this plant include Fawn's Breath, Dropwort, False Ipecac, Indian Hippo, Ipecacuanha, and Three-Leaved Spiraea. • This plant is reputed to have medicinal value similar to **American Ipecac** (p. 150).

Dwarf Cinquefoil
Potentilla canadensis

DENNIS HORN

GENERAL: Low, reclining perennial to 4 in. tall, with silver-hairy stems and runners (stolons) to 18 in. long. **LEAVES:** Alternate, palmately compound; **5 leaflets,** 0.5–1.5 in. long, are rounded and toothed at the extremity, but wedge-shaped and **without teeth on the lower ¹/₂. FLOWERS:** Solitary, yellow, about 0.5 in. wide, 5 rounded petals; borne on stalks arising from the leaf axils, the **first flower usually from the axil of the first well-developed stem leaf.** March–May. **FRUITS:** Aggregate of smooth, brown achenes. **WHERE FOUND:** Fields and woods throughout the eastern U.S. and Canada. From the Central Basin east in TN, also in Cheatham County. Frequent.

NOTES: The genus name *Potentilla* means "little powerful one" and is the diminutive form of the Latin *potens*, "powerful." • Cinquefoils are also called "starflowers" or "five fingers," in reference to the 5 leaflets on plants in this genus. • In herbal medicine, Native Americans used tea made of the pounded roots of this plant to treat diarrhea. Many cinquefoils are considered to be astringent, with tannins playing an active role.

DENNIS HORN

Sulphur Cinquefoil, Rough-Fruited Cinquefoil · *Potentilla recta**

GENERAL: Showy roadside perennial with stout erect stems to 30 in. tall; stems and leaves are hairy. **LEAVES:** Alternate, palmately compound with **5–7 narrow, toothed leaflets,** 1–4 in. long, which are widest at the tip and taper to the base. **FLOWERS:** Pale yellow, about 1 in. across, 5 broad petals are shallowly indented; in **showy clusters** at the ends of leafy branches. May–July. **FRUITS:** Aggregate of achenes; achenes are striped and have low, curved ridges, accounting for the common name "rough-fruited." **WHERE FOUND:** Introduced from Europe. Roadsides and dry fields throughout most of the U.S. In TN, from the Western Highland Rim eastward, also Carroll and Shelby counties in West TN. Frequent. **SIMILAR SPECIES:** ROUGH CINQUEFOIL (*P. norvegica*) has strawberry-like **leaves with 3 leaflets** scattered along the stem; smaller yellow **flowers only 0.4 in. across.** Roadsides and waste places. Scattered throughout the U.S., including TN. Frequent. May–September.

NOTES: The species name *recta* means "upright," referring to the erect stems. "Sulphur" in the common name points out the pale yellow color of the flowers. **Sulphur Cinquefoil** is also called Septfoil and Tormentil. • The fruits, whether dark purple and fully ripe or red, are considered pleasant tasting.

KURT EMMANUELE

Common Cinquefoil
Potentilla simplex

GENERAL: Short perennial to 12 in. tall, emerging erect in the spring and later extending over the ground to form wide mats; stems are slender with long internodes and smooth or covered with fine, long hairs. **LEAVES:** Alternate, palmately compound, **5 obovate leaflets,** 1–3 in. long, are **toothed ⅔ of the way from the tip.** **FLOWERS:** Yellow, about 0.5 in. across, 5 rounded petals; borne singly on long, thin stalks in the leaf axils, the **first flower usually from the axil of the second well-developed stem leaf.** April–June. **FRUITS:** Aggregate of achenes, borne on a raised receptacle. **WHERE FOUND:** Dry woods and fields throughout the eastern U.S., Canada, and TN. Common.

NOTES: The name "cinquefoil" literally means "five-leaf," which refers to the 5 leaflets that extend radially from a common point, like the fingers of a hand. This plant is sometimes called Decumbent Five-Finger or Old Field Cinquefoil. • In 1785, Manasseh Cutler wrote that this plant was "mildly astringent and antiseptic. A decoction of it is used as a gargle for loose teeth and spungy gums."

Three-Toothed Cinquefoil
Potentilla tridentata

GENERAL: Low perennial herb to 12 in. tall, from a woody base. **LEAVES:** In a mat, mostly near the base; each leaf is palmately divided into **3 oblanceolate leaflets**, 0.6–1.6 in. long, and **each with 3 shallow teeth** near the blunt tip. **FLOWERS:** White, 0.4–0.6 in. across, 5 petals; borne on thin, wiry stems 2–12 in. long. May–October. **FRUITS:** Aggregate of achenes on a raised receptacle; achenes are covered with long, fine hairs. **WHERE FOUND:** Rock crevices and balds at **high elevations**. Primarily a tundra plant of Canada and Greenland, extending southward to TN and GA. In the mountains from Carter, Johnson, and Unicoi counties in East TN. Rare. *Sibbaldiopsis tridentata*.

NOTES: The species name *tridentata* means "three-toothed" in reference to the leaves with 3 leaflets and 3 teeth at the tip of each leaflet. • Of note, the flowers of **Golden Cinquefoil** (*P. aurea*) have insect-attracting patterns that are only visible to insects—or to humans under ultraviolet light.

KURT EMMANUELE

Carolina Rose, Pasture Rose
Rosa carolina

GENERAL: Low, slender, wild rose to **36 in. tall**, with **straight, narrow thorns** below the stipules and else-where along the stem. **LEAVES:** Alternate, pinnately compound, **5–7 dull green**, elliptic, **coarsely toothed** leaflets, 0.6–1.6 in. long. **FLOWERS:** Usually **solitary, pink, about 2 in. wide**, 5 petals, many yellow stamens in the center. May–June. **FRUITS:** Aggregate of ach-enes in red, pulpy hips, 0.3–0.5 in. thick; sepals persistent. **WHERE FOUND:** Dry woods, pastures, and fence rows. Found in most of the eastern and cen-tral U.S. and throughout TN. Common.

NOTES: The *Rosa* genus includes perennial shrubs and woody vines with showy flowers. Wild roses have 5 petals, while cultivated roses have flowers with many overlapping layers of petals. Seven species are found in TN. • Many parts of various *Rosa* species are edible, including the young shoots, petals, and the false fruits or **rose hips**, which may vary in size and flavor. Some rose hips taste sweet like raspberries, while others are bitter. Rose hips soften after a frost and generally acquire a sweet, acid, and aromatic flavor. To extract the pleasant-tasting pulp, gently press the hip between the fingers and the pulp will come out at the base; it is delicious raw.

DAVID DUHL

Multiflora Rose · *Rosa multiflora**

GENERAL: Colonial shrub with slender, **arching canes to 5 ft. tall**; stems are thorny.
LEAVES: Alternate, pinnately compound with about **7 elliptic leaflets**, 0.8–1.5 in. long; **deeply fringed leaf-like appendages (stipules)** at the base of leaf stalks. **FLOWERS:** Numerous, **white, about 1.25 in. wide**, 5 triangular petals are shallowly indented; borne in clusters. May–June. **FRUITS:** Aggregate of achenes in red, ellipsoid hips, about 0.3 in. long; sepals persistent. **WHERE FOUND:** Introduced from Asia. Roadsides, fence rows, and pastures. Naturalized over much of the eastern U.S. and TN. Frequent.

NOTES: An eastern Asia introduction for use as a "living fence" around farm buildings and ponds, this rose has become an invasive pest. • The rose represents love, magic, hope, and joy. Its name is from the Latin *rosa*, "red." • Rose oil is distilled from the petals of 2 hybrid Asian species: *R*. x *alba* and *R*. x *bifera*, and is one of the most expensive of all essential oils, as 1 ton of fresh petals yields only ½ pint of oil.

DENNIS HORN

Swamp Rose · *Rosa palustris*

GENERAL: Bushy shrub, 2–7 ft. tall; **canes have curved or hooked thorns. LEAVES:** Alternate, pinnately compound with about **7 dull green, finely toothed, elliptic leaflets**, 1–2 in. long; leaf stalks have long, **narrow, wing-like stipules** at the base. **FLOWERS: Pale pink, to 2 in. wide**, 5 petals are broad and notched at the blunt tip; often **solitary** at the ends of leafy stems. June–August. **FRUITS:** Aggregate of achenes with gland-tipped hairs in red, ovoid hips, 0.3–0.5 in. across. **WHERE FOUND:** Swamps and low ground in most of the eastern U.S. and TN. Frequent. **SIMILAR SPECIES: VIRGINIA ROSE (*R. virginiana*)** has **shiny, dark green leaflets with coarse teeth; wider, leaf-like stipules; flowers occur in small clusters.** Thickets and meadows from the North Atlantic states inland to MO. In TN, in Maury, Montgomery, and Sumner counties in Middle TN. Rare. May–June.

NOTES: Swamp Rose is also called **Marsh Rose** for its favored habitat, and notably, it will tolerate standing water and constantly wet soil. • Swamp Rose is the only wetland rose that has 7 leaflets and large, pink flowers. The fruit is an important food source for deer and other wildlife.

OTTO R. HIRSCH

Prairie Rose · *Rosa setigera*

GENERAL: Climbing or trailing perennial with **canes to 12 ft. long**; smooth canes have widely spaced, curved thorns. **LEAVES:** Alternate, pinnately compound, **3** (sometimes 5) **glossy, dark green**, finely toothed, lanceolate **leaflets**, 1–3 in. long; **stipules are quite narrow and glandular. FLOWERS:** Numerous, **showy, rich pink,** 5 wide petals, about 1 in. long, are notched at the tip; reflexed sepals fall early; often occur in **flat-topped clusters.** May–June. **FRUITS:** Aggregate of glandular-hairy achenes in brown-green to red, ovoid hips, about 0.4 in. long. **WHERE FOUND:** Open woods, thickets, and clearings. Introduced into the northeastern U.S. Found in the southeastern U.S. and most of TN. Frequent.

NOTES: Rose petals can be added raw to salads, beverages, and desserts, and can be used as an edible decoration. In the Middle East, the petals are sometimes made into jam, and in China, rose petals are used to flavor black tea. Some species have been used to make preserves, honey, and vinegar. Rose water, the by-product of distillation, has been used medicinally as an eyewash and skin tonic.

DENNIS HORN

Southern Blackberry · *Rubus argutus*

GENERAL: Smooth **canes ascending** 3–6 ft. tall (not rooting at the tip), with **straight, spreading prickles**; petioles and flowering branches have smaller, curved prickles. **LEAVES:** Alternate, compound with 3–5 toothed, lanceolate leaflets, 2–5 in. long. **FLOWERS:** White, about 1 in. wide, 5 petals are longer than sepals; borne in a loose, raceme-like cyme. May–June. **FRUITS:** Black, seedy berries are actually aggregates of small drupelets; **edible berries are sweet** and juicy when ripe; **fruit and receptacle separate from the stem as a unit. WHERE FOUND:** Thickets and clearings. Widespread in the southeastern U.S. and TN. Common. **SIMILAR SPECIES:** BLACK RASPBERRY (**R. occidentalis**) has **arching canes,** conspicuously whitened, and **hooked prickles**; petals and sepals about 0.25 in. long; **edible, purple-black, seedy fruit separates from the receptacle.** Disturbed areas in the eastern U.S. and most of TN. Frequent. May–June. WINEBERRY (**R. phoenicolasius***) is **covered with wine-colored, glandular bristles**; petals much shorter than sepals; **red, raspberry-like fruit.** Introduced from eastern Asia. Throughout the eastern U.S. Mostly in the eastern ½ of TN. Occasional. May–June.

DENNIS HORN

NOTES: Southern Blackberry is also known as **Sawtooth Blackberry** and **Prickly Florida Blackberry.** • The fruits can be harvested for eating, baking, and preserving into jams and jellies. Raspberries and blackberries contain vitamins A and C, pectin, essential oils, and organic acids (citric, malic). The seeds are spread by birds and other animals. • There are presently 12 species of *Rubus* listed for TN. Many are difficult to separate.

Purple-Flowering Raspberry • *Rubus odoratus*

GENERAL: Bushy **shrub** to 5 ft. tall; reddish brown, **thornless stems have sticky hairs. LEAVES:** Alternate, broad, 4–8 in. wide, toothed, **resembling maple leaves** with 5 pointed lobes and a heart-shaped base. **FLOWERS:** Showy, **pink-purple, to 2 in. wide,** 5 broad, rounded petals, numerous yellow stamens; borne in small clusters at the ends of the branches, making this shrub very easy to identify. June–July. **FRUITS:** Shallow, cup-shaped, red berries are actually aggregates of small drupelets; **fruit is dry and tasteless;** drupelets fall separately. **WHERE FOUND:** Borders of rich woods and along roadsides. From the northeastern U.S. and Canada, south in the mountains to AL and GA. In TN, in the Blue Ridge Mountains, also Marion, Hamilton, and Hancock counties. Occasional.

JERRY DROWN

NOTES: As with other blackberry and raspberry species, the young shoots are edible and the leaves can be used to make tea.

Canadian Burnet, American Burnet • *Sanguisorba canadensis*

GENERAL: Smooth perennial herb to 6 ft. tall, from a thick rhizome; erect stem is simple below, often branching above. **LEAVES:** Alternate, compound, up to 20 in. long, lower **leaves pinnately divided** into 7–15 toothed leaflets, each 1–3 in. long; leaves reduced in size upward. **FLOWERS:** White, showy, 4 petal-like sepals, 0.15 in. long; petals absent; white, flattened, **club-shaped filaments** 0.3–0.4 in. long; borne in **cylindric spikes,** 2–6 in. long. August–September. **FRUITS:** Achenes, enclosed in a 4-angled calyx tube. **WHERE FOUND:** Prairies, fens, seeps, and wet meadows in Canada and the northern U.S., south in the mountains to GA. In TN, found only in Carter and Johnson counties in the Blue Ridge Mountains. Rare.

NOTES: *Sanguisorba* means "to absorb blood," from this plant's earlier use in folk medicine to stop bleeding. It was also used by the Cherokee and other tribes to make a red dye for baskets and as a skin stain. • The *Sanguisorba* genus includes about 25 species found mostly in the northern hemisphere.

B. EUGENE WOFFORD

Steeplebush, Hardhack · *Spiraea tomentosa*

GENERAL: Sparsely branched, **low shrub**, about 3 ft. tall. **LEAVES:** Alternate, simple, 1–2 in. long, toothed, elliptic, tapering at both ends, **undersides light brownish-woolly** with conspicuous veins. **FLOWERS:** Pink, 0.12–0.25 in. across, 5 petals, reflexed sepals; **steeple-shaped inflorescence**, which gives the plant its name, flowers open from the top down. June–August. **FRUITS:** Capsules with dense woolly hairs (tomentose); small seeds. **WHERE FOUND:** Wet meadows and swamps. Throughout eastern Canada and the eastern U.S. In TN, from the Western Highland Rim eastward. Occasional. **SIMILAR SPECIES: JAPANESE SPIRAEA (*S. japonica**)** has a **flattened inflorescence** of **pink flowers**; individual flower stems and **cups are quite hairy**. Introduced from Japan and spread from cultivation throughout the eastern U.S. In TN, thinly scattered from the Eastern Highland Rim eastward, also in Davidson and Cheatham counties. Occasional. June–July. **APPALACHIAN SPIRAEA (*S. virginiana*)** is a native shrub much like Japanese Spiraea, but has **smooth flower cups** and **white petals**. Rocky banks along mountain streams from PA and OH, south to GA and LA. In TN, from the Cumberland Plateau eastward. Infrequent. June.

DENNIS HORN

NOTES: *Spiraea* species are shrubs of the Northern Hemisphere, with about 70 species documented. Several varieties are cultivated as border plants in landscaping. • Medicinally, Native Americans used an infusion of **Steeplebush** leaves and stems as a tea to treat dysentery, sickness during pregnancy, and to ease childbirth.

Barren Strawberry
Waldsteinia fragarioides

GENERAL: Low perennial **resembles a strawberry, but lacks runners**; flowers and leaves occur on separate stalks. **LEAVES:** Basal, long-petioled, compound with 3 blunt leaflets, 1–3 in. long, toothed, sometimes shallowly lobed, wedge-shaped at the base. **FLOWERS:** Yellow, about 0.5 in. across, 5 petals; borne in small clusters; similar to **Indian Strawberry** (p. 147), but without the 3-toothed bracts and with petals generally longer than sepals. April–June. **FRUITS:** Hairy, red achenes are **dry and inedible**. **WHERE FOUND:** Rich woods and clearings. Southeastern Canada and the northeastern U.S., extending south in the mountains and highlands to AL, GA, and AR. In TN, from the Eastern Highland Rim eastward, also Davidson County in Middle TN. Occasional.

DENNIS HORN

NOTES: The genus name *Waldsteinia* represents a genus of creeping herbs named in honor of Franz Adam (1759–1823), the Count of Waldstein-Wartenberg and a German botanist; *fragarioides* means "resembling a strawberry" after *Fragaria*, the genus of the true **Wild Strawberry** (p. 148). Although **Barren Strawberry** resembles Wild Strawberry, the flowers of Barren Strawberry are yellow and the fruits are dry or "barren."

Bean or Pea Family (Fabaceae)

The Bean or Pea Family is large, with species of herbs, shrubs, vines, and trees mostly found in temperate, cold, and tropical regions. Most members of this family (also called Leguminosae) are readily identifiable by their 5-parted, pea-like flowers. The upper petal is large and referred to as the "standard," 2 smaller side petals are the "wings," and the lower 2 petals (which may be fused) are referred to as the "keel." Leaves are pinnately compound with 3 to many leaflets, often with prominent stipules. The fruit is a legume containing bean-like seeds. There are 44 genera and 129 species listed for TN.

Many beans, also called peas, are economically important, providing food, forage, dyes, gums, resins, oils, and medicines. Specifically, food products include garden peas, peanuts, beans, and soybeans; forage includes clover, alfalfa, and sweet clover; ornamentals are lupine, redbud, sweet pea, and wisteria; and dyes include indigo.

1a. Shrubs or woody vines 2
  2a. Shrubs . . . . ***Lespedeza***
  2b. Vines 3
    3a. Leaves trifoliate (the uppermost rarely 1-foliate) . . . . ***Pueraria***
    3b. Leaves 1-pinnate with 7 or more leaflets; petals bluish or rarely white . . . . ***Wisteria***
1b. Herbs, not woody 4
  4a. Leaves simple . . . . ***Crotalaria***
  4b. At least some leaves compound 5
    5a. Leaves, bipinnately compound (subfamily Mimosoideae) 6
      6a. Stamens 5, whitish; stems without prickles . . . . ***Desmanthus***
      6b. Stamens 9–13, pinkish; stems with prickles . . . . ***Mimosa (Schrankia)***
    5b. Leaves either 2–3-foliate, or 1-pinnate with numerous leaflets 7
      7a. Leaves 2-foliate or 1-pinnate with more than 3 leaflets .8
        8a. Leaves 2-foliate, the terminal leaflet modified into a tendril . . . . ***Lathyrus***
        8b. Leaves 1-pinnate, tendril present or absent 9
          9a. Leaves odd-pinnate (with a terminal leaflet) 10
            10a. Inflorescence umbel-like . . . . ***Coronilla***
            10b. Inflorescence a raceme 11

Amphicarpaea
p. 161

Baptisia
pp. 164–55

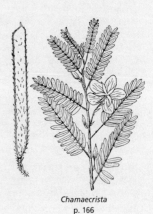

Chamaecrista
p. 166

11a. Twining vines, usually more than 40 in. long . . . . ***Apios***

11b. Plants erect, decumbent or trailing, but not twining,
rarely up to 40 in. long **12**

    12a. Inflorescence axillary, flowers bilaterally symmetric,
and of uniform color . . . . ***Astragalus***

    12b. Raceme terminal or lateral and opposite the leaves;
flowers either large, bilaterally symmetric and bicolored,
or smaller, radially symmetric, and of uniform color **13**

        13a. Flowers large, strongly bilaterally symmetric and pink-cream
bicolored; leaves not dotted with glands . . . .***Tephrosia***

        13b. Flowers smaller, apparently radially symmetric,
and of uniform color (blue, purple, or white);
leaves dotted with glands . . . . ***Dalea***

9b. Leaves even-pinnate (excluding tendrils, if present) **14**

    14a. Flowers yellow; radially symmetric or nearly so; tendrils absent
(subfamily Caesalpinoideae) **15**

        15a. Stamens all with normal anthers;
pod elastically dehiscent . . . . ***Chamaecrista***

        15b. Upper 3 stamens sterile; pods indehiscent or essentially so . . . . ***Senna***

    14b. Flowers white, pink, purple, blue, or rarely yellowish;
bilaterally symmetric; tendrils present **16**

        16a. Leaflets averaging less than 0.4 in. wide . . . .***Vicia***

        16b. Leaflets averaging more than 0.4 in. wide . . . . ***Lathyrus***

7b. Leaves palmately or pinnately 3-foliate **17**

17a. Leaflet margins with sharp or rounded teeth **18**

18a. Inflorescence a dense head, short spike, or head-like raceme;
petals mostly persistent and attached to the staminal tube;
terminal leaflet usually sessile or subsessile . . . . ***Trifolium***

18b. Inflorescence an elongate, slender raceme; petals soon deciduous and
free from the staminal tube; terminal leaflet distinctly stalked . . . . ***Melilotus***

Coronilla
p. 167

Clitoria
p. 167

Desmanthus
p. 170

Desmodium
p. 170

17b. Leaflets entire 19

 19a. Leaves palmately 3-foliate 20

  20a. Stamens distinct 20

   21a. Fruits flat; flowers yellow . . . . *Thermopsis*

   21b. Fruits inflated; flowers white, blue, or yellow . . . . *Baptisia*

  20b. Stamens united . . . . *Trifolium*

 19b. Leaves pinnately 3-foliate 22

  22a. Flowers 1 in. long or more 23

   23a. Calyx lobes shorter than the tube . . . . *Clitoria*

   23b. Calyx lobes longer than the tube . . . . *Centrosema*

  22b. Flowers less than 1 in. long 24

   24a. Fruits 1-seeded or of 2–several, 1-seeded segments 25

    25a. Leaves dotted with glands . . . . *Orbexilum* (*Psoralea*, in part)

    25b. Leaves not dotted with glands 26

     26a. Petals bluish; pod 1-seeded . . . . *Pediomelum* (*Psoralea*, in part)

     26b. Petals yellow, white, pink, or purplish (at least not bluish);
      pod 1-seeded, or of 2–several, 1-seeded segments 27

      27a. Stipules united to the petiole, forming a sheath that
       encircles the stem; flowers bright yellow or orange . . . . *Stylosanthes*

      27b. Stipules free; flowers variously colored 28

       28a. Fruit with 2–several segments, usually with hooked hairs;
        leaflet stipules usually present . . . . *Desmodium*

       28b. Fruit 1-seeded, lacking hooked hairs;
        leaflet stipules absent . . . . *Lespedeza*

   24b. Fruits 2–many-seeded and never segmented 29

    29a. Leaflets 4 in. long or more, an exotic woody vine . . . . *Pueraria*

    29b. Leaflets less than 4 in. long, native herbaceous vines 30

     30a. Calyx cylindric, not subtended by a pair of small bracts . . . . . *Amphicarpaea*

     30b. Calyx flared, subtended by a pair of small bracts 31

      31a. Keel petals nearly straight; style smooth . . . . *Galactia*

      31b. Keel petals strongly curved upward;
       style hairy along the upper surface . . . . *Strophostyles*

Mahler, W.F. 1970. Manual of the legumes of Tennessee. *Journal of the Tennessee Academy of Sciences.* 45:65–96.

Orbexilum
p. 175

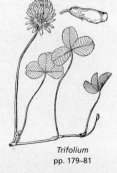

Trifolium
pp. 179–81

Vicia
pp. 181–82

Hog Peanut · *Amphicarpaea bracteata*

GENERAL: Annual, or sometimes short-lived perennial, slender, **twining vine** to 5 ft. long. **LEAVES:** Alternate, compound with 3 thin, mostly ovate leaflets, 1–3 in. long, with broadly rounded bases, and appressed-straight hairs on both surfaces. **FLOWERS:** Pale lilac to white, pea-like, 0.5–0.7 in. across; borne in simple, nodding racemes on long stalks from the leaf axils; **second set of flowers without petals are produced at the base of the vine**. August–September. **FRUITS:** Normal flowers produce flattened, usually twisted legumes, 1.5–2.0 in. long, generally with three seeds; flowers without petals produce 1-seeded fruits, often subterranean. **WHERE FOUND:** Dry or damp woodlands and especially streambanks throughout most of the eastern U.S. and TN. Common.

THOMAS G. BARNES

NOTES: Other names for this plant include American Licorice and Wild Peanut. • The ripe seeds are a good source of protein and are delicious when added to cereals. • Beans are legumes and are rich in carbohydrates, but must be cooked fully because they contain trypsin inhibitors, which left uncooked prevent digestive enzymes from doing their work.

Groundnut · *Apios americana*

GENERAL: Herbaceous perennial **trailing vine** to 10 ft. long, from **many fleshy tubers** about 0.4–0.8 in. across; stem usually smooth. **LEAVES:** Alternate, pinnately compound, 4–8 in. long; 5–7 leaflets are ovate-lanceolate, 1–2 in. long, usually smooth; stipules minute. **FLOWERS:** Purple-brown, pea-like, **strongly fragrant**, about 0.5 in. wide, 1–2 from each swollen node; borne in dense axillary racemes. June–August. **FRUITS:** Linear legumes, 2–4 in. long, about 0.25 in. wide, many-seeded. **WHERE FOUND:** Moist woods and streambanks, from Québec to ND, south to FL and TX. Throughout TN. Common.

NOTES: The many names of this plant, such as Chocolate, Rabbit Vine, Traveler's Delight, and White Apples, are strong clues that it is edible. The fleshy and pale underground tubers, also known as "turkey peas," make a good substitute for potatoes, are quite nutritious, and were prized by Native Americans as a source of food. They were first mentioned as a food in 1590 in an account by Thomas Hariot, a member of an expedition sent by Sir Walter Raleigh to what is now NC. Hariot later became the author of the first book to be written in English in America.

DAVID DUHL

PAUL SOMERS

Price's Potato Bean · *Apios priceana*

GENERAL: Herbaceous perennial **trailing vine** to 10 ft. long, from a **solitary, large, underground tuber** to 4 in. thick. **LEAVES:** Alternate, pinnately compound, 5–9 leaflets are ovate-lanceolate, entire, to 2.5 in. long. **FLOWERS:** Pinkish purple to greenish white, pea-like, approximately 1 in. long, **standard terminates in a spongy projection at the apex**; borne in compact axillary racemes. July–August. **FRUITS:** Linear legumes, 5 in. long or more, 2 halves of legume twist after dehiscence. **WHERE FOUND:** Rocky slopes. Known only from IL, KY, TN, and northern AL and MS. In TN, recorded from about 10 counties in Middle TN. Infrequent.

NOTES: This species was named for its discoverer, Sarah Frances Price (1849–1903) of Kentucky. • The common name tells the story of this plant's edibility. Plants in the *Apios* genus are called "groundnuts" because their rhizomatous roots are edible. It is said that one year, when Henry David Thoreau's potato crop had failed, he dug up some groundnuts and roasted them, just as the Native Americans had first done, and the Pilgrims after them. Mr. Thoreau reportedly took pleasure in the groundnuts' nutty flavor and found them nourishing. • The large flowers are known to be pollinated by honey bees, bumblebees, and long-tailed skippers.

DENNIS HORN

Pyne's Ground Plum
Astragalus bibullatus

GENERAL: **Smooth** perennial herb, 4–6 in. tall. **LEAVES:** Alternate, pinnately compound, 3–4 in. long, with about 24 leaflets. **FLOWERS:** Pale purple, pea-like, 0.5–0.75 in. long; borne in a **compact raceme** of flowers. April. **FRUITS:** Smooth, bicolored pods, red above and yellow below, somewhat **resemble plums that have an enlargement, or "spare tire," around the middle**; pods usually lay flat on the ground. **WHERE FOUND:** A TN Central Basin cedar glade endemic. Currently known only from Rutherford County. Rare.

NOTES: The genus name *Astragalus* is the Greek word for "dice," in reference to the sound of rattling seeds in the inflated pod. • Another name for this plant is Limestone Glade Milk Vetch. This plant was first described in 1987 and is named for the contemporary botanist who discovered it, Milo Pyne. It is a close relative of the **Prairie Ground Plum (A. crassicarpus)** of the Upper Midwest and Great Plains. While the flowers are borne on upright stalks, as the fruits develop, the stalks bend down toward the ground. • Although many plants in the Bean or Pea Family are edible, some of the plants in the *Astragalus* genus can be **toxic to animals**.

Canada Milk Vetch
Astragalus canadensis

GENERAL: Robust, erect perennial herb, 4–6 ft. tall. **LEAVES:** Alternate, pinnately compound, 13–29 leaflets are oblong, 0.5–1.25 in. long. **FLOWERS:** White or **yellowish**, pea-like, 0.5–0.75 in. long; borne in an **elongate raceme**. July–August. **FRUITS:** 2-celled legumes (pods), sometimes with short hairs; pods are numerous, crowded, and erect. **WHERE FOUND:** Open woods and riverbanks throughout most of the U.S. and southern Canada. In TN, sparsely scattered from the Western Highland Rim eastward. Occasional.

NOTES: This plant is also called Little Rattlepod because Native American children used the ripe seedpods for rattles. • There is a folktale that milk vetches could increase a cow's or goat's flow of milk. • This species is a larger and less hairy plant than **Tennessee Milk Vetch**, described below. • The boiled root of **Canada Milk Vetch** has been used to treat fever, back pain, and coughs. A poultice of chewed roots was used to treat cuts.

MILO PYNE

Tennessee Milk Vetch
Astragalus tennesseensis

GENERAL: Low perennial herb, 4–16 in. tall, with silky, soft, **spreading hairs**. **LEAVES:** Alternate, pinnately compound. Leaflets, from 15–25, are narrow, elliptic to oblong, hairy and 0.5–0.75 in. long. **FLOWERS:** Yellowish white, pea-like, 0.5–0.75 in. long; borne in a **dense raceme**. April–May. **FRUITS:** Curved, hairy, yellow, indehiscent legumes that lie on the ground. **WHERE FOUND:** In cedar glades and calcareous barrens from IL to northern AL. In Middle TN, in Robertson, Davidson, Wilson, Williamson, Rutherford, Maury, Marshall, and Bedford counties. Infrequent.

DAVID DUHL

NOTES: Some milk vetches are used as forage crops owing to their high protein content. Although **Tennessee Milk Vetch** is not a forage plant, like many species in the Bean Family it increases nitrogen levels in the soil, acting as a fertilizer. • The root of another *Astragalus* species, Huang-Qi (*A. membranaceus*), has been used in China as a medicine for many ages. It has been used to stimulate the immune system, to treat congestive heart failure, and has also been shown to have beneficial antiviral properties.

White Wild Indigo · *Baptisia alba*

GENERAL: Erect perennial herb 2–4 ft. tall, with mostly **horizontal branches**. **LEAVES:** Alternate on upright stems with 3 elliptical leaflets, 1–2 in. long. Leaves blacken in fall. **FLOWERS:** Numerous, white, **pea-like**, 0.5–0.75 in. long; borne in a tall raceme that extends above the leaves. May. **FRUITS:** Inflated, ellipsoid, light brown pods, each with a short beak; 1–8 (variable) kidney-shaped seeds, tan or dark brown when dry. **WHERE FOUND:** Dry, sandy woods, from NY to MN, south to FL and TX. In TN, from the Western Highland Rim westward. Occasional. **SIMILAR SPECIES:** SPIKED INDIGO (*B. albescens*) is **smaller**, to 3 ft. tall, the branches mostly ascending; inflorescence is shorter with **fewer white flowers**, but each flower is larger. Rich woods, from VA and TN, south to FL. In TN, from the Cumberland Plateau eastward in Van Buren, Bledsoe, Cumberland, Fentress, Johnson and Polk counties. Infrequent. May. Probably not distinct from *B. alba*.

NOTES: The species name *alba* means "white," referring to the flowers. **White Wild Indigo** is also called **White Baptisia**. • White Wild Indigo is pollinated by bumblebees and other insects, which push their way into the hooded flowers.

HUGH & CAROL NOURSE

Blue False Indigo, Blue Wild Indigo · *Baptisia australis*

GENERAL: Erect perennial herb, 4–5 ft. tall, highly branched. **LEAVES:** Alternate, trifoliolate, with **obovate leaflets** 1–3 in. long; **stipules**, 0.3–0.8 in. long, **may persist until flowering**. **FLOWERS:** Deep blue-violet, pealike, 0.8–1.0 in. long; borne in a long raceme that extends above the leaves. May–June. **FRUITS:** Dry, woody legumes are dark brown and brittle. **WHERE FOUND:** Thin, moist woods, edges, glades, and barrens, in rocky soil, from southern NY to northern GA, west to NE and TX. In Middle and East TN, in Davidson, Rutherford, Maury, Marshall, Coffee, Hamilton, Scott, and Hancock counties. Infrequent.

NOTES: The genus name *Baptisia* is from the Greek *bapto*, which means "to dye"; these blue-flowering plants were used as a substitute for the blue dye that, since ancient times, has been extracted from the roots of Asian Indigo (*Indigofera tinctoria*). Many false indigos were also used to treat malaria.

OTTO R. HIRSCH

Cream Wild Indigo
Baptisia bracteata var. *leucophaea*

LUIS C. PRIETO JR.

GENERAL: Erect perennial herb, 16–32 in. tall, branched and hairy throughout. **LEAVES:** Alternate, trifoliolate with oblanceolate leaflets 0.5–1.5 in. long. **FLOWERS:** Numerous, **creamy yellow** to nearly white, **pea-like**, 0.8–1.1 in. long; borne in a mostly **1-sided raceme, usually solitary** and declining. April–May. **FRUITS:** Thick-walled, hairy legumes, 1–2 in. long. **WHERE FOUND:** Open woodlands and meadows, from southern MI to southern MN to western NE, south to TX and MS, and east to TN and KY. In TN, in Stewart County. Rare. **SIMILAR SPECIES: YELLOW WILD INDIGO (*B. tinctoria*)** has an inflorescence consisting of **many small racemes** with **brilliant yellow flowers** to 0.5 in. across. Dry, open woods and fields. A mostly northeastern U.S. species extending south to TN and GA. In TN, from the Eastern Highland Rim eastward, also Maury County. Occasional. April–August.

NOTES: *Baptisia* species are native to open prairies and can live for decades. Their strong, fleshy root systems allow them to withstand dry conditions and heat. • Plants in this genus, **Yellow Wild Indigo** in particular, were commonly used to make antiseptic poultices for gangrenous wounds, especially those accompanied by fever. • The young shoots of many *Baptisia* species resemble those of asparagus, and while some are edible when properly prepared, caution should be used as some species are **poisonous.**

Spurred Butterfly Pea
Centrosema virginianum

KURT EMMANUELE

GENERAL: **Trailing or climbing** hairy perennial herb, to 6 ft. long. **LEAVES:** Alternate, compound, with 3 entire leaflets that are ovate to lanceolate, about 2 in. long. **FLOWERS:** **Deep pink to lavender**, usually white in the center, **pea-like**, 1.0–1.4 in. wide; **rounded standard is much larger** than other petals and is flat across the face; unlike most pea-like flowers, **standard is lowermost** and has a **small spur at the base**; borne in axillary clusters of 1–4 flowers. July–August. **FRUITS:** Linear, flattened legumes with a beak-like style; many-seeded. **WHERE FOUND:** Woods, sandy soils, and disturbed sites throughout most of the southeastern U.S. and TN, but more prevalent in East TN. Occasional.

NOTES: This plant is also called **Climbing Butterfly Pea.** Its common names include the word "butterfly" because of the resemblance of the flower to the insect. • The stamens and pistil are in the white part of the flower, called the "keel." The large, flag-like petal that is flat and round is appropriately called the "standard."

DENNIS HORN

Partridge Pea
Chamaecrista fasciculata

GENERAL: Erect, arching **annual** to 3 ft. tall.
LEAVES: Alternate, pinnately compound, with
5–18 pairs of linear-oblong leaflets to 0.8 in.
long; leaves are **light sensitive, folding at
night. FLOWERS: Yellow,** to 1.5 in. wide, **not
pea-like, 5 petals are somewhat unequal in
size,** 4 of the petals have a reddish mark at
the base, **10 stamens,** 4 of the anthers are
yellow, the others dark reddish; borne in
short racemes of 1–6 flowers from the
upper leaf axils. June–September. **FRUITS:**
Dehiscent legumes, smooth to densely hairy,
up to 3 in. long. **WHERE FOUND:** Wet to dry
open meadows, roadsides, and waste places
in the eastern ⅔ of the U.S. and throughout
TN. Common. ***Cassia fasciculata.***

NOTES: Other common names for this
plant include Dwarf Cassia, Locust Weed,
and Sleeping Plant. • The flowers of this
species are not "pea-like." Instead, they are
more loose or open, and the petals are
distinctly separate. One petal, which
would be the "standard" in other pea
flowers, is larger than the other 4 petals.

DENNIS HORN

Wild Sensitive Plant
Chamaecrista nictitans

GENERAL: Erect, arching **annual** to 24 in. tall.
LEAVES: Alternate, pinnately compound, with
7–20 pairs of linear-oblong leaflets, to 0.4 in.
long, that are **light and touch sensitive.**
FLOWERS: Yellow, about 0.5 in. wide, **not pea-
like, 5 unequal petals, 5 stamens;** usually solitary in the upper leaf axils. July–September.
FRUITS: Dehiscent legumes, densely short-hairy,
up to 2 in. long. **WHERE FOUND:** Open places
with acidic soils in most of the eastern U.S.
and throughout TN. Common. ***Cassia nictitans.***

NOTES: The species name *nictitans* means
"blinking, moving." Both the species and
common names of **Wild Sensitive Plant**
indicate that it is sensitive to touch or disturbance and imply that the plant would
react quickly. In fact, the name is deceptive,
and the leaves react disappointingly slowly
to disturbance, eventually folding. • **Partridge
Pea** (see above) is a more robust plant with
larger, showier flowers and **10 stamens.**

Butterfly Pea · *Clitoria mariana*

GENERAL: Erect to **twining**, smooth perennial herbaceous **vine** to 3 ft. long. **LEAVES:** Alternate, pinnately compound with 3 leaflets that are entire, ovate to lanceolate, 1.2–2.5 in. long. **FLOWERS:** Light blue to **pinkish lavender**, darker purple in the center, 5 petals; **obovate, concave standard**, to 2 in. long, is **beneath the much smaller wings and keel**; on stalks originating from the leaf axils, either singly or in small clusters of 2–3 flowers. June–August. **FRUITS:** Flattened legumes, the 2 valves twisting during dehiscence; enclosed seeds are sticky. **WHERE FOUND:** Open areas, and well-drained soils. Most of the eastern U.S. and found throughout TN. Common.

NOTES: Butterfly Pea is the only species of the *Clitoria* genus that is widespread in North America, although Pigeon Wings (*C. fragrans*) grows in the Florida sandlands. • Upon maturing, the flowers often turn upside down, providing a landing pad for pollinating insects. • **Spurred Butterfly Pea** (p. 165) has a **round, flat standard**, and the calyx has a short tube and longer lobes (these are reversed in Butterfly Pea).

NITA R. HEILMAN

Crown Vetch
*Coronilla varia**

GENERAL: Smooth, **vine-like** perennial herb, 12–18 in. tall. **LEAVES:** Alternate, sessile, pinnately compound, with 11–21 oblong-obovate leaflets, 0.5–0.75 in. long. **FLOWERS:** Pink, rose, or purplish, **pea-like**, 0.4–0.6 in. long; borne in **dense umbels** of 10–20 flowers. May–September. **FRUITS:** Linear legumes, 4-angled with up to 7 segments, each separating individually. **WHERE FOUND:** Introduced from Europe. Roadsides and waste places throughout most of the U.S. In TN, from the Western Highland Rim eastward. Occasional.

JERRY DROWN

NOTES: The genus name *Coronilla* means "small crown," in reference to the shape of the inflorescence; *varia* means "variable," for the multicolored flowers. Other common names are Axseed, for the shape of the pods, and Hive Vine, perhaps because it attracts large numbers of bees. • This plant was originally introduced as a ground cover and was extensively planted along highways to stabilize soil. The Tennessee Exotic Pest Plant Council and similar organizations in many states now list this plant as a "significant threat" to native plant communities.

DENNIS HORN

Showy Rattlebox · *Crotalaria spectabilis* *

GENERAL: Annual, **3–4 ft. tall**, with erect stems. **LEAVES:** Alternate, simple, 2–6 in. long, **obovate**, tapering to the base; **small stipules** form an "arrowhead" pointing down the stem. **FLOWERS:** Deep yellow, pea-like, 1 in. long; borne in a long, **showy, many-flowered raceme**. March–October. **FRUITS:** Inflated legumes to 2.5 in. long; seeds rattle in the inflated, ripened pod. **WHERE FOUND:** Introduced from the Old World tropics. Fields and roadsides. Scattered throughout the southeastern U.S. Widely scattered across TN, in Shelby, Madison, Henry, Knox, Jefferson, and Grainger counties. Infrequent.

SIMILAR SPECIES: ARROWHEAD RATTLEBOX (**C. sagittalis**) is only **12–24 in. tall**; leaves are **widest near the middle**, tapering at both ends, with spreading hairs; **conspicuous stipules**; inflorescence is a **few-flowered** raceme of pale yellow flowers, 0.5 in. long. Dry fields and waste places throughout the eastern U.S. and TN. Frequent. May–September.

NOTES: The genus name *Crotalaria* means "like a rattle," for the sound made by the dried seeds; *spectabilis* means "spectacular, showy," in reference to the inflorescence. **Showy Rattlebox** is also called **Showy Crotalaria**. • All parts of these plants, especially the seeds, are **poisonous** if ingested. • The characteristic leaves of Showy Rattlebox, which are widest at the apex and taper to the base, along with the tall, many-flowered racemes, help to distinguish this plant from other *Crotalaria* species. • Showy Rattlebox is considered a weed of agronomic crops in the southern states.

PAUL SOMERS

White Prairie Clover · *Dalea candida*

GENERAL: Erect, smooth perennial herb, 12–36 in. tall. **LEAVES:** Alternate, pinnately compound, with 5–9 leaflets, 0.4–1.2 in. long, that are **narrow to oblong**, flat or folded. **FLOWERS:** Small, **white**; borne in 1 to few **dense, cylindric heads**, 1–3 in. long and less than ½ as wide; flowering progresses from bottom to top. June–July. **FRUITS:** Indehiscent legumes, usually enclosed by the calyx. **WHERE FOUND:** Dry calcareous barrens and margins of upland woods. A mostly western prairie species extending east into KY and SC. In TN, in Davidson, Wilson, Rutherford, Franklin, Overton, and Meigs counties. Rare. **Petalostemon candidus**.

NOTES: The *Dalea* genus was named in honor of Dr. Samuel Dale (1659–1739), an English botanist and author; *candida* means "shining or pure white," referring to the flowers. • Other *Dalea* species from the western U.S. are edible: the roots of Purple Dalea (*D. lasiathera*) and Woolly Prairie Clover (*D. lantana* var. *terminalis*), and the seeds of White Dalea (*D. emoryi*, now *Psorothamnus emoryi*). • Native Americans extracted a yellow dye from the twigs and flower heads of White Dalea that was used for decorating basketwork.

Leafy Prairie Clover · *Dalea foliosa*

GENERAL: Smooth **perennial** herb, 12–30 in. tall. **LEAVES:** Alternate, pinnately compound, with 19–31 **oblong to elliptic** leaflets, 0.2–0.4 in. long. **FLOWERS:** **Roseate, fading to white,** tiny, **not pea-like,** but more open; in a **dense, cylindric head,** 1–2 in. long, that flowers from bottom to top. July. **FRUITS:** Indehiscent legumes, usually enclosed by the calyx. **WHERE FOUND:** Cedar glades and calcareous barrens from northeastern IL to northern AL, but found only in IL, AL, and TN. In TN, in the Central Basin in Sumner, Davidson, Wilson, Williamson, Rutherford, Maury, and Marshall counties. Infrequent. *Petalostemon foliosus.* **SIMILAR SPECIES:** FOXTAIL PRAIRIE CLOVER (**D. leporina**), also known as HARE'S-FOOT PRAIRIE CLOVER, is an **annual; leaflets are wider toward the tip;** inflorescence is hairy; **flowers are whitish and pea-like.** Western prairies and disturbed sites in the eastern U.S. In TN, in Humphreys and Davidson counties. Rare. June–August.

DAVID DUHL

NOTES: Leafy Prairie Clover is also known as Purple Prairie Clover and Cedar Glade Prairie Clover. It is listed federally as an endangered species. The U.S. Fish and Wildlife Service has recorded only 9 viable populations of Leafy Prairie Clover in TN, most with fewer than 50 individual plants.

Gattinger's Prairie Clover, Purpletassels · *Dalea gattingeri*

GENERAL: Prostrate, **aromatic** perennial herb with many spreading branches to 12–36 in. long. **LEAVES:** Alternate, numerous, pinnately compound, to 3 in. long, each with 3–5 narrow, rolled leaflets, 0.4–0.8 in. long. **FLOWERS:** Tiny, **deep purple;** borne in a **long, cylindric head** resembling a bottlebrush; flowering progresses from bottom to top. July–September. **FRUITS:** Indehiscent legumes, usually enclosed by the calyx. **WHERE FOUND:** Dry, calcareous, rocky glades. A southeastern U.S. endemic found in MO, TN, northern AL, and northwestern GA. In TN, in the Central Basin and surrounding counties, also Hamilton and Meigs counties in East TN. Occasional. *Petalostemon gattingeri.* **SIMILAR SPECIES:** PURPLE PRAIRIE CLOVER (**D. purpurea**) is upright, 12–36 in. tall; rose to crimson flowers occur in a round head that matures to a **short, cylindric head.** Dry barrens, open glades. A mostly northern and western prairie species that extends south and east to Middle TN in Davidson, Wilson, and Rutherford counties. Rare. June–July. *Petalostemon purpureus.*

KURT EMMANUELE

NOTES: Gattinger's Prairie Clover is a herbaceous species found throughout the limestone glades in the Central Basin in Middle Tennessee. • Plants need nitrogen to grow, but although nitrogen makes up 78 percent of the atmosphere, it is in a form plants cannot use. Many clovers have a symbiotic relationship with certain types of soil bacteria, which form nodules on the roots and fix atmospheric nitrogen.

DENNIS HORN

Prairie Mimosa · *Desmanthus illinoensis*

GENERAL: Erect perennial herb, 3–6 ft. tall. **LEAVES:** Alternate, bipinnately compound with numerous oblong leaflets, 0.25–0.5 in. long. **FLOWERS:** Tiny, white, not pea-like; borne in a round, powder-puff-shaped cluster, 0.5 in. wide, resembling the inflorescence of **Mimosa** or **Silk Tree** (*Albizia julibrissin*). June–July. **FRUITS:** Dehiscent, sickle-shaped legumes (pods), turning brown in **twisted clusters**; often found at the same time as the flowers. **WHERE FOUND:** Dry soil, fields, and especially cedar glade edges, from PA to ND, south to FL and NM. Scattered throughout TN. Occasional.

NOTES: The genus name *Desmanthus* is from the Greek *desme*, "a bundle," and *anthos*, "flower," referring to the inflorescence. • *Desmanthus* species bear a striking resemblance to the Mimosa or Silk Tree in both the compound leaves and the inflorescence. • Native Americans made the leaves into a poultice infused in hot water to treat earaches. The fresh root was chewed as a remedy for toothaches.

JERRY DROWN

Naked-Flowered Tick Trefoil
Desmodium nudiflorum

GENERAL: Smooth, erect perennial with flowers on a **leafless (naked) scape** to 3 ft. tall. **LEAVES:** 4–7, trifoliolate, clustered at the end of a sterile stalk about 12 in. tall; leaflets broadly ovate, about 3 in. long. **FLOWERS:** Rose-purple, pea-like; borne in a loose raceme on a leafless scape about 3 times the length of the leaf stalk. July–August. **FRUITS:** Flattened legumes with deeply notched lower margins are covered with small, hooked hairs; legumes break into several 1-seeded segments when mature. **WHERE FOUND:** Rich woods in the eastern U.S. and throughout TN. Common. **SIMILAR SPECIES: SMALL-LEAF TICK TREFOIL (D. ciliare)** is an erect perennial with a **downy stem**; leaves have 3 small, **elliptic leaflets**, also hairy. Dry, sandy areas. Eastern U.S. and the eastern ³⁄₄ of TN. Frequent. July–August. **PANICLED TICK TREFOIL (D. paniculatum)** is usually **multi-stemmed**, 2–4 ft. tall; many rose to purple flowers in panicles at the top. Dry woods. Eastern U.S. Throughout TN. Common. July–August. **PROSTRATE TICK TREFOIL (D. rotundifolium)** is prostrate, with stems to 3 ft. long; **round leaflets**; purple flowers. Dry woods. Eastern U.S. Throughout TN. Common. July–September.

NOTES: The genus name *Desmodium* is from the Greek *desmos*, meaning "a band or chain," in reference to the bead-like seedpods; *nudiflorum* is a reference to the "nude" or leafless flower stalk. The "tick" in the common name refers to the sticky seedpods that attach and cling like ticks. • Of the 17 *Desmodium* species that occur in TN, all but 2 are reasonably common.

Hairy Milk Pea
Galactia volubilis

GENERAL: Perennial herbaceous plant with **climbing and twining stems**, up to 5 ft. long, with spreading hairs. **LEAVES:** Compound, 2–3 per node, 3 leaflets to 2 in. long are ovate to oblong or elliptic; lower leaf surface has spreading hairs. **FLOWERS:** Pink-purple, pea-like, 0.3–0.4 in. wide, on stalks about 0.15 in. long; borne in **loose racemes** to 4 in. long with 1–3 flowers at each node. July–August. **FRUITS:** Compressed legumes, 2.5 in. long, densely short-hairy. **WHERE FOUND:** Dry, sandy soils, upland woods, and barrens, from NY to KS, south to FL and TX. Throughout TN. Common.

NOTES: The genus name *Galactia* comes from *gala*, meaning "milk," and is so named because it was once thought that the branches of plants in this genus contained a milky sap. This plant is also known as **Downy Milk Pea** and **Climbing Milk Pea**. • This species is a host for the Tropical Striped Blue butterfly. The butterfly lays one egg on each flower bud, and when hatched, the caterpillars eat the flowers and seedpods. Ants tend the butterfly larvae and feed on their sugary secretions.

THOMAS G. BARNES

Everlasting Pea • *Lathyrus latifolius**

OTTO R. HIRSCH

GENERAL: Perennial with **trailing or climbing stems** up to 7 ft. long and **broadly winged**. **LEAVES:** Alternate, **winged petioles**; 2 opposite, lanceolate to elliptic leaflets to 3 in. long; terminal leaflet is modified into a branched tendril. **FLOWERS:** Showy, **reddish purple to pink or white**, pea-like, to 1 in. long; occur in clusters of 4–10 flowers. June–August. **FRUITS:** Smooth pods, 2–4 in. long. **WHERE FOUND:** Introduced from southern Europe. Now well established in waste places, often persisting near old homesites throughout the U.S. Scattered throughout TN, but more prevalent in the central and eastern regions. Frequent. **SIMILAR SPECIES:** HAIRY PEA (*L. hirsutus**) is an **annual** with **winged stems** and **smaller flowers**, about 0.5 in. long; **hairy pods**. Introduced from Europe. Escaped to roadsides and waste places in the southeastern U.S. Thinly scattered in TN. Occasional. April–July. The following 2 species **without winged stems** are native perennials with leaves of 4 or more leaflets and **purple flowers** about 0.7 in. long: MARSH PEA (*L. palustris*) has **4–8 leaflets; racemes of 2–6 flowers**. Wet woods and meadows. A northern species, found only in Coffee, Warren, Anderson, and Knox counties in TN. Rare. June–July. VEINY PEA (*L. venosus*) has **8–12 leaflets; dense racemes of 10–20 flowers**. Dry woods of the northeastern U.S., south to GA and NM. Thinly scattered across TN. Infrequent. June–July.

NOTES: Everlasting Pea is also called **Perennial Pea**, as it is a long-lived perennial (to 10 years). • This species has been established as a garden plant in the U.S. since 1720. Thomas Jefferson sowed it in his garden at Monticello in 1807.

OTTO R. HIRSCH

Narrowleaf Lespedeza
Lespedeza angustifolia

GENERAL: Slender, stiffly ascending perennial **herb** to 40 in. tall. **LEAVES:** Alternate, almost sessile, compound, with 3 **linear leaflets**, 1.0–2.5 in. long. **FLOWERS:** Whitish with a purple base, about 0.3 in. wide; borne in **dense, compact, long-stalked spikes** to 1.2 in. long. August–September. **FRUITS:** Densely short-hairy, 1-seeded legumes (only 1 segment). **WHERE FOUND:** Barrens and open areas. Mostly in the Coastal Plain from MA to FL to LA. Disjunct populations in Lincoln, Coffee, and Warren counties in Middle TN. Rare. **SIMILAR SPECIES:** SHRUBBY LESPEDEZA (**L. bicolor ***) is a **woody shrub** to 10 ft. tall, much-branched; numerous pink flowers at branch tips. Introduced from Japan. Planted for wildlife food and now escaped. Scattered throughout the eastern U.S. and TN. Frequent. July–October.

NOTES: Narrowleaf Lespedeza is also called **Narrowleaf Bush Clover.** • Lespedezas are commonly planted to improve soils because they act as nitrogen-fixers and are also used for hay. Eleven species are known in TN.

Roundhead Bush Clover · *Lespedeza capitata*

THOMAS G. BARNES

GENERAL: Erect perennial, to 5 ft. tall, **densely hairy.** **LEAVES:** Alternate, compound, with 3 thickish, **oblong to elliptic leaflets** to 2 in. long, with dense white hairs. **FLOWERS: Cream-colored** with a purple spot at the base; borne in dense, almost **round heads** on short stalks from the leaf axils. August–September. **FRUITS:** Densely short-hairy, 1-seeded legumes (only 1 segment), faintly nerved. **WHERE FOUND:** Dry woods, barrens, fields, and roadsides in most of the eastern U.S. and Middle and East TN. Occasional. **SIMILAR SPECIES:** The 3 *Lespedeza* species that follow are found throughout the eastern U.S. and are frequent statewide, though less prevalent in West TN. SERICEA LESPEDEZA (**L. cuneata***) grows to 36 in. tall; **white flowers with purple veins** occur in the leaf axils. Introduced from Asia. Planted on roadsides and escaped to areas outside the original plantings. WANDLIKE BUSH CLOVER (**L. intermedia**) grows to 36 in. tall; **violet purple flowers** are borne on **short peduncles.** Dry, open woods. SLENDER BUSH CLOVER (**L. virginica**) grows to 40 in. tall; **violet purple flowers** occur in **sessile clusters.** Dry, open woods and barrens. August–September (all 3 species).

NOTES: Roundhead Bush Clover is named for its rounded, clover-like flower heads and the clover-like foliage. The species name *capitata* means "in heads," also referring to the rounded inflorescences. • The seeds of Roundhead Bush Clover are a valuable food source for Bobwhite quail, as are many bush clovers.

Hairy Bush Clover · *Lespedeza hirta*

GENERAL: Perennial herb, 24–36 in. tall, **stems erect and hairy. LEAVES:** Alternate, trifoliolate, on hairy petioles about 0.5 in. long; 3 **rounded, elliptic leaflets**, 0.75–1.5 in. long and over 1/2 as wide, **stalk of terminal leaflet thickened**, densely hairy at the summit. **FLOWERS: Yellowish white** with a purple spot, about 0.3 in. long; hairy calyx lobes; flowers are numerous on short spikes, about 1 in. long, extending above the leaves on long stalks; inflorescence is much like **Roundhead Bush Clover** (p. 172), but the clusters are less dense. July–October. **FRUITS:** Somewhat hairy, elliptic legumes, 0.2–0.4 in. long; 1-seeded segment. **WHERE FOUND:** Dry, open places, and thin woods throughout eastern U.S., west to KS and TX. Throughout TN, but less frequent in the Central Basin and in West TN. Common.

NOTES: Lespedezas are often called "bush clovers." • The *Lespedeza* genus was named in honor of the 18th-century Spanish Governor of Florida, Vicente Manuel de Céspedes, by the French botanist André Michaux (1746–1802), who collected widely in North America. Céspedes' name was later misspelled and published as de Lespedez. • Bush clovers provide food for birds, rabbits, and deer and are cultivated as forage crops.

DENNIS HORN

Smooth Creeping Bush Clover

Lespedeza repens

GENERAL: Trailing perennial, to 4 ft. long, that sends up erect or nearly erect flower branches; slender **stems are nearly smooth to finely appressed (flattened) hairy. LEAVES:** Alternate, often with flattened, fine hairs, compound, with 3 oval to obovate leaflets, 0.4–0.8 in. long and 1/2 as wide; leaf stalks shorter than the leaflets. **FLOWERS: Pink-purple, pea-like**, about 0.5 in. long; borne in **clusters of 2–8 flowers** at the top of long, filiform stalks. June–September. **FRUITS:** Appressed-hairy, 1-seeded legumes (only 1 segment). **WHERE FOUND:** Dry open woods and roadsides throughout most of the eastern U.S. and TN. Common. **SIMILAR SPECIES:** DOWNY CREEPING BUSH CLOVER (*L. procumbens*), also called TRAILING BUSH CLOVER, has noticeably **spreading, hairy stems**; inflorescence has **8–12 flowers**. Throughout most of the eastern U.S. Frequent across TN, but less prevalent in the western part of the state. Frequent. August–September.

NOTES: The species name *repens* means "having creeping or rooting stems," which is appropriate for **Smooth Creeping Bush Clover**. It is also known as **Creeping Lespedeza**. • **Downy Creeping Bush Clover** is nearly identical to Smooth Creeping Bush Clover, but has somewhat thicker stems that are spreading-hairy, not smooth or with flattened hairs.

DENNIS HORN

JERRY DROWN

White Sweet Clover · *Melilotus albus**

GENERAL: Biennial herb, 3–6 ft. tall, highly branched. **LEAVES:** Alternate, trifoliolate, with 3 lanceolate leaflets 0.5–1.0 in. long. **FLOWERS:** White, pea-like, 0.25 in. long; borne in narrow, loose racemes. April–October. **FRUITS:** Dark brown to black legumes with a reticulated surface; usually 1-seeded. **WHERE FOUND:** Introduced from Europe and cultivated as a forage crop. Fields, roadsides, and waste places throughout the U.S., Canada, and TN. Frequent. *M. alba.* **SIMILAR SPECIES:** YELLOW SWEET CLOVER (*M. officinalis**) has **yellow flowers.** Introduced from Europe. Throughout the eastern U.S. and TN. Frequent. April–October.

NOTES: The genus name *Melilotus*, meaning "honey plant," is a reference to the **sweet-smelling flowers** containing coumarin, a fragrant organic compound. Other common names for **White Sweet Clover** are Honey Lotus, Sweet Lucerne, and Trebol. • **Yellow Sweet Clover** is also called King's Clover. It was used as a warm poultice to treat sores and ulcers of the skin.

DENNIS HORN

Sensitive Brier · *Mimosa microphylla*

GENERAL: Trailing perennial herb to 3 ft. long. **LEAVES:** Alternate, bipinnately compound with many, oblong leaflets to 0.25 in. long; **leaves and stems have small, hooked thorns. FLOWERS:** Tiny, pink-purple, not pea-like; borne in a **round, powder-puff-shaped cluster,** 0.75 in. wide, resembling the inflorescence of **Mimosa** or **Silk Tree (***Albizia julibrissin*). June–September. **FRUITS:** Dehiscent legumes, conspicuously prickly and quadrangular. **WHERE FOUND:** Dry, open areas. A generally southern species extending north to KY and VA. Found over much of TN, except the far western and eastern counties and the Central Basin of Middle TN. Frequent. *Schrankia microphylla, M. quadrivalvis.*

NOTES: If touched, especially along the spiny stem, **this plant's leaves will fold** quickly enough to be easily observed. This plant is also called **Littleleaf Sensitive Brier** and **Sensitive Plant.** • This species is commonly pollinated by bees and provides a favorite perch for the Virgin Tiger Moth. Curiously, one tall African *Mimosa* relative is pollinated by giraffes. • *Mimosa* leaves often fold at sunset or during a rainstorm and unfold when the sun shines.

Sampson's Snakeroot
Orbexilum pedunculatum

GENERAL: Slender, **glandular**, branched perennial herb to 3 ft. tall. **LEAVES:** Alternate, compound, 3 **lanceolate to narrowly oblong leaflets**, 1.25–2.75 in. long and **less than 0.8 in. wide**, gradually narrowing to a blunt tip. **FLOWERS:** Lilac purple, **pea-like**, about 0.25 in. wide; borne well above the foliage in a **spike-like raceme** to 2.5 in. long. May–June. **FRUITS:** Smooth, strongly ribbed, heavily dotted, indehiscent legumes. **WHERE FOUND:** Dry open woods, barrens, and fields, from OH to KS southward. Throughout most of TN. Frequent. *Psoralea psoralioides*. **SIMILAR SPECIES:** SAINFOIN (*O. onobrychis*) differs in having **no glands** on its foliage or fruit; broadly acuminate; leaflets, 2–4 in. long and **more than 0.8 in wide**; flower stalks barely exceed the tops of leaves. Open woods and moist barrens, from OH to IA, south to AR and SC. In TN, from the Ridge and Valley eastward, also in Montgomery County in Middle TN. Infrequent. June–July. *Psoralea onobrychis*.

DENNIS HORN

NOTES: **Sampson's Snakeroot** is also called Leather Root and False Scurf-Pea. It clumps profusely at the base and spreads from short rhizomes, eventually forming a broad mat.

Nashville Breadroot
Pediomelum subacaule

GENERAL: Semi-prostrate perennial to 12 in. tall, often with several **silvery-haired** leaf stalks originating from a single root, giving a whorled appearance to the plant. **LEAVES:** Deep green to blue-green, **palmately compound**, with 5–8 narrowly obovate leaflets, 1–2 in. long, with **whitish margins**. **FLOWERS:** Blue-purple (rarely white), **pea-like**; borne in dense racemes, about 3 in. long, at the tips of the flower stalks. April–May. **FRUITS:** Indehiscent legumes, enclosed in the calyx except for a projecting beak. **WHERE FOUND:** Calcareous cedar glade areas of KY, AL, GA, and TN. In TN, known from Davidson, Wilson, Williamson, Rutherford, Maury, Marshall, and Bedford counties in the Central Basin, also Meigs County in the Ridge and Valley. Infrequent. *Psoralea subacaulis*.

RICHARD CONNORS

NOTES: The genus name *Pediomelum* is from the Greek *pedion*, meaning "a plain or clearing," for the habitat preference of these plants, and *melum*, "apple"; the species name *subacaule* means "without much of a stem," because this squat plant appears to not have a stem. • This plant's common name indicates the edibility of the starchy root. It is also known as **Whiterim Scurf-Pea** in reference to the light-colored leaf edges.

DAVID DUHL

Kudzu • *Pueraria lobata**

GENERAL: Herbaceous, **trailing or climbing, sprawling perennial vine**, 30–100 ft. long, hairy when young. **LEAVES:** Alternate, compound, typically with 3 broadly ovate to almost round leaflets, 4–6 in. long, that are often somewhat lobed and hairy beneath. **FLOWERS:** Reddish purple, **pea-like**, to 1 in. long; borne in **racemes, 4–8 in. long**, that have the **rich aroma** of Concord grapes. July–October. **FRUITS:** Laterally compressed, brownish, hairy legumes; usually does not set fruit in our range. **WHERE FOUND:** Introduced from Japan. Roadsides, woods, and fields. Widespread in the southeastern U.S. and TN. Occasional. *P. montana* var. *lobata*.

NOTES: This Japanese native is easily established in most soils, where it will usually shade out, and thereby kill, virtually all nearby plant life. It is a rampantly growing vine introduced by the U.S. Department of Agriculture to help prevent erosion, but has become a **serious exotic pest plant**. • Medicinally, this plant was used by the Chinese to prevent excessive drinking and to normalize blood pressure. It is currently under study as a treatment for alcoholism.

OTTO R. HIRSCH

Southern Wild Senna

Senna marilandica

GENERAL: Erect perennial herb, 3–6 ft. tall. **LEAVES:** Alternate, pinnately compound, with 4–8 pairs of narrowly elliptic leaflets, 1–2 in. long; **short, rounded gland** at base of leaf stalks. **FLOWERS:** Yellow, **not obviously pea-like**, 0.5 in. long, petals open to expose the stamens; borne in a raceme. July–August. **FRUITS:** Smooth or slightly hairy legumes; **legume segments are nearly 2x as wide as long. WHERE FOUND:** Open woods, fields, and cedar glades throughout most of the eastern U.S. and TN. Frequent. **Cassia marilandica. SIMILAR SPECIES:** NORTHERN WILD SENNA (**S. hebecarpa**), also called AMERICAN SENNA, has **club-shaped glands**; pods have **joints that are nearly square**. Moist, open woods. In the northeastern U.S. south to TN and NC. Thinly scattered across TN. Occasional. July–August. *Cassia hebecarpa*.

NOTES: Southern Wild Senna is also called **Maryland Senna, Locust Plant**, and **Teaweed**. This plant is used as a potent laxative and traditionally has been considered an inexpensive alternative to "true Alexandrian Senna" (*S. alexandrina*) of the Middle East, which has been used in commercial laxatives.

Sicklepod · *Senna obtusifolia**

GENERAL: Annual, to 3 ft. tall, with an unpleasant odor. **LEAVES:** Alternate, pinnately compound with 2–3 pairs of elliptic to obovate leaflets, each leaflet 1–2 in. long; **terminal leaflets always obovate**. **FLOWERS:** Dull yellow, 5 slightly unequal petals about 0.5 in. long that never seem to open fully; 1–2 flowers in axillary clusters. July–September. **FRUITS:** Narrow legumes, strongly curved and 4-angled. **WHERE FOUND:** An introduced subtropical species. Moist to dry open woods and roadsides. Range now extends north to NE, IL, and NY. Scattered throughout TN. Occasional. *Cassia obtusifolia*.

NOTES: This plant is also called **Coffee Weed** and **Java Bean** as the seeds of a related species, Sickle Senna (*S. tora*), were roasted as a coffee substitute and eaten during times of famine. • Tea made from the seeds of **Sicklepod** was traditionally used to treat headaches, fatigue, stomachaches, hepatitis, herpes, and arthritis. The seeds are **poisonous** if ingested.

DENNIS HORN

Pink Wild Bean
Strophostyles umbellata

GENERAL: Trailing to climbing perennial to 10 ft. long; stem usually hairy. **LEAVES:** Alternate, compound, 3 somewhat leathery leaflets are oblong to narrowly ovate, to 2 in. long, never lobed. **FLOWERS:** Pink, pea-like, to about 0.5 in. across; **keel petal strongly incurved**, enclosing the 10 stamens and style within; borne in racemes with few to several flowers on a **long, naked stalk**, often held about 12 in. above the vine. June–September. **FRUITS:** Legumes, 3 in. long, with appressed hairs. **WHERE FOUND:** Dry open woodlands or open fields. A mainly Coastal Plain species found from NY to FL and TX, and north in the interior to southern IN. Throughout TN. Frequent. **SIMILAR SPECIES:** WILD BEAN (*S. helvula*) is an annual; **leaflets usually have 1–2 lateral lobes**; pink to purple flowers fade to green. Dry soil. Throughout the eastern U.S. and TN. Occasional. June–September. **SMALL-FLOWERED WILD BEAN (*S. leiosperma*)** is an annual; **leaflets are lobed** and heavily covered with stiff hairs; **smaller pink flowers** about 0.33 in. wide. Dry or moist soil in the central ⅔ of the U.S. In West TN, also Montgomery and Stewart counties. Infrequent. June–September.

DENNIS HORN

NOTES: The genus name *Strophostyles* comes from the Greek *strophe*, "turning," and *stylos*, for "style," referring to the style that is twisted within the keel petal. • **Pink Wild Bean** is also called Trailing Wild Bean or Pink Fuzzy Bean for the hairy fruit.

DENNIS HORN

Pencil Flower · *Stylosanthes biflora*

GENERAL: Wiry-stemmed, branching perennial, reclining, ascending, or erect, 6–18 in. tall, from a taproot. **LEAVES:** Alternate, trifoliolate with narrow lanceolate, bristle-tipped leaflets, 0.75–1.5 in. long. **FLOWERS:** Yellow-orange, pea-like, 5 petals, **nearly round standard** about 0.3 in. wide; in spikes of 2–6 flowers at the ends of the leafy branches. June–August. **FRUITS:** Indehiscent, 2-segmented legumes with a beak; lower segment is usually sterile and stalk-like. **WHERE FOUND:** Dry, rocky woods and barrens from NY, IL, and KS, south to FL and LA. Throughout TN. Common.

NOTES: This plant's common name refers to the stalk-like, hollow calyx tube that surrounds the pistil of the flower, a characteristic also indicated by the genus name *Stylosanthes*, from the Greek *stylos*, "style" and *anthos*, "flower"; the species name *biflora* means "two-flowered." It is also known as **Sidebeak Pencil Flower.** • **Pencil Flower** is frequented by bees, butterflies, and a variety of insects, and is a host plant for the Barred Sulphur and Little Sulphur butterflies.

JERRY DROWN

Goat's Rue

Tephrosia virginiana

GENERAL: Hairy perennial herb, 12–24 in. tall, from a tough rootstock. **LEAVES:** Alternate, pinnately compound, **15–25 leaflets** are narrowly oblong to elliptic, 1 in. long. **FLOWERS:** Pea-like, **pale yellow to cream standard, pink wings**, 0.75 in. long; borne in a terminal raceme. June–July. **FRUITS:** Densely hairy, dehiscent legumes, 2.5–3.0 in. long. **WHERE FOUND:** Open woods and fields. Throughout most of the eastern U.S. and TN. Common. **SIMILAR SPECIES:** SOUTHERN GOAT'S RUE (*T. spicata*) has **9–17 oval leaflets**; flowers **nearly white** upon opening, **becoming reddish purple** with maturity; some racemes not terminal. Open fields and barrens, from southern DE to FL, west to TN and LA. Middle and East TN. Occasional. June–July.

NOTES: These plants get their common names because they smell of goat. • Though **Goat's Rue** is **toxic** to grazing animals, the seeds are eaten by birds and turkeys. The shoestring-like roots are the source of the insecticide, rotenone, which was used by Native Americans to poison and catch fish by stunning the fish so they floated to the surface. The use of rotenone as a fish poison was a key element in the 1954 film *Creature from the Black Lagoon*—a tank of rotenone was dumped into the water to subdue the monster so that it could be captured.

Hairy Bush Pea, Aaron's Rod
Thermopsis villosa

JERRY DROWN

GENERAL: Erect, hairy perennial herb, 24–36 in. tall. **LEAVES:** Alternate, each with 3 broad leaflets, 1.5–3.0 in. long; **broad stipules**, to 2 in. long, the basal lobes **clasping the stem. FLOWERS:** Yellow, pea-like, 0.6 in. long; borne in a **dense raceme. FRUITS:** Flattened legumes, usually erect and persistently hairy. **WHERE FOUND:** Open woods and clearings, from ME, south to AL. Thinly scattered in Middle and East TN. Infrequent. **SIMILAR SPECIES: PIEDMONT BUSH PEA (*T. mollis*)** has **narrow stipules that do not clasp the stem**; inflorescence has **fewer flowers**. Open woods from southern VA to GA in the uplands. In TN, thinly scattered from the Cumberland Plateau eastward, in Franklin, Marion, Hamilton, Blount, Sevier, and Grainger counties. Infrequent. May.

NOTES: The genus name *Thermopsis* is from the Greek *thermos*, "lupine," and *opsis*, meaning "like," in reference to the lupine-like flower heads of these plants. Members of the *Thermopsis* genus resemble the yellow-flowered species of *Baptisia* as well, but can be distinguished by their flattened pods.

Low Hop Clover
*Trifolium campestre**

DENNIS HORN

GENERAL: Annual herb, 4–12 in. high. **LEAVES:** Alternate, trifoliolate, the **terminal leaflet on a long stalk**; leaflets are oblong-ovate, 0.25–0.75 in. long. **FLOWERS:** Yellow; borne in a **small head of 20–40 flowers**. April–October. **FRUITS:** Single-seeded legumes, slightly exserted from the calyx. **WHERE FOUND:** Introduced from Eurasia. Fields, roadsides, lawns, and waste places throughout much of North America, including TN. Common. *T. procumbens**. **SIMILAR SPECIES: LEAST HOP CLOVER (*T. dubium**)** has only **3–15 flowers per head**. Introduced from Europe. Scattered throughout much of North America, including TN. Occasional. April–October. **GOLDEN HOP CLOVER (*T. aureum**)** has a **terminal leaflet that is not stalked**. Introduced from Eurasia. Throughout the northeastern U.S. In TN, only in Shelby and Sevier counties. Rare. May–September. *T. agrarium*.

NOTES: As the flower head of **Low Hop Clover** dries, the individual florets become light brown and fold downward, resembling dried hops, thus accounting for the common name. This species was introduced to North America as fodder and for soil improvement.

OTTO R. HIRSCH

Crimson Clover
Trifolium incarnatum＊

GENERAL: Annual herb, 12–24 in. tall. **LEAVES:** Alternate, trifoliolate with obovate leaflets to 1 in. long. **FLOWERS:** Tiny, **crimson**; inflorescence is an **elongated head** of flowers, 1–2 in. long. May–August. **FRUITS:** 1-seeded legumes, sessile in the calyx. **WHERE FOUND:** Introduced from Europe. Old fields, pastures, and roadsides throughout most of the eastern U.S. Scattered across TN. Occasional.

NOTES: The genus name *Trifolium* means "three leaves"; *incarnatum* means "flesh-colored." This plant is also called **Carnation Clover.** Interestingly, in England it was named Napoleon and Bloody Triumph, supposedly because Napoleon's battles turned bloody. • This species is often planted as a cover crop for hay. Also, it provides good forage for many animals. A showy display of this species is a pleasure to behold!

DENNIS HORN

Red Clover · *Trifolium pratense*＊

GENERAL: Short-lived perennial herb, 12–24 in. tall. **LEAVES:** Alternate, trifoliolate with lanceolate to elliptical leaflets about 1 in. long; each leaflet has a prominent pale green "V." **FLOWERS:** Tiny, **pink, sessile**; borne in a **round head**, 1 in. across. May–August. **FRUITS:** 1-seeded legumes. **WHERE FOUND:** Introduced from Europe. Fields, roadsides, lawns, and waste places throughout most of temperate North America, including TN. Frequent. **SIMILAR SPECIES:** BUFFALO CLOVER (**T. reflexum**) has **stalked flowers** with a **bright red standard** (brighter than Red Clover), the remaining flower parts whitish pink. **Native species** of upland woods and barrens. Throughout most of the eastern U.S. In TN, in Madison, Lewis, Montgomery, and Davidson counties. Rare. May–June.

NOTES: **Red Clover** is also called Cowgrass, Honeysuckle Clover, Suckles, and Sugar Plums. Some of these names refer to the sweet nectar that is produced by the flowers. It is the state flower of Vermont. • The flowers, leaves, and young stems of Red Clover are edible. The flowers have been used in folk remedies for cancer, and the dried leaves have been used to make a tea for treating whooping cough, bronchitis, and other ailments of the lungs.

White Clover • *Trifolium repens**

GENERAL: Creeping perennial herb with stems 4–16 in. long. **LEAVES:** Alternate, trifoliolate with obovate leaflets about 0.75 in. long; each leaflet has a pale green "V." **FLOWERS:** Tiny, **white or pink-tinged**; borne in a round head, 1 in. in diameter; **flower stalk without leaves**. April–September. **FRUITS:** Legumes, exserted from the calyx; 3–4 seeds. **WHERE FOUND:** Introduced from Eurasia. Fields, roadsides, lawns, and waste places throughout most of temperate North America, including TN. Occasional. **SIMILAR SPECIES:** ALSIKE CLOVER (**T. hybridum***) has **flower heads with leafy stalks**. Introduced from Eurasia. In fields and along roadsides throughout most of temperate North America and TN. Occasional. April–September. RABBIT'S-FOOT CLOVER (**T. arvense***) has a **fuzzy, long head of tiny, grayish pink flowers**. Introduced from Eurasia. Along roadsides, often on sandy soils, throughout much of the U.S. and southern Canada. Scattered throughout TN in Shelby, Fayette, Hardeman, Bedford, Montgomery, White, Knox, Grainger, and Carter counties. Infrequent. May–September.

KURT EMMANUELE

NOTES: White Clover is also called Honeystalks, Purplewort, and White Trefoil. Another name, Lamb-Sucklings, was given because this plant is sweet forage for sheep, as well as cattle. • White Clover is the **common clover of lawns and rich pastures**. Many clovers were introduced from Eurasia and are cultivated as forage crops.

Wood Vetch • *Vicia caroliniana*

GENERAL: Short, sparse, climbing to **sprawling perennial** to 30 in. long, often with 2–4 stems arising from the same base. **LEAVES:** Alternate, pinnately compound with **5–9 leaflet pairs**; leaflets elliptic to oblong-lanceolate, to 0.8 in. long; tendrils terminate each leaf. **FLOWERS:** White with a bit of purple, to 0.5 in. long; borne in loose racemes to 4 in. long. April–May. **FRUITS:** Flattened, dehiscent legumes; 5–8 seeds. **WHERE FOUND:** Open, dry oak woods in most of the eastern U.S. and Middle and East TN. Frequent. **SIMILAR SPECIES:** NARROWLEAF VETCH (**V. sativa ssp. nigra***), also called GARDEN VETCH and COMMON VETCH, is a slender, erect to climbing **annual**, to 3 ft. tall; leaves have **3–5 leaflet pairs** that are mostly linear; **rose-purple flowers** are 0.5-0.75 in. wide; black fruits. Introduced from Europe. Roadsides and fields throughout the eastern U.S. and TN. Frequent. March–June. **V. angustifolia**.

NOTES: As indicated by the species name, *caroliniana*, **Wood Vetch** is also called **Carolina Vetch**, as well as **Pale Vetch**. • Wood Vetch is a host plant for the Silvery Blue butterfly.

KURT EMMANUELE

JERRY DROWN

Smooth Vetch
Vicia dasycarpa*

GENERAL: Annual or biennial with trailing to climbing stems to 3 ft. long, **mostly smooth** or appressed-hairy. **LEAVES:** Alternate, pinnately compound with 5–10 pairs of leaflets, 0.5–1.0 in. long, narrowly oblong to lanceolate-linear. **FLOWERS:** Blue-purple, to 0.8 in. long; typically **5–15 flowers** in dense, one-sided racemes with **short-appressed hairs** and long peduncles. May–August. **FRUITS:** Smooth to somewhat hairy, compressed legumes up to 2 in. long. **WHERE FOUND:** Introduced from Europe. Escaped to roadsides, fields, and waste places throughout most of the U.S., including TN. Frequent. *V. villosa* ssp. *varia*. **SIMILAR SPECIES:** HAIRY VETCH (*V. villosa* ssp. *villosa**) has **hairy stems**; **10–40 flowers on racemes with long-spreading hairs**. Introduced. Roadsides and fields. Scattered throughout most of the U.S., southern Canada, and TN. Occasional. June–August.

NOTES: The genus name *Vicia* is Latin for "vetch"; *dasycarpa* means "hairy fruit," which is not entirely accurate considering the fruits can be smooth or hairy. • Another species of *Vicia*, the Broad Bean (*V. faba*), is one of the earliest plants known to have been grown by humans and is still cultivated as a winter vegetable.

DENNIS HORN

American Wisteria · *Wisteria frutescens*

GENERAL: High-climbing **woody vine**, 6–30 ft. long. **LEAVES:** Alternate, pinnately compound with 9–15 leaflets about 2 in. long, oval, tapering to a point. **FLOWERS:** Blue-purple, 0.6–0.8 in. long; borne in a **compact raceme, 3–6 in. long**. April–May. **FRUITS:** Smooth legumes up to 6 in. long; segments appear slightly beaded. **WHERE FOUND:** Moist woods and river-banks, from VA to FL, west to AR and TX. Throughout TN, but more prevalent in West TN. Frequent. **SIMILAR SPECIES:** JAPANESE WISTERIA (*W. floribunda**) has an inflorescence that is a **loose, hanging raceme to 20 in. long**; flowers open sequentially from the top down; **pods are velvety**. Introduced and escaped. Throughout most of the southeastern U.S. Thinly scattered in TN. Infrequent. April–May. **CHINESE WISTERIA** (*W. sinensis**) has leaves with 7–13 leaflets; **racemes to 8 in. long**; flowers, approximately 1 in. long, open simultaneously; **pods are velvety**. Introduced and sometimes escapes from cultivation. In most of the southeastern U.S. Thinly scattered in TN. Infrequent. April–May.

NOTES: Wisteria is named for Dr. Caspar Wistar (1761–1818) of Philadelphia, a professor at the University of Pennsylvania, president of the Philosophical Society, and a renowned anatomist. • Most *Wisteria* species grown in gardens are from China or Japan; **American Wisteria** is the only native. For gardeners, this native wisteria is a good alternative to the fast-growing, often aggressive introduced wisterias.

Swamp Loosestrife
Decodon verticillatus

GENERAL: **Multi-stemmed shrub**, stems slender and **arching**, to 9 ft. long, rooting at the tips. **LEAVES:** Whorled to opposite, lanceolate, 4–6 in. long. **FLOWERS:** Magenta, usually 5 narrow petals, 0.4–0.6 in. long; 10 stamens, 5 long exserted; borne in **clusters from the upper leaf axils.** July–August. **FRUITS:** Nearly spherical, dark brown capsules, about 0.3 in. across; reddish seeds. **WHERE FOUND:** Sloughs, swamps, and wet soils, often on the bases of trees or on stumps. A mostly Coastal Plain species found from ME to FL and LA, and inland in the Mississippi River Valley to IN and MO. In TN, in Lake, Obion, Rutherford, Coffee, Warren, White, Blount, and Jefferson counties. Infrequent.

NOTES: The genus name *Decodon* means "ten teeth" in reference to the 10-parted calyx. The species name *verticillatus* means "whorled," referring to the leaves and inflorescence. • This plant is also called Swamp Willow Herb, Redroot, Slinkweed, and Water Willow. The seeds are eaten by waterfowl.

NITA R. HEILMAN

Winged Loosestrife
Lythrum alatum

GENERAL: Smooth, erect **wetland perennial herb** to 3 ft. tall with a **4-angled stem. LEAVES:** Lower leaves opposite, upper leaves mostly alternate; lanceolate, to 1.6 in. long, becoming smaller toward the top of the plant. **FLOWERS:** Dainty, **lavender to pale purple**, to 0.5 in. across, **6 petals**; occur in the axils of the upper leaves. July–September. **FRUITS:** Capsules with numerous seeds. **WHERE FOUND:** Swamps and marshes throughout most of the eastern U.S. In TN, from the Eastern Highland Rim westward, also Hamilton and Bradley counties in East TN. Occasional.

NOTES: The genus name *Lythrum* is from the Greek *lythron*, meaning "blood," in reference to the color of the flowers. The species name *alatum* means "winged," referring to the 4-angled stems. • The popular shrub or small tree, Crepe Myrtle (*Lagerstroemia indica*), is in the **Loosestrife Family**. Other members of this family are the source of certain dyes, including henna from the Mignonette Tree (*Lawsonia inermis*), a red dye from Dhataki (*Woodfordia fruticosa*), and a yellow dye from Pacari (*Lafoensia pacari*).

OTTO R. HIRSCH

Purple Loosestrife
Lythrum salicaria*

GENERAL: Stout, erect perennial to 5 ft. tall, with clustered stems from a spindle-shaped rootstock. **LEAVES:** Mostly opposite or whorled, dark green, lanceolate, to 3 in. long, heart-shaped or rounded at the base, becoming smaller toward the top of the plant. **FLOWERS:** Red-purple, showy, usually **6 narrow, wrinkled petals**, 0.3–0.5 in. long; borne in spikes from the axils of the upper leaves. June–September. **FRUITS:** Capsules with numerous seeds. **WHERE FOUND:** Introduced from Eurasia. Wet areas throughout the eastern U.S. Thinly scattered across TN, in Decatur, Sumner, Clay, Warren, Marion, Scott, Roane, and Unicoi counties. Infrequent.

NOTES: Considered a highly invasive weed, this plant is also called Kill Weed and Rosy Strife. Too often seen in cultivation, this Eurasian plant has escaped and become a **devastating pest plant** in northern wetlands. It should not be planted locally because it is a **threat to Tennessee wetlands**. In fact, the Tennessee Department of Agriculture has listed this plant as a "noxious weed." Though it is said that the plants sold in nurseries are sterile, this may not always be the case. This species is known to hybridize with native plants of the *Lythrum* genus, creating even more potential for wetland degradation.

PAUL SOMERS

Enchanter's Nightshade
Circaea lutetiana ssp. *canadensis*

GENERAL: Smooth, unbranched perennial herb, 12–36 in. tall, from a rhizome. **LEAVES:** Opposite, long-stalked, ovate, 2–4 in. long, **shallowly and irregularly toothed**. **FLOWERS:** Numerous, **white** (or pinkish), **2 deeply notched petals** less than 0.2 in. long, 2 reflexed sepals; usually **well spaced** in terminal racemes to 8 in. long; one of only a few plants with 2-petaled flowers. June–August. **FRUITS:** Small, nut-like pods, indehiscent at maturity. **WHERE FOUND:** Rich, moist woods. Scattered throughout the eastern U.S. and TN. Frequent. **SIMILAR SPECIES:** ALPINE ENCHANTER'S NIGHTSHADE (**C. alpina**) only grows to 12 in. tall; **coarsely toothed leaves**, 1.0–2.5 in. long; open **flowers are crowded** at the top of the raceme. Moist, rich woods. A northern plant, extending south at higher elevations to NC and TN. In TN, from the Cumberland Plateau eastward. Infrequent. June–September.

NOTES: The genus name *Circaea* and the common names for these plants are derived from the mythological enchantress, Circe, who allegedly used a poisonous species from this genus in her sorcery.

THOMAS G. BARNES

Fireweed · *Epilobium angustifolium*

GENERAL: Perennial herb, 3–10 ft. tall, usually single-stemmed. **LEAVES:** Numerous, **alternate**, **entire**, 2–6 in. long, **sessile**, lanceolate, pale beneath. **FLOWERS:** Numerous, **magenta to white**, 4 roundish petals, 0.4–0.8 in. long, are short-clawed; 4 purplish sepals; 8 stamens; **4-lobed stigma**; drooping flower buds; borne in a long, spike-like raceme; buds, flowers, and seedpods occur on the plant simultaneously. July–September. **FRUITS:** Narrow, purplish capsules, 1–3 in. long, angle upward; down-tufted seeds are wind dispersed. **WHERE FOUND:** Widespread in open or burned areas in Canada and the western and northeastern U.S. In TN, in high-elevation, burned areas in Carter and Unicoi counties. Rare. *Chamerion angustifolium.* **SIMILAR SPECIES:** PURPLELEAF WILLOW HERB (*E. coloratum*) is a perennial, freely branched, to 3 ft. tall; stem and branches are often purplish, with hairs occurring in lines; leaves mostly **opposite**, **short petioled**, **distinctly toothed**, narrowly lanceolate, and may be marked with purple; numerous, white or pink **flowers about 0.3 in. wide**, **stigma grooved (not lobed)**; seedpods are numerous and angle upwards, with brown seed hairs. Marshes and wet ground from the Great Plains eastward. In TN, from the Western Highland Rim eastward. Frequent. June–September.

NOTES: **Fireweed** is so called because it often invades disturbed areas such as those where fire or logging has recently occurred. • The young leaves and shoots of Fireweed are edible when cooked, and the gelatinous material inside the stalks (pith) can be dried and used for making a type of ale.

Biennial Gaura · *Gaura biennis*

GENERAL: Coarse **winter annual or biennial** to 6.5 ft. tall, commonly hairy, glandular in the inflorescence. **LEAVES:** Alternate, lanceolate, slightly toothed, to 4 in. long and **1 in. wide**. **FLOWERS:** White, turning pink with age, 4 divergent, clawed petals to 0.6 in. long; **sepals reflexed in pairs**; protruding style has a 4-lobed stigma; 8 long, conspicuous stamens have large anthers; flowers are borne on wand-like spikes, 1–8 in. long; **buds are less than 0.8 in. long.** July–October. **FRUITS:** Hard, 4-angled, nut-like pods, 0.2–0.35 in. long, indehiscent and short-hairy. **WHERE FOUND:** Fields, barrens, roadsides, and disturbed areas, from MA to MN, south to GA and MS. Thinly scattered across TN. Occasional. **SIMILAR SPECIES:** SOUTHERN GAURA (*G. longiflora*) is a **perennial** with slender **leaves to 0.4 in. wide**; **flower buds over 0.8 in. long.** pink flowers open near sunset and fade the next day. Open woods, roadsides, and fields, mostly in the midwestern U.S., south to AL and TX. In TN, in Fayette, Hardeman, Madison, and Shelby counties. Rare. May–September.

NOTES: *Gaura* (rhymes with Laura) is from the Greek *gauros*, which means "superb," in reference to the striking flowers; *biennis* means "biennial," indicating that the plant lives for 2 years, usually flowering and producing fruit in the second year. • **Biennial Gaura** is also called **Biennial Beeblossom.** Look for the flowers early in the day, as they wilt rapidly in full sun.

Slender Gaura · *Gaura filipes*

GENERAL: Clumped perennial to 7 ft. tall. **LEAVES:** Numerous, to 3 in. long, linear to linear-oblanceolate, entire or with a few coarse teeth; leaves are crowded in the lower 1/3 to 2/3 of the stem. **FLOWERS:** White, turning pink with maturity, 4 slender, spreading **petals to 0.4 in. long**; protruding style has a 4-lobed stigma; 8 long, reflexed stamens; **sepals separately reflexed**; inflorescence is long, wand-like, and branching with short appressed hairs. August–September. **FRUITS:** Sharply 4-angled pod, 0.2–0.4 in. long, indehiscent and thinly hairy, on a **slender stalk**, 0.1 in. long; 1–2 seeds. **WHERE FOUND:** Barrens, fields, and open woods, from southern IN to SC, south to FL and LA. Thinly spread across TN, mostly in the southern half. Occasional. **SIMILAR SPECIES:** SMALL-FLOWERED GAURA (**G. mollis***) is a soft and downy **annual or biennial** to 6 ft. tall, coarse, erect, and **single-stemmed**; small, white flowers with **petals 0.12 in. long** are borne on 1 or more distinctive, very long, many-flowered spikes. Fields, pastures, and streambanks. A species of the western U.S., now naturalized eastward. Known only from Knox County in TN. Rare. July–October. **G. parviflora**.

NOTES: Slender Gaura is also known as **Slender-Stalked Gaura** and **Slender-Stalked Beeblossom**. It is most easily identified by its unusual flowers, and is the only *Gaura* species with a distinct stalk on both flower and fruit.

DENNIS HORN

Seedbox
Ludwigia alternifolia

GENERAL: Perennial to 4 ft. tall, erect and usually freely branched, from thickened roots. **LEAVES:** Alternate, 2–4 in. long, lanceolate, entire, sparsely hairy, patterned on both sides. **FLOWERS:** Solitary, bright yellow, 0.5–0.75 in. wide; 4 petals, 4 wide, green sepals not reflexed and about the same length as the petals; borne on short peduncles from the upper leaf axils. May–October. **FRUITS:** Cube-shaped capsules ("seedboxes"), about 0.25 in. wide, with 4 narrow wings; capsule is rounded at the base and opens by a terminal pore. **WHERE FOUND:** Marshes, ditches, and wet soil throughout most of the eastern U.S. and TN. Common. **SIMILAR SPECIES:** WINGSTEM WATER PRIMROSE (**L. decurrens**) is an **annual** with a 4-angled stem, commonly 4-winged resulting from the **decurrent leaf bases**; yellow **flowers about 1 in. across**; narrowly pyramidal fruits. Open wet areas from PA to IL, south to FL and TX. Throughout TN. Frequent. June–October.

NOTES: Seedbox gets its name from the almost perfectly box-shaped fruits. It has a 4-petaled flower typical of the Evening Primrose Family. • When touched, shaken, or disturbed, the flowers of Seedbox easily lose their petals. The degree of hairiness (pubescence) varies on the stems and leaves, with some plants being completely smooth (glabrous).

DENNIS HORN

Spindleroot, Hairy Water Primrose
Ludwigia hirtella

DENNIS HORN

GENERAL: Erect perennial herb to 3 ft. tall from fleshy, fibrous roots; plant is densely hairy throughout. **LEAVES:** Alternate, **lanceolate**, up to 2 in. long, entire, rounded at the base and sessile, erect or ascending. **FLOWERS:** Light yellow, 4 rounded **petals to about 0.6 in. long**, 4 stamens; petals exceed sepals; base of the style is enlarged; originate from axils of the upper leaves. June–September. **FRUITS:** Capsules, 4-angled and narrowly winged. **WHERE FOUND:** Open ditches and wet areas from VA and KY, south to FL and TX. In TN, in Fentress, Cumberland, Bledsoe, Van Buren, Warren, Cannon, Franklin, Coffee, and Lewis counties. Infrequent. **SIMILAR SPECIES: NARROWLEAF WATER PRIMROSE (L. linearis)** is a perennial with **linear leaves** to about 0.2 in. wide and 2 in. long; brilliant yellow **flowers to 0.5 in. wide**; cylindric fruits are somewhat widened above. Ditches and wet open areas. A primarily Coastal Plain species. In TN, in Moore, Franklin, Coffee, Warren, Putnam, and Cumberland counties. Infrequent. July–September.

NOTES: Spindleroot is also called **Hairy Ludwigia.** This genus was named after Christian Gottlieb Ludwig (1709–73), professor of botany at the University of Leipzig, Germany. The species name *hirtella* means "hairy," referring to the overall pubescence of the plant. • Another native *Ludwigia* species, **Water Purslane** (**L. palustris**), has been used medicinally to treat asthma, chronic coughs, and tuberculosis.

Creeping Water Primrose
Ludwigia peploides

J. & D. RICHARDSON

GENERAL: Smooth perennial with horizontally creeping or floating stems that root at the nodes, often forming **large, solid mats. LEAVES:** Alternate, to about 3 in. long, lanceolate to obovate, narrowing to a short petiole. **FLOWERS:** Brilliant yellow, **5 petals, 0.4–0.6 in. long**, 10 stamens, anthers less than 0.07 in. long. May–September. **FRUITS:** Smooth, cylindric capsules, 0.8–1.6 in. long. **WHERE FOUND:** Pools, mudflats, and ditches, from NC to southern IN to KS, south to LA and TX. In TN, mostly found in West TN, very thinly scattered elsewhere in the state. Occasional. **SIMILAR SPECIES: SHOWY WATER PRIMROSE (L. uruguayensis)** is **hairy** throughout; flowers with **petals 0.6–1.0 in. long** and anthers 0.1–0.14 in. long. Sluggish streams, pools, and marshes. A typically southern species extending north to TN and NC. In TN, known from Montgomery, Stewart, and Sumner counties. Rare. May–September.

NOTES: Many plants in the *Ludwigia* genus, also known as water primroses and primrose willows, grow immersed in water, in shallow marshy areas, and ditches. They range in size from a few inches to 6 ft. tall. Most have yellow flowers that bloom throughout the season.

JERRY DROWN

Common Evening Primrose
Oenothera biennis

GENERAL: Biennial or short-lived perennial, **to 6 ft. tall**, usually branching only near the top; leafy, rough-hairy, often reddish-stemmed. **LEAVES:** Alternate, sessile, lanceolate, to 8 in. long, crisped, slightly toothed. **FLOWERS:** Light yellow, 4 roundish **petals to 1 in. long**, attached to a **calyx tube** (hypanthium), **1–2 in. long**, 4 reflexed sepals, 8 stamens, X-shaped stigma; borne in a rigid terminal spike; **flowers open at dusk**. June–October. **FRUITS:** Nearly cylindric capsules, 4 times longer than broad. **WHERE FOUND:** Dry, open places in most of the U.S. and southern Canada. Throughout TN. Frequent. **SIMILAR SPECIES: LARGE-FLOWERED EVENING PRIMROSE (O. grandiflora)** has larger, **obovate petals, 1.2–2.4 in. long**. Woods and meadows. A Southern Coastal Plain species known only from Marion County in TN. Rare. May–October.

NOTES: There are many names for **Common Evening Primrose**, some of which refer to its medicinal uses: Cure-All, Fever-Plant, and King's Cure-All. This species is the source of a pain-relieving compound for headaches and a remedy for venereal disease and eruptions of the skin. The seed oil is being used experimentally for treating a wide variety of conditions from migraines to arthritis and alcoholism. The roots, when boiled, are said to be wholesome and nutritious; the young shoots, fruits, and seeds can also be eaten. • Species in the *Oenothera* genus have flowers with 4 showy petals and 4 reflexed sepals, all separated from the ovary by a slender calyx tube (hypanthium), 8 stamens, and a long style with a 4-lobed stigma.

NORVAL ZIEGLER

Sundrops · *Oenothera fruticosa*

GENERAL: Perennial herb, 12–36 in. tall, typically with spreading hairs above. **LEAVES:** Alternate, **lanceolate**, entire, approximately 2.5 in. long. **FLOWERS:** Brilliant yellow, 4 veiny petals, to 1 in. long, notched at the ends, 8 orange stamens; generally several flowers in a dense inflorescence. June–August. **FRUITS:** Strongly ribbed capsules, 0.2–0.4 in. long, about 2x as long as wide. **WHERE FOUND:** Dry to wet, mostly rocky places, thin woods, or open areas in most of the eastern U.S. In TN, mostly from the Western Highland Rim eastward. Frequent. **O. tetragona**. **SIMILAR SPECIES:** THREADLEAF SUNDROPS (**O. linifolia**) is an **annual** to 24 in. tall; dense, **filament-like stem leaves** to 1.5 in. long; yellow **flowers to 0.4 in. wide**, in a long terminal raceme. Rocky ledges and sandy barrens from NC to western FL, west to eastern TX and eastern KS. Thinly scattered across TN. Infrequent. April–June.

NOTES: Sundrops is called **Wild Beet** in West Virginia and has been used as a potherb. • The yellow flowers of Sundrops, unlike most *Oenothera* species, open during the day and close on cloudy days and at night. Other Evening Primrose species, relatives of Sundrops, have flowers that open at night and close around noon the following day.

Cutleaf Evening Primrose
Oenothera laciniata

ED HONICKER

GENERAL: Weak-stemmed **annual or biennial** to 36 in. tall, usually branching from near the base. **LEAVES:** Alternate, lanceolate to oblanceolate, to 3 in. long, **shallowly toothed to deeply lobed.** **FLOWERS:** Yellow (to reddish), sessile, 4 **notched petals, 0.3–0.7 in. long,** reflexed sepals; flowers arise from axils of the upper leaves. May–October. **FRUITS:** Cylindric capsules, 0.8–1.5 in. long, slightly curved and hairy. **WHERE FOUND:** Dry fields, gardens, and waste places throughout the eastern U.S. and TN. Frequent. **SIMILAR SPECIES: LITTLE SUNDROPS (O. perennis)** is a **perennial** to 24 in. tall; lanceolate, petioled leaves to 2.5 in. long; notched, yellow **flowers to 0.4 in. wide** open singly; inflorescence mostly nodding. Wet or dry fields, meadows, and open woods. A mostly northeastern species extending south in the uplands to TN and SC. In TN, in Johnson, Morgan, and Scott counties. Rare. June–August.

NOTES: The genus name *Oenothera* is derived from the Greek *oinos*, "wine," and *thera*, "pursuing" or "imbibing." The story goes that when the root was eaten, a person had the capacity to drink a greater quantity of wine. Another story tells that the roots were combined with wine.

Missouri Evening Primrose
Oenothera macrocarpa

GENERAL: Perennial herb, either with no aboveground stem (leaves and flowers arising from the rootstock) or with a trailing to erect stem to 24 in. long. **LEAVES:** Linear-lanceolate, to 4 in. long, entire, narrowed at both ends; alternate on aboveground stem. **FLOWERS:** Exceptionally **large, solitary, yellow, 4 broad, obovate petals to 3 in. long,** shallowly notched, attached to a slender **calyx tube** (hypanthium), **3–4 in. long;** open at dusk and wilt rapidly upon morning sun. May–July. **FRUITS:** Capsules, 2–3 in. long; **pods are 4-winged** with wings up to 1 in. across. **WHERE FOUND:** Dry, rocky barrens and prairies, in calcareous soil. A mostly western species found in Rutherford and Wilson counties in TN. Rare. *O. missouriensis.*

DAVID DUHL

NOTES: The species name *macrocarpa* means "big fruit," lending another common name, **Bigfruit Evening Primrose.** This plant is often cultivated as a showy ornamental.

• The flowers of this species open at dusk in advance of the night. It is one of the primroses that is synchronized with the nocturnal habits of their pollinators, Sphinx Moths. It is not uncommon for a plant that opens at night to send out a fragrant scent only at that time to attract pollinators.

LUIS C. PRIETO, JR.

Showy Evening Primrose
Oenothera speciosa*

GENERAL: Erect to spreading short-lived perennial to 24 in. tall. **LEAVES:** Alternate, oblong-lanceolate to linear, to 3 in. long; lower leaves irregularly toothed or narrowly lobed, especially near the base. **FLOWERS:** White to pink with a yellow center, 1.5–3.0 in. wide, 4 broad, notched **petals with prominent veins**; flower buds nodding; several flowers from the upper leaf axils. March–August. **FRUITS:** Ellipsoid capsules, slightly angled or winged, 8-ribbed. **WHERE FOUND:** Introduced to TN. Prairies, plains, roadsides, and waste places, mostly from MO to KS, south to TX; naturalized eastward. In Middle TN, also in Shelby, Hardeman, McNairy, and Madison counties in West TN, and McMinn, Loudon, Blount, and Knox counties in East TN. Occasional.

NOTES: This plant flowers continuously from March to August and tolerates extreme heat, sun exposure, and a wide soil pH range (5.0–6.5 or higher), making it a hardy, drought-resistant, and showy ornamental. However, use caution, as this species has a tendency to take over a garden.

DENNIS HORN

Three-Lobed Evening Primrose
Oenothera triloba

GENERAL: Annual to short-lived perennial, 3–5 in. tall, unusual in having **no aboveground stems**, with the leaves and flowers arising from a stout rootstock. **LEAVES:** In a radial cluster separated by very short internodes; oblanceolate and **pinnatifid** to nearly the midrib, to 8 in. long. **FLOWERS:** Pale yellow, turning white with age, 4 obovate petals to 1 in. long; **flowers open at dusk**. May–June. **FRUITS:** Hard, woody capsules are 4-winged, long-persistent, grouped into a "cone" at ground level. **WHERE FOUND:** Dry, often calcareous soils and barrens from NY and VA, west to KS and TX. In Middle TN (especially the Central Basin), also Knox, Blount, and Hamilton counties in East TN. Occasional.

NOTES: This plant is also known as **Stemless Evening Primrose** owing to its lack of upright stems. • Like **Missouri Evening Primrose** (p. 189), the flowers of **Three-Lobed Evening Primrose** are timed to open for their nocturnal pollinators, which include Sphinx Moths. • All evening primroses originate from the Western Hemisphere. Among the first recorded collections of American native plants was the garden of John Bartram (1699–1777), a Quaker gardener and botanist. Established near Philadelphia, PA, in 1729, his collection included 12 different types of evening primroses.

Maryland Meadow Beauty
Rhexia mariana

GENERAL: Perennial herb to 24 in. tall; weakly square stem is **glandular-hairy**. **LEAVES:** Opposite, hairy, lanceolate, typically 1–2 in. long and ⅓ as wide, 3-nerved, short-petioled; on close examination, leaves have spots of red pigment throughout the season, most noticeable in fall; each tooth on the leaf margins has a red hair projecting from it. **FLOWERS:** Pale pink, 4 slightly recurved petals, 0.5–0.7 in. long, 8 stamens; **prominent, curved, yellow anthers**. May–October. **FRUITS:** Sticky capsules, somewhat hairy and **urn-shaped**, with a long neck that is sometimes longer than the body. **WHERE FOUND:** Wet marshes and fields throughout most of the eastern U.S. and TN. Common.

NOTES: Meadow beauties can be mistaken for evening primroses because of the 4 large petals that surround a showy cluster of 8 long, yellow stamens. However, they lack the evening primroses' characteristic cross-shaped stigma at the tip of the pistil. Another method of telling these species apart is to look for the unique urn-shaped fruits that appear only on meadow beauties.

DENNIS HORN

Virginia Meadow Beauty
Rhexia virginica

GENERAL: Perennial to 24 in. tall rising from thick, spongy rhizomes; **4-angled stem** is simple or lightly branched, somewhat hairy with slender wings. **LEAVES:** Opposite, ovate or lanceolate, usually 1–3 in. long and ⅓ to ½ as wide, 3–5-nerved, sparsely hairy. **FLOWERS:** Rose pink to purplish; 4 recurved petals, 0.6–0.8 in. long, 8 stamens; **prominent, curved yellow anthers**. July–September. **FRUITS:** Sticky, urn-shaped capsules with large teeth; neck is shorter than body. **WHERE FOUND:** Wet marshes and fields throughout the eastern U.S., southeastern Canada, and TN. Frequent.

NOTES: The genus name *Rhexia* is from the Greek *rhexio*, meaning "to rupture." • The tuberous, thickened rootstock is edible and can be eaten raw; the young leaves are sweetish and slightly sour, and can be eaten raw added to salads. • Meadow beauties have also been called Deer Grass, Handsome Harry, and Robin Hood. • Except for *Rhexia*, most genera in the Meadow Beauty Family are tropical.

OTTO R. HIRSCH

Bastard Toadflax
Comandra umbellata

GENERAL: Perennial, branched, herbaceous **root parasite**, 8–15 in. tall, from a rhizome. **LEAVES:** Alternate, entire, narrowly oblong to oval, 1–3 in. long, blunt or nearly acute, green above, paler beneath; mid and lateral veins are yellowish. **FLOWERS:** Perfect, calyx with **5 whitish, petal-like lobes** about 0.1 in. long, petals absent, 5 stamens; borne in **corymbs** of 3–5 flowers, alternate in the axils of the upper leaves, **appearing as panicles.** April–May. **FRUITS:** Spherical, fleshy drupes, about 0.25 in. wide. **WHERE FOUND:** Dry, open woods and roadsides. Widespread in North America. Scattered across TN. Frequent.

NOTES: The genus name *Comandra* comes from the Greek *komê*, meaning "hair," and *andros*, meaning "man," referring to the tufts of calyx-lobe hair attached to the stamens. • The fully-grown, but scarcely ripe, green "nuts" (fruits) were used as food by Native Americans. The seeds are sweet and oily.

DENNIS HORN

Allegheny Spurge
Pachysandra procumbens

GENERAL: Low-growing perennial herb with stems to 12 in. long, often decumbent at the base. **LEAVES:** Alternate, **mottled, evergreen**, long-stalked, crowded on the stem, broadly ovate, 1.5–3.0 in. long, scalloped along the upper edge; new leaf shoots at a very early stage resemble **Indian Pipe (p. 128). FLOWERS:** Small; white stamens and pistils on separate flowers; **petals and sepals absent;** inflorescence is a **spike**, 2–4 in. long, the **flowers grouped tightly** on low stalks from the previous year's growth. March–April. **FRUITS:** Hairy capsules, typically fleshy, with 3 horn-like structures. **WHERE FOUND:** In rich woods, usually on slopes in calcareous soils from KY to NC, south to western FL and southern LA. In Middle and East TN. Frequent.

JERRY DROWN

NOTES: The genus name *Pachysandra* comes from the Greek *pachys*, "thick," and *andros*, "stamen," in reference to the thick stamens of these plants. • The similar **Japanese Spurge (*P. terminalis**)** has narrow leaves and terminal inflorescences and is used as an ornamental ground cover. It sometimes may be found growing wild in the northeastern U.S.

Prostrate Spurge, Spotted Sandmat · *Chamaesyce maculata*

GENERAL: Prostrate annual weed, often forming **flat, circular mats**, 12–24 in. across; stems hairy, usually dark red, **sap milky. LEAVES:** Opposite, sessile, oblong, about 0.4 in. long, dark green with purple blotches, minute, inconspicuous teeth on margins. **FLOWERS:** Small, inconspicuous "flowers," each with 4–5 white or pink, petal-like attachments below the single spherical ovary; borne in an **involucral inflorescence** (cyathium). June–October. **FRUITS:** Tiny, 3-sided capsules; 4-angled seeds. **WHERE FOUND:** Gardens, lawns, and waste places throughout the eastern U.S. and TN, but less frequent in West TN. Common. *Euphorbia maculata, E. supina.* **SIMILAR SPECIES:** EYEBANE (*C. nutans*) is a somewhat **larger, more upright plant; larger, reddish** "flowers" with white margins. Dry or moist soils in waste places throughout the eastern U.S. and TN. Common. June–October. *E. nutans, E. preslii.*

NOTES: The name "spurge" comes from the Old French *espurgier*, which means "to purge," alluding to one of this plant's medicinal usages. **Prostrate Spurge** is commonly called **Creeping Spurge** and **Milk Purslane** for its milky sap. Other less common names that refer to its medicinal values include Emetic Weed, Eyebright, and Wart Weed. It also was reputedly used to treat inflammations of the eye. • Prostrate Spurge and **Eyebane** often occur together.

Woolly Croton

Croton capitatus

GENERAL: Erect, silvery to **tan-colored annual**, 6–24 in. tall, scarcely branched above, covered with dense, **branching hairs. LEAVES:** Alternate, petioled, mostly oblong, 1.5–4.0 in. long. **FLOWERS:** Numerous, **diminutive, whitish**; staminate above with 5 petals and sepals, pistillate below and without petals; borne in a compact terminal inflorescence about 1 in. wide. June–October. **FRUITS:** Capsules, usually with 3 glossy brown seeds. **WHERE FOUND:** Most of the southeastern U.S. In glades and barrens on shallow limestone soils in the western 1/2 of TN. Occasional.

NOTES: This plant is also called **Hogwort.** • It is an important food source for doves and quails and is sometimes browsed by deer. However, it is considered **poisonous to cattle.** • The Spurge Family, to which this plant belongs, provides rubber (from *Hevea brasiliensis*), castor oil (from *Ricinus communis*), and food (from *Manihot esculenta*, the Cassava plant, used to make tapioca).

DENNIS HORN

Prairie Tea
Croton monanthogynus

GENERAL: **Annual** to 12 in. tall, branched above; somewhat weedy tendency, usually several plants growing together. **LEAVES:** Alternate, **entire**, ovate to oval, 0.5–1.0 in. long, blunt or obtuse, rounded at the base, **silvery green**, covered with **branched hairs.** **FLOWERS:** Minute, **tawny to whitish**; male (staminate) flowers have 3–5 tiny petals and sepals; female (pistillate) flowers have 5 sepals, petals absent; both flower types grow together in a short inflorescence. June–October. **FRUITS:** 1-seeded capsules. **WHERE FOUND:** In glades and barrens throughout most of the southeastern U.S. and TN. Frequent. **SIMILAR SPECIES:** TOOTHED CROTON (*C. glandulosus* var. *septentrionalis*) has **coarsely toothed leaves** with 2 saucer-shaped glands at the base. Dry, sandy soils. Found east of the Rocky Mountains. Thinly scattered across TN. Occasional. May–October.

NOTES: Although the common name indicates that this plant could be used as a tea, this should be avoided. Though some *Croton* species were used medicinally by Native Americans to induce vomiting, and Chaparral Tea (*C. corymbulosus*) was used as a bitter tea, many plants in this genus are considered **poisonous**. **Prairie Tea** has been reported to cause skin irritation on contact.

Wood Spurge • *Euphorbia commutata*

GENERAL: Smooth, **almost succulent** perennial, 8–16 in. tall, with **reddish stems** often branched near the base. **LEAVES:** Stem leaves alternate, numerous, mostly obovate below, about 0.6 in. long; upper leaves sessile, ovate; inflorescence leaves are smaller, often fused at the base. **FLOWERS:** Minute, without sepals and petals; **crescent-shaped, yellow glands in the involucre give the "flowers" their color**; borne in an umbel-like arrangement, usually with 3 primary forks that are further divided; involucral inflorescence (cyathium) at the end of each floral branch. April–June. **FRUITS:** Smooth, 3-lobed capsules, 0.12 in. long; gray seeds. **WHERE FOUND:** Moist, rich woods from PA to MN, south to FL and TX. In TN, from the Western Highland Rim eastward. Frequent.

NOTES: Thirteen native and introduced species of *Euphorbia* are found in TN. The specialized involucral inflorescence, called the "cyathium," which simulates a single flower, contains several staminate flowers (each consisting of a single stamen) at the outer edge of the involucral cup and a stalked, solitary pistillate flower (consisting of a single pistil having a 3-celled ovary) attached to the inside of the cup. • Some *Euphorbia* species may cause **poisoning** if ingested.

OTTO R. HIRSCH

Flowering Spurge
Euphorbia corollata

GENERAL: Conspicuous, erect perennial, 20–40 in. tall, smooth to coarsely hairy, branched numerously above (like an umbel or a panicle); **milky sap.** **LEAVES:** Stem leaves are alternate, linear or elliptic, 1.2–1.5 in. long, below the numerous branches; leaves at stem branches are whorled. **FLOWERS:** Small "flowers" consist of a cup (cyathium) lined with usually 5 **showy, white "petals" (appendages)**; "flowers" terminate the many branches, forming a loose cyme up to 12 in. wide. July–September. **FRUITS:** 3-lobed capsules, central in the "cup" and stalked; shallowly pitted seeds. **WHERE FOUND:** Fields, roadsides, barrens, and open woods. Widespread over the eastern U.S. and TN. Common.

JERRY DROWN

NOTES: This plant is also known as Apple Root and Wild Hippo. Other names, such as Emetic Root, Go Quick, and Purging Root reflect this plant's medicinal use, with a doctor reporting (in 1817) that it "must undoubtedly be ranked among the most efficient medicines of the evacuating class." The leaves of this species reportedly were used by Native Americans as a tea to treat diabetes • Use caution when handling this plant as the milky juice may cause **blistering** upon contact with skin.

Wild Poinsettia, Fire-on-the-Mountain
Euphorbia cyathophora

GENERAL: Smooth, erect **annual** to 36 in. tall, usually branched. **LEAVES:** Typically alternate, highly variable, entire, serrate to lobed, linear to broadly oblong to ovate; **upper leaves typically lobed**, with a **reddish** or sometimes white **marking** at the base, giving the plant its color. **FLOWERS:** Actual flowers, like other *Euphorbia* species, are inconspicuous and without petals or sepals; clusters of **greenish involucres** each have a solitary, 2-lipped, cup-shaped gland that is typically wider than high. June–October. **FRUITS:** Smooth, 3-lobed capsules, about 0.25 in. across. **WHERE FOUND:** Moist soil in shady areas, from MN, IN, and VA, south to FL, TX, and CA. In TN, recorded only from Davidson and Shelby counties, but likely more common. Rare. *E. heterophylla.* **SIMILAR SPECIES:** TOOTHED SPURGE (*E. dentata*) has leaves that are mostly paired and **not marked or blotched.** Dry soil and roadsides from NY, IA, and CO southward. In the eastern ⅔ of TN. Frequent.

DENNIS HORN

NOTES: The genus *Euphorbia* is named for Euphorbes, the personal physician of King Juba of Numidia, about 2000 years ago; *cyathophora* means "cup bearing," in reference to the cup-shaped gland of the involucre. • **Wild Poinsettia** is cometimes called Painted Leaf. • The somewhat similar Christmas Poinsettia (*E. pulcherrima*) is a native of Mexico and Central America and is cultivated as an ornamental.

NITA R. HEILMAN

Snow-on-the-Mountain
*Euphorbia marginata**

GENERAL: Erect annual, 12–30 in. tall, densely softly hairy and highly branched above. **LEAVES:** Alternate stem leaves are sessile, typically broadly ovate to elliptic, 1.5–4.0 in. long; smaller **inflorescence leaves are outlined with white or entirely white**. **FLOWERS:** Cymes crowded with hairy involucres that have 5 unevenly fringed lobes and **5 white appendages**. July–November. **FRUITS:** 3-lobed capsules with brownish, warty seeds. **WHERE FOUND:** Waste places. A mostly western species introduced eastward as a cultivar. In TN, in Stewart, Montgomery, Knox, and Blount counties. Rare.

NOTES: The juice of this plant is **toxic** and can cause redness, swelling, and blistering of the skin on contact. A story is told that the sap is such an irritant that it was once used in Texas for branding cattle. Bees that visit the flowers often produce **poisonous honey**. Most *Euphorbia* species contain an acrid milky sap that causes **dermatitis** in susceptible individuals. It has been reported that the sap of Leafy Spurge (*E. esula*) and Sun Spurge (*E. helioscopia*), which were introduced from Europe, can cause blindness if it comes in contact with eyes.

DENNIS HORN

Cumberland Spurge, Mercury Spurge · *Euphorbia mercurialina*

GENERAL: Perennial, 8–15 in. tall, the stem branched above; milky sap. **LEAVES:** Lower stem leaves are alternate, small, scale-like; leaves of branches are whorled or opposite, narrowly elliptic, 1–3 in. long, with fine hairs on the margins. **FLOWERS:** "Flowers" on long peduncles have a slender ring of **5 white-margined, green "petals" (appendages)** terminating the central stem or each branch at each fork; floral cup, about 0.3 in. across, has a number of small staminate flowers (single stamens) with **yellow anthers**; solitary pistillate flower is borne on a stalk extending from the center of the cup. April–September. **FRUITS:** 3-lobed capsules. **WHERE FOUND:** Rich woods in the Cumberland Plateau region from southern KY to northern AL and northwestern GA. In Middle and East TN. Frequent.

NOTES: *Euphorbia* species have colorful "appendages" on the outer edge of the involucral cup that look like petals. They attract pollinators to the tiny flowers in the center of the floral cup. • Many spiny succulents that are native to the deserts of Africa and Asia are in the *Euphorbia* genus, though they can be difficult to identify and may be mistaken for plants in the Cactus Family (Cactaceae).

New Jersey Tea · *Ceanothus americanus*

GENERAL: Clumpy, **low shrub to 3 ft. tall**, dying partly back annually. **LEAVES:** Alternate, ovate, 1.5–3.0 in. long, 3-nerved, glandular-serrate on the margins, rounded to almost heart-shaped at the base. **FLOWERS: White**, tiny, 5 wide-spreading petals, 0.05 in. long; borne in **axillary or terminal panicles** on branches of the current season; panicles are cylindric to ovoid, 0.6–1.6 in. across, on peduncles 2–10 in. long. May–August. **FRUITS:** Fleshy, 3-lobed capsules. **WHERE FOUND:** Open woods, roadsides, and waste areas throughout the eastern U.S. and TN. Common.

NOTES: This plant is **conspicuous in flower** and has a subtle, **sweet aroma.** • The fresh or dried leaves were once used in the U.S. as a substitute for the heavily taxed oriental tea that precipitated the Boston Tea Party of colonial days. • The rootbark of this plant has been used as an astringent and a sedative. • Plants in the *Ceanothus* genus are also called wild lilacs because of the perfumed fragrance of the flowers, and they make good honey plants. The flowers foam into a lather when crushed in water.

JERRY DROWN

Common Yellow Flax
Linum medium var. *texanum*

GENERAL: Erect, delicate perennial with solitary stems to 3 ft. tall, the upper branches stiffly ascending. **LEAVES:** Opposite or alternate, 0.5–1.0 in. long, smooth, entire, lowest leaves spatulate, upper leaves narrowing to become linear or linear-elliptical. **FLOWERS: Yellow**, about 0.6 in. wide, **5 petals; inner sepals contain several prominently stalked glands;** inflorescence is a **corymb**. June–September. **FRUITS:** Capsules, typically splitting into 10 segments. **WHERE FOUND:** Upland woods, fields, and barrens in most of the eastern U.S. Throughout most of TN. Frequent. **SIMILAR SPECIES:** VIRGINIA YELLOW FLAX (**L. virginianum**) has **divergent inflorescence branches; inner sepals** typically have several diminutive, **sessile glands.** Upland woods and clearings in most of the eastern U.S. and TN, except the Coastal Plain and the Central Basin. Occasional. June–September. COMMON FLAX (**L. usitatissimum***) is an annual to 3 ft. tall; **showy, blue flowers** about 1 in. across. Introduced from Europe. Escaped to fields and roadsides throughout the U.S. In TN, in Shelby, Davidson, and Knox counties. Rare. May–September.

THOMAS G. BARNES

NOTES: The seeds of **Common Flax** are used to make linseed oil, while fibers of the stem have been used in the production of linen cloth since at least 3000 BCE. This plant has also been used as a poultice for skin inflammations and sunburns. • The 5 flax species that are native to Tennessee are all yellow-flowered perennials.

DENNIS HORN

Drumheads, Crossleaf Milkwort
Polygala cruciata

GENERAL: Erect **annual** to 12 in. tall, weakly branched. **LEAVES:** Usually in **whorls of 4**, linear to oblanceolate or narrowly elliptic, entire, 0.5–1.5 in. long. **FLOWERS:** Diminutive, **pinkish**; packed into a **dense, cylindric raceme**, 0.4–2.4 in. long and 0.4–0.6 in. wide, forming a compact head **similar to clover**. July–September. **FRUITS:** Capsules with black seeds; seeds usually have an aril with 2 lobes. **WHERE FOUND:** Marshes and meadows. Along the Coastal Plain from ME to FL and TX, extending inland from OH to MN. In TN, from the Eastern Highland Rim eastward, also Lawrence and Lewis counties. Occasional.

NOTES: The genus name *Polygala* is from the Greek *poly*, meaning "much," and *gala*, for "milk," in reference to the reputation that these plants increased the secretion of milk of nursing mothers and livestock. The species name *cruciata* is a reference to the cross-shaped whorl of four leaves. • *Polygala* flowers have 3 small outer sepals and 2 larger inner sepals or "wings" that are colored and petal-like. The corolla has 2 upper petals and a keel-shaped lower petal that is crested on the back. The petals are fused to the filaments at the base to form a tube. • There are 12 *Polygala* species listed for TN.

DENNIS HORN

Curtiss' Milkwort • *Polygala curtissii*

GENERAL: Erect **annual** to 16 in. tall, freely branched. **LEAVES:** Alternate, linear, linear-oblong, or narrowly oblanceolate, to 0.8 in. long and 0.15 in. wide. **FLOWERS:** Diminutive, **pink to whitish, yellow-tipped keel and upper petals**; occur in a **compact but loose raceme**, 0.4–0.8 in. long and **0.3–0.5 in. wide**, with the buds forming a small cone at the apex of the inflorescence; bracts endure after lower flowers mature and fall away. June–September. **FRUITS:** Capsules with black, hairy seeds; seeds have an aril with 2 inconspicuous lobes. **WHERE FOUND:** Dry soils. From DE to OH, south to SC and MS. In TN, from the Eastern Highland Rim eastward, also Lawrence, Lewis, Dickson, Henry, Carroll, and Fayette counties. Frequent. **SIMILAR SPECIES:** NUTTALL'S MILKWORT (*P. nuttallii*) is smaller and more slender, with stems to 12 in. tall; racemes less than 0.25 in. wide. Dry soils from MA to GA, west to AR. In TN, only in Coffee and Hickman counties. Rare. July–September.

NOTES: The open flower heads with mature flowers appearing loose, and the alternate leaves are distinctive features of **Curtiss' Milkwort**.

Field Milkwort (p. 200) is similar, but has much more compact flower heads without individually distinct flowers, and there is no yellow on the keel or petals.

Pink Milkwort · *Polygala incarnata*

GENERAL: Erect annual to 24 in. tall, with weakly branched, narrow, smooth, glaucous stems. **LEAVES: Alternate**, linear, ascending, to 0.5 in. long. **FLOWERS: Rose purple**, 0.3–0.4 in. long, corolla is nearly 3 times longer than the petal-like wings; borne in a **slender, compact raceme**; flowers open from the bottom, only a few at a time. June–August. **FRUITS:** Capsules with black seeds; aril on the seed is confined to the base. **WHERE FOUND:** Dry fields and barrens throughout most of the eastern U.S. Thinly scattered in West and Middle TN. Occasional. **SIMILAR SPECIES: WHORLED MILKWORT (*P. verticillata*)** usually has **lower leaves in whorls**; greenish white or **pinkish white flowers** in a slender, **conical raceme**. Moist areas, grasslands, and woods in the eastern U.S. Widespread across TN. Frequent. July–October.

NOTES: The species name *incarnata* means "flesh-colored," in reference to the color of the flowers, which resembles flushed cheeks. • **Pink Milkwort** is also called **Procession Flower** and **Rogation Flower**. In the Catholic Church, Rogation Sunday is the fifth Sunday after Easter, followed by Rogation Week, the time when this plant is typically in full flower. Traditionally, the flowers were woven into garlands and carried in church processions.

NITA R. HEILMAN

Dwarf Milkwort, Candyroot · *Polygala nana*

GENERAL: Erect biennial to 6 in. tall. **LEAVES:** Typically in a **basal rosette**, **spatulate**, entire, 1–2 in. long; stem leaves smaller, alternate, and few. **FLOWERS:** Small, **yellow**, petal-like wings up to 0.3 in. long; borne in a **compact raceme** 0.4–1.4 in. long and 0.5–0.8 in. wide. March–October. **FRUITS:** Capsules with black, hairy seeds; seeds have a 2-lobed aril. **WHERE FOUND:** Moist, open, sandy areas or pine barrens. A southern species extending north into TN and NC. In TN, known from Rhea and Warren counties. Rare.

NOTES: The species name *nana* means "dwarf," in reference to the diminutive size of both the flowers and the plant itself. It is also called **Bachelor's Button**. • The **Milkwort Family** includes herbs and woody plants that grow in a wide variety of surroundings on every continent, except Antarctica. In many *Polygala* species, the inflorescence is a tight cluster of flowers that form a compact, cylindric head, somewhat like that of a clover.

KURT EMMANUELE

Gaywings
Polygala paucifolia

GENERAL: Perennial herb, 3–6 in. tall, occurring in colonies. **LEAVES:** Stems have alternate, scale-like leaves near the base, becoming oval, 0.6–1.6 in. long near the apex. **FLOWERS:** Showy, **rose purple** to white, obovate **wings to about 0.6 in. long**, fringe-tipped corolla tube is about the same length as the wings; borne in a short terminal raceme or corymb of 1–4 flowers. April–May.

FRUITS: Capsules; brown seeds have a 3-lobed aril. **WHERE FOUND:** Moist, rich woods. A northeastern species extending south in the mountains to TN and GA. In TN, from the Cumberland Plateau eastward. Occasional.

NOTES: The species name *paucifolia* means "few-leaved." • The flowers of this plant resemble birds in flight, giving rise to the alternate common name **Bird-on-the-Wing**. • All *Polygala* flowers have 3 petals that form a tube and are flanked by 2 petal-colored sepals called wings. This is most notable in **Gaywings**, but other milkworts have these characteristics as well, although in tinier versions. These flowers have a pollination mechanism that is activated when an insect lands on the fringed bottom petal.

Field Milkwort
Polygala sanguinea

GENERAL: Erect **annual**, 4–16 in. tall, branched above. **LEAVES:** Alternate, linear, or narrowly elliptic, 0.5–1.5 in. long. **FLOWERS:** White to pinkish, **wings are 0.12–0.2 in. long, 2x as long as the corolla; bracts endure** as the lower flowers mature and fall; occur in a nearly **flat-topped**, compact, tight, **cylindric raceme**, 0.4–0.8 in. long and 0.4 in. wide. July–September. **FRUITS:** Capsules with black, hairy seeds; seeds have a 2-lobed aril. **WHERE FOUND:** Fields, barrens, and meadows from Nova Scotia to MN, south to GA and TX. Scattered throughout most of TN. Occasional. **SIMILAR SPECIES:** MARYLAND MILKWORT (*P. mariana*) has bracts that fall early with the flowers; **corolla is almost as long as the wings**. Dry soil. A mostly Coastal Plain species found from NJ to FL and TX, and inland to KY. In TN, known presently from Bradley, Decatur, and Hardin counties, and historically from Franklin, Lawrence, McNairy, Montgomery, and Wayne counties. Rare. June–September.

NOTES: Field Milkwort is also called **Blood Milkwort** and **Purple Milkwort**. More than one flower color is often present on this plant. • **Curtiss' Milkwort** (p. 198) is similar to **Field Milkwort**, but the raceme is pointed (conical) on top.

Seneca Snakeroot · *Polygala senega*

MIRIAM WEINSTEIN

GENERAL: Perennial, to 20 in. tall, with several unbranched stems arising from a single base. **LEAVES:** Alternate, narrowly lanceolate, 1–3 in. long, on the upper stem becoming smaller toward the base. **FLOWERS:** Tiny, greenish white; elliptic wings, about 0.15 in. long, exceed the corolla; borne in a loosely compact raceme, 0.6–1.6 in. long and 0.3 in. across. May–June. **FRUITS:** Capsules with black seeds; seeds have 1-lobed aril. **WHERE FOUND:** Dry or moist woods and barrens throughout most of the eastern U.S. and southern Canada. In TN, from the Western Highland Rim eastward. Frequent. **SIMILAR SPECIES:** BOYKIN'S MILKWORT (*P. boykinii*) has longer, narrower racemes; majority of **leaves** occur in whorls. On barrens. From TN, south to FL and LA. In TN, known from Bedford and Rutherford counties. Rare. March–August.

NOTES: **Seneca Snakeroot** has a long history of medicinal use. Native Americans used it as a diuretic, sweat inducer, to regulate menses, and to treat heart problems. It was also used to treat asthma, coughs, pneumonia, and pulmonary conditions. The roots contain methyl salicylate and were used to relieve pain and treat rheumatism. However, this native North American plant is more widely used for these purposes in Japan and Germany than in the U.S.

Illinois Wood Sorrel · *Oxalis illinoensis*

OTTO R. HIRSCH

GENERAL: Showy, **tuberous perennial** herb, 12–36 in. tall, with stems that are erect, simple, or sparingly branched; colonial from **runners** (stolons). **LEAVES:** Alternate, trifoliolate with **shamrock-like leaflets**, up to 2 in. wide, usually with a **shallow terminal notch** and **no colored margin**. **FLOWERS:** Yellow, 5 petals, 0.5–0.75 in. long; cyme-like inflorescence often same height as leaves. May–June. **FRUITS:** Longitudinally dehiscent capsules; partitions contain red seeds. **WHERE FOUND:** Rich calcareous soils of the Interior Low Plateau in southern IL and IN, western KY, and Middle TN. Occasional. **SIMILAR SPECIES:** LARGE YELLOW WOOD SORREL (*O. grandis*) is colonial from stout **rhizomes**; **leaflets have narrow, reddish brown margins** and a **prominent terminal notch**; flowers usually extend above the leaves. Widespread in rich, more acidic soils from PA to IN, south to GA and MS. In TN, from the Cumberland Plateau eastward. Occasional. May–June.

NOTES: The genus name *Oxalis* is from the Greek *oxys* for "sharp or sour," in reference to the flavor of the leaves, which contain sour-tasting oxalic acid. • Plants of this genus have leaf blades divided into 3 leaflets, each notched and heart-shaped, forming a "shamrock." The leaflets fold down at times, especially at night, as if protecting the plant. The flowers are radially symmetric with 5 separate petals, often notched. At maturity, the fruit capsules open explosively when touched. Seven species are found in TN.

Mountain Wood Sorrel
Oxalis montana

GENERAL: Low, stemless perennial, 3–6 in. tall, from a slender rhizome. **LEAVES:** All basal, long-stalked, in a whorl of **3 heart-shaped leaflets, resembling clover. FLOWERS:** 5 white petals heavily veined with pink with a yellow spot at the base, notched at the tip (sometimes quite deeply), 0.5 in. long; occur singly on stalks 3–6 in. long. May–August. **FRUITS:** Longitudinally dehiscent capsules, tapered to a point; seeds have a large basal aril that aids in seed dispersal. **WHERE FOUND:** Rich northern woods, especially spruce-fir forests, from southeastern Canada southward in the mountains to northern GA. In TN, in the Blue Ridge Mountains of East TN and the northern Cumberland Plateau counties. Infrequent. **O. acetosella.**

NOTES: Sorrel is German for "sour," which refers to the pleasantly sour taste of the leaves. Wood sorrels are commonly called sour grasses and sour clovers. • Being rich in vitamin C, the leaves are a popular addition to salads and have been used in the past to treat scurvy. In recent times, however, it has been discovered that ingesting too much oxalic acid, the ingredient responsible for the sourness, inhibits calcium absorption, so wood sorrels should be taken in moderation.

DAVID KOCHER

Price's Wood Sorrel
Oxalis priceae

GENERAL: Showy perennial, 4–12 in. tall, normally hairy and much-branched below. **LEAVES:** Alternate, **3 shamrock-like leaflets,** each 0.25–0.6 in. wide. **FLOWERS:** 5 yellow petals are **red near the base,** 0.5–0.8 in. long; umbel-like inflorescence scarcely surpasses the leaves. April–May. **FRUITS:** Longitudinally dehiscent, hairy capsules; seeds have a large basal aril that aids in seed dispersal. **WHERE FOUND:** Open calcareous areas from KY, south to FL and MS. In TN, in the limestone barrens and cedar glades of the Central Basin in Giles, Maury, Marshall, Bedford, Rutherford, Wilson, Davidson, and Sumner counties, also Cocke County in East TN. Infrequent. **O. macrantha.**

NOTES: This plant is also known as **Tufted Yellow Wood Sorrel.** Since the flowers open around Easter, it is sometimes called Alleluia "because it appeareth about Easter when Alleluia is sung again." • Iron Cross Oxalis (*O. deppei*), native to Mexico, is cultivated for its edible tubers.

DENNIS HORN

Common Yellow Wood Sorrel
Oxalis stricta

GENERAL: Perennial to 15 in. tall, highly variable and **weedy**; stems hairy, **erect or reclining, but not creeping**. **LEAVES:** Alternate, 0.4–0.8 in. wide, 3 heart-shaped leaflets form a **shamrock-type leaf**; long petioles angle upward. **FLOWERS:** Funnel-shaped, **yellow**, 5 distinct petals about 0.25 in. long; cyme or umbel-like inflorescence contains up to 9 flowers per node. April–September. **FRUITS:** Longitudinally dehiscent, hairy capsules are cylindric, pointed, 0.4–1.0 in. long, and generally angle upward; seeds have a large basal aril that aids in seed dispersal. **WHERE FOUND:** Cosmopolitan weed found throughout the U.S. and TN. Common. *O. dillenii*, *O. europaea*, *O. filipes*, *O. florida*, *O. fontana*. **SIMILAR SPECIES:** CREEPING WOOD SORREL (*O. corniculata**) has **trailing stems that root at the nodes**; purplish stems and leaves. Introduced from the tropics. Now an abundant weed in the southeastern U.S. and in greenhouses. In TN, recorded from Hardin, Davidson, and Polk counties. April–October. *O. repens*.

DENNIS HORN

NOTES: Common Yellow Wood Sorrel is also called **Sourgrass**. • **Creeping Wood Sorrel** has been used to make tea to treat fevers, urinary infections, and scurvy. Historically, the leaves were chewed to treat nausea, mouth sores, and sore throats. However, caution should be used because when taken in large doses, this plant and others in the *Oxalis* genus are **poisonous**.

Violet Wood Sorrel · *Oxalis violacea*

GENERAL: Low, colonial, **stemless perennial**, 4–8 in. tall, from a bulbous base and slender stolons. **LEAVES:** Basal, smooth, trifoliolate; leaflets 0.25–0.5 in. long, notched at the tip, **tinged with purple** on the backside. **FLOWERS:** Purple to pink to white, 5 petals, 0.4–0.7 in. long; each **sepal has an orange gland** at the tip; several flowers in umbel-like clusters on stalks 4–8 in. tall that extend well beyond the leaves. April–June. **FRUITS:** Longitudinally dehiscent, spherical capsules; seeds have a large basal aril that aids in seed dispersal. **WHERE FOUND:** In dry woods, rocky places, pinelands, and barrens throughout most of the eastern U.S. and TN. Common.

PAUL SOMERS

NOTES: This plant arises from rose-colored underground bulbs. A thin, icicle-like water storage organ may lie beneath the bulbs. • In 1753, Carl von Linne (Linnaeus), the Swedish father of modern biological taxonomy, first described **Violet Wood Sorrel**. • Wood sorrels are also known as "wild shamrocks." The shamrock became associated with St. Patrick's Day through an Irish legend. According to legend, the missionary St. Patrick finally succeeded in explaining the concept of the Holy Trinity to a tribal chief by picking up a shamrock leaf and showing him "three in one."

STANLEY SIMS

Carolina Cranesbill
Geranium carolinianum

GENERAL: Weedy, bushy-branched, hairy **winter annual or biennial**, 6–20 in. tall. **LEAVES:** Both basal and stem leaves; upper stem leaves opposite with 3–7 long, **linear-oblong lobes**, deeply toothed at the apex; leaves are round in outline, to 3 in. wide. **FLOWERS: Pale pink** or whitish, less than 0.5 in. wide, 5 petals, 10 stamens, 1 pistil; borne in terminal clusters. May–August. **FRUITS:** Capsules (schizocarps) with a narrow beak about 0.7 in. long; reticulate seeds; capsule breaks into 5 long-tailed mericarps at maturity. **WHERE FOUND:** Weed of disturbed habitats, gardens, fields, pastures, and roadsides. Throughout most of the U.S., southern Canada, and TN. Common.

NOTES: The genus name *Geranium* is from the Greek word *geranos*, meaning "crane," alluding to the long, slender beak of the fruit. *Geranium* species are also called cranesbills. When ripe, the capsules split open at the base into 5 separate threads that recoil upward, ejecting the seeds. Each seed has a tail that coils or uncoils, depending on its moisture content, allowing it to burrow into the soil. • The **Geranium Family** has 2 genera and 9 species listed for TN. Most of the common garden and houseplants that are called geraniums actually belong to the South African genus *Pelargonium*.

STANLEY SIMS

Wild Geranium • *Geranium maculatum*

GENERAL: Showy, widespread, **common woodland perennial**, 12–24 in. tall. **LEAVES:** Purplish green, 4–5 in. wide, **3–5 narrow lobes**, deeply toothed at the tips, rough-hairy; basal leaves long-petioled; stem leaves (1 pair) opposite, short-petioled. **FLOWERS:** Showy, **pink to rose purple** (rarely white), 1.0–1.4 in. across, 5 petals, 10 stamens, 1 pistil; borne in loose terminal clusters of 2–5 flowers. April–June. **FRUITS:** Capsules with a slender beak to 1 in. long; seeds finely reticulate. **WHERE FOUND:** Rich, open, wooded slopes throughout most of the eastern U.S. and TN. Common.

NOTES: This plant is also called Astringent Root, Chocolate Flower, Crowfoot, Dove's Foot, Old Maid's Nightcap, and Shameface. • The thick, horizontal roots are tannin-rich and have been used as an astringent and to stop bleeding; they were reportedly used by Native Americans to treat venereal disease. Historically, this species was also called Alum Root and the roots were used in the Appalachian Mountains in the early 1800s to treat the "flux," a disease that afflicted children. • This species is easily propagated by seeds sown in spring or autumn.

Dove's Foot Cranesbill
Geranium molle *

GENERAL: Naturalized, **annual** hairy weed, 8–20 in. tall, mostly spreading and branched from the base.
LEAVES: Basal leaves are **palmately 5–9-lobed**, shallowly toothed at the apex, nearly round, 1–2 in. across, on long, hairy petioles that appear attached to the center of the leaf; stem leaves reduced in size, upper leaves alternate.
FLOWERS: Numerous, **bright pink**, **5 deeply notched petals** are about 0.25 in. long, 10 stamens, 1 pistil; usually in pairs from the upper nodes. April–September. **FRUITS:** Capsules with a slender beak about 0.4 in. long; finely reticulated seeds. **WHERE FOUND:** Introduced from Eurasia. Pastures and disturbed habitats. Occurs sporadically throughout the eastern U.S., and in Middle and East TN. Occasional. **SIMILAR SPECIES:** HERB ROBERT (**G. robertianum**) has **pinnately 3–5-lobed** leaves, deeply dissected, the **end segment stalked**; leaves have a strong odor when crushed; bright pink to red-purple **petals are not notched**. Moist, rich woods. A northern species known in TN only from a bluff along the Cumberland River in Smith County. Rare. May–September.

NOTES: **Dove's Foot Cranesbill** is also known as Pigeon Foot, for the shape of the leaves. • In 1597, in *The Herball or General Historie of Plantes* (London), John Gerard wrote that when the foliage and roots of this plant were dried and ground into a fine powder and taken at bedtime with red wine, the mixture would "cureth miraculously ruptures or burstings," presumably referring to a sore throat or stomach ulcers.

Spotted Touch-Me-Not, Jewelweed · *Impatiens capensis*

GENERAL: Annual, 3–5 ft. tall, often forming large colonies in wet or moist open habitats; **smooth stems**, branching above, are **translucent** and often succulent.
LEAVES: Alternate, soft, ovate to elliptic, 1–4 in. long, crenate to serrate margins.
FLOWERS: Orange-yellow, about 1 in. long, hanging from a thread-like stalk; 2 tiny sepals and 1 large, cone-shaped, **sac-like sepal**, heavily spotted with reddish brown, that narrows to a **forward-curving spur** beneath the sac; 1 hood-like upper petal and 2 lobed, lateral petals are located at the opening of the large sepal; anthers are united above the stigma. May–frost.
FRUITS: Green capsules, about 0.75 in. long; when touched, mature capsules instantly explode elastically into 5 coiled sections. **WHERE FOUND:** Wet woods and roadsides, streambanks and swamps, from southern Canada south to FL and TX. Throughout TN. Common.

NOTES: Water droplets standing on the leaves of this plant reflect the light and appear jewel-like, hence the common name **Jewelweed**. • Juice from the mashed leaves and stems can be applied as a poultice to skin **to alleviate irritation from poison ivy and the sting of nettles**. • Long-tongued butterflies, such as Spicebush Swallowtail and Eastern Tiger Swallowtail, are attracted to this plant for its nectar.

Pale Touch-Me-Not · *Impatiens pallida*

GENERAL: Annual, 4–6 ft. tall, often forming large colonies in wet or moist open areas; **smooth stems**, branching above, are **translucent** and often succulent. **LEAVES:** Soft leaves, ovate to elliptic, 1–4 in. long, with crenate to serrate margins. **FLOWERS: Pale yellow**, lightly spotted with reddish brown, 1.0–1.5 in. long; **sac-like sepal** is nearly as wide as long and is constricted abruptly into a **spur that curves down at a right angle**. July–September. **FRUITS:** Green capsules, to 0.75 in. long; when touched, mature capsules elastically explode into 5 coiled sections. **WHERE FOUND:** Moist, shady sites in woods and along streams. Widespread from southern Canada south to NC, TN, and OK. Across the eastern ⅔ of TN. Frequent.

NOTES: Other common names for this plant include Quick-in-the-Hand, Snapweed, and Weathercock. It is sometimes called Silverweed because of the appearance of the leaves when submerged in water. • The juices of this plant are a soothing and medicinal remedy for nettle stings, poison ivy, and other skin irritations and rashes. • The herbage, habitat, and general flower shape of this species are very similar to that of **Spotted Touch-Me-Not** (p. 205).

JERRY DROWN

Spikenard · *Aralia racemosa*

GENERAL: Coarse perennial herb to 4 ft. tall, smooth-stemmed, from a **large, aromatic root**. **LEAVES:** Several **alternate compound leaves**, pinnately divided into 5–21 ovate or cordate leaflets, 2–6 in. long, with sharp tips. **FLOWERS:** Tiny, **greenish white**, 5 petals about 0.04 in. long, overlapping in bud; borne **in large panicles** of many small umbels from the leaf axils. June–August. **FRUITS:** Dark purple drupes, about 0.2 in. across. **WHERE FOUND:** Rich, moist woods, from Québec to MN, south to GA and TX. In TN, from the Western Highland Rim eastward, also Shelby and Tipton counties in West TN. Frequent. **SIMILAR SPECIES: WILD SARSAPARILLA (*A. nudicaulis*)** is smaller, to 2 ft. tall; **single compound leaf** has 3 primary forks, each with 3–5 leaflets; greenish flowers usually in **3 small umbels on a separate stalk**. Rich woods from the northern U.S., south in the mountains to GA. Extreme eastern TN counties. Infrequent. May–July.

JERRY DROWN

NOTES: *Aralia* species are small, usually herbaceous plants with large, aromatic roots. The spicy roots of both **Spikenard** and **Wild Sarsaparilla** were used by Native Americans to make a tea and have been used as an ingredient in root beer. The roots were also made into a poultice and applied to sores and burns. • There are 3 genera and 6 species of the Ginseng Family in TN.

American Ginseng
Panax quinquefolius

JERRY DROWN

GENERAL: Perennial herb, 8–24 in. tall, with an unbranched stem arising from a tuber-like root. **LEAVES: Single whorl** of 3–4 long, stalked, **palmately compound leaves** that radiate from the top of the stem; each leaf usually has **5 stalked leaflets** that are oval, pointed, toothed, 2–5 in. long. **FLOWERS:** Tiny, greenish white or **yellow-green**, 5 petals; borne in a solitary umbel on a short stalk that grows from the top of the stem, yet **usually stays below the leaves.** May–July. **FRUITS:** Crimson red, berry-like drupes, 0.4 in. across, 2–3 seeded; develop in late summer. **WHERE FOUND:** Cool, moist, rich woodlands and mountains throughout most of the eastern U.S. and eastern Canada. Scattered across TN. Frequent, but threatened in the wild because of over-collecting.

NOTES: Few plants have been the subject of more folklore than this species, much of which attributes not only cures, but magical properties to the roots. One of its common names is **Cure-All**, which would seem appropriate as the genus name *Panax* is derived from two Greek words: *pan* and *akos*, which mean "all" and "cure." Ginseng has many heralded curative properties, not the least of which is the ability to give one a sense of overall wellness, good spirits, and longevity. It has been said that ginseng can "cure the sick, strengthen the weak, rejuvenate the aged, and revitalize the dying" (Shin Ying Hu, 1976).

Dwarf Ginseng
Panax trifolius

DAVID DUHL

GENERAL: Similar to **American Ginseng** (see above) but smaller, 4–8 in. tall. **LEAVES: Whorl** of 3 **palmately compound leaves**; each leaf usually has 3–5 coarsely toothed, **sessile leaflets** to 3 in. long. **FLOWERS:** Tiny, **white**, 5 petals; borne in a solitary, somewhat spherical, umbel that **rises above the leaves.** April–June. **FRUITS:** Yellow, berry-like drupes with 2–3 seeds. **WHERE FOUND:** Rich woods from southeastern Canada and northeastern U.S., south in the mountains to GA. In TN, from the Cumberland Plateau eastward. Occasional.

NOTES: The name "ginseng" derives from the Chinese *jen-shen*, which means "man-like," in reference to the branching root. • The **Ginseng Family** includes perennial herbs, vines, shrubs, and trees with leaves that may be simple or compound. The numerous small flowers are usually white or greenish white and arranged in umbels. Members of this family include ivy (species of *Hedera*) and **Wild Sarsaparilla** (p. 206), used in making root beer and diet drinks.

Carrot or Parsley Family (Apiaceae)

The Carrot or Parsley Family includes vegetables, such as carrots, celery, and parsnips, and seasonings, such as anise, caraway, chervil, coriander, cumin, dill, fennel, and parsley. However, some of the deadliest plants on earth are also in this family, such as Water Hemlock (*Cicuta maculata*) and Poison Hemlock (*Conium maculatum*), which are lethal when consumed. Take a close look at the flowers, and you may be surprised at the variety of insects that can be found on each inflorescence. Since the flowers are shallow and numerous, many smaller and short-legged pollinators such as beetles and small bees specialize in collecting nectar from these flowers.

Plants in this family usually have hollow stems, and the flowers are typically arranged in umbels, or umbrella-like clusters. Branches arise from a central point, like the spokes of a wheel, each with a small umbellet, and form a large compound umbel. Leaf stalks (petioles) usually have a broad, sheathing base. Fruits in this family are schizocarps, which split between the carpels into single-seeded "nutlets." There are 33 genera and 59 species in TN.

1a. Leaves all simple 2

  2a. Petals yellow; leaves perfoliate . . . . **Bupleurum**

  2b. Petals white, greenish, or bluish; leaves not perfoliate 3

    3a. Flowers in simple umbels; leaves nearly round . . . . **Hydrocotyle**

    3b. Flowers in dense heads; leaves various, but not rounded . . . . **Eryngium**

1b. At least some leaves compound or deeply dissected 4

  4a. Ovary and fruits with dense bristles or prickles; stems hairy 5

    5a. Bracts pinnately divided; bristles of fruits in simple rows . . . . **Daucus**

    5b. Bracts simple, linear, or occasionally absent; bristles of fruits not in simple rows . . . **Torilis**

  4b. Ovary and fruits smooth or hairy, but not bristly or prickly; stems smooth 6

    6a. Leaflets or leaf segments thread-like, less than 0.04 in. wide,
flowers white . . . . **Ptilimnium**

    6b. Leaflets or leaf segments more than 0.04 in. wide 7

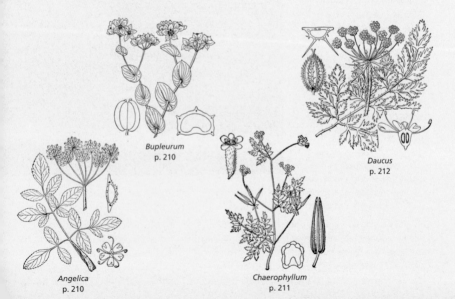

Bupleurum
p. 210

Daucus
p. 212

Angelica
p. 210

Chaerophyllum
p. 211

7a. Fruits 2.5x or more longer than wide and not winged; leaves ternately or ternate-pinnately decompound **8**

    8a. Fruits with stiff, appressed hairs; ultimate leaf segment more than 0.4 in. wide; mature fruits 0.6–1.0 in. long . . . . ***Osmorhiza***

    8b. Fruits smooth or softly hairy; ultimate leaf segment less than 0.4 in. wide; mature fruits less than 0.6 in. long . . . . ***Chaerophyllum***

7b. Fruits less than 2.5x as long as wide or winged **9**

    9a. Petals yellow, rarely maroon; leaflets toothed, ternately compound **10**

        10a. Central flower of each umbellet sessile; fruits not winged . . . . ***Zizia***

        10b. All flowers on pedicels; fruits winged . . . . ***Thaspium***

    9b. Petals white or greenish white **11**

        11a. Plants less than 6 in. tall, delicate, from small underground tubers; flowering stem leafless . . . . ***Erigenia***

        11b. Plants more than 6 in. tall; flowering stem leafy **12**

            12a. Stem leaves much dissected, the ultimate divisions usually less than 0.4 in. wide **13**

                13a. Stem red-spotted; fruits with "warts" . . . . ***Conium***

                13b. Stem without red spots; fruits without "warts"; petioles not winged . . . . ***Thaspium***

            12b. Stem leaves not much dissected, instead divided into distinct, uniform leaflets usually more than 0.6 in. wide **14**

                14a. Leaves 1-ternate or 1-pinnate **15**

                    15a. Upper petioles dilated, 0.4 in. or more wide; fruits 0.4 in. wide, with 4 dark lines on each side . . . . . ***Heracleum***

                    15b. Upper petioles not dilated, less than 0.4 in. wide; fruits 0.12–0.24 in. wide, without dark lines; leaf margins entire or with fewer than 5 coarse teeth on each side . . . . ***Oxypolis***

                14b. Leaves pinnately decompound, with many divisions **16**

                    16a. Upper petioles 0.4 in. wide or more when flattened; mature fruits smooth or hairy and prominently winged . . . . ***Angelica***

                    16b. Upper petioles less than 0.4 in. wide; fruits smooth, wings absent or narrow; fruits ribbed . . . . ***Cicuta***

Zizia
p. 218

Hydrocotyle
p. 215

Eryngium
pp. 213–14

Osmorhiza
p. 215

JERRY DROWN

Mountain Angelica, Filmy Angelica · *Angelica triquinata*

GENERAL: Perennial to 5 ft. tall, **smooth reddish stem, not downy. LEAVES:** Pinnately or bipinnately divided, to 12 in. long, with the larger leaf segments about 3 in. long and coarsely toothed; **sheaths at base of the petioles** partially enclose the stem; upper leaves are reduced to tubular sheaths, or sheaths that are longer than the leaf blades. **FLOWERS:** Tiny, **greenish white**, 5 petals; borne in **compound umbels**, 3–6 in. wide, smooth, with 12–25 spreading rays. July–September. **FRUITS:** Smooth capsules (schizocarps), strongly flattened, 2 lateral wings. **WHERE FOUND:** Mountain woods or balds at high elevations. In the Appalachian Mountains from PA to NC and the Blue Ridge in East TN. Infrequent. **SIMILAR SPECIES:** HAIRY ANGELICA (**A. venenosa**) has **downy stems, inflorescences, and fruits.** Woodland margins and roadsides. In most of the eastern U.S. In Middle and East TN, also Carroll and McNairy counties in West TN. Frequent. June–August.

NOTES: The species name for **Hairy Angelica**, *venenosa*, means "poisonous." • Although many members of the Carrot or Parsley Family are edible and are the source of many common vegetables, herbs, and spices, extreme caution should be used because there are several **extremely poisonous** plants in this family, including **Water Hemlock** (p. 211) and **Poison Hemlock** (p. 212).

MILO PYNE

Hare's Ear, Thoroughwax
Bupleurum rotundifolium*

GENERAL: Annual, 12–24 in. tall; stems hollow, purplish-tinged, smooth, and glaucous. **LEAVES:** Alternate, broadly ovate, 1–2 in. long; lower leaves sessile, upper leaves perfoliate. **FLOWERS:** Tiny, **mustard yellow**, 5 petals, nearly sessile, in umbellets surrounded by **5 pointed bractlets** about 0.5 in. long; striking inflorescence of **compound umbels** comprised of several umbellets. May–June. **FRUITS:** Ellipsoid capsules (schizocarps) with inconspicuous ribs. **WHERE FOUND:** Introduced from Europe. Now naturalized over most of the eastern U.S. In TN, in cedar glades and barrens in Davidson, Wilson, Rutherford, Maury, Marshall, and Bedford counties in the Central Basin of Middle TN, also in Knox, Hawkins, Washington, and Cocke counties in East TN. Infrequent.

NOTES: The species name *rotundifolium* and the common name **Hare's Ear** are in reference to the roundish, pointed leaves that stand upright. The young leaves of this plant are edible raw or cooked and are sometimes used as a pot-herb. They are also used as a spice. • The showy bracts attract pollinators to the flowers.

Southern Chervil, Wild Chervil
Chaerophyllum tainturieri

GENERAL: Downy, weedy annual to 30 in. tall, typically branched above. **LEAVES:** Alternate, 3-pinnately compound, to 5 in. long and almost as wide; leaflets elliptic to narrowly oblong, dissected into small segments, pointed, hairy beneath. **FLOWERS:** Small, white; borne in compound umbels with 3–10 flowers per umbellet, umbels are terminal or lateral, typically with 3 branches; umbellar bracts are strongly reflexed upon fruiting. March–April. **FRUITS:** Smooth capsules (schizocarps) with a distinct beak on the nutlets. **WHERE FOUND:** Moist to dry soil. Widespread in the southeastern U.S. and TN. Common. **SIMILAR SPECIES:** SPREADING CHERVIL (*C. procumbens*) has stems that are more divergent, smoother, and typically branched basally; umbel bracts are divergent upon fruiting. Moist woods and alluvial soil throughout most of the eastern U.S. Primarily in Middle TN, but also thinly scattered across the state. Occasional. March–April.

DENNIS HORN

NOTES: The genus name *Chaerophyllum* is from the Greek *chairo,* "to please," and *phyllon,* "leaf," referring to the pleasant aroma of the leaves of **Southern Chervil**. It is also referred to as **Hairyfruit Chervil**, though the stem is hairy rather than the fruit. • Turniproot Chervil (*C. bulbosum*), originally from Europe, is widely grown in vegetable gardens for its large, fleshy, delicately flavored root. However, some *Chaerophyllum* species can cause **skin irritation**.

Water Hemlock, Spotted Cowbane
Cicuta maculata

GENERAL: Smooth perennial, 3–7 ft. tall, the stems usually mottled with purple and relatively stout, upper branches not whorled. **LEAVES:** Alternate, 2–3-pinnately compound with thin, serrate leaflets, 1–3 in. long; lateral veins from the midvein of each leaflet can be traced to the valleys between the teeth at the leaf margin. **FLOWERS:** Tiny, white, 5 petals; 1–3 linear bracts (or none); borne in numerous compound umbels, 2–5 in. wide, both terminal and lateral on the thick stem. May–August. **FRUITS:** Capsules (schizocarps) with prominently ribbed nutlets. **WHERE FOUND:** Swamps, streambanks, marshes, and wet meadows. Widespread in eastern North America and TN. Frequent. **SIMILAR SPECIES:** AMERICAN LOVAGE (*Ligusticum canadensis*) has whorled upper stem branches; lateral veins of each leaflet terminate at the points of the teeth. Edges of streams and rich woods in the uplands from PA and MO, south to GA and AR. Throughout TN. Frequent. June–July.

DENNIS HORN

NOTES: The fleshy, finger-like roots of **Water Hemlock** have an odor of parsnip, but are **very poisonous** and can be **fatal** even if ingested in small amounts. Although most reports consider the whole plant to be **deadly poisonous**, cattle can apparently eat the leaves and fruit without ill effect. **Do not confuse this plant with other members of the Carrot or Parsley Family, some of which are harmless.**

Poison Hemlock · *Conium maculatum**

GENERAL: Coarse, taprooted **biennial**, to 9 ft. tall, with a freely branched, **purple or dark-spotted hollow stem**; usually emits a **pungent, foul odor**. **LEAVES:** Alternate, sometimes more than 12 in. long, purple-spotted, broadly triangular, 3–4-pinnately compound (carrot-like); hairless, ovate-oblong leaflets, to 0.4 in. long, are toothed and incised. **FLOWERS:** Tiny, **white**; usually several umbels, 1.5–2.5 in. wide, mostly terminal, often 2–4 at the uppermost node; umbels have several narrow, deciduous bracts at the base. May–June. **FRUITS:** Capsules (schizocarps) with strongly ribbed nutlets. **WHERE FOUND:** Introduced from Eurasia. Roadsides, fencerows, waste places, and along railroad tracks throughout most of the U.S. In Middle TN, also Carroll and Unicoi counties. Occasional.

NOTES: All parts of this plant are very poisonous, especially the flowers, fruit, and leaves. It is the same species that was used to execute Socrates and is not related to hemlock trees. • This plant has been used as a remedy for cancer, a narcotic and sedative, an analgesic, and an anti-aphrodisiac. • Contact with this plant may cause **dermatitis**.

OTTO R. HIRSCH

Queen Anne's Lace, Wild Carrot

Daucus carota*

GENERAL: Slender **biennial** to 5 ft. tall, from a heavy taproot. **LEAVES:** Alternate, compound, 8–10 in. long, generally rough-hairy, much dissected, with the ultimate divisions linear to lanceolate. **FLOWERS:** Tiny, white, 5 petals, sometimes **1 central, dark purple flower**; borne in umbels, 3–5 in. wide; umbels are surrounded at the base by spreading or **reflexed bracts**, 1–2 in. long, rough at the base, **pinnately divided** into narrow segments. May–September. **FRUITS:** Schizocarps; bristles on the nutlets have downward-directed barbs. **WHERE FOUND:** Introduced from Europe. Dry fields, roadsides, and waste places. Widespread in most of North America, including TN. Common. **SIMILAR SPECIES:** AMERICAN WILD CARROT (*D. pusillus*) is an **annual**; bracts are **appressed** to the umbel and **smooth basally**. Dry open places. A southern species extending north to VA and MO. In TN, in Wayne, Lewis, Marshall, Williamson, and Davidson counties. Rare. May–June.

NOTES: A story goes that the name **Queen Anne's Lace** is in reference to a time when a queen was

KURT EMMANUELE

sewing lace and she pricked her finger. The purple central flower in the inflorescence is where a drop of royal blood from the queen's finger dripped onto the lace. • The root of Queen Anne's Lace, when young, is sweet and tender. This plant contains high amounts of vitamin A. In fact, the cultivated carrot was derived from this species.

Harbinger-of-Spring
Erigenia bulbosa

HUGH & CAROL NOURSE

GENERAL: Delicate perennial herb, **1–4 in. tall** at flowering, from a nearly round, edible tuber. **LEAVES:** 1–2, compound, membranous, 4–8 in. long at maturity (smaller during flowering), arising from the base of the non-leafy flowering stem; leaves divided 2–3 times into 3 segments each, terminal leaflets linear; 1 similar compound leaf occurs just below the inflorescence. **FLOWERS:** White, 5 petals, 0.12 in. long, **5 stamens with purplish brown anthers**; terminal compound umbel has 2–4 umbellets with leaf-like bractlets. February–April. **FRUITS:** Purplish black capsules (schizocarps), about 0.2 in. wide, broader than long and notched at the apex. **WHERE FOUND:** Rich, moist deciduous woods. Widespread in the eastern U.S. and TN. Frequent.

NOTES: This plant is one of the first herbs to flower in the spring and is often called **Pepper-and-Salt** because the purplish brown anthers and white petals give the inflorescence a bicolored appearance. Taking advantage of spring sunshine, this plant sometimes produces fruit before the leaves have fully opened. • The round and tuberous root can be eaten raw or cooked. • This is the only species of the *Erigenia* genus.

Prostrate Eryngo, Creeping Eryngo • *Eryngium prostratum*

DENNIS HORN

GENERAL: Perennial with fibrous roots and **stems that creep along on the ground**; often **takes root at the leaf nodes**. **LEAVES:** Alternate, but appearing whorled, a few at each node, ovate to lanceolate, 1.0–1.5 in. long, toothed or lobed, on leaf stalks often as long as the blade. **FLOWERS:** Minute, **pale blue**, sessile, subtended by a minute bract; in a rounded, **cylindric head** about 0.25 in. across with narrow bracts, 0.25 in. long, at the base. May–October. **FRUITS:** Capsules (schizocarps) with no ribs, but covered with scales. **WHERE FOUND:** Wet areas such as low meadows, moist and sandy ditches, and along the margins of ponds and lakes throughout the southeastern U.S. In the western 1/2 of TN, and rare in East TN. Occasional. **SIMILAR SPECIES:** ERYNGO (**E. integrifolium**) is an **erect branching** perennial to 3 ft. tall from a single stem; leaves and inflorescences are generally larger; **stem leaves usually sessile**, not veined; **hemispherical flower heads** to 0.4 in. across. Wet pinelands, meadows, and savannas. A southern Coastal Plain species. In TN, in Benton, Coffee, Warren, and White counties. Rare. August–October.

NOTES: *Eryngium* is a Greek reference to the prickly or spiny herbs in this genus. • Members of this genus are unique in the Carrot and Parsley Family because they have dense flower heads rather than the characteristic umbels. The flowers, with their elongated nectar tubes, are uniquely suited to long-tongued bees and butterflies.

DENNIS HORN

Rattlesnake Master
Eryngium yuccifolium

GENERAL: Coarse, erect perennial to 4 ft. tall. **LEAVES:** Alternate, numerous lower leaves are silvery green, 6–30 in. long, **narrow, parallel-veined, sharp-tipped,** and have spine-like serrations; upper leaves are fewer and smaller but otherwise similar. **FLOWERS:** Minute, **white to greenish;** few **spherical flowering heads,** almost 1 in. across, in widely branching umbels; bracts and bractlets lanceolate, sharp-tipped, and short, not extending beyond flower heads. June–August. **FRUITS:** Capsules (schizocarps); nutlets are covered in scales. **WHERE FOUND:** Dry soils, open woods, barrens, and road-sides, from MN to northern VA, south to FL and TX. Widespread in TN. Occasional.

NOTES: The species name *yuccifolium* is a reference to the yucca-like, sword-shaped leaves. The common name comes from this plant's reputation as a cure for snakebites, especially those of rattlesnakes. A poultice was made from the leaves and roots and applied to the wound. This plant has also been used as a stimulant and diuretic.

KURT EMMANUELE

Cow Parsnip · *Heracleum maximum*

GENERAL: Large, woody, **rank-smelling,** unbranched perennial herb, 3–10 ft. tall; **stout stem is grooved,** hairy or woolly. **LEAVES:** Alternate, 3 broadly ovate leaflets, each 4–12 in. long, pinnately or palmately lobed and coarsely toothed; petioles swollen at base into sheaths sometimes 2 in. wide. **FLOWERS:** Small, **white,** tinged with purple; borne in **compound umbels,** 4–8 in. wide, with 15–30 rays; outer flowers of the umbel often larger and irregular. June–August. **FRUITS:** Ovate capsules (schizocarps) with conspicuous oil-tubes extending barely to the middle. **WHERE FOUND:** Moist woods, roadsides, and meadows across Canada and the northern U.S., south in the mountains to GA. In TN, in the Blue Ridge Mountains of East TN and Stewart County in Middle TN. Infrequent. *H. lanatum.*

NOTES: Despite its common name, the foliage of this plant is **poisonous** to livestock, and the acrid juice can cause **blisters** or **burns** on contact, owing to the photosensitizing furanocoumarins it contains. • As a food source, Native Americans would boil the young roots, shoots, and leaves in several changes of water. The petioles and young stems were peeled carefully before being eaten. The strongly aromatic fruits can be used in moderation as a condiment. • In herbal medicine, the roots were used widely by Native Americans to treat colic, cramps, headaches, sore throats, colds, coughs, and flu. They were also made into a poultice that was applied to bruises, swellings, and boils.

Water Pennywort
Hydrocotyle umbellata

GENERAL: Perennial herb with slender, sometimes **floating stems**; flowers and leaves arise separately from the same nodes; spreads horizontally to **form dense mats**. **LEAVES:** **Peltate**, 1–3 in. across, shallowly lobed, petiole is attached to lower surface of blade. **FLOWERS:** Tiny, **white**, 5 petals; borne in **simple umbels**, about 1 in. wide, 10 or more flowers per umbel, on **peduncles taller than the leaves**. July–September. **FRUITS:** 2 connected carpels form kidney-shaped fruits, 0.1 in. long, deeply notched at the base. **WHERE FOUND:** Ditches, pond edges, and other wet places throughout much of the eastern U.S. In TN, in Coffee, Cumberland, Hamilton, Henderson, and Shelby counties. Rare. **SIMILAR SPECIES:** WHORLED WATER PENNYWORT (*H. verticillata*) has an inflorescence that is an interrupted spike of tiny **flowers below the leaves**. Southern U.S. Southeastern TN. Rare. June–August. **MARSH WATER PENNYWORT** (*H. americana*) has **non-peltate leaves** that are **shallowly lobed**; umbels are almost sessile. Northeastern U.S. Sporadic in East TN. Rare. June–September. **FLOATING WATER PENNYWORT** (*H. ranunculoides*) has **non-peltate leaves** that are **lobed to the middle**; umbels are on long peduncles. Southern U.S. In TN, only in Lake and Obion counties. Rare. May–August.

NOTES: Some species of *Hydrocotyle* are called navelworts, an allusion to their cup-shaped leaves. • **Water Pennywort** stems are capable of rooting at the nodes and may also be floating. The identifying characteristics of this plant are the **round leaves with scalloped margins** and the **umbrella-like heads of small, white flowers.**

Sweet Anise, Aniseroot
Osmorhiza longistylis

GENERAL: Erect perennial to 3 ft. tall with thick, **fragrant, anise-scented roots** and essentially **smooth stems**; stems, leaves, and fruits also have the anise or licorice scent. **LEAVES:** Alternate, **compound, fern-like**, to 12 in. long, somewhat hairy, lower leaves with long petioles, upper leaves mostly sessile; leaflets are somewhat oval, with margins that are serrate or lobed, 0.5–1.0 in. wide. **FLOWERS:** Tiny, **white; styles, about 0.1 in. long, are much longer than the 5 petals**; borne in few-branched, compound umbels with 3–6 rays and 1–3 narrow involucral bracts; 5–20 flowers per umbellet. April–June. **FRUITS:** Capsules (schizocarps) with slightly flattened nutlets. **WHERE FOUND:** Moist woods, from southern Canada south to GA, TX, and CO; more prevalent south and west. Widespread in TN. Frequent. **SIMILAR SPECIES:** SWEET CICELY (*O. claytonii*) has **stems that are quite hairy** and the anise scent is weaker; flower **styles are shorter than the white petals**. Rich, moist woods. A mostly northeastern species extending south to GA, AL, and AR. In Middle and East TN. Frequent. April–June.

NOTES: In herbal medicine, Native Americans made a tonic from the roots of **Sweet Anise** that was used to treat upset stomach. The roots were also pounded into a poultice and applied to boils and skin wounds, and made into a tea that was used as an eyewash.

DENNIS HORN

Cowbane · *Oxypolis rigidior*

GENERAL: Smooth perennial herb to 5 ft. tall, stem with few branches and leaves, arising from slender, spindle-shaped roots to 8 in. long. **LEAVES:** Alternate, pinnately divided into 5–9 sessile leaflets, 2–5 in. long, lanceolate to narrowly obovate; **leaflets have no teeth on margins**, or teeth are widely spaced above the middle of the leaflet. **FLOWERS:** Tiny, **white**; borne in compound umbels, 3–6 in. across, with **no bracts or up to 4 narrow bracts** at the base. August–October. **FRUITS:** Ridged capsules (schizocarps); flattened nutlets are winged and rounded at both ends. **WHERE FOUND:** Swamps, wet meadows, and streambanks. Wide-spread in most of the eastern U.S. In Middle and East TN. Frequent. **SIMILAR SPECIES:** WATER PARSNIP (*Sium suave*) has pinnately compound leaves with **7–17 leaflets having numerous fine teeth**; compound **umbel has 6–10 narrow bracts** at the base. Wet meadows and swamps throughout the U.S. Thinly scattered across TN. Infrequent. June–August.

NOTES: Cowbane is also called **Stiff Cowbane**. As the common name suggests, the roots and leaves are **poisonous to cattle**. There are reports of dermatitis caused by allergic reactions from handling the leaves. • **Water Parsnip** is also considered to be **poisonous to cattle**.

NITA R. HEILMAN

Big Mock Bishop's Weed
Ptilimnium costatum

GENERAL: Erect branching annual, 2–5 ft. tall. **LEAVES:** Alternate, 2–6 in. long, pinnate, divided into many **thread-like (filiform) leaflets**; leaflets are crowded on the main leaf axis, the primary ones **appearing whorled**. **FLOWERS:** Small, **white**; compound umbel, 2–3 in. wide, has **undivided, thread-like bracts**. July–August. **FRUITS:** Capsules (schizocarps) with prominently ribbed nutlets. **WHERE FOUND:** Streambanks, wet meadows, and swamp margins. Scattered throughout the south-eastern U.S. In Middle TN, also Hamilton and Bradley counties in East TN. Infrequent. **SIMILAR SPECIES:** ATLANTIC MOCK BISHOP'S WEED (*P. capillaceum*) has **less crowded leaflets** that **do not appear whorled**; umbel **bracts usually 3-parted**. Wet soil, from NY to KS, south to FL and TX. West and Middle TN. Occasional. June–October. OZARK MOCK BISHOP'S WEED (*P. nuttallii*) has **fewer and longer leaflets**; umbel **bracts undivided**. Wet soil. From KY to KS, south to AL and TX. Thinly scattered across TN. Occasional. June–July.

NOTES: The Greek translation of the genus name *Ptilimnium* is "mud feather," in reference to the finely divided leaves and typical habitat of these plants; the species name *costatum* means "ribbed," in reference to the prominent ribs on the fruit.

Hairyjoint Meadow Parsnip · *Thaspium barbinode*

JERRY DROWN

GENERAL: Perennial herb to 3 ft. tall, branched above, with **minute, stiff hairs circling the upper nodes**. **LEAVES:** Basal and alternate stem leaves typically 2-ternately compound, lanceolate to ovate **leaflets**, 1–2 in. long, are **toothed** and incised. **FLOWERS:** Small, **brilliant yellow**; borne in compound umbels, typically 1.2–2.5 in. across, the stalks of the umbellets about equal; **each umbellet has a distinctly stalked central flower**. May–June. **FRUITS:** Capsules (schizocarps); nutlets are ribbed, winged, and **smooth**. **WHERE FOUND:** Woods and barrens. Widespread in most of the eastern U.S. In TN, from the Cumberland Plateau eastward. Frequent. **SIMILAR SPECIES: CHAPMAN'S MEADOW PARSNIP (*T. chapmanii*)** has **pale yellow flowers** and **hairy fruits**. Limestone bluffs and rocky woods of the southeastern U.S. Mostly in Middle TN. Occasional. May–June. **CUTLEAF MEADOW PARSNIP (*T. pinnatifidum*)** has **finely divided leaf segments** and **creamy white flowers**. Mountain woods of the southeastern U.S. In TN, in Hamilton and Cocke counties. Rare. May–June. **YELLOW PIMPERNEL (*Taenidia intergerrima*)** has **smooth stems** and **leaflets with entire margins**. Dry woods and road banks on basic soils. Throughout the eastern U.S. Middle and East TN. Frequent. April–June.

NOTES: Both the common name and species name *barbinode*, which means "with beards at the nodes or joints," draw attention to the hairs at nodes on the stem of **Hairyjoint Meadow Parsnip**.

Smooth Meadow Parsnip
Thaspium trifoliatum

HUGH NOURSE

THOMAS G. BARNES

GENERAL: Perennial herb to 3 ft. tall; **smooth, weakly branched, hollow stem** with strongly defined ridges; 2 varieties of this species are encountered: the yellow-flowered variety (upper photo), **Yellow Meadow Parsnip (*T. trifoliatum var. flavum*)**, and the purple-flowered variety (lower photo), **Purple Meadow Parsnip (*T. trifoliatum var. trifoliatum*)**. **LEAVES:** Basal leaves are long-petioled, finely toothed, heart⁺- to kidney-shaped, and simple; upper leaves are alternate, compound with 3 toothed leaflets (sometimes 5), lanceolate to ovate; leaves have a **transparent border**. **FLOWERS:** Small, **purple** or **yellow**; borne in compound umbels, to 3 in. wide, long-peduncled, without basal leaves; **each umbellet has a distinctly stalked central flower**. April–June. **FRUITS:** Oval capsules (schizocarps), to 0.16 in. long, with ribs prominently winged. **WHERE FOUND:** Moist woods and streambanks of the eastern and central U.S. **Yellow Meadow Parsnip** (upper photo), is more frequently found in the western part of the species range. Throughout TN. Common. **Purple Meadow Parsnip** (lower photo), occurs more often in the eastern part of the species range. In the mountains of East TN and in several counties near the KY border. Infrequent.

NOTES: This plant is also called **Woodland Meadow Parsnip**. • Some species of golden alexanders (*Zizia* spp., p. 218), are remarkably similar in appearance to **Yellow Meadow Parsnip**, but the central flower of each umbellet is sessile.

DENNIS HORN

Field Hedge Parsley · *Torilis arvensis**

GENERAL: **Weedy annual** to 3 ft. tall, highly branched, from a taproot. **LEAVES:** Alternate, 1–3 times pinnate, leaflets coarsely toothed, linear-lanceolate, the central leaflet largest and up to 2 in. long, lower leaflets usually stalked and ovate to lance-ovate. **FLOWERS:** Small, **white**; borne in terminal and lateral compound umbels on **peduncles 1–8 in. long; 5–9 umbellets are spreading** or ascending on stalks about 1 in. long. June–July. **FRUITS:** Capsules (schizocarps) covered with barbed bristles; slightly flattened nutlets. **WHERE FOUND:** Introduced from Europe and established in much of the eastern U.S. Fields and roadsides. Widespread in TN. Occasional. **SIMILAR SPECIES:** KNOTTED HEDGE PARSLEY (*T. nodosa**) has a **dense, head-like inflorescence** on a **short peduncle**, less than 0.8 in. long. Introduced from Eurasia. Waste places. GA, AL, and MS. In TN, in Davidson, Maury, and Knox counties. Rare. May.

NOTES: The genus name *Torilis* means "engraved," in reference to the grooves in the fruit hidden beneath the bristles; the species name *arvensis* means "cultivated fields," for this plant's favored habitat. **Field Hedge Parsley** is also known as **Spreading Hedge Parsley.** • Although caution should be used, the roots of Field Hedge Parsley are peeled and eaten raw in Asia, and the young leaves, after careful preparation, are eaten as greens.

JERRY DROWN

Common Golden Alexanders · *Zizia aurea*

GENERAL: Smooth, branching perennial to 3 ft. tall, from a thickened root cluster. **LEAVES:** Basal leaves are **compound**, usually 2-ternate; **finely toothed leaflets** are ovate to lanceolate; upper leaves are alternate, nearly stalkless, compound, with 3 finely toothed leaflets. **FLOWERS:** Small, **bright yellow**; in compound umbels, 2–3 in. wide, without bracts; umbel usually has more than 10 primary rays; **central flower of each umbellet is stalkless.**

April–June. **FRUITS:** Smooth capsules (schizocarps) are ribbed but not winged. **WHERE FOUND:** Moist woods and meadows in the eastern U.S. Primarily in the middle counties of TN. Occasional. **SIMILAR SPECIES:** HEART-LEAVED GOLDEN ALEXANDERS (*Z. aptera*) has **simple, heart-shaped basal leaves** on long stalks. Low meadows and open woods in the eastern U.S. and the eastern ⅔ of TN. Frequent. May–June. MOUNTAIN GOLDEN ALEXANDERS (*Z. trifoliata*) has **compound basal leaves**, usually with only **3 coarsely toothed leaflets**; umbel usually has less than 10 primary rays. Mountain woods from VA and KY, south to GA. In TN, mainly in the Blue Ridge Mountains of East TN and Dickson, Williamson, and Lawrence counties of Middle TN. Occasional. May–June.

NOTE: Common Golden Alexanders, like many plants of the Carrot or Parsley Family, is **toxic.** However, ethnobotanists recognize that the difference between a poison, a medicine, and a narcotic is often just a matter of dosage. Traditionally, both Native Americans and colonists used this plant medicinally for a variety of purposes, from a mood enhancer to treating fevers. • In *Zizia* species, the central floret of each umbellet is sessile, while in meadow parsnips (*Thaspium* spp., p. 217) the central floret is stalked.

Yellow Jessamine · *Gelsemium sempervirens*

GENERAL: Smooth, trailing or **high-climbing vine**; stems slender, wiry, and freely branched. **LEAVES:** Opposite, somewhat evergreen, lanceolate, smooth, entire, 1.5–2.5 in. long, base rounded or tapered. **FLOWERS: Funnel-shaped**, fragrant, **rich yellow**, 1.0–1.5 in. long, with 5 spreading corolla lobes; solitary or 2–3 in axillary clusters, on short pedicels with scaly bracts. April–May. **FRUITS:** Ellipsoid capsules about 0.75 in. long; a partition separates the 2 few-seeded carpels. **WHERE FOUND:** Woods and thickets, from VA to AR, southward. In Marion, Hamilton, Bledsoe, and Rhea counties in East TN and Obion County in West TN. Rare.

NOTE: This plant is also called **Carolina Jessamine, Evening Trumpet Flower**, and Yellow Jasmine. • All parts of this plant are **extremely poisonous** and contain poisonous alkaloids; eating just one flower has been **fatal to children**. Contact can cause **dermatitis**, lending the name Cow Itch. The ornamental Butterfly Bush (*Buddleia*) is included in this family, as well as many extremely poisonous plants, including the Strychnine Tree (*Strychnos nux-vomica*), from whose seeds the deadly poison **strychnine** is obtained.

DENNIS HORN

Mitrewort, Lax Hornpod
Mitreola petiolata

GENERAL: Annual, 8–20 in. tall, with an unbranched stem, topped by a branched inflorescence. **LEAVES:** Opposite, 0.5–2.0 in. long, ovate, entire with narrowed bases; lower leaves have a short petiole, upper leaves sessile. **FLOWERS: Tiny, white**, 5-lobed; in stalked cymes with **secund (1-sided) branches** of flowers terminating the stem and branches of the uppermost leaf nodes. July–September. **FRUITS:** Capsules with black, grooved seeds. **WHERE FOUND:** Barrens, meadows, open streambanks, and lakeshores. Mainly a Coastal Plain species found from southeastern VA to FL to Mexico and inland to AR and TN. In TN, in Giles, Wilson, Rutherford, Bedford, Coffee, Warren, White, Sequatchie, Hamilton, and Bradley counties. Infrequent. *Cynoctonum mitreola*.

NOTES: The **Logania Family** consists of herbs and woody plants mostly from tropical and subtropical climates, with about 20 genera and 500 species worldwide. TN has 5 genera, each with a single species.

DENNIS HORN

Indian Pink · *Spigelia marilandica*

GENERAL: Unbranched perennial herb, 12–28 in. tall. **LEAVES:** Opposite, sessile, ovate to lanceolate, 2–4 in. long, acute or acuminate at the tips with bases usually rounded. **FLOWERS:** Tubular corolla about 2 in. long, **scarlet outside, greenish yellow inside**, with **5 conspicuous**, flaring, pointed **lobes**; narrow sepals; borne on a terminal, **secund (1-sided) cyme.** May–June. **FRUITS:** Swollen capsules with irregularly angled, black seeds that catapult before the capsule appears to be ripe. **WHERE FOUND:** Rich, moist woodlands, and forests in most of the southeastern U.S., north to IL and IN. Throughout TN. Common.

NOTES: The genus *Spigelia* was named for Adrian van den Spiegel (1578–1625), professor of anatomy at the University of Padua and a writer on botany. This plant is also known as **Pinkroot, Woodland Pinkroot**, and **Wormgrass.** • This species is a nectar plant for hummingbirds. It contains the **poisonous alkaloid**, spigeline, and the root has been used as a vermifuge (dewormer) in the past. This showy plant's poisonous side effects have prevented it from being over-collected.

JERRY DROWN

American Columbo
Frasera caroliniensis

GENERAL: Erect, glabrous, short-lived perennial herb; one of the tallest TN wildflowers, growing 3–10 ft. tall; consists primarily of a basal rosette of leaves increasing in numbers each year until the plant flowers and then dies. **LEAVES:** Basal leaves to 24 in. long, in a rosette; **stem leaves usually in whorls of 4**, progressively reduced in size upward. **FLOWERS:** Numerous, **greenish white sprinkled with purple**, about 1 in. wide, **4 lobes**, each with a large, round, **green gland** below the middle; borne in terminal, panicle-like clusters. May–June. **FRUITS:** Beaked capsules with brown, winged seeds. **WHERE FOUND:** Rich woods and limestone glades, from western NY to MI and IL, south to northern GA and MS. Thinly spread across TN, more prevalent in Middle TN. Frequent. *Swertia caroliniensis*.

NOTES: This plant is also commonly called **Green Gentian** and **Columbo Root** and is less commonly called Deer's Ears, Indian Lettuce, Meadow Pride, Pyramid Flower, and Yellow Gentian. • Traditionally, a tea made from the roots was used to treat colic, cramps, dysentery, diarrhea, stomachaches, lack of appetite, and nausea. The plant also was made into a tonic, and the powdered plant was applied as a poultice to sores and skin ulcers.

OTTO R. HIRSCH

Soapwort Gentian · *Gentiana saponaria*

GENERAL: Erect perennial herb to 24 in. tall with smooth stem and leaves. **LEAVES:** Opposite, lanceolate to narrowly elliptic, 2–4 in. long, acute at both ends. **FLOWERS:** Tubular corolla, 1–2 in. long, the **5 lobes usually closed** at the tips, a **bright blue** color that varies as the flower ages; borne in clusters at the apex and leaf axils. September–October. **FRUITS:** Elongated capsules; numerous seeds to 0.1 in. long. **WHERE FOUND:** Wet meadows and roadsides, from southern NY to FL, irregularly westward to IL and eastern TX. In TN, mainly in the eastern ⅔ of the state. Occasional. **SIMILAR SPECIES: APPALACHIAN GENTIAN (G. decora)** has **hairy stems; flowers somewhat open,** tubes white with blue lobes. Moist mountain woods from WV to GA. High elevations of East TN. Infrequent. September–November.

NOTES: Soapwort Gentian gets its common name from its soapy sap. Other names include Bluebells, Calathian Violet, and **Harvest Bells.** • The vessel-shaped flowers are visited by bumblebees, which have to push their way into the narrow opening, though they sometimes resort to chewing a hole in the side of the flower in pursuit of the nectar. Once the flower is pollinated, the petals start to turn a dusty purplish color. • Seven *Gentiana* species are listed for TN, 2 are endemic to the southern Appalachian Mountains.

HUGH NOURSE

Pale Gentian, Striped Gentian
Gentiana villosa

GENERAL: Perennial herb to 20 in. tall with erect, **smooth stems.** **LEAVES:** Opposite, sessile, narrowly obovate to elliptic, 2–4 in. long, acute tips, tapered to the base; several dark green, shiny leaves at the base of the inflorescence. **FLOWERS:** Tubular corolla, 1–2 in. long, **greenish white,** often purple-striped, the **5 lobes partially open;** borne in terminal clusters with a few in the leaf axils. September–October. **FRUITS:** Elongated capsules to 1 in. long; oblong, brown, wingless seeds. **WHERE FOUND:** Open woods and oak-pine forests in most of the eastern U.S. from PA southward. Throughout TN. Frequent. **SIMILAR SPECIES: BOTTLE GENTIAN (G. clausa)** has **smooth stems;** slender, pointed leaves; **dark blue flowers; corolla lobes typically do not open.** Moist meadows, woods. A northeastern species extending south in the mountains to TN and NC. In TN, in Carter, Unicoi, Johnson, and Washington counties in East TN. Rare. September–October. **BLUE RIDGE GENTIAN (G. austromontana)** has **hairy stems;** lanceolate to ovate leaves; **white flowers with tightly closed blue lobes.** Upper-elevation grassy balds of the NC, VA, and TN mountains. In TN, in Washington, Carter, Unicoi, and Johnson counties. Rare. September–October.

PAUL SOMERS

NOTES: The *Gentiana* genus is named for the 6th-century king of Illyria, Gentius, who discovered that the roots of the Yellow Gentian (*G. lutea*) had a healing effect on his malaria-stricken troops. The species name *villosa* means "covered with soft hairs," though the stems of **Pale Gentian** are smooth.

KURT EMMANUELE

Stiff Gentian · *Gentianella quinquefolia*

GENERAL: Annual, 10–30 in. tall with stiff, 4-ridged stems, usually branched. **LEAVES:** Stem leaves opposite, sessile, lanceolate to ovate, 1–3 in. long, with acute tips and rounded at the base; basal leaves spatulate. **FLOWERS:** Narrow, tubular, violet-blue to lilac, about 1 in. long, **closed at the tip**, appear pointed; a profusion of flowers occurs in dense terminal clusters. September–October. **FRUITS:** Elongated capsules, 0.6–1.0 in. long; round, yellowish seeds. **WHERE FOUND:** Rich woods, wet fields, and mountain slopes in the Appalachian region from ME to MN, south to GA and AR. In TN, from the Cumberland Plateau eastward, also Cannon and Smith counties. Occasional.

SIMILAR SPECIES: PRAIRIE GENTIAN (***Gentiana puberulenta***) is 8–24 in. tall; blue-purple-striped, **broadly tubular flowers**, 1.4–2.4 in. long; corolla lobes acute and divergent, **wide open in full sun**. Meadows, prairies, and barrens. A mostly Midwestern species with disjunct populations in Coffee and Rutherford counties in Middle TN. Rare. September–October.

NOTES: Stiff Gentian is also known as **Ague Weed** and Five-Flowered Gentian. • A story is told that pioneers added a little piece of gentian to gin or brandy to stimulate the appetite and to aid in digestion. This habit caught on and there are still several aperitifs that include an extract made from gentian.

KURT EMMANUELE

Pennywort · *Obolaria virginica*

GENERAL: Small, smooth perennial herb, 3–6 in. tall, with a mostly unbranched, **fleshy stem and thick leaves**. **LEAVES:** Lower leaves opposite and bract-like; upper floral leaves obovate, 0.3–0.6 in. long, with a wedge-shaped base, green with a purplish tint. **FLOWERS:** White or purplish white, 0.5 in. long, nearly sessile; funnel-shaped corolla cleft to about the middle, with **4 pointed lobes**; borne in upper leaf axils, as well as terminal in clusters of 1–3 flowers. March–April. **FRUITS:** Swollen capsules about 0.25 in. long; translucent, yellowish seeds. **WHERE FOUND:** Rich hardwood forests, from NJ to southern IL, south to FL and TX. Throughout TN. Common.

NOTES: The genus name *Obolaria* is from the Greek *obolos*, meaning "a small coin," referring to the thick, roundish leaves, also implied in the common name. Sometimes called **Virginia Pennywort**, this plant is often overlooked in leaf litter because of its small size. • **Pennywort** contains little chlorophyll and is dependent on mycorrhizal fungi. This is the only species of the genus.

Rose Pink · *Sabatia angularis*

GENERAL: Smooth, erect **biennial**, 12–36 in. tall, with many **opposite branches** and a 4-angled, **winged stem**. **LEAVES:** Opposite, sessile, ovate, 0.5–1.6 in. long, rounded to nearly heart-shaped at the base, often clasping; basal leaves often absent during flowering. **FLOWERS:** Rose pink (rarely white), about 1 in. wide, with a distinctive **greenish yellow center** bordered by a thin, red line, 5 divergent lobes; borne in a loose, terminal cyme. July–August. **FRUITS:** Oblong, angled capsules to 0.4 in. long; blackish brown seeds. **WHERE FOUND:** Moist or dry open areas and roadsides in most of the eastern U.S. Throughout TN. Common. **SIMILAR SPECIES:** SMALL ROSE PINK (*S. brachiata*) is smaller, to 24 in. tall, with several erect, **opposite branches**; stem leaves oblong; basal leaves present during flowering; **stems not typically winged**; pink flowers with a greenish yellow eye. In much of southeastern U.S. and southern Middle TN. Occasional. June–July. SLENDER MARSH PINK (*S. campanulata*) is a **perennial**; stem has **alternate branches**; **leaves are linear**. A Coastal Plain species found locally inland. In TN, from the Eastern Highland Rim eastward, also in Dickson and Hickman counties. Occasional. July–August.

JOHN OATES

NOTES: Other common names for **Rose Pink** are **Bitter Bloom**, **Common Marsh Pink**, Pink Bloom, Red Century, Square-Stemmed Sabatia, and Wild Succory. • In herbal medicine, Rose Pink was prescribed to treat yellow fever, stomachaches, nausea, and a variety of other ailments.

Appalachian Rose Gentian
Sabatia capitata

GENERAL: Annual to 24 in. tall, usually with few branches; hollow stems with vertical lines. **LEAVES:** Opposite, 1–2 in. long, lanceolate with acute tips, sessile or somewhat clasping. **FLOWERS:** Showy, **7–12 bright pink petals**, 0.5–1.0 in. long, fused at the base, **yellow center with a border of red marks**; calyx lobes are narrow and erect; a few nearly sessile flowers occur in **tight terminal clusters** or in the upper leaf axils. June–August. **FRUITS:** Ellipsoid capsules with small seeds. **WHERE FOUND:** Forest openings, roadsides, and meadows on sandstone ridges of the Cumberland Plateau and the Ridge and Valley of AL, GA, and TN. In TN, known only from Hamilton and Sequatchie counties. Rare.

AL GOOD

NOTES: The genus name *Sabatia* honors Liberato Sabbati, an 18th-century curator of the botanic garden in Rome, Italy. The species name *capitata* refers to the head-like flower clusters. This plant is also known as **Upland Sabatia** and **Cumberland Rose Gentian**, in reference to the area where it grows. • Of the 4 species of *Sabatia* that occur in TN, only this species has flowers with more than 5 petals.

JERRY DROWN

Eastern Blue Star
Amsonia tabernaemontana var. *tabernaemontana*

GENERAL: Loosely branched perennial herb to 3 ft. tall; smooth stems contain a **milky sap**. **LEAVES:** Alternate, 3–6 in. long, **1.2–2.5 in. wide**, elliptic to ovate with narrowed tips and a dull surface. **FLOWERS:** Pale blue corolla is **5-lobed**, with short, hairy lobes that open in the shape of a star, approximately 0.5 in. across; numerous, in terminal clusters. April–May. **FRUITS:** Paired, erect, linear follicles, 2–4 in. long. **WHERE FOUND:** Bluffs, woodlands, and streambanks, from NY to KS, south to FL and TX. Throughout TN. Frequent. **SIMILAR SPECIES:** GATTINGER'S BLUE STAR (*A. tabernaemontana* var. *gattingeri*) has **narrower, lanceolate leaves, less than 1.2 in. wide**. Generally found in gravel bars and limestone cedar glades in KY and TN, primarily the Central Basin in TN. Infrequent. April–May.

NOTES: **Eastern Blue Star** is also called Blue Dogbane and Willow Amsonia for its willow-like leaves. • Members of the **Dogbane Family** have leaves with entire margins, flowers with 5 corolla lobes, and fruits that are in 2 pods. Plants of this family, which are related to the milkweeds, also contain a milky sap. Four genera and 6 species are found in TN.

DICK SOOY

Indian Hemp
Apocynum cannabinum

GENERAL: Erect, branching perennial herb to 4 ft. tall, with milky sap. **LEAVES:** Opposite, entire, elliptic to ovate, 2–4 in. long, smooth above and often hairy beneath. **FLOWERS:** Greenish white, urn-shaped, 0.1–0.2 in. long, 5-lobed; in open axillary clusters, not extending beyond the foliage. May–August. **FRUITS:** Slender follicles, usually paired, about 4 in. long; smooth seeds. **WHERE FOUND:** Roadsides, fields, and woodland margins throughout the U.S. and TN. Common.

SIMILAR SPECIES: SPREADING DOGBANE (*A. androsaemifolium*) has showy, **fragrant, bell-shaped, white or pink flowers**. Upland woodland margins in most of the U.S. In TN, in Franklin, Sequatchie, Bledsoe, Blount, Cocke, and Polk counties. Infrequent. June–August.

NOTES: The species name *cannabinum* means "hemp-like," referring to the fibrous stems, which are similar to hemp and were used for making rope. Rope made from this plant reportedly was "stronger and kept longer in water than that made of common hemp." • **Indian Hemp is poisonous**, and should not be confused with **Common Milkweed** (p. 229) when gathering edible wild foods. • Medicinally, the fresh root was used by Native Americans to induce vomiting and to treat syphilis.

Climbing Dogbane
Trachelospermum difforme

DENNIS HORN

GENERAL: High, **twining, woody vine** with smooth, reddish brown stems; our only climbing member of the Dogbane Family. **LEAVES:** Opposite, thin-stalked, 2–4 in. long, entire, ovate-lanceolate, acute at the tips. **FLOWERS:** Pale yellow or cream-colored, **funnel-shaped corolla tube**, about 0.25 in. long, has **5 divergent lobes**; multi-flowered cyme arises from a single axil of the paired leaves. June–August. **FRUITS:** Slender follicles, 5–9 in. long. **WHERE FOUND:** Moist woods, streambanks, and swamp margins. In the Coastal Plain from DE to TX, and interior in the Mississippi River Valley to southwestern IN and southeastern MO. In West TN, also Robertson, Rutherford, Giles, and Hamilton counties. Occasional.

NOTES: The Dogbane Family name, Apocynaceae, is from the Greek *apocynum*, meaning "away dog," because these plants were considered to be poisonous to dogs, but apparently they are not as poisonous as once thought. The word "bane" signifies that the plant is **poisonous.** • As is often the case, plants that are poisonous also may contribute important medicinal compounds. For example, in the 18th century, it was discovered that roots of some plants in this family contain cymarin, a cardiac glycoside and a potential remedy for heart disease shown to have digitalis-like activity, as well as the alkaloid reserpine.

Periwinkle • *Vinca minor**

ED HONICKER

GENERAL: Trailing, **semi-woody, mat-forming vine**. **LEAVES:** Opposite, **lanceolate to elliptic**, 1–2 in. long, smooth, shiny, dark **evergreen**, entire. **FLOWERS:** Blue or lavender blue, **0.8–1.2 in. across**, slender 5-lobed corolla tube, 0.3–0.5 in. long; axillary on the erect stalks. April–May. **FRUITS:** Follicles, usually paired and erect; rough seeds. **WHERE FOUND:** Introduced from Europe. Old home sites, cemeteries, and waste ground. Widespread in the eastern U.S. and across TN. Occasional. **SIMILAR SPECIES:** GREATER PERIWINKLE (*V. major**) is stouter with flowering stems up to 20 in. tall; **deciduous** to semi-evergreen, **triangular-ovate leaves**; lavender blue **flowers, 1.4–2.0 in. across**, with corolla tubes 0.6–0.8 in. long. Introduced from Europe. Escaped in the southeastern U.S. as far north as NY and IL. Thinly spread across TN. Occasional. April–May.

NOTES: Periwinkle is also commonly known as **Myrtle**, and less commonly as Hundred Eyes, Joy-of-the-Ground, and Running Myrtle. • In herbal folklore, it was used to treat stomach ailments, to stop nose bleeds, and for certain wounds. It also was used as an aphrodisiac. • Both *V. minor* and *V. major* have showy flowers, but often escape and become troublesome weeds.

Bluntleaf Milkweed, Curly Milkweed • *Asclepias amplexicaulis*

GENERAL: Perennial herb, 18–36 in. tall, with a stout, erect stem. **LEAVES:** Opposite, 3–6 in. long, ovate to oblong, **wavy with a clasping base.** **FLOWERS:** Rose purple, 0.5–0.7 in. long; 5 corolla lobes, 0.3–0.4 in. long; **pink "hoods" are shorter than "horns"**; borne in large umbels, usually solitary. May–July. **FRUITS:** Follicles, 4–6 in. long, dehiscent along 1 suture; seeds have silky tufts of hair that aid in dispersal. **WHERE FOUND:** Dry soil, fields, thin woods, roadsides, and barrens throughout the eastern U.S. Scattered across TN. Occasional.

NOTES: Milkweeds are sometimes called "swallowworts." Many *Asclepias* species are edible after careful preparation. • Members of the **Milkweed Family** are perennial herbs that usually contain a milky sap. The unusual flowers occur in umbels. The corolla is deeply divided into 5 lobes that are bent backward. It supports a crown of 5 incurved, erect, or spreading "hoods," each usually containing a slender, incurved "horn." Seeds are produced in pods and are attached to soft downy tufts of hair. The soft down was used by Native Americans for the absorption of waste in papoose carriers. There are 13 species of milkweeds in TN.

HUGH & CAROL NOURSE

Poke Milkweed, Tall Milkweed
Asclepias exaltata

GENERAL: Erect, mostly smooth perennial herb, 3–5 ft. tall. **LEAVES:** Broadly elliptic, 4–8 in. long, mostly smooth, thin, tapered at each end, resembling those of **Pokeweed** (p. 72), except that milkweed leaves are opposite. **FLOWERS:** White tinged with green or lavender; 5 corolla lobes, 0.3–0.4 in. long; **"horns" are longer than "hoods"**; loosely flowered with drooping umbels; flower clusters emerge from upper leaf axils. June–July. **FRUITS:** Smooth, erect follicles, 5–6 in. long, dehiscent along 1 suture; seeds have silky tufts of hair that aid in dispersal. **WHERE FOUND:** Upland woods, dry clearings, and rich forest margins. A northeastern U.S. species extending south in the uplands to GA. In TN, from the Cumberland Plateau eastward, also in Giles, Maury, and Sumner counties. Occasional.

NOTES: The dewy fresh flowers of this plant exude a sweet sugar. The young pods of some milkweed species can be blanched and then fried. The buds, young shoots, and flowers can be cooked as pot-herbs in several changes of water and added to soups. • In folklore, the dried sap was collected and used as chewing gum, but there are warnings that it can be **toxic.**

JERRY DROWN

Prairie Milkweed · *Asclepias hirtella*

GENERAL: Erect or reclining perennial herb to 3 ft. tall. **LEAVES:** Numerous, **mostly alternate**, 4–6 in. long, **linear to oblong**, roughish. **FLOWERS: Greenish white or slightly purple, very slender,** 0.3–0.35 in. long, 5 reflexed corolla lobes, 0.2 in. long; borne on slightly hairy stalks; inflorescences arise from the leaf axils in nearly spherical umbels. June–August. **FRUITS:** Erect, smooth follicles, dehiscent along 1 suture; seeds have silky tufts of hair that aid in dispersal. **WHERE FOUND:** Prairies, barrens, and glades, from WV to MN, south to GA and LA. In TN, in Montgomery, Stewart, Lewis, Franklin, Coffee, Warren, Bledsoe, and Bradley counties. Infrequent.

NOTES: The silky material inside milkweed pods is useful for more than simply dispersing seeds. During World War II, it was collected and used as stuffing for lifejackets because it is 5 or 6 times more buoyant than cork. It is also warmer than wool and 6 times lighter. A few pounds of this silky "floss" stuffed into a jacket could float a 150-pound pilot if he crashed into the sea and would keep him warm as well.

DENNIS HORN

Swamp Milkweed
Asclepias incarnata

GENERAL: Erect perennial herb, 2–5 ft. tall; stems are slender, branched above, and smooth. **LEAVES:** Opposite, numerous to the top of the stem, 3–6 in. long, petioled, linear-lanceolate to slightly ovate, hairy beneath. **FLOWERS: Pink to deep rose,** 5 reflexed corolla lobes about 0.2 in. long, "hoods" about 0.1 in. long; borne in numerous umbels, 1–2 in. across, terminal and in the upper leaf axils. June–August. **FRUITS:** Erect follicles, dehiscent along 1 suture; **pods on erect stalks;** seeds have silky tufts of hair that aid in dispersal. **WHERE FOUND:** Moist meadows, ditches, and marshes in most of eastern and central U.S., southern Canada, and throughout TN. Frequent.

NOTES: One of our showiest milkweeds, this plant is also called Flesh-Colored Silkweed, Rabbit Milk, Rose Milkweed, Silkplant, Water-Nerve Root, and White Indian Hemp. • Native Americans would harvest the ripe plant and rub it to separate the fibers to use as fishing line and sewing thread. The roots were used medicinally for asthma and dysentery. It was also added to liquor to make bitters.

KURT EMMANUELE

Aquatic Milkweed
Asclepias perennis

GENERAL: Erect perennial herb to 3 ft. tall with slender stems. **LEAVES:** Opposite, 2–6 in. long, thin, oblong, acute at both ends, on thin petioles. **FLOWERS:** Sparse, white to light pink, 5 reflexed corolla lobes, 0.1–0.16 in. long, "hoods" about 0.1 in. long, shorter than "horns"; borne in umbels about 1 in. across. July–August. **FRUITS:** Erect follicles, dehiscent along 1 suture; seeds lack silky tufts of hair; mature fruits are pendant. **WHERE FOUND:** Swamps, marshes, and riverbanks along the Coastal Plain from SC to TX, and interior in the Mississippi River Valley to southern IN and southern MO. In TN, from the Western Highland Rim westward. Occasional.

NOTES: This plant is also known as White Milkweed for the flowers, Smoothseed Milkweed for the lack of silky hair on the seeds, and Wetland Milkweed for its favored habitat. The genus name *Asclepias* is derived from the name of the Greek god of medicine, Asklepios, indicating the medicinal uses of plants in this genus. • Insects that feed on milkweeds include bees, wasps, flies, beetles, and butterflies.

MILO PYNE

Purple Milkweed
Asclepias purpurascens

GENERAL: Stout perennial herb to 3 ft. tall, with soft, downy stems. **LEAVES:** Opposite, simple, elliptic or oblong, 3–5 in. long, entire, on short leaf stalks, hairy beneath. **FLOWERS:** Deep red-purple; 5 reflexed corolla lobes, 0.3–0.4 in. long; "horns" shorter than "hoods," which are 0.2–0.3 in. long; numerous flowers in 1–3 umbels, 1.6–3.0 in. across. June–July. **FRUITS:** Erect, somewhat downy follicles, dehiscent along 1 suture; seeds have silky tufts of hair that aid in dispersal. **WHERE FOUND:** Roadsides, rocky ground, and dry fields, from NH to SD, south to GA and TX. In TN, in Montgomery, Stewart, Williamson, and Greene counties. Rare.

NOTES: Butterflies and hummingbirds are attracted to the reddish purple flowers of milkweeds, including this species and especially **Butterfly Weed** (p. 230). The umbels of milkweeds are a perfect perch for many butterfly species, including the Monarch, Red-Spotted Purple, and swallowtails. They drink the nectar and move from plant to plant, unknowingly distributing pollen. The Monarch butterfly lays its eggs on the leaves of milkweeds. When the larvae hatch, they feed voraciously on the leaves and buds for 10 to 14 days before forming a gold-banded, green chrysalis on a stiff stem or branch. In a few weeks, a Monarch butterfly emerges.

DENNIS HORN

Fourleaf Milkweed · *Asclepias quadrifolia*

GENERAL: Slender, unbranched perennial herb with stems 12–20 in. tall. **LEAVES:** Lanceolate, sessile, 2–6 in. long, slightly hairy underneath; middle leaves usually in **whorls of 4**, upper and lower leaves smaller and opposite. **FLOWERS:** Light pink, 5 reflexed corolla lobes about 0.2 in. long, **white "hoods,"** 0.16–0.2 in. long, are **longer than incurved "horns"**; hemispherical umbels, 1.5–2.0 in. across, are terminal or from the upper leaf nodes. May–June. **FRUITS:** Erect, smooth follicles, 4–5 in. long, dehiscent along 1 suture; seeds have silky tufts of hair that aid in dispersal. **WHERE FOUND:** Dry upland woods and forest edges from NH to MN. south in the uplands to GA, AL, and AR. In TN, from the Western Highland Rim eastward. Frequent.

NOTES: Both the common name and the species name *quadrifolia*, meaning "four leaves," refer to the mid-level leaves that are often in whorls of 4. • During fall when the seedpods are conspicuous, the pods will burst open and release hundreds of seeds on silken parachutes. Goldfinches use these silken seeds to line their nests.

JERRY DROWN

Common Milkweed · *Asclepias syriaca*

GENERAL: Erect, colonial perennial herb, 3–5 ft. tall, with stout, hairy stems. **LEAVES:** Opposite, oblong to slightly oval, 4–6 in. long, acute at the tip, hairy beneath, smooth above. **FLOWERS:** Numerous, **fragrant, grayish lavender or dull rose**, 5 reflexed corolla lobes, 0.3–0.4 in. long; **"horns" equal to "hoods,"** which are about 0.2 in. long; borne in umbels, 2–4 in. across. June–August. **FRUITS:** Spiny follicles, **erect on recurved stalks**, several ascending the stem. **WHERE FOUND:** Fields, roadsides, and meadows from southern Canada and the eastern U.S., west to the Great Plains. In TN, along the Western Highland Rim eastward, also in Shelby County in West TN. Frequent.

NOTES: The young leaves, buds, flowers, and seedpods of this species are considered edible, but must be boiled several times to eliminate the milky, **toxic sap.** The buds are a good substitute for broccoli. If the young sprouts are carefully prepared, they can be eaten like asparagus. • At one time, the root was used as a contraceptive by the native peoples of Québec, and the Shawnees used the white sap to remove warts. Medicinally, this plant was also used to treat dysentery and asthma. • The milky juice in the stem protects the plants from ants: their feet puncture the stem and get caught in the sticky, white sap.

JERRY DROWN

Butterfly Weed, Pleurisy-Root
Asclepias tuberosa

GENERAL: Attractive perennial herb to 24 in. tall; although a true milkweed, the **milky sap is absent**. **LEAVES:** Alternate, numerous, 2–4 in. long, sessile or short-petioled, linear to lanceolate, acute or sometimes rounded at the tips, hairy, coarse. **FLOWERS:** Showy, **orange or orange-red** (rarely yellow), 5 reflexed corolla lobes about 0.3 in. long; **erect "hoods" are longer than "horns"**; borne in hemispheric terminal umbels, 1–2 in. wide, usually abundant. June–August. **FRUITS:** Follicles, 3–5 in. long, dehiscent along 1 suture, **erect on drooping stalks**. **WHERE FOUND:** Roadsides, prairies, and dry, open sandy soils in southeastern Canada and in most of the eastern and central U.S. Throughout TN. Common.

NOTES: This beautiful plant is often taken from the wild for home gardens, which has extirpated it from some areas. It should be grown from seed or obtained through nurseries. • The relationship between the Monarch butterfly and **Butterfly Weed** is mutually beneficial. In addition to providing nectar, Butterfly Weed contains a cardiac glycoside that passes from the caterpillar into the butterfly and subsequently to any bird that feeds on the insect. If a bird eats the butterfly, it will suffer nausea and vomiting and learn to be cautious about eating another Monarch. In exchange, the butterfly pollinates the plant, ensuring its survival.

White Milkweed · *Asclepias variegata*

GENERAL: Erect perennial herb to 3 ft. tall, with an unbranched stem. **LEAVES:** Opposite, 4–6 pairs of broad, ovate-oblong leaves, 3–5 in. long, dark green above, pale and hairy beneath. **FLOWERS:** White with a purple band around the center, 5 reflexed corolla lobes, about 0.3 in. long; **inward-turned "horns" are shorter than "hoods"**; borne in dense umbels, 1–2 in. wide, stalked and mainly terminal. May–June. **FRUITS:** Erect follicles, 4–5 in. long, dehiscent along 1 suture, on **stalks that are bent downward**; seeds have silky hairs. **WHERE FOUND:** Thin, dry upland woods and woodland margins throughout most of the eastern U.S. and TN. Common.

NOTES: This showy species is also called **Variegated Milkweed**, after the species name *variegata*, which refers to the multicolored flowers. • Although this plant may not attract as many butterflies as other milkweeds, it does attract a wide variety of sizable flying insects. • The white flowers and ovate leaves are distinctive characteristics of this species. It is most easily distinguished from **Poke Milkweed** (p. 226) because the flower clusters are erect, not drooping.

Whorled Milkweed · *Asclepias verticillata*

GENERAL: Erect perennial herb 10–20 in. tall, stem often branched near the top, from rhizomes and fleshy roots. **LEAVES:** In whorls of 3–6 around the slender stem, numerous, **linear**, 1–2 in. long. **FLOWERS:** Greenish white, 5 corolla lobes, 0.15–0.2 in. long; white divergent "hoods," prominent, **incurved "horns" longer than hoods**; small umbels, 1–2 in. wide, on stalks arising from leaf axils. June–August. **FRUITS:** Narrow, spindle-shaped follicles, 2–3 in. long, on **erect stalks**, dehiscent along 1 suture. **WHERE FOUND:** Roadsides, upland woods, and barrens, from VT to FL, west to MT and AZ. In TN, along the Western Highland Rim eastward, also McNairy County in West TN. Frequent.

NOTES: This plant is also known as **Whorled Leaf Milkweed**, in reference to the arrangement of the leaves. This interesting milkweed is easily overlooked as it blends with the surrounding vegetation. However, when seen, it is one of the easiest milkweeds to identify because of its characteristic thread-like, whorled leaves.

MILO PYNE

Green Milkweed
Asclepias viridiflora

GENERAL: Perennial herb 12–30 in. tall with slightly hairy stems, erect or reclining, sometimes prostrate, rarely branched. **LEAVES:** Opposite, 2–4 in. long, linear-lanceolate to elliptic to ovate-oblong, entire, thick, edges rough, slightly hairy beneath. **FLOWERS:** Pale green, 5 **strongly reflexed corolla lobes**, 0.25–0.3 in. long; **narrow, erect "hoods"** about 0.2 in. long, **"horns" absent**; borne in dense hemispheric umbels, 1.0–1.5 in. wide, emerging from the upper leaf nodes. July–August. **FRUITS:** Erect follicles, 5–6 in. long, dehiscent along 1 suture. **WHERE FOUND:** Dry upland woods, barrens, prairies, cedar glades, and sandy soils in most of the eastern and central U.S., more common westward. Thinly scattered across TN. Occasional.

NOTES: This species, also known as **Green Comet Milkweed**, is unusual because of the greenish color and the lack of horns on the flowers. • Milkweeds have an interesting method of cross-pollination. Pollen sacs (pollinia) occur in pairs and are hidden within the flower hoods. When a pollinating insect visits a flower, the sacs become attached to the insect's legs. Upon visiting another plant, the sacs are dislodged and new ones are picked up.

DENNIS HORN

Antelope-Horn Milkweed
Asclepias viridis

GENERAL: Perennial herb, 10–30 in. tall, reclining or ascending. **LEAVES:** Numerous, **alternate**, ovate-oblong to lanceolate, 2–5 in. long, rounded at the base, short-petioled. **FLOWERS:** Greenish, about 1 in. wide, **purple center**, on erect stalks, 5 **ascending or spreading corolla lobes, not reflexed**; "hoods" about 0.2 in. long, **"horns" absent**; in several clusters. May–June. **FRUITS:** Follicles, dehiscent along 1 suture; seeds have silky hairs to aid in dispersal. **WHERE FOUND:** Prairies, barrens, and limestone glades, from OH to NE, south to FL and TX. In TN, in Davidson, Rutherford, Wilson, Giles, Hamilton, and Rhea counties. Infrequent.

KURT EMMANUELE

NOTES: The name of this perennial is inconsistent with its structure, as the flower is without horns and does not look like a typical milkweed. It is also called **Spider Milkweed** for the white Crab Spider, which makes its home on the plant and is well camouflaged when on the flowers. The spider preys on insects that visit the flower clusters, and when the flowers are in bloom, it can eat enough prey to increase its mass tenfold (from 40 mg to 400 mg) in 2 weeks.

Common Anglepod
Matelea gonocarpos

GENERAL: Perennial **twining vine** with a downy stem and **milky sap. LEAVES:** Opposite, **heart-shaped**, to 4 in. long and ½ as wide, each leaf on a stalk up to the length of the blade. **FLOWERS:** Smooth, **star-shaped, greenish purple**, about 1 in. wide, 5 narrow lobes; clustered on long stalks; **conical flower buds.** June–July. **FRUITS:** Smooth, **angled** follicles, 3–5 in. long, dehiscent along 1 suture. **WHERE FOUND:** Moist, rich woods, thickets,

DENNIS HORN

and waste places, from southeastern VA to FL and TX; in the Mississippi River Valley to southern MO and southern IN. Throughout TN. Frequent. **SIMILAR SPECIES:** SPINYPOD (*M. carolinensis*), also known as **MAROON CAROLINA MILKVINE**, has **dark maroon flowers** that are glandular-hairy with **lobes 0.3–0.4 in. long** and nearly ½ as wide; **round flower buds; spiny follicles**. Rich woods and thickets, from DE to southern MO, southward. Mostly in Middle TN. Occasional. June–July. **CLIMBING MILKVINE** (*M. obliqua*) also has dark maroon flowers, but the **lobes are 0.4–0.6 in. long** and ¼ as wide; **conical flower buds**. Rocky woods and clearings, usually on calcareous soils, from PA to MO, south to GA and MS. Widely scattered across TN. Occasional. June–July.

NOTES: Common Anglepod is also referred to as **Angularfruit Milkvine** and is best identified by its large, heart-shaped leaves, vining habit, and greenish, star-shaped flowers.

Jimsonweed · *Datura stramonium**

GENERAL: Coarse, **strongly scented, weedy annual**, 2–5 ft. tall, with a mostly smooth, purplish, branched stem. **LEAVES:** Alternate, broadly lanceolate, 3–6 in. long, petioled, coarsely toothed. **FLOWERS:** Very showy, **white to lavender**, 2.5–4.0 in. long, **funnel-shaped with pleated lobes**; terminal and solitary, usually opening in the late afternoon. June–August. **FRUITS:** Dry, **spiny**, ovoid capsules, 1–2 in. long, with numerous black, flattened seeds. **WHERE FOUND:** Sunny, disturbed ground, farm lots and barnyards, fields, and roadsides. Introduced from Asia and presently scattered throughout the majority of temperate North America and TN. Occasional.

DENNIS HORN

NOTES: Another common name, **Thorn Apple**, indicates that this plant is both edible and poisonous. It was said that a person could eat a small amount of the root with wine to have "not unpleasant fantasies," but if too much was taken, it could be **lethal**. The rank smell is another clue that it can be **poisonous**. • The **Potato Family** includes many commonly cultivated plants: potatoes, tomatoes, eggplants, peppers, tobacco, and petunias. It is a highly variable family, but all species have 5-parted flowers. Five genera and 19 species are listed for TN.

Apple-of-Peru
Nicandra physalodes*

GENERAL: Smooth **annual**, 1–4 ft. tall, with a single, ridged, succulent, stout, highly branched stem. **LEAVES:** Alternate, 4–8 in. long, thin, mostly lanceolate-ovate, long petioled, coarsely toothed. **FLOWERS:** Pale blue, **open bell-shaped**, about 1.5 in. wide; sepals deeply 5-parted, veiny, about 0.5 in. long, much longer when in fruit; solitary from leaf axils, usually opening late in the after-

NITA R. HEILMAN

noon. July–September. **FRUITS:** Dry berries, 0.5–0.8 in. across, enclosed by an enlarged **papery calyx**, resembling a tomatillo. **WHERE FOUND:** Introduced from Peru. Disturbed ground and fields in most of the eastern U.S. Thinly scattered throughout TN. Occasional.

NOTES: The *Nicandra* genus was named in honor of Nikander of Colophon (200–130 BCE), a Greek poet who wrote about plants and their medicinal uses. The species name *physalodes* means "like a bladder," referring to the inflated calyx of the fruit designed to protect it from pests and the elements. This plant is **very poisonous** and historically was used as fly poison, giving it another name, Shoofly Plant.

Angular Ground Cherry
Physalis angulata

GENERAL: Smooth, highly branched **annual**, 12–36 in. tall. **LEAVES:** Alternate, ovate to lanceolate-ovate, 2–4 in. long, irregularly and **coarsely toothed**. **FLOWERS:** Yellowish, **not dark in the center**, broadly bell-shaped, about 0.5 in. wide, 5 shallow lobes; fruiting calyx is sunken at the base and smooth, about as wide as long, typically purple-veined and 10-ribbed. July–September. **FRUITS:** Pulpy or mealy berries with numerous seeds, enclosed in a lantern-like, **papery calyx**. **WHERE FOUND:** Fields, roadsides, and open woodlands. A southern U.S. species extending north to VA, IL, and KS. Thinly scattered across the western ⅔ of TN. Occasional. **SIMILAR SPECIES:** DOWNY GROUND CHERRY (*P. pubescens*) has an **upper stem with soft, spreading hairs**; leaves shallowly toothed; yellow flowers with a dark center. Moist soil, from VT to MN, southward. Scattered throughout TN. Frequent. May–September.

NOTES: Nine species of ground cherries (*Physalis* spp.) are found in TN, all fairly similar in appearance with yellow, bell-like flowers, usually solitary, and often brown at the corolla base. The united sepals form an inflated bladder (calyx) around a small, tomato-like berry. When the fruits are green, the berries, like the young leaves, are **poisonous**. However when the fruits are fully ripe, they have traditionally been used in jams or pies. **Use extreme caution.**

RICHARD CONNORS

Virginia Ground Cherry · *Physalis virginiana*

GENERAL: Perennial herb, 12–24 in. tall, from rhizomes, stem with short hairs. **LEAVES:** Alternate, narrowly lanceolate to ovate, 1–4 in. long, toothed or entire, with **spreading hairs, tapering at the base** to a narrow, winged petiole. **FLOWERS:** Yellow with brown spots **in the center**, bell-shaped, drooping, about 0.75 in. wide, 5 shallow lobes, yellow anthers; fruiting calyx is sunken at the base, 5-angled, considerably longer than wide, with spreading hairs; usually solitary in the upper leaf axils. May–August. **FRUITS:** Red-orange, tomato-like berries surrounded by a **papery husk**. **WHERE FOUND:** Dry woods, fields, and clearings, from ME to ND, south to GA and NM. Throughout TN. Frequent. **SIMILAR SPECIES:** LONGLEAF GROUND CHERRY (*P. longifolia*) has **leaves with minute hairs or none; greenish yellow berries**. Fields and open woods throughout the U.S. Widespread across TN. Common. July–August. CLAMMY GROUND CHERRY (*P. heterophylla*) has **stems with sticky hairs; leaves with heart-shaped base** and **spreading hairs; yellow berries**. Upland woods and barrens throughout most of the eastern and central U.S., southeastern Canada, and TN. Frequent. June–September.

DENNIS HORN

NOTES: Virginia Ground Cherry has also been called Hog Plum, Husk Tomato, and Lance-Leaved Ground Cherry. • Native Americans ate the fully ripe fruit raw and used it in sauces. Extracts from this plant have been shown to have anticancer properties, and an infusion of the whole plant has been used to treat dizziness.

Horse Nettle
Solanum carolinense

GENERAL: Erect to sprawling, deep-rooted perennial herb, 12–36 in. tall, **covered with prickles. LEAVES:** Alternate, ovate, 3–5 in. long, with branched hairs on both surfaces and a few coarse teeth or shallow lobes on each margin. **FLOWERS: Pale violet to white**, about 0.75 in. wide, star-shaped with 5 lobes; long yellow anthers form a central cone; borne in lateral cluster. May–September. **FRUITS:** Yellow-orange berries, 0.5 in. across, **deadly poisonous** if ingested. **WHERE FOUND:** Weed of waste places, fields, and gardens throughout the eastern U.S. and TN. Common. **SIMILAR SPECIES: SILVERLEAF NIGHTSHADE (S. elaeagnifolium)** has **silvery foliage, small, weak spines**, and **lavender flowers**. Dry soil throughout the southern U.S. In Obion, Madison, and Shelby counties of West TN. Rare. June–September. **BUFFALO BUR (S. rostratum*)** is a **spiny annual** with **yellow flowers**; berries are enclosed by a spiny calyx. Dry areas. A native of the Great Plains, now naturalized throughout the U.S. Thinly scattered across TN. Infrequent. July–September.

NOTES: Other common names for **Horse Nettle** are Apple-of-Sodom, Bull Nettle, Poisonous Potato, Thorn Apple, and Tread Softly, indicating the danger of the prickly stems and the plant's inedibility. Although native, this species is a stubborn weed closely related to the cultivated potato.

Bittersweet Nightshade
Solanum dulcamara*

GENERAL: Woody vine, shrubby down low, but trailing or climbing to 9 ft. long. **LEAVES:** Alternate, smooth, ovate, 2–4 in. long; variable, some with a **pair of basal lobes. FLOWERS: Blue or violet**, about 0.75 in. wide, 5 narrow lobes, **each lobe with 2 green dots at the base**, bright yellow anthers surrounding the style; borne in drooping clusters of 10–25 flowers. June–September. **FRUITS: Bright red, oval berries**, about 0.4 in. long, are well liked by birds, but **poisonous** to humans. **WHERE FOUND:** Introduced from Eurasia. Moist, disturbed ground, open woods, and cliffs. Throughout most of the northern U.S. In TN, in Davidson, Hawkins, and Carter counties. Rare.

NOTES: Bittersweet Nightshade is also known as **Climbing Nightshade**, Blue Bindweed, Fellenwort, Myrtlevine, and Violet Bloom. Names that indicate its medicinal and inedible properties are Fevertwig, Poison Berry, Poison Flower, Snakeberry, and Wolf Grape.
• Historically, the roots of Bittersweet Nightshade were used to treat venereal diseases, as well as rheumatism, bronchitis, and various skin ailments.

OTTO R. HIRSCH

Common Nightshade, Black Nightshade · *Solanum ptychanthum*

GENERAL: Erect **annual** to 24 in. tall, with **smooth stems and leaves**, not hairy, prickly, or spiny. **LEAVES:** Alternate, ovate to deltoid, 2–4 in. long, irregularly blunt-toothed or almost entire, long-petioled. **FLOWERS:** White or pale violet, to 0.4 in. wide, 5 pointed lobes, yellow anthers united in a central cone; inflorescence is short-peduncled and umbel-like with 2–5 flowers lateral from the nodes. May–October. **FRUITS:** Ripe berries are black and edible; unripe berries are poisonous. **WHERE FOUND:** Cosmopolitan weed of disturbed habitats throughout the eastern and central U.S. and TN. Frequent. *S. americanum*, *S. nigrum*.

NOTES: This plant is also called **Deadly Nightshade**, Blueberry, Bonewort, Morel, and Stubbleberry. Note that the **leaves and unripe berries are poisonous**. In Madagascar, the ripe berries of a closely related Eurasian species are very popular cooked in sauces and eaten with chicken and rice. In herbal medicine, Common Nightshade berries were used to treat stomachaches, nervous afflictions, inflammations of mucous membranes, syphilitic eruptions, and as a narcotic.

KURT EMMANUELE

Hedge Bindweed
Calystegia sepium

GENERAL: Twining **perennial herbaceous vine** to 6 ft. long. **LEAVES:** Alternate, triangular to oblong with sagittate or hastate bases, 2–4 in. long, long-stalked. **FLOWERS:** Solitary, white to rose pink, funnel-shaped, 1.5–3.0 in. long and broad, 5 shallow lobes; large involucral bracts, to 0.8 in. long, mostly ovate, hide the calyx. May–August. **FRUITS:** 2-chambered capsules. **WHERE FOUND:** Thickets, roadsides, and disturbed areas throughout most of temperate North America and TN. Frequent. *Convolvulus sepium*. **SIMILAR SPECIES:** LOW BINDWEED (*C. spithamaea*) is more erect and has less tendency to vine; leaves velvety, on short petioles. Fields and roadsides from ME to MN, south to AL and GA. Scattered across TN. Occasional. May–July. FIELD BINDWEED (*Convolvulus arvensis**) lacks the bracts covering the calyx; smaller flowers. Introduced from Europe and now a weed throughout the U.S. and TN. Occasional. May–September.

NOTES: Other names for **Hedge Bindweed** include Creepers, Devil's Vine, Hellweed, and Woodbind, mostly referring to this plant's twining characteristic. The species name *sepium* means "of hedges" for its habit of using shrubs and hedges as support. • The bindweed species mentioned here are **poisonous**. • The family name, Convolvulaceae, is from the Latin *convolvere*, which means "to twine around," an apt name for the plants in this group.

Common Dodder, Love Vine
Cuscuta gronovii

GENERAL: Parasitic, twining herb, slender with pinkish yellow to **orange, smooth stems**; twining stems often form a dense, **tangled mat on low-growing vegetation**; lacks both leaves and chlorophyll. **LEAVES:** None. **FLOWERS:** White, waxy, bell-shaped, 0.10–0.16 in. wide, 5 short, pointed lobes; borne in compact clusters. August–October. **FRUITS:** Irregularly dehiscing capsules with 2–4 seeds. **WHERE FOUND:** Low ground, fields, and thickets throughout most of the eastern and central U.S. and TN. Frequent.

NOTES: The name **Love Vine** comes from the characteristic of the stems to twine around themselves and the host plant. Once attached, it invades the host plant's stem to extract nourishment from it. The seeds germinate in soil, but the roots soon die as the plant attaches to its host plant. • Plants of this genus are parasitic on various herbaceous plants and occasionally on woody plants as well. Six *Cuscuta* species are listed for TN, but separating them is difficult. They sometimes are placed in their own family, the Dodder Family (Cuscutaceae).

NITA R. HEILMAN

Small Red Morning Glory · *Ipomoea coccinea*⁕

GENERAL: Smooth **twining annual herbaceous vine**, 3–9 ft. long. **LEAVES:** Alternate, typically **heart-shaped**, 2–4 in. long, entire, may occasionally be coarsely toothed or angularly lobed. **FLOWERS:** Scarlet, **trumpet-like** (salverform), to 1.4 in. long and 0.8 in. across, 5 shallow lobes, **yellow throat**; few to many in raceme- or cyme-like clusters at the apex of long, axillary stalks. August–October. **FRUITS:** 4-valved capsules. **WHERE FOUND:** Introduced from tropical America. Moist soil and waste places. Escaped from cultivation and naturalized in most of the eastern U.S. and in the eastern ¾ of TN. Frequent.

OTTO R. HIRSCH

NOTES: All parts of this plant are **poisonous** and contain substances that can cause hallucinations. Plants in the *Ipomoea* genus are called "morning glories" because the flowers bloom early in the day, near dawn, and close a few hours later. They wilt rapidly when exposed to full sun. • The 7 *Ipomoea* species listed for TN are twining vines, with funnel-shaped to bell-shaped or trumpet-like flowers that have entire, angled, or shallowly lobed margins.

DAVID DUHL

Ivyleaf Morning Glory · *Ipomoea hederacea**

GENERAL: Annual, twining, hairy vine, 3–6 ft. long. **LEAVES:** Alternate, 2–5 in. long, usually **distinctively 3-lobed** (atypically 5-lobed to entire) and pointed. **FLOWERS:** White, pale blue or pink, funnel-shaped, 1–2 in. long, usually about as wide as long; hairy sepals have narrow, curved-back tips; 1–3 flowers on stalks shorter than leaf petioles. July–October. **FRUITS:** Flattened, 2-valved capsules. **WHERE FOUND:** Introduced from tropical America. Naturalized to disturbed areas, fencerows, fields, and waste places throughout the eastern U.S. and TN. Frequent. **SIMILAR SPECIES: SCARLET CYPRESS VINE** (*I. quamoclit**) is a **smooth** annual vine, 3–16 ft. long; **leaves pinnately divided into very narrow segments**; funnel-shaped, **scarlet flowers** to 1.4 in. long and 0.8 in. across. Introduced from tropical America. Escaped from cultivation in most of the eastern U.S. In TN, in Shelby, Williamson, and Blount counties. Rare. August–October.

NOTES: The genus name *Ipomoea* is from the Greek meaning "worm-like," which is appropriate since the viny stems of these plants wind or "worm" their way up the stalks of other plants. Subsequently, the large leaves of **Ivyleaf Morning Glory** block the sunlight of surrounding species, causing damage to crops such as corn, cotton, and soybeans.

DENNIS HORN

Small White Morning Glory · *Ipomoea lacunosa*

GENERAL: Annual twining vine, 3–9 ft. long, smooth or sparsely hairy. **LEAVES:** Alternate, ovate, 1.5–3.0 in. long, **margins typically maroon**; leaf base is **heart-shaped with 2 small lobes** or sometimes unlobed. **FLOWERS:** White or sometimes pink, funnel-shaped, to 0.9 in. long and not as wide; 1–3 flowers on stalks from the leaf axils shorter than the leaf petioles. August–October. **FRUITS:** 2-valved capsules with hairs at the top. **WHERE FOUND:** Disturbed areas, fencerows, fields, and waste places, from NY to IA and KS, south to FL and TX. Widespread in TN. Frequent.

NOTES: Interestingly, a morning glory always twines around its support in the same direction, typically clockwise, without variation, regardless of heat, cold, light, climate, or even hemisphere. In comparison, honeysuckle (*Lonicera*) and bindweed (*Calystegia*) can twist in either direction, even on the same plant. • The first morning glories that were found in Mexico were sent to Spanish monasteries and later appeared as part of the painted borders of many manuscripts.

Wild Potato Vine
Ipomoea pandurata

KURT EMMANUELE

General: Smooth, perennial, **trailing, herbaceous vine** to 15 ft. long, arising from a **large, vertical tuber-like root**. **Leaves:** Alternate, 2–6 in. long, somewhat variable, usually ovate and entire with a heart-shaped base and pointed tip. **Flowers: White with a purple center, funnel-shaped,** 2–3 in. long, typically about as wide as long; 1–5 flowers on stout stalks from the leaf axils, stalks usually longer than leaf petioles. May–July. **Fruits:** 2-valved capsules; seeds hairy on the angles. **Where Found:** Open, dry areas throughout most of the eastern U.S. and TN. Common.

Notes: This plant is also called **Man-of-the-Earth**, Man Root, and Wild Rhubarb in reference to the giant root, which can weigh up to 30 pounds and be as long as 4 ft. or more. The **edible roots** are similar to those of the related cultivated Sweet Potato (*I. batatas*), though they are more bitter. **Wild Potato Vine** was an important food source for Native Americans.

Common Morning Glory · *Ipomoea purpurea**

WILLIAM F. RAINEY, JR.

General: Hairy, **twining annual vine** to 15 ft. long. **Leaves:** Alternate, 2–5 in. long, widely heart-shaped, entire. **Flowers: White, blue, pink, purple, or variegated, funnel-shaped**, 1.4–2.5 in. long and typically about as wide, 1–5 flowers on stalks from the leaf axils, stalks are about the same length as leaf petioles. July–October. **Fruits:** Nearly spherical, 3-valved capsules, about 0.4 in. wide. **Where Found:** Introduced from tropical America. Escaped from gardens into disturbed areas, fencerows, fields, and waste places. Widely established in most of the eastern and central U.S. Widespread in Middle and East TN, and Shelby County in West TN. Occasional.

Notes: Also called **Tall Morning Glory** and Blue Morning Glory, this plant is native to tropical America and was introduced to Britain around 1629. At that time, it was known as Indian Bindweed. • To see these glorious flowers, look for them in the morning before the sun has fully risen and the flowers close. The striking profusion of color of this plant has made an impression for many years. An example occurs in *Old Herbaceous* (1951), by Reginald Arkell. When Mrs. Charteris sees morning glories on the French Riviera, she exclaims that it is "as though someone had torn great masses out of a morning sky. It was so blue, so blue that it positively hurt."

DENNIS HORN

Hairy Phlox · *Phlox amoena*

GENERAL: Erect, **finely hairy** perennial herb to 12 in. tall, stems erect or reclining at the base. **LEAVES:** Opposite, 1–2 in. long, narrowly oblong to lanceolate and ascending. **FLOWERS:** Red-purple (also lavender to white), 0.6–0.8 in. across, **tubular with 5 divergent lobes; style short**, not reaching the lowest anthers; anthers remain inside the flower tube and are not visible upon flowering; **compact inflorescence** with a **hairy calyx.** April–June. **FRUITS:** Papery, dehiscent, 3-valved capsules, 0.25 in. long; 1–4 seeds per chamber. **WHERE FOUND:** Dry woods and fields from southern KY to western NC, south to northern FL and eastern MS. Middle and East TN. Frequent.

NOTES: Phloxes, sometimes referred to as "sweet williams," are popular because for a minimum of effort, gardeners can have a striking, sweet-smelling, long-lasting display of flowers. Most of the 50 to 60 species are native and are found only in North America, with a few additional species in northern Asia. Species of *Phlox* were exported to Europe and not cultivated in North America until they were reintroduced by European horticulturists. • Because *Phlox* species often hybridize in the wild, they can be difficult to identify. There are 11 species listed for TN.

PAUL SOMERS

Glade Phlox
Phlox bifida ssp. *stellaria*

GENERAL: Perennial with stiff reclining or ascending stems, flowering branches usually erect to 12 in. tall; often found in clusters. **LEAVES:** Opposite, linear to narrowly lanceolate, stiff, 0.6–1.6 in. long. **FLOWERS:** **Pale blue-violet to white**, 0.6–0.8 in. across, tubular with 5 divergent, **deeply notched corolla lobes**; **long style**, **anthers and style visible** upon full flowering; borne in few-flowered cymes. April–May. **FRUITS:** Papery, 3-valved capsules, 0.25 in. long. **WHERE FOUND:** Dry, sandy soils from southern MO and southern IN, south to TN. In TN, in the cedar glades of Davidson, Rutherford, and Wilson counties. Rare. **SIMILAR SPECIES:** MOSS PINK (*P. subulata*), also called **MOSS PHLOX**, is **densely matted** with numerous, shorter, hairy, clustered leaves and **shallowly notched corolla lobes**. Dry sandy or rocky areas. A mostly northeastern species that extends south in the uplands to TN and NC. Thinly scattered in Middle and East TN. Infrequent. April–May.

NOTES: The flowers of *Phlox* species have been described by botanists as salverform, or "tray-shaped," because of the flat surface formed by the 5 lobes at the end of the funnel tube. • The wide variety of *Phlox* species have evolved in different ways to specialize for specific pollinators, including bee flies, bees, beetles, butterflies, flies with long probosces, hummingbirds, moths, and owlet moths. Some are even pollinated by bats, and others are able to self-pollinate.

Wild Blue Phlox, Woodland Phlox
Phlox divaricata

DENNIS HORN

GENERAL: Perennial herb to 20 in. tall, with spreading, erect basal shoots. **LEAVES:** In **widely spaced pairs**, ovate-lanceolate to oblong, 1.2–2.0 in. long, widest below the middle, sharp-tipped. **FLOWERS:** Pale blue to red-purple (to white), 0.8–1.2 in. across, tubular with 5 divergent lobes; smooth corolla tube encloses the **short style**, which does not reach the lowest anthers, anthers also remain inside the flower tube and are not visible upon full flowering; borne in a loose, branched cyme with flowers on well-defined stalks. April–June. **FRUITS:** 3-valved capsules, 0.25 in. long. **WHERE FOUND:** Rich, moist woods from VT to MN, south to FL and TX. Throughout TN. Common. **SIMILAR SPECIES: MOUNTAIN PHLOX (*P. latifolia*)**, also called **WIDEFLOWER PHLOX**, has elliptic to obovate leaves; style is long; **anthers and style are visible** at the apex of the corolla tube. Open woods and thickets, mostly in the mountains from PA and IN, south to AL and GA. In northeastern TN, in Knox, Grainger, Hancock, Sevier, Cocke, and Greene counties. Infrequent. May–June. *P. ovata*.

NOTES: The name *Phlox* is Greek for "flame," referring to the bright color of the flowers in this genus; *divaricata* means "widely spreading," for the spreading inflorescence of **Wild Blue Phlox**. • Phlox flowers traditionally symbolized sweet dreams and a proposal of love.

Smooth Phlox • *Phlox glaberrima*

KURT EMMANUELE

GENERAL: Perennial herb, 20–48 in. tall, branched near the top of the stem, usually entirely **smooth and erect**. **LEAVES:** Opposite, 2–5 in. long, **firm, linear to narrowly lanceolate**, narrowed to a tapering tip. **FLOWERS:** Red-purple to pinkish, 0.6–0.8 in. wide, long, thin corolla tube with 5 spreading lobes; long style, **anthers and style show at the end of the corolla tube**; borne in compact cymes, located at the apex and axillary at the upper leaf axils. May–July. **FRUITS:** Capsules up to 0.25 in. long. **WHERE FOUND:** Wet woods and barrens from MD to southern WI, south to FL, LA, and OK. Throughout TN. Frequent. **SIMILAR SPECIES: FALL PHLOX (*P. paniculata*)**, also called **GARDEN PHLOX**, is larger, to 7 ft. tall; inflorescence, leaf margins, and **corolla tube finely hairy**; lateral **leaf veins prominent**. Rich, moist areas from ME to MN, south to northern GA and AR. Throughout TN. Common. July–September. **BROADLEAF PHLOX (*P. amplifolia*)** is much like Fall Phlox, but smaller, to 5 ft. tall; **glandular-hairy inflorescence; smooth corolla tube**. Dry or moist woods, from southern IN and MO, south to GA and MS. Middle and East TN. Occasional. June–September.

NOTES: The native **Smooth Phlox** has fragrant flowers and attracts hummingbirds and butterflies. • **Fall Phlox**, also known as **Summer Phlox**, is the ancestor of the popular cultivated ornamental of gardeners' perennial borders. The species name *paniculata* refers to the flowers, which are borne in panicles or loosely bunched clusters.

JERRY DROWN

Wild Sweet William · *Phlox maculata*

GENERAL: Smooth, erect perennial, 12–36 in. tall, the **stems usually dotted with red**. **LEAVES:** Opposite, linear-lanceolate to lanceolate or narrowly oblong, 2–5 in. long. **FLOWERS:** Red-purple, 0.5–1.0 in. wide, tubular with 5 spreading lobes, **long style, anthers and style show** at the end of the corolla tube; borne in elongated terminal and several axillary cymes that are densely and minutely hairy. June–July. **FRUITS:** 3-valved capsules, up to 0.25 in. long. **WHERE FOUND:** Wet woods and meadows, from ME to MN, south to GA and MS. In TN, from the Eastern Highland Rim eastward, also Dickson and Wayne counties. Occasional.

NOTES: The name that many people associate with *Phlox* species is that of Thomas Drummond (1790–1835), a Scottish naturalist and indefatigable collector of plants in Canada and the U.S. In all, he sent nearly 750 plant and 150 bird specimens to London. After leading a rather tortuous life and suffering numerous near-death tragedies, the annual Drummond's Phlox (*P. drummondii*) was one of the last plants he sent home before dying in Cuba from unrecorded causes. Sir Joseph Hooker of Kew Gardens named this plant in his honor to "serve as a frequent memento of its unfortunate discoverer." This was one of the plants that Victorian gardeners hybridized and later sent back to North America.

DENNIS HORN

Downy Phlox · *Phlox pilosa*

GENERAL: Perennial herb, 12–24 in. tall. **LEAVES:** Opposite, linear to ovate-lanceolate or ovate, 1.5–3.0 in. long, narrowed to a tapering tip. **FLOWERS:** Usually **pale purple** (to white), 0.6–0.8 in. across; **hairy corolla tube** with 5 spreading lobes; **short style** does not reach the lowest anthers, anthers remain inside the flower tube and are not visible upon full flowering; borne in a **loose, branched cyme with flowers on distinct pedicels**. April–June. **FRUITS:** 3-valved capsules to 0.25 in. long. **WHERE FOUND:** Dry, open woods, prairies, and roadsides throughout most of the eastern and central U.S. and TN. Frequent.

NOTES: The species name *pilosa* means "covered with long soft hairs," in reference to the hairy corolla tube. • In herbal medicine, the leaves of *Phlox* species were often crushed and added to water, which then was used to treat stomachaches, sore or irritated eyes, various skin diseases, and as a laxative. Butterflies, especially skippers, and moths frequent the flowers for nectar, while hover flies feed on the pollen.

Creeping Phlox · *Phlox stolonifera*

GENERAL: **Mat-forming** perennial herb with sterile **basal runners** (stolons) and divergent stems to 16 in. long. **LEAVES:** Opposite; runner and **lower stem leaves spatulate**, 1–2 in. long, gradually narrowed to a petiole-like base; upper stem leaves lanceolate to oblong and almost sessile. **FLOWERS:** **Pale bluish to red-purple**, 1.0–1.2 in. wide, tubular with 5 divergent corolla lobes; **long style**, **anthers and style show** at the apex of the corolla tube; few-flowered, glandular hairy cymes are loose and open. April–May. **FRUITS:** 3-valved capsules to 0.25 in. long. **WHERE FOUND:** Moist woods from ME and southern OH, south to AL and GA, mostly in the mountains but also in the Piedmont. In TN, limited to the Blue Ridge Mountains in Polk, Blount, Sevier, Cocke, Unicoi, Carter, and Johnson counties. Infrequent.

NOTES: The species name *stolonifera* means "having stolons or rooting runners," referring to this plant's method of spreading by leafy horizontal stems. • It is a showy roadside plant in the Smoky Mountains in mid- to late April. A popular garden plant, a large number of varieties of this species are available in nurseries.

DAVID DUHL

Greek Valerian, Jacob's Ladder
Polemonium reptans

GENERAL: Perennial herb, 10–20 in. tall, with one to many erect or ascending slender stems. **LEAVES:** Alternate, **pinnately compound** with a terminal leaflet and 3–8 lateral pairs of elliptic leaflets, 0.5–1.5 in. long. **FLOWERS:** **Lavender** (to white), **bell-shaped**, about 0.4 in. long, 5 lobes are about ½ the length of the corolla; **cream-colored stamens** are shorter than corolla; borne in a loose, few-flowered panicle. April–May. **FRUITS:** Capsules enclosed by the calyx, which enlarges after flowering. **WHERE FOUND:** Rich, moist woods from NH to MN, south to GA, MS, and eastern OK, and most abundant west of the Appalachian Mountains. Throughout TN, often along streambanks. Frequent.

NOTES: The long, ladder-like compound leaves with rung-like leaflets give this plant one of its common names, **Jacob's Ladder**. This name is also applied to *P. van-bruntiae*, a northeastern Appalachian species that does not occur in TN. • Medicinally, **Greek Valerian** was reported to cure consumption, and an infusion of the root in wine was used to treat coughs, colds, and a variety of complaints of the lungs.

DENNIS HORN

Appendaged Waterleaf
Hydrophyllum appendiculatum

GENERAL: Densely **hairy biennial**, 12–24 in. tall, from a taproot.
LEAVES: Alternate, broad, 3–6 in. long and wide, palmately 5-lobed (maple-leaf-shaped), the lobes broad, toothed, and pointed.
FLOWERS: Lavender, **bell-shaped**, about 0.5 in. long, 5 lobes about ½ the length of the corolla, **stamens extend 0.1 in.** beyond the corolla; loosely flowered **cymes extend above the leaves.** May–June. **FRUITS:**
Rounded capsules; 1–3 tan-colored seeds, wrinkled on the surface (reticulate). **WHERE FOUND:** Rich woods. A northern species extending south from Ontario and MN to AL and AR. Primarily in Middle TN. Occasional. **SIMILAR SPECIES:** BROADLEAF WATERLEAF (*H. canadense*) is a mostly **smooth perennial**, 12–20 in. tall; **leaves** with 5–7 palmate lobes **extend above the flowers**; white to pale purple flowers about 0.5 in. long; **stamens protrude 0.2 in.** beyond the corolla. Rich, moist woods from VT to southern Ontario and MI, south to northern GA, and northern AL. Scattered across most of TN. Occasional. May–June.

NOTES: The name "waterleaf" refers to plants of the genus *Hydrophyllum*, which have watery (*hydro*) stems or leaves (*phyllum*), and may also refer to the mottled leaves that appear water-stained. • The Waterleaf Family, with about 250 species, is found throughout much of the world, but is best represented in western North America. It is closely related to the Phlox and Forget-Me-Not families. The flowers are blue, purple, or white, and the corolla has 5 lobes and 5 stamens extending beyond the corolla. In TN, plants in the Waterleaf Family tend to be hairy with lobed leaves.

Largeleaf Waterleaf
Hydrophyllum macrophyllum

GENERAL: Perennial herb, 12–24 in. tall, and **very hairy**.
LEAVES: Alternate, 4–10 in. long and ½–⅔ as wide, **mottled, pinnately divided** with **7–13 coarsely toothed lobes**.
FLOWERS: White or pinkish, 0.3–0.5 in. long, 5 lobes ½ the length of the corolla tube, stamens extending another 0.33 in.; first appear as a round cluster of hairy buds. May–June. **FRUITS:** Rounded capsules surrounded by the calyx; 1–3 seeds with wrinkled surface. **WHERE FOUND:** Rich, moist woods from PA to IL, south to GA and AR. In Middle and East TN. Occasional. **SIMILAR SPECIES:** VIRGINIA WATERLEAF (*H. virginianum*) has stem and leaves only **sparsely hairy**; mottled **leaves with 3–7 lobes**; white to **dark violet** flowers. Rich, moist woods from New England to southern Manitoba, south to NC, TN, and OK. In East TN, in Knox, Sevier, Greene, Unicoi, Carter, Johnson, and Sullivan counties. Infrequent. May–June.

NOTES: The species name *macrophyllum* means "large leaf," and accurately describes **Largeleaf Waterleaf**, with its large, hairy leaves. Notice the blotchy, light green, mottled pattern, characteristic of waterleaf species. • **Virginia Waterleaf** has juicy leaves that are edible raw or cooked. It is also called **Shawnee Salad**, Indian Salad, and John's Cabbage.

Baby Blue Eyes · *Nemophila aphylla*

GENERAL: Small, diffusely branched, weak-stemmed **annual**, 4–16 in. tall, from a taproot. **LEAVES:** Alternate, long-petioled, 0.5–1.2 in. long, triangular in outline, **deeply divided** into 3–5 lobes, these again lobed and toothed. **FLOWERS:** White to pale blue, upward-turned, **bell-shaped, only 0.12 in. wide**, 5 rounded lobes; borne singly on long, thin stalks from the leaf nodes. March–May. **FRUITS:** Hairy capsules; 1–2 light brown seeds with a pitted surface. **WHERE FOUND:** Moist woods and river bottoms, from MD and KY, south to FL and TX. In Middle and East TN, also Shelby County in West TN. Frequent. ***N. microcalyx***, ***N. triloba***.

NOTES: The genus name *Nemophila* is from the Greek *nemos*, "a glade," and *phileo*, "to love," alluding to the spreading habit of some of these annual species. It is also known as **Smallflower Baby Blue Eyes**. • Members of the *Nemophila* genus are low, sprawling plants that grow in sun or partial shade.

OTTO R. HIRSCH

Purple Phacelia · *Phacelia bipinnatifida*

GENERAL: Biennial, 8–24 in. tall, with **hairy stems**. **LEAVES:** Alternate, long-petioled, mottled, hairy, **pinnately lobed** or divided, 2–4 in. long, coarsely toothed, emitting a distinctly musty odor when crushed. **FLOWERS:** Dusty purple with a white center, saucer-shaped, 0.4–0.6 in. wide, 5 rounded corolla lobes, **hairy stamens project beyond the corolla**; in a terminal inflorescence of helical cymes; very colorful when found en masse. April–May. **FRUITS:** Capsules with 2–4 black seeds. **WHERE FOUND:** Widespread in moist woods and on rocky slopes from PA to IA, south to GA and AR. Middle and East TN. Common. **SIMILAR SPECIES:** BLUE PHACELIA (***P. ranunculacea***) is a smaller, weak-stemmed **annual**; small tubular to funnel-shaped flowers, about 0.2 in. long; **smooth stamens included**. Rich, moist alluvial woods, from OH to MO, south to NC and AR. In TN, in Stewart, Montgomery, Lake, Obion, Lauderdale, and Shelby counties. Infrequent. April–May.

JERRY DROWN

NOTES: The genus name *Phacelia* comes from the Greek *phacelos*, meaning "a fascicle," in reference to the tightly coiled inflorescence when in bud. The species name *bipinnatifida* is a reference to the mottled leaves that are twice pinnately divided. • Phacelias are also called "scorpionweeds" because of the cluster of young flowers that coils like a scorpion's tail at the end of the stem. These plants are favored by bees, and their flowers yield a flavorful honey.

DENNIS HORN

Glade Phacelia
Phacelia dubia var. *interior*

GENERAL: Multi-stemmed **annual**, 4–15 in. tall, with weak and hairy stems. **LEAVES:** Alternate, short-petioled (or upper leaves sessile), **pinnately lobed**, to 2.5 in. long, with 3–11 toothed to entire segments. **FLOWERS: Pale blue to white**, 0.25–0.5 in. wide, resembling **Miami Mist** (p. 247), except the **petals are not fringed; sepals obovate-oblong**; borne in terminal clusters. April–May. **FRUITS:** Capsules with 4–6 brown seeds. **WHERE FOUND:** Cedar glades and barrens. Endemic to the Interior Low Plateau of TN. Found only in Montgomery, Sumner, Cheatham, Wilson, Davidson, Williamson, Rutherford, Maury, Giles, and Marshall counties in Middle TN. Infrequent. **SIMILAR SPECIES:** APPALACHIAN PHACELIA (*P. dubia* var. *dubia*), also known as **SMALL-FLOWERED SCORPION WEED**, has **lanceolate sepals**. Along roadsides, in fields and woods, and on rock outcrops from NY to OH, south to GA and LA. In East TN, in Polk, Monroe, Blount, Roane, Knox, Grainger, Cocke, Unicoi, and Carter counties. Infrequent. April–June.

NOTES: The species name *dubia* means "doubtful." Linnaeus originally placed **Glade Phacelia** in the genus *Polemonium*, but apparently had some reservations about this decision. • **Appalachian Phacelia**, like Glade Phacelia, depends on seeds for yearly reproduction. Studies have shown that the seeds may remain ungerminated, yet viable, for up to 7 years before eventually germinating in the fall. This strategy helps to ensure the survival of the species by conserving the seeds if a year is unfavorable to flowering or seed production.

BILL M. CAMPBELL, MD

Fringed Phacelia
Phacelia fimbriata

GENERAL: Annual, 8–16 in. tall, with weak and hairy stems. **LEAVES:** Alternate, lower leaves petioled, upper leaves sessile, to 1.5 in. long, 5–9 **pinnate lobes**, slightly broader than those of **Miami Mist** (p. 247). **FLOWERS: White, cup-shaped**, about 0.5 in. wide, 5 **deeply fringed lobes**; each inflorescence has 5–15 flowers; inflorescence is hairy, the **hairs spreading**. April–June. **FRUITS:** Capsules with 2–4 seeds. **WHERE FOUND:** Rich mountain woods in southwestern VA and western NC to northern AL. In East TN, in Blount, Sevier, Washington, Unicoi, and Carter counties. Rare, but locally abundant.

NOTES: This plant is also known as **Fringed Scorpionweed**, named for the fringe on the petals. This Appalachian endemic can be found in the Smoky Mountains from mid to high elevations, where massive displays look like snow. Whether seen en masse or singly, its blossoms make a handsome display. • Almost every part of North America, from the Yukon to the Florida coast, has at least one native representative of this large genus of nearly 200 species, with the majority occurring in southern California.

Miami Mist
Phacelia purshii

GENERAL: Annual, 6–20 in. tall with hairy stems. **LEAVES:** Alternate, lower leaves petioled, upper leaves sessile, about 1.5 in. long, coarsely **pinnately lobed**. **FLOWERS:** Cup-shaped, **pale lavender** or sometimes blue with a **white center**, about 0.5 in. wide, 5 **deeply fringed lobes**; inflorescence has 10–30 individual flowers; stem and inflorescence are hairy, the **hairs appressed**. April–June. **FRUITS:** Capsules with 2–4 seeds. **WHERE FOUND:** Rich woods, moist fields, and along roadsides from PA to MI, south to GA, AL, and OK. Primarily in Middle TN, but also in Claiborne, Monroe, Blount, Sevier, and Johnson counties in East TN. Occasional.

STANLEY SIMS

NOTES: This species was named after its discoverer, Frederick Traugott Pursh (1774–1820), a German explorer, collector, horticulturist, and author who made distinguished contributions in all his fields during the 21 years he resided in North America. • **Miami Mist** is remarkably similar to **Fringed Phacelia** (p. 246), but Fringed Phacelia is generally smaller, with weaker stems and white flowers.

Wild Comfrey · *Cynoglossum virginianum*

GENERAL: Erect, unbranched hairy **perennial** herb, 15–30 in. tall. **LEAVES:** Basal leaves are thick, hairy, 4–8 in. long, ovate to elliptic, tapering to a long, winged petiole; alternate stem leaves are **sessile, often clasping**, progressively smaller upward. **FLOWERS:** Light blue, 0.3–0.4 in. wide, 5 round, overlapping lobes; in a raceme-like, **forked inflorescence** extending well above the leaves. April–June. **FRUITS:** 4 uniformly bristly nutlets, separating at maturity. **WHERE FOUND:** Upland woods and woodland edges throughout the eastern U.S. and TN. Common. **SIMILAR SPECIES:** HOUND'S TONGUE (**C. officinale***), also called **GYPSY FLOWER**, is a **weedy biennial**, leafy throughout, including the inflorescence; **dull purplish red flowers**. A Eurasian native, found in fields, roadsides, and open areas. Now widely established in the eastern U.S. and westward. Thinly scattered in Middle and East TN in Cheatham, Davidson, Sumner, White, Bledsoe, Cumberland, Fentress, and Knox counties. Infrequent. May–July.

DENNIS HORN

NOTES: The genus name *Cynoglossum* means "hound's tongue" from the Greek *kynos*, "dog," and *glossa*, "a tongue," in reference to the broad, rough leaves. • In herbal medicine, **Wild Comfrey** had many uses, including the treatment of wounds, digestive disorders, and respiratory infections. It was also used as a mild sedative.

MIRIAM WEINSTEIN

Viper's Bugloss · *Echium vulgare**

GENERAL: Hairy **biennial**, 12–30 in. tall, from a taproot.
LEAVES: Basal rosette, stalked, oblanceolate, 3–10 in.
long; stem leaves alternate, oblong to narrowly lanceolate, becoming progressively smaller and sessile upward.
FLOWERS: Attractive and distinctive, **blue changing to
pink, funnel-shaped**, 0.5–0.8 in. long, 5 **unequal lobes,
protruding stamens**; borne in helical cymes on the
upper portion of the erect stem. June–October. **FRUITS:**
4 wrinkled nutlets, separating at maturity. **WHERE
FOUND:** Introduced from southern Europe. Waste places,
roadsides, and meadows. Widely established throughout the U.S. In Middle and East TN, in Hickman, Rutherford, Roane, Cumberland, Scott, Hawkins, Sullivan,
Washington, Carter, and Unicoi counties. Infrequent.

NOTES: This plant is also called Adder's Wort, Blue
Devil, Blue Thistle, Cat's Tails, and Viper's Grass.
These names indicate that the plant was used medicinally to treat snakebites. The seed is "like the head
of an adder or viper," and the spots on the stem
resemble the spots on some snakes. • Many farmers
consider this plant an invasive weed, and the bristly
hairs on the leaves and stem can cause **dermatitis**
upon contact with skin.

OTTO R. HIRSCH

Turnsole, Indian Heliotrope
*Heliotropium indicum**

GENERAL: Annual herb, 12–30 in. tall, **sparsely
hairy** leaves and stems, from a taproot. **LEAVES:**
alternate, ovate, or elliptic, 1–4 in. long,
abruptly tapering to narrow wings on the long
petiole. **FLOWERS:** Lavender blue, funnel-shaped,
0.12–0.16 in. wide, 5 rounded lobes; solitary
terminal **helical spikes** elongate as the **2 rows
of tiny flowers** open on the 1-sided helix.
July–November. **FRUITS: 2-lobed**, the lobes
maturing to nutlets. **WHERE FOUND:** Introduced
from tropical Asia or Brazil. Moist, disturbed
areas, roadsides, and ditches, from OH and
MO, south to FL and TX. Middle and West TN.
Frequent. **SIMILAR SPECIES:** EUROPEAN HELIOTROPE
(**H. europaeum**) is densely hairy; light blue or
white flowers in 2–5 spikes; **4-lobed fruits**.
Introduced from Europe. Disturbed areas.
Widely established in the southeastern U.S. and
occasionally north to NY and IL. In TN, in Shelby
and Wayne counties. Rare. June–September.

NOTES: Turnsole is a much sought after plant by Tiger butterflies because the plant contains
the chemical lycopsamine, which is needed by the butterflies to produce the pheromones
necessary for attracting a mate and reproducing. • Most *Heliotropium* species are tropical.
• Garden Heliotrope (*H. arborescens*), native to Peru, is valued for the vanilla-like fragrance
of its purple flowers.

Slender Heliotrope
Heliotropium tenellum

GENERAL: Hairy, many-branched **annual**, 4–16 in. tall. **LEAVES:** Alternate, linear, entire, averaging 1 in. long. **FLOWERS:** White, about 0.4 in. wide, **5-lobed**; solitary at the ends of leafy branches. June–August. **FRUITS:** 4-lobed, splitting into 4 1-seeded nutlets. **WHERE FOUND:** Calcareous soils, dry woods, and barrens, from WV to IA, south to GA and TX. In cedar glades of the Central Basin of Middle TN in Davidson, Wilson, Williamson, Maury, Marshall, Rutherford, and Giles counties and the Western Highland Rim counties of Decatur and Perry. Infrequent.

NOTES: The genus name *Heliotropium* comes from the Greek *helios,* "sun," and *trope,* meaning "to turn," referring to the idea that these flowers turn to follow the sun. The leaves and flowers of many plants turn toward or away from light and are known as heliotropic. The species name *tenellum* means "tender, delicate," referring to the tiny white flowers and the overall fragile nature of these plants. • **Slender Heliotrope** is the only native *Heliotropium* in TN and is distinctive because its flowers are solitary and therefore do not appear in a coiled cyme (like a scorpion's tail).

DENNIS HORN

Hoary Puccoon
Lithospermum canescens

GENERAL: Softly hairy perennial with up to 5 usually unbranched stems 4–16 in. long, from a thick taproot. **LEAVES:** Alternate, lanceolate to narrowly oblong, about 2 in. long, softly and densely hairy. **FLOWERS:** Showy, **orange to golden yellow**, 0.5 in. wide or less, 5-lobed; numerous in leafy cymes. April–May. **FRUITS:** 4 shiny, smooth, yellowish nutlets, separating at maturity. **WHERE FOUND:** Rocky open areas, usually over limestone, from southern Canada, NY and ND, south to GA and TX. Widespread in Middle and East TN, also Hardin, Decatur, and Fayette counties. Frequent.

NOTES: Puccoon is a name given by Native Americans to many plants that yield a red or yellow dye. Medicinally, the root of **Hoary Puccoon** was used to treat swellings and aches, especially those of the joints. It was also used by Native Americans to make body paint and to dye garments. • There are 3 *Lithospermum* species in TN. Plants in this genus are also called "gromwells."

KURT EMMANUELE

OTTO R. HIRSCH

Southern Stoneseed
Lithospermum tuberosum

GENERAL: Hairy perennial herb, 12–20 in. tall, arising from a tuber-like root; forked stems curl at first, straightening only after the flowers open. **LEAVES:** Mostly in a **basal rosette**, obovate to oblong, 2–4 in. long; stem leaves alternate, smaller, and sessile. **FLOWERS:** Pale yellow, funnel-shaped, 5-lobed, 0.25 in. wide; solitary in the congested upper leaf axils. May–June. **FRUITS:** 4 nutlets separating at maturity; nutlets are slightly pitted, otherwise smooth and shiny. **WHERE FOUND:** Calcareous woods from KY to FL and LA. Widespread in TN, more prevalent in Middle TN. Occasional. **SIMILAR SPECIES:** AMERICAN GROMWELL (*L. latifolium*) has pale yellow flowers, but is taller (16–32 in.) and **lacks the basal rosette.** Woods and woodland edges. A northern species extending south into TN and AR. In Middle TN, also Shelby, Hamilton, and Claiborne counties. Occasional. May–June. CORN GROMWELL (*Buglossoides arvensis**) is an **annual; white or pale bluish white flowers; seeds are wrinkled or pitted** all over. Introduced from Eurasia. In disturbed areas in most of the U.S. Throughout TN. Frequent. April–July. *L. arvense.*

NOTES: Southern Stoneseed is also known as **Tuberous Stoneseed** for its tuber-like root. • The genus name *Lithospermum* means "stone seed," alluding to the hard nutlets of these plants.

KURT EMMANUELE

Virginia Bluebell • *Mertensia virginica*

GENERAL: Smooth perennial herb, 12–30 in. tall. **LEAVES:** Alternate, pale green, elliptic to obovate or oblanceolate; stem leaves rounded at the tip, mostly tapering to the base, 2–6 in. long; leaves wither soon after flowering occurs. **FLOWERS:** Showy, nodding, **pale blue** (rarely pink or white), about 1 in. long, **tubular, abruptly enlarged at the tip** into a cup with 5 shallow lobes; **flower buds pink;** in 1-sided helical cymes terminating the stem and branches; no similar species occur in TN. March–May. **FRUITS:** 4 wrinkled nutlets, separating at maturity. **WHERE FOUND:** Moist or wet woods, meadows, bottomlands, and thickets, often forming spectacular colonies. Throughout most of the eastern U.S. In TN, from the Western Highland Rim eastward, also Shelby County in West TN. Frequent.

NOTES: This plant is also called **Virginia Cowslip**, and was named when the English still referred to Massachusetts as North Virginia. • The *Mertensia* genus is named in honor of Franz Carl Mertens (1764–1831), a distinguished German botanist and professor at Bremen Polytechnic College. • The stems of this species are nearly hollow, making the plant somewhat fragile. This striking plant will form large colonies and is often cultivated for its display of showy flowers in early spring. After flowering, the foliage turns yellow and the entire plant will seem to disappear, going dormant until the following spring.

Scorpion Grass · *Myosotis macrosperma*

GENERAL: Hairy perennial, 10–30 in. tall, with a few wand-like branches. **LEAVES:** Basal and alternate; sessile stem leaves 1–3 in. long, simple, narrowly spatulate at the base, elliptic and progressively smaller upward. **FLOWERS:** White, only 0.12 in. wide, 5-lobed; in tight helical racemes at the ends of the branches; flower stalks spread outward as fruits mature. April–May. **FRUITS:** 4 sharply angled nutlets, 0.07 in. long, separating at maturity. **WHERE FOUND:** Moist woods with calcareous soil, from PA to MO, south to FL and TX. Throughout TN. Common. **SIMILAR SPECIES: EARLY SCORPION GRASS (M. verna)** is a **winter annual, 6–16 in. tall,** with **erect fruit stalks** and small, white flowers. Dry, open woods. Widespread over most of the U.S. and TN. Occasional. April–June.

NOTES: The botanical name *Myosotis* comes from the Greek *mus*, "mouse," and *otis*, "ear," alluding to the short, soft leaves of some plants in this genus that are shaped like mouse ears. • This plant is called **Scorpion Grass** because the flowers grow on one side of the helical (coiled) flower stalk, somewhat resembling a scorpion's tail. • Following the Doctrine of Signatures (the belief that what a plant looked like, it could cure), some people thought that Scorpion Grass could cure scorpion bites.

True Forget-Me-Not
*Myosotis scorpioides**

GENERAL: Perennial with appressed-hairy, **creeping stems,** 8–24 in. long, often stoloniferous (rooting from nodes). **LEAVES:** Alternate, lower leaves to 3 in. long, narrow, broader toward the tip, becoming elliptic and progressively smaller upward. **FLOWERS: Pale blue with a yellow eye, 0.3 in. wide,** corolla has a short tube and 5 spreading lobes; inflorescence is a coil of stalked flowers. May–September. **FRUITS:** 4 black, shiny nutlets, separating at maturity. **WHERE FOUND:** An introduced wetland species from Europe. Throughout most of the U.S. and northeastern TN. Infrequent. **SIMILAR SPECIES:** The native **SMALL FORGET-ME-NOT (M. laxa)** has **smaller flowers,** about 0.2 in. wide; **stems do not creep.** Moist soils and shallow water in Canada and the northern U.S., south to AL and GA. Northeastern TN. Infrequent. May–September.

NOTES: True Forget-Me-Not is also called Love Me, Mouse-Ear Scorpion Grass, and Snake Grass. It was believed that a person who wore a forget-me-not flower would not be forgotten by his or her lover. The best-known legend is about a German knight who picked forget-me-nots for his lady as they strolled beside a riverbank. He slipped and fell into the water, but before drowning he tossed the flowers to her and cried, "Vergiss mir nicht!" which is the German name of the flower. • Alpine Forget-Me-Not (*M. alpestris*) is the state flower of Alaska.

NITA R. HEILMAN

False Gromwell
Onosmodium molle ssp. *molle*

GENERAL: Many-stemmed perennial, to 4 ft. tall, **hairy throughout**, from a woody root. **LEAVES:** Alternate, numerous, uniform, sessile, lanceolate to narrowly ovate, 1–3 in. long. **FLOWERS:** Dull white to greenish white, tubular, 0.3–0.6 in. long, 5 triangular corolla lobes, not spreading; borne in terminal, **leafy, helical cymes**, elongating at maturity. June–July. **FRUITS:** 4 shiny, smooth nutlets, sometimes surface-pitted, separating at maturity. **WHERE FOUND:** Dry calcareous glades and barrens, from NY to MT, south to VA, GA, and NM. In Middle TN, in Sumner, Trousdale, Davidson, Wilson, Williamson, Rutherford, Maury, Giles, Coffee, and Franklin counties. Infrequent.

NOTES: The 3 other subspecies of *O. molle* are listed for protection in TN because of their rarity. The separation of subspecies within *O. molle* concerns characteristics of the nutlets and the hairiness of the stem, which may be difficult to determine in the field. • False gromwells (*Onosmodium* spp.), also called "marbleseeds," have a coiled arrangement of flowers, but differ from other genera with coiled inflorescences by having leafy bracts among the flowers, and styles that protrude conspicuously from the flowers, giving them a distinctive appearance.

DENNIS HORN

Rose Vervain · *Glandularia canadensis*

GENERAL: Perennial herb, 12–24 in. tall, with **hairy, bushy stems**, often sprawling. **LEAVES:** Opposite, ovate to lanceolate, 1–3 in. long, **pinnately lobed** or incised, coarsely toothed. **FLOWERS:** Rose purple, turning pink with age, 0.4–0.6 in. wide, nearly radially symmetric, corolla tube about 1 in. long, 5 spreading **lobes notched**; bracts are shorter than calyx; borne in dense, rounded clusters at the ends of the stems. March–September. **FRUITS:** 4 nutlets, separating at maturity; nutlets have a white, warty inner surface. **WHERE FOUND:** Cedar glades, sandy barrens, and rocky areas, from southern PA to MN, south to FL and NM. West and Middle TN. Occasional. *Verbena canadensis*. **SIMILAR SPECIES:** BIG-BRACT VERBENA (*Verbena bracteata*), also called PROSTRATE VERVAIN, has small, sessile, **lavender flowers, 0.12 in. across**, in a spike 4–6 in. long at the top of the stem; **conspicuous bracts** are longer than calyx and corolla. Fields, roadsides, and waste places throughout the U.S. and southern Canada. In TN, in Shelby, Tipton, Lauderdale, Obion, Chester, Carroll, Benton, and Montgomery counties. Infrequent. April–October.

NOTES: Rose Vervain is also known as **Rose Verbena**. All *Verbena* species are good nectar sources for butterflies. • *Verbenae*, in Latin, were the sacred boughs of laurel, olive, or myrtle used in holy ceremonies. • Traditionally, vervains have held an important place in folk medicine and were used to treat jaundice and a variety of illnesses of the stomach, kidneys, and bladder. • There are 5 genera and 14 species of the **Vervain Family** found in TN.

Lopseed · *Phryma leptostachya*

GENERAL: Perennial herb, 15–36 in. tall, with hairy, 4-angled, purplish stems. **LEAVES:** Opposite, simple, ovate, 2–6 in. long and 1/2 as wide, petioled, hairy, serrate. **FLOWERS:** Small, **pale purple, pink, or white**, bilaterally symmetric corolla, about 0.25 in. long, upper lip straight and notched, lower lip longer and 3-lobed, 4 stamens; flowers are **opposite and horizontal**, on interrupted spike-like racemes at the end of the stem or from the axils of upper leaves; after flowering, the **hardened calyx becomes closely reflexed** against the main flowering stem, giving the appearance that the fruit has "lopped" down. June–August. **FRUITS:** Drooping achenes, about 0.15 in. long, held in the persistent calyx. **WHERE FOUND:** In rich, mesic woods throughout the eastern U.S., southeastern Canada, and TN. Common.

NOTES: Lopseed flowers open 2 at a time, traveling up the stem. The common name refers to the manner in which the seeds hang against the stem. • For years, this species was placed in its own family, the Lopseed Family, composed of only one genus with just this single species from eastern North America. Recently, taxonomists have placed the genus *Phryma* in the Vervain Family.

OTTO R. HIRSCH

Lanceleaf Fogfruit · *Phyla lanceolata*

GENERAL: Prostrate perennial herb to 15 in. tall, with erect branches. **LEAVES:** Opposite, lanceolate, 1–2 in. long, short-petioled, 5–8 coarse teeth per side above the middle of the leaf. **FLOWERS:** Small, **pinkish white**, 4-lobed; **compact, beehive-shaped flower heads**, about 0.5 in. wide, on long stalks from the upper leaf axils; flowers open a few at a time in a ring at the bottom of the head and progress upward. May–October. **FRUITS:** 2 yellowish nutlets, rounded on one side, flattened on the other. **WHERE FOUND:** Moist, open areas from Ontario to SD, south to FL, CA, and Mexico. Throughout TN. Frequent. *Lippia lanceolata*.

NOTES: This plant, sometimes called **Frogfruit** and **Northern Fogfruit**, is named for its preferred moist habitat and is commonly found growing along the shores of rivers and lakes, and grows even in water. • A wide variety of insects visit this plant for its nectar, but the largest recorded group of pollinators are small to medium-sized flies (*Syrphidea*), which hover motionless in the air. These flies mimic

KURT EMMANUELE

bees or wasps and often have black and yellow stripes along the abdomen. With short proboscis (the slender, tubular feeding and sucking organ), the flies visit the small, shallow flowers where nectar is accessible through short nectar tubes.

KURT EMMANUELE

Narrowleaf Vervain · *Verbena simplex*

GENERAL: Smooth or slightly hairy perennial herb, **6–24 in. tall**, with **4-angled**, branching stems. **LEAVES:** Opposite, linear to narrowly oblong, 1–4 in. long, coarsely toothed, short-stalked. **FLOWERS: Pale lavender** (rarely white), about 0.25 in. wide, 5 spreading lobes; borne in a slim spike at the apex of each branch. May–September. **FRUITS:** 4 brown, well-developed nutlets with a white, warty surface on the inner side; nutlets separate at maturity. **WHERE FOUND:** Dry fields and roadsides throughout the eastern U.S. and TN. Common. **SIMILAR SPECIES:** WHITE VERVAIN (**V. urticifolia**) is a **weedy plant to 5 ft. tall**, often branched near the base; **leaves are broadly lanceolate** to oblong-ovate, 2–6 in. long, stalked, coarsely and somewhat doubly toothed; **tiny, white flowers** grow in slender spikes that terminate the stem and branches. Fields and waste places throughout most of the eastern U.S. and TN. Common. June–September.

NOTES: The genus name *Verbena* is derived from the word "vervain"; *simplex* means "simple," referring to the erect, unbranched stem. The elongated leaves with their bases tapering to the stem are characteristic of **Narrowleaf Vervain**, as indicated by its common name. Only a few flowers open on each spike at one time.

DENNIS HORN

Hoary Vervain · *Verbena stricta*

GENERAL: Perennial, 12–48 in. tall, with a densely **white-haired, 4-angled stem. LEAVES:** Opposite, **ovate to elliptic**, 2–4 in. long, hairy, coarsely toothed, **sessile. FLOWERS: Pink-purple**, about 0.4 in. across, 5-lobed; occur on 1 or more blunt-tipped spikes. June–September. **FRUITS:** 4 brown nutlets, with or without a white, warty inner surface; nutlets separate at maturity. **WHERE FOUND:** Dry prairies and roadsides. A primarily northern and western species introduced into the Southeast. In West TN, in Shelby, Tipton, Dyer, Obion, Weakley, Henry, and Carroll counties, as well as Pickett County in Middle TN. Infrequent. **SIMILAR SPECIES:** BLUE VERVAIN (**V. hastata**) has **narrower leaves on short stalks**; smaller **flowers are violet blue**. Meadows and wet areas throughout most of the U.S. and southern Canada. Thinly scattered across TN. Occasional. June–September.

NOTES: **Hoary Vervain** is named after its hairy appearance, and is sometimes referred to as Mullein-Leaved Vervain for the downy leaves similar to those of **Common Mullein** (p. 291). Another name, Feverweed, came from its use in treating fevers, especially those associated with malaria. • The leaves and seeds of **Blue Vervain** were used as food by Native Americans, with the seeds, after several soakings, being dried, roasted, and then ground into flour. Medicinally, Blue Vervain is used to reduce early-stage fevers, reduce chest and throat congestion, and to treat insomnia and menopausal hot flashes.

Mint Family (Lamiaceae)

General characteristics of the Mint Family are leaves that are simple and opposite, usually square stems, usually 2-lipped corollas, either 2 or 4 stamens, and fruits that are 4-seeded nutlets. Many plants in this family contain essential oils that are used in flavoring foods and making teas, and many have medicinal value. Culinary herbs include basil, lavender, marjoram, mint, rosemary, sage, savory, and thyme. Many of these plants may be identified by their mint odor and square stem. Mints are represented by 34 genera and about 80 species in TN.

1a. Anther-bearing stamens 4 2

  2a. Ovary deeply 4-lobed; nutlets basally attached; style basal 3

    3a. Central lobe of corolla lower lip entire, notched, or wavy-margined 4

      4a. Woody shrub with diffuse, decumbent branches,
         endemic to Cumberlands . . . .***Conradina***

      4b. Herbs, stems ascending or trailing and mat-forming, more widespread 5

        5a. Stems, at least the sterile, trailing and mat-forming .6

          6a. Leaves heart-shaped at base . . . .***Glechoma***

          6b. Leaves wedge-shaped at base . . . .***Ajuga***

        5b. Stems erect or ascending, not trailing 7

          7a. Calyx bilaterally symmetric, the lobes distinctly unequal 8

            8a. Calyx bearing a dorsal scoop-shaped shield or crest . . . .***Scutellaria***

            8b. Calyx lacking a dorsal scoop-shaped shield or crest 9

              9a. Corolla 0.2–1.0 in. long 10

                10a. Inflorescence axillary, a raceme, or raceme-like flower clusters,
                   not headlike 11

                  11a. Fruiting calyx asymetrically swollen; the pedicel appearing to
                     attach to the calyx laterally . . . .***Perilla***

                  11b. Fruiting calyx not asymetrically swollen;
                     the pedicel attached to the calyx basally . . . .***Calamintha***

                10b. Inflorescence terminal, dense, and headlike . . . . .***Pycnanthemum***

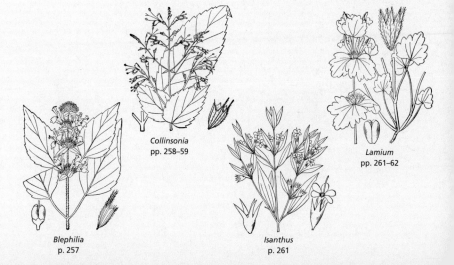

Collinsonia
pp. 258–59

Lamium
pp. 261–62

Blephilia
p. 257

Isanthus
p. 261

9b. Corolla 1.0–1.6 in. long . . . .*Synandra*

7b. Calyx radially symmetric or nearly so; the lobes equal or essentially so **12**

12a. Anthers with stiff hairs . . . .*Lamium*

12b. Anthers smooth or with short hairs **13**

13a. Inflorescence headlike . . . .*Pycnanthemum*

13b. Inflorescence a raceme or axillary **14**

14a. Flowers single in the axil of each bract . . . .*Physostegia*

14b. Flowers 2–several in the axil of each bract . . . .*Stachys*

3b. Central lobe of corolla lower lip irregularly torn or cut **15**

15a. Pedicels conspicuous in an open thyrse;
stamens exserted more than 0.2 in. . . . .*Collinsonia*

15b. Pedicels hidden within a dense spike or head; stamens included . . . .*Prunella*

2b. Ovary slightly 4-lobed; nutlets laterally or obliquely attached; style terminal **16**

16a. Corolla upper lip greatly reduced, ¹/₁₀ or less the length of the lower . . . .*Teucrium*

16b. Corolla upper lip about the same length as the lower . . . .*Trichostema*

1b. Anther-bearing stamens 2 . . . .**17**

17a. Corolla lower lip irregularly torn or cut; stamens exserted more than 0.2 in. . . . . .*Collinsonia*

17b. Corolla lower lip variously lobed, but not irregularly torn or cut;
stamens included or exserted 0.2 in. or less **18**

18a. Calyx bilaterally symmetric **19**

19a. Flowers creamy, pale blue to lavender, with purple spots,
10 or more in each headlike cluster . . . .*Blephilia*

19b. Flowers blue to violet, 10 or fewer in each open whorl . . . .*Salvia*

18b. Calyx radially symmetric or nearly so **20**

20a. Calyx 0.16 in. long or more . . . .*Monarda*

20b. Calyx less than 0.14 in. long **21**

21a. Flowers sessile . . . .*Lycopus*

21b. Flowers on pedicels . . . .*Cunila*

Contributed by J.L. Collins

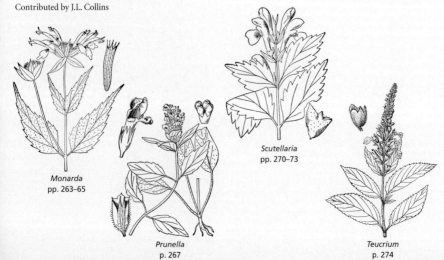

Monarda
pp. 263–65

Prunella
p. 267

Scutellaria
pp. 270–73

Teucrium
p. 274

Carpet Bugle · *Ajuga reptans**

GENERAL: Normally **smooth**, evergreen to semi-evergreen, low-growing perennial herb, 4–12 in. tall, with erect flowering stems; **spreads aggressively by leafy runners** to form loose mats. **LEAVES:** Smooth, stem leaves opposite, obovate to elliptic, 1–2 in. long, tapering to a nearly stalkless base, **bronze or purplish**, darker beneath. **FLOWERS:** Bright blue, corolla about 0.5 in. long, 2-lipped, short upper lip is 2-lobed, longer lower lip 3-lobed, 4 stamens protrude beyond the upper lip; borne in leafy whorls. April–June. **FRUITS:** Dark brown, oval, 1-seeded nutlets, 0.1 in. long, reticulate. **WHERE FOUND:** Introduced from Eurasia. Fields, roadsides, and lawns from Canada, south to GA and TX. Recorded only in a few counties of TN, but likely more widespread. Rare. **SIMILAR SPECIES: ERECT BUGLE (A. genevensis*)** has **downy stems** and **lacks runners**. Introduced from Eurasia. In the northeastern U.S. Not yet recorded from TN, but likely present. May–July.

ALAN S. HEILMAN

NOTES: The flowers of **Carpet Bugle** are specially adapted with their lipped structure for cross-pollination by bees, which seek the nectar at the base of the tube of the corolla. • Also called **Bugleweed** and **Carpetweed**, Carpet Bugle is a popular ground-cover plant sold in nurseries. It escapes cultivation and grows in lawns and at old homesites. • Usually, members of the **Mint Family** have square stems and many have a minty aroma. There are 34 genera and 88 species, varieties, and crosses in TN.

Downy Wood Mint · *Blephilia ciliata*

GENERAL: Erect perennial herb, 16–32 in. tall, with a **finely hairy stem** appearing gray or whitish. **LEAVES:** Opposite, lanceolate to ovate, 1.2–2.5 in. long, entire or with a few shallow teeth, **narrowed to the base and almost sessile**. **FLOWERS:** Small, **purplish**, corolla is 2-lipped, the upper lip entire and the lower 3-lobed, stamens protrude beyond corolla; 2-lipped calyx has teeth with hairy fringes; flowers are **crowded into axillary and terminal whorls** about 1 in. across. May–July. **FRUITS:** Segments of the fruit break at maturity into 4 one-seeded nutlets (mericarps) that are black, smooth, and shiny. **WHERE FOUND:** Dry woods and openings, from NH to WI, south to GA and AR. West and Middle TN, also Knox County in East TN. Frequent. **SIMILAR SPECIES: HAIRY WOOD MINT (B. hirsuta)** has leaves that are rounded at the base with **petioles at least 0.4 in. long**. Moist woods from Québec to MN, south to GA and AR. Throughout TN. Frequent. May–August.

OTTO R. HIRSCH

NOTES: The genus name *Blephilia* comes from the Greek *blepharis*, meaning "eyelash," in reference to the hairy fringe of the bracts and calyx teeth. **Downy Wood Mint** is also called **Downy Pagoda Plant**. • The Mint Family contains culinary and medicinal herbs such as lavender, rosemary, sage, thyme, mint, balm, marjoram, savory, and basil.

B. EUGENE WOFFORD

Glade Savory · *Clinopodium glabellum*

GENERAL: Perennial herb, 10–24 in. tall; **smooth stem is often reclining at the base** with ascending branches.
LEAVES: Opposite, lower primary leaves are linear to narrowly elliptic, 1–2 in. long, short-petioled, reduced in size upward, entire or sparingly toothed. **FLOWERS:** Pinkish, **odoriferous,** 0.3–0.6 in. long, tubular, distinctly 2-lipped, the lower lip spreading and 3-parted; flowers grow in clusters in the axils of leaf-like bracts. May–August.
FRUITS: Black, smooth, roundish nutlets. **WHERE FOUND:** Open limestone glades and barrens in TN, KY, and VA. In Middle TN, in Dickson, Cheatham, Davidson, Wilson, Williamson, and Rutherford counties. Infrequent. *Calamintha glabella, Satureja glabella.* **SIMILAR SPECIES:** BASIL THYME (*Calamintha nepeta**) has **more erect and hairy stems,** often with tufts of smaller leaves in the axils of larger leaves. Introduced from Europe. Fields and roadsides from NY to KY, south to GA and AR. Middle and East TN. Occasional. June–September. *Satureja calamintha.*

NOTES: Glade Savory, also called **Ozark Calamint,** has a limited range but is well known in the cedar glades of the Central Basin in TN. • Many mint species contain essential oils and are used universally for flavoring foods, making fragrant teas, and medicinally for a variety of purposes such as treating stomachaches, headaches, and to induce relaxation and sleepiness. In most cases, the flowering tops and leaves are used for these purposes.

THOMAS G. BARNES

Northern Horse Balm, Richweed
Collinsonia canadensis

GENERAL: Stout, nearly smooth, **erect perennial** herb, 12–36 in. tall; thick rootstock, 2–6 in. long, is hard and rhizome-like. **LEAVES:** Opposite, 3 or more pairs of oval leaves, spaced rather evenly along the stem; **blades generally longer than 4 in., with 15–40 teeth on each margin; leaf stalks less than ½ the blade length. FLOWERS:** Yellow, lemon-scented, about 0.5 in. long, 2-lipped corolla, upper lip 2-lobed, lower lip 3-lobed, lower central lobe is longer than other lobes and fringed; **2 protruding stamens;** borne in a panicle. July–September. **FRUITS:** Smooth, dark brown, roundish nutlets, about 0.1 in. long. **WHERE FOUND:** Rich, moist woods throughout the eastern U.S. and TN. Common.

NOTES: The lemon-scented flowers account for another common name, **Citronella.** Still another name, **Stoneroot,** refers to the thick, hard rootstock, which has been used in medicine to stimulate, cleanse, and tone the mucous membranes of the digestive system and to treat urinary tract ailments, kidney stones, and gastroenteritis accompanied by diarrhea. This plant was also used to treat painful and swollen limbs by rubbing a poultice made from the leaves and roots on the afflicted areas.

Southern Horse Balm
Collinsonia tuberosa

GENERAL: Spreading or **reclining perennial** herb, 12–36 in. tall, from a tuber-like rootstock about 2 in. long. **LEAVES:** Opposite, 4 or more pairs of oval leaves, **2–3 in. long**, 5–15 teeth on each edge; leaf stalks more than ½ the length of the blade. **FLOWERS:** Pale yellow to cream, about 0.5 in. long, **thin purple streaks**, 2-lipped corolla, lower lip fringed and much longer than the upper, **2 stamens are long exserted**; borne in a panicle. July–August. **FRUITS:** Smooth, round, solitary nutlets. **WHERE FOUND:** Moist woods, usually on neutral soils. NC and TN, south to GA and LA. In TN, in Wayne, Lewis, Hickman, Marion, and Sequatchie counties. Rare.

NOTES: **Deepwoods Horse Balm** is another name for this plant. This species closely resembles **Northern Horse Balm** (p. 258), and it may not be worthy of separate species status. However, the distribution of Southern Horse Balm is more southern. • The genus is named in honor of Peter Collinson (1694–1768), a British botanist, cloth merchant, and naturalist who collected many new plants from North America for his own garden and for his friends in England.

DENNIS HORN

Whorled Horse Balm
Collinsonia verticillata

GENERAL: Stiff perennial herb, 10–20 in. tall. **LEAVES:** Opposite, ovate to oblong-obovate, 3–8 in. long, hairy margins, petioles 0.5–1.5 in. long; in 2–3 pairs, usually near the base of the inflorescence, giving a **whorled appearance**. **FLOWERS:** Pink-tinged, 0.6–0.8 in. long, 2-lipped corolla, lower lip fringed and longer than upper lip, **4 stamens**; borne in a panicle with 1 long axis that rises above the leaves, with 3–6 flowers at each node, the branches of the inflorescence with dense glandular hairs. May–June. **FRUITS:** Smooth, round, solitary nutlets. **WHERE FOUND:** Rich mesic woods from southern VA to OH, south to FL and AL. In TN, from the Cumberland Plateau eastward. Occasional.

NOTES: Other common names for this plant are **Early Stoneroot** and Whorled Stoneroot, which refer to the hard, thickened rhizome. • Several *Collinsonia* species were reportedly given the name "horse balm" because horses liked to eat the plants and the plants were also used to treat the animals' sore backs.

KURT EMMANUELE

MARGRET RHINEHART

Cumberland Rosemary
Conradina verticillata

GENERAL: **Low shrub**, 10–20 in. tall, evergreen, with widely spreading branches and **shredding bark**.
LEAVES: Stiff, **needle-like**, 0.6–0.8 in. long, **glandular-pitted** on the upper surface; in clustered pairs, appearing whorled; when crushed, the leaves release a strong, distinct rosemary scent. **FLOWERS: Pinkish to lavender**, 0.6–0.7 in. long, **heavily spotted**; 2-lipped corolla, upper lip weakly 2-lobed, lower lip deeply 3-lobed, 4 stamens beneath the upper lip; in clusters of 1–3 flowers, terminally or in the upper leaf axils. May–June. **FRUITS:** Nutlets, usually up to 4 per calyx; nutlets fall out when the calyx falls from the plant. **WHERE FOUND:** Rocky and sandy streambanks. Endemic to the sandy banks of larger Cumberland Plateau streams in KY and TN. In TN, in White, Cumberland, Morgan, Fentress, and Scott counties. Rare.

NOTES: This plant's common name refers to its resemblance to the culinary herb, Rosemary (*Rosmarinus officinalis*), which is also in the Mint Family. Given the strong rosemary odor of the crushed stems and leaves, the presence of this species in its natural habitat is sometimes detected by the nose before the plant is observed. • **Cumberland Rosemary** is federally listed as threatened by the U.S. Fish and Wildlife Service.

TERRY LIVINGSTONE

Ground Ivy, Gill-over-the-Ground · *Glechoma hederacea**

GENERAL: Fibrous-rooted perennial herb with **trailing stems** to 16 in. long that root at the nodes and **form mats**; flowering stems erect, to 8 in. tall, with hairy leaf nodes. **LEAVES:** Opposite, evergreen, **often purplish**, 0.5–1.5 in. long, petiolate, roundish with blunt-lobed teeth, may be either smooth or hairy. **FLOWERS: Purplish blue**, 0.5–0.9 in. long; 2-lipped corolla, upper lip shallowly 2-lobed, lower lip larger, deeply 3-lobed, and spotted; **stamens do not protrude beyond corolla**; produced in the leaf axils, usually 3 per node. April–June. **FRUITS:** Reddish brown, slightly pimpled nutlets. **WHERE FOUND:** Introduced from Eurasia. Moist woodlands and open areas throughout most of the U.S. and TN. Frequent.

NOTES: Ground Ivy is so named because it spreads quickly and grows near the ground. Other common names for this plant are Runaway-Robin, Creeping Charlie, Field Balm, Robin-Run-in-the-Hedge, and Scarlet Runner. An aromatic oil is released when the plant is crushed. • This species has been used to make ale, reportedly helping those who drank it to extend their lives, and cure headaches, pains, inflammations, coughs, and many other ailments. It is frequented by bees, which make good honey from this plant's nectar.

False Pennyroyal, Fluxweed
Isanthus brachiatus

GENERAL: Annual, 6–16 in. tall, the stem finely hairy and often branched. **LEAVES:** Opposite, short-stalked, **lanceolate to elliptic**, 1.0–1.5 in. long, acute at the tip, **3-veined. FLOWERS:** Pale lavender to blue, about 0.2 in. long, **5 nearly symmetric corolla lobes**, **4 stamens are straight; 5 calyx lobes** about 0.12 in. long and **regular; flowers occur in groups of 1–3**, from the axils of leaves and upper bracts, **borne on stalks to 0.4 in. long**. July–September. **FRUITS:** Nutlets, to 0.12 in. long, minutely hairy at the top. **WHERE FOUND:** Dry glades and barrens, from VT to MN, south to FL and AZ. In TN, in East and Middle TN, usually on limestone. Frequent. *Trichostema brachiatum*. **SIMILAR SPECIES:** AMERICAN PENNYROYAL (*Hedeoma pulegioides*), also called AMERICAN FALSE PENNYROYAL, has **nearly sessile flowers in groups of 3–11, calyx lobes unequally cleft, only 2 stamens**; strongly aromatic. Dry soils throughout the eastern U.S. and TN. Common. July–September.

MILO PYNE

NOTES: For years, **False Pennyroyal** was placed in the *Isanthus* genus. It was then moved to the genus *Trichostema*, but recently was returned to *Isanthus*. Unlike most members of the Mint Family, False Pennyroyal has nearly regular flowers and straight stamens. • The Pennyrile Region of southern KY, an extension of the Highland Rim in TN, is named for **American Pennyroyal**.

Henbit • *Lamium amplexicaule**

GENERAL: Reclining, weedy **annual**, 4–16 in. tall, from a short taproot, the base usually branched; stems inconspicuously hairy, occasionally smooth. **LEAVES:** Opposite, **rounded upper leaves sessile** (generally subtending the flowers), horizontally oriented, **clasping**, about 0.6 in. long; lower leaves have long petioles and coarse, rounded teeth. **FLOWERS:** Pinkish purple, tubular, to 0.7 in. long, 2-lipped corolla is **dilated at the throat**, the **lower lip spotted**, densely hairy calyx has long, narrow, converging teeth; borne in clusters in a few axillary whorls (verticils). March–June. **FRUITS:** Smooth, shiny, brownish, 3-angled nutlets. **WHERE FOUND:** Introduced from Eurasia. A weed of open areas, lawns, fields, and waste places throughout the U.S. and TN. Frequent.

NOTES: The genus name *Lamium* is Greek for "dead nettle"; *amplexicaule* means "clasping the stem," in reference to the upper leaves.
• Although this invasive plant is a cool-weather weed, it manages to set seed late in summer and is ready to flower again the following spring. The seeds are a food source for many bird species. In many areas, Henbit is considered a **bothersome weed**.

DENNIS HORN

DENNIS HORN

Purple Dead Nettle
Lamium purpureum*

GENERAL: Weedy, taprooted **annual**, 4–16 in. tall, with reclining stems. **LEAVES:** Opposite, **petioled**, 0.5–1.0 in. long, **heart-shaped** with coarse rounded teeth, **upper leaves crowded, overlapping**, bend downward at a slight angle, and are progressively reduced in size upward. **FLOWERS: Pinkish purple**, 0.4–0.6 in. long, 2-lipped; corolla tube has a ring of hairs inside, near the base; calyx teeth diverge; in whorls arising from the upper leaf axils. March–June. **FRUITS:** 3-angled nutlets, less than 0.1 in. long. **WHERE FOUND:** Introduced from Eurasia. A weed of open areas, fields, lawns, and waste places throughout most of the U.S. and TN. Frequent.

NOTES: This plant also is known as **Red Dead Nettle**. Use caution when planting because this plant is **invasive** and is very difficult to remove once established. • Plants in the *Lamium* genus are called "dead nettles," and although they may have nettle-like leaves, they lack the sting. • The overlapping leaf and flower pattern of **Purple Dead Nettle** somewhat resembles a Japanese pagoda.

THOMAS G. BARNES

Cutleaf Water Horehound
Lycopus americanus

GENERAL: Colonial perennial herb, 12–24 in. tall, spreading by stolons or rhizomes. **LEAVES:** Opposite, lanceolate, 1–3 in. long, tapering to a short petiole, lower leaves **pinnately lobed near the base**. **FLOWERS: White**, tubular, 0.1–0.15 in. long, 4-lobed, **corolla slightly longer than calyx; sharply pointed calyx teeth overtop the mature nutlets**; borne in clusters in the leaf axils. June–September. **FRUITS:** Nutlets less than 0.1 in. long with corky ridges. **WHERE FOUND:** Moist areas throughout most of the U.S., southern Canada, and TN. Frequent. **SIMILAR SPECIES: TAPERLEAF WATER HOREHOUND (L. rubellus)** also has **calyx teeth longer than the nutlets; leaves not lobed**, just toothed; 5-lobed **corolla is 2x the calyx length**. Moist ground, from NH to MI and MO, south to FL and TX. Throughout TN. Frequent. June–September. **VIRGINIA WATER HOREHOUND (L. virginicus)** has **lower leaves that are toothed, not lobed; calyx teeth have blunt points and do not overtop the mature nutlets**. Moist areas throughout the eastern U.S. and TN. Common. June–September.

NOTES: Cutleaf Water Horehound is also called American Water Horehound, American Bugleweed, and Gypsywort. • *Lycopus* species have toothed or lobed leaves and small, white flowers that grow in dense whorls in the leaf axils. The 4–5-lobed flowers are more bell-shaped than 2-lipped, in contrast to most members of the Mint Family. • Some *Lycopus* species have been used in folk medicine to treat thyroid conditions. Three species are found in TN.

Eastern Bergamot
Monarda bradburiana

GENERAL: Perennial herb, 12–24 in. tall, with a **smooth stem**. **LEAVES:** Opposite, nearly **sessile**, 2–4 in. long, **rounded** or nearly heart-shaped **at the base**, the veins hairy underneath. **FLOWERS: Deep lavender (to white)**, about 1 in. long, **dotted with purple**, 2-lipped corolla; calyx is hairy in the throat and its narrow lobes often have glandular hairs; **floral bracts usually tinged pink or purple**; inflorescence heads about 1 in. thick. May–June. **FRUITS:** Smooth nutlets. **WHERE FOUND:** Dry bluffs, ravines, and open woods, from southern IN to IA, south to AL and TX. In TN, in the Western Highland Rim, also Coffee County. Occasional. *M. russeliana*.

NOTES: The *Monarda* genus is named after Nicolas Monardes (1493–1588), a Spanish physician and botanist. He was the author of the first European book on American medicinal plants. *Monarda* species are also called "horsemints" and "bee balms." **Eastern Bergamot** is sometimes called White Horsemint. • As indicated by "bergamot" in the common name, a pleasant tea can be made from the leaves of several *Monarda* species. Oil of bergamot is one of the ingredients in Earl Grey tea. A tea made from the leaves of Eastern Bergamot has been used to treat fevers, upset stomach, digestive gas, and as a cold and cough remedy. • There are 7 *Monarda* species in TN.

Lemon Mint • *Monarda citriodora*

GENERAL: Annual, 12–24 in. tall, stem simple or branching, **minutely hairy**. **LEAVES:** Opposite or whorled, lanceolate, 1–3 in. long, margin remotely toothed, **base narrowed to a short petiole**. **FLOWERS: Lavender to pink**, about 0.75 in. long; 2-lipped corolla, upper lip narrow and arching above the wider lower lip; **stamens not exserted beyond the upper corolla lip**; calyx teeth long-linear; borne in **2 or more whorls** at apex of the stem, each whorl subtended by hairy purple to whitish bracts. June–August. **FRUITS:** 1-seeded nutlets, about 0.05 in. long. **WHERE FOUND:** Prairies and roadsides, from MO and KS, southwest to Mexico; introduced eastward. In TN, in Cannon, Marshall, Rutherford, and Trousdale counties in Middle TN, and Anderson and Meigs counties in East TN. Infrequent.

NOTE: Both the common name and the species name *citriodora*, "lemon-scented" refer to the aroma of this species. • In TN, plants in the *Monarda* genus are erect herbs with toothed leaves and large, attractive, 2-lipped flowers that are borne in terminal heads or whorls in the upper leaf axils. Variously colored, leaf-like bracts often surround the flower heads.

JAMES I. 'BUS' JONES

DENNIS HORN

Basil Bee Balm
Monarda clinopodia

GENERAL: Perennial, simple or branched, 18–36 in. tall; stem smooth or slightly hairy. **LEAVES:** Opposite, ovate, 2–5 in. long, acuminate tip, shallowly toothed margins, base usually rounded; leaf stalk 0.4–1.2 in. long. **FLOWERS:** White or cream, about 1 in. long, **fragrant**; 2-lipped corolla, upper lip narrow and erect above the wider lower lip, tip of upper lip without a tuft of hairs; floral bracts are green to whitish; borne in a **solitary terminal head**. May–August. **FRUITS:** Yellowish brown, 1-seeded nutlets, about 0.05 in. long. **WHERE FOUND:** Moist woods in the eastern U.S. from VT to MI, south to AL. Throughout Middle and East TN. Frequent.

THOMAS E. HEMMERLY

NOTES: **Basil Bee Balm** is also called **White Bergamot**. The name "bee balm" implies that this plant is attractive to bees. Although bees do visit this plant, the long, tubular flowers make the nectar less accessible to bees, but more easily reached by long-tongued butterflies and flies. • The fresh or dried leaves and flower heads can be brewed into a tea. They also blend well with other teas.

Crimson Bee Balm, Oswego Tea • *Monarda didyma*

GENERAL: Perennial herb, 30–60 in. tall, with hairy nodes. **LEAVES:** Opposite, **stalked**, ovate to deltoid-ovate to lance-olate, 3–6 in. long, serrate along the margins and nearly rounded at the base, sometimes slightly tapered. **FLOWERS:** Showy, **scarlet to crimson, odorless**, 1.0–1.6 in. long; 2-lipped corolla, upper lip narrow, nearly straight, upper lip does not have an obvious tuft of hairs; **showy, reddish bracts**; in terminal flower heads. July–September. **FRUITS:** Dark brown, ellipsoid nutlets, 0.1 in. long. **WHERE FOUND:** Moist mountain woods and bottomlands. A mostly northeastern species extending south in the mountains to TN and GA. In TN, in the Blue Ridge Mountains in Polk, Monroe, Blount, Sevier, Cocke, Greene, Unicoi, Carter, and Johnson counties, and the Cumberland Plateau counties of Cumberland and Scott. Occasional.

JERRY DROWN

NOTES: This plant is a favorite of hummingbirds owing to the color of the blossoms and the tubular flowers. Not many kinds of butterflies are attracted to this plant, although long-tongued butterflies including the Cloudless Sulphur and Eastern Tiger Swallowtail are exceptions. Their tongues are sufficiently long to extract the nectar. • The Boston Tea Party in 1773 led to a shortage of tea in America, and this plant's leaves were used widely as a substitute for imported tea. It is often cultivated for its showy flowers.

Wild Bergamot · *Monarda fistulosa*

GENERAL: Branched, rhizomatous perennial herb, 24–48 in. tall, the upper stem slightly hairy. **LEAVES:** Opposite, 2–4 in. long, on **petioles 0.4–0.6 in. long**, deltoid-lanceolate, tapering at the tip, slightly tapered to truncate at the base, margins somewhat serrated; may be conspicuously hairy. **FLOWERS: Pale to bright lavender, aromatic**, about 1 in. long, 2-lipped, **tip of the straight upper lip has a tuft of hairs**; inside of corolla tube has white hairs; **floral bracts often pale green to lilac-tinged**; inflorescence is head-like, to 1.6 in. across, terminating the stem and branches. June–September. **FRUITS:** Shiny, oblong nutlets, 0.06 in. long. **WHERE FOUND:** Dry clearings and borders of woods in most of the U.S. and southern Canada. Throughout TN. Common. **SIMILAR SPECIES:** PURPLE BERGAMOT (*M. media*) has **deep reddish purple flowers** and **dark purple floral bracts**. Roadsides and open woods in the mountains, from ME to southern Ontario, south to GA and AL. In East TN, in Polk and Monroe counties. Rare. July–August.

DENNIS HORN

NOTES: The leaves of **Wild Bergamot** and **Purple Bergamot** can be enjoyed as a pleasant tea for casual drinking, as indicated by "bergamot" in the common name. • Wild Bergamot was used medicinally to treat pain in the stomach and intestines, as were many species of the Mint Family. • Purple Bergamot has intermediate characteristics between **Crimson Bee Balm** (p. 264) and Wild Bergamot and is possibly a hybrid of the two.

Horse Mint · *Monarda punctata*

GENERAL: Perennial, 12–36 in. tall with tough crowns; stem simple or branching, **somewhat hairy**. **LEAVES:** Opposite, lanceolate, 1–3 in. long, toothed margins, wedge-shaped base tapering to a petiole, 0.2–1.0 in. long. **FLOWERS: Pale yellow spotted with purple**, 0.6–1.0 in. long, 2-lipped corolla, **stamens do not exceed the arching upper lip**; short calyx teeth; in **2–7 whorls** at the top of stem, each whorl subtended by **greenish or purple-tinged bracts**. July–September. **FRUITS:** Brown to blackish nutlets, 0.06 in. long. **WHERE FOUND:** Dry, sandy soil, from VT to MN, south to FL and NM. In East TN, in Washington and Unicoi counties. Rare.

DENNIS HORN

NOTES: This plant also is known as **Spotted Horse Mint**, in reference to the purple spots in the flower. • Native Americans used a tea made from the leaves of this plant to treat flu, colds, and fever, and to increase sweating. Essential oils collected from **Horse Mint** are high in thymol, an effective fungicide and bactericide that can also be used to expel hookworms. Today, thymol is manufactured synthetically. • The flowers of Horse Mint display a row of dots as guides for pollinators. Studies have shown that flowers with guide marks are more successful in attracting bees and wasps than those without marks.

DENNIS HORN

Beefsteak Plant
Perilla frutescens*

GENERAL: Erect, branching, coarse, **aromatic annual**, 12–36 in. tall. **LEAVES:** Opposite, ovate, 3–6 in. long, often reddish purple, coarsely toothed, tapering at the base to a long petiole. **FLOWERS: White or purplish**; about 0.2 in. long, 5 short, rounded corolla lobes; 4 stamens; hairy calyx tube has upper lip with 3 teeth, lower lip with 2 teeth; calyx is shorter than corolla, but elongates in fruit; borne in 1-sided racemes, 2–6 in. long, terminal or from upper leaf axils. August–September. **FRUITS:** Spherical, reticulated (veiny) nutlets. **WHERE FOUND:** Introduced from India. A weed of roadsides and waste places over most of the eastern U.S. Throughout TN. Frequent.

NOTES: This plant is also called Rattlesnake Weed, for the dried seed cases that rattle. The name **Beefsteak Plant** refers to the reddish purple leaves, which can be used as a condiment to season meat. **Caution: ingesting large amounts can cause fluid on the lungs**. • In herbal medicine, the leaves were made into a tea to treat abdominal pain, diarrhea, vomiting, coughs, fevers, and colds. An application of fresh leaves rubbed on a wart for 10 to 15 minutes a day can remove warts in 2 to 6 days. Perilla oil, obtained from the crushed seeds, has been used as a substitute for linseed oil. The seeds are a rich source of omega-3 essential fatty acid and alpha-linolenic acid.

JERRY DROWN

Obedient Plant, False Dragonhead
Physostegia virginiana

GENERAL: Smooth, erect perennial herb to 1–4 ft. tall, sometimes branched at the top, with 4-angled (square) stems. **LEAVES:** Opposite, sessile, 2–5 in. long, narrowly lanceolate and sharply toothed. **FLOWERS: Bright pink with purple lines**, tubular, about 1 in. long, somewhat suggestive of snapdragons; 2-lipped corolla, the upper lip hooded, the lower spreading and 3-lobed; borne in terminal racemes, 2–6 in. long, **flowers closely spaced, often in vertical ranks**. July–September. **FRUITS:** Oblong nutlets, about 0.14 in. long, finely beaded, shiny, sharply angled. **WHERE FOUND:** Open, moist areas throughout eastern North America. Scattered across most of TN, but more common in the eastern ½ of the state. Occasional.

NOTES: The flowers of this plant are long lasting when cut. They especially make good flowers for arrangements because when the flowers are repositioned on the stem, they are "obedient" and retain the new position, providing the name **Obedient Plant**. The name **False Dragonhead** is a reference to the pinkish red, mouth-like flowers. • This plant is often cultivated because of the showy flowers and its unusual "obedient" character, however, use caution because this plant can be an **aggressive colonizer**, especially on rich, moist sites.

Heal All, Selfheal · *Prunella vulgaris**

GENERAL: Erect or creeping perennial herb, 6–20 in. tall; often forms large colonies. **LEAVES:** Opposite, lanceolate or elliptic, 1–3 in. long, entire or sometimes with fine teeth, lower leaves on long stalks. **FLOWERS:** Violet or purplish, 0.4–0.6 in. long, 2-lipped, upper lip hooded, arching over the 4 stamens; lower lip 3-lobed, bent downward, the **middle lobe whitish and fringed**; borne in a **short, cylindric, terminal spike**, 1–2 in. tall and about 0.75 in. across, flowers crowded among **fringed bracts**. May–September. **FRUITS:** Dark brown, shiny, ribbed nutlets, about 0.1 in. long. **WHERE FOUND:** Introduced from Europe. Now established in disturbed soil throughout most of North America, including TN. Common.

HUGH NOURSE

NOTES: This species has long been used for the treatment of a variety of ailments. For example, a leaf tea was used as a gargle for sore throats and mouth sores as well as to treat fevers and diarrhea. Externally, this plant has been used to treat wounds, bruises, sores, and ulcers. Research indicates the presence of antibiotic, anti-tumor, and hypertensive compounds. It contains the antioxidant substance rosmarinic acid in larger quantities than found in Rosemary (*Rosmarinus officinalis*) itself.

Loomis' Mountain Mint
Pycnanthemum loomisii

GENERAL: Loosely branched, leafy, erect perennial, 12–36 in. tall; stem has short hairs. **LEAVES:** Opposite, **short-stalked**, ovate to lanceolate, 1–2 in. long, toothed; **upper leaves and bracts hoary (white-haired) on both sides as if dusted with white powder**; lower leaves hoary beneath only. **FLOWERS:** White or purple-spotted, about 0.2 in. long, 2-lipped, 4 stamens; borne in relatively **loose heads**, 0.75–1.5 in. across. July–September. **FRUITS:** Smooth nutlets, 0.05–0.06 in. long. **WHERE FOUND:** Upland woods and roadsides from VA to IL, southward. Throughout TN. Common. **SIMILAR SPECIES:** SOUTHERN MOUNTAIN MINT (**P. pycnanthemoides**) has **pitted nutlets**. Woods, from PA to IL, southward. Scattered across TN. Occasional. July–August. SHORT-TOOTHED MOUNTAIN MINT (**P. mutilum**) has **nearly sessile leaves**, **dense flower heads**, and **bracts without fringe**. Damp woods and meadows in the eastern U.S., west to TX. In TN, primarily on the Eastern Highland Rim and Cumberland Plateau. Occasional. June–August. THINLEAF MOUNTAIN MINT (**P. montanum**) also has **dense flower heads**, but the **bracts are fringed**. Mountain woods from WV to northern GA. In TN, in the Blue Ridge Mountains. Infrequent. July–August.

JERRY DROWN

NOTE: The genus name *Pycnanthemum* translates as "compact flower," referring to the dense flowering heads and inflorescence of many members of this genus. Mountain mints usually have a strong minty flavor. There are 10 *Pycnanthemum* species in TN.

MILO PYNE

Narrowleaf Mountain Mint
Pycnanthemum tenuifolium

GENERAL: Smooth, leafy perennial 12–36 in. tall, much branched above; **lacks the strong, minty fragrance. LEAVES:** Opposite, **linear,** 1–2 in. long, about 0.12 in. wide, entire, nearly sessile, generally **not hoary** (white-haired). **FLOWERS:** White, 0.2–0.3 in. long, 2-lipped corolla; **numerous compact flower heads,** 0.2–0.4 in. wide; borne in showier clusters than most other mountain mints. June–July. **FRUITS:** Tiny, black, oblong nutlets, 0.05 in. long. **WHERE FOUND:** Meadows, prairies, and pastures throughout the eastern U.S. and TN. Common. **SIMILAR SPECIES: HAIRY MOUNTAIN MINT (*P. verticillatum* var. *pilosum*)** is **taller (to 5 ft.),** with **hairy stems; narrowly lanceolate leaves; leaves and bracts hairy above.** Woods, thickets, and clearings, from the midwestern U.S., south to GA and AR. In TN, from the Western Highland Rim westward, also Anderson and Rhea counties in East TN. Occasional. July–September. **VIRGINIA MOUNTAIN MINT (*P. virginianum*)** is similar to *P. verticillatum*, but the **leaves and bracts are smooth above.** Moist prairies and forest edges in the eastern U.S. Thinly scattered across TN. Infrequent. June–August.

NOTES: Medicinally, the leaves of many mountain mints are used in poultices to treat headaches, and as a tea to treat fevers, colds, and coughs. Many hikers and backpackers know that a quick way to make a refreshing and calming tea is to place the leaves in hot water and let them steep for a few minutes before drinking.

OTTO R. HIRSCH

Blue Sage · *Salvia azurea* var. *grandiflora*

GENERAL: Erect perennial herb, **2–5 ft. tall,** stem simple or branched above and minutely hairy. **LEAVES:** Opposite, linear to elliptic, 1–3 in. long, tapering to the base, minutely hairy on both sides. **FLOWERS: Blue, tubular,** about 0.75 in. long; 2-lipped corolla, upper lip hood-like, lower lip broad and 3-lobed with **2 white marks near the throat;** hairy calyx about 0.25 in. long; bracts are minute or absent; borne in dense, spike-like racemes, 10 or fewer flowers per node. August–October. **FRUITS:** Olive brown nutlets are glandular-resinous and dull. **WHERE FOUND:** A western prairie and barrens plant found from NE to TX, extending eastward to OH and GA. In TN, along the western Tennessee River Valley in Stewart, Henry, Decatur, Perry, and Hardin counties. Rare. *S. pitcheri*.

NOTES: *Salvia*, the old Latin name for sage, means "healthy" or "safe," indicating that these plants have many medicinal properties. • Most plants in the *Salvia* genus are good honey plants and are frequently visited by bees. The flowers in this genus are produced in a terminal, spike-like inflorescence or in whorls with 1–3 (or more) flowers per node. The calyx is 2-lipped, the upper lip 3-lobed or entire, and the lower lip is 2-lobed.

Lyreleaf Sage · *Salvia lyrata*

DENNIS HORN

GENERAL: Erect, single-stemmed, fibrous-rooted perennial herb, 12–24 in. tall. **LEAVES:** Mostly in a **basal rosette, lyre-shaped**, oblong or obovate-oblong, 4–8 in. long, pinnately lobed into rounded segments; petioles 1–4 in. long. **FLOWERS: Pale blue to lavender**, tubular, about 1 in. long; 2-lipped corolla, the upper lip shorter than the broad lower lip; inflorescence is a terminal raceme, 4–12 in. long; flower clusters few, widely separated, usually with 6 flowers per node. April–June. **FRUITS:** Dull, pimpled, dark brown nutlets. **WHERE FOUND:** Dry, open woods, clearings, sandy meadows, and fields from CT to IL and MO, south to FL and TX. Throughout TN. Common. **SIMILAR SPECIES: BLOOD SAGE (*S. coccinea*),** also called **TEXAS SAGE**, is a perennial with ovate, **mostly stem leaves** that are **toothed (not lobed)** and a **scarlet corolla**. Sandy soils of the Coastal Plain from SC to TX. Not recorded from TN. May–October. **KITCHEN SAGE (*S. officinalis**),** also called **COMMON** or **GARDEN SAGE**, is a **shrubby** plant; **leaves are downy, soft gray-green, aromatic**, elliptic; **lavender blue flowers**. Introduced from Eurasia. Used for cooking and occasionally escapes. In TN, in Davidson County. May–July.

NOTE: Lyreleaf Sage is also called Cancerweed because of its medicinal properties. It was made into a salve that was considered a cure for warts and cancer. The leaves and seeds were ingredients in an ointment that was used to cure wounds and sores. • This native species is **often invasive** in open habitats. The flowers are visited by hummingbirds, bumblebees, and some long-tongued flies.

Nettleleaf Sage · *Salvia urticifolia*

KURT EMMANUELE

GENERAL: Perennial herb, **12–24 in. tall**, with one to a few hairy stems, from a woody rhizome. **LEAVES:** Opposite, deltoid, to 3 in. long, coarsely crenate-serrate-toothed and winged (leaf tissue extends along the petiole from the blade toward the stem). **FLOWERS: Deep lavender to blue**, tubular, 0.4–0.6 in. long; 2-lipped corolla, upper lip hood-like, much shorter than the broad, **white-striped, 3-lobed lower lip; calyx,** about 0.2 in. long, is **shorter than corolla tube;** inflorescence is a terminal raceme, 4–8 in. long, with 6–10 flowers per node. April–June. **FRUITS:** Smooth, shiny, dark brown, ellipsoid nutlets. **WHERE FOUND:** Dry woods and barrens on calcareous soils, from PA to KY, south to FL and MS. In TN, from the Western Highland Rim eastward, also Decatur and McNairy counties in West TN. Occasional. **SIMILAR SPECIES: LANCELEAF SAGE (*S. reflexa*)** is an **annual**; narrow leaves 1–2 in. long and about ¼ as wide; blue to lilac flowers about 0.5 in. long; **corolla tube is about equal to calyx in length.** Dry prairies of the northern and western U.S. In TN, only in the cedar glades of Davidson County. Rare. June–September.

NOTES: Both the species name *urticifolia*, meaning "nettle-leaved," and the common name refer to this plant's hairy stems and nettle-like leaves.

Hairy Skullcap · *Scutellaria elliptica*

GENERAL: Erect perennial herb with hairy stems 12–24 in. tall, occasionally branched above; 2 varieties are recognized by differences in the stem pubescence: *S. elliptica* var. *elliptica* has fine, **short, ascending stem hairs**; *S. elliptica* var. *hirsuta* (see photo) has fine, **spreading, glandular stem hairs**. **LEAVES:** Opposite, 2–3 in. long, short-petioled, mostly rhombic-ovate, crenate leaf margins. **FLOWERS:** Blue to violet, 0.6–0.8 in. long; 2-lipped corolla, upper lip hood-like, broader **lower lip marked with white**; calyx has spreading, glandular hairs; racemes about 4 in. long are borne from the upper 1–3 pairs of leaf axils. May–June. **FRUITS:** Tuber-like nutlets, less than 0.05 in. long. **WHERE FOUND:** In dry upland woods and barrens, from NY to MI, south to FL and TX. Throughout TN, except in the westernmost counties. Common.

NOTES: The origin of the genus name *Scutellaria* is *scutella*, meaning "a small dish," alluding to the crest on the fruiting calyx. The common name, Skullcap, also refers to the hump of the upper lip of the calyx. • There are 16 skullcap species and varieties listed for TN. All have strongly 2-lipped, tubular flowers. The upper lip forms an arching "hood" that hides the 4 stamens. The lower lip has a broad central lobe, notched at the tip, and 2 small lateral lobes partially attached to the base of the upper lip.

Downy Skullcap · *Scutellaria incana*

GENERAL: Single-stemmed perennial herb, 24–36 in. tall, with a minutely hairy stem. **LEAVES:** Opposite, 2–4 in. long, ovate, obtuse at the tip, **rounded at the base**, crenate, may be hairy above, on **stalks 0.5–1.2 in. long**. **FLOWERS:** Blue, 0.75–1.0 in. long; 2-lipped corolla, upper lip hood-like, **lower lip with a white center**; **calyx** has appressed hairs **without glands**; several racemes may terminate the stem and may also grow from upper leaf axils. June–August. **FRUITS:** Warty nutlets, less than 0.05 in. long. **WHERE FOUND:** Upland forests and fields, from NY to WI, south to GA, AL, and KS. Throughout TN. Frequent. **SIMILAR SPECIES:** HEARTLEAF SKULLCAP (*S. ovata*) has broader, **heart-shaped leaves**, 2–6 in. long, with crenate margins, on **stalks 1–3 in. long**; blue corolla, 0.6–1.0 in. long, with a whitish lower lip; **glandular calyx**; 1 to few racemes about 4 in. long. Mesic forests from MD to MN, south to FL and TX. In TN, from the Ridge and Valley westward. Occasional. May–July.

NOTES: *Scutellaria* species were once believed to cure hysteria, convulsions, and other nervous disorders. Interestingly, modern science has found that an extract from the flowers contains scutellaine, an effective sedative and antispasmodic agent.

Hyssopleaf Skullcap
Scutellaria integrifolia

GENERAL: Erect perennial herb, 12–24 in. tall, with finely hairy stems, sometimes branched above. **LEAVES:** Opposite, **middle and upper leaves entire**, lanceolate to oblanceolate, 1.0–2.5 in. long, obtuse at the tip, and short petioled. **FLOWERS: Blue, pink, or white**, 0.6–1.0 in. long; 2-lipped corolla, upper lip hood-like, wider **lower lip with a pair of white marks**; racemes terminate the stem and branches; inflorescence has both flowers and bracts, the latter smaller upward. May–July. **FRUITS:** Warty, dark brown nutlets, 0.05 in. long. **WHERE FOUND:** Fields, barrens, and open woods. Primarily a Coastal Plain species, from MA to FL and TX, but also inland to OH and MO. Throughout TN, but more often from the Eastern Highland Rim eastward. Frequent.

NOTES: The species name *integrifolia* refers to the entire or uncut upper leaves. • **Hyssopleaf Skullcap** produces 1–several stems from a somewhat woody base and occurs in populations of low density. The flowers are scentless and the foliage is not aromatic. • Medicinally, the properties of this plant provide similar relief to nervous conditions as **Mad-Dog Skullcap** (see below), but because Hyssopleaf Skullcap is more bitter, it is less commonly used.

MARGRET RHINEHART

Mad-Dog Skullcap
Scutellaria lateriflora

GENERAL: Erect perennial herb 1–2 ft. tall, from slender rhizomes, the solitary stem freely branched, **smooth** or hairy in lines. **LEAVES:** Opposite, ovate, or narrowly ovate, 1–3 in. long, with a rounded base and pointed tip, toothed, pinnately veined, petioled. **FLOWERS: Blue or pink**, to 0.4 in. long, the tube nearly straight; 2-lipped corolla, lower lip longer than upper; borne in numerous, axillary, **1-sided racemes**, 1–4 in. long, the **flowers often paired**. July–September. **FRUITS:** Round, pimpled nutlets, flattened on the side, about 0.05 in. across. **WHERE FOUND:** Moist to wet areas over much of the U.S. and Canada. Throughout TN, usually in small populations. Frequent.

NOTES: The leaves of this plant were made into a tea that was once used as a folk remedy to treat rabies. A potent tea was also used as a sedative, nerve tonic, and antispasmodic for a variety of nervous conditions, including anxiety, epilepsy, and insomnia.

THOMAS G. BARNES

Large-Flowered Skullcap · *Scutellaria montana*

GENERAL: Perennial herb, about 12 in. tall, with a simple, erect, **hairy stem**. **LEAVES:** Opposite, mostly ovate, 2–4 in. long, crenate, sparsely **glandular-hairy**, rounded or wedge-shaped bases, on petioles to 0.75 in. long. **FLOWERS:** Whitish, showy, 1.0–1.5 in. long, 2-lipped corolla with a **lavender lower lip**; bracts longer than calyx; borne in a solitary terminal raceme, 2–6 in. long. May–June. **FRUITS:** Nutlets, usually dark brown to black; surfaces of nutlets appear pimpled. **WHERE FOUND:** Rocky, dry mountain slopes in northern GA and southern TN. In TN, in Marion, Sequatchie, and Hamilton counties. Rare. **SIMILAR SPECIES: SHOWY SKULLCAP (S. serrata)** is 12–24 in. tall, with 1 to several stems from a common base, the **stems normally smooth** below the inflorescence; **leaves essentially smooth** on both sides; flowers are whitish blue to pale lavender, showy, about 1 in. long; racemes normally solitary. Rich woods and slopes from NY to OH, south to FL and MS. In TN, only in Morgan, Greene, Washington, Unicoi, and Sullivan counties in East TN. Rare. May–June.

NOTES: Although **Large-Flowered Skullcap** is a federally listed rare plant, it is locally abundant in populations that grow in ravines and gorges of the southern Cumberland Plateau in TN. It grows on dry to slightly moist rocky slopes primarily under mature hardwoods of oaks and hickories. Trees on these sites are 70 to over 200 years old, depending on the site. The most significant threat to the Large-Flowered Skullcap is habitat destruction, such as logging, wildfires, livestock grazing, and residential development.

Small Skullcap · *Scutellaria parvula*

GENERAL: Small perennial herb **only 4–8 in. tall**, often with several stems together arising from a thin rhizome; 4-angled **stems have spreading glandular hairs**. **LEAVES:** Opposite, hairy, sessile, **to 0.6 in. long**, ovate to nearly round, **obscurely toothed**, 3–5 veins on each side of the midrib. **FLOWERS: Blue to violet** corolla, to 0.3 in. long, with **dark spots** on the inside of the lower lip; calyx usually reddish and glandular hairy; flowers arise from the axils of foliage leaves. April–June. **FRUITS:** Dark brown nutlets, dull and flattened on the sides. **WHERE FOUND:** Cedar glades, prairies, and upland woods, from Québec to ND, south to FL and TX. In TN, primarily the Central Basin and Western Highland Rim, thinly scattered elsewhere. Occasional. **SIMILAR SPECIES: VEINED SKULLCAP (S. nervosa)** is taller (to 24 in.); **stem minutely hairy; leaves** ovate to round-ovate, **0.8–1.8 in. long, prominently toothed**, rounded to nearly cordate at the base. Moist woods, from NY to IA, south to GA and LA. In TN, in the Western Highland Rim, also Clay, Hamilton, Roane, Scott, Union, and Knox counties. Occasional. May–June.

NOTES: The species name *parvula* means "very small, insignificant," in reference to the size of the overall plant, as well as the diminutive size of the flowers. **Small Skullcap** also is called **Little Skullcap**. This plant is the smallest of the skullcaps in our area and can easily be overlooked because of its size.

Southern Showy Skullcap
Scutellaria pseudoserrata

GENERAL: Perennial herb, 12–18 in. tall, with erect, **hairy stem**, usually solitary. **LEAVES:** Opposite, lanceolate to ovate, 2–3 in. long, acute tip, toothed margins, rounded or wedge-shaped base; **both surfaces are glandular, but normally smooth** (without hairs), on petioles 0.5–0.75 in. long. **FLOWERS:** Blue and white to lavender, showy, 1.0–1.5 in. long, **2 darker lines near the center of the lower lip**; inflorescence is a simple terminal raceme. May–June. **FRUITS:** Brown nutlets. **WHERE FOUND:** Rich, rocky mountain woods from TN and NC, south to AL, GA, and SC. Found in 12 counties of southeastern TN. Occasional.

NOTES: This plant is also called **Falseteeth Skullcap**, which presumably is a translation of *pseudo*, meaning "false" and *serrata* meaning "toothed," in reference to the toothed margins of the leaves.

DENNIS HORN

Smooth Hedge Nettle, Common Hedge Nettle • *Stachys tenuifolia*

GENERAL: Simple, **smooth-stemmed** perennial herb 12–36 in. tall; occasionally **slightly hairy on the angles of the square stem**. **LEAVES:** Opposite, **lanceolate to narrowly elliptic**, 3–6 in. long, pointed, toothed, obtuse at the base, **usually smooth**, petioles 0.3–1.0 in. long. **FLOWERS:** White to pink to lavender, to 0.5 in. long, 2-lipped corolla, upper lip hooded, hiding the 4 stamens, lower lip 3-lobed; occur in **clusters of 6** in the axils of the upper leaves or reduced bracts. June–August. **FRUITS:** Nutlets about 0.07 in. long. **WHERE FOUND:** Moist soil in the shade, from the Great Plains eastward. Throughout TN. Frequent. **SIMILAR SPECIES:** NUTTALL'S HEDGE NETTLE (*S. nuttallii*), also called HEARTLEAF HEDGE NETTLE, is **glandular-hairy on the sides of the stem; stem angles have short, stiff hairs; ovate, coarsely hairy leaves, petioles less than 0.3 in. long**. Moist woods and meadows, from NY to IL, south to GA and AL. Middle and East TN. Occasional. June–August. *S. riddellii, S. cordata.* CLINGMAN'S HEDGE NETTLE (*S. clingmanii*) has **stem angles with long, spreading hairs; sides of the stem are not glandular-hairy; hairy leaves with petioles 0.4–1.2 in. long**. Mountain woods and meadows mostly at high elevations in the Appalachian Mountains, also IN and AR. In TN, in Monroe, Blount, and Sevier counties in the Blue Ridge Mountains of East TN. Rare. June–August.

JERRY DROWN

NOTES: Smooth Hedge Nettle flowers are pollinated primarily by long-tongued bees looking for nectar. Short-tongued bees sometimes collect the pollen, as do flower flies, but neither species is a very effective pollinator. The bitter foliage of this and other *Stachys* species is not generally eaten by larger mammals.

DENNIS HORN

Guyandotte Beauty, Synandra
Synandra hispidula

GENERAL: Erect perennial herb, 8–24 in. tall, the **stem with long, soft, curved hairs. LEAVES:** Opposite, 2–3 pairs of stem leaves 1.5–3.0 in. long, **toothed, heart-shaped at the base**, pointed, hairy, the petiole often longer than the blade. **FLOWERS:** Showy, **greenish yellow or greenish white with purple lines on the lower tip**, to 1.5 in. long; strongly 2-lipped with the **corolla tube much dilated**, upper lip hooded, lower lip broadly 3-lobed; 4 stamens; calyx is nearly regular; 4–12 flowers are solitary in the axils of small sessile leaves, forming a terminal spike. April–June. **FRUITS:** Smooth, bi-convex nutlets. **WHERE FOUND:** Rich mesic woods, from WV to southern IL, south to TN and northern AL. In TN, thinly scattered from the Western Highland Rim eastward, but more prevalent in northern Middle TN. Occasional.

NOTES: The genus name *Synandra* comes from the Greek *syn*, "together," and *andr*, "man," in reference to the anthers that are joined in pairs. This plant is also called **Hairy Synandra** and **Wyandotte Beauty**. • This species is somewhat threatened by land-use conversion, habitat fragmentation, and forest management practices that open the canopy by logging. • *Synandra* is a monotypic genus, meaning that it contains only one species.

OTTO R. HIRSCH

American Germander, Wood Sage • *Teucrium canadense*

GENERAL: Erect perennial herb, 12–36 in. tall, from a rhizome, the hairy stems solitary. **LEAVES:** Opposite, lanceolate-ovate to oblong, 2–5 in. long, toothed, petioles 0.2–0.6 in. long. **FLOWERS:** Pale rose purple, 0.5–0.75 in. long; 2-lipped corolla, **upper lip much shorter than the long, lobed lower lip, 4 stamens** diverge from the corolla, **arching over the lower lip**; borne in a crowded, spike-like, terminal raceme, 2–8 in. long. June–August. **FRUITS:** Yellowish brown, ellipsoid nutlets, 0.08 in. long. **WHERE FOUND:** Moist to wet soils, swamps, and wet barrens in most of U.S. and southern Canada. Throughout TN. Common.

NOTES: The genus *Teucrium* was named in honor of Teucer, the first king of Troy, who first used this plant in medicine. • **American Germander**, also called **Canada Germander**, has been used since ancient times to heal sores and ulcers of the skin. A tea made from the leaves has been used to induce menstruation, urination, and sweating. This herb is sometimes sold commercially as **Pink Skullcap**.

Bluecurls
Trichostema dichotomum

GENERAL: Annual, 8–28 in. tall, with a densely glandular, hairy stem, usually branched. **LEAVES:** Opposite, narrow, oblong to elliptic, 1–2 in. long, less than 5 times as long as wide, usually evident lateral veins. **FLOWERS:** Blue, about 0.25 in. long; 2-lipped corolla with 5 lobes, the 4 upper lobes ascending, the lower curved downward; 4 prominent stamens, about 0.6 in. long, with arching filaments; irregular calyx; grow in leaf axils of both large and small leaves. August–October. **FRUITS:** Distinctly veiny nutlets, 0.08 in. long. **WHERE FOUND:** Open, dry soil in fields, cliffs, glades, and barrens, from ME to MI, south to FL and TX. In most of TN, but absent in the Central Basin and most of West TN. Frequent. **SIMILAR SPECIES:** LINEARLEAF BLUECURLS (*T. setaceum*) has 1-nerved linear leaves to 0.2 in. wide, at least 6 times longer than wide. Dry sites. A chiefly Coastal Plain species, from CT to FL and TX and irregularly inland to MO and OH. In TN, in Fayette, Franklin, Rhea, and Roane counties. Rare. August–October.

NOTES: The genus name *Trichostema* means "hairy stamen"; *dichotomum* means "forked in pairs," referring to the arching stamens of this plant. **Bluecurls** is also called Blue Gentian and Heart's Angel for the striking beauty of the flowers. • *Trichostema* species are called bluecurls for their distinctively curled, blue-stalked stamens.

Bracted Plantain • *Plantago aristata*

GENERAL: Hairy, taprooted annual or short-lived perennial, 4–12 in. tall. **LEAVES:** In a basal rosette, linear or very narrowly elliptic, to 5 in. long, may be hairy or smooth. **FLOWERS:** Whitish, translucent, about 0.15 in. wide, 4-lobed, 4 short stamens; long floral bracts are linear, more or less hairy, extending well past the flowers; borne on densely flowered spikes, 1–3 in. long. May–July. **FRUITS:** 2-seeded capsules; seeds brown, horizontally grooved, up to 0.12 in. long. **WHERE FOUND:** Waste places and disturbed sites. Native from IL to LA and TX, but now naturalized over most of the eastern U.S. and adjacent Canada. Throughout TN. Common. **SIMILAR SPECIES:** DWARF PLANTAIN (*P. pusilla*) is also an annual, but smaller; linear leaves only to 3 in. long; minute bracts and flowers. Dry, sandy soil in most of the eastern U.S. Thinly spread across TN. Occasional. April–June.

NOTES: The very narrow leaves and long, hairy bracts separate **Bracted Plantain**, also known as **Largebracted Plantain**, from the other *Plantago* species. • Most *Plantago* species, known as plantains, have basal leaves and flowers that are densely crowded in spikes on basally naked scapes. Each flower is sessile in the axil of a bract, and the corolla is long persistent. The fruit capsule separates into two halves at or below the middle. Where Bracted Plantain has become naturalized beyond its native range, it is considered a weed.

PAUL SOMERS

English Plantain · *Plantago lanceolata**

GENERAL: Fibrous-rooted perennial, 6–25 in. tall, with a stout root crown. **LEAVES:** In a basal rosette, **narrowly lance-olate** to oblanceolate, 4–12 in. long, only 1/6 as wide, tapering at both ends; 3 to several nerved. **FLOWERS:** Whitish, translucent, 4 corolla lobes spreading to reflexed, about 0.08 in. long; protruding style and stamens; flowers open first at the bottom of the dense spike which may be 3 in. long at maturity; buds at the top give the **spike a rounded, conical appearance.** May–October. **FRUITS:** Capsules with 1–2 blackish, shining seeds. **WHERE FOUND:** Introduced from Eurasia, now a cosmopolitan weed of lawns and waste places throughout the eastern U.S. and TN. Common. **SIMILAR SPECIES:** AMERICAN PLANTAIN (*P. rugelii*) is a fibrous-rooted perennial with scapes to 10 in. tall; **broadly elliptic to ovate, smooth leaves with reddish stalks** separate this species from the others. Lawns and waste places through-out the eastern U.S. and TN. Frequent. May–October. HOARY PLANTAIN (*P. virginica*) is a small, taprooted **annual or biennial**; oblanceolate to elliptic, slightly hairy leaves; mod-erately to **densely hairy scape**, normally less than 6 in. tall; erect corolla lobes enclose the fruit. Dry soil, often weedy. Throughout the eastern U.S. and TN. Common. April–June.

NOTES: Many plantains are **weedy and vigorous growers** and are a nuisance to gardeners and lawn keepers. They also are edible, with the very young leaves being rich in vitamins A and C, as well as iron. • Medicinally, all of the plantains contain a high level of tannin, which causes the leaves to have an astringent property, making them useful for treating skin condi-tions such as sores, cuts, inflammations, and bites.

DENNIS HORN

Fringe Tree, Old Man's Beard · *Chionanthus virginicus*

GENERAL: **Showy shrub** or small deciduous **tree**, 5–15 ft. tall. **LEAVES:** Opposite, simple, entire, elliptic to obovate, 3–8 in. long, taper-ing at the base to long petioles; one of the last woody plants to produce leaves in spring. **FLOWERS:** White, showy, **fragrant**, corolla has **4 linear lobes**, each 0.6–1.2 in. long, separate nearly to the base; borne in many-flowered panicles in **drooping clusters.** May–June. **FRUITS:** Ellipsoid, purple or dark blue drupes, 0.4–0.6 in. long; 1–3 seeds. **WHERE FOUND:** Moist woods, streambanks, and bluffs from NY to MO, south to FL and TX. Mostly in East TN and the Cumberland Plateau and High-land Rim of Middle TN. Frequent.

NOTES: The genus name *Chionanthus* is from the Greek *chion*, "snow," and *anthus*, "a flower," referring to this tree's showy white flowers. • In herbal medicine, the bark has been used as a diuretic and to treat fevers. • Members of the Olive Family are shrubs or trees with opposite leaves. Ash trees, lilac, privet, and forsythia are examples.

Figwort Family (Scrophulariaceae)

The Figwort Family, sometimes called the Snapdragon Family, is large and contains mostly herbs and a few shrubs and trees, primarily found in temperate regions and tropical mountains. It contains many recognizable ornamentals, including louseworts (*Pedicularis*), mulleins (*Verbascum*), pentemons/beardtongues (*Penstemon*), snapdragons (*Antirrhinum*), speedwells (*Veronica*), and monkeyflowers (*Mimulus*). Some plants in this family are partial parasites, including louseworts (*Pedicularis*) and Indian paintbrushes (*Castilleja*). Some members of the Figwort Family are edible, and others provide herbal treatments for fever, stomach sickness, skin irritations, liver ailments, and venereal diseases.

1a. Stem leaves alternate **2**

  2a. Flowers nearly radially symmetric; corolla lobes longer than the tube . . . . . . ***Verbascum***

  2b. Flowers bilaterally symmetric; corolla lobes equal to or shorter than the tube **3**

    3a. Corolla spurred; calyx lobes 5 . . . . ***Linaria***

    3b. Corolla not spurred; calyx lobes 4, or united and bearing 2 lateral appendages **4**

      4a. Bract-like leaves 3-parted, usually scarlet . . . . ***Castilleja***

      4b. Bract-like leaves pinnately divided, not scarlet . . . . ***Pedicularis***

1b. Stem leaves opposite or whorled (bract-like leaves sometimes alternate) **5**

  5a. Leaves whorled . . . . ***Veronicastrum***

  5b. Leaves opposite **6**

    6a. Calyx lobes 4, or united and bearing 2 lateral appendages **7**

      7a. Stamens 2; corolla tube much shorter than the lobes . . . . ***Veronica***

      7b. Stamens 4; corolla tube equal to or longer than the lobes **8**

        8a. Flowers axillary; leaves mostly entire; seeds 4 per capsule . . . . ***Melampyrum***

        8b. Flowers in terminal spikes; leaves pinnately divided;
            seeds numerous . . . . ***Pedicularis***

    6b. Calyx lobes 5 . . . . **9**

      9a. Fertile stamens 2 . . . . ***Gratiola***

      9b. Fertile stamens 4 (additional sterile stamen sometimes present) **10**

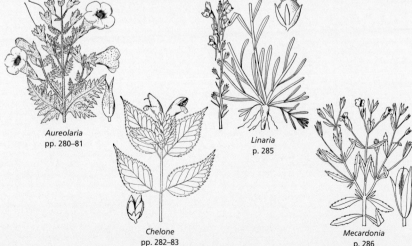

Aureolaria
pp. 280–81

Chelone
pp. 282–83

Linaria
p. 285

Mecardonia
p. 286

10a. Flowers yellow, corolla weakly bilaterally symmetric,
plants parasitic on oak trees **11**

11a. Anthers hairy, calyx lobes usually longer than the tube . . . . . **Aureolaria**

11b. Anthers smooth, calyx lobes equaling or
shorter than the tube . . . . **Dasistoma**

10b. Flowers not yellow, primarily either
white, pink, purple, blue, or greenish **12**

12a. Sterile stamen (staminode) present **13**

13a. Flowers sessile in dense terminal spikes;
sterile stamen smooth . . . . **Chelone**

13b. Flowers on pedicels, in panicles or racemes;
sterile stamen hairy . . . . **Penstemon**

12b. Sterile stamen (staminode) absent
(or reduced to a callous knob in *Collinsia*) **14**

14a. Corolla strongly bilaterally symmetric **15**

15a. Corolla tube more than 0.5 in. long . . . . **Mimulus**

15b. Corolla tube less than 0.5 in. long **16**

16a. Upper leaves sessile; flowers blue and white . . . . **Collinsia**

16b. Upper leaves nearly sessile to short-petioled;
flowers purple, at least partly . . . . **Mazus**

14b. Corolla weakly bilaterally symmetric **17**

17a. Flowers pink; inflorescence a raceme; leaves linear . . . . . . **Agalinis**

17b. Flowers blue or purple, rarely white; flowers axillary or in terminal
spikes; leaves elliptic to ovate to oblanceolate **18**

18a. Sepals distinct nearly to the base . . . . **Mecardonia**

18b. Sepals fused to form a lobed tube . . . . **Buchnera**

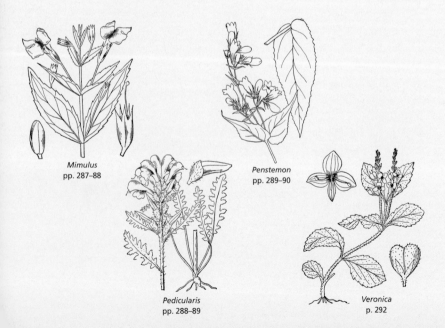

Mimulus
pp. 287–88

Penstemon
pp. 289–90

Pedicularis
pp. 288–89

Veronica
p. 292

Smooth Purple Gerardia · *Agalinis purpurea*

GENERAL: Simple to much-branched **annual**, 16–48 in. tall, with squarish **smooth stems**. **LEAVES:** Primary leaves are opposite, dark green or purplish, linear, 0.5–1.5 in. long, to 0.1 in. wide; prominent clusters of small leaves (**fascicles**) in the leaf axils are **lacking** or poorly developed. **FLOWERS:** Pink to purplish, 0.8–1.6 in. long; tubular corolla with 5 spreading lobes, **throat is hairy within** and lined with yellow; borne on stout pedicels less than 0.2 in. long. August–October. **FRUITS:** Roundish capsules with dark seeds. **WHERE FOUND:** Dry to moist areas and wetland margins. Widely scattered across the eastern U.S. and TN. Frequent. **SIMILAR SPECIES:** FASCICLED PURPLE GERARDIA (*A. fasciculata*) has a **rough stem** and **clusters of small leaves** in the primary leaf axils. Dry soil, from NY to FL and TX, north in the interior to IN and MO. In West and Middle TN. Occasional. August–October.

NOTES: Smooth Purple Gerardia is also called **Purple False Foxglove.** • Members of this genus are annual herbs that are often parasitic on the roots of native grasses, as are Indian paintbrushes, yellow rattles, and a few other members of the Figwort Family. • *Agalinis* species were formerly combined with the *Aureolaria* genus in the unwieldy (now rejected) genus *Gerardia*. The 10 species in TN are difficult to distinguish without careful observation.

DENNIS HORN

Slender Gerardia · *Agalinis tenuifolia*

GENERAL: Smooth, much-branched **annual**, 12–24 in. tall; **stem and leaves dark green** to purplish, specimens drying dark. **LEAVES:** Opposite, linear, 0.8–2.0 in. long, to 0.15 in. wide, **leaf clusters not present** in leaf axils. **FLOWERS:** Pink to purplish, tubular, about 0.5 in. long; 5-lobed **corolla is smooth within**, the **upper lip arching over the stamens; calyx is not net-veined**; on slender, divergent pedicels 0.4–0.8 in. long; occur in terminal racemes from the upper leaf axils. August–October. **FRUITS:** Rounded capsules. **WHERE FOUND:** Dry to moist open areas throughout the eastern U.S. and TN. Common. **SIMILAR SPECIES:** GATTINGER'S GERARDIA (*A. gattingeri*) has a few small leaves and is profusely branched; slender, **pale greenish branches** usually terminate with a single flower; spreading corolla is pink, 0.5–0.7 in. long; **calyx tube is net-veined**. Open forests and barrens, from southern Ontario to MN, south to AL and TX. Primarily in Middle TN. Occasional. August–October. EARLEAF FALSE FOXGLOVE (*A. auriculata*) has rough, **wide**, lanceolate-ovate, **toothed leaves, some lobed**

DENNIS HORN

(auricled). Open woods and barrens, from PA to MN, south to AL and TX. In TN, in Bledsoe, Carroll, Montgomery, Roane, and Tipton counties. Rare. August–September. *Tomanthera auriculata*.

NOTES: The flowers of **Slender Gerardia** are short-lasting, opening in the morning and closing in the afternoon. • Even though *Agalinis* species are able to survive on their own, if the opportunity arises, they will take nourishment from the roots of other plants.

THOMAS E. HEMMERLY

Smooth False Foxglove
Aureolaria laevigata

GENERAL: Perennial herb, 2–5 ft. tall, usually with **smooth, green stems. LEAVES:** Opposite, narrowly lanceolate, 2–4 in. long, **lower leaves generally lack lobes** or teeth and taper to a sharp point. **FLOWERS:** Yellow, **funnel-shaped**, to 1.4 in. long, 5 corolla lobes are shorter than the tube; **flower stalks 0.12 in. long or shorter**; solitary from the upper leaf axils. July–September. **FRUITS:** Smooth capsules with winged seeds. **WHERE FOUND:** Upland woods from PA to southern OH, south to GA and MS. In TN, from the Cumberland Plateau eastward. Occasional. **SIMILAR SPECIES:** YELLOW FALSE FOXGLOVE **(A. flava)** usually has **glaucous (waxy), purplish stems; lower leaves pinnately divided**, upper leaves lobed or toothed; **flower stalks are 0.15–0.4 in. long** and curved upward; often found under oak trees (*Quercus* spp.) of the red or black oak group. Dry, upland woods throughout the eastern U.S. and TN. Frequent. August–September.

NOTES: *Aureolaria* species are also known as "oak-leeches." They are native annual or perennial herbs and are partly parasitic on the roots of native oak trees. **Mullein Foxglove** (p. 284) is closely related, but its flowers are much smaller and are densely hairy inside. • Five *Aureolaria* species are listed for TN.

DENNIS HORN

Spreading False Foxglove • *Aureolaria patula*

GENERAL: Sparsely hairy, widely branched perennial herb, 2–4 ft. tall. **LEAVES:** Opposite, 3–6 in. long, upper leaves lanceolate, **lower leaves coarsely lobed. FLOWERS:** Yellow, tubular, about 1.5 in. long, 5 rounded corolla lobes; calyx lobes are longer than tube; **on stalks 0.4–0.6 in. long.** July–September. **FRUITS:** Smooth, ovoid capsules; winged seeds. **WHERE FOUND:** Restricted to river bluffs and related habitats in calcareous regions from central KY to northern GA and AL. In TN, in Stewart, Montgomery, Davidson, Franklin, Pickett, Morgan, Roane, and Claiborne counties. Infrequent. **SIMILAR SPECIES: DOWNY FALSE FOXGLOVE (A. virginica)** is mostly **downy throughout; flower stalks 0.15 in. long or less**; hairy fruits; parasitic on white oaks. Dry woods in most of the eastern U.S. In TN, from the Western Highland Rim eastward, also Carroll County in West TN. Frequent. June–September.

NOTES: The flowers of plants in the *Aureolaria* genus generally resemble those of the garden plant, Foxglove (*Digitalis purpurea*), hence the common name. • Native Americans used some *Aureolaria* species medicinally for cleansing wounds and reducing swelling.

Southern Fernleaf False Foxglove · *Aureolaria pectinata*

GENERAL: Much-branched, **glandular-hairy annual** to 36 in. tall. **LEAVES:** Opposite, 1.0–2.5 in. long, lanceolate to triangular, finely **pinnately divided and fern-like**, their divisions sharp-pointed. **FLOWERS: Yellow tinged with brown**, funnel-shaped, to 1.6 in. long, 5 corolla lobes are shorter than the tube; calyx lobes toothed, calyx tube short and hemispheric. July–October. **FRUITS:** Ovoid, glandular-hairy capsules; wingless seeds. **WHERE FOUND:** Dry upland woods and barrens. A southeastern species extending north into VA, KY, and MO. Widespread across TN, but absent in the westernmost counties of West TN and most of the counties near the KY border. Frequent.

JERRY DROWN

NOTES: The name "foxglove" may come from the story that fairies gave the flowers to foxes to wear as gloves so that they would not be caught raiding chicken coops. Another version of this story is that children were told not to pick the flowers or they would offend the fairies, probably to keep the children away from this **poisonous** plant. • Plant specimens that have been gathered and dried for use in herbarium collections turn black.

Blue Hearts · *Buchnera americana*

GENERAL: Rarely branched, hairy perennial herb, 16–36 in. tall, with a hard rootstock. **LEAVES:** Mostly on the **lower ½ of the stem**, opposite (upper ones sometimes alternate), 1–3-veined, 2–4 in. long, lanceolate with a few coarse teeth, lower leaves much wider than upper. **FLOWERS: Purple** (rarely white), **5 flaring corolla lobes**, 0.2–0.3 in. long; hairy calyx is persistent; borne in spikes that gradually lengthen to 6 in. long. July–September. **FRUITS:** Mostly long, ovoid, many-seeded capsules, opening at the end. **WHERE FOUND:** Open fields and barrens in most of the eastern U.S. In TN, primarily in the Highland Rim and Cumberland Plateau. Occasional.

OTTO R. HIRSCH

NOTES: The *Buchnera* genus is characterized by purple-blue flowers and a tubular corolla with nearly equal spreading lobes. These plants are partly parasitic on various hosts and blacken upon drying. They resemble some *Verbena* species, but this latter genus has fruits with 4 distinct nutlets rather than a many-seeded capsule. • **Blue Hearts** is the only species of this genus found in TN.

Indian Paintbrush
Castilleja coccinea

GENERAL: Parasitic, **annual or biennial** herb, 8–20 in. tall, with a usually unbranched, hairy stem. **LEAVES:** Basal rosette; stem leaves alternate, 1.0–1.6 in. long; leaves and bracts are 3–5-lobed. **FLOWERS: Greenish yellow**, about 1 in. long, 2-lipped corolla is slightly longer than the **red-colored calyx**; borne in dense terminal spikes; **red-orange bracts** are usually more deeply colored than the actual flowers. May–August. **FRUITS:** Ellipsoid capsules. **WHERE FOUND:** Moist meadows, prairies, and barrens, from ME to MN, south to FL and LA. In TN, in Lewis, Coffee, Grundy, Van Buren, Bledsoe, Cumberland, Morgan, Roane, Sevier, and Jefferson counties. Infrequent.

NOTES: The *Castilleja* genus is named in honor of Domingo Castillejo (1744–93), a Spanish botanist; *coccinea*, appropriately, means "scarlet." Species of this genus are sometimes called "painted cups." Other names for this plant include Indian Blanket, Nosebleed, and Prairie Fire, all referencing the showy-colored calyx, inside of which is the actual greenish yellow corolla. • This plant is pollinated by hummingbirds. • TN has only one *Castilleja* species, but there are many others in the western U.S. The terminal inflorescence combines yellow to reddish tubular flowers mixed with longer, similarly colored bracts in a spreading cluster. It is partly parasitic, as are many members of the Figwort Family.

White Turtlehead
Chelone glabra

GENERAL: Smooth perennial herb, 20–36 in. tall; may be simple or branched. **LEAVES:** Opposite, short-stalked or sessile, 4–6 in. long, **relatively narrow**, lanceolate with serrate margins. **FLOWERS: Dull white to often pink-tipped** (some regional variation in color), to 1.4 in. long, **2-lipped corolla resembles the head of a turtle**; borne in short terminal spikes. July–September. **FRUITS:** Broadly ovoid capsules, 0.4 in. long. **WHERE FOUND:** Moist ground and along streams. Widespread in wetlands of the eastern U.S., south to GA and AR. Widespread across TN, but generally absent from the Central Basin and much of West TN. Common.

NOTES: Native Americans used a strong decoction of this plant to treat skin diseases, hemorrhoids, constipation, and ulcers. It also has some folk-medicinal uses as a bitter tonic and itch-reliever. • Turtleheads are usually found in moist or wet places. Three species are listed for TN.

Red Turtlehead · *Chelone lyonii*

GENERAL: A primarily southern Appalachian perennial herb, 16–40 in. tall, stems erect. **LEAVES:** Opposite, **ovate to ovate-lanceolate**, 3–5 in. long, **widest below the middle**, rounded or squared-off base, serrated margins; on **well-developed petioles**, 0.6–1.6 in. long. **FLOWERS:** Reddish purple, 1.2–1.6 in. long, 2-lipped corolla, lower lip with a prominent yellow beard; borne in short, terminal spikes. July–September. **FRUITS:** Broadly ovoid capsules, 0.4 in. long. **WHERE FOUND:** Rich coves and open streambanks in the Appalachian Mountains of TN, NC, and SC; escaped from cultivation and naturalized in the northeastern U.S. In TN, in Blount, Sevier, Cocke, Greene, Unicoi, Carter, Warren, Grundy, and Marion counties. Infrequent. **SIMILAR SPECIES: NARROWLEAF RED TURTLEHEAD (*C. obliqua*)** has **narrower leaves, widest near the middle, on shorter petioles**; pink to reddish purple corolla. Wet woods and swamps in the Coastal Plain of the southeastern U.S., north in the interior to MI and MN. In TN, in Lewis, Madison, and Obion counties. Rare. August–October.

HUGH & CAROL NOURSE

NOTES: Plants in the *Chelone* genus are commonly called "turtleheads" for their 2-lipped flowers, which resemble a tortoise's or turtle's head in shape. Species in this genus have also been called Snake Mouth and Fish Mouth because the flowers resemble the heads of these animals.

Blue-Eyed Mary · *Collinsia verna*

GENERAL: Weak stemmed **annual**, 8–16 in. tall. **LEAVES:** Stem leaves below the inflorescence are opposite, sessile, triangular-ovate, to 2 in. long; lower leaves petiolate. **FLOWERS:** Striking, **bicolored**, 0.5 in. wide; 4 corolla lobes evident, **upper 2 lobes white**, **lower 2 lobes bright blue**, 5th lobe is folded and disappears between the lower 2, creating a pouch that contains the style and 4 stamens; in 1–3 whorls of 4–6 flowers each. April–May. **FRUITS:** Capsules, usually with 4 seeds. **WHERE FOUND:** On slopes and in rich woods, especially in deep soil of small stream floodplains, from NY to WI, south to VA, TN, and OK. Widespread north of TN. In TN, native populations occur in Clay and Sumner counties in Middle TN; naturalized at the Chattanooga Nature Center. Rare.

DICK DOUB

NOTES: The *Collinsia* genus is named in honor of Zaccheus Collins (1764–1831), a botanist from Philadelphia. • This plant is also known as Blue-Bonnet-White-Apron, Innocence, and Lady-by-the-Lake. • Erect and slender annuals of the *Collinsia* genus have opposite leaves and axillary flower clusters. Only one species is known in TN, and its distribution is restricted. This American genus includes several western species.

THOMAS G. BARNES

Mullein Foxglove · *Dasistoma macrophylla*

GENERAL: Somewhat **hairy**, robust, partially **parasitic** perennial herb, 3–6 ft. tall. **LEAVES:** Opposite, 4–8 in. long, lower leaves broadly ovate and deeply lobed, upper leaves progressively reduced in size, becoming lanceolate and entire. **FLOWERS:** Yellow, about 0.6 in. long, smooth externally but **woolly inside**; funnel-shaped corolla tube is longer than the 5 lobes, which are all alike and widely spreading; borne in an elongated, leafy, interrupted spike. June–September. **FRUITS:** Capsules, each of the 2 halves with a short triangular beak. **WHERE FOUND:** Partly parasitic on tree roots. Rich, moist open woods and limestone glades, from PA to WI and NE, south to GA and TX. Widespread in Middle TN, also Shelby, Tipton, Lauderdale, Obion, and Hardin counties in West TN and Claiborne County in East TN. Occasional. **Seymeria macrophylla.**

NOTES: The *Dasistoma* genus is monotypic, containing only this one species. The common name, **Mullein Foxglove**, reveals that this plant closely resembles false foxgloves in the *Aureolaria* genus and bears a similarity to mullein species (*Verbascum*).

THOMAS G. BARNES

Clammy Hedge Hyssop
Gratiola neglecta

GENERAL: Annual, 4–12 in. tall, **glandular-hairy**, stems usually branched near the base. **LEAVES:** Opposite, sessile, about 2 in. long, narrowly rhombic, **widest beyond the middle**, tapering to a narrow base, often toothed toward the tip. **FLOWERS:** Tubular, about 0.4 in. long, **yellowish with 5 white lobes, 2 stamens**, 5 narrow sepals at the base and 2 bractlets below; solitary on **slender axillary pedicels, 0.4–0.8 in. long**. April–July. **FRUITS:** Ovoid capsules, 0.1–0.2 in. long. **WHERE FOUND:** Wet places, ditches, and pond margins throughout the U.S. and southern Canada. Primarily in Middle and West TN. Common. **SIMILAR SPECIES:** ROUND-FRUIT HEDGE HYSSOP (**G. virginiana**) is smooth; white corolla with purple lines; **stout pedicels about 0.2 in. long**. Wet woods in the southeastern U.S. Throughout TN. Frequent. April–September. SHAGGY HEDGE HYSSOP (**G. pilosa**) is a **hairy perennial**; broad-based **ovate leaves; white corolla**. Shady woods in the southeastern U.S. In Middle and East TN. Occasional. June–September. STICKY HEDGE HYSSOP (**G. brevifolia**) is a **glandular perennial**; thick, linear leaves with 1–3 teeth per side; **yellow corolla with white lobes**. Wet areas. In the southeastern U.S. and a few counties in central TN. Rare. April–August.

NOTES: The genus name *Gratiola* is Latin for "agreeableness or pleasantness," in reference to the medicinal properties of some plants in this genus. The species name *neglecta* refers to the fact that this plant is often overlooked or "neglected." • **Clammy Hedge Hyssop** is also known as **American Hedge Hyssop.**

Blue Toadflax · *Linaria canadensis*

GENERAL: Slender, smooth, tap-rooted **biennial or winter annual**, 8–24 in. tall, with an erect, almost leafless flowering stem arising from a basal rosette of prostrate, leafy stems. **LEAVES:** Linear, 0.4–1.0 in. long, alternate on flowering stem, opposite on prostrate stems. **FLOWERS:** Blue to lavender, 0.2–0.5 in. long; 2-lipped corolla with a **narrow spur**, lower lip has a **double-humped, white palate** and much exceeds the upper lip; borne in 1 to several racemes. April–May. **FRUITS:** Nearly spherical capsules, 0.1–0.15 in. long; prism-like seeds. **WHERE FOUND:** Roadsides, fields, and thin soil of rock outcrops. Widespread in eastern North America and the Pacific Coast states. Widely scattered across TN. Occasional. ***Nuttallanthus canadensis***.

NOTES: Plants in the *Linaria* genus are also called "toadflaxes" because the flower opens its mouth like a toad when it is squeezed in a certain way. The *Linaria* genus is comprised mostly of plants from Eurasia, a number of them cultivated. The North American species have blue (rather than yellow) flowers with a lower lip that is greatly enlarged relative to the upper one. They are often placed in the genus *Nuttallanthus*.

DENNIS HORN

Butter-and-Eggs, Yellow Toadflax
Linaria vulgaris*

GENERAL: Erect, finely hairy perennial herb, 12–36 in. tall, from a rhizome; typically colonial. **LEAVES:** Numerous, alternate, pale blue-green, narrow, 1–2 in. long, **uniformly distributed on the stem** up to the inflorescence. **FLOWERS:** Bright yellow, about 1 in. long including the **prominent, stout spur**; 2-lipped corolla, both lips about equal in size, **lower lip with an orange palate**; borne in a congested raceme at the top of the stem. May–October. **FRUITS:** Round-ovoid capsules 0.3–0.5 in. long; winged seeds. **WHERE FOUND:** Introduced from Europe. Escaped throughout eastern North America, spreading from plantings to roadsides and waste places. Thinly scattered across TN, from the Western Highland Rim eastward. Occasional.

NOTES: This plant takes its common name **Butter-and-Eggs** from the yellow-and-orange flowers. It is also called Gallweed because it was fed to chickens to rid them of gallstones. • Toadflax flowers have markings known as "color guides" that lead potential pollinators to their source of nectar located in the long spur, usually reached only by long-tongued insects and hummingbirds.

DICK SOOY

Japanese Mazus
*Mazus pumilus**

GENERAL: Creeping, low-growing, several-stemmed **annual**, to 6 in. long. **LEAVES:** Mostly basal, opposite, spatulate; uppermost leaves become alternate, to 0.6 in. long. **FLOWERS:** Blue-violet, 0.3–0.4 in. long; 2-lipped corolla, upper lip short, 2-toothed, lower lip larger and 3-lobed with an **orange-and-white palate**; borne in terminal racemes. April–November. **FRUITS:** Small capsules with several seeds. **WHERE FOUND:** An introduced Asian species, escaped and spread into lawns and open places across the milder regions of eastern North America. Thinly scattered across TN. Infrequent. ***M. japonicus***.

NOTES: The genus name *Mazus* is Greek for "a teat," alluding to the 2 tubercles closing the mouth of the corolla of these low-growing herbs. • The only member of this introduced genus in TN, this plant can be seen in the lawn of the Sugarlands Visitor Center at the Great Smoky Mountains National Park headquarters.

Mecardonia, Axilflower
Mecardonia acuminata

GENERAL: Smooth perennial herb with an erect stem, 8–20 in. tall, with few branches; stems and leaves usually blacken upon drying. **LEAVES:** Opposite, oblanceolate, serrate above the middle, about 1.5 in. long. **FLOWERS:** White, 5-lobed, tubular corolla, about 0.4 in. long, with **purple lines on the lower lip**; 4 fertile stamens; solitary from the leaf axils on ascending pedicels, 0.5–1.2 in. long, with 2 linear bractlets at the base of each pedicel. June–September. **FRUITS:** Ellipsoid capsules. **WHERE FOUND:** Moist woods, open wetlands, and seepage areas in limestone glades. A species of the southeastern U.S., extending north to DE and MO. Widespread across the western 2/3 of TN. Frequent.

NOTES: *Mecardonia* species can be easily confused with those of *Lindernia* or *Gratiola*, but technically, they are distinguished from these genera by having 4 fertile stamens. Additionally, they are distinguished from *Lindernia* by having 2 bractlets at the base of the pedicel. **Mecardonia** has longer pedicels than most *Gratiola* species in TN, and whitish lavender, not yellowish, flowers. • Only this single *Mecardonia* species is found in TN.

Cow Wheat
Melampyrum lineare

GENERAL: Small **annual,** 4–16 in. tall, usually branched. **LEAVES:** Opposite, mostly short-stalked, linear to lanceolate-ovate, 1.0–2.5 in. long. **FLOWERS:** Distinctive 2-lipped corolla, 0.25–0.5 in. long, **white with a yellow palate,** slightly widened toward the end, with the lips about equal in size; **4 paired stamens** stay inside the upper lip; solitary from the upper leaf axils. May–July. **FRUITS:** Flattened capsules with 4 smooth seeds. **WHERE FOUND:** Open upland woods, swamps, or wet soil, mostly north of TN. A northern U.S. and southern Canada species extending south in the uplands to GA. In TN, in the Blue Ridge Mountains of East TN, and Fentress, Grundy, and Wayne counties in Middle TN. Occasional.

NOTES: The genus name *Melampyrum* is from the Greek *melas,* "black," and *pyros,* "wheat," because when Cow Wheat seeds were mixed with grains of wheat and ground into flour, the resulting bread often appeared black; *lineare* refers to the narrow leaves. It is also known as **Narrowleaf Cow Wheat.** In the northern part of its range, this species tends to have narrower leaves and is less likely to be branched. • This plant can be parasitic on the roots of many woody and herbaceous plants, taking nutrients from them.

Sharpwing Monkey Flower • *Mimulus alatus*

GENERAL: Perennial herb, 2–4 ft. tall; **square stems have flanges ("wings") along the edges.** **LEAVES:** Opposite, lanceolate to ovate, 2–4 in. long, coarsely toothed, on petioles 0.4–0.8 in. long, the upper leaves nearly sessile. **FLOWERS:** Lavender to rarely white, 0.8–1.0 in. long; strongly 2-lipped corolla, upper lip 2-lobed and erect, lower lip spreading and 3-lobed with a **2-ridged palate;** solitary in the leaf axils on **stalks shorter than the calyx.** July–August. **FRUITS:** Capsules enclosed by the persistent calyx; numerous yellow seeds. **WHERE FOUND:** In marshes and other wetlands throughout most of the eastern U.S. and TN. Common.

NOTES: The genus name *Mimulus* is the Latin diminutive of *mimus* and means "little actor," in reference to the corolla "acting" or looking similar to a monkey's face. The name "monkey flower" also refers to this characteristic. The species name *alatus* means "winged," referring to the 4-angled and winged stem.

Square-Stemmed Monkey Flower • *Mimulus ringens*

GENERAL: Perennial herb, 2–4 ft. tall; **square stems** with rounded angles, **lacking evident flanges ("wings")** on the edges. **LEAVES:** Opposite, lanceolate, 2–4 in. long, sessile, often clasping the stem, obscurely crenate margins. **FLOWERS:** Lavender, 0.8–1.2 in. long; 2-lipped corolla, throat with a raised palate shaded with yellow; spreading **flower stalks are conspicuously longer than the** calyx, to nearly 2 in. long, and arise from the leaf axils. June–September. **FRUITS:** Ellipsoid capsules enclosed by the calyx; numerous yellow seeds. **WHERE FOUND:** Marshes and other wetlands throughout the central and eastern U.S., slightly more northern in distribution. In TN, from the Eastern Highland Rim eastward, also in Benton, Carroll, Dickson, Hardin, and Henry counties. Frequent.

NOTES: This plant is also referred to as **Monkey Flower** and **Allegheny Monkey Flower**. If a monkey flower is squeezed, it looks as if it is "laughing." • Plants in the *Mimulus* genus have a "face-like" corolla with an erect, 2-lobed upper lip, a downward-trending, 3-lobed lower lip, and a raised palate that closes the corolla tube. About 90 *Mimulus* species are found in the U.S., mostly in the western states.

Wood Betony, Forest Lousewort • *Pedicularis canadensis*

GENERAL: Colonial, upright, **hairy** perennial herb, 6–16 in. tall, from short rhizomes. **LEAVES:** Basal or alternate on the stem, dark green, lanceolate to elliptic, 2–6 in. long, deeply pinnately lobed, stalked below, reduced upwards, **deeply divided and fern-like. FLOWERS: Pale yellow to deep maroon, may be bicolored**; 2-lipped corolla has a hood-like upper lobe; borne in a spike with small, leaf-like bracts, the flowers appearing whorled. April–June. **FRUITS:** Dry capsules to 0.7 in. long. **WHERE FOUND:** Moist to dry woods and barrens throughout southern Canada, the central and eastern U.S., and TN. Common.

NOTES: The genus name *Pedicularis* is from *pediculus*, meaning "a louse," which provides the generic name "lousewort." Folklore says livestock that fed on European Lousewort (*P. palustris*) soon would be covered in lice. • **Wood Betony** also is known as Red Helmet, Elephant Head, Walrus Head, and Indian Warrior as a tribute to the unusual flower. • This plant has a symbiotic relationship with a root fungus that helps it gather nutrients and therefore should not be disturbed. • There are 2 *Pedicularis* species in TN.

Swamp Lousewort · *Pedicularis lanceolata*

GENERAL: Short-lived, erect, **smooth** perennial herb, 12–30 in. tall, with few branches; usually solitary. **LEAVES:** Generally opposite, 2–4 in. long, sessile or short-stalked, **pinnately lobed**. **FLOWERS: Creamy yellow**, about 1 in. long; 2-lipped corolla with a helmet-like upper lobe; borne in terminal spikes from the leaf axils. August–September. **FRUITS:** Dry capsules to 0.5 in. long. **WHERE FOUND:** Marshes and open wetlands. A mostly northern species extending south into GA and AR. In TN, in Bledsoe, Bradley, Coffee, Crockett, Cumberland, Greene, Stewart, Union, and Warren counties. Infrequent.

NOTES: The flower of this plant forces a bee to lift the right side of the flower's upper lip, which causes the pollen-receptive stigma to dip down and touch the bee's pollen-laden body. At the same time, the stamens place new pollen on the insect's back. When the bee visits the next flower, the exact same spot on the bee's back will be touched by the new stigma, and the pollen will be transferred to the new plant. Although louseworts do not have nectar, the pollen is enough to attract bees.

DENNIS HORN

Longsepal Beardtongue
Penstemon calycosus

GENERAL: Perennial herb, 12–36 in. tall; flowering stem is usually smooth and often tinged with purple. **LEAVES:** Basal rosette; stem leaves are opposite, lanceolate or lance-ovate to narrowly oblong, 2–4 in. long. **FLOWERS: Bright purple**, usually much paler inside, 1.0–1.4 in. long; 2-lipped corolla ends in 5 spreading lobes, the tube basal portion narrow, abruptly expanding into the open throat; narrow, **long-pointed sepals, 0.2–0.5 in. long**; 4 fertile stamens and 1 bearded sterile stamen; panicle-like inflorescence has **stalked glands**. May–June. **FRUITS:** Brown capsules, 0.3 in. long. **WHERE FOUND:** Roadsides, meadows, and woodland margins throughout most of the eastern U.S. In TN, from the Eastern Highland Rim westward, also in Cumberland and Marion counties. Frequent. **SIMILAR SPECIES:** SMOOTH BEARDTONGUE (*P. laevigatus*), also called **EASTERN BEARDTONGUE**, has smaller flowers, 0.6–0.8 in. long; **sepals only 0.1–0.2 in. long**. Rich woods across the eastern U.S. and TN. Frequent. May–June.

KURT EMMANUELE

NOTES: The common name "beardtongue" arises from a large, sterile, fifth "stamen" (staminode) that often has a "beard" or tuft of hairs. • While the *Penstemon* genus is distinct, with trumpet-shaped flowers up to 1.4 in. long in a terminal cluster, individual species can be difficult to distinguish. Careful observation of a variety of characteristics is necessary to tell them apart. All 10 TN species have a basal rosette of leaves and opposite, sessile stem leaves.

Foxglove Beardtongue
Penstemon digitalis

GENERAL: Perennial herb, 24–60 in. tall, flowering stem usually has a few glandular hairs, but is **shiny and smooth below**, often glaucous. **LEAVES:** Basal rosette; stem leaves opposite, lanceolate or lance-ovate to narrowly triangular, 3–6 in. long, smooth or slightly hairy. **FLOWERS:** White, more than 1 in. long, often with purple lines inside; tubular, weakly 2-lipped, tubular **corolla expands abruptly** from the narrower basal portion into the open throat with 5 almost equal, flaring lobes; in a terminal panicle-like inflorescence on erect to strongly ascending branches, often glandular. May–July. **FRUITS:** Brown capsules to 0.5 in. long. **WHERE FOUND:** Moist, open woods and meadows. Widespread in the central and eastern U.S. Thinly scattered across TN. Occasional. **SIMILAR SPECIES:** GRAY BEARDTONGUE (*P. canescens*) is a perennial to 30 in. tall; **stem and leaves finely hairy**; distinctly 2-lipped **corolla**, 0.8–1.2 in. long, **only gradually widening** from the basal neck, with a large, open but **ridged throat**. Upland woods from PA to IL, south to GA and northern AL, chiefly in the uplands. In TN, primarily from the Eastern Highland Rim eastward. Frequent. May–June.

NOTES: The genus name *Penstemon* comes from the Greek word *pente*, "five," and *stemon*, "stamen," indicating the 5 stamens found in these flowers. The species name *digitalis* is from the Latin *digitus*, for "finger," referring to the shape of the flower that is like a finger-glove. • This plant is the host plant for the Buckeye butterfly and is mostly pollinated by bees. • The majority of *Penstemon* species are found in the western U.S.

Slender Whiteflower Beardtongue
Penstemon tenuiflorus

GENERAL: Perennial herb, 12–24 in. tall, with 1 or more soft-hairy stems arising from a basal rosette. **LEAVES:** Mostly basal or opposite on the lower part of the stem, narrowly lanceolate to oblanceolate, 2–4 in. long, **entire** or finely serrated, **permanently soft-hairy**, greatly reduced in size and number upward. **FLOWERS:** White to yellowish, 0.8–1.2 in. long, distinctly 2-lipped corolla, throat is more or less closed by **2 ridges on the lower lip**. May–June. **FRUITS:** Capsules to 0.5 in. long. **WHERE FOUND:** Dry woodlands, barrens, and glade margins from southern KY to northern MS and northern AL. In TN, often found in the limestone cedar glades of Middle TN, west to Hardeman, Chester, Carroll, and Henry counties in West TN. Occasional. **SIMILAR SPECIES:** HAIRY BEARDTONGUE (*P. hirsutus*) has **pale violet flowers** with whitish lobes; flowering stem is finely hairy and often glandular; **leaves are usually toothed, becoming smooth with age**. Dry woods, openings, and rocky hillsides. Widespread in the northeastern U.S. In TN, in Hickman, Montgomery, Cheatham, Davidson, Sumner, Trousdale, Smith, and Pickett counties of Middle TN. Infrequent. May–July.

NOTES: Slender Whiteflower Beardtongue is also known as **Eastern Whiteflower Beardtongue** and Glade Beardtongue. • **Hairy Beardtongue** and several *P. hirsutus* varieties are commonly sold in nurseries.

Moth Mullein · *Verbascum blattaria**

DAVID DUHL

GENERAL: Slender **biennial**, 2–4 ft. tall; stem and leaves more or less smooth, but with glandular hairs in the inflorescence. **LEAVES:** Flat basal rosette; alternate stem leaves are lanceolate, 3–6 in. long, coarsely toothed. **FLOWERS: Yellow or white**, about 1.2 in. wide, nearly regular, 5-lobed; 5 fertile stamens with **purple, woolly filaments**; calyx with 5 narrow lobes; loosely distributed on pedicels 0.3–0.6 in. long; borne in a terminal, generally unbranched raceme. May–June. **FRUITS:** Dry, spherical capsules covered with glandular hairs. **WHERE FOUND:** Introduced from Eurasia. Disturbed sites. Naturalized and widespread across the U.S. and TN. Frequent.

NOTES: The flower of this plant is said to resemble a moth, the stamens and style mimicking the insect's antennae and tongue. • Curiously, mulleins are not as generous with their pollen as other plants. The long hairs and knobs on the stamens give insects the impression of masses of pollen, when in fact there is only a small amount. This strategy attracts pollinators without the flower having to produce copious amounts of pollen. • Mulleins have a large rosette of leaves at the end of the first year, followed the second year by a prominent flowering stalk with alternate leaves and a terminal raceme of flowers. • There are 3 *Verbascum* species listed for TN.

Common Mullein · *Verbascum thapsus**

JERRY DROWN

GENERAL: Densely woolly biennial, 3–6 ft. tall in its second year, with a stout, upright, mostly unbranched stem. **LEAVES: Pale green**, broadly oval, feel like thick flannel, grow to 12 in. long from a basal rosette the 1st year; 2nd-year stem leaves are alternate, the bases extending down the stem. **FLOWERS: Yellow** with an **orangy center**, 0.5–0.8 in. wide, tubular corolla with 5 rounded, spreading lobes; flowers occur irregularly in a thick terminal spike. June–September. **FRUITS:** 2-valved capsules with longitudinally ridged seeds. **WHERE FOUND:** Introduced from Europe. Naturalized along roadsides and in disturbed areas across temperate North America and throughout TN. Frequent. **SIMILAR SPECIES:** CLASPINGLEAF MULLEIN (**V. phlomoides***), also called ORANGE MULLEIN, has **dark green leaves**, widest in the middle and **somewhat clasping**; flowers are 1 in. wide or more. Introduced from Europe; now a roadside weed from ME to MN, south to TN and SC. In TN, in Knox County. Rare. May–June.

NOTES: Common Mullein is also called **Woolly Mullein**, Flannel Plant, Hag's Taper, Candle Wick and many other fanciful and utilitarian names. The name Quaker Rouge arose from women rubbing the leaves on their cheeks to make them glow. • Common Mullein has been used medicinally since the time of the Roman Empire as a folk remedy that called for smoking the leaves to treat coughs and asthma. The stout stalks dipped in tallow provided candlelight for an extended time. More recently, hikers and backpackers have found the soft leaves valuable as "emergency" toilet paper or as added cushioning for tired feet.

MIRIAM WEINSTEIN

Common Speedwell, Gypsyweed · *Veronica officinalis**

GENERAL: Low, mat-forming, hairy perennial herb, 4–8 in. tall; branch tips ascending. **LEAVES:** Opposite, elliptic, 1–2 in. long, toothed, rather thick. **FLOWERS:** Pale lavender or blue, about 0.25 in. wide, often with darker lines; 4-lobed corolla, upper lobe slightly wider and lower lobe narrower than the 2 lateral lobes; 2 stamens; borne in erect axillary racemes from the upper leaf axils. April–July. **FRUITS:** Heart-shaped, triangular capsules, 0.16 in. long. **WHERE FOUND:** Introduced from Europe. Lawns and disturbed areas. Scattered throughout the northern and eastern U.S. and the eastern ½ of TN. Occasional. **SIMILAR SPECIES:** BIRD'S-EYE SPEEDWELL (*V. persica**) is a hairy annual; leaves less than 1 in. long; bright blue flowers, about 0.4 in. wide, with a distinctive pale center. Introduced from southwestern Asia. Throughout North America. Thinly scattered across Middle and East TN. Occasional. April–August. IVYLEAF SPEEDWELL (*V. hederifolia**) is an annual; leaves 3–5-lobed; pale blue flowers only about 0.16 in. wide. Introduced from Europe. Primarily in the east-central U.S. Widely scattered across TN. Occasional. April–May.

NOTES: The genus name *Veronica* means "true image." It is told that Saint Veronica was the woman who wiped Jesus' face when he fell carrying the cross on the road to Calvary, and her cloth preserved the "true image" of his face. In Europe, speedwells grow along waysides, perhaps greeting travelers on their journeys. • *Veronica* species are small annual or perennial herbs with a 4-lobed corolla, one lobe being smaller. Of 12 species credited to TN, only 4 are native, and 3 of these are rare.

OTTO R. HIRSCH

Culver's Root · *Veronicastrum virginicum*

GENERAL: Distinctive perennial herb, 24–60 in. tall. **LEAVES:** Lanceolate, 2–6 in. long, toothed, in whorls of 3–7, on petioles 0.1–0.4 in. long. **FLOWERS:** Numerous, white (rarely pinkish, purple, or blue), about 0.3 in. long, tubular, 2 protruding stamens; borne in several showy spikes, 3–8 in. long, terminal or arising from the upper leaf whorls. June–September. **FRUITS:** Ovoid or ellipsoid capsules to 0.1 in. long. **WHERE FOUND:** Barrens, roadsides, meadows, and wet to almost dry soils, from ME to Manitoba and ND, south to FL and TX. In TN, primarily in the Western Highland Rim and the Cumberland Plateau, also McNairy and Henderson counties in West TN, Hamilton and Roane counties in East TN, and Rutherford County in the Central Basin. Occasional. *Leptandra virginica, Veronica virginica.*

NOTES: A tea made from the dried roots of this plant was used by Native Americans as a laxative, cathartic, liver stimulant, and diuretic. However, caution should be used as it is potentially toxic. • This plant is the only species of this genus in North America; one other is found in Siberia.

Squaw Root, Cancer Root · *Conopholis americana*

GENERAL: Stout, yellowish brown, perennial **root-parasite** with unbranched stems, 2–8 in. tall and 1 in. thick. **LEAVES:** Overlapping, **brown, fleshy, scaly,** ovate to broadly lanceolate, to 0.8 in. long, **lacking chlorophyll. FLOWERS:** Whitish to yellowish, 0.4–0.5 in. long; 2-lipped corolla, upper lip notched, lower lip shorter and 3-lobed; many of the stems are actually spike inflorescences, crowded with flowers and scaly bracts. April–June. **FRUITS:** Ovoid capsules; dark, angled, shiny seeds. **WHERE FOUND:** Rich woodlands from Nova Scotia to WI, south to FL and MS. In TN, from the Western Highland Rim eastward, chiefly in the uplands. Frequent.

NOTES: This species usually occurs in clumps under oak trees, which it parasitizes. • The common name **Squaw Root** indicates that this plant was collected by Native Americans as a source of food. It is also a favorite food of bears. • All members of the **Broomrape Family** are root-parasitic herbs that lack chlorophyll and have scale-like leaves. There are 3 genera and 5 species listed for TN.

Beechdrops · *Epifagus virginiana*

GENERAL: Many-branched perennial **root-parasite**, 6–18 in. tall; thin, ascending stems are pale brown with brownish purple streaks. **LEAVES:** Scaly, lacking chlorophyll, alternately arranged, triangular-ovate, 0.1–0.15 in. long. **FLOWERS:** Inconspicuous, white with brown-purple stripes, 2-lipped; upper flowers male, 0.4 in. long, produce pollen; lower flowers female, 0.2 in. long; borne in a panicle. September–November. **FRUITS:** Brown capsules with yellowish white seeds. **WHERE FOUND:** Parasitic on and subsequently found beneath or in the vicinity of beech trees. Rich woods throughout the eastern U.S., southeastern Canada, and TN. Common.

NOTES: This plant is also called Cancer Drops, Clapwort, and Virginia Broomrape. In herbal medicine, it is has been used to treat dysentery, cancer, and gonorrhea (also called the "clap").

• Although common, **Beechdrops** are often overlooked because the slender plants blend with the brown leaves on the forest floor, usually under American Beech trees (*Fagus grandifolia*), and the flowers are not showy.

One-Flowered Cancer Root · *Orobanche uniflora*

GENERAL: Perennial **root-parasite**, often found in groups; stems mostly underground, each plant producing 1–3 slender, leafless stalks, 2–6 in. tall, covered with glandular hairs. **LEAVES:** Brown, overlapping **scales** at the base of the naked flower stalk (scape). **FLOWERS:** Solitary, **white to pale lavender**, about 0.75 in. long; 5-lobed, lightly veined, tubular corolla. April–May. **FRUITS:** Brown capsules about 0.5 in. long; veiny seeds. **WHERE FOUND:** Rich woods and streambanks throughout the U.S. and southern Canada. In TN, from the Western Highland Rim eastward. Occasional. **SIMILAR SPECIES: PRAIRIE BROOMRAPE (O. ludoviciana)** has **numerous flowers** in a spike or spike-like raceme. Sandy to silty soil. A mostly western species found east to OH and VA and south to TN. In TN, only in Lauderdale County. Rare. June–August.

NOTES: The genus name *Orobanche* means "vetch strangler" and refers to this plant's habit of taking nutrients from other plants; the species name *uniflora* means "one-flowered," in reference to this plant's single-flowered stalks. • **One-Flowered Cancer Root** is also called **Naked Broomrape**, Pipes, and Squirrel's Grandfather. Another name, Squawdrops, alludes to its use by Native Americans as a food source.

Branched Foldwing, Dicliptera · *Dicliptera brachiata*

GENERAL: Coarsely branched perennial herb, 12–24 in. tall, erect or somewhat reclining. **LEAVES:** Opposite, ovate or lanceolate-ovate, 2–4 in. long, entire, acuminate tips, slender petioles. **FLOWERS: Pale purple or pink**, 0.6 in. long, tubular, **deeply 2-lipped corolla** with leaf-like bracts borne in axillary clusters. August–October. **FRUITS:** Flattened, brown capsules, 0.2 in. long. **WHERE FOUND:** Moist lowlands and rich woods, from VA to KS, south to FL and TX. In TN, in the Central Basin, the Western Highland Rim, and also Smith, Hamilton, and Shelby counties. Occasional.

NOTES: This plant is also called **Wild Mudwort.** • Another southeastern U.S. species, **Sixangle Foldwing (D. sexangularis)**, is found in TX and in saltwater hammocks in FL. The corolla is crimson. • The **Acanthus Family** is a pantropical family of perennial herbs, shrubs, woody vines, and trees, and includes more than 2000 species. The 3 genera and 7 species in TN are all perennial herbs.

JERRY DROWN

OTTO R. HIRSCH

American Water Willow · *Justicia americana*

GENERAL: Colonial, smooth perennial herb with stout stems, 18–36 in. tall, from rhizomes. **LEAVES:** Numerous, opposite, **linear to lanceolate**, 3–6 in. long, sessile or with short petioles. **FLOWERS:** Bluish white, to 0.5 in. long; 2-lipped corolla, upper lip shallowly notched, lower lip 3-lobed, the center lobe **heavily marked with purple**; in a dense, **head-like cluster** on ascending peduncles, 2–6 in. long, arising from upper leaf axils. June–September. **FRUITS:** Brown capsules with 4 **rough seeds**. **WHERE FOUND:** Abundant, dense colonies often occur in shallow streams and rivers, and around the margins of reservoirs and other impoundments. Throughout the eastern U.S. and TN, but mostly absent from West TN. Frequent. **SIMILAR SPECIES: COASTAL PLAIN WATER WILLOW (*J. ovata*)** has **ovate leaves**; flowers in **loose spikes** (not head-like); **smooth seeds**. Mud and shallow water. A Coastal Plain species found from southeastern VA to FL and TX, and inland in the Mississippi River Valley to southeastern MO and southwestern KY. In West TN and Humphreys County in Middle TN. Occasional. June–September.

TERRY LIVINGSTONE

NOTES: The genus *Justicia* was named in honor of James Justice (1698–1763), a Scottish horticulturist; *americana* indicates that this plant is native to North America. • Although **American Water Willow** is not related to true willows (*Salix*), its name is deserved, owing to the leaf shape and its preferred wet habitats. This colonial species provides good cover for amphibians, fish, reptiles, and other wildlife.

Hairy Ruellia
Ruellia caroliniensis

GENERAL: Hairy, erect perennial herb, 6–30 in. tall. **LEAVES:** Opposite, simple, entire, lanceolate to ovate, 1.5–4.0 in. long, tapered to a **short petiole**. **FLOWERS:** Bluish violet, funnel-shaped, 1–2 in. long, sessile; corolla has 5 nearly equal lobes; 4 stamens, in pairs; **linear calyx lobes, 0.04 in. wide or less**; borne in the leaf axils. May–September. **FRUITS:** Smooth capsules, 0.5–0.6 in. long; brown seeds. **WHERE FOUND:** Moist or dry woods, from NJ to southern IL, south to FL and TX. Throughout TN. Common. **SIMILAR SPECIES: GLADE WILD PETUNIA (*R. humilis*)** has hairy, **sessile leaves**. Dry soils, glades, and open woods from PA to southeastern MN, south to FL and TX. In TN, from the Western Highland Rim to the Ridge and Valley, also Decatur and McNairy counties in West TN. Occasional. May–July.

KURT EMMANUELE

Notes: Hairy Ruellia is also called **Carolina Wild Petunia**. • The hairs on the stem of this plant are usually denser on 2 opposite sides of the stem than on the other 2 sides. • Plants in the *Ruellia* genus are perennial herbs with large, showy, funnel-shaped flowers and are mostly found in the tropics. TN has 4 species. Variability and hybridization often make identification difficult.

DENNIS HORN

Smooth Ruellia · *Ruellia strepens*

GENERAL: Perennial herb, 12–36 in. tall, stems nearly **smooth**. **LEAVES:** Opposite, 2–6 in. long, ovate, entire, tips pointed, base tapers to a stalk, 0.25–0.75 in. long. **FLOWERS:** Lavender blue, to 2 in. long, 5-lobed, **funnel-shaped like petunias;** lanceolate **calyx lobes 0.1–0.15 in. wide at the base; flower stalks, 0.2–0.6 in. long,** have leafy bracts at the flower base; usually solitary from the leaf axils in the central portion of the stem. May–July. **FRUITS: Smooth capsules** with brown seeds. **WHERE FOUND:** Moist woods, from NJ to NE, south to FL and TX. Throughout TN. Frequent. **SIMILAR SPECIES:** PURSH'S WILD PETUNIA (*R. purshiana*) has **flower stalks up to 1.5 in. long; calyx lobes about 0.04 in. wide at the base;** minutely **hairy capsules.** Dry woods, from MD and WV, south to GA and AL. In Blount, Cocke, and Hawkins counties in East TN. Rare. May–September.

NOTES: Smooth Ruellia is also called **Smooth Wild Petunia** for its general lack of hairs on the stems and leaves, and **Limestone Wild Petunia** for locations where it can be found. The flowers last for one day only, but the plant produces petunia-like flowers for an extended period of time.

ALICE JENSEN

Cross Vine · *Bignonia capreolata*

GENERAL: Woody perennial **vine** that uses its tendrils to climb trees or rock cliffs to a height of 50 ft. or more. **LEAVES:** Opposite, smooth, pinnately compound, composed of **2 lower leaflets** that are elliptic to lanceolate, 2–6 in. long, base heart-shaped, other leaflets are modified into a **terminal, branched tendril; semi-evergreen,** often persisting through winter. **FLOWERS:** Showy, trumpet or bell-shaped corolla, 2.0–2.5 in. long; **reddish maroon or dark red outside** with 5 flaring **yellow lobes;** 4 stamens in 2 pairs; borne in clusters. April–June. **FRUITS:** Flattened capsules, 5–7 in. long, 1 in. wide. **WHERE FOUND:** Low, moist woods and barrens in most of the eastern U.S., from OH to MO, southward. Throughout TN. Common. *Anisostichus capreolata*.

NOTES: The *Bignonia* genus is monotypic, meaning that this plant is the only species in the genus. It derives its common name from the cross that can be seen in a cross-section of a stem. • Plants of the mostly tropical **Trumpet Creeper Family** may be woody vines or trees with opposite leaves that are simple or pinnately compound. The ovary is superior, and capsules have numerous winged seeds. There are 3 genera and 4 species in TN.

Trumpet Creeper, Trumpet Vine · *Campsis radicans*

JERRY DROWN

GENERAL: Woody perennial **vine without tendrils**, climbing or trailing to 50 ft. high by aerial roots. **LEAVES:** Opposite, smooth, **pinnately compound** with 7–15 ovate, coarsely toothed leaflets, 1–3 in. long. **FLOWERS:** Showy, **trumpet-shaped, red-orange**, 3–4 in. long, corolla slightly 2-lipped with 5 flared, rounded lobes; 4 stamens in 2 pairs; borne in clusters. June–September. **FRUITS:** Capsules, 4–7 in. long, 1.0–1.25 in. wide; winged seeds. **WHERE FOUND:** Aggressive in woodlands and waste places, especially common along fencerows. Throughout most of the central and eastern U.S. and TN. Common.

NOTES: Another name for this plant is **Cow-Itch Vine** as the wet foliage can irritate sensitive skin. • **Trumpet Creeper** is sometimes cultivated, but it can become **weedy**. The deep trumpet-shaped flowers are frequented by hummingbirds. The genus *Campsis* has only 2 species—our native species and Chinese Trumpet Creeper (*C. grandiflora*) from eastern Asia. **Cross Vine** (p. 296) is similar in appearance, but has leaves with tendrils and bicolored flowers that open in spring.

Horned Bladderwort · *Utricularia cornuta*

KURT EMANUELE

GENERAL: Finely branched **terrestrial** herb, 4–10 in. tall, with minute **leaves, stems, and bladders underground**. **LEAVES:** Minute, linear or dissected, with tiny bladders; usually underground and seldom seen. **FLOWERS:** Yellow, 2-lipped corolla, **lower lip at least 0.5 in. long** with a **downward-pointing spur** 0.3–0.5 in. long and an **elevated palate**; 2–5 flowers on erect, green, leafless stalks (scapes), 4–10 in. tall. July–August. **FRUITS:** Capsules, 0.1–0.14 in. wide; veiny seeds. **WHERE FOUND:** Wet soils, primarily along the Great Lakes and coastal areas from Canada to TX. In TN, only in Coffee County. Rare. **SIMILAR SPECIES:** ZIGZAG BLADDERWORT (*U. subulata*) is also **terrestrial**; smaller yellow flowers with **lower lip only 0.25 in. long**. Wet soil, mostly in the southeastern U.S. Middle and East TN. Infrequent. April–August. HUMPED BLADDERWORT (*U. gibba*) is **aquatic; bladders well developed**; yellow flowers with lower lip 0.2–0.4 in. long. Shallow ponds. Eastern U.S. West and Middle TN. Occasional. June–September. *U. biflora*. LAVENDER BLADDERWORT (*U. resupinata*) is terrestrial or aquatic; **pinkish lavender flowers** about 0.4 in. long. Mud or shallow ponds. Scattered throughout the eastern U.S. In TN, in Cumberland and Greene counties. Rare. July–September.

NOTES: The genus name *Utricularia* comes from the Latin word *utriculus*, meaning "a little bladder." • Bladderworts are terrestrial or aquatic **carnivorous** plants that trap tiny aquatic organisms using very small bladder traps. Terrestrial species are difficult to find unless they are in flower. Aquatic species have a fine network of stems and bladder-bearing leaves, which form floating mats in quiet acidic ponds. Six species occur in TN.

JERRY DROWN

Tall Bellflower • *Campanula americana*

GENERAL: Erect **annual or biennial**, 2–6 ft. tall, coarse, mostly smooth, freely branched. **LEAVES:** Alternate, lanceolate, 3–6 in. long, toothed margins. **FLOWERS: Blue, about 1 in. wide**; **corolla face flat**, not bell-shaped, 5-lobed with a pale ring in the throat; long, distinctly curved style; borne in a loose terminal raceme, flowering from the bottom of the raceme upward. July–frost. **FRUITS:** Capsules with brown, shiny, ellipsoid seeds. **WHERE FOUND:** Moist woods and streambanks, from Ontario to MN, south to FL and OK. Throughout TN. Common. ***Campanulastrum americanum.*** **SIMILAR SPECIES: MARSH BELLFLOWER (*C. aparinoides*)** is a **reclining perennial** with 3-angled stems to 2 ft. long; leaves are narrowly lanceolate or linear to 3 in. long, reduced progressively on the upper stem; flowers are **solitary, white**, 5-lobed, **bell-shaped, to 0.35 in. long**, on long pedicels. Wet meadows, from Nova Scotia to Saskatchewan, south to GA, MO, and CO. In TN, scattered from the Eastern Highland Rim eastward, in Coffee, Cumberland, Fentress, Blount, Greene, Unicoi, Carter, and Johnson counties. Infrequent. June–August.

NOTES: Although the name *Campanula* means "little bell" in Latin, **Tall Bellflower** does not have the characteristic bell shape of most *Campanula* species. It also is called **American Bellflower** and is self-seeding, sowing its own seeds at a productive rate. • In herbal medicine, Native Americans used the leaves of Tall Bellflower to make a tea for treating coughs and tuberculosis. • There are 4 *Campanula* species in TN.

HUGH & CAROL NOURSE

Southern Harebell
Campanula divaricata

GENERAL: Freely branched, rather weak-stemmed perennial herb, 1–3 ft. tall. **LEAVES:** Alternate, linear-lanceolate, 1–3 in. long, margins coarsely toothed. **FLOWERS: Pale blue, bell-shaped, about 0.3 in. long**; 5-lobed, tips of the **lobes curled back; style protrudes** about 0.25 in. from the bell; **calyx lobes ascending**; borne in a panicle. July–September. **FRUITS:** Top-shaped capsules, 0.2 in. long; brown, ellipsoid seeds. **WHERE FOUND:** Rocky woods at lower elevations, from western MD to eastern KY, south to GA and AL. In TN, from the Cumberland Plateau eastward. Occasional. **SIMILAR SPECIES: CREEPING BELLFLOWER (*C. rapunculoides**)** is a perennial, 1–3 ft. tall; alternate, narrowly oval, toothed leaves taper to a point; 5-pointed, **bell-shaped flowers about 1 in. long** hang on one side of a vertical stem; **calyx lobes spreading** or reflexed. Introduced European weed. Naturalized in lawns and along roadsides in the northern U.S. In TN, found only in Davidson and Knox counties. Rare. July–August.

NOTES: Southern Harebell is also known as **Small Bonny Bellflower**, as well as Southern Bellflower and Southern Bluebell. • A related cultivated species, Spreading Bellflower (*C. patula*), has a common method of attracting pollinators by increasing the intensity of the scent toward the base of the flower, where the nectar resides. Because of its open structure, it is visited and pollinated by a wide variety of insects.

Gattinger's Lobelia
Lobelia appendiculata var. *gattingeri*

GENERAL: Smooth-stemmed, erect **annual, 6–12 in. tall. LEAVES:** Alternate, elliptic, 1–2 in. long, toothed to nearly entire. **FLOWERS: Light blue to lavender,** to 0.4 in. long; 2-lipped corolla, upper lip 2-lobed and much smaller than 3-lobed lower lip; borne in a 1-sided raceme. May–June. **FRUITS:** Capsules with yellowish brown seeds. **WHERE FOUND:** Endemic to the cedar glades and barrens of KY and TN. In TN, in Montgomery, Wilson, Davidson, Williamson, Rutherford, Maury, Marshall, and Bedford counties of Middle TN. Infrequent.

NOTES: **Gattinger's Lobelia** is named for the early Tennessee physician and botanist, Dr. Augustin Gattinger (1825–1903), who came to Tennessee during the Civil War. He played an important role in identifying cedar glades as botanically important areas. • *Lobelia* species are easily distinguished by their bilaterally symmetric flowers, which have a 2-lipped corolla, the upper lip with 2 lobes and the lower lip with 3 spreading lobes. All 5 stamens are united into a tube, at the end of which is the pollen. When *Lobelia* plants are visited by pollinators such as bees, the pollen is dropped onto the pollinator's back. • There are 9 *Lobelia* species listed for TN.

DAVID DUHL

Canby's Lobelia · *Lobelia canbyi*

GENERAL: Branched perennial herb, 16–36 in. tall. **LEAVES:** Alternate, **linear,** to 2 in. long, margins entire. **FLOWERS:** Pale lavender to blue, to 0.5 in. long, on short stalks; 2-lipped corolla, **lower lip bearded toward the base within;** borne in a raceme. July–August. **FRUITS:** Club-shaped capsules, longer than wide. **WHERE FOUND:** Swamps, wet fields, and barrens. An Atlantic Coastal Plain species found from NJ to SC, also inland in northern GA and Middle TN. In TN, in Franklin, Coffee, Grundy, Warren, Van Buren, and Cumberland counties. Infrequent. **SIMILAR SPECIES: NUTTALL'S LOBELIA (L. nuttallii)** has a **lower corolla lip that is smooth inside** and has **2 green spots.** Moist soil. A Coastal Plain species found from NY to FL and LA, and inland in the uplands to southern KY. In TN, along the Cumberland Plateau in Cumberland, Fentress, Morgan, Marion, Grundy, Van Buren, and White counties, also Roane County in the Ridge and Valley. Infrequent. July–September.

NOTES: **Canby's Lobelia** grows to 3 ft. tall, which may seem tall for *Lobelia* species in this region. However, these plants can reach tree-like heights of up to 30 ft. in subtropical areas or may be as small as 2–6 in. tall.

DENNIS HORN

Cardinal Flower · *Lobelia cardinalis*

GENERAL: Erect, typically unbranched perennial herb, 24–48 in. tall. **LEAVES:** Alternate, lanceolate, 2–6 in. long, toothed margins. **FLOWERS:** Intensely **red or scarlet** (rarely pink or white), 0.75–1.5 in. long; 2-lipped corolla, lower lip smooth within; borne in a showy raceme; the **bright red flowers are unique among *Lobelia* species** in our flora. July–September. **FRUITS:** Ovoid or spherical capsules with brown seeds. **WHERE FOUND:** Wet soil, streambanks, and roadside ditches throughout the eastern and southwestern U.S., southeastern Canada, and TN. Common.

NOTES: This plant's common name comes from the scarlet flowers, which are the color of the robes worn by cardinals of the Roman Catholic Church. • A favorite of hummingbirds, the flowers are also visited by long-tongued butterflies such as the Spicebush Swallowtail, Eastern Tiger Swallowtail, and Cloudless Sulphur. • Native Americans used the roots to treat a variety of illnesses, but especially to rid the body of worms. Although this plant has been used as a medicine, it is also **very poisonous**, and extracts of the leaves and fruit can produce vomiting, sweating, pain, and eventually death.

JERRY DROWN

Indian Tobacco · *Lobelia inflata*

GENERAL: Erect, branched **annual**, 6–30 in. tall, usually **hairy** throughout. **LEAVES:** Alternate, mostly sessile, 2–3 in. long, ovate, toothed margins. **FLOWERS:** Light **blue to white**, to 0.3 in. long, short-stalked; 2-lipped corolla, lower lip bearded within; **base of the flower (ovary) inflates** markedly when in fruit; borne in a terminal or lateral raceme; flowers and fruit often occur at the same time on a single plant. July–October. **FRUITS:** Inflated, ellipsoid capsules. **WHERE FOUND:** Fields, roadsides, and open woods throughout most of the eastern U.S. and TN. Common.

NOTES: This plant is also called **Wild Tobacco** because the leaves taste of tobacco. It was one of the most frequently used medicinal herbs in the U.S. during the 19th century. Its use as an emetic during this period accounts for the colloquial names Pukeweed and Vomitwort. It was also used to treat stomach ailments and colds, and to encourage perspiration. • This plant is **poisonous** owing to its high concentration of alkaloids and **should not be ingested or smoked**. It contains lobeline, related to nicotine, and is used in some "stop smoking" products.

JERRY DROWN

Downy Lobelia · *Lobelia puberula*

GENERAL: Erect perennial herb, 1–4 ft. tall, with hairy stems. **LEAVES:** Alternate, oblong to lance-olate, 2–4 in. long, toothed margins; lower leaves obtuse or rounded; upper leaves smaller and acute. **FLOWERS:** Blue, 0.6–0.75 in. long, nearly sessile; 2-lipped corolla, lower lip smooth within; calyx lobes lanceolate, 0.2–0.4 in. long; borne in a 1-sided raceme. August–October. **FRUITS:** Capsules, 0.3 in. long. **WHERE FOUND:** Damp or dry soil, woods, and clearings, from southern NJ to southern IL, south to FL and TX. Throughout TN. Common. **SIMILAR SPECIES:** SOUTHERN LOBELIA (*L. amoena*) has smooth stems; leaves are elliptic-lanceolate, 2–6 in. long. Marshes, streambanks, and wet cliffs in the Coastal Plain from VA to LA, and in the mountains of the western Carolinas, TN, and northern GA. In TN, in Polk and Monroe counties in the Blue Ridge Mountains of East TN. Rare. August–October.

NOTES: The species name *puberula* means "with tiny hairs," referring to the hairy stems of **Downy Lobelia.** • All *Lobelia* species should be considered **toxic.** Studies have shown that the levels of active alkaloids vary, making lobelias unpredictable when used medicinally.

JERRY DROWN

Great Blue Lobelia
Lobelia siphilitica

GENERAL: Robust, erect perennial herb, 2–4 ft. tall. **LEAVES:** Alternate, elliptic to lanceolate, 3–5 in. long, toothed margins. **FLOWERS:** Blue (rarely white in some populations), to 1 in. long; 2-lipped corolla, tube is striped beneath and somewhat inflated; borne in a raceme; leafy bracts in the inflorescence are gradually reduced upward. August–September. **FRUITS:** Ovoid to spherical capsules; yellowish brown seeds. **WHERE FOUND:** Swamps, streambanks, and roadside ditches, from ME to Manitoba and WY, south to GA and TX. Throughout TN. Frequent.

NOTES: The species name *siphilitica* is Latin for "of syphilis," referring to the use of the root as a treatment, albeit an ineffective one, for syphilis. This plant is also called Blue Cardinal Flower and Highbelia. • Most *Lobelia* species are pollinated by bees, which land on the lower lip and then crawl into the corolla tube.

JERRY DROWN

DENNIS HORN

Pale-Spiked Lobelia · *Lobelia spicata*

GENERAL: Erect perennial herb, 12–36 in. tall; stem is typically unbranched and hairy on the lower portion. **LEAVES:** Alternate, ovate-lanceolate, 2–4 in. long, toothed margins. **FLOWERS: Pale blue to white,** 0.3–0.4 in. long, nearly sessile; 2-lipped corolla, lower lip bearded within; **calyx lobes** lanceolate, **0.1–0.15 in. long;** borne in a slender, crowded terminal raceme. May–August. **FRUITS:** Capsules, less than 0.25 in. wide. **WHERE FOUND:** Meadows, glades, barrens, and thickets, from Nova Scotia to MT, south to GA and TX. In TN, from the Western Highland Rim eastward, also McNairy County in West TN. Frequent.

NOTES: Native Americans used this plant for several medicinal purposes. They brewed a tea that was used as an emetic, to treat trembling, and as a wash for "bad blood." However, like other species of *Lobelia*, it should be considered **poisonous.** • **Pale-Spiked Lobelia** is highly variable, and has produced several recognized varieties.

HUGH NOURSE

Venus' Looking Glass
Triodanis perfoliata

GENERAL: Erect **annual,** 10–30 in. tall, with fibrous roots. **LEAVES:** Alternate, clasping, round, 0.75–1.0 in. long, toothed margins. **FLOWERS: Star-shaped, purple;** 5-lobed **corolla is flat,** not bell-shaped, about 0.5 in. wide; 5 stamens; borne singly in the leaf axils. May–August. **FRUITS:** Capsules; **seeds are dispersed through roundish pores or "windows"** in the sides of the capsules; each pore is covered by a valve or "door" that coils open as the capsule matures. **WHERE FOUND:** Open woods, fields, and roadsides throughout the U.S., southern Canada, and TN. Common. *Specularia perfoliata.*

NOTES: The genus name *Triodanis* means "three seeds." This plant is also called Clasping Bell-flower. The common name comes from the Latin name of a similar European species, *Legousia speculum-veneris,* with *speculum* meaning "looking glass," in reference to the shiny seeds. It was said of this plant: "When the long capsule opens, the looking-glasses of the Virgin or Venus are revealed, the seeds of which are oval or elliptical, pale brown, exquisitely polished, and pellucid like a speculum" (Geoffrey Grigson, *The Englishman's Flora,* 1955).

Buttonbush
Cephalanthus occidentalis

GENERAL: Shrub or occasionally a small tree, 3–9 ft. tall. **LEAVES:** Opposite or occasionally whorled, ovate to elliptic, 2–5 in. long, entire, usually smooth on short petioles. **FLOWERS:** Numerous, small, white, tubular, 4-lobed; **styles protrude** well beyond the end of the corolla, stigmas often covered with pollen; borne in **compact, spherical heads,** 1.0–1.5 in. wide, on long stalks terminating the branches or from the upper leaf axils. June–August.

NITA R. HEILMAN

FRUITS: Angular nutlets, 0.15–0.25 in. long. **WHERE FOUND:** Low areas and margins of ponds, lakes, and marshes throughout the eastern U.S., southeastern Canada, and TN. Common.

NOTES: Native Americans used the leaves, roots, and bark of this plant to make teas that were used to treat a variety of ailments. However, caution is required because the leaves have caused **livestock poisoning.** • The **Madder Family** contains important plants such as coffee (*Coffea*) and quinine (*Cinchona*), and ornamental shrubs such as gardenias (*Gardenia*). This family includes over 6000 species worldwide, mostly tropical and subtropical.

Rough Buttonweed
Diodia teres

GENERAL: Annual, 12–24 in. tall, with spreading or ascending stems. **LEAVES:** Opposite, sessile, linear to narrowly lanceolate, 0.8–1.6 in. long, stiff, rough, bristle-tipped; stipules have bristles. **FLOWERS:** Pinkish, about 0.25 in. wide, funnel-shaped corolla with 4 spreading lobes; **calyx has 4 sepals; style undivided**; sessile, usually solitary from the upper leaf axils. June–September. **FRUITS:** Capsules with stiff hairs and a prominent furrow. **WHERE FOUND:** Dry soil in fields and waste places throughout most of the eastern and southern U.S. and TN. Common.

NOTES: This plant is also known as **Poor Joe,** as it is often found in poor soil and eroded fields. • **Rough Buttonweed** and **Virginia Buttonweed** (p. 304) are creeping or erect branched annuals, often weedy. The leaves are opposite, narrowly lanceolate, with stipules. The flowers are axillary, small, tubular, and 4-lobed, with persistent sepals that form a crown on the capsule.

HUGH & CAROL NOURSE

Virginia Buttonweed
Diodia virginiana

GENERAL: **Annual** with branched and spreading stems, 8–32 in. long, hairy along the stem angles. **LEAVES:** Opposite, thin, narrowly elliptic, 1–2 in. long, with linear stipules to 0.2 in. long. **FLOWERS:** Trumpet-shaped, **white**, about 0.4 in. wide; 4 narrow, spreading lobes; narrow tube about 0.4 in. long; **calyx has 2 linear sepals; style has 2 thread-like stigmas;** flowers sessile, usually solitary from the leaf axils.

DENNIS HORN

June–August. **FRUITS:** Hairy capsules with prominent ribs. **WHERE FOUND:** Wet ground, ditches, and shorelines, from southern NJ to southern IL and KS, south to FL and TX. Throughout TN. Common.

NOTES: This plant is also known as Large Buttonweed. Although a native species, it can become **a troublesome weed**, forming dense mats on low, damp ground and in waste places. It is distinguished from the other *Diodia* species in TN by its long, thin, white corolla and the 4 hairy lobes.

Cleavers, Bedstraw • *Galium aparine*

GENERAL: **Annual** with **4-angled stems**, 12–36 in. long, with **harsh, downward-curved bristles** on the angles. **LEAVES:** Narrowly oblanceolate, 1–3 in. long, mostly in **whorls of 8**. **FLOWERS:** Tiny, white, 4-lobed; usually borne in 3-flowered cymes on long stalks from the leaf axils. April–May. **FRUITS:** Dry carpels with bristles. **WHERE FOUND:** Moist ground, woodlands, and disturbed places, usually in the shade. Throughout temperate North America and TN. Common. **SIMILAR SPECIES:** FRAGRANT BEDSTRAW (**G. triflorum**) is a perennial; **leaves in whorls of 6; slightly bristly stems;** sweet **vanilla scent.** Woods throughout the U.S. and TN. Common. June–August. WILD LICORICE (**G. circaezans**), also called FOREST BEDSTRAW, has **leaves in whorls of 4;** mostly **sessile flowers** in clusters at the upper 2–3 leaf nodes only. Rich woods throughout the eastern U.S. and TN. Common. June–July. HAIRY BEDSTRAW (**G. pilosum**) has **leaves in whorls of 4**; white to greenish maroon **flowers on pedicels** and in clusters, usually at the upper 6–12 leaf nodes. Dry woods throughout the eastern U.S. and TN. Common. June–August.

DENNIS HORN

NOTES: This plant is named **Cleavers** because the bristles "cleave" or adhere to birds, animals, or people, aiding seed dispersal. The name **Bedstraw** indicates that early Americans may have used it as a mattress filler because the stems remain flexible when dried. • The *Galium* genus includes plants with weak, reclining, slender, 4-angled stems and whorled leaves. The flowers are small, white, usually 4-lobed, and occur in loose clusters. The fruits are a pair of small, dry, 1-seeded, bristly carpels. There are 16 *Galium* species in TN.

Quaker Ladies, Innocence
Houstonia caerulea

THOMAS E. HEMMERLY

GENERAL: Delicate perennial herb, 2–7 in. tall, with a slender, **erect stem**; often occurs in thick stands. **LEAVES:** Mostly **basal**, spatulate, 0.2–0.5 in. long; stem leaves opposite, **nearly sessile**, and greatly reduced. **FLOWERS:** Sky blue to white, about 0.5 in. across with a **yellow eye**; narrow **corolla tube is smooth within**, 4 lobes abruptly spreading; solitary on long stalks, terminal or from the upper leaf axils. April–May. **FRUITS:** Flattened, 2-chambered capsules, about 0.15 in. wide; round seeds. **WHERE FOUND:** Open deciduous woodlands, meadows, and grassy places, from Nova Scotia to WI, south to GA and LA. Throughout TN. Common. *Hedyotis caerulea.*

NOTES: The species name *caerulea* means "sky blue," alluding to the color of the flowers. This plant is also known as **Bluets**, as well as Blue-Eyed Babies, Bright Eyes, Nuns, Quaker Bonnets, and Star Violet. • The Cherokee used the leaves to make a tea to prevent bed-wetting. • *Houstonia* species are small plants with tubular, 4-lobed flowers and opposite or whorled leaves. They spread by slender rhizomes, often forming large colonies that appear as a blue or white blanket of color. There are 7 species found in TN.

Venus' Pride
Houstonia purpurea var. *calycosa*

DENNIS HORN

GENERAL: Fibrous-rooted perennial herb, 6–20 in. tall, with several stems. **LEAVES:** Opposite, sessile, oblong-lanceolate, 1–2 in. long, **less than 0.5 in. wide, rounded at the base, 3–5-nerved. FLOWERS:** Funnel-shaped, white or purplish, about 0.35 in. long; 4 spreading corolla **lobes about ½ the tube length; sepals 0.15–0.25 in. long** at flowering; borne in a flat cluster on pedicels less than 0.2 in. long. April–July. **FRUITS:** Round, 2-parted capsules, about 0.15 in. across. **WHERE FOUND:** Moist or dry, rocky, open woods or bluffs, from the eastern U.S., west to MO and AR. Widespread across TN. Frequent. *Hedyotis purpurea* var. *calycosa.* **SIMILAR SPECIES:** LONGLEAF BLUET (*H. longifolia*) is usually smaller; **linear-oblong leaves, tapering to the base, 1-nerved; sepals less than 0.1 in. long** at flowering. Dry woods and open areas, from ME to Saskatchewan, south to FL, MS, and OK. Widely scattered across the eastern ½ of TN, also Carroll County in West TN. Occasional. June–August. *Hedyotis longifolia.*

NOTES: The *Houstonia* genus was named in honor of Dr. William Houston (1695–1733), a Scottish physician and botanist who, as a ship's surgeon, collected and wrote about plants in Mexico and the West Indies. **Venus' Pride** is also known as **Purple Bluets**.

Roan Mountain Bluet
Houstonia purpurea var. *montana*

GENERAL: Erect, fibrous-rooted perennial herb, 4–12 in. tall; 1–several branching stems with **smooth internodes**. **LEAVES:** Opposite, 0.4–1.2 in. long, ovate, **rounded to heart-shaped at the base, 3–5 main veins**. **FLOWERS:** Funnel-shaped, **deep purple**, about 0.35 in. long; 4 spreading corolla **lobes about ½ the tube length**; numerous flowers on short pedicels in terminal cymes. April–June. **FRUITS:** Round, 2-parted capsules, about 0.15 in. across. **WHERE FOUND:** At high elevations on rock outcrops in the Blue Ridge Mountains of NC and TN. In TN, only in Carter County. Rare. *H. montana, Hedyotis purpurea* var. *montana*.

SIMILAR SPECIES: GLADE BLUET (*Hedyotis nigricans*), also called DIAMOND FLOWERS, is a taprooted perennial; **1-nerved linear leaves**, often with clusters of small leaves in the axils; numerous funnel-shaped flowers, some sessile; **corolla lobes about ⅔ the tube length**. Dry soil and barrens, from MI to NE, south to FL and Mexico. In TN, thinly scattered from the Western Highland Rim to the Ridge and Valley. Occasional. June–August. *Houstonia nigricans*.

NOTES: Roan Mountain Bluet was named for Roan Mountain, located on the NC–TN border. This plant is on both the U.S. and TN endangered species lists. • **Glade Bluet** is the only bluet species of TN that remains in the *Hedyotis* genus.

Large Bluet, Summer Bluet
Houstonia purpurea var. *purpurea*

GENERAL: Erect, fibrous-rooted perennial, 6–20 in. tall; 1–several branching stems with **hairy internodes**. **LEAVES:** Basal, absent at flowering time; stem leaves opposite, ovate, 1–2 in. long, **greater than 0.5 in. wide, rounded to heart-shaped at the base, 3–5 main veins**. **FLOWERS:** Funnel-shaped, **white to lavender**, about 0.35 in. long; 4 spreading corolla lobes **about ½ the tube length**; numerous flowers on short pedicels in terminal cymes. April–July. **FRUITS:** Round, 2-parted capsules, about 0.15 in. across. **WHERE FOUND:** Open, dry woods, slopes, and rocky places, from NY to IA, south to FL and TX. In TN, from the Western Highland Rim eastward, also Hardeman County in West TN. Common. *Hedyotis purpurea.* **SIMILAR SPECIES:** FRINGED BLUET (*H. canadensis*) has **basal leaves fringed with hairs, present at flowering**; stem leaves narrow; **flowers purple** and few. Hillsides and rocky woods in the northeastern U.S. Scattered across most of TN. Occasional. May–June. *Hedyotis canadensis*.

NOTES: Large Bluet is also called **Large Houstonia.** • More than 2 dozen species of bluets are found in North America, but their subtle differences make them difficult to identify. Some bear clusters of flowers at the tops of branching stems, while others bear 1–2 flowers atop each stem.

Small Bluet
Houstonia pusilla

DENNIS HORN

GENERAL: Annual, 2–4 in. tall, with a slender, branched, smooth, erect stem. **LEAVES: Mostly basal**, ovate to elliptic, 0.2–0.4 in. long, on short petioles; stem leaves smaller, opposite, often sessile. **FLOWERS: Blue or purple** 0.2–0.3 in. across, with a **reddish eye**, corolla has a smooth, narrow tube with 4 abruptly spreading lobes; solitary on long stalks, terminal or from the upper leaf axils. March–April. **FRUITS:** Flattened, 2-chambered capsules, about 0.15 in. wide. **WHERE FOUND:** Fields, meadows, and open woods, usually dry places. In the Coastal Plain from DE to TX, and inland to IL and KS. In TN, primarily from the Western to the Eastern Highland Rim, also thinly scattered in West and East TN. Frequent. *H. patens, Hedyotis crassifolia*.

NOTES: The species name *pusilla* means "insignificant or weak." The diminutive size of **Small Bluet** lends the other common names **Tiny Bluet** and **Least Bluet**. • The easiest way to identify this plant is to look for the reddish-centered flowers. • Bluets are pollinated by butterflies, as well as several species of bees.

Creeping Bluet, Mountain Bluet • *Houstonia serpyllifolia*

DENNIS HORN

GENERAL: Perennial, 4–8 in. tall, with smooth, diffusely branched, **creeping stems** and numerous erect branches arising from a base of prostrate runners. **LEAVES:** Ovate to roundish, less than 0.3 in. long, **short-petioled**. **FLOWERS:** Blue-violet 0.4–0.5 in. across, with a **light yellow eye**; 4 abruptly spreading corolla lobes, **narrow tube is hairy within**; solitary on long stalks, terminal or from the upper leaf axils. April–June. **FRUITS:** Flattened, 2-chambered capsules to 0.2 in. wide. **WHERE FOUND:** Streambanks, rich woods, and wet slopes, from PA to GA in the mountains. In TN, in the Blue Ridge Mountains in Monroe, Blount, Sevier, Unicoi, Carter, and Johnson counties, also Van Buren County in Middle TN. Infrequent. *Hedyotis michauxii*.

NOTES: This plant is also called **Thymeleaf Bluet**, from the species name *serpyllifolia*, which means "thyme leaf," referring to the shape of the leaves. • **Quaker Ladies** (p. 305) is similar, but lacks the prostrate runners, the stem leaves are elongate-ovate without a distinct petiole, and the corolla tube is smooth within.

Partridgeberry
Mitchella repens

GENERAL: Small, **creeping, evergreen,** perennial herb; stems often rooting at the nodes; plants often form a mat on hummocks or small banks in the woods. **LEAVES:** Opposite, round to ovate, dark, **leathery,** 0.3–0.75 in. long, petioled. **FLOWERS: Fragrant, white, trumpet-shaped,** about 0.5 in. long; 4 (occasionally 3, 5, or 6) spreading lobes are fuzzy inside; **occur in pairs** on terminal peduncles with their ovaries united, forming a **single berry that bears the marks where the 2 corollas were attached.** May–June. **FRUITS: Scarlet berries** about 0.25 in. wide; may remain until the next flowering season if not eaten by birds. **WHERE FOUND:** Rich deciduous woods on acidic soil, throughout the eastern U.S., southeastern Canada, and TN. Common.

NOTES: The species name *repens*, meaning "spreading or creeping," refers to the trailing growth habit of this plant. • It was told that the berries were the "beloved food" of partridges, hence the common name. It is also known as Chicken Berry, Eyeberry, Hive Vine, Mountain Tea, Pudding Plum, and Squaw Plum, many of which are references to this plant's edibility and medicinal properties. It was taken before childbirth and used as a diuretic and a tonic to invoke overall general wellness. The berries are **edible** and were sometimes used to flavor milk.

Field Madder
Sherardia arvensis*

GENERAL: Annual, 4–16 in. tall, erect or reclining, much-branched, **rough, square stems;** often **forms dense mats. LEAVES:** In **whorls of 6,** ovate to linear, hairy, sharp-pointed, 0.2–0.6 in. long. **FLOWERS: Tiny, pinkish to lavender;** 4-lobed corolla, tube about 0.12 in. long, 3x longer than the spreading lobes; occur in heads surrounded by a whorl of involucral leaves. April–August. **FRUITS:** Dry, rough, twin, 1-seeded carpels, topped by persistent sepals. **WHERE FOUND:** Introduced from Eurasia. Now naturalized in fields, lawns, roadsides, and waste places throughout the eastern U.S. and TN. Occasional.

NOTES: The genus name commemorates Dr. William Sherard (1659–1728), an English botanist. The species name *arvensis*, "of cultivated land," as well as the common name, refer to the habit of this plant of growing in farm fields and resembling Madder (*Rubia tinctorum*). This species is also known as **Blue Field Madder.**

Southern Bush Honeysuckle · *Diervilla sessilifolia*

GENERAL: Shrub, 2–6 ft. tall, branchlets smooth, twigs round. **LEAVES:** Opposite, sessile, **smooth**, lanceolate to narrowly ovate, 3–6 in. long, **margins toothed, not ciliate**. **FLOWERS:** Tubular, **light yellow**, 0.5–0.8 in. long, **5-lobed**. June–August. **FRUITS:** Capsules about 0.5 in. long, contracted at the tip to an elongated beak. **WHERE FOUND:** Bluffs and woodland borders. A southern Appalachian species extending north from GA and AL to VA. In TN, in Unicoi, Cocke, Sevier, Blount, Monroe, Polk, Hamilton, and Marion counties. Infrequent. **SIMILAR SPECIES:** MOUNTAIN BUSH HONEYSUCKLE (**D. rivularis**) has **densely hairy** branchlets and lower leaf surfaces. Bluffs and mountain woods in NC, GA, AL, and East TN. Infrequent. June–August. NORTHERN BUSH HONEYSUCKLE (**D. lonicera**) has **short-petioled leaves** with toothed, **ciliate margins**. Forests with dry, rocky soil and moist, rocky gorges. A northern species extending south to GA and FL. In TN, in Cheatham, Marion, Hamilton, Polk, Roane, Anderson, and Johnson counties. Infrequent. June–July.

NOTES: The genus name *Diervilla* was named in honor of Dr. N. Dièreville, a French surgeon who traveled in Canada from 1699 to 1700 and brought **Bush Honeysuckle** to a French botanist. • Honeysuckles are appropriately named, since a person must suckle the flower to taste the honey-like nectar.

Japanese Honeysuckle
Lonicera japonica*

GENERAL: Widespread trailing or high-climbing **woody vine**. **LEAVES:** Opposite, ovate to oblong, rounded or broadly wedge-shaped at the base, 1.5–3.0 in. long, **leaves of new shoots often lobed**. **FLOWERS:** White, cream, or rarely pink, sweet fragrance, 1–2 in. long; **strongly 2-lipped corolla; occur in pairs**. April–June. **FRUITS:** Glossy, **black berries** with black, shiny seeds. **WHERE FOUND:** Introduced from eastern Asia. Woods and fields. A weed of thickets, borders, and roadsides throughout the eastern and southern U.S. and TN. Common. **SIMILAR SPECIES:** AMERICAN FLY HONEYSUCKLE (**L. canadensis**) is a loosely branched shrub to 5 ft. tall; leaves ovate, entire, 2–4 in. long, sparsely hairy beneath; **pale yellow flowers** are **weakly 2-lipped**; **red berries**. Cool woodlands. A northeastern species extending south to GA in the mountains. In TN, in Carter, Meigs, and Sevier counties in East TN. Rare. May–June.

NOTE: The genus name commemorates Adam Lonitzer (1528–86), a German botanist. • The introduced **Japanese Honeysuckle** is **a serious threat to native plants** because it spreads into woodland areas, growing over and wrapping around native plants and even trees in a strangling manner. More than likely, with the help of birds who eat the small black seeds and deposit them far and wide, Japanese Honeysuckle can be found in every county in TN.

Trumpet Honeysuckle
Lonicera sempervirens

GENERAL: Smooth woody, twining vine, to 15 ft. long, stems trailing or climbing. **LEAVES:** Opposite, elliptic to ovate, 1–3 in. long, **whitened or waxy beneath**; uppermost pair of stem leaves just below the flowers, **fused and surrounding the stem. FLOWERS:** Bright red or yellow with **yellow inside the throat**; narrowly tubular corolla, 1–2 in. long, with 5 short, flaring, **nearly equal lobes**; yellow stamens and style protrude slightly; borne in terminal clusters on new branches. May–July. **FRUITS:** Red, few-seeded berries. **WHERE FOUND:** Woods, thickets, and fencerows, often escapes from cultivation. Widespread in the eastern U.S. and throughout TN. Frequent. **SIMILAR SPECIES:** YELLOW HONEYSUCKLE (*L. flava*) has **strongly 2-lipped, golden to orange flowers; leaves not whitened or waxy beneath**. Rocky woods, from southern MO to OH, south to GA and AR. In TN, in Hamilton, Franklin, and Lewis counties. Rare. April–May. MOUNTAIN HONEYSUCKLE (*L. dioica*) has **strongly 2-lipped, pale yellow to purplish flowers; fused leaves whitened and waxy beneath**. Moist woods and thickets. A northern species extending south in the uplands to GA. Thinly scattered in the eastern ½ of TN, also Lewis County. Occasional. May–June.

DENNIS HORN

NOTES: Trumpet Honeysuckle is also called **Coral Honeysuckle** and **Woodbine**. The tubular flowers are a favorite nectar source for hummingbirds, and the seeds are sought by Bobwhites, Northern Cardinals, Pine Siskins, Purple Finches, goldfinches, and sparrows. • Medicinally, the juice from the plant has been used to treat bee stings.

Common Elderberry
Sambucus canadensis

GENERAL: Colonial shrub to 10 ft. tall with numerous stems, forming thickets; stems have a white pith. **LEAVES:** Opposite, compound, usually with 7 lanceolate to ovate, sharply serrate leaflets, 2–4 in. long. **FLOWERS:** Numerous, white; corolla about 0.2 in. wide, with 5 equal lobes; in **flat-topped or convex terminal cymes**, 4–8 in. across. July–August. **FRUITS:** Edible, **black or purple berries**, 4-seeded. **WHERE FOUND:** Moist woods, fields, and roadsides throughout the central and eastern U.S., southeastern Canada, and TN. Common. *S. nigra* ssp. *canadensis*. **SIMILAR SPECIES:** RED ELDERBERRY (*S. racemosa* ssp. *pubens*) bears its flowers in **elongated, panicle-like inflorescences; red berries; stems have a brown pith**. Rich woods and mountain openings. A northeastern species extending south to GA. In TN, in the Blue Ridge Mountains, also Marion, Grundy, and Van Buren counties. Infrequent. May–June. *S. racemosa* var. *racemosa*.

DENNIS HORN

NOTES: The flowers of **Common Elderberry** add lightness to pancakes, while the berries are good for jelly or sauce, are used to make wine, and are high in vitamin C. • Common Elderberry has many medicinal properties, and is used to treat colds and flu, headaches, and as a poultice applied to cuts, sores, and swollen limbs. The unripe berries, stems, and roots may cause an **upset stomach** if ingested. The berries are a highly valued food source for wildlife.

Yellow Horse Gentian
Triosteum angustifolium

GENERAL: Perennial herb, 12–36 in. tall, with hairy stems. **LEAVES:** Opposite, entire, elliptic, lanceolate, or oblanceolate, 3–6 in. long, **over 3x as long as wide**, narrowed below the middle to a sessile base. **FLOWERS:** Greenish yellow, tubular, 0.5–0.6 in. long, with 5 unequal lobes; sepals with stiff hairs; usually solitary in the leaf axils. April–June. **FRUITS:** Roundish, red-orange drupes, to 0.4 in. long, **capped with 5 prominent, linear sepals that persist**. **WHERE FOUND:** Rich, low woods. Widespread in the eastern U.S. and throughout TN. Frequent.

NOTES: The genus name *Triosteum* comes from the Greek words *treis*, "three," and *osteon*, "a bone," in reference to the 3 bony seeds of these herbs. The species name *angustifolium* means having "narrow leaves," which is a characteristic of **Yellow Horse Gentian**. This plant is also called **Yellow-fruited Horse Gentian** and Yellow Tinker's Weed. • Plants in the genus *Triosteum* are erect perennials with large, opposite leaves, tubular flowers with 5 unequal lobes, 5 sepals persistent in fruit, and 5 stamens. There are 3 species in the U.S. and TN.

OTTO R. HIRSCH

Orange-Fruited Horse Gentian · *Triosteum aurantiacum*

GENERAL: Coarse perennial herb, 16–36 in. tall with stiff-hairy stems. **LEAVES:** Opposite, ovate or elliptic, 4–10 in. long, tapering to a narrow, sessile base, **generally wider than 2 in. and shorter than 3x the width**. **FLOWERS:** Purplish red, tubular, 0.6–0.8 in. long, 5 unequal corolla lobes. May–July. **FRUITS:** Bright red-orange drupes, about 0.5 in. long, capped with narrow, persistent sepals. **WHERE FOUND:** Rich woods in the

ALAN S. HEILMAN

northeastern U.S. Thinly scattered in Middle and East TN. Occasional. **SIMILAR SPECIES:** FEVERWORT or WILD COFFEE (*T. perfoliatum*) has the **middle pairs of leaves joined at the base; purplish to greenish yellow flowers; orange-yellow fruits**. Rich woods in the eastern U.S. Thinly scattered in Middle and East TN. Infrequent. May–July.

NOTES: The species name *aurantiacum* means "orange-colored," referring to the fruits.• The fruits of **Feverwort** can be dried, roasted, and ground for use as a coffee substitute. In herbal medicine, Native Americans used the roots of these *Triosteum* species as a purgative and to treat fevers. A poultice was made from the roots and applied to sores and swellings. In large doses, it is a powerful laxative and can induce vomiting.

Mapleleaf Viburnum
Viburnum acerifolium

GENERAL: Colonial **shrub**, 3–7 ft. tall, usually with runners (stolons). **LEAVES:** Opposite, petioled, shallowly **3-lobed, maple-leaf-shaped**, 2–4 in. long, serrated margins; lower leaf surfaces covered with star-shaped hairs. **FLOWERS:** Numerous, **whitish, 5-lobed**, about 0.2 in. wide; borne in a stalked, terminal cyme, about 2 in. across. May–June. **FRUITS:** Ellipsoid, **purple-black drupes**, about 0.4 in. long. **WHERE FOUND:** Moist or dry woods throughout the eastern U.S. In TN, from the Eastern Highland Rim eastward, also Davidson, Sumner, and Macon counties. Frequent. **SIMILAR SPECIES:** SWAMP HAW (*V. nudum* var. *nudum*), also called **POSSOM HAW**, has **shiny, unlobed leaves**, elliptic-ovate, mostly entire; **cymes on stalks 1–2 in. long.** Wet woods and swamps throughout the southeastern U.S. and in West TN, the Eastern Highland Rim, and the Cumberland Plateau. Occasional. May–July. **WILD RAISIN** (*V. cassinoides*) has **dull, unlobed leaves**, with **shallow rounded teeth; cymes on stalks 2–10 in. long.** Wet or dry sites throughout most of the eastern U.S. In TN, from the Cumberland Plateau eastward. Occasional. May–June. *V. nudum* var. *cassinoides.*

NOTES: The attractive flowers in spring and colorful autumn foliage have made **Mapleleaf Viburnum** a popular landscape shrub. The fruits are eaten by birds and mammals. Native Americans used a bark tea made from Mapleleaf Viburnum, prepared in a lengthy process, to treat diabetes. • **Swamp Haw** is also called **Southern Wild Raisin.**

Witch Hobble, Hobblebush
Viburnum lantanoides

GENERAL: Shrub, 3–12 ft. tall, branches reclining and often rooting. **LEAVES:** Opposite, petioled, 4–7 in. long, nearly round with **fine teeth, noticeably veined**, base distinctly heart-shaped, covered in rusty brown hairs when young. **FLOWERS:** Numerous **whitish, 5-lobed, fertile** flowers, about 0.2 in. wide, in the center of the inflorescence; **large, showy, sterile** flowers, about 1 in. wide, **around the outside**; borne in a **sessile cyme** about 4 in. across. April–June. **FRUITS:** Ellipsoid, **red drupes** to 0.4 in. long, turning dark when mature. **WHERE FOUND:** Moist woods and cool habitats. A northeastern species extending south in the mountains to GA. In East TN, in the Blue Ridge Mountains. Infrequent. *V. alnifolium.* **SIMILAR SPECIES:** SOUTHERN ARROWWOOD (*V. dentatum*) has **coarsely toothed leaves, stalked cymes without sterile flowers**, and nearly spherical, **blue-black fruits**, about 0.2 in. wide. Low woods throughout the eastern U.S. and the eastern ½ of TN. Occasional. May–July. SOUTHERN BLACK HAW (*V. rufidulum*) has **fine-toothed leaves; rusty brown hairs cover the petioles**, leaves, and inflorescence branches; **nearly sessile cymes lack sterile flowers.** Woods and thickets throughout the southeastern U.S. and TN. Common. April–May.

NOTES: Witch Hobble is also known as Hobbleberry and is valued for its berries, which produce a kaleidoscope of colors as they ripen. Also adding to this species' value as a landscape plant, the spring flowers resemble those of some hydrangeas, such as Ashy Hydrangea, Wild Hydrangea, and Silverleaf Hydrangea (all listed on p. 140). Additionally, the foliage of Witch Hobble turns attractive colors in the fall.

Large-Flowered Valerian
Valeriana pauciflora

GENERAL: Perennial herb, 12–30 in. tall, from a slender rhizome. **LEAVES:** Petioled, 2 distinct leaf types; basal leaves heart-shaped, simple, 2–3 in. long; **stem leaves opposite, pinnately divided** into 3–7 segments, terminal segment is ovate or deltoid, much larger than the lateral segments. **FLOWERS:** Pink, 0.6–0.7 in. long, **slender, tubular corolla with 5 short, nearly equal lobes;** calyx small at flowering, the tip expanding into about 10 long, plume-like bristles at maturity; inflorescence is initially compact, with short branches that lengthen with age. April–May. **FRUITS:** Oblong achenes, about 0.2 in. long, thinly hairy when young. **WHERE FOUND:** Rich, moist woods, often on basic soils, from PA to IL, south to VA and AL. In TN, in both the Western and Eastern Highland Rims. Occasional.

NOTES: The genus name *Valeriana* comes from the Latin *valere*, "to be healthy." The species name *pauciflora* means "few flowered." • The tubular flowers of this plant make it a favorite source of nectar for many species of butterflies. • The **Valerian Family** contains mostly herbs and shrubs, including the popular garden shrub Red Valerian or Pretty Betsy (*Centranthus ruber*).

DENNIS HORN

Beaked Corn Salad
Valerianella radiata

GENERAL: Erect **annual** to 30 in. tall, with forking stems. **LEAVES:** Opposite, narrowly spatulate to elliptic-lanceolate, about 2.5–3.0 in. long. **FLOWERS:** White, less than 0.08 in. long, tubular corolla with 5 short, nearly equal lobes; sparsely **fringed bracts;** borne in clusters at the ends of the stems. April–May. **FRUITS:** Nutlets, twice as long as broad. **WHERE FOUND:** Open disturbed sites, from NY to OH to KS, south to FL and TX. Throughout most of TN. Common. **SIMILAR SPECIES:** NAVEL CORN SALAD (*V. umbilicata*) has larger white flowers, 0.12–0.20 in. wide, in a loosely flowered inflorescence with long branches; **bracts without fringe;** nutlets are as broad as long. In open disturbed sites, from southern NY to IL, south to SC and AL. Middle TN. Occasional. April–May. **EUROPEAN CORN SALAD** (*V. locusta******), also called **LAMB'S LETTUCE,** has **pale blue flowers.** Introduced from Europe. Fields and roadsides in the eastern and western U.S. Primarily Middle and East TN. Occasional. April–May. *V. olitoria*.

DENNIS HORN

NOTE: The leaves of **Beaked Corn Salad** make an excellent salad or cooked greens. • The 4 *Valerianella* species found in TN are succulent annuals with forked stems and opposite, sessile stem leaves with entire margins or a few basal teeth. The inflorescence is cyme-like with bracts and tiny, 5-lobed flowers.

Teasel
*Dipsacus fullonum**

GENERAL: Coarse **biennial**, 2–6 ft. tall, few branched with **prickly stems**. **LEAVES:** Basal leaves oblanceolate with shallow, rounded teeth, withering early in the 2nd season; stem leaves opposite, lanceolate, 4–12 in. long, entire, sessile or grown together, prickly on the mid-vein beneath. **FLOWERS:** **Slender, white corolla tube,** 0.4–0.6 in. long, with **4 short, pale lavender to pink lobes;** silky calyx; in ovoid to **cylindric heads** terminating the stems, heads are 1.25–4.0 in. long, with **numerous flowers and stiff, prickly awns.** July–September. **FRUITS:** Nutlets, 0.1 in. long. **WHERE FOUND:** Introduced from Europe. Now naturalized throughout most of North America in waste places and along roadsides. An increasingly common weed on major roadways. Middle and East TN. Occasional. ***D. sylvestrus.***

NITA R. HEILMAN

NOTES: Other common names for this plant are Adam's Flannel, Church Broom, Prickly Back, and Water Thistle. The names Clothier's Brush and Gipsy Combs indicate that the dried seed heads were used as combs. In fact, early wool manufacturers fastened the seed heads to a spindle to "tease" (comb) cloth to raise the nap. This brushing of the nap produced air pockets that provided added insulation and gave the wool a softer surface and more pleasing appearance.

Aster or Sunflower Family (Asteraceae)

The Aster or Sunflower Family is the second largest family of flowering plants (after the Orchid Family) in the world, with over 21,000 species (also called "composites") of herbs, shrubs, climbers, and a few trees. Composites can be recognized by their inflorescence, which is often mistaken for a single large flower, but actually consists of numerous, tiny disk flowers surrounded by longer ray flowers, clustered together on the broadened top of the stem. Usually, central disk flowers are surrounded by more showy ray flowers, but a plant may have only ray or disk flowers. There are 82 genera and 322 species known in TN.

The Aster Family has a significant economic value and includes edible plants, such as lettuce (*Lactuca*), globe artichoke (*Cynara*), endive and chicory (*Cichorium*), and sunflower seeds (*Helianthus*). Popular ornamentals included are asters, bachelor's button, chrysanthemums, coneflowers, cosmos, dahlias, daisies, marigolds, sunflowers, and zinnias.

1a. Heads with ray flowers only; juice milky . . . . **Key A**
1b. Heads with disk flowers; ray flowers present or absent; juice watery **2**
  2a. Heads with both ray and disk flowers **3**
   3a. Rays yellow or orange . . . . **Key B**
   3b. Rays white, pink, or purplish, not yellow or orange . . . . **Key C**
  2b. Heads with disk flowers only (the outermost disk flowers
     sometimes enlarged and different from the inner ones) . . . . **Key D**

Key A

1a. Pappus of scales or none, no bristles present **2**
  2a. Corollas blue to pink or white . . . . *Cichorium*
  2b. Corollas yellow or orange; involucral bracts in 1 series; pappus usually present . . . . *Krigia*
1b. Pappus of bristles, at least in part **3**
  3a. Pappus bristles simple, not plumose **4**
   4a. Achenes flattened . . . . *Lactuca*
   4b. Achenes rounded to angular in cross-section, not flattened **5**
    5a. Flowers white, pink or cream; heads usually nodding . . . . *Prenanthes*
    5b. Flowers bright yellow to orange or orange-red; heads erect **6**
     6a. Achenes beakless or with a short, stout beak less than 1/2 as long as
       the achene body **7**
      7a. Involucral bracts in 1 series . . . . *Krigia*
      7b. Involucral bracts in more than 1 series, the outer series
        frequently very short . . . . *Hieracium*
     6b. Achenes with a long, slender beak from 1/2 as long to longer
       than the achene body **8**
      8a. Plants with only a leafless flowering stem (scape),
        each scape with a solitary head . . . . *Taraxacum*
      8b. Plants with a leafy stem, usually branched above
        and with several heads . . . . *Pyrrhopappus*
  3b. Pappus bristles plumose **9**
   9a. Involucral bracts in 1 series; leafy-stemmed plants with grass-like leaves . . . . *Tragopogon*
   9b. Involucral bracts in more than one series; leaves not grass-like;
     receptacle with thin, dry scales . . . . *Hypochaeris*

Key B

1a. Receptacle with thin, dry scales (or only bristly in *Gaillardia*) **2**

  2a. Disk flowers sterile, with undivided style **3**

    3a. Leaves lobed or dissected; achenes only slightly flattened; pappus absent . . . . . .**Polymnia**

    3b. Leaves usually not lobed or dissected; achenes flattened; pappus present or absent **4**

      4a. Rays 5 or 6, 0.3–0.6 in. long; leaves with winged petioles . . . .**Chrysogonum**

      4b. Rays more than 6, more than 0.6 in. long; leaves sessile or petioles wingless . . . . .**Silphium**

  2b. Disk flowers fertile, with divided style **5**

    5a. Involucral bracts in 2 distinct series (or 3 in *Gaillardia*),
the outer ones more or less spreading **6**

      6a. Ray flowers 3-cleft (if present; rarely absent); leaves alternate . . . .**Gaillardia**

      6b. Ray flowers entire, not 3-cleft; leaves opposite (in our spp.),
perhaps appearing whorled **7**

        7a. Achenes wing-margined; pappus awns, if present,
without backward-pointing barbs . . . .**Coreopsis**

        7b. Achenes not wing-margined; pappus awns usually
with backward-pointing barbs . . . .**Bidens**

    5b. Involucral bracts all similar, not in 2 distinct series **8**

      8a. Leaves all alternate **9**

        9a. Receptacle strongly conic or columnar; pappus a low crown or none **10**

          10a. Ray flowers subtended by receptacular bracts; leaves pinnatifid . . . . .**Ratibida**

          10b. Ray flowers not subtended by receptacular bracts;
leaves pinnatifid or entire . . . .**Rudbeckia**

        9b. Receptacle merely convex; pappus of 2 or 3 awns or scales **11**

          11a. Achenes strongly flattened; stem winged
with extended petiole bases . . . .**Verbesina**

          11b. Achenes not flattened; stem not winged . . . .**Helianthus**

      8b. Leaves, at least the lower, opposite **12**

        12a. Rays persistent on the achenes and becoming papery; pappus none . . . . .**Heliopsis**

        12b. Rays deciduous from the achenes at maturity; pappus present, of 2 awns **13**

          13a. Achenes strongly flattened **14**

            14a. Stem winged, erect, receptacle flat to short-conic . . . .**Verbesina**

            14b. Stem not winged, decumbent, rooting at the nodes;
receptacle elongated . . . .**Acmella (=Spilanthes)**

          13b. Achenes not flattened; stem not winged . . . .**Helianthus**

1b. Receptacle without thin, dry scales **15**

  15a. Pappus of scales, or a few firm awns **16**

    16a. Pappus of 2–several firm, deciduous awns, not of scales . . . .**Grindelia**

    16b. Pappus of evident scales, these sometimes awn-tipped **17**

      17a. Involucral bracts erect and appressed; heads small, disk about 0.2 in. wide or less,
rays only 0.12–0.2 in. long . . . . .**Amphiachyris (=Gutierrezia, Xanthocephalum)**

      17b. Involucral bracts spreading or deflexed, heads larger,
disk about 0.24–1.2 in. wide, rays 0.2–1.2 in. long **18**

        18a. Style branches with an awl-shaped appendage . . . .**Gaillardia**

        18b. Style branches truncate, without an awl-shaped appendage . . . . . .**Helenium**

  15b. Pappus of capillary bristles **19**

    19a. Involucral bracts all of equal length, in 1 series
(sometimes with a few much shorter ones at base) **20**

20a. Disk flowers fertile, with divided style; stems more or less leafy . . . . *Senecio*

20b. Disk flowers sterile, with undivided style; stems merely bracteate . . . . . . *Tussilago*

19b. Involucral bracts overlapping, in several series **21**

21a. Pappus of 2 series of bristles,
the outer ones much shorter than the inner . . . . *Heterotheca*

21b. Pappus not differentiated into an inner and an outer series;
fibrous-rooted perennial from a caudex or rhizome **22**

22a. Leaves more or less glandular-dotted; rays more numerous than
disk flowers, inflorescence a flat-topped cyme . . . . *Euthamia*

22b. Leaves not glandular-dotted (except *S. odora*); plants with rays less numerous than
disk flowers or inflorescence not a flat-topped cyme . . . . *Solidago*

Key C

1a. Receptacle without thin, dry scales **2**

2a. Pappus all or in part of capillary bristles **3**

3a. Involucral bracts in 1 series, occasionally with a few short basal ones **4**

4a. Rays less than 0.08 in. long, taprooted annual . . . . *Conyza*

4b. Rays more than 0.08 in. long, annual or perennial . . . . *Erigeron*

3b. Involucral bracts overlapping, in several series (like shingles) **5**

5a. Rays less than 0.2 in. long, white . . . . *Solidago* (*S. bicolor*)

5b. Rays more than 0.2 in. long, white, blue or pink **6**

6a. Pappus bristles not in 2 distinct series **7**

7a. Disk flowers as well as rays white to straw-colored . . . . *Sericocarpus*

7b. Disk flowers typically yellow, changing to red, brown, or purplish;
rays various; involucral bracts in several series, more or less leaf-like,
at least at the tip . . . . *Aster* (**most species key here**)

6b. Pappus in 2 series, the outer of short, sharp-pointed bristles **8**

8a. Inner pappus-bristles club-shaped at the tips;
involucral bracts thin, leathery, without herbaceous tips,
shorter than the height of the disk . . . .*Doellingeria*

8b. Inner pappus bristles uniformly filiform their entire width;
involucral bracts equal to the height of the disk . . . . . .*Aster* (*A. linariifolius*)

2b. Pappus not of capillary bristles, of awns, or a short crown, or none **9**

9a. Pappus a short crown or none; heads solitary or few **10**

10a. Heads solitary, rays white, leaves toothed . . . .*Chrysanthemum*

10b. Heads solitary or few, rays pale purplish, leaves entire . . . .*Astranthium*

9b. Pappus of 2–4 short awns; heads several in a corymb . . . .*Boltonia*

1b. Receptacle with thin, dry scales **11**

11a. Leaves, or many of them, opposite . . . .*Polymnia*

11b. Leaves alternate **12**

12a. Rays 0.8–3.0 in. long . . . .*Echinacea*

12b. Rays less than 0.8 in. long **13**

13a. Rays more than 8 . . . .*Anthemis*

13b. Rays 1–5 . . . .**14**

14a. Leaves pinnately dissected . . . .*Achillea*

14b. Leaves merely lobed, toothed, or nearly entire **15**

15a. Disk flowers sterile, with undivided style; stem not winged . . . .*Parthenium*

15b. Disk flowers fertile, with divided style;
stem winged with extended petiole bases . . . .*Verbesina*

Key D

1a. Plants thistles, with more or less spiny-margined leaves, usually also with a spiny involucre; heads purple, blue, pink, or white, rarely yellowish; pappus of bristles only 2

   2a. Pappus of plumose bristles . . . . **Cirsium**

   2b. Pappus of simple capillary bristles . . . . **Carduus**

1b. Plants not thistles, the leaves not spiny-margined 3

   3a. Pappus partly or wholly of capillary bristles 4

      4a. Receptacle with thin, dry scales or bristly . . . . **Centaurea**

      4b. Receptacle without thin, dry scales 5

         5a. Heads yellow . . . . **Senecio**

         5b. Heads white, tan, greenish, or pink to purple, not yellow 6

            6a. Pappus distinctly double, with an inner series of long bristles and an outer series of very short bristles . . . . **Vernonia**

            6b. Pappus simple, of similar bristles 7

               7a. Pappus bristles barbed or plumose 8

                  8a. Corollas whitish . . . . **Kuhnia**

                  8b. Corollas purplish . . . . **Liatris**

               7b. Pappus bristles smooth or scabrous, but not plumose 9

                  9a. Involucre of 4 bracts; twining vines . . . . **Mikania**

                  9b. Involucre of more than 4 bracts; erect or scrambling, but not twining 10

                     10a. Involucre of 1 series of uniform bracts, sometimes with a few much smaller ones at the base 11

                       11a. Leaves lanceolate, pinnately veined . . . . **Erechtites**

                       11b. Leaves kidney-shaped or deltoid, palmately veined 12

                           12a. Leaves mostly basal, plants of high-elevation forest openings of the Great Smoky Mtns . . . . **Rugelia**

                           12b. Leaves basal and along the stem, reduced upward; plants more widespread . . . . **Cacalia**

                     10b. Involucre of more than 1 series of bracts 13

                       13a. Leaves chiefly or wholly basal, forming a basal mat . . . . **Antennaria**

                     13b. Leaves chiefly or all cauline, not forming a basal mat 14

                         14a. Stems and lower leaf surfaces white-woolly . . . . . . **Gnaphalium**

                       14b. Stems and lower leaf surfaces not white-woolly 15

                           15a. Flowers all perfect and fertile; leaves, at least the lower, usually opposite or whorled 16

                             16a. Corollas bluish purple, rarely white, not pinkish . . . . **Conoclinium**

                             16b. Corollas white to creamy to purplish 17

                               17a. Involucral bracts all approximately the same length, in 1–2 series . . . .**Ageratina**

                               17b. Involucral bracts of different lengths, strongly overlapping . . . .**Eupatorium**

                           15b. Outer flowers of head pistillate; leaves alternate, plants with a distinctive odor . . . .**Pluchea**

3b. Pappus of a few awns or scales, or absent 18

   18a. Heads unisexual; pistillate involucre nut-like or bur-like . . . .**Ambrosia**

   18b. Heads bisexual; involucre various 19

19a. Receptacle with thin, dry scales or bristly; corollas yellow, orange, white or blue, not pinkish purple **20**

    20a. Involucral bracts in 2 series, the outer ones spreading . . . .***Bidens***

    20b. Involucral bracts in 1–several series, all bracts similar **21**

        21a. Involucral bracts with a modified tip . . . .***Centaurea***

        21b. Involucral bracts without a modified tip **22**

            22a. Heads white, pink, or blue . . . .***Marshallia***

            22b. Heads dull yellow or greenish . . . .***Polymnia***

19b. Receptacle without thin, dry scales; corollas pinkish purple . . . . . .***Elephantopus***

Adapted primarily from: Cronquist, A. 1980. *Vascular Flora of the Southeastern United States. Vol. I, Asteraceae.* University of North Carolina Press: Chapel Hill, NC.

Subdivision of *Aster* (e.g. *Doellingeria, Sericocarpus*) adapted from: Small, J.K. 1933. *Manual of the Southeastern Flora.* University of North Carolina Press: Chapel Hill, NC.

Aster
pp. 324–27

Coreopsis
pp. 336–37

Ambrosia
p. 321

Cirsium
pp. 333–34

Eupatorium
pp. 342–46

Hieracium
pp. 358–59

Liatris
pp. 362–65

Helianthus
pp. 350–55

Krigia
pp. 360–61

Parthenium
p. 366

Prenanthes
p. 368

Rudbeckia
pp. 370–72

Solidago
pp. 378–82

Vernonia
p. 386

Yarrow, Milfoil · *Achillea millefolium*

GENERAL: Aromatic perennial herb, often rhizomatous, 12–36 in. tall, with sparsely to densely hairy stems. **LEAVES:** Both basal and alternate on the stem, 2–6 in. long, finely dissected with a **feathery appearance**. **FLOWERS:** Ray flowers white (occasionally pink), usually 5, **3-toothed**, 0.08–0.12 in. long; disk whitish, 10–30-flowered, 0.1–0.15 in. wide; involucral bracts to 0.2 in. long, overlapping; heads radiate, numerous in flat-topped clusters that terminate flowering stems. May–November. **FRUITS:** Compressed achenes; pappus absent. **WHERE FOUND:** Both native and introduced subspecies occur in North America. Fields, lawns, and disturbed places throughout the U.S., southern Canada, and TN. Common.

NOTES: Since the primary medicinal use of this plant was to stop bleeding, it is sometimes referred to as Bloodwort, Deadman's Daisy, Nosebleed Plant, Staunchgrass, and Woundwort. • The genus name *Achillea* pays honor to Achilles, who is said to have used this plant in the Trojan War to help his wounded soldiers. It was thought to be particularly helpful when a wound was caused by iron, so it was used as recently as the American Civil War, when the crushed plant was applied to bullet and shrapnel wounds. The Navajo refer to it as "life medicine" because of its many healing properties. It contains at least 100 biologically active compounds, with more than 12 identified as anti-inflammatory agents.

OTTO R. HIRSCH

Creeping Spotflower
Acmella oppositifolia var. *repens*

GENERAL: Smooth to hairy, **colonial** perennial herb with reclining stems to 24 in. long; routinely roots at the lower nodes. **LEAVES:** Opposite, broadly lanceolate, 1–3 in. long, 0.2–1.2 in. wide, toothed, petioles to 0.8 in. long. **FLOWERS:** Ray flowers **yellow, 8–12, 3-toothed**, 0.12–0.4 in. long; **disk dark yellow**, 0.2–0.4 in. wide, **domed** at first, elongating to conical with age; heads radiate, few, on leafless stalks. June–October. **FRUITS:** Black achenes with lighter warts and white ciliate margins; pappus of 1–2 short awns or absent. **WHERE FOUND:** Low, moist, alluvial woods, swamps, and wetlands. A Coastal Plain species found from NC to TX, and north along the Mississippi River Valley to MO. In TN, in Shelby, Haywood, Lauderdale, and Tipton counties in West TN, and Rutherford County in Middle TN. Rare. ***Spilanthes americana***.

DENNIS HORN

NOTES: The species name *oppositifolia* refers to the leaves that occur in opposite pairs, which accounts for another common name, **Oppositeleaf Spotflower**. A more charming but less commonly used name is Button of Gold.

White Snakeroot · *Ageratina altissima*

GENERAL: Robust perennial herb, 1–4 ft. tall, smooth or short-hairy. **LEAVES:** Opposite, ovate to heart-shaped, to 7 in. long and 5 in. wide, palmately veined; tips acuminate; margins **sharply serrate; petioles over 1 in. long, but always shorter than the blade. FLOWERS:** Ray flowers absent; **disk flowers bright white**, 12–24; involucral bracts about 0.2 in. long, acuminate to obtuse, rarely white-margined; inflorescence a flat or rounded corymb-like cluster. July–October. **FRUITS:** Achenes, usually about 5 per head, about 0.1 in. long; pappus a tuft of whitish, hair-like bristles. **WHERE FOUND:** Rich woodlands throughout the central and eastern U.S. and across TN. Common. *Eupatorium rugosum.* **SIMILAR SPECIES:** AROMATIC SNAKEROOT (*A. aromatica*) has leaves that are thicker, with **rounded teeth** and **petioles less than 1 in. long**; achenes at least 9 per head. In drier sites in the eastern U.S. and the eastern 2/3 of TN. Frequent. August–October. *E. aromaticum.* LUCY BRAUN'S SNAKEROOT (*A. luciae-brauniae*) is a delicate perennial; **petioles about as long as leaf blades**. An endemic of "rockhouse" habitats of the Cumberland Plateau in northern TN and southern KY. Rare. September. *E. luciae-brauniae.*

NOTES: White Snakeroot contains **toxins** that can pass from cattle to humans through milk, which in pioneer days caused severe illness and often death. This "milksick" disease is thought to have killed Abraham Lincoln's mother. • White Snakeroot was included in preparations made by several Native American tribes to treat fever, diarrhea, and problems of the urinary tract.

Common Ragweed · *Ambrosia artemisiifolia*

GENERAL: Weedy annual with branched stems, 1–4 ft. tall, taller in rich soil; stems become woody late in the season. **LEAVES:** Opposite on lower stem, alternate on upper stem, 2–4 in. long, **deeply pinnately dissected. FLOWERS:** Inconspicuous, greenish, separate male (staminate) and female (pistillate) flower heads present on the same plant; ray flowers absent; male heads saucer-shaped, about 0.1 in. wide, disk flowers 5-lobed, borne in terminal spikes; female heads roundish, 1 fertile flower without corolla, clustered in the upper leaf axils below the male spikes. August–October. **FRUITS:** Brown achenes, beaked and with short, erect spines; pappus absent. **WHERE FOUND:** Fields and disturbed places throughout the U.S. and TN. Frequent. **SIMILAR SPECIES:** GREAT RAGWEED (*A. trifida*) is a coarse, weedy annual, 3–12 ft. tall; all opposite **leaves with only 3–5 lobes**. Moist soils and waste places throughout the U.S. and TN. Frequent. July–October. LANCELEAF RAGWEED (*A. bidentata*) has spreading hairs on the stem and **lanceolate leaves** with a single pair of coarse teeth near the base. Prairies and fields in the eastern U.S. Thinly scattered across TN. Occasional. July–October.

NOTES: The genus name *Ambrosia* refers to the "food of the gods that imparted immortality." **Common Ragweed** is also referred to as Bitterweed, Hayfever Weed, Stickweed, and Wild-Wormwood. • Although Common Ragweed has a fragrant smell, its wind-borne pollen is one of the worst causes of hayfever. • **Great Ragweed** is said to have been cultivated by several Native American tribes as a food or medicinal plant. A red dye was obtained by crushing the flower heads.

Prairie Broomweed, Common Broomweed
Amphiachyris dracunculoides

GENERAL: Annual, 1–3 ft. tall, with a thin, brittle, **broom-like stem** with resinous sap; freely and many-branched above, bush-like and rounded. **LEAVES:** Alternate, numerous, entire, linear, to 2.5 in. long and 0.1 in. wide, **peppered with glandular depressions. FLOWERS:** Ray flowers yellow, 5–10; **disk flowers yellow**, staminate, 10–30; involucral bracts about 0.2 in. long, tan base, blunt, green tip, overlapping, sticky; heads radiate, about 0.5 in. across, numerous in terminal cymes. July–October. **FRUITS:** Cylindric achenes, several-nerved; pappus a tiny, toothed crown. **WHERE FOUND:** Prairies and roadsides in the southwestern U.S., naturalized eastward. In Middle TN, in cedar glades. Infrequent. *Gutierrezia dracunculoides, Xanthocephalum dracunculoides.*

NOTES: The species name *dracunculoides* signifies the resemblance that broomweeds have to Tarragon (*Artemisia dracunculus*). This plant is also known as Broom Snakeweed. • The name "broom" comes from the shape of the plant, which resembles an upended broom. • Studies have shown that this species is spreading, as it was only in 1973 that Dr. Robert Kral of Vanderbilt University noted the plant had become common in the cedar glades in the Central Basin of TN.

OTTO R. HIRSCH

Plantainleaf Pussytoes
Antennaria plantaginifolia

GENERAL: Perennial herb, 4–16 in. tall, spreading by stolons, which may be leafy or only bracteate. **LEAVES:** Basal and alternate on the stem; basal leaves 1–3 in. long; **widely spatulate**, entire, most are 3-nerved, **pale green above** and **woolly beneath**; stem leaves narrow and smaller. **FLOWERS:** Dioecious (male and female flowers on different plants); ray flowers absent; **disk flowers white or purplish**, numerous; female plants have involucral bracts 0.2–0.3 in. long, white-tipped with a purplish base; male involucral bracts are smaller with broad, conspicuous, white tips; heads discoid, in **clusters of 3–21**. April–June. **FRUITS:** Shiny, brown, resin-dotted achenes; pappus a tuft of whitish bristles. **WHERE FOUND:** Dry soils of open woods and roadsides throughout the eastern U.S. and TN. Common.

NOTES: The common name "pussytoes" comes from the resemblance of the flower heads to cats' paws. Other evocative common names include Dog's Toes, Ladies' Chewing Tobacco, Love's Test, Mouse's Ear, Pincushions, and Poverty Weed. • In folk medicine, this plant was used to make a tea for treating lung ailments, was boiled in milk to treat diarrhea and dysentery, and the chewed leaves were applied to bruises, sprains, and swellings. It has been rumored that for a small fee, Native Americans would allow themselves to be bitten by a rattlesnake, and then cure themselves with this herb.

DENNIS HORN

Solitary Pussytoes
Antennaria solitaria

GENERAL: Perennial herb, 4–10 in. tall, spreading by slender, nearly naked stolons. **LEAVES:** Basal, **narrowly spatulate**, 2–4 in. long, mostly 3-nerved, **purplish above** and **white-woolly beneath**. **FLOWERS:** Dioecious (male and female flowers on different plants); ray flowers absent; **disk flowers white or purplish**, tubular, numerous; involucral bracts of pistillate heads 0.3–0.5 in. long; **solitary, large head** at the end of each nearly naked flower stalk. April–May. **FRUITS:** Ellipsoid, resin-dotted achenes; pappus a tuft of whitish bristles. **WHERE FOUND:** Dry woods and clearings from PA to IL, south to GA and LA. In TN, from the Western Highland Rim eastward, also Henderson County in West TN. Frequent.

NOTES: *Antennaria* is a highly variable genus that even confuses experts, who variously recognize as few as 6 and as many as 32 species in eastern North America. All members of this genus have rounded, basal leaves and flower heads that bear fluffy whitish or grayish bristles. Only 2 species are listed for TN. One association with the genus name *Antennaria*, from the Latin *antenna*, is that the pappus of male flowers resembles an insect's antennae. • Members of this genus are dioecious, with male and female flowers on separate plants. These herbs are mat forming, or colonial, and have runners (stolons). The lower leaf surfaces are covered with soft, white wool or silky down.

DENNIS HORN

Mayweed, Dog Fennel · *Anthemis cotula* *

GENERAL: Malodorous, taprooted **annual**, 6–24 in. tall, with branched stems. **LEAVES:** Alternate, 1.0–2.5 in. long, 2–3 times pinnately dissected giving the plant a **lacy appearance**. **FLOWERS:** Ray flowers white, 10–18, 0.2–0.4 in. long, **3-toothed, sterile; disk yellow**, 0.2–0.4 in. wide; heads radiate, single head terminates each flowering stalk. May–August. **FRUITS:** Rounded achenes, obscurely 10-ribbed, surface is glandular; pappus a short crown or absent. **WHERE FOUND:** Introduced from Europe. Fields and disturbed areas throughout the U.S. and TN. Frequent. **SIMILAR SPECIES:** CORN CHAMOMILE (**A. arvensis***) is **not ill-scented; ray flowers** are female and **fertile** (produce seed); smooth, 4-angled achenes. Also introduced from Europe. Fields and disturbed areas. Widespread in the U.S. and TN. Occasional. May–August.

NOTES: Other common names that allude to the unpleasant odor of **Mayweed** are Fetid Chamomile, Pigstye Daisy, Poison Daisy, **Stinking Chamomile**, and Stinkweed. It was also called Chigger Weed because it was thought that chiggers, troublesome mites that burrow under the skin, would breed or hide in the flower heads. • One reputed medicinal use for Mayweed is to rub the leaves on insect stings, but beware, **touching or ingesting the plant may cause an allergic reaction**. • These are the only 2 *Anthemis* species in TN.

OTTO R. HIRSCH

DENNIS HORN

Eastern Silvery Aster
Aster concolor

GENERAL: Smooth (or slightly silky), wand-like perennial herb, 12–36 in. tall, with slender, usually unbranched stems. **LEAVES:** Alternate, numerous, oblong, ascending, entire, **silvery-silky**, sessile (slightly clasping), 1.5–2.0 in. long. **FLOWERS:** Ray flowers **blue or lavender**, 8–16, to 0.5 in. long; **disk flowers pale yellow; involucral bracts** narrow, 0.2–0.4 in. long, **overlapping, silky**; heads radiate, about 0.75 in. wide, in a narrow, elongated, terminal cluster. September–October. **FRUITS:** Brown achenes, 0.1 in. long; pappus a tuft of white bristles, 0.3 in. long. **WHERE FOUND:** Dry, open, sandy areas, from NY, south to KY, LA, and FL. Widely scattered across TN. Occasional. *Symphyotrichum concolor.* **SIMILAR SPECIES:** BARRENS SILKY ASTER (*A. pratensis*) is a southeastern U.S. species with **larger flower heads** spaced farther apart and **spreading floral bracts**. Dry, open areas and barrens from VA and KY, south to FL and TX. In TN, in Decatur, Coffee, Cumberland, and Roane counties. Rare. August–September. *Symphyotrichum pratense.*

NOTES: Aster is the Greek word for "star," referring to the shape of the flower heads; *concolor* means "of one color." • Members of the *Aster* genus have flower heads that include yellow disk flowers that often change to purple and are surrounded by rays that vary from white to blue or purple. Plants of the *Aster* genus are so similar and numerous that identification to species is often difficult. There are 34 *Aster* species listed for TN.

JERRY DROWN

White Wood Aster
Aster divaricatus var. *divaricatus*

GENERAL: Colonial perennial herb, 12–36 in. tall, spreading by rhizomes; nearly smooth, **zigzag stems**. **LEAVES:** Alternate, toothed, lower leaves heart-shaped, petioled, 2–4 in. long, upper stem leaves reduced in size. **FLOWERS:** Ray flowers white, **10 or fewer**, 0.4–0.6 in. long; **disk yellow**, about 0.2 in. wide; involucral bracts 0.2–0.3 in. long, rounded at the tip, overlapping; heads radiate, in a flat or rounded corymb. July–October. **FRUITS:** Smooth to sparingly hairy achenes; pappus a tuft of white bristles. **WHERE FOUND:** Dry woods. A mostly northeastern species extending south in the uplands to northern GA and northern AL. In TN, from the Eastern Highland Rim eastward, also Hardin County. Frequent. *Eurybia divaricata.* **SIMILAR SPECIES:** LOWRIE'S ASTER (*A. lowrieanus*) has toothed, heart-shaped **leaves with winged petioles**; white or whitish rays. Woods. Middle and East TN. Occasional. July–September. *Symphyotrichum lowrieanum.* **WHORLED WOOD ASTER** (*A. acuminatus*) has toothed, **lanceolate leaves** arranged so they **appear whorled**; white or whitish rays. Woods. Blue Ridge of East TN. Infrequent. July–October. *Oclemena acuminata.* Both are northeastern U.S. species extending south in the uplands to GA.

NOTES: Herbal legends claim that Shakers used asters in a paste to improve their complexions, and ancient Greeks put them to use as an antidote for snakebites. • Asters symbolize elegance and refinement and were considered the flower of love.

Stiffleaf Aster • *Aster linariifolius*

GENERAL: Erect, colonial perennial herb, 12–24 in. tall, from a stout root crown, rarely rhizomatous; clumped **stems are wiry, stiff-hairy, mostly unbranched**. **LEAVES:** Alternate, numerous, **stiff, linear, entire**, 0.5–1.5 in. long, with a single prominent vein. **FLOWERS: Ray flowers blue to violet**, 10–20, broad, showy, to 0.5 in. long; **disk yellow or reddish**, 0.25–0.5 in. wide; heads radiate, several, solitary at the ends of flower stalks. September–October. **FRUITS:** Hairy achenes; pappus of 2 types of bristles, long inner and short outer. **WHERE FOUND:** Dry prairies, rocky ledges, open woods, and other dry sites, throughout the eastern U.S. In TN, from the Western Highland Rim eastward, also McNairy and Carroll counties in West TN. Occasional. *Ionactis linariifolius*. **SIMILAR SPECIES:** BUSHY ASTER (*A. dumosus*) is a **branched, bushy plant**; usually **smaller, pale blue to white ray flowers**; linear, **bract-like leaves on the flowering branches** are much reduced compared to those on the main stem. Mesic to dry areas throughout the eastern U.S. and TN. Common. August–October. *Symphyotrichum dumosum*.

DENNIS HORN

NOTES: The bluish flowers of **Stiffleaf Aster** and **Bushy Aster** attract butterflies and bees. Asters are sometimes called Michaelmas Daisies and Christmas Daisies because they bloom late in the year. Michaelmas (the Feast of St. Michael) is a church festival celebrated on September 29th.

New England Aster • *Aster novae-angliae*

GENERAL: Perennial herb, 2–6 ft. tall, with a stout root crown or thick, short rhizome; clustered stems, usually with spreading hairs. **LEAVES:** Alternate, sessile, **entire, lanceolate**, 1–4 in. long, with pointed **lobes at the base that conspicuously clasp the stem**. **FLOWERS: Ray flowers violet, rose, or magenta**, showy, more than 50, to 0.8 in. long; **disk yellow**, 0.6–0.8 in. wide; **involucral bracts** spreading, green to purplish, **sticky, glandular**; heads radiate, borne in a leafy, many-headed panicle. August–October. **FRUITS:** Achenes with dense, silky hairs obscuring the nerves; pappus a tuft of hair-like bristles. **WHERE FOUND:** Moist meadows and thickets in

THOMAS G. BARNES

most of the U.S. Thinly spread across TN. Occasional. *Symphyotrichum novae-angliae*. **SIMILAR SPECIES:** The following asters all have violet or blue (sometimes white) rays, heart-shaped leaves, and are found in woods and clearings in the eastern U.S.: LARGELEAF ASTER (*A. macrophyllus*) has **toothed basal leaves, 5–8 in. wide**, and is **glandular in the inflorescence**. Middle and East TN. Occasional. August–September. *Eurybia macrophylla*. HEARTLEAF ASTER (*A. cordifolius*) has a **smooth stem and smaller toothed leaves with a deep notch at the base**. Throughout TN. Frequent. August–October. *S. cordifolium*. SHORT'S ASTER (*A. shortii*) has **smooth stems and narrow, entire leaves**. Middle and East TN. Frequent. August–October. *S. shortii*. WAVYLEAF ASTER (*A. undulatus*) has a **hoary stem** and rough leaves that are wavy margined or slightly toothed with **winged petioles that clasp the stem**. Middle and East TN. Frequent. August–November. *S. undulatum*.

NOTES: Compared to other native asters, the flowers of **New England Aster** tend to be more numerous and have a more intense purple color. • New England Aster is a critical late-season nectar plant for butterflies, especially Monarchs, that stock up for their long migration to Mexico.

Southern Prairie Aster
Aster paludosus ssp. *hemisphericus*

GENERAL: Smooth perennial herb, 12–24 in. tall, from stout rhizomes. **LEAVES:** Alternate, **widely spaced on the stem**, **thick**, **linear**, 2–6 in. long, usually concentrated toward the base of the plant. **FLOWERS: Ray flowers blue or violet**, showy, 15–30, 0.6–1.0 in. long; **disk yellow**; involucre bell-shaped to hemispheric; heads radiate, 1–2 in. wide, in a long, raceme-like inflorescence, with flower heads borne in leaf axils. August–October. **FRUITS:** Smooth to slightly hairy achenes; pappus a tuft of hair-like bristles. **WHERE FOUND:** Barrens, roadsides, and open woods, less often in moist to wet sites. A southern species from FL to TX, extending north to KY and MO. West and Middle TN, also Hamilton and Rhea counties in East TN. Frequent. *A. hemisphericus*, *Eurybia hemispherica*. **SIMILAR SPECIES:** AROMATIC ASTER (*A. oblongifolius*) has hairy or sticky stems that are stiff and bushy, to 36 in. tall; rough, stiff, toothless, **oblong leaves**, 1–3 in. long, are **slightly clasping**; flower heads 1–2 in. wide; 15–40 blue or purple rays. Open, dry places. Widespread across the central U.S. and in Middle and East TN. Occasional. September–October. *Symphyotrichum oblongifolium*.

NOTES: **Southern Prairie Aster** is also known as **Tennessee Aster** and **Southern Swamp Aster**. • As the common name suggests, the leaves of **Aromatic Aster** are fragrant when crushed. This species provides one of the latest displays of fall flowers.

Late Purple Aster · *Aster patens*

GENERAL: Perennial herb, 12–36 in. tall, from a stout root crown. **LEAVES:** Alternate, oblong, **entire**, **rough**, **hairy**, 1–5 in. long, the **base of each almost encircling the hairy stem**. **FLOWERS: Ray flowers deep blue or purple**, 15–25, about 0.6 in. long; **disk yellow or reddish**, 0.3–0.4 in. wide; involucral bracts glandular and/or short-hairy; heads radiate, solitary at the ends of side branches. August–October. **FRUITS:** Achenes covered with short, silky hairs; pappus a tuft of hair-like bristles. **WHERE FOUND:** Dry, open places and forests in most of the eastern U.S. Throughout TN, except for the Mississippi River Valley. Common. *Symphyotrichum patens*. **SIMILAR SPECIES:** The following asters have similar flower heads and lanceolate leaves that clasp the stem: SMOOTH ASTER (*A. laevis*) has **smooth, greenish stems** and **smooth, mostly entire leaves**. Dry, open places throughout the eastern U.S. Middle and East TN. Occasional. August–October. *S. laeve*. PURPLE-STEMMED ASTER (*A. puniceus*) has **purplish stems** and **rough, toothed leaves**. Swamps and wet meadows throughout the eastern U.S. East TN and Carroll county in West TN. Infrequent. August–October. *S. puniceum*.

NOTES: In Greek mythology, the goddess Astraea was the last immortal to leave the Earth. She wept as she ascended to the heavens to become the constellation Virgo. Her tears fell as stardust, and where they touched the earth, asters sprouted. Considered a sacred plant, wreaths and bouquets were made of asters and placed in temples and shrines to honor gods and goddesses.

White Heath Aster
Aster pilosus

GENERAL: Perennial herb, 2–5 ft. tall, from a stout root crown; upper stems extensively branched. **LEAVES:** Basal leaves oblanceolate, petioled, 1–4 in. long; alternate stem leaves linear to elliptic, becoming sessile upward; **margins entire** to slightly toothed; basal and lower leaves wither early. **FLOWERS:** Ray flowers white, usually **15–30**, 0.2–0.4 in. long; **disk yellow to reddish**, 0.2–0.3 in. wide; urn-shaped involucre; heads small, radiate, on short branches with narrow, pointed, bract-like leaves; open, diffuse inflorescence may have 100 or more heads. September–October. **FRUITS:** Hairy achenes, tapered from the base upward; pappus a tuft of hair-like bristles. **WHERE FOUND:** Old fields throughout the eastern U.S. and TN. Common. *Symphyotrichum pilosum*. **SIMILAR SPECIES:** CALICO ASTER (*A. lateriflorus*), also called STAR ASTER, has **coarsely toothed leaves; flower heads have 9–14 rays; disk is usually purple**. Open, dry areas. Widespread over the eastern 1/2 of the U.S. Throughout TN. Frequent. August–October. *S. laterifolium*.

NOTES: White Heath Aster is also called **Awl Aster** because of its narrow, pointed involucral bracts, and is sometimes called **Hairy Aster**, as indicated by the species name *pilosus*, meaning "covered with long, soft hairs."

Western Daisy
Astranthium integrifolium

GENERAL: Low-growing, branched **annual**, 4–18 in. tall, with stems sparsely to densely hairy at the base. **LEAVES:** Alternate, entire, narrowly oblanceolate, to 3 in. long; upper leaves smaller, linear to elliptic. **FLOWERS:** Ray flowers pale bluish or pinkish with white bases, 8–30, 0.25–0.5 in. long; **disk yellow**, 0.2–0.4 in. wide; heads radiate, small, flat, at the tips of long side branches. April–July. **FRUITS:** Minutely glandular-hairy achenes; pappus absent. **WHERE FOUND:** Prairies, roadsides, and often sandy soils, from TX to southeastern KS, east to KY and northwestern GA. In TN, roadsides, and in limestone glades and barrens in Middle TN, also Hamilton County in East TN. Occasional. *Bellis integrifolia*.

NOTES: This plant is also known as Wild Daisy and **Entireleaf Western Daisy**, and is a good garden plant for attracting butterflies, as it is a favored early-flowering nectar plant. **Western Daisy** is a distinctive plant of Middle TN, and one of several spring-flowering members of the Aster Family (the majority flower in summer and autumn).

OTTO R. HIRSCH

Nodding Bur Marigold
Bidens cernua

GENERAL: Annual, possibly short-lived perennial, 12–40 in. tall; stems usually smooth or with short, rough hairs. **LEAVES:** Opposite, lance-linear to lance-ovate, coarsely toothed to almost entire, 2–8 in. long, 0.2–1.8 in. wide, **sessile, or often with bases grown together around the stem. FLOWERS:** Ray flowers yellow, **6–8,** to 0.6 in. long, or none; **disk yellow,** hemispheric, 0.5–1.0 in. wide; outer involucral bracts leafy, typically surpassing the disk; heads radiate or discoid, nodding (at least at maturity), at the ends of slender side branches. August–November. **FRUITS:** Achenes; **pappus of 4 barbed awns. WHERE FOUND:** Low, wet places, sometimes in shallow water, in most of temperate North America. Thinly spread across TN. Occasional. **SIMILAR SPECIES:** BEGGAR-TICKS (*B. frondosa*), also called STICK TIGHT, is a smooth **annual,** 24–48 in. tall; **leaves stalked and compound** with 3–5 toothed leaflets; generally 8 green bracts surpass the **yellow-orange rayless disks;** achenes with a **pappus of 2 barbed awns.** Damp waste places throughout the U.S. and TN. Common. August–October.

NOTES: The genus name *Bidens* is from the Latin *bis,* "two," and *dens,* "teeth," in reference to the bristled awns of the fruit. Plants in the *Bidens* genus are called Bur Marigold, Beggar-Ticks, and Harvest Lice, mostly referring to the barbed fruit, some of which have 2 curved awns, much like antennae.

DENNIS HORN

Ozark Tickseed Sunflower
Bidens polylepis

GENERAL: Annual or biennial, 12–60 in. tall; green or reddish, erect stems are branched, mostly smooth or slightly hairy; may not be distinct from *B. aristosa.* **LEAVES:** Opposite, pinnately divided or compound, 2–6 in. long, short-hairy; petioles 1–2 in. long. **FLOWERS:** Ray flowers yellow, **typically 8,** to 1 in. long; **disk yellow; outer involucral bracts** curled and twisted, usually stiff-hairy, **longer than inner bracts; heads showy,** radiate, slightly fragrant, few, on slender side branches. August–October. **FRUITS:** Achenes; **pappus of usually 2 barbed awns. WHERE FOUND:** Wet areas in full sun. A western prairie species extending eastward across TN. Frequent. **SIMILAR SPECIES:** MIDWESTERN TICKSEED SUNFLOWER (*B. aristosa*) has **outer involucral bracts shorter than the inner.** Wet areas, often in the shade, from ME to MN, south to GA and TX. Throughout TN. Common. August–November. SPANISH NEEDLES (*B. bipinnata*) has **inconspicuous ray flowers;** linear, needle-like achenes with a **pappus of usually 3–4 awns.** Disturbed habitats. Widespread across the eastern U.S. and TN. Frequent. July–October.

NOTES: Ozark Tickseed Sunflower is also known as Coreopsis Beggar-Ticks and Long-Bracted Tickseed Sunflower. It is a weedy species with flowers that are popular with many kinds of insects, including bees, wasps, flies, butterflies, skippers, and beetles. The seeds are eaten by small rodents and various birds, including the Ring-Necked Pheasant, Bobwhite, Swamp Sparrow, and Purple Finch. Occasionally, the foliage is eaten by the Cottontail Rabbit.

False Aster · *Boltonia asteroides*

GENERAL: Short-lived, much-branched perennial herb, 12–40 in. tall, with or without rhizomes. **LEAVES:** Alternate, **broadly linear to lanceolate**, 2–5 in. long, progressively smaller upward. **FLOWERS: Ray flowers white, pink or purplish**, 20–30, **0.3–0.6 in. long**; disk yellow, 0.25–0.4 in. wide; involucral bracts overlapping; heads radiate, usually numerous, in an intricately branched, leafy corymb. July–October. **FRUITS:** Achenes; pappus of usually 2 well-developed awns and several minute bristles. **WHERE FOUND:** Moist to wet sites, from ME to ND, south to FL and TX. Widely scattered in West and Middle TN. Occasional. **SIMILAR SPECIES: DOLL'S DAISY (B. diffusa)** has mainly **very narrow, bract-like leaves**; more scattered, smaller flower heads with **white or lilac rays, 0.2–0.3 in. long.** Wet to moist to sometimes dry areas, from NC to southern IL, west to OK and eastern TX. Widely scattered in West and Middle TN. Occasional. July–September.

NOTES: The *Boltonia* genus was named in honor of James Bolton (1750–99), a self-taught English naturalist and natural history illustrator. • *Boltonia* species are slender, wiry, branching, perennial herbs with narrow, sessile leaves. The flowering heads are smaller than those of true *Aster* species, the rays are white or lilac, and the disk flowers are yellow. Two species are listed for TN.

Pale Indian Plantain
Cacalia atriplicifolia

GENERAL: Fibrous-rooted, perennial herb, 3–9 ft. tall; stout, **smooth, round stems** have faint raised ridges. **LEAVES:** Basal and alternate on the stem, petioled, 2–6 in. long, slightly wider than long, shallowly lobed, pale green on the upper side, whitish beneath. **FLOWERS:** Ray flowers absent; **disk flowers whitish, 5 per head**, involucral bracts 5, about 0.3 in. long; heads discoid, to 0.2 in. wide, numerous; inflorescence broadly flat-topped. June–September. **FRUITS:** Ellipsoid achenes about 0.2 in. long; pappus a tuft of hair-like bristles. **WHERE FOUND:** Woods and pastures, from NY to southern MN, south to western FL and OK. In TN, from the Western Highland Rim eastward, also in Henderson and Weakley counties in West TN. Frequent. *Arnoglossum atriplicifolium*. **SIMILAR SPECIES: GREAT INDIAN PLANTAIN (C. muehlenbergii)** has green **stems, conspicuously grooved** and slightly angled; leaves are green on the underside; 5 disk flowers per head. Open woods from NJ to southern MN, south to GA and MS. Thinly scattered across TN. Occasional. June–September. *A. muehlenbergii*. **SWEET-SCENTED INDIAN PLANTAIN (C. suaveolens)** has **halberd-shaped (hastate) leaves; 25–30 disk flowers per head.** Moist, low woods from NY to MN, south to GA. In TN, in the Western Highland Rim in Middle TN. Infrequent. July–September. *Hasteola suaveolens*.

NOTES: The leaves of **Pale Indian Plantain** are noticeably thick and leathery. In times of little rain and drought, this plant often is found wilted, but revives rapidly. In heavily wooded areas, it may not flower, but is often represented by its large basal leaves.

Nodding Thistle · *Carduus nutans**

GENERAL: Biennial, 2–7 ft. tall; **stem prickly-winged**, smooth or sparsely hairy. **LEAVES:** Alternate, pinnately lobed, to 10 in. long and 4 in. wide, smooth or hairy on the lower veins, **very spiny**. **FLOWERS:** Ray flowers absent; **disk flowers purplish**, numerous; involucres purplish, outer bracts reflexed, rigid, and spine-tipped, inner bracts softer and more erect; **heads usually solitary**, about 2 in. across, **nodding**, at the ends of long stalks. May–November. **FRUITS:** Ribbed achenes; pappus a tuft of hair-like bristles. **WHERE FOUND:** Roadsides, pastures, and waste places. Introduced from Eurasia. Now spreading across the U.S. and considered a pest. Scattered throughout TN. Frequent.

NOTES: The "thistle" genera *Carduus* and *Cirsium* share many similarities. They are mostly biennial herbs with simple, alternate, elliptic to lanceolate, prickly leaves, often pinnately lobed or dissected. The flower heads are large with spiny involucres, numerous disk flowers, usually purple to red (or yellow), and smooth achenes. The primary difference is the pappus, with feather-like bristles in *Cirsium* and hair-like bristles in *Carduus*. • The species name *nutans* means "nodding" or "drooping," in reference to the flowers that droop when mature. This plant is also known as **Musk Thistle** and Nodding Plumeless Thistle. • Each plant may produce thousands of seeds, sometimes resulting in a spiny, impenetrable thicket of thistle. This species was first discovered in Davidson County, TN, in 1942 and has been declared a **noxious weed** in many states.

DENNIS HORN

Bachelor's Button · *Centaurea cyanus**

GENERAL: Downy **annual**, 12–36 in. tall; grooved, **silky white stem**. **LEAVES:** Alternate, **linear**, mostly entire, 2–5 in. long, white-hairy when young. **FLOWERS:** Ray flowers absent; **disk flowers bright blue, pinkish (or white)**, numerous, **marginal florets enlarged and divided into sharply pointed segments**; involucres bell-shaped, 0.4–0.6 in. long, bracts fringed; heads discoid, terminating slender side branches. July–September. **FRUITS:** Shiny, blue-gray achenes, 0.2 in. long; pappus a ring of brown bristles, to 0.2 in. long. **WHERE FOUND:** Introduced from the Mediterranean. Now found along roadsides, fields, and other open places throughout the U.S. and TN, but less common in West TN and the Cumberland Plateau. Occasional. **SIMILAR SPECIES:** YELLOW STAR-THISTLE (**C. solstitialis***) has yellow **flower heads** and the **marginal florets are not enlarged**; involucral bracts with spines 0.5 in. long or more. Also naturalized from Europe; now an invasive weed of fields and waste places throughout the U.S., except the Southeast. In TN, recorded only from Davidson County in Middle TN. Rare. June–August.

ALAN S. HEILMAN

NOTES: Bachelor's Button is called Bluebottle, and more commonly **Cornflower**, because it grows wild in the grain fields of southern Europe. • When Napoleon forced Queen Louise of Prussia from Berlin, she hid her children in a cornfield and kept them entertained and quiet by weaving wreaths of these flowers. One of her children, Wilhelm, later became the first kaiser (emperor) of Germany. • The blue (also pink or white) flowers were boiled and used as a tonic and stimulant by herbalists, but contain a bitter substance called centaurin. The flowers were also used in an eyewash and made into a cordial to counteract the poison of scorpions and spiders.

Spotted Knapweed · *Centaurea maculosa**

GENERAL: Short-lived perennial herb, 12–48 in. tall; minutely roughened stems covered with downy hairs. **LEAVES:** Alternate, simple, 4–8 in. long, **pinnatifid** with linear segments, downy-hairy, minutely roughened. **FLOWERS:** Ray flowers absent; **disk flowers lavender to pinkish,** numerous, central flowers narrow, bisexual, **marginal flowers enlarged,** 0.4–0.6 in. long, falsely radiate, sterile, **with linear segments; involucres urn-shaped,** about 0.5 in. high, with overlapping, ribbed bracts tipped with a blackish fringe; heads are terminal on numerous side branches. June–October. **FRUITS:** Blackish, shiny, hairy achenes; pappus of a few short bristles. **WHERE FOUND:** Introduced from Europe. Along fields, roadsides, and waste places. Scattered throughout most of the U.S. and across TN. Frequent. **C. biebersteinii.**

MARGRET RHINEHART

NOTES: The genus name *Centaurea* is an ancient Greek name meaning "of the Centaur," which in Greek mythology is a race of half-man and half-horse famed for the gift of healing. • A single plant of this species can produce over 1000 seeds that are mostly wind dispersed but are also spread by the animals and birds that eat them. The seeds can remain viable in soil for over 5 years, germinating in a wide variety of conditions. • This plant produces a **toxin,** cnicin, in its foliage and roots, which when released retards the growth of surrounding plants. This allows **Spotted Knapweed** to spread more rapidly with less competition for sun, water, and nutrients.

Oxeye Daisy · *Chrysanthemum leucanthemum**

GENERAL: Rhizomatous perennial herb, 12–30 in. tall, with smooth or inconspicuously hairy stems. **LEAVES:** Mainly basal, narrowly spatulate, 2–6 in. long, **usually lobed and toothed,** becoming linear and reduced in size upward on the stem. **FLOWERS:** Ray flowers white, 15–35, 0.5–0.8 in. long; **disk yellow,** 0.5–0.8 in. wide; involucral bracts narrow, brown-margined; heads radiate, **showy,** solitary at the ends of leafless flower stalks. May–October. **FRUITS:** 10-ribbed achenes; pappus a short crown or absent. **WHERE FOUND:** Introduced from Europe. Now naturalized in temperate North America. Fields and roadsides throughout most of North America and TN. Common. **Leucanthemum vulgare.**

JERRY DROWN

NOTES: The genus name *Chrysanthemum* is Greek for "golden flower," though the species name *leucanthemum* means "white flower." Notice that this plant is called a daisy, along with Painted Daisy and Shasta Daisy, which are also *Chrysanthemum* species. • Vast displays of **Oxeye Daisy** can be found along roadsides in TN in late May to early June. • Historically, infusions of the petals and leaves have been made into wine and medicine, and the dew collected from them was taken to promote longevity. Oxeye Daisies are used freely in many countries, except Italy, where they are associated with the dead and funerals and are not accepted in any other context.

Green-and-Gold
Chrysogonum virginianum var. *australe*

GENERAL: Low-growing perennial herb to **5 in. tall**, with hairy stems and leaves; **mat-forming, stoloniferous. LEAVES:** Opposite, ovate, 1–3 in. long, hairy, petiolate, tip acute, base truncate, margins have shallow teeth. **FLOWERS: Ray flowers bright yellow,** usually **5, broad,** 0.3–0.6 in. long; **disk bright yellow,** 0.3–0.4 in. wide; involucres with 5 wide outer bracts, 0.2–0.4 in. long, and 5 smaller inner bracts; heads radiate, 1.0–1.5 in. across, solitary or few on slender flowering stalks. March–July. **FRUITS:** Flattened, black to brown achenes; pappus a 5-lobed crown. **WHERE FOUND:** Rich woods from NC and TN, south to FL and LA. In TN, in Polk, Scott, Claiborne, and Greene counties. Rare. *C. virginianum* var. *brevistolon*. **SIMILAR SPECIES:** The more northern variety of **GREEN-AND-GOLD** (*C. virginianum* var. *virginianum*) grows in **clumps to 16 in. tall** and is **not stoloniferous.** Woodlands from NY to KY, south to SC. Not yet recorded in TN. March–July.

NOTES: The genus name *Chrysogonum* originates from the Greek *chrysos,* "golden," and *gonu,* "knee," referring to the yellow rays and bent stem (a misnomer). • **Green-and-Gold** is rare in the wild but can be seen frequently in gardens. It spreads rapidly, rooting wherever a runner touches the ground at a leaf node, is easy to grow, and makes a bright addition to any garden or woodland edge. • This genus has only one species.

Chicory • *Cichorium intybus**

GENERAL: Perennial herb, 1–5 ft. tall, from a long taproot; freely branched stems have **milky sap. LEAVES:** Alternate, oblong, 3–10 in. long, toothed or pinnately lobed, becoming smaller and entire upward on the stem; basal leaves typically withered at flowering time. **FLOWERS: Ray flowers blue (rarely white),** to 1 in. long, 5 teeth at the tip; disk flowers absent; involucre cylindric, 0.4–0.6 in. long; heads ligulate, 1–3 in upper leaf axils, usually **open only in the morning.** June–October. **FRUITS:** Achenes; pappus of many minute scales. **WHERE FOUND:** Introduced from Eurasia and naturalized along roadsides, and in fields and disturbed areas throughout the U.S. and TN. Occasional.

NOTES: The genus name *Cichorium* is a Greek and Latin name of Arabic origin; *intybus* is from the Egyptian *tybi,* meaning "January," the month in which it was normally eaten. • This plant originated in southern Europe and western Asia. • The young leaves can be eaten raw in salads or cooked, and the light blue ray flowers can be pickled and added to salads. It is also called Coffeeweed for the roots, which are roasted and ground as a coffee substitute or flavoring. **Chicory** contains vitamins A, B, C, and K, as well as rutin (a bioflavonoid), proteins, and minerals.

KURT EMMANUELE

HUGH NOURSE

Carolina Thistle, Spring Thistle
Cirsium carolinianum

GENERAL: Slender, fibrous-rooted **biennial herb, 2–5 ft. tall; stem without wings,** smooth or softly hairy when young. **LEAVES:** Stem **leaves few,** alternate, 3–6 in. long, 1 in. wide, smooth above but **white-woolly below, margins spiny** or with irregular lobes, reduced in size upward; basal leaves similar but larger. **FLOWERS:** Ray flowers absent; **disk flowers pink-purple,** numerous; involucres 0.6–0.8 in. high, bracts appressed, only outer bracts have short spines; heads discoid, solitary to several at ends of long stalks. May–June. **FRUITS:** Smooth achenes; pappus a tuft of plumose hairs. **WHERE FOUND:** Open woodlands and dry soil from southern OH and southern MO, south to GA and TX. In TN, in the Western Highland Rim and from the Cumberland Plateau, eastward. Occasional.

THOMAS G. BARNES

NOTES: *Cirsium* is the Greek name of a thistle used for healing varicose veins known as *kirsion*, from *kirsos*, "swollen veins." • This plant provides seeds for birds, such as goldfinches, and a home for the caterpillar of the Thistle, or Painted Lady, butterfly. The prickly "wings" (bracts) protect the flowers from predators, such as ants, as well as people who try to pick them.

Field Thistle • *Cirsium discolor*

GENERAL: Stout **biennial,** 3–7 ft. tall, the **stem leafy,** hairy, **without wings. LEAVES:** Alternate, elliptic, 4–8 in. long, reduced in size upward, smooth or slightly scabrous above, **white-woolly below, deeply pinnately lobed, very spiny. FLOWERS:** Ray flowers absent; **disk flowers pink-purple,** numerous; involucres 1.0–1.5 in. tall, bracts appressed, outer and middle bracts with distinct spines; heads discoid, few to many, on leafy stalks, with the **uppermost leaves just below the head.** July–October. **FRUITS:** Smooth achenes; pappus a white tuft of plumose bristles. **WHERE FOUND:** Open woodlands, thickets, bottoms, and pastures, from Quebec to Manitoba, south to GA and LA. Throughout TN. Frequent. **SIMILAR SPECIES:** TALL THISTLE (**C. altissimum**) grows to **9 ft. tall; leaves only toothed to shallowly lobed,** with smaller, weaker spines. Fields and clearings throughout most of the eastern U.S. In TN, from the western Highland Rim, eastward, also Carroll County in West TN. Occasional. July–October.

NOTES: The young shoots, stems, leaves, and flower receptacles of almost all thistles can be eaten either raw or cooked. The seeds, however, contain alkaloids, which can be **toxic** if eaten. • Many thistles are not only nectar plants for butterflies, but are also used as host plants.

KATHY WALLACE

DENNIS HORN

Swamp Thistle · *Cirsium muticum*

GENERAL: Coarse **biennial**, 3–7 ft. tall, with branching stems and several stout roots. **LEAVES:** Basal and alternate on the stem, ovate to elliptic, 4–10 in. long, 1–2 in. wide, **pale green underside**, deeply pinnately lobed into lanceolate or oblong, entire, lobed or dentate segments, weakly spiny; reduced in size upward. **FLOWERS:** Ray flowers absent; **disk flowers purple, pink or lavender** (rarely white), **large**; **involucres 1.0–1.4 in. tall**, sticky bracts lack spines; heads discoid, inflorescence well branched. July–October. **FRUITS:** Smooth achenes; pappus a tuft of plumose bristles. **WHERE FOUND:** Swamps, wet meadows, and moist woods throughout most of the eastern U.S. In TN, thinly scattered from the Western Highland Rim, eastward. Occasional. **SIMILAR SPECIES:** CANADA THISTLE (**C. arvense***) is a colonial **perennial** herb; **green lower leaf surfaces**; more numerous, **smaller flower heads (involucre less than 0.8 in. tall)**; bracts either lack spines or bear only very weak ones. A **noxious weed** of fields and pastures introduced from Eurasia into the northern U.S. and southern Canada. A major problem to eradicate because of its habit of spreading from creeping roots. In TN, thinly scattered from the Western Highland Rim, eastward. Infrequent. July–August.

NOTES: The Swamp Metalmark butterfly feeds only on **Swamp Thistle**, which has led to the butterfly's threatened status. • Owing to the invasiveness of **Canada Thistle**, it is illegal in 37 states to have it growing on one's land.

DENNIS HORN

Bull Thistle · *Cirsium vulgare**

GENERAL: Weedy biennial, 3–7 ft. tall; **stem with spreading hairs, conspicuously spiny-winged from extended leaf bases. LEAVES:** Alternate, elliptic, lower leaves 3–12 in. long and 1–4 in. wide, upper leaves smaller, leaf surface rough above and thinly hairy below, **pinnately dissected, strongly spiny**; bases extend down the stem. **FLOWERS:** Ray flowers absent; **disk flowers purple**, numerous; involucres 1.0–1.5 in. tall, appressed to spreading **bracts, all have distinct, yellowish spines**; heads discoid, few to many on leafy stalks. June–October. **FRUITS:** Smooth achenes; pappus plumose and tan. **WHERE FOUND:** Introduced from Eurasia. Pastures, roadsides, and waste ground. Widely established throughout the U.S. Scattered throughout TN. Frequent. **SIMILAR SPECIES:** SPINY THISTLE (**C. horridulum**), also called YELLOW THISTLE, has **large** yellowish, tan, or purple heads to 2 in. wide; involucre, to 2 in. tall, is surrounded by a whorl of narrow, strongly **spiny leaves**. Sandy soils and roadsides. Chiefly a Coastal Plain species found from ME to FL to TX. In TN, in Stewart, McNairy, Hardin, Wayne, Henderson, Decatur, and Bradley counties. Infrequent. May–August.

NOTES: The Scots Thistle (*Onopordum acanthium*) is the national emblem of Scotland. Legend says that a Viking invader stepped on a thistle and yelled, alerting the Scots and allowing them to defend themselves from the Norsemen. The superstition continues today that whoever wears the thistle will be safe from harm.

Mistflower
Conoclinium coelestinum

DAVID DUHL

GENERAL: Perennial herb, 1–3 ft. tall, spreading from rhizomes; stem short-hairy, becoming hairier and more glandular in the inflorescence. **LEAVES:** Opposite, **broadly ovate-deltoid** to heart-shaped, 2–4 in. long, 1–2 in. wide, palmately veined, short-hairy to smooth, tips acute, margins crenate-serrate, bases broadly tapering to heart-shaped; petioles shorter than blades. **FLOWERS:** Ray flowers absent; **disk flowers blue-purple, 35–70;** involucral bracts awl-shaped, purple-tipped, nearly smooth, about 0.2 in. long; heads discoid, numerous in terminal corymbs. July–October. **FRUITS:** Glandular achenes less than 0.1 in. long; pappus a tuft of whitish bristles. **WHERE FOUND:** Moist woods, wet meadows, and other low areas, from NY to IL and NE, south to FL and TX. Throughout TN. Common. *E. coelestinum.* **SIMILAR SPECIES:** PINK THOROUGHWORT (*Fleischmannia incarnata*) has **pink-purple flowers,** with **fewer flowers (18–24) per head;** stems are typically weak, giving the plant a lax habit. Moist woodlands and thickets, from VA to southern IL to OK, south to FL and TX. Throughout TN. Common. August–October. *E. incarnatum.*

NOTES: The species name *coelestinum* means "heavenly," in reference to the color of the flowers. **Mistflower** is often grown in gardens, although it can become a pest because of its long, white, creeping underground stems and wind-dispersed fruits.

Horseweed · *Conyza canadensis*

DENNIS HORN

GENERAL: Weedy annual, 1–5 ft. tall; stem normally unbranched to the inflorescence. **LEAVES:** Alternate, numerous, hairy, stem leaves **linear** to narrowly elliptic, 1–4 in. long, **lower leaves soon deciduous. FLOWERS:** Ray flowers white or pinkish, 25–40, **inconspicuous,** mostly concealed by involucral bracts; disk about 0.1 in. wide, few-flowered; involucres 0.10–0.15 in. long, bracts overlapping; **heads radiate, tiny, numerous,** in panicles terminating the stem. July–October. **FRUITS:** Yellowish, shiny, ribbed achenes, about 0.05 in. long; pappus a tuft of hair-like bristles. **WHERE FOUND:** Roadsides, fields, and waste places throughout the U.S., southern Canada, and across TN. Frequent. *Erigeron canadensis.* **SIMILAR SPECIES:** DWARF FLEABANE (*C. ramosissima*) is **shorter, to 12 in. tall, diffusely branched** from near the base. Weed of dry fields and waste places throughout the central U.S. In TN, thinly spread from the Cumberland Plateau westward. Occasional. July–September. *E. divaricatus.*

NOTES: Horseweed is also called Bitterweed, Colt's Tail, Hogweed, and Squaw Weed. The young leafy seedlings are boiled and eaten in Japan. The leaves have a sharp flavor and an aromatic taste similar to tarragon. • Native Americans used Horseweed when in flower as a diuretic and to treat diarrhea and internal hemorrhages.

JERRY DROWN

Lobed Tickseed
Coreopsis auriculata

GENERAL: Hairy perennial herb, 8–24 in. tall, with erect or ascending stems, leafy below; often **forms colonies via stolons. LEAVES:** Mostly basal, petioled, ovate to **broadly elliptic, to 3 in. long** and 1.6 in. wide, **usually with a pair of small lateral lobes at the base of the blade. FLOWERS: Ray flowers 8, yellow,** to 1 in. long, tips deeply 4-lobed; **disk yellow,** 0.3–0.6 in. wide, corollas 5-toothed; about 8 outer involucral bracts to 0.4 in. long; heads radiate, solitary or few on long leafless stalks. April–June.

FRUITS: Achenes with narrow wings; pappus of 2 tiny, deciduous scales. **WHERE FOUND:** Open woods across most of the southeastern U.S. In TN, from the Eastern Highland Rim, eastward, also Sumner County. Occasional. **SIMILAR SPECIES:** LANCELEAF COREOPSIS (**C. lanceolata**), also know as LANCELEAF TICKSEED, lacks stolons; longer, narrower leaves, 8 in. long, 0.8 in. wide, mostly **near the base of the usually smooth plant; larger flowers** to 2.5 in. across. Dry, open, often sandy soils. Most of the central and eastern U.S. Widespread across TN. Frequent. April–June. HAIRY TICKSEED (**C. pubescens**) is generally **hairy and leafy throughout**; leaves are more rounded. Sandy woods from VA to southern IL to KS, south to FL and TX. Scattered across TN. Occasional. June–September.

NOTES: The species name *auriculata* means "with basal lobes, shaped like a mouse ear," in reference to the ear-like lobes at the base of the leaves, and gives **Lobed Tickseed** another common name, **Mouse Ear Coreopsis.** • An orange to reddish orange dye can be obtained from the flowers and stems of Lobed Tickseed.

OTTO R. HIRSCH

Whorled Coreopsis
Coreopsis major

GENERAL: Rhizomatous perennial herb, 20–36 in. tall, with hairy stems. **LEAVES:** Opposite, with several sets along the stem, sessile, hairy, **compound with 3 narrow, elliptic leaflets,** 1–3 in. long, the leaves appearing as **whorls of 6. FLOWERS: Ray flowers 8, yellow,** 0.6–1.0 in. long, may be slightly toothed; **disk yellow,** about 0.3 in. wide; outer involucral bracts 0.2–0.3 in. long, about equaling inner bracts; heads radiate, 1–2 in. across, in a loosely branched corymb. June–July. **FRUITS:** Black, narrowly winged achenes; pappus of minute, inconspicuous awns. **WHERE FOUND:** Dry, open forests from NY to IN, south to FL and LA. Middle and East TN, also Carroll County in West TN. Frequent.

NOTES: This species is also called **Greater Coreopsis** in recognition of its large (for coreopsis) flowers and tall stems. • *Coreopsis* flowers have heads with 7–10 (usually 8) yellow rays, each typically with 3–6 teeth at its tip. The flower buds are usually spherical. The plants are generally smaller and more delicate than sunflowers (*Helianthus* spp.) and wingstems (*Verbesina* spp.), and most flower earlier. Eight species are found in TN.

Garden Coreopsis
Coreopsis tinctoria

GENERAL: Taprooted **annual**, 1–3 ft. tall, with smooth, **leafy**, abundantly branching stems. **LEAVES:** Opposite, 2–4 in. long, **very narrow (linear)** segments, **1–2 times pinnatifid. FLOWERS:** Ray flowers yellow, reddish brown at the base, 8, 0.4–0.8 in. long; **disk reddish brown**, 0.2–0.5 in. wide, corollas 4-toothed; heads radiate, 1.5–2.0 in. wide, in a loosely branched corymb. June–September. **FRUITS:** Black, wingless achenes; pappus absent. **WHERE FOUND:** Open and disturbed sites. Native to the Great Plains, south to TX and LA, but widely cultivated, escaped, and irregular throughout the U.S. Widely scattered in TN. Frequent.

MIRIAM WEINSTEIN

NOTES: This plant is also called Golden Tickseed, Rocky Mountain Flower, and **Plains Tickseed**. Another name, **Calliopsis**, is New Latin for "having beautiful eyes," referring to the flower's reddish central disk. It is the only TN *Coreopsis* with reddish brown at the base of each yellow ray. • Native Americans used this plant to make a root tea to induce vomiting and to treat diarrhea. A red dye was extracted from the ray flowers.

Tall Coreopsis · *Coreopsis tripteris*

GENERAL: Perennial herb, often 8–9 ft. tall (**our tallest coreopsis**), from a short rhizome; solitary stems, usually smooth and somewhat glaucous. **LEAVES:** Opposite, **petioled, each divided into 3 narrowly elliptic leaflets**, 2–4 in. long. **FLOWERS:** Ray flowers 8, yellow, 0.5–1.0 in. long, rounded at tips; **disk yellow, turning brown**, to 0.4 in. wide, corollas 5-toothed; involucre with usually 8 narrow, spreading outer bracts about 0.1 in. long and broader, longer, appressed inner bracts; heads radiate, 1.0–1.5 in. across, in a loosely branched corymb. July–August. **FRUITS:** Brown achenes with narrow wings; pappus absent. **WHERE FOUND:** Thickets and meadows throughout most of the central and eastern U.S. Throughout most of TN, but largely absent from the Ridge and Valley and the Blue Ridge of East TN. Frequent.

NOTES: The genus name *Coreopsis* is from the Greek *koris*, which means "bedbug," and *opsis*, meaning "similar to," referring to the appearance of the hard, flat, insect-like fruits. • Early pioneers reportedly stuffed their mattresses with the seeds to repel bedbugs and fleas. • The nectar of *Coreopsis* flowers feeds butterflies, and the seeds are favored by finches and sparrows. • The arrangement of involucral bracts in this plant is typical for most *Coreopsis* species.

DENNIS HORN

DENNIS HORN

Tall Flat-Topped White Aster
Doellingeria umbellata

GENERAL: Large, bushy perennial herb, 3–7 ft. tall, from well-developed rhizomes; stems smooth or nearly so. **LEAVES:** Alternate, sessile, entire, narrow, linear to lanceolate or elliptic, 2–6 in. long, with prominent, fine veins beneath. **FLOWERS:** Ray flowers white, 7–14, 0.2–0.3 in. long; disk flowers pale yellow when young, 20–40; heads radiate, 0.5–0.75 in. wide, numerous, in a **dense corymb**, rounded or flat-topped. August–October. **FRUITS:** Softly hairy achenes; pappus a cluster of hair-like bristles, outer bristles shorter and inner bristles longer. **WHERE FOUND:** Roadsides, fields, and edges of woodlands. A northern species from Newfoundland to ND, extending south in the uplands to GA and northern AL. Scattered across TN, but found mostly on the Eastern Highland Rim and Cumberland Plateau. Occasional. *Aster umbellatus*. **SIMILAR SPECIES:** APPALACHIAN FLAT-TOPPED WHITE ASTER (*D. infirma*) is smaller, to 4 ft. tall, with an **open cluster of fewer heads**; 5–12 white rays, 0.6–0.8 in. long; wider, more rounded leaves; smooth achenes. Open woodlands from MA to KY, south to FL and MS. Widely scattered across Middle and East TN. Frequent. August–October. *A. infirmus*.

NOTES: Tall Flat-Topped White Aster is also commonly known as **Parasol Whitetop**, in reference to the umbrella-like inflorescence. • The *Doellingeria* genus has only 3 species, all native to eastern North America. This genus was recognized as distinct from the *Aster* genus in the late 1800s and early 1900s, but subsequently was again included in the *Aster* genus until recently.

DENNIS HORN

Pale Purple Coneflower
Echinacea pallida

GENERAL: Perennial herb, 24–40 in. tall, from a strong taproot; coarse hairs on stems and leaves. **LEAVES:** Mostly basal, petioled, 4–8 in. long, narrow, coarsely hairy, **lacking teeth, parallel-veined**. **FLOWERS:** Ray flowers **pale lavender (to pinkish or white)**, 13–21, **drooping**, narrow, 1.5–3.0 in. long; **disk purplish, conic**, to 1.2 in. wide, **greenish white pollen**; spiny bracts longer than corollas; heads radiate, solitary. June–July. **FRUITS:** Quadrangular achenes; pappus a short, toothed crown. **WHERE FOUND:** Dry, open places. Scattered from ME to NE, south to GA and TX. In TN, in Montgomery, Coffee, and Franklin counties. Rare.

NOTES: The genus name *Echinacea* comes from the Greek *echinos*, "hedgehog" or "sea urchin," referring to the prickly bracts of the flower head; *pallida* means "pale." Other common names are Black Susan, Comb Flower, Droops, and Scurvy Root. This plant was given the name Snakeroot because it was used as an antidote for snakebite and other venomous bites and stings. • *Echinacea* species are similar to those of the genus *Rudbeckia*, but have purplish or pink rays. They are mainly found in the midwestern prairies, but are scattered eastward. Four *Echinacea* species occur in TN. **Pale Purple Coneflower** is closely related to **Prairie Purple Coneflower** (p. 339), which has distinctly **yellow pollen**.

Purple Coneflower
Echinacea purpurea

BILL M. CAMPBELL, MD

GENERAL: Perennial herb, 24–36 in. tall, with hairy stems; from a stout root crown or short, stout rhizome. **LEAVES:** Alternate, petioled, **lanceolate**, 2–6 in. long, **large-toothed**, mostly hairy, tapering to a sharp point. **FLOWERS: Ray flowers purplish, reflexed**, 15–20, 1–2 in. long; **disk orange**, 0.6–1.4 in. wide, spiny bracts; heads radiate, solitary. June–October. **FRUITS:** 4-angled achenes; pappus a short, bluntly toothed crown. **WHERE FOUND:** Moist woods and prairies, from NY to WI and KS, south to FL and TX. Sometimes escapes from cultivation. Thinly scattered across Middle and East TN, also McNairy County in West TN. Occasional.

NOTES: The rhizomes of many *Echinacea* species were commonly used by Native Americans to treat infections, chronic wounds, fever sores, eczema, and to relieve pain, swelling, and inflammation. Today, many commercial pharmaceuticals contain *Echinacea*, and its immunostimulatory properties have been confirmed by scientific studies.

Prairie Purple Coneflower
Echinacea simulata

DNH/MILO PYNE

GENERAL: Perennial herb, 24–36 in. tall, from a stout root crown or rhizome; stems and leaves coarsely spreading-hairy. **LEAVES: Mostly basal**, petioled, 4–8 in. long, narrow, **parallel-veined, without teeth. FLOWERS: Ray flowers pink (to purplish)**, 13–21, narrow, **drooping**, 1.5–3.0 in. long; **disk purplish, conic**, to 1.2 in. wide, spiny bracts, **yellow pollen**; heads radiate, solitary. June–July. **FRUITS:** 4-angled achenes; pappus a short, toothed crown. **WHERE FOUND:** Cedar glades and dolomite bluffs from southeastern MO and southern IL, south to central TN. In TN, only in Rutherford County. Rare.

NOTES: All coneflowers were once classified in the genus *Rudbeckia*. However, the purple coneflowers were reclassified because of their distinctly different structure, with spiny bracts (chaff) among the disk flowers. • This species is closely related to **Pale Purple Coneflower** (p. 338), which has distinctly greenish white pollen. • The dead flower heads of coneflowers are often visited by goldfinches, which feed on the seeds.

Tennessee Coneflower
Echinacea tennesseensis

GENERAL: Perennial herb, 24–36 in. tall, from a stout root crown or short rhizome; stem and leaves coarsely spreading-hairy. **LEAVES:** Mostly basal, petioled, 4–8 in. long, narrow, **parallel-veined, without teeth**. **FLOWERS:** Ray flowers purplish (to pinkish to white), 8–15, to 2 in. long, narrow, **spreading, pointing slightly forward or upward**; disk dark purplish, to 1.2 in. wide, **yellow pollen**; heads radiate, solitary. May–October. **FRUITS:** 4-angled achenes; pappus a short, toothed crown. **WHERE FOUND: Endemic** to the cedar glades of Davidson, Rutherford, and Wilson counties in the Central Basin in TN. Rare.

NOTES: This species was the first plant from TN to qualify as a federally endangered species. It is found nowhere else in the world except the Central Basin of the state. The extreme endemism of this species may be partially explained by the inability of its seeds to be easily dispersed from one open cedar glade to others nearby. • The consistent upward or forward pointing ray flowers aid in the identification of this species. The ray flowers rarely, if ever, appear reflexed or bent back.

KURT EMMANUELE

Leafy Elephant's Foot
Elephantopus carolinianus

GENERAL: Fibrous-rooted perennial herb, 12–36 in. tall; stems densely hairy, usually highly branched. **LEAVES: Basal leaves few or absent**; stem leaves alternate, well developed, broadly elliptic to obovate, 4–10 in. long, 1–4 in. wide, softly hairy beneath, margins crenate; leaves are reduced in size upward. **FLOWERS:** Ray flowers absent; **disk flowers pale pink to lavender, 5-lobed**, 2–5, arranged in a circle and **resembling ray flowers**; involucres about 0.4 in. high, with 4 pairs of alternating bracts, bracts acuminate and thinly hairy with a resinous coating; heads discoid, in compact clusters with **usually 3 leafy, triangular-ovate bracts at the base, resembling a single head**, at the ends of spreading stem branches. August–September. **FRUITS:** Ribbed achenes; pappus of 5 slender bristles with dilated, narrowly triangular bases. **WHERE FOUND:** Open, dry woods from NJ to KS, south to FL and TX. Throughout TN. Common. **SIMILAR SPECIES: DEVIL'S GRANDMOTHER** (**E. tomentosus**), also known as **ELEPHANT'S FOOT**, has a **rosette of large basal leaves that lie flat on the ground**; stem leaves are greatly reduced, usually to small bracts. Open woods throughout the southeastern U.S. and TN. Frequent. August–September.

LUIS C. PRIETO, JR.

NOTES: The large lower leaves provide the inspiration for the common name of "elephant's foot." When trying to identify elephant's foot species, look for the distinctive pale pink to lavender flowers, located in compact clusters within the 2–3 leafy bracts.

Pilewort
Erechtites hieraciifolia

DENNIS HORN

GENERAL: Robust, **rank-smelling**, fibrous-rooted, **weedy annual**, 2–8 ft. tall; erect, smooth stems, sometimes with spreading hairs. **LEAVES:** Alternate, 2–8 in. long, irregularly lobed, sharply serrate with stiff teeth; lower leaves mostly oblanceolate and stalked; upper leaves mostly elliptic, sessile or clasping. **FLOWERS:** Ray flowers absent; **disk whitish**, 0.2–0.4 in. wide; involucral bracts, 0.4–0.6 in. long, tinted reddish purple; heads discoid, **cylindric**, numerous, in clusters terminating the stem and branches. August–September. **FRUITS:** 10–12-ribbed achenes, about 0.1 in. long; pappus a tuft of soft, **bright white bristles** that carry each achene on the wind. **WHERE FOUND:** Old fields, open woods, and disturbed places, from Newfoundland to FL, west to SD and TX, also on the West Coast. Throughout TN. Common. *E. hieracifolia*.

NOTES: This plant is often abundant in fire-swept areas, thus its other common names, **Fireweed** and **American Burnweed**. • Though the young leaves may be added to salad or cooked as greens, the offensive odor of the herbage may suggest that a taste for this plant must be acquired.

Common Fleabane, Philadelphia Fleabane
Erigeron philadelphicus

STANLEY SIMS

GENERAL: Biennial to short-lived hairy perennial herb, 12–30 in. tall. **LEAVES:** Basal leaves narrowly oblanceolate, 2–6 in. long, coarsely toothed; stem leaves alternate, narrower, smaller, with **bases clasping the stem**. **FLOWERS:** Ray flowers white to pink to pale rose-purple, **usually more than 150**, 0.2–0.4 in. long; **disk yellow**, 0.3–0.6 in. wide; heads radiate, 0.5–1.0 in. across, usually numerous, in a corymb. April–July. **FRUITS:** Slightly compressed, ribbed achenes; pappus a tuft of hair-like bristles. **WHERE FOUND:** Occupies a variety of habitats. Widespread in North America. Throughout TN. Common. **SIMILAR SPECIES:** The following fleabane species are weedier, with **heads having fewer than 100 white ray flowers**, and lanceolate **leaves that do not clasp the stem.** DAISY FLEABANE (*E. annuus*) has **stems with long, spreading hairs** and **numerous toothed leaves.** Disturbed areas in the central and eastern U.S. May–October. **LESSER** DAISY FLEABANE (*E. strigosus*) has **stems with short, appressed hairs** and **fewer, mostly entire leaves.** Disturbed areas throughout most of the U.S. May–August. Both species are found throughout TN. Common.

NOTES: Native Americans used **Common Fleabane** to treat menstrual problems and bad vision, as a diuretic, and as a poultice for headaches. • Fleabanes are downy, often weedy herbs with alternate, sessile leaves. The flower heads have yellow disks and numerous, very narrow, white rays. Most begin flowering in spring. There are 4 species in TN.

DENNIS HORN

Robin's Plantain · *Erigeron pulchellus*

GENERAL: Hairy perennial herb, 8–24 in. tall, from a fibrous root crown, **spreading by runners**, often forming colonies. **LEAVES:** Basal leaves hairy, oblanceolate, 1–5 in. long, rounded teeth, tapering to a narrow base; stem leaves alternate, ovate to lanceolate, progressively smaller upward. **FLOWERS:** Ray flowers white to pale lilac to violet, **50–100**, 0.4–0.6 in. long; **disk yellow**, 0.4–0.8 in. wide, corollas about 0.2 in. long; heads usually 2–5, terminating the hairy stem. April–June. **FRUITS:** Shiny, ribbed achenes; pappus a tuft of tan bristles with minute, downward-pointing barbs. **WHERE FOUND:** Along roadsides and streambanks throughout the eastern U.S. In TN, from the Western Highland Rim eastward, also Hardin, Shelby, and Haywood counties in West TN. Common.

NOTES: The genus name *Erigeron* is from the Greek words *eri*, "early," and *geron*, "old man," referring to the early flowering phenology and hairiness being reminiscent of an unshaven old man. • When burned, fleabanes were reputed to drive away flies, gnats, fleas, or "any venomous thing." It was once common practice to hang fleabane inside houses to rid them of fleas and bedbugs.

DENNIS HORN

Tall Thoroughwort
Eupatorium altissimum

GENERAL: Perennial herb, 2–6 ft. tall, from branching rhizomes; stems stout, solid, densely soft-hairy throughout. **LEAVES:** Opposite, elliptic-lanceolate, 2–6 in. long, 0.3–1.2 in. wide, **palmately 3-nerved**, serrate above the middle, tapering toward the tip and base, with resinous dots below. **FLOWERS:** Ray flowers absent; **disk flowers 5, white to cream-colored**; involucral bracts rounded, overlapping; heads discoid, about 0.25 in. high, numerous, in flat-topped corymbs, 4–8 in. across. August–October. **FRUITS:** Resinous-glandular achenes; pappus a tuft of white bristles. **WHERE FOUND:** Open woodlands and fields from NY to southern MN, south to FL and TX. In TN, from the Western Highland Rim, eastward, also in Weakley County in West TN. Occasional. **SIMILAR SPECIES:** SMALLFLOWER THOROUGH-WORT (*E. semiserratum*) has **smaller flower heads**; leaves are toothed above the middle with **lateral veins emerging from the mid-vein rather than the base**. Low, wet woods and clearings from VA and MO, south to FL and TX. In the southern counties of Middle and West TN. Infrequent. July–September.

NOTES: The genus *Eupatorium* was named after Mithridates Eupator, king of Parthia, 132–63 BCE, who discovered the medicinal uses for *Eupatorium* species. The species name *altissimum* means "towering," though this species is not as tall as some plants in this genus. • *Eupatorium* species are perennial herbs, mostly with simple leaves, opposite or whorled, entire or toothed, often glandular below. The inflorescences are flat-topped or rounded corymbs with numerous small heads (under 0.5 in. high) composed of discoid (tubular), bisexual flowers with a whitish (or purplish) pappus and overlapping bracts. There are 17 species in TN.

Dog Fennel · *Eupatorium capillifolium*

GENERAL: Perennial herb, 3–6 ft. tall; **stems shaggy-hairy,** especially above. **LEAVES:** Opposite below, alternate above, 1–3 in. long, 2–4 times pinnately divided into **very narrow (filiform) segments. FLOWERS:** Ray flowers absent; **disk flowers greenish white, 3–6;** involucre smooth, with acute outer bracts and longer, acuminate inner bracts; **heads discoid, numerous, tiny (0.1 in. long),** in a long panicle. September–October. **FRUITS:** Achenes; pappus a tuft of cream-colored bristles. **WHERE FOUND:** Open woods, fields, and pastures. A mostly Coastal Plain species found from NJ to FL and TX, and in the interior to MO and KY. Scattered across TN, mostly in the southern counties. Occasional. **SIMILAR SPECIES:** YANKEE WEED (*E. compositifolium*), also called DOG FENNEL, has **wider leaves (linear, but not filiform).** Fields, pastures, and sandy soils. Primarily a Coastal Plain species found north to KY and AR. Recorded only from Knox County in TN. Rare. September–October.

NOTES: It has long been reputed that an extract of **Dog Fennel** is effective against insect bites. This species can be quite aggressive in areas with disturbed ground.

DENNIS HORN

Hollow Joe-Pye Weed · *Eupatorium fistulosum*

GENERAL: Robust perennial herb, 3–7 ft. tall; **stems smooth, purple-glaucous and hollow. LEAVES: In whorls of 4–7,** lanceolate, 4–12 in. long, petioled, pinnately veined, smooth to slightly hairy below, tapering to tip and base, margins crenate. **FLOWERS:** Ray flowers absent; **disk flowers pink to purple, usually 5–7;** involucral bracts rounded to acute; heads discoid, small, numerous; inflorescence **large, dense, rounded, corymb** with densely hairy branches. July–September. **FRUITS:** Achenes less than 0.25 in. long; pappus a tuft of purplish bristles. **WHERE FOUND:** Wet meadows and marshes throughout the eastern U.S. and TN. Frequent. **SIMILAR SPECIES:** SWEET JOE-PYE WEED (*E. purpureum*) has a **smooth, green, solid stem,** purple only at the nodes; **leaves in whorls of 3–4; heads with 4–7 flowers.** Calcareous, open woods in the eastern U.S. Widespread in TN. Frequent. July–September. SPOTTED JOE-PYE WEED (*E. maculatum*) has **solid stems, purple-spotted** or deep purple, **seldom glaucous; inflorescence flat-topped** with many flowers; **heads with 10–16 flowers.** Moist, calcareous soils in the northern U.S. Thinly scattered in TN. Infrequent. July–September. STEELE'S JOE-PYE WEED (*E. steelei*) is similar to *E. purpureum* but the **stem is spreading glandular-hairy.** Mountain woods of KY, VA, NC, and East TN. Infrequent. July–September.

NOTES: Joe-Pye weeds were widely used during the 19th century to treat kidney stones and fever. Joe Pye was an herb doctor in colonial times who advocated the medicinal use of plants that he had learned from Native Americans. The story goes that Joe Pye used species of *Eupatorium* to treat spotted fever and diarrhea.

JERRY DROWN

JERRY DROWN

Hyssopleaf Thoroughwort
Eupatorium hyssopifolium

GENERAL: Erect perennial herb, 20–40 in. tall; stems rough-hairy, especially above. **LEAVES: Usually in whorls of 4** but occasionally in 3s, opposite or alternate, simple, linear to narrowly elliptic, 1–3 in. long, 3-veined, rough-hairy beneath, especially on the veins, entire or with a few teeth, tapering toward the tip and base, with resinous dots below; **conspicuous clusters of tiny leaves in leaf axils. FLOWERS:** Ray flowers absent; **disk flowers 5, white to cream-colored**; involucral bracts rounded to acute; heads discoid, about 0.25 in. high, numerous, in a broad, flat-topped corymb. August–October. **FRUITS:** Resinous-glandular achenes; pappus a tuft of white bristles. **WHERE FOUND:** Open woodlands, barrens, and fields, usually sandy soil, from MA to MO, south to FL and TX. Throughout TN. Frequent. **SIMILAR SPECIES:** JUSTICE WEED (*E. leucolepis*) has white, slender-tipped involucral bracts; **opposite, narrow leaves folded lengthwise**; small flower heads. Wet meadows. A Coastal Plain species ranging from MA to TX. In TN, known only from Coffee County. Rare. July–October.

NOTES: Herbal folklore endows **Hyssopleaf Thoroughwort** with many curative powers, including that of an antivenin to be used against the "bite of reptiles and insects by bruising and applying to the wound," as reported by Jacobs and Burlage in their *Index of Plants of North Carolina with Reputed Medicinal Uses* (1958).

DENNIS HORN

Boneset· *Eupatorium perfoliatum*

GENERAL: Erect perennial herb, 2–5 ft. tall; **stems shaggy-hairy.** **LEAVES:** Opposite, **bases united around the stem (connate-perfoliate)**, lanceolate, 3–8 in. long, 0.6–1.8 in. wide, resin-dotted, pinnately veined, sparsely hairy on the upper surface, densely hairy beneath, tips acuminate, margins crenate-serrate. **FLOWERS:** Ray flowers absent; **disk flowers white, usually 9–23**; involucral bracts acute to acuminate, hairy, glandular, often white-margined; heads discoid, numerous, in a flat-topped corymb with opposite, soft-hairy branches. August–October. **FRUITS:** Resinous-glandular achenes; pappus a tuft of white bristles. **WHERE FOUND:** Bottomland woods, wet meadows, and other low places throughout the eastern and central U.S., southeastern Canada, and TN. Frequent.

NOTES: This plant was given the name **Boneset**, because it relieved "the deep-seated pain in the limbs" caused by influenza (*King's American Dispensatory*, 1898). Other common names include Ague Weed, Feverwort, Indian Sage, Sweating Plant, and Wild Isaac. • The leaves and flowers were widely used by Native Americans and European settlers to induce nausea and vomiting, as well as for treating fevers, epilepsy, arthritis, malaria, and other ailments. • Some *Eupatorium* species are called "thoroughworts" because the stem of the most renowned species, Boneset, appears to grow through the leaves.

Roundleaf Thoroughwort
Eupatorium rotundifolium

JERRY DROWN

GENERAL: Perennial herb, 1–5 ft. tall, from a short rhizome or root crown; stems short-hairy. **LEAVES: Opposite, ovate to cordate,** sessile or nearly so, 1–4 in. long, 0.4–2.4 in. wide, palmately veined, softly hairy and glandular on both surfaces, tips acute, margins crenate to serrate, bases broadly tapering to truncate. **FLOWERS:** Ray flowers absent; **disk flowers 5, white;** involucral bracts acute to obtuse, softly hairy and glandular, often white-margined; heads discoid, numerous, in a flat-topped **corymb with opposite, hairy branches.** July–September. **FRUITS:** Resinous-glandular achenes; pappus a tuft of white bristles. **WHERE FOUND:** Woodlands, fields, and meadows, from ME to MO, south to FL and TX. Widespread across Middle and East TN. Frequent. **SIMILAR SPECIES: HAIRY THOROUGHWORT** (*E. pilosum*) is very closely related (sometimes considered a variety), but is distinguished by the **narrower, ovate-lanceolate leaves**; upper leaves and **inflorescence branches tend to be alternate.** Wetter habitats from NY to FL, west to KY and LA. In TN, from the Eastern Highland Rim, eastward. Occasional. August–September.

NOTES: *Eupatorium* species are food plants for a wide variety of butterflies. Thoroughworts add masses of tiny white flowers to fields and roadsides in late summer.

Late-Flowering Thoroughwort
Eupatorium serotinum

DENNIS HORN

GENERAL: Perennial herb, 2–6 ft. tall; stems densely soft-hairy, especially above. **LEAVES:** Opposite, distinctly petioled, lanceolate to ovate, 2–8 in. long, 0.6–4.0 in. wide, palmately nerved, sparsely hairy, with resinous dots below, tips acuminate to acute, margins sharply serrate, bases tapered. **FLOWERS:** Ray flowers absent; **disk flowers white, 9–15;** involucral bracts rounded to acute, white-margined, overlapping; heads discoid, about 0.25 in. tall, numerous; inflorescence a flat-topped corymb with gray, hairy branches. August–October. **FRUITS:** Resinous-glandular achenes; pappus a tuft of white bristles. **WHERE FOUND:** Moist to dry open woods, fields, and waste places throughout the central and eastern U.S. Throughout TN. Common.

NOTES: Aptly, the species name *serotinum* means "late in flowering or ripening." This plant is also known as **Late-Flowering Boneset.**

Upland Boneset
Eupatorium sessilifolium

General: Single-stemmed, erect perennial herb, 2–6 ft. tall; stem hairy at the top, but **smooth below the inflorescence. Leaves:** Opposite, sessile, narrowly lanceolate, 3–6 in. long, **rounded at the base**, tapering to a pointed tip, **margin finely toothed**, 1 main vein. **Flowers:** Ray flowers absent; **disk flowers 5–6, white; involucral bracts blunt-tipped**; heads discoid, small, densely clustered in a flat-topped corymb. July–September. **Fruits:** Achenes, 0.2 in. long; pappus a tuft of whitish bristles, 0.3 in. long. **Where Found:** Woodlands, usually sandy, acidic soils, from NH to MN, south to GA and AR. Throughout Middle and East TN, also Madison County in West TN. Frequent. **Similar Species:** WHITE-BRACTED THOROUGHWORT (*E. album*) has **hairy lower stems**; **leaves coarsely toothed with a tapering base**; **white-margined involucral bracts tapering to a narrow tip**. Dry, open woods, fields, and meadows from NY to IN, south to FL and LA. In TN, from the Western Highland Rim, eastward, also Henry County in West TN. Frequent. July–September.

Notes: The species name *sessilifolium* from *sessile*, "stalkless," and *folium*, "leaf," refers to the stalkless leaves. • German researchers have reported that some *Eupatorium* species contain immunologically active polysaccharides (a type of carbohydrate).

Mississippi Valley Flat-Topped Goldenrod
Euthamia leptocephala

General: Rhizomatous, smooth perennial herb, 16–40 in. tall, upper stem branched; plant **sparsely resinous. Leaves:** Alternate, sessile, entire, **linear**, 1–3 in. long, 10–20 times as long as wide, **1–3-nerved, inconspicuously resin-dotted. Flowers:** Ray flowers yellow, **10–14**, short; **disk flowers yellow, 3–5**, about 0.15 in. long; involucre cylindric, 0.2 in. long; heads small, numerous, in a flat-topped corymb. August–October. **Fruits:** Hairy, several-nerved achenes; pappus a tuft of white capillary bristles. **Where Found:** Open, moist sites in southern MO to KY, south to TX and western FL. In TN, in Coffee, Lincoln, Obion and Shelby counties. Rare. *Solidago leptocephala*. **Similar Species:** GREAT PLAINS FLAT-TOPPED GOLDENROD (*E. gymnospermoides*) is **copiously resinous**. Open, moist to dry areas, from the Great Plains, scattered eastward. In TN, in Hardeman, Lawrence and Coffee counties in TN. Rare. August–October. *S. gymnospermoides.* COMMON FLAT-TOPPED GOLDENROD (*E. graminifolia*) has somewhat **wider leaves, the larger usually 5–7-nerved**, and **larger heads with 20–35 flowers.** Open, moist ground in the northern U.S., widely scattered southward. In TN, primarily from the Cumberland Plateau, westward. Occasional. August–October. *S. graminifolia.*

Notes: *Euthamia* species, also called "grassleaf goldenrods," generally have erect stems that bear linear, grass-like leaves, with 1–7 well-developed veins and flower heads borne in clusters.

Firewheel, Blanket Flower
*Gaillardia pulchella**

DENNIS HORN

GENERAL: Freely branched **annual** or short-lived perennial, 6–24 in. tall; stems with **glandular hairs**. **LEAVES:** Alternate, hairy, narrowly oblanceolate, 1–3 in. long, variable, toothed, pinnately lobed, or entire. **FLOWERS: Ray flowers bright reddish purple, usually yellow-tipped**, 0.4–0.8 in. long; **disk purplish**, 0.4–1.0 in. wide; involucre broadly bell-shaped; heads radiate, showy, solitary, terminating stem branches. May–September. **FRUITS:** Pyramidal achenes with a tuft of long hairs at the base; pappus of 5–7 awned scales. **WHERE FOUND:** In western prairies and sandy soils in the South, over most of the U.S., except the Northwest. Not native to TN, but occasionally escapes from cultivation. In TN, reported only from Warren and Roane counties. Rare.

NOTES: The genus is named in honor of Gaillard de Charentonneau, an 18th-century French patron of botany. • The name **Blanket Flower** refers to this plant's frequent occurrence in large, spreading colonies. *Gaillardia* species are commonly called "Indian blankets." These plants are popular in cultivation as the flowers last a long time.

Rabbit Tobacco, Sweet Everlasting
Gnaphalium obtusifolium

JERRY DROWN

GENERAL: Annual or winter annual, 12–36 in. tall; **stem white-woolly. LEAVES:** Alternate, numerous, sessile, very woolly, linear-lanceolate, 1–3 in. long. **FLOWERS:** Ray flowers absent; **disk flowers whitish or yellow**, 75–125, **fragrant; involucre off-white to purple-tinged**, bell-shaped, with several rows of overlapping bracts; heads discoid, numerous, about 0.25 in. tall, in dense terminal clusters. August–October. **FRUITS:** Smooth achenes; pappus of **separate capillary bristles. WHERE FOUND:** Old fields, pastures, sandy waste places, and open woods throughout the central and eastern U.S. and TN. Common. ***Pseudognaphalium obtusifolium.*** **SIMILAR SPECIES: PURPLE CUDWEED** (*G. purpureum*) is a smaller plant with **brown or purplish bracts** surrounding more sparse heads; spatulate or oblanceolate leaves; **capillary pappus bristles** on the achene are **united at the base.** Sandy soil and waste places throughout the U.S. and TN. Common. April–October. ***Gamochaeta purpurea.*** **HELLER'S CUDWEED** (*G. helleri*) has **greenish, glandular, sticky stems**. Dry, sandy soils in the southeastern U.S., scattered northward. In TN, in Franklin, Grundy, Roane, Blount and Polk counties. Rare. August–October. ***Pseudognaphalium helleri.***

Notes: Rabbit Tobacco is also known as **Catfoot**, Balsam, Fuzzy-Guzzy, and Moonshine. It is also called Feather Weed because impoverished people used the flower heads to fill beds, as a substitute for feathers. Four species are listed for TN.

Lanceleaf Gumweed
Grindelia lanceolata

GENERAL: Taprooted **biennial** or short-lived perennial herb, 12–48 in. tall. **LEAVES:** Alternate, mostly lanceolate, 1.5–4.0 in. long, margins usually with **bristle-tipped teeth**. **FLOWERS:** Ray flowers yellow, 15–30, 0.4–0.6 in. long; disk yellow, 0.4–0.8 in. wide; **involucral bracts slightly resinous**, slender, loose and spreading but **not reflexed** or markedly overlapping; heads radiate, terminating the stems and branches. June–September. **FRUITS:** 4-angled, nerved achenes; pappus of 2 deciduous awns. **WHERE FOUND:** Dry, open places, often on limestone, from OH to KS, south to AL and NM. In TN, in the Central Basin of Middle TN, also Chester, Franklin, and Knox counties. Infrequent. **SIMILAR SPECIES:** CURLYCUP GUMWEED (**G. squarrosa***) has **leaves with teeth that are blunt or rounded; involucral bracts highly resinous, distinctly reflexed at the tip** and overlapping. Dry, open sites. A northern and western U.S. species introduced into TN, in Knox County. Rare. July–September.

NOTES: The genus *Grindelia* is named for David Hieronymus Grindel (1776–1836), a professor of botany at Riga, Latvia. • **Lanceleaf Gumweed** is also called Gumplant for the resinous bracts. In late summer, look for the bright yellow flowers in the limestone cedar glades of Middle TN, a preferred habitat.

Bitterweed
Helenium amarum

GENERAL: Smooth annual, 8–20 in. tall, from a taproot; single, stout stem is much branched above. **LEAVES:** Alternate, **numerous**, linear to **linear-filiform**, 1–3 in. long, usually less than 0.1 in. wide, dotted with resinous glands. **FLOWERS:** Ray flowers yellow, **5–10**, reflexed, wedge-shaped, 0.2–0.5 in. long, with **3 lobes at the tip**; disk yellow, spherical, 0.25–0.5 in. wide; heads radiate, extending above the leaves on slender, leafless stalks. August–October. **FRUITS:** Brown, hairy achenes; pappus of 6–8 spine-tipped scales. **WHERE FOUND:** Overgrazed pastures and along roadsides, from MO to TX, introduced eastward. Throughout most of TN, generally absent from the Northeast. Frequent. **H. tenuifolium**.

NOTES: **Bitterweed** was given its name because the milk of cows that eat this plant has a bitter taste. • *Helenium* species are also called "sneezeweeds," because Native Americans used the powdered flower heads as snuff to induce violent sneezing to rid the body of evil spirits. Plants in this genus have narrow, alternate leaves with resinous glands.

KURT EMMANUELE

DENNIS HORN

Autumn Sneezeweed, Common Sneezeweed
Helenium autumnale

GENERAL: Fibrous-rooted perennial herb, 2–5 ft. tall, with **winged stems**. **LEAVES:** Alternate, numerous, **narrowly lanceolate**, mostly toothed, 1.6–6.0 in. long, 0.2–1.6 in. wide, **base extends as a "wing" down the stem; lower leaves withered at flowering**. **FLOWERS:** Ray flowers yellow, 13–21, 0.6–1.0 in. long, slightly reflexed, widely spaced, wedge-shaped, with **3 shallow lobes** at the tip; **disk yellow, hemispheric**, 0.3–0.8 in. wide; heads radiate, 1–2 in. across, numerous on leafless stalks. September–October. **FRUITS:** Light brown, hairy achenes; pappus of spine-tipped scales. **WHERE FOUND:** Low, moist places throughout the U.S. In TN, from the Western Highland Rim, eastward. Common.

NOTES: Other common names for this plant include False Sunflower, Staggerwort, Swamp Sunflower, and Yellow Star. • Native Americans reportedly made the dry, mature flower heads into a snuff that was used for colds, and an infusion of the leaves was taken as a laxative.

Purple-Headed Sneezeweed
Helenium flexuosum

GENERAL: Fibrous-rooted perennial herb, 10–36 in. tall; **stem hairy-winged** from extension of leaf bases. **LEAVES:** Alternate, sessile, mostly oblong to linear-lanceolate, 1–5 in. long, 0.2–0.8 in. wide, not much reduced upward, so **plant has leafy appearance**. **FLOWERS:** Ray flowers bright yellow, 8–13, about 0.6 in. long, 3-lobed at the tip; **disk red-brown or purplish**, mostly **spherical**, 0.3–0.6 in. wide; heads radiate, usually numerous, in an open corymb with leafy bracts. June–August. **FRUITS:** Brown, hairy achenes; pappus of spine-tipped scales. **WHERE FOUND:** Moist soil in open meadows and fields. Widespread in the central and eastern U.S. and southeastern Canada. Throughout TN, but largely absent from the Central Basin of Middle TN. Common. ***H. nudiflorum*. SIMILAR SPECIES: SHORTLEAF SNEEZEWEED (*H. brevifolium*)** has smooth **lower stems; fewer leaves** and flower heads; **rounded pappus scales**. Swamps and moist woods, from southeastern VA to TN, south to FL and LA. In TN, in Cumberland and Morgan counties. Rare. May–June.

Notes: *Helenium* species contain helenalin, a compound that is **poisonous** to various animals, but has anti-cancer properties. • **Purple-Headed Sneezeweed** is often found standing undisturbed in pastures as cows will not eat it. The best way to identify this plant is to look for the heavily winged stems and the brown, spherical disk.

HUGH & CAROL NOURSE

Narrowleaf Sunflower
Helianthus angustifolius

GENERAL: Fibrous-rooted perennial herb, 2–5 ft. tall, with crown buds and a solitary stem, highly branched and **mostly hairy**, especially below. **LEAVES:** Opposite on the lower stem, alternate upward, sessile, **linear**, 2–6 in. long, 10–30 times as long as wide, **undersides pale** and may have sessile glands, **margins revolute**. **FLOWERS:** Ray **flowers yellow**, 8–21, **narrow**, 0.6–1.2 in. long; **disk purple, flattened**, 0.6–0.8 in. wide; involucral bracts with narrow, pointed tips; heads radiate, solitary or few on long, slender stalks. August–October. **Fruits:** Dark brown achenes; pappus of 2 deciduous awns or scales. **WHERE FOUND:** Moist to wet sites, occasionally dry sites, from NY to IN and MO, south to FL and TX. Widespread across TN. Frequent.

NOTES: This species is frequently seen in the late summer along roadsides and in fallow fields and pastures throughout most of TN. • *Helianthus* species, also called "sunflowers," are mostly tall, coarse plants whose flowers have yellow, typically overlapping rays. These plants are common in western prairies and in barrens and open woods of TN. Twenty species are listed for TN.

DAVID DUHL

Common Sunflower
Helianthus annuus

GENERAL: Annual with coarse, stout, rough, branched, **hairy stems** from a taproot; cultivated varieties up to 10 ft. tall, but wild plants seldom more than 5 ft. tall. **LEAVES:** Mostly **alternate**, rough, **heart-shaped**, toothed, long-petioled, 2–8 in. long and nearly as wide. **FLOWERS:** Ray flowers yellow, 20 or more, 1–2 in. long; **disk reddish brown or yellow**, 1–2 in. or more across, to 6 in. or wider in cultivated varieties; involucre 1–4 in. wide, bracts ovate with a long, narrow tip; heads radiate, several to many, fewer and larger in domesticated varieties. July–October. **FRUITS:** Striped, finely hairy achenes; pappus of 2 deciduous awns.

WHERE FOUND: Introduced from the Great Plains and now widely naturalized elsewhere. Moist, low ground and roadsides throughout the U.S. Widely scattered across TN. Occasional.

NOTES: This plant, the state flower of Kansas, is grown for its oil-rich seeds. Native Americans used ground sunflower seeds as flour and oil from the seeds for cooking, mixing paints, and grooming their hair. Teas made from the leaves and flowers were taken for fevers, lung ailments, and insect bites. American settlers used fibers from the stalks for making cloth, and the leaves were dried and smoked like tobacco. The seeds were also ground and used as a coffee substitute. The yellow ray flowers were used to make a permanent dye.

Woodland Sunflower
Helianthus divaricatus

GENERAL: Perennial herb, 2–7 ft. tall, from long rhizomes; stems smooth, often glaucous below the inflorescence. **LEAVES:** Opposite, sessile (or nearly so), lanceolate, rough above, not glaucous beneath, 2–6 in. long, 3 veins from the broadly rounded base. **FLOWERS:** Ray flowers yellow, 8–15, 1.0–1.5 in. long; disk yellow, 0.4–0.6 in. wide; involucral bracts lanceolate, 0.4–0.6 in. long, hairy along margins, loose, often with reflexed tips; heads radiate, 2–3 in. across, usually several on stiff branches. July–September. **FRUITS:** Blackish achenes; pappus of 2 deciduous awns. **WHERE FOUND:** Dry woods and open places throughout the eastern U.S. In TN, from the Western Highland Rim eastward, also Haywood and Weakley counties in West TN. Frequent. **SIMILAR SPECIES: PALELEAF WOODLAND SUNFLOWER** (*H. strumosus*) has **thick, stalked, narrow leaves less than 1.5 in. wide,** lower surfaces pale, **base tapers.** Woods and open places throughout the eastern U.S. and TN. Frequent. July–August. **THINLEAF SUNFLOWER** (*H. decapetalus*) also has **stalked leaves** that are pale beneath, **base tapers,** but **generally over 1.5 in. wide, thin,** sharply toothed, **upper leaves usually alternate.** Moist woods and thickets in the eastern U.S. Middle and East TN. Occasional. August–October.

THOMAS G. BARNES

NOTES: The species name *divaricatus* means "spreading," referring to this plant's habit of spreading from rhizomes. • **Woodland Sunflower** is one of the most common and widespread plants in its range.

Tennessee Sunflower, Eggert's Sunflower
Helianthus eggertii

GENERAL: Perennial herb, 3–6 ft. tall, with long rhizomes; **stems smooth,** waxy, and usually **glaucous;** often forms colonies. **LEAVES:** Mostly **opposite, blue-waxy, sessile,** lanceolate, 3–6 in. long, 0.6–1.4 in. wide, entire or serrate, smooth (or nearly so) above; **undersides very smooth and strongly glaucous. FLOWERS:** Ray flowers yellow, 10–14, to 0.8 in. long; disk yellow, 0.5–0.8 in. wide; involucral bracts firm, tapering, about equaling the disk, hairy on margins; heads radiate, showy, to 3 in. across, usually few on long stalks. August–September. **FRUITS:** Achenes; pappus of 2 deciduous awns or scales. **WHERE FOUND:** Endemic to dry, rocky hills and open, silty flats of the Highland Rim and Cumberland Plateau of TN and adjacent central KY and northern AL. In TN, in Dickson, Davidson, Williamson, Maury, Lawrence, Lewis, Giles, Coffee, Franklin, and Marion counties. Infrequent.

DENNIS HORN

Notes: Although federally listed in 1997 under the Endangered Species Act as a threatened species, this plant has made a recovery and is likely to be removed from the list. Numbers have increased in specially managed sites. **Tennessee Sunflower** is more resilient than first thought and has been found growing along roadsides and under power lines.

DENNIS HORN

Stiff-Haired Sunflower
Helianthus hirsutus

GENERAL: Perennial herb, 2–6 ft. tall, from long rhizomes; **stems covered with stiff hairs. LEAVES:** Mostly **opposite, short-petioled**, lanceolate to ovate, 3–6 in. long, 0.8–2.5 in. wide, serrate to entire, 3 primary veins from the base, coarsely **hairy on both sides. FLOWERS:** Ray flowers yellow, 10–15, 0.6–1.4 in. long; **disk yellow**, 0.6–0.8 in. wide; involucral bracts slender, long-pointed, often with loose or reflexed tips, conspicuously hairy on the margins and often on the back; heads radiate, 2–3 in. across, usually several on stiff branches. July–October. **FRUITS:** Dark brown achenes, hairy toward the top; pappus of deciduous awns or scales. **WHERE FOUND:** Dry wooded or open places, especially barrens, throughout the central and eastern U.S. Throughout TN, except the Blue Ridge. Common.

Notes: Sunflowers generally face the sun. Since light inhibits growth of the stem, the side of the stem in the shade grows faster, thus turning the flower head toward the sun. • Sunflowers have been reported growing as tall as 40 feet in the Padua Botanic Garden in Italy.

DENNIS HORN

Maximilian's Sunflower
Helianthus maximiliani

GENERAL: Perennial herb, 2–10 ft. tall, with short rhizomes and crown buds; **stems with short, appressed, white hairs**, especially upward. **LEAVES:** Alternate, lanceolate, 3–8 in. long, 0.4–1.2 in. wide, short-petioled, strongly scabrous, entire or slightly toothed, **some leaves partially folded along the midrib**, pinnately veined (not 3-nerved). **FLOWERS:** Ray flowers yellow, 10–25, 1.0–1.6 in. long; **disk yellow**, 0.6–1.0 in. wide; involucral bracts narrow, firm, with short, white hairs, loose, often much exceeding the disk; heads radiate, large, showy, usually several in an elongated raceme. July–October. **FRUITS:** Brown to black, smooth achenes; pappus of 2 deciduous awns. **WHERE FOUND:** Prairies, barrens, and waste ground. Primarily from the Great Plains, but naturalized over most of the U.S. In TN, from the Western Highland Rim, eastward, as an extension of its natural range. Occasional.

NOTES: This species was named in honor of Prince Maximilian zu Wied (1782–1867), who held the rank of major general in the Prussian army before devoting his life to natural history, ethnology, and exploration. From 1832 to 1834, he traveled in North America, along the Missouri River, and spent the winter in what is now Bismarck, ND, with the Mandan and Minnetaree peoples.

Small-Headed Sunflower
Helianthus microcephalus

GENERAL: Perennial herb, 3–7 ft. tall, with crown buds and short rhizomes; **stem smooth and usually glaucous.**
LEAVES: Opposite, lanceolate to lance-ovate, 3–6 in. long, 0.8–2.0 in. wide, mostly scabrous above, resin-dotted, usually short-hairy beneath, entire or toothed; abruptly narrowed to a petiole, 0.4–1.0 in. long. **FLOWERS:** Ray flowers yellow, 5–8, 0.4–0.6 in. long; **disk yellow,** 0.2–0.4 in. wide; involucral bracts few, acuminate, smooth with hairy margins; heads radiate, **numerous, small,** on long, slender stalks. August–September.
FRUITS: Brown to black achenes; pappus of 2 deciduous awns. **WHERE FOUND:** Roadsides and woods from NJ to southern MN, south to northwestern FL and southeastern LA. Throughout TN. Common.

NITA R. HEILMAN

Notes: In North America, sunflowers are grown and sold widely as bird food, providing seeds that are high in protein and minerals. It has been said of the seeds that they were "set as though a cunning workman had of purpose placed them in very good order, much like the honeycombs of Bees" (*The Herball or General Historie of Plantes*, 1597, John Gerard).

Hairy Sunflower, Downy Sunflower
Helianthus mollis

GENERAL: Colonial perennial herb, 20–40 in. tall, from a stout rhizome; densely and **softly hairy throughout.**
LEAVES: Opposite, **sessile,** ovate to broadly lanceolate, 2–5 in. long, bases rounded or slightly heart-shaped.
FLOWERS: Ray flowers yellow, 20–30, 1.0–1.5 in. long; disk yellow, about 1 in. wide; involucral bracts lanceolate, white-hairy, glandular; heads radiate, 2.5–4.0 in. wide, few or solitary on hairy stalks. July–September.
FRUITS: Black, densely hairy achenes; pappus of deciduous awns. **WHERE FOUND:** Dry sites and prairies of the Midwest, but may be found eastward to the Atlantic Coast. Widely scattered across TN. Occasional.

Notes: The *Helianthus* genus takes its name from the Greek words *helios*, "sun," and *anthos*, "flower." In mythology, Helios, the Greek god of the sun, was raised to the sky and became the sun after being drowned by his uncles, the Titans. • The soft and densely hairy stems and leaves give **Hairy Sunflower** a silvery appearance, accounting for another common name, **Ashy Sunflower.**

DENNIS HORN

Western Sunflower
Helianthus occidentalis

GENERAL: Perennial herb, 24–48 in. tall, from rhizomes and often stoloniferous; sparsely hairy stems are mostly without leaves. **LEAVES: Mostly basal or near the base of the stem,** 2–6 in. long, ovate to lanceolate, entire, long-petioled; a few, small, opposite or 3-whorled leaves present on the largely naked upper stem. **FLOWERS: Ray flowers yellow,** 10–15, 0.6–1.2 in. long; **disk yellow,** 0.4–0.6 in. wide; heads radiate, 2–3 in. across, terminating stems and branches. August–October. **FRUITS:** Achenes; pappus of 2 deciduous awns or scales. **WHERE FOUND:** Dry soil and barrens throughout much of the eastern U.S. Thinly scattered across TN, in Weakley, Decatur, Stewart, Montgomery, Rutherford, Franklin, Bledsoe, Hamilton, Meigs, Roane, and Knox counties. Occasional.

NOTES: The species name *occidentalis* means "western," hence the common name **Western Sunflower.** • Sunflowers are native only to North America. There are about 50 species and many hybrids. • The sunflower has been called the "consummate American plant: tenacious, brash, bright, open, varied, optimistic, and cheerful, it might well be considered the true American flower" (Carlton B. Lee).

Ozark Sunflower
Helianthus silphioides

GENERAL: Perennial herb, 3–10 ft. tall, usually with **several stems** arising from a short rhizome or root crown. **LEAVES:** Opposite, 2–6 in. long, broadly ovate, hairy petioles with narrow wings are generally 1/3 or less the length of the blade; **leaves often present above the middle of the stem,** upper leaves alternate, greatly reduced in size. **FLOWERS: Ray flowers yellow,** 10–15, about 1 in. long; **disk dark purple,** 0.4–0.6 in. wide; heads radiate, to 3 in. across, showy, several on long, leafless stalks in a flat-topped corymb. July–October. **FRUITS:** Achenes; pappus of 2 deciduous awns or scales. **WHERE FOUND:** Dry, open woods, primarily in the Ozark Mountains, but extending eastward into KY and TN, south to AL and LA. In TN, as far east as the Cumberland Plateau. Occasional. **SIMILAR SPECIES: APPALACHIAN SUNFLOWER (H. atrorubens)** has **stems that are typically solitary; leaves are mostly basal** with longer petioles, more than 1/3 the length of the blade, with wings that broaden near the blade. From VA to KY and western TN, south to northern FL and southeastern LA. In TN, from the Western Highland Rim, also Henderson and Rutherford counties, and from the Cumberland Plateau, eastward. Frequent. July–October.

NOTES: The species name *silphioides* means "looks like *Silphium*," another genus in the Aster Family. • **Ozark Sunflower** is colonial. In the field, this plant is most easily identified by its leaves, which are on the lower and middle parts of the stem but reduced in size upward, the flower heads with dark centers, and the rounded involucral bracts.

Jerusalem Artichoke
Helianthus tuberosus

GENERAL: Perennial herb, 3–10 ft. tall, with well-developed, **tuberous rhizomes** and **hairy stems**. **LEAVES:** Alternate (upper) and opposite (lower), thick, rough, toothed, broadly lanceolate, 4–8 in. long, winged petioles. **FLOWERS:** Ray flowers yellow, 10–20, 1.0–1.5 in. long; disk yellow, 1.0 in. wide; involucral bracts lanceolate; heads radiate, numerous, in a typically flat-topped corymb. August–October. **FRUITS:** Mottled light and dark brown achenes; pappus of deciduous awns or scales. **WHERE FOUND:** Disturbed sites throughout most of the central and eastern U.S. and TN. Common. **SIMILAR SPECIES:** TALL SUNFLOWER (*H. giganteus*) has **rough, dull, reddish stems**; narrower, more sharply pointed leaves. Moist places in the eastern U.S. In TN, in Davidson, Rutherford and Scott counties. Rare. August–October. **SAWTOOTH SUNFLOWER** (*H. grosseserratus*) has **smooth, whitish, glaucous stems**; narrower, more sharply pointed leaves. Damp prairies in the central and northeastern U.S. In TN, in Shelby, Henderson, Carroll, Meigs, Van Buren, Scott, and Hamblen counties. Infrequent. July–October.

NOTES: Jerusalem Artichoke seems misnamed as it is different from French artichokes and has no connection to the city of Jerusalem. However, the word "Jerusalem" actually comes from the Italian word *girasole*, which means "turns to the sun." It has also been named Canada Potato and Earth Apple because of its edibility. Native Americans cultivated the plant for its large tubers, which can be eaten like potatoes.

Oxeye, False Sunflower
Heliopsis helianthoides

GENERAL: Stout, fibrous-rooted perennial herb, 2–5 ft. tall, with a **smooth, erect stem**. **LEAVES:** Opposite, ovate-lanceolate, 2–6 in. long, petioled, serrated, smooth or rough, generally shorter and wider than those of sunflowers. **FLOWERS:** Ray flowers golden yellow, 8–16, 0.6–1.6 in. long, **fertile** with a forked pistil at the base; disk yellow, 0.4–1.0 in. wide; involucres hemispheric, bracts oblong, smooth, tips spreading; heads radiate, showy, solitary or several on slender stalks. July–September. **FRUITS:** 4-angled, slightly hairy achenes; pappus absent or a few short scales. **WHERE FOUND:** Thickets, woodlands, and streambanks from the midwestern prairies to the Atlantic Coast. Widespread in TN. Frequent.

NOTES: The alternate name for this species, **False Sunflower**, suggests the resemblance of this plant to sunflowers (*Helianthus* spp.).
• Only the disk flowers of sunflowers form seeds (actually achenes), but both the disk and ray flowers of **Oxeye** plants form seeds.

DENNIS HORN

Prairie Golden Aster
Heterotheca camporum

GENERAL: Taprooted perennial herb, 16–36 in. tall, spreading by creeping rhizomes; **stems with coarse, spreading hairs**. **LEAVES:** Alternate, numerous, narrowly oblanceolate, 1–3 in. long, 0.3–0.8 in. wide, mostly entire. **FLOWERS:** Ray flowers yellow, 21–34, about 0.4 in. long; **disk yellow**, 0.5–1.0 in. wide; involucre 0.3–0.4 in. long; heads radiate, loosely clustered at the top of the stem. July–September. **FRUITS:** 6–12-nerved achenes; double pappus of capillary bristles, long inner bristles within a ring of short outer bristles. **WHERE FOUND:** Fields and roadsides. A prairie species of the Midwest, recently introduced into the southeastern U.S. Middle and East TN. Frequent and spreading. *Chrysopsis camporum*.

NOTES: Golden asters (*Heterotheca* spp.) have been placed in three genera: *Chrysopsis*, *Heterotheca*, and *Pityopsis*. They have been reclassified several times, and even for the trained botanist, it is a taxonomically difficult group. Golden asters may be identified in various manuals by a number of different names. All species described here have showy, radiate flower heads with a yellow disk and yellow rays. Seven species in these 3 genera are found in TN.

JERRY DROWN

Grassleaf Golden Aster
Heterotheca graminifolia

GENERAL: Fibrous-rooted perennial herb, 12–36 in. tall, often with stolon-like rhizomes; branched **stems covered with silky, appressed hairs**. **LEAVES:** Alternate, mostly at the base of the plant, **silvery-silky**, linear, grass-like, largest to 12 in. long, reduced upward. **FLOWERS:** Ray flowers yellow, 10–30, about 0.5 in. long; **disk yellow**, about 0.3 in. wide; involucre bell-shaped, 0.3 in. long, bracts linear, appressed, glandular; heads radiate, top- to bell-shaped, several to many, terminating the branches. August–September. **FRUITS:** Linear, tan achenes; pappus of tan bristles. **WHERE FOUND:** Dry sites, from DE to southern OH, south to FL and TX. In TN, from the Cumberland Plateau eastward, also Hardeman, McNairy, and Hardin counties in West TN. Frequent. *Chrysopsis graminifolia*, *Pityopsis graminifolia*. **SIMILAR SPECIES:** CREEPING GRASSLEAF GOLDEN ASTER (*H. adenolepis*) is **strongly stoloniferous**. Dry woodlands. Inner Coastal Plain from NC to SC and inland to TN. Polk County in East TN. Rare. August–September. Perhaps not distinct from **Grassleaf Golden Aster**. *C. adenolepis, P. adenolepis*.

NOTES: The genus name *Heterotheca* is a Greek word meaning "different case," referring to the varying achenes or "seeds"; the species name *graminifolia* means "grass-like," for this plant's linear leaves. **Grassleaf Golden Aster** is also called **Narrowleaf Silkgrass** and simply Silk Grass, because of the very soft or "silky" leaves. As a garden plant, the silver, grassy leaves provide an interesting contrast to other plants. A native plant, it tolerates drought and is adaptable to a wide variety of growing conditions.

Maryland Golden Aster · *Heterotheca mariana*

DENNIS HORN

GENERAL: Fibrous-rooted, erect, short-lived perennial herb, 8–32 in. tall, with **woolly stems**. **LEAVES:** Basal rosette, oblanceolate to elliptic, petioled, 2–6 in. long, 0.4–1.4 in. wide, **woolly with long slender hairs** when young, less hairy at maturity; stem leaves alternate, gradually reduced upward, mostly sessile. **FLOWERS:** Ray flowers bright yellow, 13–21, 0.4–0.6 in. long; **disk yellow**, 0.4–0.8 in. wide; involucre hemispheric, 0.3–0.4 in. long, bracts lanceolate, appressed, glandular; heads radiate, in a dense cluster. August–October. **FRUITS:** Reddish brown achenes; pappus of tan bristles. **WHERE FOUND:** Old fields, open woods, and dry soils, from southern NY to southern OH, south to FL and TX. Across most of TN, but generally absent from the Central Basin and counties near the Mississippi River. Frequent. *Chrysopsis mariana*. **SIMILAR SPECIES:** HAIRY GOLDEN ASTER (*H. pilosa*) is an **annual** with erect, **hairy (not woolly) stems**, 12–48 in. tall; stem leaves oblanceolate to elliptic, spreading, hairy on both surfaces, serrate, sessile, to 4 in. long, 0.2–1.2 in. wide, reduced and entire upward; 10–25 rays, 0.6–1.0 in. long; hemispheric involucres, to 0.5 in. wide; corymb-like inflorescence. Barrens, from southern VA to KS, south to FL and TX. In TN, in Lawrence, Giles, and Stewart counties. Rare. July–October. *C. pilosa*.

Notes: **Maryland Golden Aster** is similar to **Grassleaf Golden Aster** (p. 356), but has a basal rosette of woolly, wider, dark green leaves.

Ruth's Golden Aster · *Heterotheca ruthii*

GENERAL: Compact perennial herb, **less than 12 in. tall**; clustered stems are leafy up to the flower heads. **LEAVES:** Alternate, **linear**, 1–3 in. long, **basal leaves shorter than stem leaves**; **covered with silky hairs** that give a silvery appearance. **FLOWERS:** Ray flowers yellow, about 12, 0.35 in. long; **disk yellow**; involucral bracts awl-shaped, glandular; heads radiate, several, about 0.75 in. wide. September–October. **FRUITS:** Linear achenes, tapered at both ends; tan pappus bristles in a head resembling dandelion fruits, but about 1/2 as large. **WHERE FOUND:** Soil-filled cracks of boulders in areas with little shade. Endemic to the Hiwassee River and Ocoee River gorges of TN, only in Polk County. Rare. *Pityopsis ruthii*, *Chrysopsis ruthii*. **SIMILAR SPECIES:** CAMPHORWEED (*H. subaxillaris*), an erect **weedy biennial** or **annual**, 12–60 in. tall; stems are spreading-hairy, glandular above; **leaves are ovate** to oblong, toothed to almost entire, the lower stalked and upper sessile and **clasping**, 1–4 in. long, 0.4–1.2 in. wide; 15–30 yellow rays, 0.4–0.8 in. long; hemispheric involucres to 0.5 in. wide; corymb-like inflorescence; achenes of the ray flowers hairy, those of the disk smooth. Dry open areas, from NY to CA, south to FL, TX, and Mexico. In TN, in Knox, Hamilton, Shelby, Tipton, Madison, Marshall, Sumner, and Davidson counties. Infrequent. July–September.

NITA R. HEILMAN

NOTES: **Ruth's Golden Aster** is a federally endangered plant, mostly because of its restricted distribution and habitat, which has been affected by degraded water quality and controlled water levels. Other potential threats are damage from toxic chemical spills and trampling from recreational activities.

JANIE COOPER FINCH

King Devil
*Hieracium caespitosum**

GENERAL: Perennial herb, 10–36 in. tall, from rhizomes and often with short stolons; **stems with black, glandular hairs** above. **LEAVES:** Basal, sometimes 1–2 leaves low on the stem, densely and softly hairy on both sides, oblanceolate to elliptic, 3–10 in. long. **FLOWERS:** Ray flowers yellow; disk flowers absent; involucre with blackish, gland-tipped hairs; **heads ligulate, 5–30, 0.5–0.75 in. wide, in a compact corymb.** May–September. **FRUITS:** Rounded to several-angled achenes, strongly ribbed, without beak; pappus a tuft of white bristles. **WHERE FOUND:** Introduced from Europe. Fields, pastures, and roadsides. Now widespread in the northeastern U.S. and southeastern Canada, extending south in the highlands to northern GA. In northeastern TN, in Union, Sevier, Cocke, Hawkins, Sullivan, Washington, Unicoi, Johnson, and Carter counties. Infrequent. *H. pratense*.

NOTES: *Hieracium* species, also called "hawkweeds," are perennials containing milky juice, with leaves that are simple, alternate, and pinnately veined. The heads are composed entirely of 5-toothed ray flowers, and involucres are 0.3–0.4 in. tall with slightly overlapping bracts. Flowers are yellow to orange-red, with 20–40 per head. Seven species are found in TN.

THOMAS G. BARNES

Hairy Hawkweed · *Hieracium gronovii*

GENERAL: Perennial herb, 12–60 in. tall, without stolons; stems mostly solitary with long, spreading hairs, top ½ of stem usually without leaves. **LEAVES:** Basal, **hairy**, oblanceolate, 2–8 in. long; stem leaves alternate, progressively smaller upward. **FLOWERS:** Ray flowers yellow, **20–40**; disk flowers absent; involucre 0.3 in. long, often glandular; heads ligulate, about 0.5 in. wide, numerous, in a long, cylindric panicle. July–October. **FRUITS:** Achenes, 0.1–0.15 in. long, narrowed toward the top; pappus a tuft of tan bristles. **WHERE FOUND:** Dry, open woods and fields, from MI to KS and TX, eastward. Throughout TN. Common. **SIMILAR SPECIES:** PANICLED HAWKWEED (*H. paniculatum*) has mostly **smooth leaves**, evenly distributed on the stem; achenes lack tapering tip. Woods. A northeastern species extending south to GA and AL in the uplands. In TN, from the Cumberland Plateau, eastward. Occasional. July–September. ROUGH HAWKWEED (*H. scabrum*) is a rough-hairy plant with stem leaves reduced in size upward; **40–100 rays per head**. Dry, open woods. A northeastern U.S. species, found south to GA and AR. In TN, in Pickett, Morgan, Union, Jefferson, Carter, and Johnson counties. Infrequent. July–September.

Notes: The species name *gronovii* honors Johan Gronovius (1690–1762) of Leyden in the Netherlands. A physician and botanist, he was one of the celebrated scholars of his time. • Hawkweeds are visited by insects, but do not rely entirely upon them for pollination. The flowers are often self-pollinated, thus producing offspring that are a clone-like duplicate of the parent.

Rattlesnake Weed · *Hieracium venosum*

GENERAL: Perennial herb, 8–24 in. tall, **without stolons; 1–few smooth, mostly leafless stems. LEAVES:** Essentially basal, oblanceolate to elliptic, 2–6 in. long, 0.5–2.0 in. wide, **conspicuously purple-veined**, mostly smooth or with hairy margins, tips obtuse to acute, margins wavy, bases long-tapered. **FLOWERS: Ray flowers yellow**, 15–40; disk flowers absent; involucre 0.3–0.4 in. long, smooth or slightly glandular; heads ligulate, 0.5–0.6 in. wide, numerous, in a flat-topped corymb. May–July. **FRUITS:** Achenes, about 0.1–0.15 in. long; pappus a tuft of yellowish bristles. **WHERE FOUND:** Dry, open woods, from ME to MI, southward. Widespread in the eastern 1/2 of TN. Frequent. **SIMILAR SPECIES:** MOUSE-EAR HAWKWEED (*H. pilosella**) is less than 12 in. tall, **forming carpets by creeping runners;** mostly leafless **stems with spreading hairs;** leaves basal, white-woolly beneath; flower heads usually solitary, to 1 in. wide, rays yellow. Introduced from Europe. Now a weed in fields, pastures, and roadsides. In the northeastern U.S. In TN, only in Van Buren County on the Cumberland Plateau and in Sevier, Unicoi, and Johnson counties in the mountains of East TN. Rare. May–September.

OTTO R. HIRSCH

NOTES: Rattlesnake Weed is also known as Bloodwort and Veinleaf Hawkweed. The common names are derived from the pattern on the leaves, as well as from the belief that it was a reliable cure for the bite of rattlesnakes. The leaves were chewed and then applied directly to the wound.

Spotted Cat's Ear · *Hypochaeris radicata**

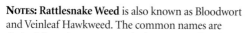

GENERAL: Perennial herb, 10–24 in. tall, from a root crown or several enlarged roots; stems are sparsely branched and mostly leafless with minute, scattered bracts. **LEAVES:** Basal, with **firm coarse hairs**, oblanceolate, **pinnatifid**, lobes rounded, 2–6 in. long, 1–2 in. wide. **FLOWERS: Ray flowers yellow**, numerous, 0.4–0.6 in. long; disk flowers absent; involucre, 0.4–0.6 in. high, has erect, overlapping, smooth or hairy bracts; heads ligulate, 2–7, showy, **dandelion-like**, about 1 in. wide, terminating the stem branches. May–September. **FRUITS:** Many-nerved achenes, usually with short beaks; pappus of barbed bristles. **WHERE FOUND:** Introduced from Eurasia. Now widely established in the U.S. along roadsides and in fields, pastures, and waste places. Scattered across TN and spreading. Occasional. *Hypochoeris radicata.*

NOTES: The genus name *Hypochaeris* is a Greek name for "cat's ear"; the species name *radicata* means "conspicuous roots." • The crisp, young leaves of this species can be eaten raw and have a pleasant flavor. The flower heads are tasty as well, and can also be eaten raw. • This plant can easily be mistaken for a dandelion or hawkweed and is best distinguished by examining the leaves and involucral bracts.

PAUL SOMERS

Two-Flowered Cynthia · *Krigia biflora*

GENERAL: Fibrous-rooted perennial herb, 8–30 in. tall, with **smooth, glaucous stems and leaves. LEAVES:** Mainly basal, oblanceolate to broadly elliptic, 2–8 in. long, 0.4–2.0 in. wide, gradually tapered to the base, blunt-tipped, margins entire to toothed or pinnately lobed; 1–2 **stem leaves are alternate, smaller, clasping,** smooth-edged. **FLOWERS: Ray flowers orangish yellow,** numerous, 0.4–0.6 in. long; disk flowers absent; involucres 0.25–0.5 in. high; heads ligulate, few, about 1 in. wide, on long, slender stalks from leaf axils. May–October. **FRUITS:** Brown, slightly ribbed achenes; pappus a tuft of 20–40 tan bristles. **WHERE FOUND:** Moist woodlands throughout the eastern U.S. and TN. Common.

NOTES: The *Krigia* genus contains annual to perennial herbs with milky juice and simple, alternate, nearly opposite or basal, pinnately veined leaves. The heads have yellow or orange ray flowers only and involucral bracts in 1 series. The beakless achenes are rounded, with several ribs; the pappus consists of scales and bristles or may be absent. Five species are found in TN.

DENNIS HORN

Oppositeleaf Dwarf Dandelion

Krigia caespitosa

GENERAL: Slender **annual,** 4–18 in. tall, with several smooth, slender, branching stems. **LEAVES:** Basal rosette, narrowly elliptic, toothed or shallowly lobed, 2–6 in. long; stem leaves alternate, **upper leaves appearing opposite. FLOWERS: Ray flowers yellow,** numerous, 0.3–0.4 in. long; disk flowers absent; involucre hemispheric, bracts 0.3–0.4 in. long; heads ligulate, 0.6–0.75 in. wide, several, solitary on long stalks from upper leaf axils. April–June. **FRUITS:** Reddish brown, obovoid achenes, 0.06 in. long; **pappus bristles absent. WHERE FOUND:** Fields and roadsides, from VA to NE, southward. Throughout TN, but more prevalent in the western ½ of the state. Frequent. ***K. oppositifolia, Serinia oppositifolia.* SIMILAR SPECIES:** MOUNTAIN DWARF DANDELION (***K. montana***) is a smooth **perennial** with **mostly basal leaves;** flower heads solitary; achenes with **15 or more pappus bristles.** Moist rock cliffs and streambanks in the mountains of NC, SC, TN, AL, and GA. In TN, only in Sevier County. Rare. May–September.

NOTES: The genus *Krigia* is named in honor of David Krieg (d. 1710), a German physician who collected plant specimens in Maryland; the species name *caespitosa* means "growing in dense clumps," in reference to the growing habit of these plants. • Unlike true dandelions (*Taraxacum* spp.), some dwarf dandelions, such as **Oppositeleaf Dwarf Dandelion,** bear more than 1 flower head on a single plant and have leafy stems that branch.

DENNIS HORN

Potato Dandelion · *Krigia dandelion*

GENERAL: Colonial perennial herb, 4–20 in. tall, from **tuberous rhizomes**; **stems smooth** and glaucous. **LEAVES:** Basal rosette, linear to narrowly oblanceolate, 2–8 in. long, 0.1–1.0 in. wide, **smooth**, glaucous, tips acute, margins entire to pinnately lobed, bases tapering. **FLOWERS: Ray flowers golden yellow**, numerous, 0.6–1.0 in. long; disk flowers absent; involucre about 0.5 in. high; **head solitary**, ligulate, showy, 1–2 in. wide. April–June. **FRUITS:** Dark brown, ribbed achenes; pappus a tuft of **20–40 tan bristles. WHERE FOUND:** Roadsides, open woods, and waste places, from NJ to IA, south to FL and TX. Throughout TN. Occasional. **SIMILAR SPECIES:** VIRGINIA DWARF DANDELION (**K. virginica**) is **annual**; **stems and leaves often hairy**; smaller flower heads, 0.5–0.75 in. wide; achenes reddish brown, ribbed, **pappus bristles 5–7**, short. Roadsides, fields, and lawns, from WI to TX, eastward. Throughout Middle and East TN, and in Henry County in West TN. Frequent. March–July.

NOTES: Potato Dandelion gets its name from its edible underground tubers, which resemble potatoes. *Krigia* species are also called "dwarf dandelions," as in **Virginia Dwarf Dandelion**, because their flower heads are smaller than those of true dandelions (*Taraxacum* spp.), and their stems and leaves are more slender.

DENNIS HORN

False Boneset · *Kuhnia eupatorioides*

GENERAL: Perennial herb, 1–4 ft. tall; stems short-hairy or nearly smooth. **LEAVES:** Alternate to nearly opposite, linear-lanceolate to elliptic-rhombic, 1–4 in. long, 0.4–1.2 in. wide, **dotted with resinous glands beneath**, sessile or lower leaves short-petioled, tips acuminate to acute, margins entire or toothed, bases wedge-shaped to rounded. **FLOWERS: Ray flowers absent; disk flowers cream-colored**, 10–12; involucral bracts lanceolate to linear, striped, overlapping; heads discoid, cylindric, 0.3–0.5 in. high, terminal in **corymb-like clusters**. August–October. **FRUITS:** Hairy achenes about 0.2 in. long, 10–20-ribbed; pappus a tuft of 20 whitish, feathery bristles. **WHERE FOUND:** Dry, open woods, glades, and barrens in most of the central and eastern U.S. Throughout TN. Frequent. *Brickellia eupatorioides*.

NOTES: The genus name *Kuhnia* honors Adam Kuhn (1741–1817), an American botanist and physician from Philadelphia, PA. • This plant resembles many *Eupatorium* species, hence the species name *eupatorioides*. Its common name alludes to the healing properties of the thoroughworts. • *Kuhnia* is often included in the genus *Brickellia*.

DENNIS HORN

THOMAS G. BARNES

Florida Blue Lettuce · *Lactuca floridana*

GENERAL: Stout **annual** or **biennial**, 2–7 ft. tall, with **milky juice**; stem smooth, usually reddish, leafy. **LEAVES:** Alternate, simple, lanceolate to triangular-ovate, 3–8 in. long, 1–4 in. wide, pinnately veined, smooth, tips pointed, margins serrate to pinnately lobed, bases tapered. **FLOWERS: Ray flowers blue (to white)**, 11–17; disk flowers absent; involucres about 0.5 in. high, bracts overlapping; heads ligulate, numerous; inflorescence long, panicle-like. June–September. **FRUITS:** Flattened, **short-beaked achenes** with several ribs on each side; pappus a tuft of white hair-like bristles. **WHERE FOUND:** Moist, open woodlands and thickets, from NY to SD, south to FL and TX. Throughout TN. Common. **SIMILAR SPECIES:** WILD LETTUCE (*L. canadensis*) lacks prickles; **pale yellow flowers; long-beaked achenes** with 1 rib on each side. Fields and roadsides across the U.S., adjacent Canada, and throughout TN. Frequent. July–September. PRICKLY LETTUCE (*L. serriola**) has **prickly foliage; yellow flowers; achenes with a thread-like beak** as long as the achene body. Introduced from Europe. Now naturalized throughout the U.S. and TN. Occasional. July–September. Frequently hybridizes with cultivated lettuce (*L. sativa*).

NOTES: The genus name *Lactuca* is Latin for "milk-giving," alluding to the milky white sap. • Common commercial lettuce is derived from *L. sativa* and its many varieties. Lettuce plants were a source of lactucarium, called "lettuce opium" because the dried sap looks and smells like opium. • The milky latex of **Wild Lettuce** was used by Native Americans as a remedy for poison ivy.

DENNIS HORN

Rough Blazing Star · *Liatris aspera*

GENERAL: Perennial herb, 2–5 ft. tall; stems short-hairy to smooth. **LEAVES:** Alternate, numerous, narrowly elliptic, short-hairy to smooth; lower leaves 4–12 in. long, 0.5–1.2 in. wide, long-petioled; upper leaves gradually reduced, becoming sessile. **FLOWERS:** Ray flowers absent; **disk flowers pinkish lavender**, 15–40; involucral bracts broadly obtuse, **margins thin, hyaline (translucent to transparent)**, whitish or pinkish, **often jagged-crispy** and **rolled inward**; heads discoid, about 0.75 in. high, sessile or short-stalked, numerous, in a spike-like inflorescence. August–October. **FRUITS:** Hairy achenes, 0.25 in. long; pappus a tuft of roughened bristles. **WHERE FOUND:** Open woodlands, barrens, and old fields, from ND to TX, east to NY and FL. In TN, mostly in the Cumberland Plateau and Ridge and Valley, thinly scattered westward. Occasional.

NOTES: Members of the *Liatris* genus, commonly called "blazing stars," are perennials that arise from thickened, corm-like rootstock. The leaves are alternate, entire, the lower larger, the upper smaller and usually sessile. Look for heads of disk flowers only, in spike-like or raceme-like inflorescences with overlapping involucral bracts. The flowers are all perfect, usually pink-purple, and the achenes are blackish, tapering from base to apex, 10-ribbed, with plumose (feather-like) or barbellate (minutely roughened) pappus bristles. Seven species are found in TN.

Cylindric Blazing Star
Liatris cylindracea

GENERAL: Perennial herb, 8–24 in. tall; stems short-hairy to smooth. **LEAVES:** Alternate, numerous, short-hairy to smooth, 4–10 in. long, 0.1–0.5 in. wide, linear to narrowly elliptic, reduced in size upward. **FLOWERS:** Ray flowers absent; **disk flowers pink-purple** (occasionally white), 10–35; **involucre cylindric, 0.5–0.8 in. high**, bracts appressed, firm, abruptly sharp-pointed; heads discoid, about 1 in. high, numerous, short-stalked or sessile, in a spike-like inflorescence. July–September. **FRUITS:** Narrow achenes to 0.3 in. long; pappus a tuft of feathery bristles. **WHERE FOUND:** Limestone glades and prairie-like barrens. A midwestern U.S. species with disjunct populations extending south to TN and AL. In TN, in Decatur, Rutherford, Franklin, Marion, Meigs, Rhea, and Roane counties. Infrequent.

NOTES: *Liatris* species are unusual because they flower from the top of the inflorescence down, rather than from the bottom up. Many species hybridize quite freely, making precise identification difficult.

HUGH NOURSE

Small-Headed Blazing Star • *Liatris microcephala*

GENERAL: Perennial herb, 12–30 in. tall, with **smooth stems. LEAVES:** Alternate, numerous, **linear, smooth**, 2–6 in. long, 0.04–0.2 in. wide, gradually reduced in size upward. **FLOWERS:** Ray flowers absent; **disk flowers lavender**, 4–5; **involucre cylindric, to 0.3 in. long**, bracts greenish, blunt-tipped, margins hyaline (translucent or transparent) and fringed; heads discoid, about 0.5 in. high, numerous, **on erect stalks** 0.1–0.6 in. long, in an elongated, raceme-like inflorescence. August–September. **FRUITS:** Achenes, 0.15 in. long, hairy along the 10 ribs; pappus a tuft of roughened bristles. **WHERE FOUND:** Open meadows, barrens, and sandy soils, from the uplands of KY to SC, GA and AL. In TN, in the Eastern Highland Rim and Cumberland Plateau, also Roane, Rhea, Hamilton, and Polk counties in East TN. Occasional.

NOTES: The species name *microcephala* is from the Greek words *micro*, "small," and *cephala*, "head," referring to the characteristic small flower heads. • The corms of some *Liatris* species were stored as winter food by Native Americans. • Butterflies frequent the pink-purple flowers.

OTTO R. HIRSCH

Dense Blazing Star
Liatris spicata

GENERAL: Perennial herb, 2–6 ft. tall; stems smooth or nearly so. **LEAVES:** Alternate, **numerous**, **linear to narrowly elliptic**, smooth or nearly so, 4–12 in. long, 0.2–0.6 in. wide, reduced in size upward. **FLOWERS:** Ray flowers absent; **disk flowers rose purple** (rarely white), 6–10 (usually 8); **involucre cylindric, to 0.4 in. long**, bracts obtuse, margins hyaline (translucent or transparent), fringed, often purplish; heads discoid, about 0.6 in. high, numerous, **sessile**, in a spike-like inflorescence. July–September. **FRUITS:** Achenes, 0.25–0.3 in. long; pappus a tuft of roughened bristles. **WHERE FOUND:** Wet or dry meadows and barrens throughout the eastern U.S. from NY to WI, southward. In TN, from the Western Highland Rim eastward, also Carroll and Shelby counties in West TN. Frequent.

NOTES: This plant is also known as Backache Root, Colic Root, Dense Button Snakeroot, Devil's Bite, **Gayfeather**, Prairie Pine, and Throatwort. Many of these common names refer to its reputed value in herbal medicine for soothing sore throats and for treating gonorrhea and other venereal diseases. In 1798, Benjamin Smith Barton wrote, "Its agreeable odour is due to Coumarin, which may be detected on the surface of its spatulate leaves." Coumarin smells like vanilla, but has a bitter taste. It was banned by the FDA as a food additive in 1940 because studies showed that it was toxic to the liver.

OTTO R. HIRSCH

Scaly Blazing Star · *Liatris squarrosa*

GENERAL: Perennial herb, 12–30 in. tall; stems smooth or hairy. **LEAVES:** Alternate, numerous, smooth or hairy, linear to narrowly elliptic, 3–10 in. long, 0.2–0.5 in. wide, somewhat reduced in size upward. **FLOWERS:** Ray flowers absent; **disk flowers lavender**, 20–45; **involucral bracts leaf-like**, lanceolate, **tips acuminate, reflexed**, firm and dark purple at flowering time, margins fringed; heads discoid, about 1 in. high, short-stalked or sessile, few or solitary in the upper leaf axils. July–August. **FRUITS:** Hairy achenes, 0.25–0.3 in. long; pappus a tuft of feathery (plumose) bristles. **WHERE FOUND:** Dry open woods and glades, often associated with limestone, from DE to SD, south to FL and TX. Throughout TN, but more common in West and East TN. Frequent.

NOTES: Blazing stars and goldenrods decorated large expanses of tallgrass prairie before the rapid conversion of the prairies to agriculture in the 1880s. Remnant prairies have been studied by Dr. Charles Allen of Louisiana State University, and in one 10-acre study area, 400–500 different plant species were found.

DENNIS HORN

Southern Blazing Star · *Liatris squarrulosa*

GENERAL: Perennial herb to nearly 5 ft. tall; **stem often softly hairy**. **LEAVES:** Alternate, smooth, lanceolate, 4–14 in. long, 0.5–2.0 in. wide, reduced in size upward. **FLOWERS:** Ray flowers absent; **disk flowers pink-purple, 14–24**; involucral bracts spreading, with broadly rounded tips; inner bracts with thin, papery margins; heads about 0.75 in. high, short-stalked or sessile, **often more than 20** in a spike-like inflorescence. July–September. **FRUITS:** Achenes, 0.15–0.25 in. long; pappus a tuft of roughened bristles. **WHERE FOUND:** Dry, open woods, roadsides, and glades, from WV to southern OH and southern MO, south to FL and TX. Widespread across TN, but more prevalent in the Western Highland Rim and southeastern counties. Frequent. **SIMILAR SPECIES:** NORTHERN BLAZING STAR (*L. scariosa*), also called **LARGE BLAZING STAR**, is usually shorter (to 3 ft. tall); **heads of 25–80 flowers, seldom more than 20 in number**. Dry, open places and barrens, from ME to WI, south to GA, MS, and AR. In TN, in Decatur, Franklin, Van Buren, Cumberland, Morgan, Roane, Polk, and Monroe counties. Infrequent. August–September.

NOTES: The species name for **Southern Blazing Star**, *squarrulosa*, means "recurved at the tip," referring to the involucral bracts. • In 1914, a passage by Melvin R. Gilmore about Native American uses of **Northern Blazing Star** reported "the corm after being chewed was blown into the nostrils of horses to enable them to run well without getting out of breath. It was supposed to strengthen and help them. The flower heads mixed with shelled corn were fed to horses to make them swift and put them in good condition."

Appalachian Barbara's Buttons
Marshallia grandiflora

GENERAL: Smooth perennial herb, 8–30 in. tall; stems single or clustered from a crown. **LEAVES:** Alternate, entire, elliptic to spatulate, 2–6 in. long, **3-nerved, mostly on the lower stem**. **FLOWERS:** Ray flowers absent; **disk flowers white to pale purple, tubular**, numerous, narrow, 5-lobed; **involucral bracts lanceolate, 0.4–0.5 in. long; heads solitary, 0.8–1.4 in. wide, terminal** on long stalks. June–August. **FRUITS:** Brownish, hairy achenes, tapered from the base to the squared tip, 0.1–0.15 in. long, 5-ribbed; pappus of 5 short, translucent scales. **WHERE FOUND:** In crevices of flooded rock shelves and along riverbanks. Historically known to grow in boggy areas. In the Appalachian region from PA, south to NC and TN. In TN, in Cumberland, Morgan, Roane, and Scott counties of the Cumberland Plateau. Rare. **SIMILAR SPECIES:** BROADLEAF BARBARA'S BUTTONS (*M. trinervia*) has stems that grow singly from short, creeping rhizomes; **leaves are distributed evenly along the stem**. Low woods and streambanks in the southeastern U.S. In TN, in Lewis, Coffee, and Grundy counties of Middle TN. Rare. May–June. **SPOONLEAF BARBARA'S BUTTONS** (*M. obovata*) has **blunt involucral bracts**. From southern VA to western FL. In TN, only in Polk County. Rare. April–June.

NOTES: **Appalachian Barbara's Buttons** is also known as **Giant Barbara's Buttons** and **Large-Flowered Barbara's Buttons**. It is listed as an endangered species in PA, KY, and TN, and as threatened in WV. In NC and MD, all previously known populations are considered extinct owing to habitat destruction.

Climbing Hempweed
Mikania scandens

GENERAL: Perennial, twining, **herbaceous vine** to 15 ft. long; stems smooth to softly hairy; often forming dense mats over herbs, shrubs, or small trees. **LEAVES:** Opposite, **deltoid-ovate**, 2–5 in. long, palmately veined, minutely glandular and occasionally hairy, tips acuminate, margins usually wavy or entire, bases heart-shaped; petioles to the length of the blade. **FLOWERS:** Ray flowers absent; **disk flowers white, pale pink or lavender**, 4; involucral bracts 4, acuminate, nearly smooth; heads discoid, about 0.1 in. high; in **compact corymbs** at the tips of long stalks (longer than leaves) from the leaf axils. July–October. **FRUITS:** Resin-dotted achenes, about 0.1 in. long; pappus a tuft of whitish bristles. **WHERE FOUND:** Moist woods and thickets, open marshy areas, and along shorelines of ponds, lakes, swamps, and reservoirs. Mostly a Coastal Plain species found from ME to FL to TX, and north in the interior to MI. Throughout West TN, thinly dispersed in Middle and East TN. Occasional.

NOTES: This plant is also called **Climbing Boneset** and twines upward in a clockwise direction. The genus *Mikania*, consisting of over 200 mostly tropical species, is named in honor of Joseph G. Mikan (1743–1814), a professor of botany in Prague. The species name *scandens* means "climbing."

Wild Quinine • *Parthenium integrifolium*

GENERAL: Perennial herb, 12–36 in. tall, with a **bitter aroma** when crushed. **LEAVES:** Basal leaves ovate to elliptic, 3–8 in. long, round-toothed, long-petioled; upper stem leaves alternate, smaller, often clasping the stem. **FLOWERS:** Ray flowers white, **5, inconspicuous**, female (pistillate), fertile; **disk white**, about 0.25 in. across, male (staminate), sterile; involucre hemispheric, 0.2 in. high, bracts hairy; heads radiate, small, numerous, in **flat-topped cluster** at the ends of the stem and branches. June–September. **FRUITS:** Blackish, obovoid, slightly flattened achenes, 0.15 in. long, 0.1 in. wide; pappus of a few small scales or absent. **WHERE FOUND:** Barrens, fields, roadsides, and dry woods, from MA to southeastern MN, south to GA and TX. Middle and East TN, also Decatur County in West TN. Frequent.

NOTES: The genus name *Parthenium* is Greek meaning "virgin," for the white flowers. • The leaves of this species were used by Native Americans as a poultice on burns, and traditionally it was thought to be useful in treating fevers similar to malaria. A study has shown that **Wild Quinine** may stimulate the immune system. **Caution** should be used because this plant may cause an **allergic reaction** or skin irritation.

Marsh Fleabane
Pluchea camphorata

GENERAL: Short-lived perennial herb, 2–5 ft. tall, with a **camphor-like odor. LEAVES:** Alternate, lance-olate, 3–10 in. long, toothed, petioled. **FLOWERS:** Ray flowers absent; **disk flowers pink or occasionally white**, numerous; involucre hemispheric, about 0.2 in. long, bracts stiff and overlapping; heads discoid, 0.1–0.2 in. wide, numerous, in rounded clusters. August–September. **FRUITS:** Tiny, densely hairy, pinkish to tan achenes; pappus a tuft of hair-like bristles. **WHERE FOUND:** Wet woods, marshes, and open reservoir shorelines, from NJ to southern IL and eastern KS, south to northern FL and TX. Throughout TN , but absent from most northeastern counties. Frequent.

NOTES: The genus *Pluchea* is named for Abbé Noël-Antoine Pluche (1688–1761), a French priest and naturalist. • Other common names such as Stinkweed and **Camphorweed** and the species name *camphorata* refer to the plant's pungent, camphor-like scent. True camphor comes from the Camphor Tree (*Cinnamomum camphora*), native to China, Japan, and Taiwan (its chief natural source). However, because the natural substance is often in short supply, camphor can also be obtained from oil of turpentine. The alcohol solution of camphor is known as spirits of camphor.

OTTO R. HIRSCH

White-Flowered Leafcup • *Polymnia canadensis*

GENERAL: Perennial herb, 30–60 in. tall; **rank smelling; upper stems hairy or glandular**; often grows in large stands. **LEAVES:** Opposite, broadly oblong, pinnately lobed, toothed, 4–12 in. long, petiole sometimes winged near the blade. **FLOWERS:** Ray flowers white, **3-lobed, few to many, fertile**, to 0.5 in. long, occasionally inconspicuous or absent; **disk pale yellow**, 0.3–0.5 in. wide, sterile; involucral bracts lanceolate, to 0.4 in. long; heads radiate, in clusters at branch tips. June–October. **FRUITS:** Mottled brown, slightly triangular achenes, **prominently 3-ribbed**; pappus absent. **WHERE FOUND:** Moist woods, especially over calcareous bedrock, from VT to MN, south to GA and AR. Middle and East TN. Frequent. **SIMILAR SPECIES: TENNESSEE LEAFCUP** (*P. laevigata*) has **smooth stems**; rays are white to cream or absent; **achenes with 4–6 ribs**. Thinly distributed in the Appalachian Plateau, the Interior Highlands, and the Coastal Plain from KY and southeastern MO, south to FL. In TN, primarily in the Eastern Highland Rim and Cumberland Plateau, thinly scattered elsewhere. Occasional. August–September.

NOTES: White-Flowered Leafcup is also called **Pale-Flowered Leafcup, Small-Flowered Leafcup**, and White Bear's Foot. • If you look closely at the disk flowers of White-Flowered Leafcup, you may see that the styles are undivided, an indication that they are sterile.

MILO PYNE

Barbed Rattlesnake Root
Prenanthes barbata

General: Perennial herb, 12–60 in. tall; stems purplish, unbranched below the inflorescence, upper stems hairy; stem exudes **milky juice** when broken. **Leaves:** Alternate, sessile, elliptic to oblanceolate, 2–4 in. long, somewhat **hairy**, variably toothed or shallowly lobed, reduced in size upward. **Flowers:** Ray flowers pinkish white, usually **11–13**; disk flowers absent; **8 principal involucral bracts**, pinkish brown, about 0.5 in. long, with **numerous stiff hairs**; heads ligulate, **bell-shaped, nodding**, inflorescence widely branched. September–October. **Fruits:** Elliptic, tan achenes; pappus a tuft of yellow bristles. **Where Found:** Prairies and floodplains, from KY, south to GA and TX. In the Western Highland Rim and Coffee County of Middle TN. Infrequent. **Similar Species:** ROAN MOUNTAIN RATTLESNAKE ROOT (*P. roanensis*) has **mostly smooth leaves**; inflorescence long and narrow; **5–6 green involucral bracts**; **5–8 yellowish ray flowers**. In the high mountains of VA, NC, and TN. In TN, only in Polk, Sevier, Greene, Unicoi, and Carter counties in East TN. Rare. August–September.

DENNIS HORN

Notes: The genus name *Prenanthes*, from the Greek *prenes*, "to face downwards," and *anthos*, "a flower," refers to the drooping flowers. The species name *barbata* means "bearded," for the stiff hairs on the flower heads of **Barbed Rattlesnake Root**.

Lion's Foot
Prenanthes serpentaria

General: Perennial herb, 2–5 ft. tall; **stems smooth** but often rough-hairy in the inflorescence. **Leaves:** Alternate, well distributed along the stem, broadly obovate, 3–6 in. long, 2–4 in. wide, mostly smooth above, usually short-hairy on the veins beneath; petioles winged, pinnately few-lobed, the lobes rounded or toothed. **Flowers:** Ray flowers yellowish white, 8–14; disk flowers absent; involucre 0.4–0.6 in. long, with **8 principal bracts** and a few long, coarse, **black-dotted hairs**; heads ligulate, nodding, at the tips of long, ascending branches; inflorescence open, panicle-like. August–October. **Fruits:** Smooth, cylindric, striated, reddish brown achenes; pappus of upwardly barbed, capillary bristles. **Where Found:** Dry mesic woods, from NH to KY, south to northern FL and MS. In TN, from the Eastern Highland Rim, eastward. Occasional. **Similar Species:** TALL RATTLE-SNAKE ROOT (*P. altissima*) has a **smooth involucre** with **4–6 principal bracts** and **5–6 ray flowers per head**. Open woods, from ME to MO, south to GA and TX Throughout TN. Frequent. August–September. **GALL-OF-THE-EARTH** (*P. trifoliolata*) has a **smooth involucre** with **7–9 principal bracts** and **9–13 ray flowers per head**. Dry woods, from ME to MI, south to GA. In the eastern ½ of TN. Occasional. August–September.

JERRY DROWN

Notes: The species name *serpentaria* means "of serpents" and refers to the historical use of the plant's milky juice as an antidote to the bite of poisonous snakes. • **Lion's Foot** is also known as **Cankerweed**, Earthgall, Joy Leaf, and Snakeweed.

False Dandelion
Pyrrhopappus carolinianus

JERRY DROWN

GENERAL: Annual or biennial, 8–36 in. tall, from a large taproot; stems and branches smooth or minutely hairy, with **milky sap**. **LEAVES:** Alternate, **simple**, oblanceolate to narrowly elliptic, 3–10 in. long, 0.4–2.5 in. wide, pinnately veined, smooth or minutely hairy; tips acute to acuminate; margins toothed to pinnatifid; bases wedge-shaped. **FLOWERS:** Ray flowers pale yellow, numerous, 0.8–1.0 in. long; disk flowers absent; involucres about 1 in. high, 1 inner series of bracts and several outer series, inner bracts with distinctive 2-lobed thickenings at the tip; **heads 1 to several** on slender stalks. June–September. **FRUITS:** Round, ribbed achenes, tapered toward each end, with a long beak tipped with short, reflexed white hairs; pappus a tuft of tan, hair-like bristles. **WHERE FOUND:** Roadsides, fields, and waste places throughout the southeastern U.S., north to MD, IN, and NE. Throughout TN. Common.

NOTES: This plant, also called Leafy False Dandelion, is similar to **Common Dandelion** (p. 383), but has stem leaves in addition to basal leaves. • **False Dandelion** is primarily visited by short-tongued bees.

Gray-Headed Coneflower
Ratibida pinnata

KURT EMMANUELE

GENERAL: Somewhat hairy perennial herb, 3–5 ft. tall, fibrous-rooted, from a woody rhizome or crown. **LEAVES:** Alternate, **pinnately compound**, deeply cut into 3–7 lanceolate leaflets, 1–2 in. long; lower leaves long-stalked; upper leaves short-stalked or sessile. **FLOWERS:** Ray flowers pale yellow, 5–10, 1–2 in. long, **strongly reflexed**; disk grayish when young, darker gray or brown with age, ellipsoid, 0.4–0.8 in. across, taller than wide; involucral bracts linear or narrowly lanceolate, few, spreading; heads radiate, several, on long, leafless stalks. June–August. **FRUITS:** Smooth, angular achenes; pappus absent. **WHERE FOUND:** Sporadically in cedar glades, barrens, and along roadsides, from southern Ontario to SD, south to GA, western FL and LA. In TN, from the Western Highland Rim, eastward, also in McNairy County. Occasional. **SIMILAR SPECIES:** LONG-HEADED CONEFLOWER (*R. columnifera*), also called MEXICAN HAT, is a prairie plant; **disk at least 2x as tall as wide**; **yellow rays** are faintly to conspicuously **marked with brownish red**. From MN to MT, south to LA and TX, introduced eastward. In TN, reported only from David-son County, but likely more widespread. June–August.

NOTES: **Gray-Headed Coneflower** is also called **Prairie Coneflower** because it is common on the midwestern prairies. Native Americans extracted a yellow-orange dye from the flowers, and made a tea from the flowers and leaves. • If you bruise or crush the flower cone of a *Ratibida* species, you may smell an anise-like aroma, which is useful for identification.

KURT EMMANUELE

Orange Coneflower
Rudbeckia fulgida

GENERAL: Variable perennial herb, 12–36 in. tall, sparsely to moderately hairy; forms large colonies through numerous stolons. **LEAVES:** Alternate, elliptic to oblanceolate, 1.5–4.0 in. long, margins entire or with a few shallow teeth, base tapering to a long petiole, gradually reduced in size and petiole length upward. **FLOWERS: Ray flowers yellow,** often **dark yellow or orange at the base,** 8–21, **0.5–0.8 in. long,** relatively blunt; **disk dark purple or brown,** hemispheric, bristly, **style forks short, blunt;** involucral bracts reflexed, 0.4–0.8 in. long; heads radiate, about 2 in. wide, long-stalked, usually solitary. July–October. **FRUITS:** Smooth, 4-angled achenes without resin dots; pappus a short crown. **WHERE FOUND:** Moist woods or open areas from MA to WI, south to FL and TX. In TN, from the Western Highland Rim eastward, also Henry and McNairy counties in West TN. Common.

NOTES: *Rudbeckia* is one of several genera called "coneflower," so named for the shape of the flower head disk. *Rudbeckia* rays are yellow and usually not as overlapping as those of sunflowers. • Native Americans used the roots of these plants to make a tea to treat worms, snakebite, and indigestion.

ROBERT VANTREASE

Black-Eyed Susan
Rudbeckia hirta

GENERAL: Biennial or short-lived perennial, 12–36 in. tall, with 1–several **bristly-hairy** stems from a root crown. **LEAVES:** Alternate, lance-ovate, **bristly-hairy;** lower leaves mostly elliptic to narrowly spatulate, 2–6 in. long, toothed or entire, with long tapering petioles; upper leaves smaller, narrower, sessile. **FLOWERS:** Ray flowers yellow, 8–21, **showy, 1.0–1.5 in. long; disk dark brown,** hemispheric, 0.5–0.8 in. wide, **style forks long, awl-shaped;** involucral bracts linear, 0.4–1.0 in. long, spreading, hairy; heads to 3 in. across, 1–several on long stalks. July–August. **FRUITS:** Blackish, angular achenes, tapering from base to tip; pappus absent. **WHERE FOUND:** Open and often disturbed sites across most of the U.S. Throughout TN. Common.

NOTES: This plant is the state flower of Maryland. • When you see a **Black-Eyed Susan,** you may think it is misnamed, because the centers are more reddish brown and not a true black. • It is pollinated by bees, wasps, beetles, flies, and many other insects, but has developed a strategic method for keeping away unwanted pests such as ants. The bristly hairs on the stems make it uncomfortable, if not impossible, for ants to pass. Few butterflies frequent this plant, but the Pearl Crescent is one species that takes advantage of the high center perch and is attracted to the yellow color.

Cutleaf Coneflower · *Rudbeckia laciniata*

JERRY DROWN

GENERAL: Perennial herb, 3–9 ft. tall, from a woody base; highly branched **stems smooth, often glaucous. LEAVES:** Alternate, to 8 in. long, petioled, **pinnately divided** into 3–7 sharply pointed lobes, uppermost leaves smaller, ovate, often entire. **FLOWERS: Ray flowers lemon yellow,** 6–16, **drooping,** to 2.5 in. long; **disk greenish yellow,** 0.4–0.8 in. wide, rounded when young, elongating with age; involucral bracts elliptic to lanceolate, 0.3–0.8 in. long, reflexed; heads radiate, several on long stalks. July–September. **FRUITS:** Brown achenes, 0.2 in. long; pappus a short crown, usually toothed. **WHERE FOUND:** Rich, moist soils, from southern Canada and throughout most of the U.S. In TN, from the Western Highland Rim, eastward, prevalent in the Appalachian Mountains, also Haywood County in West TN. Frequent.

NOTES: This species is also called **Green-Headed Coneflower.** • The genus *Rudbeckia* is named in honor of Olaf Rudbeck the Younger (1660–1740) and his father, Olaf Rudbeck the Elder (1630–1702), a Swedish botanist who taught at the University of Uppsala, Sweden. Together, they assembled a book called *Campus Elysii* (*The Elysian Fields*) that contained all the plants known at that time and was illustrated with thousands of woodcuts of the individual species. Tragically, the book was destroyed in a fire in 1702.

Sweet Coneflower
Rudbeckia subtomentosa

B. EUGENE WOFFORD

GENERAL: Perennial herb, 2–5 ft. tall, from a stout rhizome; upper stem **often downy, not bristly. LEAVES:** Alternate, **thick, firm,** petioled, deeply 3-lobed; lower leaves 3–6 in. long, upper leaves entire or toothed, with dense short hairs, especially beneath. **FLOWERS: Ray flowers bright yellow, 12–21,** 0.8–1.6 in. long; **disk dark purple or brown, hemispheric,** 0.3–0.6 in. wide; **involucral bracts sticky,** hairy, linear, **anise-scented;** heads radiate, showy, several on long stalks. August–September. **FRUITS:** 4-sided achenes with a flat base; pappus a tiny, inconspicuous crown. **WHERE FOUND:** Wet prairies and riverbanks, primarily in the Mississippi Valley from WI and MI, south to MS and TX. In TN, only in Stewart and Montgomery counties of the Western Highland Rim in Middle TN. Rare.

NOTES: Sweet Coneflower is also referred to as **Sweet Black-Eyed Susan,** and gets its common names from the flower's sweet anise scent. • The dome-shaped central disk provides nectar for butterflies and seed for goldfinches. • The flowers of **Black-Eyed Susan** (p. 370) are similar to those of **Sweet Coneflower,** but lack the sticky, scented heads. The lobed leaves of **Thinleaf Coneflower** (p. 372) are similar to those of Sweet Coneflower, but the leaves are thin and the flower heads are smaller, with only 6–12 rays.

PAUL SOMERS

Thinleaf Coneflower, Brown-Eyed Susan · *Rudbeckia triloba*

GENERAL: Short-lived, hairy perennial herb, 2–5 ft. tall; highly branched **stems usually hairy but not bristly. Leaves:** Basal leaves ovate, to 4 in. long, often 3-lobed but not deeply dissected; stem leaves alternate, **thin**, mostly toothed or entire, lanceolate, short-stalked to sessile. **FLOWERS:** Ray **flowers yellow to orange, 6–12**, 0.4–0.8 in. long; **disk dark purple or brown**, hemispheric, 0.3–0.6 in. wide; heads radiate, small, numerous, in branched clusters. June–October. **FRUITS:** Blackish achenes, equally 4-angled; pappus a tiny, inconspicuous crown. **WHERE FOUND:** Thickets and edges of damp woods throughout much of the central and eastern U.S. In TN, from the Western Highland Rim eastward, also Shelby, Haywood, Obion, and Tipton counties in West TN. Frequent.

NOTES: The species name *triloba* helps us to remember that this plant has 3-lobed leaves. However, since this plant is highly variable, this characteristic is not always reliable. Some leaves may not have lobes, and some may be toothed or smooth-edged, especially those on the upper stem. • If you see this plant in the wild, enjoy it, because the small flowers last only a short time.

MIRIAM WEINSTEIN

Rugel's Indian Plantain
Rugelia nudicaulis

GENERAL: Perennial herb, 12–20 in. tall, stems hairy and glandular above. **LEAVES:** Mostly basal, broadly ovate, 3–6 in. long, coarsely toothed, long-petioled; base may be heart-shaped, flat, or rounded; stem leaves alternate, much smaller and bract-like. **FLOWERS:** Ray flowers absent; disk pale yellow, with **protruding, 2x-forked (bifurcate) yellow stigmas**; involucral bracts 0.5 in. long; heads discoid, nodding, to 0.4 in. across. July–August. **FRUITS:** Brown, smooth, cylindric achenes, 0.25 in. long; pappus a tuft of white bristles. **WHERE FOUND:** Endemic to the Great Smoky Mountains of TN and NC. Locally abundant in forest openings at high elevations. In TN, in Blount, Cocke, and Sevier counties. Rare. *Cacalia rugelia, Senecio rugelia*.

NOTES: This plant is also called **Rugel's Ragwort** and was first placed in the ragwort genus *Senecio*, then moved to the Indian plantain genus, *Cacalia*, thus accounting for the present common name. It was finally placed in its own genus, *Rugelia*. The species name *nudicaulis* means "bare-stemmed." • This species was named for Ferdinand Rugel (1806–79), a field botanist who collected plants in the southeastern U.S. and Cuba.

Southern Ragwort, Small's Ragwort
Senecio anonymus

GENERAL: Perennial herb, 12–30 in. tall, **stem** densely and persistently **woolly at the base**, young stems sometimes slightly hairy above, but soon become smooth (glabrous). **LEAVES:** Basal leaves elliptic to oblanceolate, mostly serrate, to 12 in. long, blunt tip, base tapers to a petiole; stem leaves alternate, deeply pinnately incised, reduced upward. **FLOWERS:** Ray **flowers yellow**, 8–15, 0.2–0.3 in. long; **disk yellow**, 0.2–0.3 in. wide; involucral bracts linear, smooth, 0.2–0.3 in. long; **heads** radiate, **usually 20–100**, in a corymb-like inflorescence. May–June. **FRUITS:** Ellipsoid achenes; pappus a tuft of white bristles. **WHERE FOUND:** Uplands, meadows, pastures, roadsides, and dry open woods, from southern PA to southern IN, south to FL and MS. Throughout TN, except the northwestern counties. Common. *S. smallii, Packera anonyma*. **SIMILAR SPECIES:** **BALSAM RAGWORT** (*S. pauperculus*) has **fewer flower heads** (usually less than 20); **stem normally smooth at the base**. Moist meadows and fields. A northern species extending south to FL and MS. Thinly scattered in TN. Infrequent. May–July. *P. paupercula*.

NOTES: **Southern Ragwort** is also known as **Appalachian Ragwort** and was used by Native Americans to treat heart trouble and to prevent pregnancy. **Caution should be used** because this plant contains **toxins** that have been shown to increase blood pressure and cause uterine contractions and liver damage. Also, it may possibly contain cancer-causing compounds.

Golden Ragwort · *Senecio aureus*

GENERAL: Perennial herb, 12–30 in. tall, with **numerous stolons** and **smooth stems**. **LEAVES:** Basal leaves strongly heart-shaped at the base, long-petioled, to 5 in. long and wide, **purplish beneath**, rounded tip, blunt-toothed margins; stem leaves alternate, mostly pinnatifid, reduced and sessile upwards. **FLOWERS:** Ray flowers yellow, 10–12, 0.25–0.5 in. long; **disk yellow**, 0.2–0.5 in. wide; involucral bracts 0.2–0.3 in. long, purple-tipped; heads radiate, several on slender stalks in open clusters. April–August. **FRUITS:** Brownish, cylindric achenes; pappus a tuft of white bristles. **WHERE FOUND:** Moist woods and fields, from Labrador to MN, south to northern FL, central AR, and TX. Middle and East TN. Frequent. *Packera aurea*. **SIMILAR SPECIES:** **NEW ENGLAND GROUNDSEL** (*S. schweinitzianus*) has **basal leaves** mostly lanceolate, acute, **bases shallowly heart-shaped**, to 3 in. long, much longer than wide. A northeastern U.S. species with isolated populations in the mountains of TN and NC. In Carter and Unicoi counties in East TN. Rare. May–August. *P. schweinitziana*.

NOTES: **Golden Ragwort** is also known as Cough Weed, Female Regulator, Squaw Weed, Grundy Swallow, Life Root, and Wild Valerian. As suggested by its other names, Female Regulator and Squaw Weed, this plant was used as a "female remedy," including easing the pain of childbirth. • Ragworts are annual or perennial herbs with alternate leaves, and many small heads with yellow to orange disk and ray flowers clustered at the tops of the stalks. Ragworts are also known as "groundsels." • Species in the *Senecio* genus were historically used for medicinal purposes. • Eight *Senecio* species can be found in TN.

THOMAS E. HEMMERLY

Roundleaf Ragwort · *Senecio obovatus*

GENERAL: Smooth perennial herb, 12–24 in. tall, **spreading by runners (stolons)**. **LEAVES:** Basal leaves **rounded to obovate**, 2–4 in. long, margins shallowly toothed, tapering or abruptly narrowing to a long petiole; stem leaves alternate, reduced in size upward, becoming sessile and pinnately lobed. **FLOWERS:** Ray flowers yellow, 8–10, 0.2–0.4 in. long, irregularly spaced; **disk yellow**, 0.3–0.6 in. across; involucral bracts purple-tipped, 0.2 in. long; heads radiate, several on slender stalks in open, corymb-like clusters. April–June. **FRUITS:** Smooth achenes, 0.1 in. long; pappus a tuft of white bristles. **WHERE FOUND:** Dry woods, limestone ledges, and rocky bluffs throughout most of the eastern U.S., more common southward. Throughout Middle and East TN, also Madison and Shelby counties in West TN. Common. *Packera obovata.* **SIMILAR SPECIES:** PRAIRIE RAGWORT (*S. plattensis*) has **hairy or woolly** stem, leaves, and achenes. Prairies and dry soils of the Great Plains, scattered eastward. In TN, in Montgomery and Knox counties. Rare. May–July. *P. plattensis.*

NOTES: Roundleaf Ragwort is also known as Running Groundsel and Squaw Weed. • The genus name *Senecio* is Latin for "old man," referring to the white pappus of these herbs, which resembles gray hair. The genus includes over 1000 species worldwide, including 25 that are **poisonous**.

Butterweed, Yellowtop
Senecio glabellus

DENNIS HORN

GENERAL: Smooth, fibrous-rooted **annual**, 12–36 in. tall, with mostly unbranched, **hollow stems**. **LEAVES:** Basal leaves elliptic, 4–8 in. long, incised or simply toothed; stem leaves alternate, pinnatifid, with rounded teeth and lobes, progressively smaller upward. **FLOWERS:** Ray flowers yellow, **showy**, 10–15, 0.2–0.4 in. long; **disk yellow**, about 0.25 in. wide; about 13 or 21 involucral bracts, 0.2 in. long; heads radiate, numerous, in clusters at the tops of stems. April–June. **FRUITS:** Narrowly ellipsoid achenes, about 0.06 in. long; pappus a tuft of white bristles. **WHERE FOUND:** Moist woods, fields, and wet pastures, from SD, IL, and NC, south to FL and TX. Primarily in Middle and West TN. Frequent. *Packera glabella.* **SIMILAR SPECIES:** COMMON GROUNDSEL (*S. vulgaris**) has **heads that lack ray flowers**; outer **bracts have black tips**. Introduced from Europe. Now a weed throughout the U.S. In TN, found only in Montgomery, Davidson, Knox, and Unicoi counties, but likely more widespread. May–October.

NOTES: The name **Butterweed** refers to the smooth, yellow flowers and shiny texture. The species name *glabellus* means "somewhat smooth." Of note is the octopus-shaped network of roots that allow this plant to be easily pulled from the ground. • Butterweed is primarily pollinated by bees.

Narrowleaf White-Topped Aster
Sericocarpus linifolius

GENERAL: Smooth perennial herb, 12–24 in. tall, from a short, stout rhizome. **LEAVES:** Alternate, **linear, firm, not toothed**, 1–3 in. long, slightly smaller upward. **FLOWERS: Ray flowers white to pink, 3–6, narrow, 0.2–0.4** in. long; **disk flowers cream-colored, 5–10;** involucral bracts whitish with green tips; heads radiate, in a flat-topped inflorescence. July–September. **FRUITS:** Ellipsoid achenes, 0.1 in. long; pappus a tuft of whitish bristles. **WHERE FOUND:** Open, dry woods, from ME to IN, south to GA and LA. Throughout most of TN. Frequent. *Aster solidagineus.* **SIMILAR SPECIES: TOOTHED WHITE-TOPPED ASTER (S. asteroides)** has somewhat **broader, often toothed leaves** and **broader rays.** Open, dry woods, from ME to southern MI, south to eastern AL and northwestern FL. In TN, from the Eastern Highland Rim eastward. Occasional. June–September. *A. paternus.*

NOTES: The genus name *Sericocarpus* is from the Greek *serikos*, "silk," and *karpos*, "fruit," referring to the dry fruits that are covered with silky hairs. The species name *linifolius* means "flax-like leaves," referring to the narrow, linear leaves. • *Sericocarpus* species are closely related to our true native asters.

DENNIS HORN

Compass Plant
Silphium laciniatum

GENERAL: Coarse perennial herb, 3–10 ft. tall, with a **rough-hairy stem. LEAVES:** Basal leaves broadly elliptic to ovate, to 20 in. long, **deeply pinnately divided;** stem leaves alternate, greatly reduced in size upward, becoming entire. **FLOWERS: Ray flowers yellow,** 1–2 in. long, usually 17–25; **disk yellow,** about 1 in. wide; involucre 0.8–1.6 in. long, with ovate, stiff-haired bracts, tips spreading; heads radiate, several on the upper stem. July–September. **FRUITS:** Obovate, flattened achenes; pappus absent or of 2 small awns. **WHERE FOUND:** Prairies from NY to ND, south to AL and NM. In TN, in Haywood, Henry, Montgomery, and Carroll counties. Rare. **SIMILAR SPECIES: SOUTHERN ROSINWEED (S. asteriscus)** has **leafy, hairy stems;** lanceolate leaves, 1.5–6.0 in. long, usually coarsely toothed, but **not divided;** flower heads smaller, usually with 8 or 13 rays. A southeastern U.S. species, from VA to MO, south to FL and TX. Middle and East TN. Occasional. June–September.

NOTES: Compass Plant gets its name from the habit of the basal leaves, which align themselves in a north-south direction and thus face the sun in the morning (east) and afternoon (west). • Eleven *Silphium* species are found in TN. All are coarse perennial herbs having medium to large yellow flower heads, with coarse, wide bracts. Only the ray flowers produce seed. Sunflowers have narrow bracts and only the disk flowers produce seed.

EDWARD W. CHESTER

KURT EMMANUELE

Shaggy Rosinweed
Silphium mohrii

GENERAL: Perennial herb, 2–5 ft. tall; **densely stiff-haired stems** give the plant a "shaggy" appearance. **LEAVES:** Lower stem leaves alternate, **ovate**, 4–10 in. long, progressively smaller upward, densely covered with relatively long, **bristly hairs. FLOWERS: Ray flowers pale yellow**, about 13, 0.6–0.8 in. long; **disk yellow**, 0.6–1.0 in. wide; involucre hemispheric, 0.4–0.6 in. high, bracts lanceolate, rough-hairy; heads several, in branched clusters on the upper stem. July–October. **FRUITS:** Flattened, winged, obovate achenes; pappus absent or of 2 small awns. **WHERE FOUND:** Barrens and open woods in the Interior Low Plateau and Cumberland Plateau regions of TN, AL and GA. In southern Middle TN, also Cumberland County. Infrequent.

NOTES: Many *Silphium* species have common names that refer to their resin, also referred to as rosin, hence the name **Shaggy Rosinweed**. • It was claimed that Native Americans sometimes chewed on *Silphium* leaves, despite the turpentine-tasting resin, to cleanse their teeth and mouth.

DENNIS HORN

Cup Plant
Silphium perfoliatum

GENERAL: Coarse perennial herb, 3–8 ft. tall, with a stout **square stem**, mostly smooth. **LEAVES:** Opposite, ovate, 6–12 in. long, scabrous; upper leaves smaller, **connate-perfoliate** (stem passes through the pair of fused leaf bases), forming a "cup." **FLOWERS:** Ray flowers yellow, 0.6–1.6 in. long, **fertile**, usually 16–35; **disk yellow**, 0.6–1.0 in. wide; involucral bracts ovate, smooth, tips spreading; heads radiate, in an open inflorescence. July–September. **FRUITS:** Obovoid, winged achenes, 0.3 in. long. **WHERE FOUND:** Low, wet ground, from ME and southern Ontario to ND, south to GA and LA. Middle and West TN, also Knox and Hancock counties in East TN. Occasional. **SIMILAR SPECIES: PRAIRIE ROSIN-WEED (S. integrifolium)** has smooth stems; leaves sessile or clasping (but **not connate-perfoliate**). Prairies, roadsides, and fields from MI to WY, south to AL and NM. In TN, from the Central Basin of Middle TN, westward. Occasional. July–September.

NOTES: Cup Plant, also known as Indian Cup and Ragged Cup, is named for the fused leaf bases that form a "cup-like" depression on the upper stems. Another name, Carpenter Weed, refers to the square stem of this plant. • Although seldom used in the garden, Cup Plant should be considered for sunny locations as a backdrop for shorter perennials.

Cutleaf Prairie Dock, Tansy Rosinweed
Silphium pinnatifidum

GENERAL: Perennial herb, 3–10 ft. tall, with **smooth stems, appearing leafless. LEAVES:** Basal leaves elliptic (lower photo), 6–18 in. long and $\frac{1}{2}$ as wide, persistent, **pinnatifid, deeply incised**, long-stalked; stem leaves alternate, widely spaced, small, bract-like. **FLOWERS: Ray flowers yellow, 13–21**, about 1 in. long; **disk yellow, 0.6–1.4 in wide**; involucral bracts broad, smooth, overlapping; heads (upper photo) radiate, 2–4 in. wide, several on the upper stem. July–September. **FRUITS:** Narrowly winged, obovate achenes; pappus absent or of 2 small awns. **WHERE FOUND:** Cedar glades and barrens, from WI to OH, south to AL and GA. In Middle TN, also Bradley County in East TN. Infrequent. *S. terebinthinaceum* var. *pinnatifidum*. **SIMILAR SPECIES: BROADLEAF PRAIRIE DOCK** (*S. terebinthinaceum*) has **basal leaves that are entire, broad, and spade-shaped.** Prairies of the eastern U.S. Middle and East TN, especially the Ridge and Valley. Occasional. July–September. **LESSER PRAIRIE DOCK (S. compositum)** has **lobed basal leaves;** numerous flowering branches; **disk smaller, 0.3–0.5 in. wide, with only 5–10 rays.** Dry, sandy clearings and pine woods, from VA and WV to TN, south to FL. Found in 8 East TN counties. Infrequent. June–September.

NOTES: Cutleaf Prairie Dock is also known as Southern Prairie Dock. • The genus name *Silphium* is the ancient Greek name of another resin-producing plant in that region. The species name *pinnatifidum* means "pinnately divided" or "finely cut," in reference to the leaves.

DNH/PAUL SOMERS

DENNIS HORN

Whorled Rosinweed · *Silphium trifoliatum* var. *trifoliatum*

GENERAL: Perennial herb, 3–6 ft. tall, with **smooth, glaucous stems**, leafy to the inflorescence. **LEAVES:** Usually in **whorls of 3–4, nearly sessile**, narrowly ovate, 3–6 in. long, margins shallowly toothed or entire, bases tapering. **FLOWERS: Ray flowers yellow, 8–13**, 0.6–1.2 in. long; **disk yellow,** 0.4–0.6 in. wide; involucral bracts smooth, overlapping, margins fringed; **heads** radiate, **several.** June–September. **FRUITS:** Obovate achenes with well-developed wings ending in a tooth on each side; pappus of 2 small awns extending from the wings. **WHERE FOUND:** Prairies and roadsides from NY to IL, south in the mountains to GA and AL. In TN, primarily Middle and East TN. Frequent. **SIMILAR SPECIES:** Another variety of **WHORLED ROSINWEED (S. trifoliatum var. latifolium)** has **opposite leaves** that are wider and have longer petioles. Prairies and roadsides, from IN, OH, and southwestern VA, south to GA and LA. Thinly scattered in Middle and West TN, also Roane County. Occasional. June–September. **CUMBERLAND ROSINWEED (S. brachiatum)** has **lanceolate lower and middle stem leaves** with heart-shaped to truncate bases, **coarsely toothed, long-petioled; flower heads small, numerous, 4–6 rays.** Open woods of the Cumberland Plateau region of TN, AL, and GA. In TN, in Franklin, Grundy, Marion, and Polk counties. Rare. July–September.

THOMAS E. HEMMERLY

NOTES: Rosinweeds such as **Whorled Rosinweed** are visited by a wide variety of insects, especially bees, flies, butterflies, moths, and a few species of beetles.

Yellow Leafcup
Smallanthus uvedalius

GENERAL: Coarse perennial herb, 3–10 ft. tall; **stems usually smooth** below the inflorescence. **LEAVES: Opposite,** triangular to ovate, 4–12 in. long, **lobes mostly palmate,** broadly winged petioles. **FLOWERS: Ray flowers yellow, fertile,** 8–15, to 1 in. long; **disk bright yellow;** about 0.6 in. wide, with **sterile flowers;** involucral bracts ovate, leafy, 0.4–0.8 in. long; heads radiate, showy, several in open cymes. July–September. **FRUIT:** Blackish, rounded, swollen achenes, 0.25 in. long, faintly grooved; pappus absent. **WHERE FOUND:** Woods and meadows from NY to MO, south to FL and TX. Throughout TN. common. *Polymnia uvedalia.*

NOTES: This plant is also known as **Bear's Foot** because of the large, lobed leaves, and **Large-Flowered Leafcup** for its striking flowers. The species name *uvedalius* honors English teacher and botanist Robert Uvedale (1642–1722), because the plant was first found in his garden.

DENNIS HORN

Silverrod, White Goldenrod
Solidago bicolor

GENERAL: Perennial herb, 12–36 in. tall; solitary, **soft-hairy stems** and **bicolored flower heads. LEAVES:** Alternate, narrowly elliptic, shallowly toothed, hairy, 2–5 in. long, reduced upward. **FLOWERS: Ray flowers white,** 7–9, 0.1–0.2 in. long; **disk yellow;** involucre 0.1–0.2 in. long, bracts whitish with a pale green tip; heads radiate, in a narrow, **spike-like panicle.** July–October. **FRUITS:** Smooth achenes, 0.15–0.2 in. long, tapered from base to tip; pappus a tuft of whitish bristles, 0.3 in. long. **WHERE FOUND:** Dry woods, barrens, and open rocky areas, from Nova Scotia to WI, south to GA and LA. In TN, from the Western Highland Rim eastward, also Carroll and McNairy counties in West TN. Frequent.

NOTES: The genus *Solidago* contains perennial herbs with tiny, yellow flower heads in showy clusters. **Silverrod,** with its white rays, is the only exception. • Most *Solidago* species begin flowering in late summer, often signaling the beginning of hay fever season. However, **goldenrods do not cause hay fever,** because the pollen is too heavy to be airborne. Ragweeds (*Ambrosia* spp.) are the usual culprits, flowering at the same time. • Goldenrods have long lived and spreading root systems, with a few reports of plants living up to 100 years. • There are 32 *Solidago* species found in TN.

JERRY DROWN

Blue-Stemmed Goldenrod, Wreath Goldenrod · *Solidago caesia*

GENERAL: Slender perennial herb, 12–36 in. tall; **stems smooth, cylindric, often arching, bluish, glaucous.** **LEAVES:** Alternate, smooth, shallowly toothed, **narrowly lanceolate,** 2–5 in. long, with a tapering, **nearly sessile base.** **FLOWERS:** Ray flowers yellow, 3–4, about 0.1 in. long; **disk flowers yellow,** 5–8; involucre smooth, 0.1–0.2 in. long, bracts narrow, tips blunt; heads radiate, **clustered at the base of the leaves.** August–October. **FRUITS:** Hairy, tapered achenes; pappus a tuft of white bristles. **WHERE FOUND:** Woodlands and thickets throughout the eastern U.S. and TN. Common. **SIMILAR SPECIES: CURTIS' GOLDEN-ROD (*S. curtisii*)** has an **angled stem, not glaucous,** marked with fine, parallel lines. Woodlands from PA to KY, south to GA. In TN, from the Western Highland Rim eastward, also Carroll County in West TN. Frequent. August–October. *S. caesia* var. *curtisii*. ZIGZAG GOLDENROD (*S. flexicaulis*) has a **smooth, zigzag stem;** alternate, **broad, petioled,** toothed **leaves;** flower clusters on short stalks from the leaf axils. Woodlands of the eastern and midwestern U.S. Widespread across Middle and East TN. Frequent. July–October.

DENNIS HORN

NOTES: Another name for **Blue-Stemmed Goldenrod** is Axillary Goldenrod, referring to the flower clusters in the leaf axils. The genus name *Solidago* is from the Latin *solido*, "to make whole or cure," referring to the reputed healing power of these plants, which were used to treat urinary infections and colic.

Erect Goldenrod · *Solidago erecta*

GENERAL: Erect perennial herb, 12–48 in. tall, with **smooth stems.** **LEAVES:** Alternate, **smooth,** 3–12 in. long, narrowly spatulate to elliptic, decreasing in size upward. **FLOWERS:** Ray flowers pale yellow, 5–9, 0.1–0.2 in. long; **disk flowers pale yellow,** 6–10; involucre about 0.2 in. long, bracts yellowish, tips blunt; heads radiate, in a **narrow, elongated inflores-cence** above the principal leaves. August–October. **FRUITS:** Smooth, prominently ribbed achenes, 0.2 in. long; pappus a tuft of white bristles, 0.2 in. long. **WHERE FOUND:** Dry woods in the eastern U.S. Throughout Middle and East TN. Common. *S. speciosa* var. *erecta*. **SIMILAR SPECIES:** 2 other goldenrod species have flowers with 7–16 yellow rays in narrow, **wand-like clusters** above toothed, petioled leaves: **DOWNY GOLDENROD (*S. puberula*)** has **very small hairs on the stems and leaves.** Infrequent. Sandy or rocky open areas from OH to LA, eastward. In the mountains of East TN. August–October. **HAIRY GOLDENROD (*S. hispida*)** has **stems and leaves that are quite hairy;** flowers are deep yellow. Occasional. Dry rocky areas in the eastern U.S. and Canada. Widespread in the central 2/3 of TN. July–October.

NOTES: Erect Goldenrod is also called **Wandlike Goldenrod** and **Slender Goldenrod.** · Goldenrods have tubular disk flowers that hold pollen in goblet-shaped containers, surrounded by petal-like ray flowers.

DENNIS HORN

JERRY DROWN

Giant Goldenrod, Late Goldenrod
Solidago gigantea

GENERAL: Perennial herb, 2–7 ft. tall; **stem purplish, glaucous, and smooth** below the inflorescence. **LEAVES:** Alternate, **mostly smooth**, sharply toothed, **narrowly lanceolate**, 3–6 in. long, with 3 prominent veins; leaves reduced in size upward. **FLOWERS:** Ray flowers yellow, 10–17; disk flowers yellow, 6–12; involucre about 0.15 in. long; heads radiate, bell-shaped, in a showy, terminal, plume-like inflorescence with flowers attached along only 1 side of the recurved branches. August–October. **FRUITS:** Tapered, hairy achenes, 0.1 in. long; pappus a tuft of white bristles. **WHERE FOUND:** Moist thickets and woodland edges in most of the U.S. and southern Canada. Throughout TN. Common. **SIMILAR SPECIES:** COMMON GOLDENROD (*S. canadensis*), also called CANADA GOLDENROD, has **downy leaves**; stems are **grayish and softly hairy**. Moist or dry open places throughout the U.S. and southern Canada. Throughout TN. Common. August–October. The following 2 species also have a plume-like inflorescence, but the leaves are primarily near the base of the stem. SHARPLEAF GOLDENROD (*S. arguta*) has a **smooth, reddish brown stem** and **wide, mostly smooth, double-toothed leaves**. Dry, open woods from ME to FL and west to KS and TX. Widespread across TN. Frequent. July–October. ROUGHLEAF GOLDENROD (*S. patula*) has a **smooth, 4-angled stem** and **large, rough lower leaves**. Swamps and wet meadows in the eastern U.S. Middle and East TN. Occasional. August–October.

NOTES: The species name *gigantea* means "very large" and is derived from *giganteus*, "of or belonging to the giants." • **Late Goldenrod** is an inappropriate name for this plant, because it is one of the earlier goldenrods to flower. • **Giant Goldenrod** is also called **Smooth Goldenrod** for its smooth stem.

DENNIS HORN

Early Goldenrod
Solidago juncea

GENERAL: Early-flowering, perennial herb, 2–4 ft. tall, mostly smooth throughout. **LEAVES:** Basal leaves narrowly elliptic to lanceolate, 4–16 in. long, toothed, net-veined, tapering to long petioles; stem leaves alternate, reduced and becoming entire upward; **small leaf clusters in upper axils. FLOWERS:** Ray flowers yellow, 7–12, 0.1–0.2 in. long; disk flowers yellow, 9–14; involucre 0.1–0.2 in. long; heads radiate, in a terminal, **plume-like** inflorescence, about as broad as long, with heads attached only to the upper side of the recurved branches. Late June–August. **FRUITS:** Short-hairy achenes, 0.1 in. long; pappus a tuft of white, hair-like bristles. **WHERE FOUND:** Dry, open areas and dry woods, from Nova Scotia to MN, south to northern GA and LA. Thinly scattered throughout most of TN. Occasional. **SIMILAR SPECIES:** ROUGH-STEMMED GOLDENROD (*S. rugosa*) has **rough-hairy stems**; **leaves are prominently veined and hairy**, with deeply toothed margins. Low, open woods, meadows, and barrens, throughout the eastern U.S., southeastern Canada, and TN. Frequent. July–October.

Notes: Goldenrod (*Solidago* spp.) is the state flower of KY, where these wildflowers grow plentifully, with over 30 species. It is also the state flower of AL and NE. • **Early Goldenrod** is one of the first goldenrods to flower.

Gray Goldenrod · *Solidago nemoralis*

GENERAL: Perennial herb, 1–3 ft. tall, with **hairy, grayish stems and leaves**. **LEAVES:** Basal leaves oblanceolate, 2–5 in. long; stem leaves alternate, reduced upward; **tiny leaf clusters in the axils**. **FLOWERS:** Ray flowers **yellow, 5–9, 0.1–0.16 in.** long; **disk flowers yellow, 3–6**; involucral bracts appressed, overlapping, smooth; heads radiate, in terminal plumes with heads arranged on 1 side of grayish, finely hairy branches. September–November. **FRUITS:** Hairy achenes, 0.1 in. long; pappus a tuft of white **bristles, 0.15 in. long**. **WHERE FOUND:** Dry, sandy woodlands and in open, baked, poor soils of old fields, roadsides, and pastures throughout the eastern and central U.S. and southern Canada. Throughout TN. Common. **SIMILAR SPECIES:** SHORT-PAPPUS GOLDENROD (*S. sphacelata*) is 2–4 ft. tall; **basal leaves prominently heart-shaped**, to 5 in. long, with long petioles; stem leaves progressively smaller upward, **without axillary leaf clusters**; panicle-like inflorescence has fewer spreading branches with flowers on 1 side; **pappus bristles very small**, firm, and much shorter than the achene. Open woods and rocky places, particularly overlying limestone, from VA to IL, south to GA and MS. In TN, from the Western Highland Rim, eastward. Frequent. August–September.

THOMAS E. HEMMERLY

NOTES: Gray Goldenrod is also known as Old Field Goldenrod. Its yellow flowers are sometimes used for dying clothing and baskets, and dry well for winter bouquets.

Sweet Goldenrod · *Solidago odora*

GENERAL: Erect perennial herb, 2–5 ft. tall. **LEAVES:** Alternate, **narrowly lanceolate, anise-scented**, 2–4 in. long, **parallel-veined**, mostly smooth, sessile, entire, with **translucent glandular dots**. **FLOWERS:** Ray flowers **yellow, 3–5, 0.1–0.15 in.** long; disk flowers yellow, 3–5; involucre to 0.2 in. long, bracts appressed, smooth, yellowish; heads radiate, rather showy, in a **plume-like inflorescence** with recurved branches. June–September. **FRUITS:** Hairy to nearly smooth achenes, 0.1 in. long; pappus a tuft of white bristles, 0.15 in. long. **WHERE FOUND:** Dry soil of open woods and barrens, from NH to MO, south to FL and TX. Scattered throughout TN. Frequent. **SIMILAR SPECIES:** ELMLEAF GOLDENROD (*S. ulmifolia*) has an **inflorescence with long, spreading branches**; significantly **wider, pinnately veined leaves, not anise-scented**. From Nova Scotia to MN, south to FL and TX. Widespread in TN, but mostly absent from the Blue Ridge Mountains. Common. August–October.

DENNIS HORN

NOTES: The species name *odora* refers to the pleasant aroma of the leaves. The fresh or dried leaves can be used to make an excellent anise- or tarragon-scented tea, but use caution because a **poisonous fungus often grows on goldenrods**. • The leaves contain an essential oil and have been used medicinally to treat various stomach and digestive system ailments, colds, coughs, fevers, and measles, as well as being used to make a mild astringent and wash.

DENNIS HORN

Hardleaf Goldenrod, Stiff Goldenrod
Solidago rigida

GENERAL: Coarse, erect, **hairy-stemmed** perennial herb, 2–5 ft. tall, from a stout rhizome. **LEAVES:** Basal leaves **firm, rough,** elliptic to ovate, 3–6 in. long, finely toothed, long-petioled; stem leaves alternate, much smaller, sessile, oval, very stiff. **FLOWERS: Ray flowers yellow,** 7–14, about 0.2 in. long; **disk yellow,** 0.2–0.4 in. wide; involucre 0.2–0.3 in. high, bracts firm, rounded, appressed, striped; heads radiate, in a dense, **flat-topped plume.** August–October. **FRUITS:** Smooth, angular achenes, about 0.1 in. long; pappus a tuft of white bristles. **WHERE FOUND:** A mid-western prairie plant usually found in dry, open areas from MA to MT, south to GA and NM. In TN, thinly scattered from the Western Highland Rim, eastward. Occasional. *Oligoneuron rigidum.* **SIMILAR SPECIES:** SHOWY GOLDENROD (*S. speciosa*) has a **smooth, reddish stem; small leaf clusters in the axils; 5–6 ray flowers; heads in a dense pyramidal cluster.** Open woods and prairies, from NH to KS, south to GA and LA. Thinly scattered across TN. Occasional. August–October.

NOTES: Prairie Goldenrod is another name for **Hardleaf Goldenrod.** • Goldenrods contain small quantities of rubber, which has been studied extensively to determine if it would be feasible to produce in large quantities.

JERRY DROWN

Roan Mountain Goldenrod
Solidago roanensis

GENERAL: Perennial herb, 12–36 in. tall; **stems are smooth below,** hairy near the inflorescence. **LEAVES:** Alternate, thin, smooth, highly variable; lower leaves elliptic to obovate, 2–6 in. long, sharp tips, toothed margins, long, winged petioles; upper leaves lanceo-late, smaller, less toothed or entire, becoming sessile. **FLOWERS: Ray flowers deep yellow,** 6–9, about 0.1 in. long; **disk flowers yellow,** about 10; involucre 0.15 in. long, bracts slender; heads radiate, in a dense, **long, cylindric inflorescence.** August–October. **FRUITS:** Smooth achenes, 0.1 in. long; pappus a tuft of white bris-tles, 0.2 in. long. **WHERE FOUND:** Mountain woods from PA, south to AL and GA. In TN, from the Cumberland Plateau, eastward. Occasional. **SIMILAR SPECIES:** EARED GOLDENROD (*S. auriculata*) is **densely hairy throughout;** leaves ovate with a **winged petiole clasping the stem; plume-like inflorescence.** Dry limestone soils of the southeastern U.S. from TN, south to FL and TX. In TN, only in Franklin County. Rare. September–October. *S. notabilis.* GATTINGER'S GOLDENROD (*S. gattingeri*) is **smooth throughout; basal leaves narrowly spatulate,** long-petioled; upper leaves reduced to tiny bracts; **spreading inflorescence.** Limestone barrens and glades in MO, TN, and AR. In TN, found only in Rutherford and Wilson counties in the Central Basin. Rare. July–September.

NOTES: Roan Mountain Goldenrod is named after Roan Mountain on the NC–TN border. • Goldenrods are symbols of good fortune and treasure. • These plants are favored by bees and butterflies.

Common Dandelion
*Taraxacum officinale**

OTTO R. HIRSCH

GENERAL: Familiar perennial herb, 2–20 in. tall, with naked flower stalks. **LEAVES:** Basal rosette, oblanceolate, 2–10 in. long, **pinnately lobed, lobes backward pointing,** usually smooth above, lightly hairy beneath. **FLOWERS: Ray flowers yellow,** numerous; disk flowers absent; involucre with **reflexed outer bracts, equal in length to the inner bracts**; heads ligulate, **solitary,** 1–2 in. wide, **on a smooth, leafless, hollow stalk.** April–December. **FRUITS:** Olive brown achenes, 0.2 in. long, tapered at both ends; pappus a tuft of white, hair-like bristles. **WHERE FOUND:** Introduced from Eurasia. Now widely naturalized in lawns and disturbed places throughout the U.S. and TN. Common. **SIMILAR SPECIES:** RED-SEEDED DANDELION (*T. laevigatum**) has reddish brown achenes; more deeply incised leaves; **outer bracts are spreading and about** 1/2 **as long as inner involucral bracts.** Introduced from Eurasia. Widely established in the U.S. and southern Canada. In TN, in Hickman, Davidson, Giles, DeKalb, Knox, and Sevier counties. Infrequent. March–December. *T. erythrospermum*.

NOTES: The name "dandelion" evolved from the French *dent de lion*, for "lion's tooth," referring to the toothed leaves. • After flowering, the delicate, parachute-like appendages form an airy ball. The seeds break free and are easily dispersed by wind. A children's legend says that if a wish is made, a person can blow on the airy ball of seeds, and the wish will be carried with the wind on its way to becoming true. • Dandelion plants contain high levels of vitamins A and C. The young leaves make a nutritious addition to salads, the flowers can be used to make wine, and the root can be used as a coffee substitute.

Yellow Goatsbeard · *Tragopogon dubius**

GENERAL: Smooth **biennial,** 12–36 in. tall, with erect stems. **LEAVES:** Alternate, grass-like, 4–10 in. long, **clasping the stem. FLOWERS: Ray flowers pale yellow,** numerous; disk flowers absent; **involucral bracts extend beyond the rays**; heads ligulate, 1–2 in. across, solitary, on erect stalks; flowers open in the morning and usually close by noon. May–July. **FRUITS:** Brown, cylindric achenes, 10-ribbed, tapered to a long beak; pappus a tuft of feathery, tan bristles; fruit cluster an airy, **dandelion-like ball, 3–4 in. across** (lower photo). **WHERE FOUND:** Introduced from Europe. Dry, open sites and roadsides. Widely scattered throughout most of the U.S. and TN. Occasional. **SIMILAR SPECIES:** SHOWY YELLOW GOATSBEARD (*T. pratensis**) has **bracts that do not extend beyond the ray flowers.** Introduced from Europe. Established sporadically on roadsides and waste places in most of the U.S. Recently recorded in TN. Rare. June–October. OYSTER PLANT (*T. porrifolius**), also called **SALSIFY,** has **purple rays** and **long bracts.** Introduced from Europe. Established sporadically on roadsides and waste places in most of the U.S. In TN, in Grainger and Knox counties in East TN. Rare. May–July.

NITA R. HEILMAN

JERRY DROWN

NOTES: Yellow Goatsbeard is also called Meadow Salsify and Johnny-Go-To-Bed-At-Noon. It was given another name, Joseph's Beard, because Joseph, the Virgin Mary's husband, is usually portrayed as having a long, white beard. • The long taproots of Yellow Goatsbeard can be ground, roasted and used as a coffee substitute, much like the roots of **Common Dandelion** (see above).

EDWARD SCHELL

Coltsfoot
*Tussilago farfara**

GENERAL: Perennial herb, 2–20 in. tall, from a rhizome. **LEAVES:** Basal, heart-shaped to nearly round, 2–8 in. wide and long, firmly toothed, shallowly lobed, long-petioled, smooth above, densely **white-hairy beneath**. **FLOWERS:** Ray flowers yellow, numerous, linear, **fertile**; **disk flowers yellow**, sterile; involucre 0.3–0.6 in. long; heads radiate, solitary, about 1 in. across, on **scaly, leafless flowering stems**. March–April, **before the leaves develop**. **FRUITS:** Linear, 5–10-ribbed achenes; pappus a tuft of hair-like bristles. **WHERE FOUND:** Introduced from Europe. Disturbed places in the northeastern U.S. and southeastern Canada. In TN, in the northeastern counties, also Cheatham County in Middle TN. Occasional.

NOTES: The genus name *Tussilago* is from the Latin words *tussis*, "cough," and *agere*, "to chase," referring to its medicinal use for curing coughs. The species name *farfara* is the Latin name for "coltsfoot." • This plant is also called **British Tobacco** because of the historical use of the leaves as an herb tobacco by the British. The leaves are edible, as are the flower heads. **Caution:** this plant should only be eaten in small quantities because of its **high alkaloid content**, which has caused it to be banned as a food in several European countries. In addition to containing alkaloids, the leaves contain a resin, tannin, an essential oil, vitamin C, minerals, and an antibiotic substance.

JERRY DROWN

Wingstem • *Verbesina alternifolia*

GENERAL: Coarse perennial herb, 3–9 ft. tall; stem leafy. **LEAVES:** Alternate, narrowly lanceolate, 4–10 in. long, margins serrate to entire; **petioles with wings that extend down the stem**. **FLOWERS:** Ray flowers yellow, **2–10, irregularly spaced, reflexed**, 0.4–1.2 in. long; **disk flowers yellow, loosely arranged, forming a sphere** 0.4–0.6 in. wide; involucral bracts narrow, smooth, reflexed; heads radiate, numerous, in an open, branched inflorescence. August–September. **FRUITS:** Achenes, 0.25 in. long, 0.15 in. wide, with broad wings, usually 0.1 in. wide; pappus of 2 short awns. **WHERE FOUND:** Moist thickets and edges of woods throughout most of the eastern U.S. Throughout TN. Frequent. *Actinomeris alternifolia*. **SIMILAR SPECIES:** OZARK WINGSTEM (*V. helianthoides*) is only 24–48 in. tall; larger flower heads to 2 in. wide; **8–15 yellow rays, not reflexed**; disk flowers in **tighter clusters**. From OH to IA, south to GA and TX. West and Middle TN. Occasional. June-October.

NOTES: Wingstem is named for the winged petioles, which continue down the stem in a wing-like fashion. • Wingstems are used as host plants and for nectar by Silvery Checkerspot butterflies.

Yellow Crownbeard
Verbesina occidentalis

GENERAL: Perennial herb, 3–7 ft. tall; leafy stems are smooth below, softly hairy above. **LEAVES: Opposite**, ovate, 3–7 in. long, rough to finely hairy, serrate; **winged petioles extend down the stem. FLOWERS: Ray flowers yellow, 2–5,** 0.4–0.8 in. long; **disk yellow,** 0.25 in. wide; involucral bracts lanceolate, erect, hairy, 0.2–0.4 in. long; heads radiate, numerous in a flat-topped, open inflorescence. August–September. **FRUITS:** Blackish, hairy achenes, 0.25 in. long, not winged; pappus of 2 awns bent at an angle. **WHERE FOUND:** Moist woods, thickets, and waste places, from PA to MO, south to FL and TX. In TN, from the Eastern Highland Rim eastward, also Macon, Trousdale, Smith, Davidson, Montgomery, and Obion counties. Frequent.

OTTO R. HIRSCH

NOTES: Many *Verbesina* species have a strong, somewhat disagreeable odor. Some have the scent of "a cow pen, rotting meat, or a skunk." • In herbal medicine, *Verbesina* species were used in salves and ointments that were applied to the skin. • Four *Verbesina* species are found in TN.

White Crownbeard, Tickweed
Verbesina virginica

GENERAL: Coarse perennial herb, 3–7 ft. tall, with **winged stems. LEAVES: Alternate,** broadly lanceolate, 4–8 in. long, toothed to entire, **winged petioles. FLOWERS: Ray flowers white, 3–5,** 0.2–0.4 in. long; **disk grayish white,** 0.12–0.25 in. wide; involucral bracts lanceolate, appressed, hairy, 0.2–0.4 in. long; heads radiate, 20–200 crowded at the top of the stem. August–October. **FRUITS:** Dark brown, hairy achenes, narrowly winged; pappus of 2 small awns. **WHERE FOUND:** Along streams and roadsides, also in waste places. Primarily a southern species, ranging from MD to IA, south to FL and TX. Throughout TN. Frequent.

NOTES: White Crownbeard is distinguished from other *Verbesina* species by its distinctive white flowering heads. Another name, **Frostweed,** refers to the peculiar formation of "frost flowers" around the stem and just above the ground during cold autumn nights. This is caused when water is forced out of the stem during the first hard freeze, resulting in the ice formation. This phenomenon is observed in other plants, such as **Low Frostweed** (p. 95) and deserves further study.

DENNIS HORN

Tall Ironweed
Vernonia gigantea

JERRY DROWN

GENERAL: Perennial herb, 3–10 ft. tall; **stems usually smooth**, leafy. **LEAVES:** Alternate, simple, mostly lanceolate, 4–12 in. long and ¼ as wide, smooth above, hairy beneath, pinnately veined, serrate, tips acuminate, short-petioled. **FLOWERS:** Ray flowers absent; **disk flowers purplish, 13–30**; involucre 0.2–0.3 in. high, bracts overlapping, appressed, purplish, **apex rounded to a short tip**, usually smooth, entire, or sometimes edged with cobwebby hairs; heads numerous in terminal corymbs. August–November. **FRUITS:** Ribbed achenes, about 0.2 in. long; **pappus a tuft of hair-like bristles, purplish**. **WHERE FOUND:** Moist woods, meadows, and pastures, from western NY to IA and KS, south to FL and TX. Throughout TN. Common. *V. altissima*. **SIMILAR SPECIES: NEW YORK IRON-WEED** (*V. noveboracensis*) has **30–55 flowers per head** and **involucral bracts that terminate in a very long, slender tip**. Moist, open areas, from NH to OH, south to FL and AL. Middle and East TN. Occasional. August–September. **TENNESSEE IRONWEED** (*V. flaccidifolia*) has a **smooth, glaucous stem** and a **light tan pappus**. Upland woods in TN, northern GA, and AL. In TN, in Montgomery, Franklin, Coffee, Grundy, Marion, Sequatchie, and Hamilton counties. Infrequent. July–August.

NOTES: The *Vernonia* genus was named for the English botanist, William Vernon (d. 1711) who botanized in the United States in the late 1600s and developed an extensive plant collection in Maryland. • Native Americans used the leaves and roots to make a tea that was used during pregnancy and childbirth and to relieve postpartum pain.

Water Plantain
Alisma subcordatum

GENERAL: **Aquatic** or nearly aquatic perennial herb, 12–36 in. tall, with tufts of fibrous roots and **scapes that exceed the leaves.** **LEAVES:** In a dense basal cluster, ascending, elliptic-rounded to **almost heart-shaped** (subcordate), 2–6 in. long, on petioles as long or longer than the blades. **FLOWERS:** Whitish; **3 petals**, about 0.1 in. long; many ovaries, in a circle on a flattened receptacle; inflorescence to 24 in. long, of numerous, whorled, panicled branches. June–September or later, where waters are receding around large reservoirs. **FRUITS:** Heads

DENNIS HORN

with flattened achenes, about 0.1 in. long. **WHERE FOUND:** Shallow water along streams, in swamps, and marshes, and on muddy shorelines throughout the eastern U.S. Scattered throughout TN, often locally abundant. Frequent.

NOTES: The genus name *Alisma* is the classical Greek name for water plantain. This plant is also known as Southern Water Plantain, **American Water Plantain**, and Common Water Plantain. • The Water Plantain Family is sometimes referred to as the Arrowhead Family. It is a small family of aquatic species and marsh herbs found in temperate and tropical regions. The Water Plantain Family is represented by 3 genera and 10 species in TN, all essentially wetland species.

Creeping Burhead · *Echinodorus cordifolius*

GENERAL: Creeping perennial with arching scapes, 24–48 in. long, **becoming prostrate.** **LEAVES:** Basal, **heart-shaped**, 2–8 in. long, 1.5–6.0 in. wide, petioles often nearly 12 in. long. **FLOWERS:** White, 0.5–1.0 in. wide, **3 petals**; numerous stamens and pistils; **styles shorter than ovaries**; on slender pedicels, about 1 in. long, in several whorls of 3–10 flowers, widely spaced on the scapes. June–August. **FRUITS:** Ribbed achenes in bur-like heads, 0.4 in. wide. **WHERE FOUND:** Shallow water of marshes, swamps, and reservoir shorelines. A Coastal Plain species extending northward into the Mississippi River Valley. Middle and West TN. Occasional. Plants growing in reservoir draw-down zones are often much smaller and flower in October. **SIMILAR SPECIES:** UPRIGHT BURHEAD **(E. berteroi)**, also called TALL BURHEAD, has scapes to 24 in. tall that **remain erect; styles are longer than ovaries.** Swamps, ditches, and

OTTO R. HIRSCH

sandy soils from FL to TX and CA, north into the Midwest and Plains states. In TN, in Obion County. Rare. June–October. *E. rostratus.*

NOTES: The genus name *Echinodorus* is Greek for "sea-urchin" or "hedgehog," alluding to the round fruiting heads that are bur-like and covered in prickly spines. The species name *cordifolius* means "with heart-shaped leaves."

DENNIS HORN

Grassleaf Arrowhead
Sagittaria graminea

GENERAL: Slender, **aquatic** perennial herb, 4–20 in. tall, from short rhizomes. **LEAVES:** Basal, **linear-lanceolate** to elliptic-ovate (rarely arrowhead-shaped), 2–12 in. long, 0.2–4.0 in. wide, long-petioled. **FLOWERS:** White to pink, male and female flowers on the same plant; **3 petals**, 0.4–0.8 in. long and wide; lower flowers female (pistillate), on relatively thick, ascending pedicels; upper flowers usually male (staminate), on slender, **erect pedicels**; 2–12 whorls of 3 flowers each on simple or occasionally branched scapes. July–September. **FRUITS:** Short-beaked achenes, winged on the margins, with 1 or more facial wings. **WHERE FOUND:** Swamps, marshes, and shallow, muddy ponds, from southern Canada, south to the Gulf Coastal Plain and west to AZ. In TN, in Dickson, Fentress, and Coffee counties. Rare.

NOTES: The genus name *Sagittaria* comes from the Latin *sagitta*, "arrow," referring to the arrowhead-shaped leaves of many species in this genus. The species name *graminea* refers to the grass-like leaves. All species in this genus have flowers with 3 showy, white petals. Seven *Sagittaria* species are found in TN.

HUGH & CAROL NOURSE

Broadleaf Arrowhead, Duck Potato
Sagittaria latifolia

GENERAL: **Aquatic** perennial herb, 12–48 in. tall, with large, **edible tubers**. **LEAVES:** Basal, **commonly arrowhead-shaped**, 6–16 in. long and about 1/2 as wide, with narrow basal lobes; petioles to 12 in. long or more, usually as long as the water is deep. **FLOWERS:** White, **showy**, male and female flowers on the same plant; **3 petals** to 0.8 in. long; numerous pistils or stamens; slender, **ascending pedicels, 1 in. long or more**, longer than the subtending bracts; upper flowers staminate (male) or perfect, lower flowers mainly pistillate (female) and longer-stalked; in 2–10 whorls of 3 flowers each on erect scapes. July–September. **FRUITS:** Beaked achenes clustered in heads; the beak turned at a right angle away from the achene body. **WHERE FOUND:** Shallow water or mud, throughout the U.S. and TN. Frequent. **SIMILAR SPECIES:** SOUTHERN ARROWHEAD (*S. australis*) has wider leaves and basal leaf lobes; petioles 5-winged in cross-section; flower **pedicels are less than 0.7 in. long**, shorter than the subtending bracts; achene beaks turn upward. Springs and ponds, from NY to IA, south to FL and AR. Scattered throughout TN. Frequent.

NOTES: The common name **Duck Potato** refers to the tuberous roots that can be eaten raw or cooked and are similar to potatoes. Other names also reference its use as a food source by both people and animals: Swan Potato, Bull Tongue, Chinese Onion, Muskrat Potato, Swanroot, and Tule Potato. Native Americans gave it the name of **Wapato**, and used it as an important staple food and a product for trade or barter.

Plantainleaf Arrowhead
Sagittaria platyphylla

GENERAL: Aquatic perennial herb, 12–36 in. tall, propagating by runners (stolons). **LEAVES:** Basal, erect, lanceolate, **elliptic**, or ovate, **unlobed**, 2–6 in. long, long-petioled, longer than flower stalk. **FLOWERS:** White, **3 petals**, 0.4–0.8 in. long; in 3–8 whorls of 3 flowers each, lower 2–3 whorls have pistillate flowers with thick, **downward-curved pedicels**; inflorescence branched, 8–20 in. tall. June–August. **FRUITS:** Obovate achenes, 0.1 in. long and wide, with 1–3 slender ridges. **WHERE FOUND:** Marshes and stream edges, from VA to KS, southward. In TN, in Lake, Obion, Lauderdale, Hamilton, Fentress, and Cumberland counties. Infrequent. **SIMILAR SPECIES:** HOODED ARROWHEAD (**S. calycina**) is a robust **annual**; **arrowhead-shaped leaves**, 2–20 in. long, on long, round petioles; stout flowering stalk, 12–48. tall; **fruiting pedicels curve downward**. Marshes or ponds with alkaline water, throughout most of U.S. Thinly scattered across TN. Occasional. May–September.

DENNIS HORN

NOTES: The species name *platyphylla* comes from the Greek words *platy*, "flat" or "broad," and *phylla*, "leaf," referring to the flat leaves of this plant. **Plantainleaf Arrowhead** is also know as **Delta Arrowhead.** • Some arrowheads may cause dermatitis.

Sweetflag, Calamus · *Acorus calamus**

GENERAL: Colonial perennial herb, 2–6 ft. tall, from aromatic, fleshy rhizomes. **LEAVES:** Basal, **sword-like**, stiff, narrow, 0.3–1.0 in. wide, with a vertical midrib; very similar to cattail leaves. **FLOWERS:** Numerous, minute, **greenish brown**; inflorescence a cylindric, tapering spadix (fleshy spike), 2–4 in. long, 0.4 in. wide, angling off from a stalk 8–24 in. high; **linear, green, leaf-like spathe** (leaf-like bract) continues upward for another 4–18 in. May–July. **FRUITS:** Hard, dry, indehiscent fruits covering the spadix are gelatinous within, 1–3-seeded. **WHERE FOUND:** Marshes, riverbanks, and wet slopes, from eastern Canada, south to GA and TX. Thinly scattered in TN. Occasional.

NOTES: The genus name *Acorus* is Latin for "sweet flag," for the aromatic roots, which were used in making cosmetics and in herbal medicine. • The roots were traditionally used in teas or chewed for relieving thirst, stomach ailments, indigestion, heartburn, colds, fevers, and coughs. It is said that Native Americans also used them as a stimulant on long journeys. • Plants of the Arum Family are perennial herbs that grow in wet places (many are aquatic) from rhizomes or corms. Numerous tiny flowers are clustered on a fleshy spike or spadix, often enclosed, at least partially, by a leafy spathe. • Five genera and 7 species are found in TN.

DENNIS HORN

Green Dragon · *Arisaema dracontium*

GENERAL: Perennial herb, 12–48 in. tall, from a corm.
LEAVES: Solitary, **compound basal leaf**, long-petioled, pedately divided into **5–15 dull green leaflets**, often in a horizontal, U-shaped configuration. **FLOWERS:** Tiny, **yellow-green; male and female flowers** at the base of a **spadix** (fleshy spike) with a long, sterile tip (the "dragon's tongue" or "dragon's tail"), surrounded by a **green, sheath-like spathe** (leaf-like bract), the spadix extending 2–4 in. beyond the spathe; flowering stalk from a sheath near the base of the leaf stalk. May–June. **FRUITS: Orange-red berries**, clustered at the base of the spadix, appear in autumn (lower photo). **WHERE FOUND:** Low woods and streambanks, throughout the eastern U.S. and TN. Common.

NOTES: The genus name *Arisaema* is from the Greek *aris*, "arum," and *haima*, "blood," in allusion to the leaf color of some of the species in this genus. The species name *dracontium* is from *draco*, meaning "dragon." Other common names for this plant are **Dragonroot**, Dragon Arum, and American Wake-Robin. • The plant, especially the root, contains calcium oxalate, which causes a burning of the mouth and tongue unless the root is dried and aged before it is ingested. Native Americans used this plant for treating female disorders, and it was reputed to give those who carried it "the power of supernatural dreams."

LUIS C. PRIETO, JR. (INSET); HUGH NOURSE (TOP)

Jack-in-the-Pulpit, Indian Turnip
Arisaema triphyllum

GENERAL: Perennial herb, 12–36 in. tall, from an **acrid corm**.
LEAVES: Basal, 1–2, **compound**, with **3 ovate leaflets**, 3–6 in. long, at the tip of a sheathed stalk, overtopping and often hiding the inflorescence. **FLOWERS:** Tiny, male or female (both on one plant); inflorescence a **greenish, club-shaped spadix** (fleshy spike) with flowers at the base and a slender sterile tip ("Jack"), encircled by a flanged spathe (leaf-like bract) that surrounds and extends over the spadix to form the "pulpit"; **spathe green or purple, often striped**, sometimes nearly black inside, smooth or ridged. April–May. **FRUITS: Bright red berries**, clustered at the base of the spadix, produced in autumn. **WHERE FOUND:** Rich, moist woods, stream banks, throughout the eastern U.S. and most of TN. Common. **SIMILAR SPECIES: PRESTER-JOHN (A. quinatum)** has **lateral leaflets that are deeply 2-lobed**, giving the leaves the appearance of having 5 leaflets. Similar habitats as *A. triphyllum*, from TN and NC, south to GA and LA. In TN, in Sequatchie, Polk, Monroe, Blount, Sevier, Knox, and Unicoi counties. Infrequent. Often considered to be a variety of, or not distinct from, *A. triphyllum* in various botanical treatments.

KURT EMMANUELE

NOTES: The species name *triphyllum* is from the Greek words *tri*, "three," and *phyllum*, "leaf," referring to the plant's 3 leaflets. Other common names are Pepper Turnip, Bog Onion, Brown Dragon, Indian Cherries, Indian Cradle, Marsh Turnip, and Plant-of-Peace. • The root of **Jack-in-the-Pulpit** was a food item for Native Americans and early settlers, but caused a severe burning reaction if eaten raw because of the needlelike crystals of calcium oxalate. It had to be cooked or dried to remove its astringent qualities.

Goldenclub, Bog Torch
Orontium aquaticum

GENERAL: **Aquatic** perennial herb with a white scape (leafless flower stalk) 8–16 in. tall, erect in flower, becoming prostrate in fruit. **LEAVES:** Basal, clustered, long-petioled, **ovate**, 3–8 in. long, occasionally rising to a height of 24 in., **usually floating** on the surface of the water; leaves have a waxy epidermal layer that readily sheds water and large intercellular air pockets that add buoyancy. **FLOWERS:** Tiny, **golden yellow**, closely spaced; inflorescence a spadix (fleshy spike), 1–2 in. long, that terminates the top of the scape. March–June. **FRUITS:** Blue-green bladder-like utricle with 1 round seed. **WHERE FOUND:** Wet soil, shallow ponds, acid streams in the Atlantic and Gulf Coastal states, inland to WV and KY. Thinly scattered in TN, in Lewis, Fentress, Scott, Morgan, Roane, Johnson, Carter, Washington, Greene, and Cocke counties. Infrequent.

NOTES: The leaves of **Goldenclub** have the ability to shed water, thus accounting for another common name, Never-Wet. Like many plants in this family, it has thick, starchy roots that were boiled and eaten by Native Americans and early settlers, or pounded into flour. Although the raw fruits usually cause an unbearable burning sensation when eaten, Native Americans frequently used the fruits for food, boiling them in several changes of water or drying them.

Arrow Arum, Tuckahoe · *Peltandra virginica*

GENERAL: **Aquatic** perennial herb, 18–36 in. tall, from fleshy, fibrous roots. **LEAVES:** Basal, long-stalked, **arrowhead-shaped**, 4–12 in. long at flowering time, larger later, resembling those of Broadleaf Arrowhead (p. 388) but **pinnately** rather than palmately **veined**. **FLOWERS:** Tiny, **pale yellowish**, male or female (both on one plant); inflorescence a distinctive, slender, **club-shaped spadix** (fleshy spike) enclosed in a narrow, pointed, **green spathe** (leaf-like bract), 5–7 in. long; flower stalk erect in flower, recurved in fruit. May–June. **FRUITS:** Dark green berries, about 0.5 in. wide, turn brown after drying. **WHERE FOUND:** Wet soil, swamps, and shallow waterways, throughout the eastern U.S. In West and East TN, and Robertson County in Middle TN. Occasional.

NOTES: The genus name *Peltandra* is from the Greek *pelte*, "a small shield," and *aner*, meaning "stamen," refering to the shape of the stamens. Other names for this plant include Breadroot, Cruel-Man-of-the-Woods, Duck Corn, Hog Wampee, Poison Arum, Taw-ho, Tuckahoe, and Virginia Wake-Robin. • Eastern Native Americans boiled or roasted the stout root, and some cooked and ate the berries.

KURT EMMANUELE

KURT EMMANUELE

EDWARD SCHELL

Skunk Cabbage · *Symplocarpus foetidus*

GENERAL: Perennial herb, 12–24 in. tall, with a
skunk-like odor; from a thick rhizome. **LEAVES:**
Basal, cabbage-like, net-veined, **heart-shaped**,
entire, 10– 20 in. long and almost as wide, on
short, stout petioles; appear in late spring, after
the flowers. **FLOWERS:** Tiny, star-like, **yellowish**;
inflorescence barely rises above the ground and
has a **knob-like, ovoid spadix** (fleshy spike),
1.0–1.25 in. wide, almost hidden by the spathe
(leaf-like bract); **spathe brownish purple, hood-
like, fleshy, green-spotted or striped**, 3–6 in. tall,
open on 1 side only. February–March, before the
leaves emerge. **FRUITS:** Berry-like, in a subglobu-
lar mass to 4 in. wide, embedded with spherical seeds, about 0.4 in. thick. **WHERE FOUND:** Swamps
and wet woods. A northeastern species extending south to TN and NC in the mountains. In TN,
only known from Carter, Johnson, and Sullivan counties in the northeastern part of East TN. Rare.

NOTES: The species name *foetidus* refers to the plant's fetid or rotten odor, used to lure insects
who find the odor attractive. • Native Americans reportedly knew how to "dress" the leaves to
make them palatable so they could be smoked like tobacco. This plant is also called Polecat
Weed and Swamp Cabbage. • The spathe and spadix emerge in late winter and may be seen
growing through ice and snow. Biologist Roger Knutson found that **the flowers produce
warmth** over a period of 12–14 days, **remaining on average 36°F (20°C) above the outside
air temperature**, day and night. During this time, the plant regulates its warmth, similar to a
warm-blooded animal, and provides a warmer haven for a variety of newly emerged insects.

MILO PYNE

Irisleaf Yellow-Eyed Grass
Xyris laxifolia var. *iridifolia*

GENERAL: Perennial herb, 20–36 in. tall, arising from a bulbous base.
LEAVES: Basal, 4–10, shiny green, ascending, flat, linear (**iris-like**), 16–28 in.
long, 0.4–1.0 in. wide, usually **reddish purple at the base**. **FLOWERS:** Small,
yellow; **3 petals**, each with a narrow base (claw) and a toothed blade,
0.12 in. long; borne in a compact, ellipsoid, **head-like spike, 1.0–1.5 in.
long**, atop a naked, very smooth flowering stalk (scape); flowers open
in the early morning, but usually wither in a couple of hours. July–September. **FRUITS:** Capsules with tiny fusiform (spindle-shaped) seeds.
WHERE FOUND: Locally abundant in shallow water and around the margins of ponds, marshes, and depressions, usually in muck. A southeastern Coastal Plain species extending north into TN and AR. In TN, in
Grundy, Franklin, White, Warren, and Coffee counties. Rare. *X. iridifolia*.
SIMILAR SPECIES: BOG YELLOW-EYED GRASS (*X. difformis*) is a smaller plant
with **flower spikes only 0.2–0.6 in. long**. Low, wet, sandy soils. Atlantic and Gulf Coasts, less common inland. Thinly scattered in TN. Infrequent. July–September.

Notes: The species name *laxifolia* means "loose-leaved," and *iridifolia* means "iris-leaved,"
referring to the similarity between these leaves and those of an iris. • Surprisingly, despite
their similar appearance, yellow-eyed grasses are not related to the Grass or Iris Families, but
are more closely related to the Pineapple Family. Only 1 genus of this mostly tropical and
subtropical family occurs in North America.

Twisted Yellow-Eyed Grass · *Xyris torta*

GENERAL: Perennial herb, 8–32 in. tall; **scapes** (leafless flowering stems) are round and ribbed near the base, **twisted**, usually flattened directly below the spike. **LEAVES:** Basal, ascending, **dark green**, 8–20 in. long, 0.1–0.2 in. wide, usually **spiraled or twisted**, purplish at the base. **FLOWERS:** Yellow, tiny, **3 obovate petals** with blades to 0.16 in. long; borne in egg-shaped spikes, 0.4–1.0 in. long; flowers open during the morning. June–August. **FRUITS:** Capsules containing tiny, translucent, ellipsoid, longitudinally lined seeds. **WHERE FOUND:** Damp to wet, but often drying soil throughout most of the eastern U.S. In TN, primarily in the Western Highland Rim, Eastern Highland Rim, and Cumberland Plateau. Occasional. **SIMILAR SPECIES:** RICHARD'S YELLOW-EYED GRASS (*X. jupicai*), an **annual**, has yellow-green leaves without the purplish base; **leaves and flowering scape are usually not twisted**. Wet, sunny disturbed soils from VA to MO, south to FL and TX. In Middle TN, in Putnam, White, Warren, Van Buren, Coffee, Grundy, and Sequatchie counties. Infrequent. July–September.

NOTES: Of the 7 *Xyris* species known from TN, **Twisted Yellow-Eyed Grass** is the most likely to be encountered. However, as 4 of the 7 species are rare and often difficult to identify, all *Xyris* plants should be left undisturbed.

Asiatic Dayflower · *Commelina communis**

GENERAL: Fibrous-rooted **annual** with branched stems, 8–30 in. long, initially erect, later reclining and rooting at the lower nodes. **LEAVES:** Alternate, lanceolate-ovate, 2–5 in. long, bases sheathing the stem. **FLOWERS:** Showy, 3 petals, **upper 2 petals dark blue**, 0.3–0.6 in. long, **lower petal white**, much smaller; borne on slender pedicels from a **spathe (leaf-like bract) with edges open to the base**; each flower opens for 1 morning only. May–frost. **FRUITS:** 3-celled capsules; 2 cells each with 2 reddish brown seeds, about 0.15 in. long; upper (3rd) cell of ovary aborts. **WHERE FOUND:** Introduced from eastern Asia. Moist and shaded ground. Widespread weed across the eastern U.S. and TN. Frequent.

NOTES: The genus *Commelina* is named for the Commelins: Jan (1629–92) and his nephew Kaspar (1667–1731), who were Dutch botanists. They are represented by the 2 large petals; Kaspar's son, who died very young, is represented by the small lower petal since he passed away "before accomplishing anything in Botany" (Linnaeus). • The young leaves of this plant can be eaten raw, but older ones are better cooked. The flowers add a colorful flourish to salads. • The Spiderwort Family is a large, mostly tropical and subtropical family, represented in our flora by perennial or annual herbs. Three genera and 9 species are found in TN.

OTTO R. HIRSCH

OTTO R. HIRSCH

JERRY DROWN

Slender Dayflower
Commelina erecta

GENERAL: Perennial herb, 12–36 in. tall, from thick, fibrous roots; slender, erect, jointed stems, often branched, frequently weaken and arch or fall as the summer progresses. **LEAVES:** Alternate, linear to lanceolate, 2–6 in. long; bases form white-hairy sheaths around the stem. **FLOWERS:** Showy, 3 petals, **upper 2 petals pale blue** (rarely pink), 0.4–1.0 in. long; **lower petal white**, much smaller; borne on slender pedicels protruding from a folded spathe (leaf-like bract); **spathe edges fused for about the lower ¹⁄₃**; several spathes near the stem tip; each flower opens for 1 morning only. June–frost. **FRUITS:** Capsules with brown, smoothish seeds, about 0.12 in. long. **WHERE FOUND:** Dry soil, often along forest borders and roadsides. Scattered over the central and eastern U.S. In TN, throughout the Central Basin, thinly scattered elsewhere. Occasional.

NOTES: Spiderworts and dayflowers are quite similar, except that spiderwort flowers are never in spathes, and their 3 petals are uniform in size and color. • Many dayflower species are used in herbal medicine, made into tea to treat sore throats, colds, urinary infections, and intestinal irritations. • The roots of **Slender Dayflower** are edible.

KURT EMMANUELE

Virginia Dayflower
Commelina virginica

GENERAL: Rhizomatous perennial herb, 12–48 in. tall; stems often branched, robust, with stands of several dozen stems not unusual. **LEAVES:** Alternate, lanceolate, 4–8 in. long, 1–2 in. wide, bases sheathing the stem; sheath margins noticeably hairy with coarse, reddish hairs. **FLOWERS:** Showy, **3 pale blue petals, 0.4–0.6 in. long**, lower petal only slightly reduced; numerous terminal **spathes** (leaf-like bracts), **with lower ¹⁄₃ of margins fused**, bear a sequence of flowers; each flower opens for 1 day only. June–frost. **FRUITS:** 3-parted capsules with a few reddish brown, smooth seeds. 0.15–0.24 in. long. **WHERE FOUND:** Moist or wet woods and shaded ditches throughout the eastern U.S. from NJ to KS, southward. In TN, in West and Middle TN, and thinly scattered in East TN. Frequent. **SIMILAR SPECIES:** CREEPING DAYFLOWER (**C. diffusa**) is a highly branched, reclining **annual**; flowers have **3 small, blue petals, 0.2–0.3 in. long**; sickle-shaped (falcate) spathes, the **margins completely free (not fused)**. Damp woods and riverbanks, from VT to IL and KS, southward. West and Middle TN, also Blount and Hawkins counties in East TN. Occasional. June–October.

NOTES: The leaves of **Virginia Dayflower** are edible, especially when young, while the older leaves are better cooked. The colorful flowers can be added to salads.

Wideleaf Spiderwort
Tradescantia subaspera

GENERAL: Stout perennial herb, 16–36 in. tall; **stems clumped and succulent**. **LEAVES:** Alternate, firm, dark green, lanceolate, 4–8 in. long, **usually wider than 0.8 in.** and broader than the opened sheath. **FLOWERS:** Purplish blue, 3 ovate petals, 0.4–0.6 in. long; 3 **hairy sepals**; 0.2–0.4 in. long; on pedicels 0.4–0.8 in. long; borne in terminal and axillary cymes. June–July. **FRUITS:** 3-chambered capsules, 0.2 in. long; 1–2 seeds per chamber. **WHERE FOUND:** Rich woods and clearings, from NY to MO, south to FL and LA. Throughout TN.

HUGH & CAROL NOURSE

Common. **SIMILAR SPECIES:** OHIO SPIDERWORT (*T. ohiensis*) has smooth stems; **leaves usually less than 0.8 in. wide**, narrower than the opened sheath; pedicels and **sepals smooth**. Woods, meadows, and roadsides throughout the eastern U.S. Thinly scattered across TN. Occasional. April–July. HAIRY SPIDERWORT (*T. hirsuticaulis*) has **densely hairy stems**. Dry, rocky woods from the Gulf Coastal Plain, north to NC and AR. In TN, in Lawrence, Hickman, and Cheatham counties in the Western Highland Rim. Rare. April–July.

NOTES: The genus *Tradescantia* was named in honor of John Tradescant the Elder (c. 1570–1638), botanist and gardener to Charles I of England. Tradescant collected in Europe, Russia, Greenland, Algeria, Turkey, and the Holy Land and brought many new plants to England, including apricots.

Virginia Spiderwort, Widow's Tears · *Tradescantia virginiana*

GENERAL: Clumped perennial herb, with jointed, erect stems, 4–16 in. tall at flowering time. **LEAVES:** Alternate, linear, 0.2–0.6 in. wide, narrower than the sheath; bracts below the inflorescence are often wider and longer than the leaves. **FLOWERS:** Bluish purple, showy, 3 regular petals, 0.5–0.7 in. long; densely hairy sepals; slender, sparsely hairy pedicels, about 1 in. long; borne in terminal and axillary cymes. April–July. **FRUITS:** 3-chambered capsules with 1–2 gray seeds per compartment. **WHERE FOUND:** Rich wooded slopes, prairies, and meadows. A northeastern U.S. species extending south to GA and LA. Widespread across TN, but more frequent in Middle TN. Occasional.

DENNIS HORN

NOTES: The very young leaves of this plant are edible raw, but as the leaves get older, they must be cooked or they will be too tough to eat. • Native Americans used the roots of **Virginia Spiderwort** to make a tea to treat various stomach, kidney, and female ailments. The leaves were also mashed and made into a poultice for insect bites and skin inflammations.

Soft Rush, Common Rush · *Juncus effusus*

GENERAL: Smooth perennial herb, 12–48 in. tall, densely tufted; flowering stems erect, green, round in cross-section. **LEAVES:** Basal, consisting of reddish brown, **bladeless sheaths**, to 8 in. tall; involucral leaf extends upward from the base of the inflorescence, appearing as a continuation of the stem. **FLOWERS:** Flowers numerous, **greenish or pale brown**; 3 petals and 3 sepals, essentially alike, narrow, pointed, about 0.1 in. long; **branched inflorescence** spreads laterally from the base of the involucral leaf, with branches 2–4 in. long. July–September.

FRUITS: Brown capsules with numerous small seeds. **WHERE FOUND:** Margins of swamps and ponds throughout the U.S. and TN. Common. **SIMILAR SPECIES:** LEATHERY RUSH (*J. coriaceus*) has a **smaller inflorescence** with **fewer branches, to 1.6 in. long**, and fewer flowers; blades of **basal leaves prominent**. Swamps and wet ground throughout the southeastern U.S. and TN. Frequent. June–September.

NOTES: Soft Rush is a valued food for a wide variety of birds; muskrats use the plant for food and nesting material. Native Americans used it as a bedding material and occasionally for weaving. • Though sedge-like in appearance, **rushes have round stems and regular green or brown flowers**. There are 27 species listed for TN.

Path Rush, Poverty Rush · *Juncus tenuis*

GENERAL: Smooth perennial herb, 6–24 in. tall, somewhat tufted. **LEAVES:** Basal, narrow, 0.05 in. wide, flat or often rolled, about 1/3 to nearly as long as the flowering stems; involucral leaf, 1–4 in. long, often longer than the inflorescence, does not appear to be an extension of the stem. **FLOWERS:** Greenish or pale brown; 3 petals and 3 sepals, alike, narrow, pointed, 0.1–0.2 in. long; **loosely branched inflorescence**, each branch with 2–6 flowers. June–September. **FRUITS:** Ovoid, green or pale brown capsules, about 0.1 in. long, shorter than sepals; seeds numerous. **WHERE FOUND:** Dry or moist, often compacted soils along roads and paths throughout the U.S. and TN. Common. **SIMILAR SPECIES:** HEDGEHOG WOOD-RUSH (*Luzula echinata*) is a tufted perennial with many **hairy basal leaves and flowering stems**; branches of inflorescence widely spreading, each with a **dense flower cluster**. Woods, bluffs, and clearings, from NY to IA, south to FL and TX. Throughout TN. Common. March–August.

NOTES: Path Rush is also known as Wire Grass because of its tough stems, and as Slender Rush. • Wood-rushes of the genus *Luzula* are similar to rushes, but the capsules have only 3 seeds, and the leaves are hairy. Although rushes look similar to sedges and grasses, they have flowers with 3 petals and 3 sepals, and are more closely related to the Lily Family.

Frank's Sedge · *Carex frankii*

MILO PYNE

GENERAL: Perennial herb, 12–30 in. tall, in small, dense tufts. **LEAVES:** Alternate, grass-like, to 0.4 in. wide. **FLOWERS:** Tiny, male or female, in **erect spikes; terminal spike usually male (staminate)**, to 1 in. long and 0.1 in. wide; 3–7 dense, **greenish, cylindric, female (pistillate) spikes**, 0.5–1.5 in. long and 0.4 in. wide, **along the stem**, fruit-producing. June–September. **FRUITS:** Tiny achenes within sac-like, seed-bearing bracts (perigynia). **WHERE FOUND:** Open, wet places, from western NY to southeastern NE, south to FL and NM. Throughout Middle and East TN, and Tipton and Hardeman counties in West TN. Common.

NOTES: Many *Carex* species have a tender, whitish leaf base that is edible, having a pleasant, mild, and nutty flavor. The edible grain of Japanese Sedge (*C. kobomugi*) was used as a famine food in Eastern Asia. • Certain butterflies use grasses and sedges as host plants, including Branded Skippers (sometimes called Grass Skippers) and satyrs and their relatives. • Plants of the large Sedge Family are grass-like herbs, but unlike grasses, the stems are solid and usually triangular in cross-section. Also, sedges bear flowers in the axil of a single scale, whereas grass flowers are borne between 2 scales. • While predominantly wetland plants, sedges occur in a wide range of habitats. TN has 16 genera and over 240 species recorded. *Carex*, with over 140 species, is the largest genus of plants in TN.

Plantainleaf Sedge, Seersucker Sedge
Carex plantaginea

DENNIS HORN

GENERAL: Tufted perennial herb, 12–24 in. tall; flowering stems triangular with purple sheaths near the base. **LEAVES:** Mostly basal, **evergreen**, numerous, linear, **strap-like**, to 24 in. long and 0.5–1.0 in. wide, with **prominent parallel veins**, tinged with red-purple at the base. **FLOWERS:** Tiny, male or female, in dense, cylindric spikes; **terminal spike male (staminate)**, purplish, erect, 0.4–0.8 in. long, on a long stalk; 2–4 **erect, female (pistillate) spikes**, 0.4-1.2 in. long, scattered along the stem, **below the male spike**. April–May. **FRUITS:** Tiny achenes, sharply 3-angled, 0.15–0.2 in. long, within sac-like bracts (perigynia). **WHERE FOUND:** Rich hardwood forests from ME to MN, south in the mountains to AL and northern GA. In the eastern ½ of TN, also Wayne County. Frequent. **SIMILAR SPECIES:** FRINGED SEDGE (**C. crinita**), also called DROOPING SEDGE, is 2–5 ft. tall; grass-like leaves to 0.5 in. wide; **greenish flower spikes**, 1–3 male spikes above the 2–5 showy, **drooping female spikes**, each 1.5–4.0 in. long. Low woods and meadows from ME to MN, south to GA and TX. Across most of TN, but largely absent from the Central Basin. Common. May–June.

NOTES: The genus name *Carex* is Latin meaning "grasses with sharp leaves." The strap-like leaves of **Plantainleaf Sedge**, with the prominent veins and crinkled surface, account for the alternate common name, **Seersucker Sedge**.

JERRY DROWN

Fraser's Sedge
Cymophyllus fraserianus

GENERAL: Tufted perennial herb from a branched rhizome; scapes 4–16 in. tall at flowering. **LEAVES:** Each rhizome branch produces 1 leathery, **evergreen**, **strap-like** leaf, 0.8–2.0 in. wide and 8–20 in. long; other leaves sheath-like around the base of the stem. **FLOWERS:** Tiny, **white**, **showy**, male or female; in a **solitary spike** about 0.4 in. across, with male (staminate) flowers at the tip and female (pistillate) flowers below. March–May. **FRUITS:** Small achenes enclosed in inflated sacs (perigynia) that are ovoid, white, 3-nerved. **WHERE FOUND:** Moist ravines at lower elevations and rich woodlands, from southern PA to KY, south to northern GA. In TN, restricted to the mountainous area near the NC border in Polk, Monroe, Blount, Sevier, Cocke, Unicoi, Carter, and Johnson counties. Infrequent. *C. fraseri*, *Carex fraseri*.

NOTES: The only species in the *Cymophyllus* genus, this plant is endemic to the southern Appalachian Mountains. • The species name *fraserianus* honors John Fraser (1750–1811), a Scottish collector of North American plants who made several collecting expeditions, traveling from Newfoundland to the Carolinas. The Fraser Magnolia (*Magnolia fraseri*) was also named in his honor by his friend Thomas Walter of SC.

DENNIS HORN

False Nutsedge
Cyperus strigosus

GENERAL: Coarse, tufted, short-lived perennial herb, 6–24 in. tall, occasionally taller in robust plants; stems smooth, sharply triangular. **LEAVES:** Basal, numerous, linear, 0.1–0.4 in. wide, equal in length to the stems. **FLOWERS:** Several stalked, **cylindric spikes** arranged in a **terminal umbel**, each spike composed of 5–15 **straw-colored flowering spikelets** to 1 in. long; several long, leafy, **linear bracts** surround the base of the inflorescence. July–October. **FRUITS:** Reddish, papillose, 3-angled achenes, 0.06–0.08 in. long. **WHERE FOUND:** Open, wet places and shorelines throughout most of the U.S. and all of TN. Common.

NOTES: The genus name *Cyperus* is the Greek word for "sedge" and *strigosus* means "with stiff bristles." Plants of this genus are sometimes referred to collectively as "umbrella sedges" as individual spikes of the inflorescence radiate out from the top of the stem like the spokes of an umbrella.

Wool Grass · *Scirpus cyperinus*

PAUL SOMERS

GENERAL: Coarse, tufted perennial herb, 2–6 ft. tall, from a short rhizome; often forms dense colonies. **LEAVES:** Basal, numerous, grass-like, curving, 0.1–0.4 in. wide, to 24 in. long; alternate stem leaves shorter. **FLOWERS:** Greenish **spikelets** in large, **terminal, arching clusters**, becoming very **fuzzy** (woolly) in appearance as they mature; several long, **linear, leafy bracts, spreading and drooping**, just below the inflorescence. July–September. **FRUITS:** Yellowish, smooth, ellipsoid achenes. **WHERE FOUND:** Open, wet places and shorelines throughout the eastern and central U.S., southern Canada, and TN. Frequent.

NOTES: The genus name *Scirpus* is Latin for "bulrush" and "tule." • The stems of many *Scirpus* species were used by Native Americans for weaving baskets, mats, and seat covers. Many species are edible. Their starchy and sweetish tasting rootstocks were used as food by Native Americans, chewed raw or dried and ground. The roots are very fibrous, so they would often be sifted or passed through a food mill to remove the fibers. The pollen of various species was gathered and mixed with different flours for making cakes or other foods. • There are 6 *Scirpus* species in TN. Seven other species in TN, previously in *Scirpus*, have been moved to the genus *Schoenoplectus*.

Big Bluestem, Turkeyfoot
Andropogon gerardii

DENNIS HORN

GENERAL: Clumped, sod-forming perennial grass with erect, leafy stems, 3–8 ft. tall; **plant is bluish green** in summer, **turning light brown** in autumn. **LEAVES:** Alternate, linear, to 16 in. long and 0.2–0.4 in. wide; lower leaves and leaf sheaths often hairy. **FLOWERS:** Tiny, concealed by scales; a stalked, male (staminate) spikelet above a sessile, fertile (perfect) spikelet, arranged in pairs on a spike-like raceme, 2–4 in. long; **racemes (usually 3)** clustered in several **forked inflorescences** ("turkeyfeet") on **long peduncles**, terminal and from the upper leaf axils. August–October. **FRUITS:** Linear-ellipsoid grains, about 0.1 in. long, 1 per fertile flower. **WHERE FOUND:** Barrens, prairies, and roadsides, in the eastern and central U.S. Throughout TN. Frequent. **SIMILAR SPECIES: COMMON BROOMSEDGE (*A. virginicus*)** is 2–5 ft. tall; **racemes in pairs** on **short peduncles**. Fallow fields, open woods, and roadsides throughout most of the eastern U.S. and TN. Frequent. September–October.

NOTES: The species name *Andropogon* comes from the Greek *aner*, "man," and *pogon*, "beard," in reference to the silky hairs on the rachis (central axis of the spike) and pedicels of the inflorescence. The species name *gerardii* commemorates Louis Gerard (1733–1819), a French botanist who described the species from plants cultivated in Provence, France. • The name **Turkeyfoot** comes from the resemblance of the purplish 3-parted, finger-like flower clusters to turkey feet.

River Oats, Spangle Grass
Chasmanthium latifolium

GENERAL: Loosely colonial grass, 2–5 ft. tall, from stout rhizomes. **LEAVES:** Alternate, **narrowly lanceolate**, 4–8 in. long, 0.4–0.8 in. wide, flat, sharply fine-toothed, with smooth sheaths. **FLOWERS:** Tiny, concealed by scales, 6–17 florets in **flattened spikelets**, 0.6–1.6 in. long, 0.4–0.8 in. wide, **green, becoming tan with age**; numerous spikelets in an open, terminal, **drooping panicle**, 4–8 in. long. June–October. **FRUITS:** Dark red grains, 0.25 in. long, inside the spikelets, enclosed by flower scales. **WHERE FOUND:** Moist woods, streambanks, mesic to dry forests, and barrens, from NJ to WI and KS, south to FL and AZ. Throughout TN. Common. *Uniola latifolia.*

NOTES: The species name *latifolium* refers to the broad leaves of this plant. • **River Oats** is smaller, but otherwise resembles **Sea Oats** (*Uniola paniculata*) found on Atlantic and Gulf coastal dunes. TN has 2 other forest species of this genus, **Slender Woodoats** (*C. laxum*) and **Longleaf Woodoats** (*C. sessiliflorum*), but these both have **narrow inflorescences** with small, **erect spikelets**. • The Grass Family is a large family of mostly herbaceous plants with long, narrow leaves in 2 vertical rows, usually split leaf sheaths, and stems that are usually round and hollow between the joints. Economically, this is the world's most important plant family, providing pasture for grazing animals and grains for humans and livestock: rice, wheat, corn, oats, barley, and rye. TN has recorded 76 genera and over 260 species.

Silver Plumegrass · *Erianthus alopecuroides*

GENERAL: Tufted perennial herb with flowering stems 3–9 ft. tall, silky below the inflorescence and hairy at the leaf nodes. **LEAVES:** Alternate, linear, up to 24 in. long, 0.4–1.0 in. wide, with spreading hairs near the base. **FLOWERS:** Tiny, concealed by scales, in a spikelet with a flattened, **twisted awn, 0.4–0.6 in. long**, projecting from the tip; inflorescence of many racemes in a **dense plume**, silvery to tawny, 8–12 in. long, conspicuously **silky** from a ring of hairs around each spikelet. September-October. **FRUITS:** Reddish, ellipsoid grains, 0.1 in. long. **WHERE FOUND:** Old fields, fencerows, and woodland edges, from NJ to MO, south to FL and TX. Throughout TN. Common. *Saccharum alopecuroidum.* **SIMILAR SPECIES:** SUGARCANE PLUMEGRASS (*E. giganteus*) has a **brownish or purplish plume; nearly straight awn** is round in cross-section (not flattened). Moist soil and old fields, from NY to MO, south to FL and TX. Scattered across TN. Occasional. September–October. *S. giganteum.* RAVENNA GRASS (*E. ravennae**) is introduced from the Mediterranean, cultivated and sometimes escapes. It differs from native species by having **3 stamens (instead of 2)** and an **awn that is only 0.1–0.2 in. long**. Roadsides. Thinly scattered in the U.S. Recently naturalized in TN. Rare. August–September. *S. ravennae.*

NOTES: The genus name *Erianthus* is from the Greek words *erion*, "wool," and *anthos*, "flower," in reference to the plume-like inflorescence.

Redtop Panic Grass · *Panicum rigidulum*

GENERAL: Coarse, tufted perennial herb, 2–5 ft. tall, **without rhizomes. LEAVES:** Alternate, crowded near the base of the stems (culms), narrow, 8–16 in. long, rough margins, smooth-keeled sheaths. **FLOWERS:** Tiny, concealed by scales; **spikelets greenish purple**, about 0.1 in. long, **aligned with the pedicel;** inflorescence a narrow, pyramidal panicle, 4–12 in. tall, with **spikelets attached on 1 side** of the branches. July–September. **FRUITS:** Ellipsoid grains, 0.05 in. long. **WHERE FOUND:** Moist soils throughout the eastern U.S., west to TX. Throughout TN. Frequent. **SIMILAR SPECIES: BEAKED PANIC GRASS (*P. anceps*)** has scaly rhizomes; **spikelets are attached on 1 side** of the inflorescence branches and **set at an angle to the pedicel.** Moist soils throughout the eastern U.S., west to TX. Throughout TN. Common. July–September. **SWITCH GRASS (*P. virgatum*)** also has **rhizomes;** inflorescence an open panicle, 6–20 in. tall, with **spikelets,** 0.14–0.2 in. long, **attached on both sides** of the branches. Prairies and thin woods over most of the U.S. and TN. Frequent. July–October.

NOTES: The genus name *Panicum* comes from the Latin word *panus,* which means "an ear of millet." • **Switch Grass** is a dominant species in wet to wet-mesic barrens and in the midwestern tallgrass prairie. In TN, there are 14 *Panicum* species and 25 *Dichanthelium* (formerly *Panicum*) species.

DENNIS HORN

Yellow Indian Grass · *Sorghastrum nutans*

GENERAL: Loosely tufted perennial herb, 4–7 ft. tall, from short rhizomes; flowering stems few, smooth, with hairy nodes. **LEAVES:** Alternate, linear, glaucous, to 16 in. long and 0.2–0.4 in. wide, rough surface, sheaths smooth. **FLOWERS:** Tiny, concealed by scales, in hairy spikelets, about 0.25 in. long, each with a **bent awn, 0.3–0.6 in. long;** inflorescence a **narrow, terminal panicle,** 6–12 in. long, **turning from green to golden brown** in autumn. September–October. **FRUITS:** Flat, reddish grains, 0.1–0.15 in. long. **WHERE FOUND:** In barrens, along roadsides, and in old fields over the eastern ²/₃ of North America, also the midwestern tallgrass prairie. Throughout TN. Frequent. **SIMILAR SPECIES:** SLENDER INDIAN GRASS **(*S. elliottii*)** has a **dark brown, drooping panicle;** awns are twice bent, 0.8–1.4 in. long. Dry, sandy soil in the Coastal Plain, from MD to TX and occasionally inland. Mostly in the eastern ⅓ of TN, also Fayette County in West TN. Infrequent. September–October.

NOTES: The name *Sorghastrum* comes from the resemblance of plants in this genus to **Sorghum (*Sorghum bicolor*).** The species name *nutans* means "nodding." Oddly, although **Slender Indian Grass** has a nodding inflorescence, **Yellow Indian Grass** does not. • The flowers of Yellow Indian Grass attract bees, songbirds and small mammals eat the seeds, and deer browse the foliage. It also provides nesting sites and protective cover for pheasants, quail, and Mourning Doves.

DENNIS HORN

DENNIS HORN

Johnson Grass · *Sorghum halepense**

GENERAL: Robust, **rhizomatous perennial** herb, 2–6 ft. tall, forming dense, leafy stands; stems mostly smooth, leaf nodes hairy. **LEAVES:** Alternate, linear, tapering to a narrow tip, to 24 in. long and **0.4–0.8 in. wide**; prominent white midvein develops with maturity. **FLOWERS:** Tiny, concealed by scales, in **silky, paired spikelets**, about 0.25 in. long, each spikelet with a bent awn, 0.4–0.6 in. long; inflorescence an open, terminal, **pyramid-shaped panicle**, 5–20 in. long and ½ as wide. May–October. **FRUITS:** Reddish, flattened grains, about 0.1 in. long. **WHERE FOUND:** Introduced from southern Europe. Fields, pastures, and along roadsides throughout the U.S. and TN. Common. **SIMILAR SPECIES:** SORGHUM (*S. bicolor**), also called MILO, is an **annual** with **leaves well over 1 in. wide**. Introduced from Africa. Widely cultivated and escaped throughout the U.S. Thinly scattered across TN. Occasional. July–August.

NOTES: Plants in the *Sorghum* genus are used for making syrup and also provide a source of grain and forage. • A native of the Mediterranean region, **Johnson Grass** was introduced as a forage crop, but has become **a very troublesome and aggressive weed** in crop fields, pastures, and gardens. It spreads rapidly by seed or by vigorous rhizomes. A single mature plant may produce over 80,000 seeds and 200 feet of rhizomes. The seed can remain viable in the soil for up to 25 years and begins producing lateral rhizomes 6–9 weeks after germination.

DENNIS HORN

American Bur Reed
Sparganium americanum

GENERAL: Aquatic perennial herb, 12–36 in. tall, with sparingly branched, leafy stems; sometimes forms large stands. **LEAVES:** Alternate, **linear**, sheathing at the base, **soft, thin**, to 36 in. long and 0.2–0.7 in. wide, reduced to **spreading bracts** above. **FLOWERS:** Small, **whitish**, male or female, in **dense, sessile, spherical heads**, 0.5–0.8 in. wide (larger in fruit), along the upper stem and branches; male (staminate) heads above; female (pistillate) heads below. June–August. **FRUITS:** Dull brown achenes, 0.1–0.2 in. long, in dense, spherical heads about 1 in. wide; present from late summer until winter kill. **WHERE FOUND:** Shallow water of marshes, swamps, and streams throughout the eastern U.S. Scattered throughout TN, more prevalent on the Cumberland Plateau and spreading in Middle and West TN as beaver ponds become more plentiful. Frequent. **SIMILAR SPECIES:** BRANCHING BUR REED (*S. androcladum*) has **stiff leaves, ascending bracts**, and **shiny achenes**, 0.2–0.3 in. long. A northern species extending south to AL and TX. In TN, known only from Blount, Johnson, and Carter counties in East TN, and Grundy County in Middle TN. Rare. June–August.

NOTES: The genus name *Sparganium* is from the Greek *sparganion*, "swaddling band," referring to the long, narrow, ribbon-like leaves of plants in this genus. • The seeds of **American Bur Reed** are eaten by birds and waterfowl; muskrats are not picky and eat the entire plant.

Common Cattail, Broadleaf Cattail
Typha latifolia

THOMAS E. HEMMERLY

GENERAL: Semi-aquatic perennial herb, 3–10 ft. tall, forming dense stands from extensive rhizomes. **LEAVES:** Mostly basal, **linear**, **0.4–1.0 in. wide**, flattened, with **parallel veins**, sheathing at the base, taller than the inflorescence. **FLOWERS:** Tiny, numerous (1000s per plant) male or female; inflorescence a dense cylindric spike with 2 adjacent parts; **slender, yellow, upper spike** has male flowers only, shed soon after pollination; **lower spike wider**, 4–6 in. long, 0.8–1.2 in. thick, with female flowers only, **green when young, becoming brown with age**, persistent. May. **FRUITS:** Tiny achenes with soft bristles at the base, densely packed into fuzzy, brown cylindric spikes (cattails) that persist into winter. **WHERE FOUND:** Shallow water of ponds, ditches, and marshes throughout the U.S. and TN. Frequent. **SIMILAR SPECIES:** NARROWLEAF CATTAIL (*T. angustifolia*) is smaller with **narrow leaves, 0.2–0.4 in. wide**; male and female **flower spikes separated about 2 in**. Throughout most of the U.S. Thinly scattered across TN. Infrequent. May; cattails lasting into winter.

NOTES: Almost every part of a cattail has a practical use: the peeled rhizomes can be cooked like potatoes or dried and made into protein-rich flour; the young shoots are juicy with a nutty flavor; the base of the leaves can be eaten like an artichoke; the flowers can be eaten raw or cooked; the pollen can be used as flour without grinding or can be eaten with a little honey as dessert. The leaves are not edible, but can be woven into mats, seats, and baskets. The fluffy, white fruits have been used by hikers and campers as extra padding in shoes and as stuffing in pillows and sleeping bags. • Two species of the small Cattail Family occur in TN.

Blue Mud Plantain, Duck Salad
Heteranthera limosa

MARGRET RHINEHART

GENERAL: Smooth **aquatic annual**; flowering stems 6–12 in. tall. **LEAVES:** Basal and alternate on the stem; smooth, entire, **oblong to ovate, 1–2 in. long**, on petioles 4–6 in. long, bases sheathing. **FLOWERS: White to light blue**, 1.0–1.5 in. wide, perfect; **6 tepals**, spreading at the tip of a tube, 1.6–1.8 in. long; flowers solitary, emerging from a bladeless, sheathing spathe at the tip of the stem. July–October. **FRUITS:** 3-parted capsules with numerous seeds. **WHERE FOUND:** Shallow ponds, ditches, lakeshores, and persistently muddy areas in most of the Mississippi River drainage of the central U.S. In TN, in Henry, Stewart, Montgomery, Humphreys, and Davidson counties. Rare. **SIMILAR SPECIES:** WATER STARGRASS (*H. dubia*) is a perennial with **yellow flowers**, 0.4–0.8 in. wide; narrow **leaves are grass-like, to 6 in. long**. Throughout most of the U.S. Thinly scattered across TN. Occasional. July–frost. *Zosterella dubia*.

NOTES: The genus name *Heteranthera* comes from the Greek *heter*, meaning "various" or "different," and *anthera*, meaning "anther," for the dissimilar anthers in the original species; the species name *limosa* means "of marshy or muddy places," accurately describing this plant's favored habitat. The common name **Duck Salad** indicates that this plant is eaten by waterfowl.

DENNIS HORN

Mud Plantain
Heteranthera reniformis

GENERAL: Smooth perennial herb with flowering stems to 12 in. or longer, floating in water or trailing on mud, rooting at the nodes. **LEAVES:** Basal or alternate, entire, smooth, **kidney-shaped**, 0.4–2.0 in. wide, on petioles 1–5 in. long, bases sheathing. **FLOWERS:** **Bluish white**, about 0.5 in. wide, perfect; **6 tepals**, glandular-hairy outside, spreading at the tip of a tube, 0.2–0.4 in. long; flowers in clusters of 2–8 emerge from a folded spathe, 0.4–2.0 in. long, that forms the sheathing side or base of a leaf petiole; flowers of each cluster all open on the same day. August–frost. **FRUITS:** Capsules, 0.5–0.75 in. long, with many brown, longitudinally ridged seeds. **WHERE FOUND:** Shallow water or mud of ponds, ditches, reservoir margins, and similar habitats, in most of the eastern U.S. Scattered in Middle and West TN, also in Knox and Greene counties in East TN. Occasional.

NOTES: The species name *reniformis* means "kidney-shaped," referring to the shape of the leaves and providing another common name, **Kidneyleaf Mud Plantain**. Look for **Mud Plantain** creeping in mud or floating in shallow water, often in large colonies. • The Pickerelweed Family, sometimes called the Water Hyacinth Family, includes a small group of aquatic, usually perennial herbs, mostly of the tropics. The showy but invasive **Water Hyacinth** (***Eichhornia crassipes***), now a troublesome weed in the southeastern U.S., is included in this family. Two native genera occur in TN.

KURT EMMANUELE

Pickerelweed · *Pontederia cordata*

GENERAL: Robust **aquatic** perennial herb from thick, creeping rhizomes, often in **dense colonies**; flowering stems upright, often more than 24 in. tall, with 1 petioled leaf similar to the basal leaves. **LEAVES:** Mostly in a basal rosette, long-petioled, blades 3–7 in. long, entire, extremely variable, arrow- or heart-shaped to lanceolate. **FLOWERS:** **Lavender-blue to whitish**, funnel-shaped; **2-lipped**, each lip 3-lobed, 0.3–0.4 in. long, the **upper lip marked with yellow**; 6 stamens, 3 extending well beyond the corolla; inflorescence a dense, terminal, spike-like panicle, 2–6 in. long, with a bladeless, sheathing bract (spathe) at the base. June–frost. **FRUITS:** Achene-like, ellipsoid, with 1 red, glutinous, ovoid seed. **WHERE FOUND:** Usually in shallow water of lakes, streams, and ponds, throughout the eastern U.S. and southeastern Canada. Thinly scattered across TN in Lake, Obion, Crockett, Lewis, Rutherford, Warren, Coffee, Franklin, and Cocke counties. Infrequent.

NOTES: The species name *cordata* means "heart-shaped," referring to the shape of the leaves. • The leaf stalks of **Pickerelweed** float because they are filled with air chambers. This species is best observed in Reelfoot Lake, located in the northwestern corner of TN near Tiptonville, where dense stands commonly occur.

Lily Family (Liliaceae)

The Lily Family contains mostly perennial herbs with bulbs, rhizomes, or fleshy roots. It is known mostly for its ornamental garden plants, such as daylilies, hostas, hyacinths, lilies, and tulips. Popular garden vegetables including asparagus, leeks, and onions are also members of this Family. While many plants in the Lily Family have edible bulbs and in the past were an important food source for Native Americans, they should not be gathered because this kills the plant. Some of the plants, such as Death Camas (*Zigadenus leimanthoides*), are poisonous as they contain toxic alkaloids and glucosides.

1a. Stem leaves whorled **2**

  2a. Leaves in a single whorl; flowers solitary . . . . ***Trillium***

  2b. Leaves in 2 or more whorls; flowers 2–many **3**

    3a. Flowers 1 in. long or more . . . . ***Lilium***

    3b. Flowers less than 1 in. long . . . . ***Medeola***

1b. Stem leaves alternate, basal, or absent **4**

  4a. Flowers or flower clusters appearing axillary, leaves more than 0.4 in. wide **5**

    5a. Tepals fused . . . . ***Polygonatum***

    5b. Tepals separate **6**

      6a. Tepals recurved, pink to rarely whitish . . . . ***Streptopus***

      6b. Tepals not recurved, yellowish . . . . ***Uvularia***

  4b. Flowers solitary or in terminal inflorescences **7**

    7a. Perianth large and showy, more than 2 in. long . . . . ***Hemerocallis***

    7b. Perianth less than 2 in. long **8**

      8a. Flowers solitary or in umbellate clusters of more than 3 flowers **9**

        9a. Flowers solitary **10**

          10a. Leaves basal, stem unbranched . . . . ***Erythronium***

          10b. Leaves along stem, stem branched . . . . ***Uvularia***

        9b. Flowers 4–many, umbellate **11**

Aletris
p. 408

Allium
pp. 408–09

Chamaelirium
p. 411

11a. Plants with an onion or garlic odor . . . . ***Allium***

11b. Plants without an onion or garlic odor **12**

12a. Leaves linear, less than 2 in. wide . . . . ***Nothoscordum***

12b. Leaves oblong to obovate, 0.8–2.4 in. wide . . . . ***Clintonia***

8b. Flowers several to many, in pairs, spikes, racemes, panicles,
or at the tips or branches **13**

13a. Tepals united to the middle or beyond **14**

14a. Flowers blue or purplish . . . . ***Muscari***

14b. Flowers white **15**

15a. Perianth smooth externally; inflorescence arising from
a basal leaf sheath; ovary superior . . . . ***Convallaria***

15b. Perianth roughened externally; inflorescence arising from
a basal rosette; ovary about 1/3 inferior . . . . ***Aletris***

13b. Tepals separate to the base or nearly so **16**

16a. Stem leaves not greatly reduced upward; basal leaves absent **17**

17a. Leaves perfoliate . . . . ***Uvularia***

17b. Leaves not perfoliate **18**

18a. Tepals 4; leaves 2, rarely 3 . . . . ***Maianthemum***

18b. Tepals 6; leaves numerous **19**

19a. Flowers 1–3, terminating the branches . . . . ***Disporum***

19b. Flowers numerous, in panicles **20**

20a. Perianth white . . . . ***Smilacina***

20b. Perianth green . . . . ***Veratrum***

16b. Stem leaves greatly reduced upward; basal leaves
present and conspicuous **21**

21a. Leaves 2-ranked, iris-like; flowers white . . . . ***Tofieldia***

21b. Leaves not 2-ranked, flowers variously colored **22**

Hemerocallis
p. 415

Erythronium
pp. 414–15

Lilium
pp. 416–18

Stenanthium
p. 423

Trillium (sessile)
pp. 426–32

Trillium (pedicellate)
pp. 425–33

Uvularia
pp. 434–35

DENNIS HORN

Colicroot, White Stargrass
Aletris farinosa

GENERAL: Perennial herb, 20–40 in. tall, from a thick, short rhizome. **LEAVES:** Mostly in a **basal rosette**, narrowly lanceolate to oblanceolate, 3–8 in. long, tips acuminate; stem leaves greatly reduced or absent. **FLOWERS: Pure white**, tubular, 0.3–0.5 in. long, closely attached to the stem; 6 triangular lobes to 0.1 in. long, **outer surface mealy** (farinose); in a showy raceme, 4–8 in. long. April–June. **FRUITS:** 3-chambered capsules, tapered to a long beak; perianth persistent with fruit; seeds reddish brown, prominently ribbed. **WHERE FOUND:** Dry woodlands, grasslands, meadows, and old fields, in most of the eastern U.S. In TN, primarily in the Eastern Highland Rim, Cumberland Plateau, and the Blue Ridge; also Lewis County. Occasional.

NOTES: The scientific name is from the Greek words *aletris*, "a female slave who grinds corn," and *farinosa*, "mealy." The common name alludes to the fact that the ground root was considered a remedy for colic. This plant was also called **Unicorn-Root** because the stalk of the white flowers was thought to resemble a unicorn's horn. • The root has been used as a sedative and to soothe stomach pains.

OTTO R. HIRSCH

Wild Garlic, Canada Garlic
Allium canadense

GENERAL: Perennial herb, 8–24 in. tall, with a **strong onion odor**; lower ⅓ of the stout stem is leafy. **LEAVES:** Alternate, linear, **flat**, 4–12 in. long, 0.1–0.25 in. wide, bright green. **FLOWERS:** Small, **pink to whitish**, on pedicels to 1.2 in. long; 6 pointed tepals less than 0.25 in. long have a **magenta stripe** down the center; borne in an umbel with few flowers; **3-parted spathe** at the base has bulblets. April–May. **FRUITS:** Capsules with small, black, triangular seeds. **WHERE FOUND:** Fields, waste places, and moist woods throughout the central and eastern U.S. and TN. Frequent. **SIMILAR SPECIES: WILD ONION** or **FIELD GARLIC (A. vineale*)** has **tubular leaves** that are hollow toward the base; umbel has a wide, **unparted spathe**. Introduced from Europe. Now a problem weed of field and lawns throughout eastern U.S. and TN. Frequent. May–July.

NOTES: The word *Allium* is Latin for "garlic" or "onion." • Onions are easily recognized by their "alliaceous" odor, that is, they smell like onions or garlic. • *Allium* species arise from a bulb and have flat or tubular leaves with a sheathing base. The flowering stalk is topped by an umbel of flowers, just above very membranous or papery brown bracts. Often the flowers are replaced by bulblets. In fruit, the tepals persist as tough paper. Eight species are found in TN. • Medicinally, *Allium* species contain volatile oils and sulfur glycosides that act as a digestive stimulant and aid in expelling gas from the intestinal tract. Garlic is recommended for colds and has been shown to lower cholesterol. It contains a natural antibiotic.

Nodding Wild Onion
Allium cernuum

HUGH NOURSE

GENERAL: Perennial herb, 8–24 in. tall, with a **strong onion odor**. **LEAVES:** Several, mostly basal, linear, **flat**, glaucous, 4–16 in. long, **0.15–0.35 in. wide**. **FLOWERS:** Small, **rose to white**, on pedicels to 1.0 in. long; 6 tepals less than 0.25 in. long, rounded at the tips; in a **nodding umbel, without bulblets**, umbel stalk conspicuously bent at the top. July–September. **FRUITS:** Capsules with black, triangular seeds less than 0.1 in. long. **WHERE FOUND:** Open woods or rocky places throughout most of the U.S. Middle and East TN. Occasional. **SIMILAR SPECIES:** RAMP (**A. tricoccum**) has unusually succulent, flat-thickened leaves, **2–3 in. wide** and 12 in. long; leaf stalks, 0.75–3.0 in. long, often have a reddish cast; **flowers after leaves wither; flowers** with pale yellow to **cream tepals, 25–55 per umbel**. Rich woods of the northeastern U.S., south in the uplands to AL and GA. Middle and East TN. Occasional. July. **SMALL RAMP (A. burdickii)** has **leaves 0.8–1.6 in. wide**, usually without stalks, whitish at the base; **10–20 flowers** per umbel. Rich woods of the northeastern U.S. Thinly scattered across TN. Occasional. June.

NOTES: The species name *cernuum* is Latin for "drooping" or "nodding," referring to the hanging umbel on the bent stalk. • In some Appalachian communities, people collect the bulbs of **Ramp** and have an annual "ramp festival."

Prairie Onion, Glade Onion
Allium stellatum

THOMAS E. HEMMERLY

GENERAL: Perennial herb, 12–24 in. tall, with a straight flower stalk and a full cluster of flowers; **strong onion odor**. **LEAVES:** Few, **basal**, linear, channeled, **quite narrow** (about 0.06 in. wide), shorter than flower stalk. **FLOWERS:** Showy, **pink or lavender**, numerous; 6 tepals, 0.15–0.3 in. long; in a compact, **erect umbel**. July–August. **FRUITS:** 3-parted capsules, with 2 triangular protuberances at the tip of each compartment. **WHERE FOUND:** Rocky prairies and limestone glades of the Midwest and Great Plains. In TN, only in Davidson, Rutherford, and Wilson counties in the Central Basin of Middle TN. Rare. **SIMILAR SPECIES:** WILD LEEK (**A. ampeloprasum***) is taller, with a showy umbel of **red-purple flowers; leaves alternate** on the lower stem, **0.25–0.75 in. wide**, keeled. Introduced from Eurasia. Occasionally escapes from cultivation to roadsides in the eastern U.S. A few scattered locations in East and West TN. Infrequent. May–July. **GARLIC** (**A. sativum***) produces mostly **bulblets in the umbel**, instead of showy flowers. Introduced from Asia. Infrequent. June–July.

NOTES: **Prairie Onion** is also known as Lady's Leek and Wild Onion. The species name *stellatum* is from the Latin *stella*, "a star," referring to the flowers. It is listed as an endangered species by the Tennessee Department of Environment and Conservation. • **Wild Leek** bulbs are collected in early spring, long before the flowers appear, and are considered a delicacy. Since the species is introduced, collecting the bulbs is not a concern.

NITA R. HEILMAN

Fly Poison
Amianthium muscitoxicum

GENERAL: Bulbous perennial herb, 12–36 in. tall.
LEAVES: Predominantly basal, linear, to 16 in. long and 0.8 in. wide, forming a **dense tuft**. **FLOWERS: Showy, white**, to 0.4 in. wide, **without glands**, brownish bract beneath; 6 tepals, rounded at the tip; in a terminal raceme, 2–5 in. long, 1.0–1.5 in. wide; **flowers turn greenish** after pollination. May–July. **FRUITS:** 3-chambered capsules with 1–2 dark brown, lustrous seeds per chamber. **WHERE FOUND:** Mesic to dry woodlands, from southern NY to OK, south to FL and LA. In East TN, also scattered in southern Middle TN. Occasional.

NOTES: This monotypic genus (i.e., containing only 1 species) is easily confused with members of the genus *Zigadenus* (p. 436). It can be separated by the lack of glands on the flowers, the usually brownish inflorescence bracts, and a generally larger tuft of basal leaves. • This plant is also called Fall Poison, because it poisoned cattle that fed on it in autumn. Another name, Stagger-Grass, comes from cattle suffering the "staggers," a cerebrospinal disease, from eating the plant. The **bulb is extremely poisonous** and is a natural insecticide, but the nectar serves as food for the Silver-spotted Skipper and other butterflies.

OTTO R. HIRSCH

Wild Hyacinth • *Camassia scilloides*

GENERAL: Perennial herb, 12–36 in tall, from a bulb about 1 in. thick. **LEAVES:** In a dense **basal tuft, grass-like**, narrow, 12–30 in. long, 0.12–0.5 in. wide. **FLOWERS:** Pale blue, sometimes fading to white; 6 tepals, linear to elliptic, 0.5–0.75 in. long, joined at the base; stamens $^1/_2$–$^3/_4$ the length of the tepals, with slender filaments; styles united, tipped with a 3-cleft stigma; in a terminal raceme, 4–12 in. long, with papery bracts. April–May. **FRUITS:** Capsules with few to several seeds. **WHERE FOUND:** Rich, shady coves and slopes, wet woods, and usually on calcareous or basic soils from PA to WI, south to GA and TX. Primarily in Middle TN, also Roane, Knox, and Sullivan counties in East TN. Occasional.

NOTES: This plant is also known as Eastern Camass and Atlantic Camas. The flowers of **Wild Hyacinth** bloom from the bottom of the stem upward over a period of weeks. • **Camas** (**C. quamash**), a similar species that is common in the Northwest, is reported to have saved the Lewis and Clark expedition from starvation. • Unfortunately, the common name Camas has also been applied to the **highly poisonous Death Camas** (p. 436), and there have been instances of people wrongly ingesting Death Camas, thinking it is the edible Camas.

Fairy Wand, Devil's Bit
Chamaelirium luteum

GENERAL: Perennial herb from stout rhizomes, **plants either male or female**; male plants 12–30 in. tall, female plants up to 48 in. tall. **LEAVES:** In a **basal rosette, evergreen**, spatulate, 3–8 in. long, 0.6–2.5 in. wide, reduced upward on the stem. **FLOWERS:** Male flowers **whitish**, maturing to cream, 6 tepals 0.12–0.16 in. long, 6 showy stamens as long as the tepals; female flowers **greenish white**, 6 tepals, 0.08–0.12 in. long; flowers in spikes without bracts; **male spikes** erect at first, up to 5 in. long, **drooping at the tip when mature; female spikes** erect, less than 2 in. long at first, lengthening to 12 in. long when mature, **remaining erect** as fruits develop. May–July. **FRUITS:** Ellipsoid capsules, 2x as long as wide; seeds reddish brown, membranous at either end. **WHERE FOUND:** Mesic to dry, often open woods, in most of the eastern U.S. and southeastern Canada. Throughout TN. Frequent.

NOTES: The name **Devil's Bit** comes from an old story, which relates that the Devil bit off the end of the root for spite, and if it were not for the Devil, the plant would be useful to humans. • This plant is also known as **False Unicorn-Root**, Blazing Star, Grubroot, and Squirrel Tail.

JERRY DROWN

Bluebead Lily, Yellow Clintonia
Clintonia borealis

GENERAL: Erect perennial herb with a scape 6–15 in. tall. **LEAVES:** Basal, 2–5 (usually 3), dark **glossy green**, 4–16 in. long, oblong to elliptic, margins fringed with a few hairs. **FLOWERS:** Greenish **yellow, nodding**, similar petals and sepals (3 each), 0.6–0.7 in. long; leafless inflorescence a short, terminal raceme of **3–8 flowers**. May–June. **FRUITS:** Ellipsoid, **bright blue berries**, 0.3–0.4 in. long **WHERE FOUND:** A northeastern species extending south in the mountains to GA. In TN, only at higher elevations in the Blue Ridge Mountains of East TN, especially in spruce-fir forests in Carter, Cocke, Greene, Johnson, Monroe, Sevier, and Unicoi counties. Infrequent.

NOTES: The genus *Clintonia* is named for DeWitt Clinton (1769–1828), the 3-term governor of NY. He was responsible for the construction of the Erie Canal and was well known for writing books on natural history. • Other names for this plant include Balsam Bell, Bear Plum, Calf Corn, Canada Mayflower, Cow Tongue, and Wood Lily.

KURT EMMANUELE

KURT EMMANUELE

Speckled Wood Lily, White Clintonia · *Clintonia umbellulata*

GENERAL: Erect perennial herb, 8–15 in. tall.
LEAVES: Basal, 2–5 (usually 3), elliptic to ovate, 6–12 in. long, 1.0–3.5 in. wide, **fringed** with many long hairs near the base. **FLOWERS:** White, often with **purple spots**; similar petals and sepals (3 each), 0.3–0.4 in. long; in a terminal **umbel of 10–24 erect flowers** at the end of a leafless stalk. April–May. **FRUITS:** Ellipsoid, **blackish berries**, about 0.3 in. long, in an umbel. **WHERE FOUND:** Acidic soils of woods with rhododendron, hemlock, and sweet birch at lower mountain elevations from northern GA to central NY. In similar habitats of East TN, westward to the Cumberland Plateau in Middle TN. Occasional.

NOTES: The species name *umbellulata* means "a small umbel," for the shape of the inflorescence. It is also known as Clinton's Lily. • The young, unfurling leaves of this plant have a pleasant, cucumber-like taste and can be eaten raw. Older leaves are better cooked and eaten like spinach.

DENNIS HORN

American Lily-of-the-Valley
Convallaria majuscula

GENERAL: Perennial herb to 8 in. tall, plants generally scattered and **not densely colonial**. **Leaves:** Alternate on a short stem, usually 2–3, widely elliptic to oblance-olate, 6–12 in. long, 2–5 in. wide. **FLOWERS:** White, fragrant, **bell-shaped**, nodding; 6 united tepals, 0.25–0.4 in. long, tipped with small, recurved lobes; 1 stamen attached to the base of each tepal; in a simple **raceme that does not extend beyond the middle of the lowest leaf**, lower part of inflorescence stalk is sheathed by leaf bases, lowest bract of flower stalk at least 0.3 in. long or more. April–May. **FRUITS:** Spherical, **orange berries**, 0.3–0.4 in. across. **WHERE FOUND:** Rich upland woods, from PA to KY and GA. In TN, from the Eastern Highland Rim, eastward. Occasional. *C. montana*. **SIMILAR SPECIES:** EUROPEAN LILY-OF-THE-VALLEY (*C. majalis**) usually grows in **dense colonies**; leaves to 6 in. long and 2 in. wide; **raceme extends beyond the middle of the lowest leaf**; lowermost flower stalk bract is 0.2 in. long or less. Introduced from Europe. Escaped from cultivation and spread across the U.S. Thinly scattered in TN. Infrequent. April–May.

NOTES: The genus name *Convallaria* is Latin for "valley." Both lily-of-the-valley species are **highly poisonous** because they contain cardiac glycosides, similar to those found in Common Fox-glove (*Digitalis purpurea*), which affect muscle tissue (especially heart muscle contraction) and circulation.

Yellow Mandarin, Fairybells
Disporum lanuginosum

GENERAL: Erect perennial herb, 16–36 in. tall, with branched stems. **LEAVES:** Alternate, sessile, thin, ovate or lanceolate, 2–5 in. long, 0.8–2.0 in. wide, parallel **veins prominent. FLOWERS:** Pale yellow to greenish yellow, unspotted; similar petals and sepals (3 each), separate, spreading, 0.5–0.8 in. long; flowers, 1–3, hang like bells from the uppermost leaf axils. April–May. **FRUITS: Smooth, elliptic berries**, turning **orange**, about 0.5 in. long. **WHERE FOUND:** Moist, deciduous woods, from southern Ontario to northern AL and northern GA, mostly in the highlands. In TN, from the Eastern Highland Rim eastward, also Sumner, Davidson, Williamson, Maury, Giles, and Stewart counties. Frequent. *Prosartes lanuginosa.*

NOTES: *Disporum* is from the Greek *di*, "double," and *spora*, "seed," referring to the paired ovules found on plants in this genus. The common name **Fairybells** (also Yellow Fairybells) is descriptive of the flowers that hang like bells. • The berries, a food source for birds and rodents, are edible in moderation.

DENNIS HORN

Spotted Mandarin
Disporum maculatum

GENERAL: Erect perennial herb, 8–30 in. tall; upper stem forked, hairy when young; lower stem with sheathing bracts. **LEAVES:** Alternate, sessile, thin, elliptic or oval, 1.5–4.0 in. long, acuminate tips, **prominent parallel veins** with stiff hairs on the underside. **FLOWERS: Cream to white, peppered with purplish spots**; similar petals and sepals (3 each), 0.6–1.0 in. long; flowers, 1–3, hang like bells from the uppermost leaf axils. April–May. **FRUITS: Hairy, 3-lobed, knobby, white berries**, turning yellowish, about 0.5 in. long. **WHERE FOUND:** Rich woods over neutral or calcareous soils, from MI and OH, south in the mountains to Al and GA. In TN, from the Eastern Highland Rim, eastward. Occasional. *Prosartes maculata.*

NOTES: This plant is also known as Nodding Mandarin. • The flowers of this species are showier and somewhat larger than those of **Yellow Mandarin** (see above). It is a striking wildflower that can be easily overlooked because the flowers hang beneath the leaves. Its favored habitats are steep, wooded hillsides and rich ravines.

NITA R. HEILMAN

White Trout Lily
Erythronium albidum

GENERAL: Smooth perennial herb, 4–8 in. tall, **densely colonial**, from thickened underground stems (corms); sterile corms numerous, each producing 1 leaf; fertile corms few, each producing 2 leaves and a flower. **LEAVES:** Opposite, 2, dark green **mottled with brown**, thick, oblong, 2–8 in. long, 1–2 in. wide, tapered to base and tip. **FLOWERS:** Tepals 6, **white**, darker outside, 1–2 in. long, **strongly recurved** (spreading on sunny days); yellow anthers, stigma 3-cleft; flowers solitary, nodding. March–April. **FRUITS:** Obovoid capsules, 0.4–0.8 in. long, rather blunt-tipped; reddish brown seeds. **WHERE FOUND:** Rich, moist woods, often on basic soils, from NY to SD, south to GA and TX. Middle TN, also Shelby, Fayette, and Haywood counties in West TN and Hamilton County in East TN. Occasional. **SIMILAR SPECIES: PRAIRIE TROUT LILY (*E. mesochoreum*)** is another white-flowered species found in MO and AR, but has not yet been reported from TN. It is **seldom colonial** and the **leaves are not mottled**. Dry, open woods and prairies from IN to NE, south to TX. March–April.

NOTES: *Erythronium* species are nearly stemless perennial herbs arising from deep, solid, scaly corms, sprouting with 1 leaf when juvenile and 2 when mature. The flowers, which are large in proportion to the plant and quite showy, are always on plants with 2 leaves, and the flower stalk is bent, making the flower nod. Like other *Erythronium* species, **White Trout Lily** occurs in large colonies.

Yellow Trout Lily • *Erythronium americanum*

GENERAL: Perennial herb, 6–9 in. tall, **extensively colonial**, from thickened underground stems (corms); fertile corms each produce 2 leaves and a flower. **LEAVES:** Opposite, 2, green mottled purple-brown, elliptic, 4–6 in. long, near the base of the stem. **FLOWERS:** Tepals 6, **yellow, often red-spotted inside**, darker-colored outside, 0.8–1.6 in. long, **strongly recurved**, with strongly forked, outward-arching lateral veins; **inner tepals** with a small rounded **auricle** ("ear") just above the base; **conspicuous anthers**, yellow or red; flowers solitary, nodding. March–May. **FRUITS:** Capsules, flat, rounded, or pointed at tip when mature, but **not indented, held well off the ground**. **WHERE FOUND:** Rich woods throughout most of the eastern U.S. and southeastern Canada. Widespread in TN, but mostly absent from West TN. Common. **SIMILAR SPECIES: DIMPLED TROUT LILY (*E. umbilicatum*)** is **never colonial**; flowers lack the auricle on the inner tepals; mature **capsules are indented** at the top and **lie flat on the ground**. Rich woods and sunny, moist, moss-covered areas, from MD to KY, south to FL. East TN, also Sumner and Davidson counties in Middle TN. Occasional. March–May.

NOTES: Yellow Trout Lily has many common names including **Adder's Tongue**, **Fawn Lily**, **Dogtooth Violet**, Deer's Tongue, Rattlesnake Violet, and Yellow Snowdrop. Plants in the *Erythronium* genus are often called "dogtooth violets" because their hard, white, bulblike corms resemble canine teeth. • Trout lilies have been called "living phosphorus sinks," because their roots retrieve phosphorus from the soil and transfer it to the leaves, making it available to herbivores, such as deer. The leaves are edible to humans as well, and along with the roots, have many medicinal uses. **Warning:** The use of the leaves may cause an **allergic reaction.**

Beaked Trout Lily
Erythronium rostratum

DENNIS HORN

GENERAL: Perennial herb, 4–8 in. tall, growing in patches or colonies, from thickened underground stems (corms). **LEAVES:** Opposite, 2 on mature (flowering) plants and occasionally a small 3rd leaf, 2–4 in. long, entire, lanceolate to elliptic, smooth, green with **patches of brown and purple**, tapering to a petiole. **FLOWERS:** Tepals 6, **yellow**, 1.0–1.5 in. long, **spreading to weakly recurved; yellow anthers**; flowers solitary, nodding. March–April. **FRUITS:** Prominently **beaked capsules**; reddish brown, crescent-shaped seeds. **WHERE FOUND:** Moist, rich woods from OH to KS, south to AL and TX; a more southern and western species. In TN, in Henderson, Hickman, Wayne, Lawrence, and Marion counties. Rare.

NOTES: Trout lilies are noticeable for their **speckled leaves** and nodding flowers. They are most often found beneath bare branches of deciduous trees, taking advantage of early spring sunlight. • The name "trout lily" refers to the mottling or speckling on the leaves that resemble the markings on a trout, or perhaps the name was given to these plants because they flower in spring when trout are biting. They are also known as "fawn lilies," a reference to the spots on newborn deer.

Common Daylily, Orange Daylily
Hemerocallis fulva*

JOHN OATES

GENERAL: Perennial herb, 30–48 in. tall, arising from a tuber; **colonial**. **LEAVES:** Basal, **linear**, 24–36 in. long, rather succulent, smooth, emerging in early spring. **FLOWERS:** Tepals 6, **bright orange**, occasionally yellow or red, **without fragrance**, 3–5 in. long, flaring outward from a narrow tube at the base; large, conspicuous stamens extend just beyond the tepals; borne in 2 tight, terminal racemes, each with bracts. May–July. **FRUITS:** Rarely developing. **WHERE FOUND:** Introduced from Eurasia. Very persistent after cultivation in abandoned homesites, along roadsides and on the edges of pastures and fields. Naturalized throughout most of the eastern U.S. and TN. Occasional.

NOTES: The genus name *Hemerocallis* is from the Greek words *hemera*, "day," and *kallos*, "beauty," referring to the beautiful flowers that last only 1 day and thus accounting for the common name, daylily. The species name *fulva*, "tawny" or "reddish yellow," refers to the color of the flowers. • Despite its attractive, showy flowers, this species is a sterile triploid (having 3 sets of chromosomes) that can only reproduce vegetatively. Cultivated hybrid daylilies come in a range of colors and shapes and flower throughout summer, making them ideal ornamental plants. • The flowers and buds are edible when cooked, and the tubers can be eaten raw or cooked any time of the year.

DENNIS HORN

Canada Lily
Lilium canadense

GENERAL: Perennial herb, 2–5 ft. tall; stem smooth, branched above. **LEAVES:** In whorls of 4–12 at 6–10 stem nodes, lanceolate, 3–6 in. long, **widest at or below the middle**, tapered to both ends, rough along margins and on midvein beneath. **FLOWERS:** Tepals 6, **yellow or orange to red**, heavily spotted, 2–3 in. long, **slightly recurved or spreading**, widest toward the middle; **anthers held tightly together**, barely extending past the tepals; flowers 1–5, nodding on long stalks. June–July. **FRUITS:** 3-chambered capsules, packed with numerous flat seeds. **WHERE FOUND:** Open, moist woods and balds. A northeastern species ranging south in the uplands to GA and AL. Thinly scattered in Middle and East TN. Occasional.

NOTES: The lily has been known since the beginning of civilization. It is mentioned in both the Bible and the Talmud. In Scandinavian legend, Thor carries a lightning bolt in one hand and his scepter, crowned with a lily, in the other. • *Lilium* species are erect perennial herbs arising from scaly bulbs. The leaves are alternate or whorled and generally succulent. Sepals and petals are similar and are called "tepals," never joined but often overlapping to form a tube. The tepals are often orange to red, spotted with purple or brown. The stamens usually are slightly longer than the pistil, with brownish anthers. The stigma is 3-lobed, and the style is very long. Six *Lilium* species are found in TN.

JOHN OATES

Gray's Lily • *Lilium grayi*

GENERAL: Perennial herb, 2–4 ft. tall, with a stout, smooth stem. **LEAVES:** In whorls of 4–8 at 3–8 stem nodes, narrowly elliptic, acute- or blunt-tipped, 2–4 in. long, 0.3–1.0 in. wide, margins coarse or roughened. **FLOWERS: Bell-shaped**; 6 tepals, **red with dark spots** nearly to the tip, **flared, not recurved** or widely spreading, 1.5–2.5 in. long; anthers not usually extending beyond the tepals; flowers 1–9, held **nearly horizontal**. June–July. **FRUITS:** Capsules, 1.5–2.0 in. long. **WHERE FOUND:** Balds and openings at high elevation. Endemic to the high mountains of VA, NC, and TN. In TN, in Johnson and Carter counties of the Blue Ridge Mountains of upper East TN. Rare.

NOTES: This species is also known as Bell Lily, Roan Lily, and Roan Mountain Lily. The common name and the species name *grayi* both honor Asa Gray (1810–88), one of America's leading 19th-century botanists. • Folklore says that lilies used in church floral arrangements often had their stamens removed based on the belief that once pollinated, the aroma of the lily flower became a foul odor (H.W. Rickett).

Carolina Lily · *Lilium michauxii*

GENERAL: Perennial herb, 2–4 ft. tall, with a stout, erect stem. **LEAVES:** Mainly in whorls of 3–7, sometimes alternate on the upper stem, fleshy, **glaucous**, smooth, oblanceolate (**broadest above the middle**), 2.5–5.0 in. long, 0.6–1.0 in. wide, becoming smaller ascending the stem. **FLOWERS:** Tepals 6, **orange-red fading to yellow** in the throat, lower 1/2 purple-spotted, **strongly recurved**, lanceolate, tapering sharply to the tip, 3–4 in. long; stamens project well beyond the tepals; flowers usually 1–6, nodding from long stalks. July–August. **FRUITS:** Ellipsoid capsules, 2 in. long, 1 in. wide; flat, brown seeds. **WHERE FOUND:** Dry to moist woodlands and thickets, along the Coastal Plain from VA to TX, also in the mountains from KY and WV, southward. In TN, only recorded from the counties of the Blue Ridge Mountains in East TN. Infrequent.

NOTES: The species name *michauxii* honors André Michaux (1746–1802), a French botanist who explored extensively in North America and wrote *Flora of North America*, published posthumously in 1803. • The flowers of this species are sometimes more orange than those of **Turk's-Cap Lily** (p. 418), but color is not a reliable characteristic for distinguishing between these 2 species.

JERRY DROWN

Michigan Lily
Lilium michiganense

GENERAL: Perennial herb, 3–7 ft. tall, with a stout, erect stem, branched above. **LEAVES:** Mainly in whorls of 5–20, sometimes alternate on the upper stem, lanceolate, **widest at or below the middle**, tapering to both ends, 3–7 in. long, 0.4–1.2 in. wide, rough along the margins and on midvein beneath. **FLOWERS:** Tepals 6, **orange to red, heavily spotted with purple** from the center to beyond the middle, lanceolate, 2.2–3.2 in. long, **strongly recurved**; anthers, 0.3–0.6 in. long, on **long, divergent filaments**, extending well beyond the tepals; flowers usually 3–25, nodding on long ascending or erect stalks. June–July. **FRUITS:** Angular, 3-parted capsules, to 2 in.

HUGH & CAROL NOURSE

long. **WHERE FOUND:** Moist woods and wet meadows. A mostly midwestern species extending south to AL and MS. Primarily Middle TN, also in Anderson County in East TN. Occasional.

NOTES: This species is also known as Michigan's Turk's-Cap Lily. • This showy plant is often cultivated. Plants in cultivation often have more flowers than those growing in the wild. • Some authors list this plant as a subspecies of the **Turk's-Cap Lily** (p. 418).

Wood Lily, Prairie Lily
Lilium philadelphicum

GENERAL: Perennial herb, 12–36 in. long, with an erect stem. **LEAVES:** Mostly in whorls of 4–7, lanceolate to oblanceolate, tapering to the tip, 2–4 in. long, 0.3–1.0 in. wide. **FLOWERS:** Tepals 6, **reddish orange** to bright yellow on the lower part, **spotted, clawed**, 1.5–3.0 in. long, 0.6–1.2 in. wide, each constricted at the base to a tight, round stalk to 1 in. long, upper part spreading and tapered to a point; often only 1 **erect, terminal flower**, but may be as many as 5 flowers per stem. June–July. **FRUITS:** Capsules, to 2 in. long, less than 1 in. wide. **WHERE FOUND:** Thin woods, meadows, and along shores, from ME to MT, south to GA and NM. In TN, in Grundy, Van Buren, Sequatchie, Hamilton, Cumberland, Fentress, Morgan, Scott, and Claiborne counties. Infrequent.

NOTES: Wood Lily is the most common name for this plant in the eastern part of its range. Other common names include Fire Lily, Flame Lily, Huckleberry Lily, Orange-Cup Lily, Tiger Lily, and Red Lily, in reference to the reddish orange flowers. • This species has erect flowers, while the flowers of most other lily species droop.

Turk's-Cap Lily
Lilium superbum

GENERAL: Perennial herb, 4–8 ft. tall, with a stout, erect stems, branched above. **LEAVES:** Mainly in whorls of 5–20, becoming alternate on the upper stem, lanceolate, **widest at or below the middle**, tapering to both ends, 3–7 in. long, 0.4–1.2 in. wide, smooth or nearly so on the margins. **FLOWERS: Orange to red, liberally spotted with purple** and with a distinguishing **green "star" inside the flower tube**; 6 tepals lanceolate, 2.4–3.6 in. long, **extremely recurved**; stamens with anthers 0.6–1.0 in. long, **on spreading filaments**, extending well beyond the tepals; flowers usually 3–25 (potentially 65–70), nodding, on long, ascending or erect stalks. July–September. **FRUITS:** Angular capsules to 2 in. long. **WHERE FOUND:** Moist woods, meadows, and balds, from NH and MN, south to FL and AR, mainly in the uplands. In TN, recorded only in the Blue Ridge counties of East TN. Infrequent.

NOTES: The species name *superbum* means "superb," in reference to the striking flowers. Other common names for this plant are Nodding Lily, Martagon, Swamp Lily, and Wild Tiger Lily. • Botanist Mark Catesby (1683–1749) reported that Native Americans boiled the roots for food. • **Turk's-Cap Lily** is generally the tallest of the 6 native *Lilium* species in TN.

Canada Mayflower
Maianthemum canadense

GENERAL: Perennial herb, **2–8 in. tall**, with a single, erect stem. **LEAVES:** Alternate, 2–3, smooth, ovate, 1–3 in. long, sessile or short-stalked, with a heart-shaped base. **FLOWERS:** White; **4 tepals** (2 petals, 2 sepals), elliptic, reflexed, about 0.1 in. long; 4 stamens; in a terminal raceme, 1–2 in. long. April–May. **FRUITS:** Berries, about 0.2 in. across, **with greenish red splotches**, similar to berries of Solomon's Plume (p. 422). **WHERE FOUND:** A northern species extending south in the mountains to GA. In TN, in deciduous and mixed hemlock and white pine hardwood forests in the Blue Ridge Mountains of East TN. Infrequent.

NOTES: This plant's common name is a translation of the scientific name: *Maius* for "May" and *anthemon* for "flower"; *canadense* for "Canada." It is also called Elf Feather, Heartleaf, Muguet, One Blade, Scurvy Berries, Tobacco Berries, **Wild Lily-of-the-Valley**, and **False Lily-of-the-Valley**. As the bittersweet fruit looks like dark, translucent beads, the plant is sometimes called Bead Ruby. The berries are edible, but only in small amounts.

KURT EMMANUELE

Indian Cucumber Root
Medeola virginiana

GENERAL: Erect perennial herb, 12–30 in. tall; thin, **wiry stems** have sparse, **cottony clumps of hair**. **LEAVES:** In **1–2 whorls**, lower whorl of 5–11, smaller upper whorl of 3 (on flowering plants only); narrowly elliptic to oblanceolate, 2.5–5.0 in. long, tapering at both ends; leaves in the upper whorl usually reddened at the base. **FLOWERS:** Greenish yellow; **6 recurved tepals**, about 0.3 in. long; 3 **purplish-brown, thread-like stigmas** extend conspicuously beyond the tepals; 6 purplish stamens, 0.2-0.3 in. long; 3–9 nodding flowers on long, slender stalks from the smaller, uppermost leaf whorl. April–May. **FRUITS:** Round, **dark purple to black berries** about 0.3 in. wide. **WHERE FOUND:** Mesic hardwood or mixed coniferous-hardwood forests throughout the eastern U.S. and southeastern Canada. In TN, from the Eastern Highland Rim eastward, also in Hardeman, McNairy, Hardin, Henderson, Carroll, and Henry counties in West TN. Frequent.

NOTES: The genus name *Medeola* commemorates Medea, a sorceress in Greek mythology. • The edible rhizome is crisp and juicy, with the taste of cucumber, and was eaten by Native Americans. It is best raw or pickled.

JERRY DROWN

Bluebottle • *Muscari neglectum**

GENERAL: Perennial herb, 4–9 in. tall, from a bulb, often escaped from cultivation. **LEAVES:** Basal, linear, 4–12 in. long, narrow, grooved on 1 side, **reclining and recurved at the tip, withering soon** after the flower stalk emerges. **FLOWERS:** Urn-shaped to ellipsoid, blue to violet (rarely white), **nodding**, about 0.25 in. long; 6 tepals united nearly to the tip; stamens joined to the perianth for about ½ their length; lower flowers fertile; the few upper flowers sterile and usually lighter in color; inflorescence a **compact raceme** with bracts below each flower. April–May. **FRUITS:** 3-chambered capsules, distinctly angled, with 2 angular seeds per chamber. **WHERE FOUND:** Introduced from Europe. After cultivation, remains in abandoned lawns and waste places. Throughout the eastern U.S. Middle TN, also Henry and Shelby counties. Occasional. *M. atlanticum, M. racemosum.* **SIMILAR SPECIES:** COMMON GRAPE HYACINTH (*M. botryoides**) has **globular flowers** and **erect leaves**. Introduced from Europe. Abandoned lawns and waste places throughout most of the eastern U.S. Middle TN, also Shelby County in West TN and Knox County in East TN. Infrequent. April–May. TASSEL GRAPE HYACINTH (*M. comosum**) has a **loose, elongate raceme** with **flowers on long pedicels.** Introduced from Europe. Escaped to waste places. Widely scattered in the eastern U.S. and across TN. Rare. May.

NOTES: The genus name *Muscari* comes from the Greek *moschus*, "musky smell," referring to the sweet scent; *botryoides* means "resembling a bunch of grapes." • All *Muscari* species, commonly called "grape hyacinths," are non-native plants that often escape from cultivation.

False Garlic
Nothoscordum bivalve

GENERAL: Perennial herb, 4–12 in. tall, from a bulb; **no onion or garlic odor** (bulb sometimes has a faint onion odor when very fresh). **LEAVES:** Basal, few, linear, flat, glaucous, 4–8 in. long, 0.1–0.15 in. wide. **FLOWERS:** White, 6 tepals, 0.4–0.5 in. long, often with a **greenish yellow cast** or with a diffused green or purple midvein on the underside; stamens about ⅔ the length of tepals; in a **loose terminal umbel** of 5–12 flowers, outer flowers opening first and the inner last. March–May. **FRUITS:** 3-valved capsules with angular, black seeds. **WHERE FOUND:** Fields, open woods, pastures, and thin soil around limestone outcrops, from southeastern VA to IL and NE, southward. Middle TN, thinly scattered in East TN, mostly absent from West TN. Frequent, often abundant when encountered. *Allium bivalve.*

NOTES: The genus name *Nothoscordum* from the Greek *nothos*, "false," and *scordon*, "garlic," provide the common name **False Garlic**, referring to this plant's onion-like appearance and lack of actual onion or garlic aroma. The species name *bivalve* means "having 2 valves," in reference to the valved fruit capsule. However, False Garlic capsules have 3 valves, not 2.

Star-of-Bethlehem
Ornithogalum umbellatum*

GENERAL: Perennial herb, 4–12 in. tall, from a bulb. **LEAVES:** Linear, basal, 5–18 in. long, 0.1–0.25 in. wide, with a **white stripe on the upper surface**; withered at the time of flowering. **FLOWERS:** White, 6 **spreading tepals**, 0.6–0.8 in. long, with a **broad green stripe on the underside**; inflorescence a corymb of 3–10 flowers, elongating into a raceme as fruits develop. March–May. **FRUITS:** Obtusely 3-angled capsules with few seeds. **WHERE FOUND:** Introduced from Europe. Now widely naturalized in lawns, waste places, old fields, and alluvial woods throughout the eastern U.S. Scattered across TN. Occasional.

JERRY DROWN

NOTES: The genus name *Ornithogalum* is derived from the Greek words *ornis*, "bird," and *gala*, "milk." The genus was named and described by Dioscorides (40–90 CE) in *De Materia Medica* as having an abundance of flowers that when "opened they are like milk," forming a mass of white. Other common names for this plant are Dove's Dung, Snowdrops, Starflower, and Summer Snowflake. The names **Sleepydick** and Nap-at-Noon refer to the characteristic of the flowers to close at night or when not in full sunlight. • This species is considered **poisonous** and contains cardiac glycosides in all parts of the plant, with the bulbs having the highest amount. Sheep and other livestock have been killed by grazing on the plant.

Smooth Solomon's Seal
Polygonatum biflorum

GENERAL: Perennial herb with a single, **arching stem**, 12–48 in. long, from knotted, white rhizomes; stem is naked below, leaves on the upper stem have half-clasping bases. **LEAVES:** Alternate, in **2 rows**, elliptic to oval, 2–6 in. long, **prominent parallel veins, smooth beneath**. **FLOWERS:** Tubular, 0.5–0.9 in. long, with 6 short lobes, **greenish when young, white when mature**; 6 stamens attached at or above the middle of the tube; stigma barely 3-lobed; 1–several flowers, on short pedicels, **hang from the leaf axils** on a single stalk. April–June. **FRUITS:** Round, **blue or black berries**, about 0.4 in. across. **WHERE FOUND:** Rich, moist woods throughout the central and eastern U.S. and TN. Common. **SIMILAR SPECIES:** HAIRY SOLOMON'S SEAL (**P. pubescens**) has a shorter stem, to 36 in. tall; smaller **leaves are hairy on the underside veins**. Rich woods, from ME to MN, south to GA. In TN, from the Eastern Highland Rim, eastward. Occasional. April–June.

CALYSTA HAGLAGE

NOTES: The genus name *Polygonatum* comes from the Greek *poly*, "many," and *gony*, "knee," referring to the knotty rhizome; *biflorum* means "2 flowers." The common name "Solomon's Seal" refers to the circular scars on the rhizome that are left by each year's flower stalk and resemble wax seals. • The young shoots and rhizomes are edible. • Species referred to as King Solomon's Seal (*P. commutatum*) and Great Solomon's Seal (*P. canaliculatum*) are actually more robust forms of *P. biflorum* with double the usual number of chromosomes.

DNH/PAUL SOMERS

Sunnybells · *Schoenolirion croceum*

GENERAL: Smooth perennial herb, scapes 8–15 in. tall, arising from a bulb; stem extends below the bulb and functions as a taproot. **LEAVES:** Basal, **linear**, 8–24 in. long, 0.08–0.16 in. wide, **bright chartreuse green**. **FLOWERS:** Dark, rich yellow; 6 tepals, 0.2–0.3 in. long, united near the base; stamens slightly shorter than tepals; pistil with a short style and stigma; on pedicels 0.2–0.8 in. long; in a raceme, with a bract below each flower. March–April. **FRUITS:** Capsules with lustrous, black seeds. **WHERE FOUND:** Sandy soils and swamps, from NC and TN, south to FL and TX. In TN, locally abundant in seeps alongside limestone outcrops in the cedar glades of Davidson, Wilson, Rutherford, Marshall, and Bedford counties in the Central Basin of Middle TN. Rare.

NOTES: The genus name *Schoenolirion* is from the Greek words *schoen*, "reed" or "rope," referring to the linear leaves, and *liri*, "lily." The species name *croceum* means "saffron" or "orange color," referring to the color of the flowers. Another common name for this plant is **Yellow Sunnybells**. • State Route 840 near Murfreesboro, TN, was redirected in the 1990s to avoid destroying a population of **Sunnybells**.

Solomon's Plume, False Solomon's Seal · *Smilacina racemosa*

B. WAYNE SWILLEY

GENERAL: Perennial herb, 16–36 in. tall, with unbranched, erect, **arching stems**. **LEAVES:** Alternate, in **2 rows**, sessile, elliptic, 3–6 in. long, finely hairy beneath, **prominent parallel veins**. **FLOWERS:** White, **0.1–0.2 in. wide**; similar petals and sepals (3 each), separate; numerous flowers in a **dense terminal panicle**, 2–6 in. long. March–June. **FRUITS:** Berries, red or green with red splotches, about 0.25 in. across. **WHERE FOUND:** Moist, mostly deciduous woods throughout the U.S., southern Canada, and TN. Common. *Maianthemum racemosum*. **SIMILAR SPECIES:** STARRY

SOLOMON'S PLUME (**S. stellata**) looks like a diminutive version of **Solomon's Plume**. It differs by having fewer, showier, **larger, more star-like flowers, 0.25–0.4 in. wide**, in a **terminal raceme**; fruits are black berries. Moist woods, shores, and prairies. A northern species barely extending south to TN. In TN, along moist streambanks in Sullivan and Pickett counties. Rare. May–June. *M. stellatum*.

NOTES: According to some sources, **False Solomon's Seal** was used medicinally in the same ways as "true" Solomon's Seal (*Polygonatum*, p. 421), although others say that this plant was called "false" because it does not contain the mystical or medicinal properties of the other plant. • The fresh berries are edible, but only in small quantities. Both False Solomon's Seal and **Starry Solomon's Plume** were used as food by Native Americans.

Featherbells
Stenanthium gramineum

GENERAL: Showy perennial herb, 12–60 in. tall, arising from a bulb. **LEAVES:** Basal leaves few, not forming a dense tuft; stem leaves **alternate, linear,** 8–20 in. long, 0.2–0.6 in. wide, reduced upward on the stem. **FLOWERS:** White, usually less than 0.5 in. wide; 6 **narrow, pointed tepals;** in an **elongated panicle** with the top branch a raceme much longer than the side branches, **appearing loose and wispy.** July–September. **FRUITS:** Lanceolate capsules; brown, narrowly ellipsoid seeds, tapering at both ends. **WHERE FOUND:** Open woods and meadows from PA to MO, south to FL and TX. In TN, from the Cumberland Plateau eastward, also Davidson, Lewis, and Wayne counties in Middle TN. Occasional.

NOTES: The genus name *Stenanthium* is Greek for "narrow flower," and the species name *gramineum* means "grass," referring to the narrow tepals and leaves. • This plant is not difficult to identify when in flower, because of its showy panicles of white flowers. Immature or non-flowering plants of this species can be mistaken for grass by a casual observer.

JERRY DROWN

Rosy Twisted Stalk • *Streptopus roseus*

GENERAL: Perennial herb, 12–30 in. tall, with erect, **arching,** branched stems. **LEAVES:** Alternate, in **2 rows,** sessile, lance-ovate, 2–3 in. long, **prominent parallel veins, margins fringed** with short hairs. **FLOWERS:** Bell-shaped, **nodding, pink with darker reddish streaks;** 6 tepals, 0.3–0.4 in. long, separate, overlapping, recurved at the tips; flowers hang below leaves on thin, **zigzag stalks,** 1–2 per leaf axil. April–June. **FRUITS:** Ellipsoid, **red berries,** 0.4 in. across. **WHERE FOUND:** Rich woods in the northern U.S. and Canada, extending south in the mountains to GA. In TN, at high elevations in Carter, Johnson, Greene, Sevier, and Washington counties, especially in beech gaps and in boulder fields under Yellow Birch and Mountain Maple. Rare. *S. lanceolatus.* **SIMILAR SPECIES:** WHITE TWISTED STALK (*S. amplexifolius*) has **leaf margins that are entire** or very finely toothed; **tepals are greenish white.** Rich, moist woods. A northern species extending south to NC and TN in the mountains. In TN, known only from high-elevation beech gaps in Carter and Sevier counties. Rare. May–June.

NOTES: The genus name *Streptopus* is Greek for "twisted foot" or "stalk." The species name *roseus* means "rosy." Other common names, Liverberry and Scootberry, refer to the aftereffect of eating too many of the sweet berries: diarrhea, which was locally called "the scoots."

DENNIS HORN

DENNIS HORN

Coastal False Asphodel
Tofieldia racemosa

GENERAL: Rhizomatous perennial herb, 12–30 in. tall, with a mostly leafless, **erect, unbranched stem, covered with short,** stiff, spreading **hairs. LEAVES:** Basal, erect, linear, 6–16 in. long, 0.2 in. wide; single bract-like leaf below the middle of the flowering stem. **FLOWERS: Yellowish white**; 6 oblong, spreading tepals, 0.16 in. long; 6 stamens with flattened filaments and spherical anthers; superior ovary topped with 3 short, awl-shaped styles; in a **dense terminal raceme**, 2–6 in. long, with flowers in clusters of 3, **opening from the top down**. July. **FRUITS:** 3-parted capsules; reddish brown seeds, 0.1 in. long, with membranous white tails at either end. **WHERE FOUND:** Wet barrens. A Coastal Plain species, from NJ to FL to TX with a disjunct population in TN in Coffee County. Rare.

NOTES: The species name *racemosa* refers to the flower clusters, which are racemes. Thomas Walter (1740–89), the botanist who first named this native plant, lived in the coastal city of Charleston, SC.
• A Greek myth relating to the European plant, Asphodel (*Asphodelus ramosus*), says that it grew in Hades (the underworld), and was a favorite food of the dead. In ancient times, Asphodel was planted near gravesites.

Genus Trillium

Of the 30 or 31 *Trillium* species found in the eastern U.S., 17 are found in TN. Photographs of all are included here. *Trillium* species are divided into 2 major groups. **Toadshades**, also called sessile trilliums, have a stalkless flower attached directly above a whorl of 3 mottled leaves (7 toadshades are found in TN). **Wakerobins**, also called pedicellate trilliums, have the flower on a stalk that rises from a whorl of 3 solid green leaves (10 wakerobins are found in TN).

Here is a quick guide to the toadshades and wakerobins shown on the following pages:

Trilliums have been used medicinally for a wide range of ailments: in poultices for insect bites and stings and also in teas to treat asthma, bronchitis, and hemorrhaging from the lungs, as well as for a menstrual stimulant.

Catesby's Trillium, Rose Trillium • *Trillium catesbaei*

KURT EMMANUELE

GENERAL: Erect perennial herb, 8–20 in. tall. **LEAVES:** In a whorl of 3, **solid green**, ovate to elliptic, 3–6 in. long. **FLOWERS:** White or pink, turning pinkish rose with age, 3 petals, 1.4–2.2 in. long, recurved, with wavy margins; **somewhat twisted, outward-curved anthers** with egg-yellow pollen; **greenish white ovary**; solitary, **stalked** flowers, **nodding beneath the leaves.** April–May. **FRUITS:** Ovoid berries, 0.5 in. across. **WHERE FOUND:** Prefers more piney, upland woods than any other *Trillium* species. From southwestern GA and eastern AL to southeastern TN and central NC. In TN, in the mountains from Cades Cove in the Great Smoky Mountains to the Monteagle and Sewanee area in Franklin, Marion, Polk, McMinn, Monroe, Blount, and Sevier counties. Infrequent.

NOTES: The species name honors Mark Catesby (1683–1749), a British naturalist who made 2 trips to North America to collect flora and fauna. He wrote *The Natural History of Carolina, Florida, and the Bahama Islands.* • Another common name for this species is **Bashful Wakerobin**, referring to the nodding flower. • Though trillium flowers are very attractive and inviting, they should never be picked, as the 3 leaves below the flower are the plant's only source of food, and the trillium is likely to die or take many years to recover. In fact, it is illegal to pick trilliums in British Columbia, WA, OR, and NY.

DENNIS HORN

Sweet Betsy
Trillium cuneatum

GENERAL: Erect perennial herb, 6–15 in. tall. **LEAVES:** In a whorl of 3, **mottled**, ovate, sessile, 3–7 in. long. **FLOWERS:** Maroon, yellow, bronze or green; fruity, spicy, banana-like fragrance; 3 erect, **sessile petals**, oblanceolate, 1.0–2.5 in. long, at least 3x as long as stamens; **stamens** blunt at the tip, **without prominent, pointed projections**; flowers solitary. March–May. **FRUITS:** Maroon red, many-seeded berries, 0.5 in. long. **WHERE FOUND:** A variety of woodland habitats from the Coastal Plain of MS and AL, north to KY and southern IL, and east to the Piedmont of NC, SC, and GA. In TN, the most prevalent deciduous woodland trillium, from the Western Highland Rim, east to the western flank of the Smoky Mountains, where it is replaced by Yellow Trillium (p. 429). Frequent.

NOTES: The name **Sweet Betsy** refers to the unusual "sweet" and **fruity aroma of the flower**. This plant is sometimes called Beth Root as a variation of another name, Birthroot, which indicates its folkloric, and unproven, medicinal value. Other common names include Whippoor-will Flower, and Large Toadshade or Purple Toadshade for the similarity of the mottled leaves to toad or frog skin, as well as the arrangement of the leaves, which suggests that toads could use them for shade.

DENNIS HORN

Trailing Trillium · *Trillium decumbens*

GENERAL: Perennial herb with a partially erect, mostly **trailing stem**, to 6 in. long, densely hairy near the top. **LEAVES:** In a whorl of 3, resting on the ground, **strongly variegated**, sessile, broadly ovate, 3–4 in. long. **FLOWERS:** Maroon, **3 sessile petals**, slightly twisted, 2–3 in. long, about 4x longer than the stamens; **stamens** tipped with long, terminal, **beak-like projections**; pollen golden yellow; flowers solitary. March–April. **FRUITS:** Dark purple, ovoid, many-seeded berries, to 0.8 in. across. **WHERE FOUND:** Rich hardwood forests, usually near small creeks, from southeastern TN and northern GA, southwest into central AL. In TN, known only from the Conasauga River watershed of Polk County. Rare.

NOTES: This plant is also called **Decumbent Trillium**. The species name *decumbens* means "lying flat but with the end upturned." • Trillium seeds are plump with a white, oil-rich appendage that is very attractive to ants, and trilliums are among the few plants whose seeds are spread by ants. Upon germination, 6–7 years may be required before flowering occurs.

Red Trillium, Stinking Benjamin · *Trillium erectum*

GENERAL: Erect perennial herb, 6–15 in. tall, with an unpleasant odor. **LEAVES:** In a whorl of 3, **solid green**, broadly rhombic, 2–8 in. long and wide. **FLOWERS: Maroon or white**, occasionally green or yellow, resembling a cup and saucer in profile, with **petals and sepals** (the "saucer") nearly **at right angles to the stamens and ovary** (the "cup"); 3 petals, 1.0–2.4 in. long; stamens about as long as the pistil; round, **purplish black ovary**; flowers solitary, on erect stalks. April–May. **FRUITS:** Juicy, dark, maroon berries with numerous seeds. **WHERE FOUND:** A more northeastern species ranging from southeastern Canada, south in the mountains to GA. In TN, in the Blue Ridge, with a few isolated populations westward near Cumberland Gap and in Hamilton County. Infrequent.

HUGH NOURSE

NOTES: The species name *erectum* refers to the erect flower stalk. • This plant is also commonly called **Red Wakerobin**. The name **Stinking Benjamin**, as well as **Stinking Willie**, refers to the pungent odor of the flowers, which have been described as smelling like a wet dog. Other less commonly used names are American True-Love, Bumblebee Root, Indian Shamrock, and Threeleaf Nightshade. • In the Smoky Mountains, lower elevations tend to feature white-flowered forms, while higher elevations tend to harbor the other petal colors.

Bent Trillium, White Trillium
Trillium flexipes

GENERAL: Erect perennial herb, 8–20 in. tall. **LEAVES:** In a whorl of 3, **solid green**, sessile, rhombic, 3–6 in. long and wide. **FLOWERS:** White, rarely maroon; 3 petals, 0.8–2.0 in. long; **white to pink ovary**, protruding, flask-shaped; stamens with **creamy anthers**, longer than the white filaments; flowers solitary, on **stalks**, 1.6–5.0 in. long, **ascending to bent** under leaves, sometimes changing orientation as the fruit matures. April–May. **FRUITS:** Purplish, ovoid, juicy, fragrant berries, 6-ridged, many-seeded, to 1 in. across. **WHERE FOUND:** Rich woods from NY to SD, south into MS, AL, and GA. In TN, in limestone regions west of the Smoky Mountains to the Western Highland Rim, especially in sinkholes and on calcareous slopes. Occasional. **SIMILAR SPECIES:** Closely related to **SOUTHERN RED TRILLIUM** (*T. sulcatum*), p. 432, with which it forms hybrid swarms with interesting petal colors.

NOTES: Bent Trillium is also known as **Nodding Wakerobin**. • If you kneel close to the flower, a trillium may emit a pleasing fragrance or a musty or stale odor (or worse, the smell of carrion). Bent Trillium smells like old sneakers.

KURT EMMANUELE

DAVID KOCHER

Large-Flowered Trillium
Trillium grandiflorum

GENERAL: Erect perennial herb, 6–20 in. tall. **LEAVES:** In a whorl of 3, **solid green**, rhombic to mostly ovate, 3–6 in. long, veins prominent. **FLOWERS:** White, **turning pink with age, resembling trumpets**, with 3 petals, 1.6–3.0 in. long, flaring outward from a tightly rolled, tube-like base; stamens 0.6–1.0 in. long, with prominent **yellow anthers** readily visible; **pale green ovary**; flowers solitary on **erect to spreading stalks.** April–May. **FRUITS:** Pale green, ovoid berries, 0.5 in. long. **WHERE FOUND:** Rich, moist deciduous forests, from southeastern Canada and the northeastern U.S., south to northeastern AL and northern GA in the highlands. In the eastern ½ of TN. Frequent.

NOTES: This showy species occurs in large colonies in the Smoky Mountains at medium to low elevations. It is one of the showiest and most common trilliums in eastern North America. • After germination, a trillium first produces only 1 leaf and requires another 6–7 years before it flowers for the first time. • **Large-Flowered Trillium** is the floral emblem of the province of Ontario, Canada.

DENNIS HORN

Lanceleaf Trillium
Trillium lancifolium

GENERAL: Erect, smooth perennial herb, 6–12 in. tall, from a slender rhizome. **LEAVES:** In a whorl of 3, **mottled**, sessile, **narrowly elliptic**, 2–3 in. long, rarely more than 1 in. wide. **FLOWERS:** Maroon, rarely yellow; 3 petals, 1.0–1.5 in. long, 4x or more longer than broad; sepals spreading to recurved; **stamens curved inward** over the ovary; flowers solitary, **sessile**. April–May. **FRUITS:** Many-seeded, 6-angled (or winged) berries. **WHERE FOUND:** Rich hardwood forests on lower slopes and floodplains, from southeastern TN to SC, south to MS and FL. In TN, recorded only from Marion and Hamilton counties. Rare.

NOTES: This species, also called Lance-leaf Wakerobin, is closely related to **Prairie Trillium** (p. 430), which has strongly recurved sepals, wider leaves, and a more northern distribution. • For more information about trilliums, including their cultivation, the book *Trilliums* by Frederick Case and Roberta Case is highly recommended.

Yellow Trillium · *Trillium luteum*

GENERAL: Smooth, erect perennial herb, 6–15 in. tall. **LEAVES:** In a whorl of 3, **mottled**, sessile, ovate to elliptic, 3–6 in. long. **FLOWERS: Yellow, lemony fragrance**, lacking maroon coloration on inner parts, deepening in brilliance during flowering; 3 petals, 1.5–2.5 in. long; flowers solitary, **sessile**. April–May. **FRUITS:** Yellowish green, 6-angled, many-seeded berries. **WHERE FOUND:** Rich woods, mostly in the southern Appalachian Mountains from VA to KY, south to AL and GA. In TN, a distinctive feature of the woodlands, from the Eastern Highland Rim, eastward, but particularly showy in the Smoky Mountains. Frequent.

NOTES: The species name *luteum* means "yellow." This plant is also known as **Yellow Wakerobin** and forms hybrid swarms with **Sweet Betsy** (p. 426). • The flowers of **Yellow Trillium** are **redolent of lemons or a sweet citrus aroma**, and they range in color from yellow to various shades of green or chartreuse. • Trilliums differ from other members of the Lily Family and are often placed in their own family. They have showy petals that wither into persistent remnants and sepals that stay green through fruiting. Lilies, in contrast, have similar sepals and petals (called tepals) that fall off neatly leaving only the fruit to mature. Mature trilliums have a single flower arising from a whorl of 3 leaves at the top of the stem.

KURT EMMANUELE

Least Trillium, Dwarf Trillium
Trillium pusillum

HUGH & CAROL NOURSE

GENERAL: Erect perennial herb, 3–8 in. tall. **LEAVES:** In a whorl of 3, **solid green**, sessile, lance-ovate, 1–3 in. long, **less than 1 in. wide. FLOWERS: White, turning pink with age**; 3 petals, 0.6–1.2 in. long; stamens with a distinctive lavender color between the anther sacs; flowers solitary, on **erect stalks**. March–April. **FRUITS:** White, ellipsoid berries, 0.4–0.5 in. long. **WHERE FOUND:** Swampy, red maple–black gum woods or rocky, oak-hickory forests, from northern AL to central KY, west to the Ozarks and east to the Atlantic Coast. In TN, restricted to the Cumberland Plateau and the Highland Rim in Cumberland, Sumner, Coffee, Lincoln, Franklin, and Putnam counties. Infrequent.

NOTES: This species resembles a dwarf **Large-Flowered Trillium** (p. 428) with narrower leaves and lavender-tinged anthers. • The species name *pusillum* is Latin for "very small." It is also known as **Dwarf Wakerobin** and Ozark Wakerobin. • Variants of this species may be recognized based on distribution and morphology.

NITA R. HEILMAN

Prairie Trillium · *Trillium recurvatum*

GENERAL: Erect, perennial herb, 6–15 in. tall, from a slender horizontal rhizome. **LEAVES:** In a whorl of 3, **mottled**, 2–6 in. long, ovate to elliptic; **short petioles**, 0.2–0.4 in. long. **FLOWERS:** Maroon, rarely yellow; 3 petals, 2–3x as long as broad, with narrowed bases resembling claws; **sepals becoming sharply recurved** and extending downward between the leaf petioles; flowers solitary, **sessile**. March–April. **FRUITS:** Green (often streaked with white and purple), rhombic-ovoid, 6-angled, many-seeded berries. **WHERE FOUND:** Rich, usually calcareous woods. Mainly a midwestern species ranging southward to AL and eastern TX. In TN, persists in gardens in East TN; occurs naturally from the Cumberland Plateau, westward. The only trillium reported from the Memphis area, along the Mississippi River bluffs. Frequent.

NOTES: The species name *recurvatum* refers to the recurved sepals that reflex sharply, pointing straight down the stem between the upright petals and the stalked, spreading leaves. • **Prairie Trilliums** prefer shaded areas and moist soils and are often found growing in large colonies, rarely alone.

KURT EMMANUELE

Southern Nodding Trillium
Trillium rugelii

GENERAL: Erect perennial herb, 6–20 in. tall. **LEAVES:** In a whorl of 3, **solid green**, rhombic-ovate, 3–6 in. long and wide. **FLOWERS:** White, rarely pink or maroon; 3 petals, ovate, recurved, 1–2 in. long; stamens often bicolored with white filaments and **vivid purple anthers**; ovary usually white with purplish splotches; flowers solitary, **stalked, nodding** below the leaves. April–May. **FRUITS:** Maroon, fleshy, 6-ridged berries, to 0.8 in. across, with numerous seeds. **WHERE FOUND:** Rich hardwood forests, from TN and NC, south in the Blue Ridge and Piedmont, and in AL, GA, and SC in the Coastal Plain. In TN, generally at lower elevations in the mountains of East TN, in Blount, Sevier, Cocke, Unicoi, Carter, and Washington counties. Infrequent.

NOTES: Wakerobins in TN may be divided into 3 groups: *grandiflorum*, *erectum*, and *undulatum*. *T. catesbaei* (p. 425), *T. grandiflorum* (p. 428), and *T. pusillum* (p. 429) form the *grandiflorum* group and have petals that turn pink with age. The *erectum* group includes *T. erectum* (p. 427), *T. flexipes* (p. 427), *T. rugelii*, *T. simile* (p. 431), *T. sulcatum* (p. 432), and *T. vaseyi* (p. 433). The species in this group have rhombic leaves and 6-angled ovaries. They are distinctive in the middle of their ranges, yet readily hybridize where their ranges overlap. *T. undulatum* (p. 433) is the only TN species in the *undulatum* group, with petioled leaves and 3-angled ovaries.

Sessile Trillium
Trillium sessile

GENERAL: Erect, smooth perennial herb, 4–12 in. tall, with an unpleasant odor. **LEAVES:** In a whorl of 3, **lightly mottled**, elliptic to ovate, 2–4 in. long, sessile. **FLOWERS:** Maroon, rarely yellow, bronze or green, with a **strong carrion odor**; 3 elliptic petals, 0.7–1.4 in. long, about 2x as long as stamens; **stamens with prominent, beak-like extensions**; solitary, **sessile** flowers. March–April. **FRUITS:** Dark green, ovoid, 6-angled berries, about 0.5 in. across, with numerous seeds. **WHERE FOUND:** Rich, moist woods. Generally a more northern species extending south through central TN into northern AL. Restricted to hardwood forests in Middle TN, also Scott County in East TN. Occasional.

DAVID KOCHER

NOTES: This species is sometimes confused with **Sweet Betsy** (p. 426), but **Sessile Trillium** is a smaller plant with stinky flowers and conspicuous projections at the tips of the stamens. It is said that the scent resembles that of raw beef, which explains one of its common names, Bloody Butchers. The aroma has also been described as that of dead animal tissue and helps attract flies and beetles, which pollinate the plant.

Sweet White Trillium · *Trillium simile*

GENERAL: Erect, perennial herb 12–20 in. tall. **LEAVES:** In a whorl of 3, **solid green**, rhombic, often overlapping, 4–7 in. long and wide. **FLOWERS:** White, with a green apple fragrance when fresh; 3 ovate petals, 1.5–2.5 in. long, overlapping and forming a **cup-shaped base**; stamens longer than pistil; round, **purplish black ovary**; flowers solitary, **stalked**, held above leaves and facing horizontal. March–April. **FRUITS:** Dark purple, ovoid, many-seeded berries, 0.4–0.6 in. across. **WHERE FOUND:** In cove hardwoods and hemlock-silverbell forests in the southeastern Blue Ridge of GA, TN, NC, and SC. In TN, in Polk, Sevier, Cocke, Monroe, and Blount counties in East TN. Rare, but locally abundant.

NOTES: This species resembles the white-petaled form of **Red Trillium** (p. 427), but the flowers of Red Trillium are saucer-shaped in profile and much smaller. • The species name *simile* is from *similis*, meaning "similar or alike," in reference to this plant's likeness to other trilliums. This plant is also known as **Jeweled Wakerobin**. • **Sweet White Trillium** is often not regarded as a valid species, yet it forms pure stands, especially at lower elevations in the Smoky Mountains, where flowering begins 2 weeks earlier than that of Red Trillium.

ED HONICKER

DENNIS HORN

Twisted Trillium
Trillium stamineum

GENERAL: Erect perennial herb, 6–12 in. tall. **LEAVES:** In a whorl of 3, **obscurely mottled**, ovate to elliptic, 2–4 in. long. **FLOWERS:** Maroon, rarely yellow, with a strong carrion odor, 3 narrow, **twisted petals**, 0.8–1.4 in. long, spreading horizontally, **resembling the blades of an airplane propeller**; sepals lie horizontal and flat, purplish near the base; flowers solitary, **sessile**. March–April. **FRUITS:** Purplish, ovoid, 6-angled berries, with numerous seeds. **WHERE FOUND:** Rich woodlands, often with **Bent Trillium** (p. 427), from AL and MS, north into TN. In the western ½ of Middle TN, also Decatur and Hardin counties in West TN. Occasional.

NOTES: This plant gets its common name from the twisted or slightly twirled flower petals. • **Toadshades** in TN are generally distinctive and can be divided into 3 groups: *maculatum*, *sessile*, and *recurvatum*. Although *T. maculatum* does not occur in TN, 2 members of the *maculatum* group are found in TN: *T. cuneatum* (p. 426) and *T. luteum* (p. 429). This group does not have extended anther connectives. The *sessile* group, with extended anther connectives, includes *T. decumbens* (p. 426), *T. sessile* (p. 431), and *T. stamineum*. Members of the *recurvatum* group, *T. lancifolium* (p. 428) and *T. recurvatum* (p. 430), have reflexed sepals and incurved anthers. Where their ranges overlap, species within groups will, on occasion, cross-pollinate to form hybrids (see *T. luteum* description, p. 429).

DICK DOUB

Southern Red Trillium · *Trillium sulcatum*

GENERAL: Erect perennial herb, 12–24 in. tall. **LEAVES:** In a whorl of 3, **solid green**, rhombic, 4–8 in. long and wide. **FLOWERS:** **Deep maroon** to creamy white, resemble candle snuffers in profile; 3 ovate petals, 1.0–1.5 in. long, forming a **cup-shaped base** with recurved tips; **sepals** often maroon-tinged, **grooved or keeled at the tips; ovary usually maroon**, flask-shaped; flowers solitary, on long, **erect to spreading stalks**, 3–5 in. long. April–May. **FRUITS:** Maroon, ovoid, many-seeded berries, about 0.5 in. across. **WHERE FOUND:** Rich woods in the southern Appalachian region, from AL and GA to KY and WV. In TN, prefers hardwood and hemlock slopes of sandstone gulfs on the Cumberland Plateau, also rich hollows of the Ridge and Valley and the Eastern Highland Rim. Occasional.

NOTES: The species name *sulcatum* is Latin for "grooved or furrowed," referring to the tips of the sepals. • In 1938, Barksdale first recognized this plant as a distinct variety of **Red Trillium** (p. 427), but failed to provide a formal description. **Southern Red Trillium** is sometimes called **Barksdale Trillium**. In 1984, Thomas S. Patrick, the state botanist of GA, formally described this species while a student at the University of Tennessee.

Painted Trillium
Trillium undulatum

DAVID KOCHER

GENERAL: Erect perennial herb, 8–18 in. tall. **LEAVES:** In a whorl of 3, **bluish or coppery green**, ovate, 2–5 in. long at flowering time, sharply pointed, **short-petioled**. **FLOWERS:** White with a red, V-shaped blaze near the base (rarely pure white); 3 petals, 0.8–1.6 in. long, **wavy-margined**; flowers solitary, on **erect stalks**. April–May. **FRUITS:** Scarlet, ellipsoid to ovoid berries, 0.5–0.9 in. long. **WHERE FOUND:** Prefers cool coniferous forests or acidic woods with scattered laurel, galax, and rhododendron, from the northeastern U.S. and southeastern Canada, south to TN and GA in the mountains. In TN, restricted to the Blue Ridge Mountains in Polk, Monroe, Blount, Sevier, Cocke, Greene, Unicoi, Carter, Sullivan, and Johnson counties. Infrequent.

NOTES: The species name *undulatum* refers to the wavy or undulate margins of the petals. The bi-colored petals are a unique feature of this trillium, accounting for the common name. • Attempts to cultivate this species outside its native range are rarely successful.

Vasey's Trillium
Trillium vaseyi

JERRY DROWN

GENERAL: Erect perennial herb, 12–24 in. tall. **LEAVES:** In a whorl of 3, **solid green**, rhombic, 4–8 in. long and wide, broad with a tapering base. **FLOWERS:** Maroon, 2–5 in. across, with a strong, funereal, rose-like fragrance; 3 broadly ovate petals, 1.2–2.5 in. long, veiny, somewhat to **strongly recurved**; stamens far exceeding the length of the small, **purplish maroon ovary**; flowers solitary, **stalked**, **nodding** beneath the leaves. April–June. **FRUITS:** Dark maroon, ovoid, many-seeded berries, to 0.8 in. across. **WHERE FOUND:** Rich woods, from the mountains of TN, northern GA, southwestern NC, and northwestern SC to southwestern GA and eastern AL. In East TN, from the Smoky Mountains southward; outlier populations also occur in the rich coves of the Cumberland Mountains and the Ridge and Valley. In TN, in Morgan, Anderson, Loudon, Polk, Monroe, Blount, and Sevier counties. Infrequent.

NOTES: This is the largest flowered of our trilliums and the latest to flower. • The species name honors George Vasey (1822–93), an American botanist. • Although the flower of **Vasey's Trillium** is large, the position of the flower below the leaves and the deep maroon color make this plant easy to overlook.

DENNIS HORN

Large-Flowered Bellwort
Uvularia grandiflora

GENERAL: Erect perennial herb, 15–30 in. tall, with branched stems. **LEAVES:** Alternate, **perfoliate** (stem pierces the leaf), oval, 2–5 in. long, pointed, prominent parallel veins, minutely **hairy beneath**. **FLOWERS:** Pale to golden yellow, smooth within, similar **petals and sepals** (3 each), 1–2 in. long, separate, **twisted**, overlapping; flowers solitary and nodding from the upper leaf axils. April–May. **FRUITS:** 3-angled capsules; seeds brown, plump, sometimes puckered. **WHERE FOUND:** Rich deciduous forests, chiefly on calcareous soils, from LA to northern GA, north to southern Canada, and in most of the eastern U.S. Throughout TN. Common.

NOTES: The flowers of *Uvularia* species hang like the uvula, the bit of tissue that dangles from the soft palate in the back of the mouth. • Native Americans made a poultice from the upper vegetative parts of **Large-Flowered Bellwort** that was used to treat rheumatic pain and sore muscles. • There are 5 *Uvularia* species, all known from North America.

KURT EMMANUELE

Perfoliate Bellwort
Uvularia perfoliata

GENERAL: Erect, **colonial**, perennial herb, 8–16 in. tall, with branched stems. **LEAVES:** Alternate, **perfoliate** (stem pierces the leaf), elliptic, 2.0–3.5 in. long, **smooth beneath**. **FLOWERS:** Straw yellow with a conspicuous, **orange, granular inner surface**; 3 sepals overlap the 3 petals, all 0.7–1.0 in. long; flowers 1–3, nodding singly from upper leaf axils. April–May. **FRUITS:** Obovoid capsules, 0.3–0.4 in. long; ovoid seeds, about 0.1 in. long. **WHERE FOUND:** Thin hardwood forests and lowlands, preferring less fertile acidic soils, in most of the eastern U.S. and southern Ontario. Middle and East TN, also Hardin and McNairy counties in West TN. Common.

NOTES: This species is similar to **Large-Flowered Bellwort** (see above), but is a smaller plant, and the tepals are granular inside. • The species name *perfoliata* refers to the characteristic of the leaves surrounding or embracing the stem. Other common names for this plant include Merry Bells, Crow's Foot, Cow Bells, Haybells, Mohawk Weed, Strawbell, and Strawflower. • The roots of this species are edible after cooking and can also be made into a salve for wounds and skin lacerations. However, do not pick or disturb this plant, since disturbance is likely to threaten its survival.

Wild Oats, Sessileleaf Bellwort
Uvularia sessilifolia

GENERAL: Erect perennial herb, 6–18 in. tall, with **smooth, branched stems**; mostly found in loose clumps with 5–10 in. between stems. **LEAVES:** Alternate, **sessile**, elliptic, **glaucous**, 1.6–2.8 in. long. **FLOWERS:** Pale yellow, **smooth within**; 6 tepals, 0.1–1.0 in. long, separate, overlapping; solitary, nodding from the upper leaf axils. March–May. **FRUITS:** Sharply 3-angled capsules, 0.6–0.8 in. long; round seeds, 0.1 in. across. **WHERE FOUND:** Deciduous forests throughout the eastern U.S. and TN. Frequent. **SIMILAR SPECIES:** MOUNTAIN BELLWORT (*U. puberula*) grows in tighter clumps with 1–3 in. between the stems; **stems lined with fine hairs; shiny leaves**. Prefers drier, more upland woods with scattered pine, oak, and hickory. Mainly in the highlands from NY, south to AL and GA. In TN, in Blount, Sevier, Cocke, Carter, Washington, Sullivan, and Johnson counties in the Blue Ridge Mountains of East TN. Infrequent. March–May. *U. pudica*.

NOTES: Wild Oats is also called Cornflower or Straw Lilies. The flower has a rich, spicy fragrance. • Manasseh Cutler (1742–1823), a clergyman with an interest in natural history, wrote, "the young shoots may be eaten as asparagus. The roots are nutritious, and are used in diet-drinks."

JERRY DROWN

False Hellebore, Indian Poke • *Veratrum viride*

GENERAL: Coarse, erect, **poisonous** perennial herb, 2–6 ft. tall, with a stout stem, leafy throughout. **LEAVES:** Alternate, mostly sessile, **somewhat clasping**, oval or elliptic, 6–12 in. long and ½ as wide, **conspicuously pleated**, not significantly reduced in size upward. **FLOWERS:** Yellowish green, 6 **hairy tepals** to 0.5 in. long, tapering to the base, glandless; stamens free from the base; inflorescence a freely branched, hairy panicle, 12–24 in. tall, with the flowers on short stalks to 0.16 in. long. June–July. **FRUITS:** Ellipsoid capsules, about 1.5 in. long; yellowish brown, lanceolate seeds, winged, tapering to a point at the tip. **WHERE FOUND:** Open, moist woods and meadows. A mostly northern species extending south in the mountains to GA and AL. In TN, in Marion, Polk, Blount, Sevier, Claiborne, Hawkins, Sullivan, Carter, and Johnson counties. Infrequent. **SIMILAR SPECIES:** SMALL FALSE HELLEBORE (*V. parviflorum*) is not as robust; stem leaves narrow and much smaller upward; **smooth, green tepals**, with stamens attached to the base. Rich, wooded mountain slopes from WV and KY, south to GA and AL. In TN, from the Cumberland Plateau eastward, also Cannon County. Occasional. August–September. *Melanthium parviflorum*. WOOD'S FALSE HELLEBORE (*V. woodii*) is similar to *V. parviflorum*, but has **purple tepals**. Rich woods, from IA to OH, south to FL. In TN, in Franklin, Grundy, Hickman, and Wayne counties. Rare. July–August. *M. woodii*.

NOTES: In 1749, botanist Peter Kalm reported that Swedes in NJ called **False Hellebore** "Dollroot" as children made dolls from its corn-like stalks and leaves. • However, use caution as the thick fibrous roots of *Veratrum* species are **very poisonous**.

MIRIAM WEINSTEIN

KURT EMMANUELE

Turkeybeard · *Xerophyllum asphodeloides*

GENERAL: Perennial herb, 3–5 ft. tall, arising from simple, thick, tuberous rhizomes. **LEAVES:** Linear, grass-like; evergreen basal leaves, to 16 in. long, gracefully arch away from the crown, forming a **dense tuft** to nearly 3 ft. wide; stem leaves alternate, gradually reduced upward, forming needle-like bracts in the inflorescence. **FLOWERS:** White, showy, to 0.4 in. across, 6 lanceolate tepals; in a long, **dense, terminal raceme** opening first from the base and gradually ripening upward, forming a teardrop-shaped cluster with spent flowers at the base and buds at the top, with a nipple-like tip. May–June. **FRUITS:** 3-chambered capsules, each chamber with 3–5 glossy, brownish green seeds. **WHERE FOUND:** Dry, open, acidic soils and pine woods, from the NJ pine barrens to KY, south to GA and AL in the mountains. In the Blue Ridge of East TN, in Polk, Monroe, Blount, Cocke, Greene, Unicoi, and Washington counties. Infrequent.

NOTES: This plant is also called **Eastern Turkeybeard**.
• Native Americans, particularly in the Northwest, used the long, thin leaves of **Beargrass (*X. tenax*)**, to make clothing and decorate baskets. The baked rhizome is edible.
• There are only 2 species in the *Xerophyllum* genus, both known only from North America.

DENNIS HORN

Death Camas · *Zigadenus leimanthoides*

GENERAL: Perennial herb, 2–5 ft. tall, arising from a bulb. **LEAVES:** Linear, mostly crowded near the base, but **not forming a dense tuft**, 8–20 in. long, 0.16–0.5 in. wide; stem leaves alternate, reduced upward. **FLOWERS:** White to yellowish or greenish white; 6 ovate-elliptic **tepals, to 0.2 in. long**, each with a small, **yellow gland** at the base; in a dense panicle tipped with a raceme, 3–4 in. long, longer than the lateral racemes. June–July. **FRUITS:** Ovoid, 3-parted capsules with smooth, lustrous seeds. **WHERE FOUND:** Wet woods and fields. A Coastal Plain species found from southern NY to FL and TX, and also in southern uplands. In TN, in Coffee, Warren, Franklin, and Grundy counties in Middle TN. Rare. **SIMILAR SPECIES:** WHITE CAMAS (*Z. glaucus*) is glaucous and only 12–30 in. tall; inflorescence is panicle-like with much larger flowers; 6 **tepals, 0.4–0.5 in. long**, usually purplish near the base with a 2-lobed gland. Wet barrens with calcareous soil, in southern Canada and the northeastern U.S., south to NC and MO. In TN, only in Johnson County. Rare. July–August. *Z. elegans* ssp. *glaucus*.

NOTES: As the name suggests, these **highly poisonous** plants should not be eaten. Poisonings occur when they are confused with wild onions (*Allium* spp.). The plants contain a **toxic alkaloid** that may be twice as potent as strychnine.

Carolina Spider Lily
Hymenocallis caroliniana

GENERAL: Smooth perennial herb, 12–24 in. tall, from bulbs. **LEAVES:** Basal, linear, **strap-like**, 1.0–1.5 in. wide, to 24 in. long, surrounded at the base by tubular sheaths. **FLOWERS:** White, **showy**; 6 tepals, 2–4 in. long, narrow, spreading; **stamens and corolla unite** at the base to **form a cup-like structure** (corona) with filaments extending beyond the edge of the "cup"; in a terminal, branched umbel of 3–7 flowers. August. **FRUITS:** Capsules with 1–3 green, fleshy, round seeds, 0.6–0.8 in. long. **WHERE FOUND:** Rocky river shoals, wet meadows, and wet woodlands from southern MO and IN, south to GA and TX. Widespread across TN. Frequent. *H. occidentalis*.

JERRY DROWN

NOTES: In spite of its common name, this lovely plant has for many years been included in the Amaryllis Family. However, some authorities no longer recognize the Amaryllis Family, and instead have moved these plants to other families, such as the Lily, Iris, and Agave families; thus, **Carolina Spider Lily** would likely be placed in the Lily Family.

Yellow Stargrass · *Hypoxis hirsuta*

GENERAL: Perennial herb, 4–18 in. tall, from an underground corm; easily confused with grass when not in flower. **LEAVES:** Basal, **hairy**, **grass-like**, 4–20 in. long, 0.1–0.3 in. wide. **FLOWERS:** Star-like, yellow, 0.5–0.75 in. wide; similar petals and sepals (3 each); 6 stamens; on **hairy stalks** shorter than the leaves, in an irregular terminal umbel of 2–9 flowers. April–May. **FRUITS:** Ellipsoid capsules, 0.12–0.24 in. long, with round seeds, densely covered with pointed projections. **WHERE FOUND:** Open woods, meadows, and lawns. Widespread across the central and eastern U.S. and TN. Common.

NOTES: Members of the Amaryllis and Lily families are similar in having 3 petals, 3 sepals, and 6 stamens, but the flower stalk of an Amaryllis is always leafless and the ovary inferior. The Amaryllis Family tends to be more tropical. If the Amaryllis Family is no longer recognized, **Yellow Stargrass** would likely be placed in the Lily Family.

KURT EMMANUELE

KURT EMMANUELE

False Aloe · *Manfreda virginica*

GENERAL: Succulent, smooth perennial herb with an upright flowering stem 3–6 ft. tall. **LEAVES:** In a basal rosette, **thick**, **fleshy**, strap-like, simple, 6–16 in. long, 1.0–3.5 in. wide, with pointed tips, often with a few spiny teeth on the margin; stem leaves few, alternate, near the base, rapidly reduced to bracts upward. **FLOWERS:** Greenish tan, **not showy**, fragrant (especially at night); 6 erect, linear tepals, about 1 in. long, fused at the base over ½ their length; stamens with **large anthers**, noticeably protruding from the mouth of the flower; inflorescence a spike of several, loosely arranged flowers. June–July. **FRUITS:** Rounded, greenish capsules with black, flattened, semicircular seeds. **WHERE FOUND:** Dry soil of open woods, barrens, and fields, from MD to MO, south to FL and TX. Widespread in TN. Frequent. *Agave virginica*.

NOTES: This plant is also called Rattlesnake-Master. When the seeds are present in the dried capsules, and the stem is shaken, a sound suggestive of a rattlesnake is produced. • The 3 TN species in the small Agave Family, also called the Century Plant Family, can be recognized by the basal cluster of stiff leaves and a tall, essentially leafless, flowering stem (usually 1 per plant).

THOMAS E. HEMMERLY

Spanish Bayonet · *Yucca filamentosa*

GENERAL: Tufted, somewhat woody perennial, with an upright flower stalk often exceeding 6 ft. in height. **LEAVES:** Mainly in a basal rosette, **evergreen**, 12–24 in. long, 1–2 in. wide, **rigid**, elongated, linear-lanceolate, sharply pointed, upper surface is rough to the touch, **margins fraying** into twisting, whitish threads; flower stalk has alternate, scale-like bracts. **FLOWERS:** White, **bell-shaped, nodding**, 1.5–2.5 in. wide; 6 ovate tepals; in a **smooth, terminal panicle** with dozens of flowers, often occupying more than ½ the stalk. June–August. **FRUITS:** Capsules, to 2 in. long with numerous, flat, black seeds; dead flowering stalks with capsules often persist into winter. **WHERE FOUND:** Dry, sandy soils in open sites, from NC and TN, southward. Naturalized north to NY and WI. Thinly spread across TN. Occasional. **SIMILAR SPECIES:** The doubtfully distinct **ADAM'S NEEDLE** (*Y. flaccida*), also called **BEAR GRASS**, has long, smooth, **pliable leaves** and a conspicuously **hairy inflorescence**. Dry, usually open sites; from NC and TN, south to FL and LA; naturalized northward. Widely scattered in TN and often spreads from plantings. Occasional. June–August. *Y. smalliana*.

NOTES: Spanish Bayonet has a unique mutualism with the night-flying Yucca Moth. The female moth pollinates the plant, and in exchange, she deposits an egg in a hole in the pistil. Once the egg is hatched, the hungry larva eats some of the yucca seeds.

Huger's Carrion Flower · *Smilax hugeri*

GENERAL: Perennial herb, 12–24 in. tall, **without spines** (unlike most *Smilax* species); stem is unbranched, **not vine-like, without tendrils** or with a few weak tendrils near the tip. **LEAVES:** Alternate, appearing whorled, crowded on the upper stem, narrowly ovate, 2–4 in. long, hairy beneath, somewhat heart-shaped at the base, long-petioled. **FLOWERS:** Yellowish green, foul-smelling, male and female flowers on separate plants (dioecious); 6 tepals, 0.15–0.2 in. long; in **round umbels** on slender peduncles, from leaf axils. April–May. **FRUITS:** 3-seeded berries with red seeds, 0.1–0.2 in. long. **WHERE FOUND:** Rich, deciduous woods from KY and NC, southward. Widespread in East and Middle TN. Frequent. *S. ecirrata* var. *hugeri*. **SIMILAR SPECIES:** SMOOTH CARRION FLOWER (*S. herbacea*) is an **herbaceous vine** climbing to 9 ft., **without spines**, but with **numerous tendrils**. Low woods and thickets throughout the eastern U.S. Widespread in TN. Occasional. May–June. ROUNDLEAF GREENBRIER (*S. rotundifolia*) is a stout, **woody vine** with **green, angled stems, stout thorns,** and **shiny green leaves**. Woods and thickets throughout the eastern U.S. and TN. Common. May–June. CATBRIER (*S. glauca*) is a slender, **woody vine** with **round, wiry, thorny stems; leaves pale beneath**. Woods and thickets, from NY to KS, southward. Throughout TN. Common. May–June.

NOTES: The Greenbrier Family is primarily tropical and subtropical with 12 genera, all small except the genus *Smilax*, which contains about 300 species of mostly woody and herbaceous vines. Ten species are found in TN, though 2 may be only varieties.

Cinnamon Vine, Chinese Yam

Dioscorea polystachya*

GENERAL: Perennial, **climbing vine**, 3–12 ft. long, from a deep starchy tuber; stems twine upward from left to right. **LEAVES:** Alternate, opposite, or in whorls of 3; simple, 7–9-nerved, 2–3 in. long, about as wide as long, **halberd-shaped**, heart-shaped base; small, **potato-like, aerial tubers** (bulbils) form in the leaf axils in late summer. **FLOWERS:** White, **inconspicuous**; clustered in axillary or terminal spikes. June–August. **FRUITS:** Capsules with 3 winged lobes, rarely produced in our area. **WHERE FOUND:** Introduced from China and frequently escaped from cultivation. Fencerows and waste places, from VT to KS, south to GA and LA. Widespread throughout TN. Frequent. *D. batatas, D. oppositifolia*.

NOTES: The common name **Cinnamon Vine** is derived from the cinnamon-like fragrance of the flowers. The other name, **Chinese Yam**, indicates this plant's native region. The white, starchy, tuberous roots are edible and can weigh up to 4 lbs. This invasive vine has become **a troublesome pest** in recent years.

DENNIS HORN

DENNIS HORN

BECKY HUGHES

Wild Yam · *Dioscorea villosa*

GENERAL: Perennial, climbing **vine** with a **smooth, twining stem** to 10 ft. long, climbing upward from right to left. **LEAVES:** Alternate (on upper stem) or **whorled (on lower stem)**, 3–4 in. long, **heart-shaped**, on petioles to 3 in. long. **FLOWERS:** Tiny, whitish, 6 tepals, inconspicuous, male and female flowers on separate plants (dioecious); in loose clusters from the leaf axils; male (staminate) spikes have up to 4 flowers per node; female (pistillate) spikes have 1 flower per node. May–August. **FRUITS:** 3-winged capsules, 0.6–1.0 in. long, with flat, broadly winged seeds; clusters of dried, **papery fruits** are **conspicuous in autumn**, from October into winter. **WHERE FOUND:** Moist woods and thickets, throughout the eastern U.S. and TN. Common. **D. quaternata**.

NOTES: The showy fruit clusters are sought for dried arrangements. • As the common name indicates, the slender, tuberous roots are edible, but should be cooked. **Use caution**, because eating the plant raw may cause vomiting and other undesirable side effects. • Medicinally, the roots were used by Native Americans in a tea to relieve labor pains and by physicians to treat gastrointestinal irritations, asthma, morning sickness, and rheumatism. • **Wild Yam** contains diosgenin, used to manufacture progesterone and other steroid drugs. Interestingly, most of the steroid hormones used in modern medicine, including those in many oral contraceptives, were developed from chemical components contained in yams.

JERRY DROWN

JERRY DROWN

Blackberry Lily
*Belamcanda chinensis**

GENERAL: Perennial herb, 18–24 in. tall, from a thick rhizome. **LEAVES:** Alternate, **sword-shaped**, 12–18 in. long, oriented with 1 edge facing the stem. **FLOWERS:** Orange, **spotted with deep crimson or purple** (upper photo), 1.2–2.0 in. wide; similar petals and sepals (3 each), widely spreading; inflorescence cyme-like, widely branched. June–July. **FRUITS:** 3-lobed capsules, about 1 in. long, open at maturity, leaving a **blackberry-like mass of fleshy, black seeds** (lower photo). **WHERE FOUND:** Introduced from Asia and escaped from cultivation. Now well established in thickets, roadsides, barrens, and along the edges of open cedar glades. Widespread across the central and eastern U.S. and TN. Frequent.

NOTES: Augustin Gattinger (1825–1903), an early TN botanist, erroneously believed **Blackberry Lily** to be native. • The thin, papery covering on the mature fruit capsule splits downward, exposing numerous shiny black seeds attached to the central column, remarkably resembling a blackberry and giving the species its common name. • **The flowers last for only 1 day.**

Lamance Iris, Zigzag Iris
Iris brevicaulis

GENERAL: Perennial herb, 10–18 in. tall; stems often reclining, conspicuously zig-zagged. **LEAVES:** Numerous, sword-shaped, 12–30 in. long, 0.6–1.5 in. wide, oriented with 1 edge facing the stem. **FLOWERS:** Few, light to medium violet, 3–4 in. wide; 3 narrowly oblanceolate petals; 3 broadly spatulate-shaped sepals having a white area with purple striations at the base, surrounded by a yellow crest. June. **FRUITS:** Ellipsoid-ovoid, indehiscent capsules, 6-angled, 1–2 in. long. **WHERE FOUND:** Swamps and wet woods from OH to eastern KS, south to FL and TX. In TN, in the Tennessee River Valley separating West and Middle TN, westward, in Hardin, Humphreys, Madison, Shelby, and Stewart counties. Rare.

OTTO R. HIRSCH

NOTES: Iris flowers are large, showy, and variously colored. The genus is named for the Greek goddess Iris, who walked on the rainbow between heaven and earth, leaving a path of colorful flowers in her footsteps. • Iris flowers consist of 3 spreading, petal-like sepals, 3 erect or arching petals, and a stigma with 3 petal-like branches that arch over the 3 sepals and hide the 3 stamens. Nine *Iris* species are found in TN.

Dwarf Crested Iris · *Iris cristata*

GENERAL: Low perennial herb, 4–6 in. tall, from horizontal rhizomes; flower stalks are overtopped by sterile shoots. **LEAVES:** Light green, broadly linear, 4–8 in. long, 0.4–1.0 in. wide, oriented with 1 edge facing the stem, curved, making a gracefully arching fan. **FLOWERS:** Few, very showy, pale to deep lavender (rarely white), about 3 in. wide; 3 unmarked petals; 3 sepals with a small, fluted, yellow crest, bordered with white. April–May. **FRUITS:** Ellipsoid capsules, about 0.4 in. long, sharply 3-angled, minutely beaked; orange-brown, smooth, ovoid seeds, 0.13 in. long, appendaged. **WHERE FOUND:** Moist hillsides, ravines, and ledges in rich woods, from PA to MO, south to GA and MS. Throughout TN. Common.

NOTES: Iris is the official state flower of TN. • Irises have been bred, hybridized, and selected for more than 150 years, resulting in over 300 species and more than 1000 named hybrids and selections. The flower colors represent nearly all the colors of the rainbow. The bearded irises (*Iris* x *germanica**, p. 442) are the best known. Any of several species and varieties may occasionally escape by free seeding or from discarded garden material.

DAVID KOCHER

MARY MARTIN SHAFFNER

Copper Iris · *Iris fulva*

GENERAL: Perennial herb, from horizontal rhizomes; flowering stalks 20–40 in. tall, surpassing the leaves. **LEAVES:** Sword-shaped, 15–36 in. long, to 0.6 in. wide, oriented with 1 edge facing the stem. **FLOWERS:** Few, **reddish brown**, about 3.5 in. wide; petals (3) and sepals (3) widely spreading, spatulate sepals wider than the oblanceolate petals. May–June. **FRUITS:** Ovoid, 6-angled capsules, 2–3 in. long. **WHERE FOUND:** Swamps, in the lower Mississippi River Valley from southeastern MO and southern IL, south to FL and TX. In TN, in Shelby, Lauderdale, Fayette, Dyer, Lake, Obion, and Gibson counties, all in close proximity to the Mississippi River, also Anderson County in the Ridge and Valley. Infrequent. **SIMILAR SPECIES:** SPANISH IRIS (*I. xiphium**), also known as DUTCH IRIS, has been cultivated for centuries and is a popular cut flower. Deeply furrowed, glaucous, linear leaves to 12 in. long; **rich violet purple flowers**; each sepal has a rounded blade, 1 in. wide, narrowed and **marked with yellow or orange** toward the base; erect, oblong petals, 0.5–0.75 in. wide, are equal in length to the sepals. Introduced from Spain. Persistent from cultivation near homesites, ditches, and waste areas in TN and LA. Recorded in Wilson County of TN. Rare. April–June.

NOTES: The **Copper Iris is the only reddish iris of our area.** • The emblem known as *fleur-de-lis*, French for "flower of the lily," was designed after the floral structure of an iris, not a lily. Even more confusing, *fleur-de-lis* is a corruption of the original *fleur de Louis*, given to Louis VII during the Second Crusade (1147–49).

DENNIS HORN

Slender Blue Flag · *Iris prismatica*

GENERAL: Perennial herb, 12–36 in. tall, from creeping rhizomes; forms large, diffuse clumps. **LEAVES:** Erect, **grass-like**, 20–28 in. long, 0.12–0.25 in. wide, oriented with 1 edge facing the stem. **FLOWERS:** Dainty, **violet blue** (occasionally white), to 3 in. wide; 3 outward-arching, oblanceolate petals; 3 spatulate-shaped **sepals** have a **white area with violet lines**. May. **FRUITS:** Sharply 3-angled capsules, 1–2 in. long, opening at the tip. **WHERE FOUND:** Wet woods, roadside ditches, shorelines, and wet barrens, in the Atlantic Coastal Plain from Nova Scotia to GA, and inland in the southern Appalachian Highlands. In TN, only in Coffee and Warren counties in Middle TN. Rare. **SIMILAR SPECIES:** The familiar GERMAN IRIS (*I. germanica**), also called GARDEN IRIS, has glaucous, **sword-shaped** leaves, 0.8–1.6 in. wide, 8–18 in. long; stout stems, to 36 in. tall, are branched toward the top; flowers, 3–4 in. wide, have recurved, ovate, **violet sepals marked with yellow, white, and brown veins** at the base, and highlighted with a **long beard down the middle**; light violet, arching petals are slightly smaller than sepals. Introduced from Europe. Frequently cultivated, sometimes persisting in homesites, ditches, and waste areas across the U.S. In TN, in Shelby, Stewart, Sumner, and Williamson counties. Rare. April–May.

NOTES: **Slender Blue Flag**, also sometimes called Cubeseed Iris Bareroot, is a nectar plant for butterflies. It has clumps of grassy leaves, with clusters of 2–3 flowers that are violet blue and attractively veined.

Yellow Flag
Iris pseudacorus*

GENERAL: Showy, erect perennial herb, 24–48 in. tall, from enlarged horizontal rhizomes. **LEAVES:** Basal, elongated, **sword-like**, 24–36 in. long, about 1 in. wide, oriented with 1 edge facing the stem; leaf-like bracts on flowering stalk. **FLOWERS:** Bright yellow, slightly fragrant, about 3 in. wide; 3 short, erect petals, narrowly spatulate-shaped, about 1 in. long, unmarked; 3 sepals, 2–3 in. long, with a broad, rounded, downcurved tip and a narrow base marked with brown lines. April–June. **FRUITS:** 6-angled capsules, 2–3 in. long, with valves that open widely at maturity. **WHERE FOUND:** Introduced from Europe. Escaped from cultivation and now widely scattered across the U.S. in shallow ponds, ditches, and waste places. Thinly scattered in Middle and East TN. Occasional.

DENNIS HORN

NOTES: This plant has been transplanted into gardens all over the world and has widely escaped. It can become **a nuisance plant** if not restricted. • **Yellow Flag** is regarded as being able to remove (or absorb) metals from wastewater and has been used in sewage treatment. Spreading by underground rhizomes and seeds, this plant colonizes in large numbers and forms very dense, single-species stands. • Traditionally, the rhizomes were used as a potent laxative. The flowers have been used to make a yellow dye.

Vernal Iris, Dwarf Iris
Iris verna var. *smalliana*

GENERAL: Perennial herb to 6 in. tall, from a densely scaly rhizome. **LEAVES:** Essentially straight, narrow, bright green, to 4 in. long and 0.5 in. wide at time of flowering, later lengthening, oriented with 1 edge facing the stem. **FLOWERS:** Showy, lavender, to 2.5 in. wide; 3 erect, spatulate-shaped petals, with a narrow claw; 3 spreading or drooping sepals, with a **hairy, yellowish orange stripe, bordered with white**, but **not crested**. May. **FRUITS:** Obtusely 3-angled capsules, 0.5–1.0 in. long, with a slender beak; shiny brown seeds with a small appendage at the base. **WHERE FOUND:** Sandy or rocky, open woods, from NY to OH, south to GA and AR. In TN, from the Cumberland Plateau, eastward. Occasional.

NOTES: This plant is also known as Dwarf Violet Iris. The species name *verna* means "vernal" or "spring." This variety is named for John Kunkel Small (1869–1938), an American botanist who published the *Manual of the Southeastern Flora* in 1933.

KURT EMMANUELE

Southern Blue Flag
Iris virginica

GENERAL: Perennial herb, 20–40 in. tall, densely colonial, from thick, creeping rhizomes; stems often with 1–2 branches. **LEAVES:** Sword-shaped, pliable, erect or arching, 15–40 in. long, about 1 in. wide, oriented with 1 edge facing the stem, forming fan-like clusters. **FLOWERS:** Pale blue or lavender, about 3 in. wide, with **dark lavender or purple veins**; 3 erect petals, smaller than sepals and without markings; 3 sepals, 2–3 in. long, with broad, round, downward-arching tips, the narrow **base marked with yellow**. May–June. **FRUITS:** Obscurely 3-angled capsules, about 2 in. long and 1 in. wide. **WHERE FOUND:** Meadows, ditches, and shallow water, from NY to MN, south to FL and TX. Thinly scattered across TN. Occasional.

OTTO R. HIRSCH

NOTES: Southern Blue Flag will grow in ordinary garden soil, but prefers moist, rich soil where it forms colonies. It can also be used in water gardens. It flowers best in full sun and can be used in flower arrangements. • Southern Blue Flag can cause an **allergic reaction** in some people and should not be eaten as it is **mildly toxic**.

Pale Blue-Eyed Grass
Sisyrinchium albidum

GENERAL: Tufted, grass-like perennial herb, 4–16 in. tall. **LEAVES:** Mainly basal, **light green, linear, iris-like**, smooth, glaucous, 4–8 in. long, with 1 edge facing the stem. **FLOWERS:** White or pale blue, about 0.6 in. wide, with a **yellow center**; 6 tepals; emerging from a pair of **sessile, leaf-like bracts** (spathes) terminating the **winged scape, 0.06–0.16 in. wide**. April–May. **FRUITS:** Light tan, nearly spherical capsules, 0.1–0.2 in. long, with black seeds. **WHERE FOUND:** Open places, glades, and dry woods in most of the eastern U.S. Middle and East TN. Frequent. **SIMILAR SPECIES: SLENDER BLUE-EYED GRASS (S. mucronatum)** is **darker green**, with very slender leaves and **wiry scapes, less than 0.06 in. wide**, topped with solitary, red-purple spathes. Meadows, sandy soils, and open woods. A mainly northeastern species, south to GA and LA.

MILO PYNE

In TN, in Morgan, Knox, Polk, Bradley, Hamilton, Bledsoe, Rhea, and Franklin counties. Infrequent. May–June.

NOTES: Pale Blue-Eyed Grass is particularly common in the cedar glades of central TN. The name "blue-eyed grass" is misleading, since these plants are related to irises, not grasses. • Flowers of the *Sisyrinchium* genus are "yellow-eyed" and occur in small umbel-like clusters or singly. The petals and sepals are similar, each with a bristle tip. Flower stalks are wiry and 2-edged, 6–18 in. long. Four species are found in TN.

Eastern Blue-Eyed Grass
Sisyrinchium atlanticum

DENNIS HORN

GENERAL: Perennial herb, 6–20 in. tall, with many narrowly winged **flowering stalks, less than 0.08 in. wide**; forms large, grass-like clumps. **LEAVES:** Mostly basal, **linear**, **light green**, 3–10 in. long, smooth, glaucous, somewhat shorter than the flowering stalks, iris-like, with 1 edge facing the stem. **FLOWERS: Violet blue**, about 0.6 in. wide, with a **yellow eye**; 6 tepals, 0.3–0.5 in. long; flowering stalk terminates with a leaf-like bract from which arise 2–3 **stalked, flower-bearing spathes**. May–July. **FRUITS:** Oval, dark brown capsules, 0.1–0.2 in. wide. **WHERE FOUND:** Low, wet places. A mostly Coastal Plain species found inland to IL, MO, and AR. Widely scattered across Middle and East TN. Occasional. **SIMILAR SPECIES:** STOUT BLUE-EYED GRASS (*S. angustifolium*) has **bright green and leaves**, with **broadly winged flowering stalks more than 0.1 in. wide**. Moist places throughout the eastern U.S. and TN. Common. May–July.

NOTES: The species name *atlanticum* means "Atlantic," indicating this plant's habit of growing along the Atlantic Coast, and is the basis for another common name, Atlantic Blue-Eyed Grass. • For **Stout Blue-Eyed Grass**, the species name *angustifolium* means "narrow-leaved."

Orchid Family (Orchidaceae)

The Orchid Family is considered the largest Family, with over 23,000 species worldwide, primarily in tropical regions. Members of this family are known for their intricate flowers, beauty, and pleasing fragrance, and are identified by their bilateral symmetry, with 3 sepals (1 may be modified) and 3 petals. One petal, the labellum or lip, is often a highly specialized, complex structure used to promote cross-pollination, for example, the pouch in lady's slippers (*Cypripedium*). All orchid species are perennials and have extremely small, dust-like seeds without endosperm. Orchids found in the wild should be left in the wild, because they depend on fungi growing in the soil to supply nutrients to their roots. Tropical orchids are economically valuable to the nursery and horticultural trade. The Orchid Family is represented by 20 genera and nearly 50 species in TN.

1a. Leaves absent or withering at flowering time; flowers in spikes or racemes 2

  2a. Base of lip with a conspicuous spur . . . . **Tipularia**

  2b. Base of lip without a spur 3

    3a. Inflorescence a spike, spiraled; flowers predominately white . . . . **Spiranthes**

    3b. Inflorescence a raceme, not spiraled; flowers not white or with a whitish lip only 4

      4a. Leaf solitary, basal, withering at time of flowering . . . . **Aplectrum**

      4b. Leaves absent; plant saprophytic 5

        5a. Perianth more than 0.4 in. long . . . . **Hexalectris**

        5b. Perianth less than 0.4 in. long . . . . **Corallorhiza**

1b. Leaves present at flowering time; flowers solitary or in spikes or racemes 6

  6a. Leaf solitary 7

    7a. Leaf basal 8

      8a. Leaf broad, elliptic, or ovate . . . . **Platanthera**

      8b. Leaf narrow, grasslike . . . . **Calopogon**

    7b. Leaf along the stem 9

      9a. Flowers solitary (rarely 2 in *Pogonia*), pinkish to white .10

        10a. Sepals pink to rose; lip 1 in. long or less, with a fringed crest . . . .**Pogonia**

        10b. Sepals brownish purple; lip 1.2 in. long or more, without a fringed crest . . . . **Cleistes**

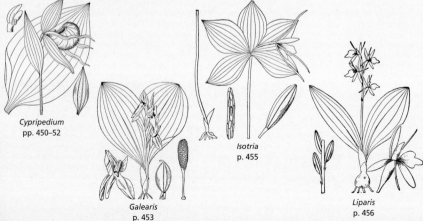

Cypripedium
pp. 450–52

Isotria
p. 455

Galearis
p. 453

Liparis
p. 456

9b. Inflorescence a multi-flowered spike; flowers orange-yellow to green **11**

    11a. Lip spurred . . . .*Platanthera*

    11b. Lip not spurred . . . .*Malaxis*

6b. Leaves 2–many **12**

    12a. Lip inflated or pouchlike **13**

        13a. Leaves uniformly green, pleated; flowers 1–3 . . . .*Cypripedium*

        13b. Leaves white-reticulate above, not pleated; flowers more than 3 . . . . .*Goodyera*

    12b. Lip not inflated or pouchlike **14**

        14a. Base of lip prolonged into an elongate spur
           or rarely short and less than 0.12 in. long **15**

           15a. Lip white, entire, the remaining perianth parts purplish . . . .*Galearis*

           15b. Lip the same color as other perianth parts,
               entire, irregularly torn or cut, or 3-parted . . . .*Platanthera*

        14b. Base of lip not prolonged into a spur **17**

           17a. Stem leaves opposite or whorled **18**

               18a. Stem leaves opposite, flowers terminal and numerous . . . .*Listera*

               18b. Stem leaves whorled, flowers solitary (usually) . . . .*Isotria*

           17b. Stem leaves alternate or the leaves predominately basal **19**

               19a. Flowers inverted, the lip uppermost **20**

                  20a. Lip bearded, flowers pink-purple, rarely white . . . .*Calopogon*

                  20b. Lip not bearded, flowers whitish green with green veins . . . . .*Ponthieva*

               19b. Flowers not inverted, the lip lowermost and not bearded **21**

                  21a. Leaves along the stem, flowers 1–6 . . . .*Triphora*

                  21b. Leaves mostly basal, flowers numerous **22**

                      22a. Leaves narrow, less than 1.2 in. wide; flowers spiraled . . . .*Spiranthes*

                      22b. Leaves elliptic to ovate, more than 1.2 in. wide;
                         flowers in a raceme . . . .*Liparis*

Luer, C.A. 1975. *The Native Orchids of the United States and Canada, excluding Florida.* New York Botanical Garden: Bronx, NY.

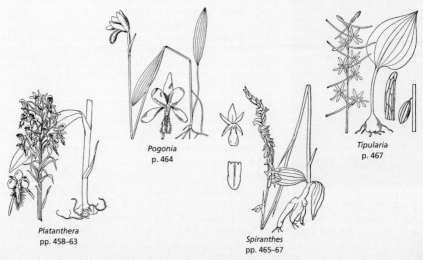

Pogonia
p. 464

Tipularia
p. 467

Platanthera
pp. 458–63

Spiranthes
pp. 465–67

JERRY DROWN

Puttyroot, Adam and Eve · *Aplectrum hyemale*

GENERAL: Perennial herb, 10–20 in. tall, from underground bulbs; flowering stalks sheathed at the base. **LEAVES:** Solitary, wintergreen, **pleated**, bluish green, oval, 4–8 in. long, with **silvery lengthwise veins**, emerging in autumn and withering by early May (before flowers develop). **FLOWERS:** Various shades of **green, yellow, and brown**; 2 arching petals; 3 spreading sepals; **whitish lip** has **pale magenta markings** and **lengthwise crests**; flowers in a loose cluster at the top of the scape; flowers often open only slightly. May–June. **FRUITS:** Hanging, ellipsoid capsules, 0.6–0.9 in. long. **WHERE FOUND:** Rich, moist soils of alluvial floodplains and deep humus pockets of mature woodlands, from northern AL and AR to the Great Lakes in most of the eastern U.S. Throughout TN. Frequent.

NOTES: This plant gets its common name, **Puttyroot**, from a sticky paste, made by crushing the bulbs and roots, that was used to mend broken pottery. The other name, **Adam and Eve**, refers to the underground bulbs or corms, which almost always occur in pairs. • Technically, the Orchid Family is defined by the fusion of pistil and stamens into a solitary column. The family name comes from *orchis*, Greek for "testicle," the name given to the European Green-Winged Orchid (*Orchis morio*) for the shape of its paired tubers. Based on the Doctrine of Signatures (the belief that whatever a plant looked like, it could cure), orchids were widely esteemed as aphrodisiacs.

OTTO R. HIRSCH

Grass Pink · *Calopogon tuberosus*

GENERAL: Erect perennial herb, usually 12–18 in. tall, but ranging from 4–48 in., from corms. **LEAVES:** Linear-lanceolate, **1–2**, strongly ribbed, 6–20 in. long, **rising vertically** from the stem base to $^1/_3$–$^1/_2$ the height of the stem. **FLOWERS:** Varying **shades of pink**, about 1.5 in. wide; 3 petals, **uppermost petal (lip)** narrow spreading to a broad, **triangular tip, with a patch of orange bristles**, bristles fading downward to yellow-tipped white hairs midway on the lip; 2 lateral petals and 3 sepals similar and usually widely spreading; 3–several flowers at the tip of a long, thin stem. June–July. **FRUITS:** Erect, cylindric to ellipsoid capsules. **WHERE FOUND:** Wet meadows and open seepage slopes, in all of the eastern U.S., southeastern Canada, and the Maritime provinces. In TN, from the Eastern Highland rim, eastward, also Lewis County in the Western Highland Rim. Occasional. **C. pulchellus**.

NOTES: The genus name *Calopogon* is derived from the Greek for "beautiful beard," in reference to the hair-like projections on the lip of the flower. The species name *tuberosus* is Latin for "tuberous," referring to the tuberous corm of this plant. Other common names include Bearded Pink, Meadow Gift, and Swamp Pink. • Thien and Marks (1972) described the pollination of **Grass Pink** as involving the attraction of recently emerged, naïve bumblebees. The bees, expecting a reward of nectar and/or pollen, land on the hairs of the upper lip, which swings down under the weight of the bee, positioning the bee on the column where pollen can be placed on the bee's back. If the bee is already carrying a load of pollen, it will contact the stigma and pollinate the plant.

Upland Spreading Pogonia · *Cleistes bifaria*

GENERAL: Erect perennial herb, 8–36 in. tall. **LEAVES:** Solitary, narrowly lanceolate, appearing above the middle of the stem, about 6 in. long; also a prominent, vertical floral bract at the top of the stem below the solitary flower. **FLOWERS:** Solitary, **pink**, somewhat **tubular**, 1.5–2.0 in. long; 3 petals, 2 lateral petals tightly overlapping and covering the lower (lip) petal, curled upward slightly at the tips; **lip** petal strongly **purple-veined**, rose red at the tip and with a yellowish central ridge; 3 slender, **spreading, purplish brown sepals**, radiating upward from the base of the petals. May–June. **FRUITS:** Narrowly cylindric capsules, 1.25 in. long. **WHERE FOUND:** Acidic soils of moist places, grassy fields, and mountainous openings from WV to KY, south to FL and TX. In TN, thinly but widely distributed from Lincoln, Moore, and Coffee counties in southern Middle TN, eastward. Occasional. *C. divaricata* var. *bifaria*.

KURT EMMANUELE

NOTES: The genus name *Cleistes* is Greek, meaning "closed," in reference to the somewhat closed shape of the flower. Only 2 species of Spreading Pogonia in North America represent this largely tropical genus.

Spotted Coralroot · *Corallorhiza maculata*

GENERAL: Smooth, erect, **saprophytic** perennial herb, 6–18 in. tall, from a branched rhizome; **reddish to purplish brown stems**, partly surrounded by a few tubular sheaths. **LEAVES:** Reduced to a few bladeless sheaths; without chlorophyll. **FLOWERS:** 3 sepals and 2 **lateral petals reddish purple**, about 0.3 in. long, widely spreading above the lip; **lower petal (lip) white with bright magenta spots**, having 2 lateral lobes and 2 parallel ridges near the base; in a loose raceme of 10–40 flowers on the upper ½ of the stem. June–August. **FRUITS:** Grooved capsules, 0.6–1.0 in. long, about 0.25 in. wide, hanging against the stem. **WHERE FOUND:** Shady coniferous or deciduous woods from Canada, south in the mountainous areas of the western and eastern U.S. In TN, in Carter, Johnson, and Washington counties in the Blue Ridge Mountains. Rare.

DENNIS HORN

NOTES: This plant is also known as **Summer Coralroot.** • The common name "coralroot" is a literal translation of the genus name *Corallorhiza* and describes the white, hard, jagged rhizomes, which are similar in appearance to bleached, white coral. • **Spotted Coralroot**, also known as Large Coralroot, lacks chlorophyll and is saprophytic, meaning that it gets its food indirectly from dead organic matter, with the assistance of mycorrhizal fungi. It takes **several years for the leafless flower stalks to develop.**

DICK SODY

Spring Coralroot • *Corallorhiza wisteriana*

GENERAL: Leafless, saprophytic perennial herb, **without chlorophyll**, 4–18 in. tall, with erect, slender flowering stems, tan below to **yellow-brown** or **reddish purple** above, sheathed around the lower portion. **LEAVES:** Reduced to a few bladeless sheaths on the lower stem; without chlorophyll. **FLOWERS:** 3 sepals and 2 lateral petals **reddish brown to greenish yellow**, often suffused with purple, converging to form a hood over the lip; **lower petal (lip) white with magenta spots**; flowers 0.25–0.33 in. long, in a loose raceme. April–May. **FRUITS:** Ovoid capsules, 0.4 in. long, 0.2 in. wide. **WHERE FOUND:** Moist woods, rich ravines and slopes, swamps, and along stream margins, in most of the central and eastern U.S. Widely scattered across TN. Frequent. **SIMILAR SPECIES:** AUTUMN CORALROOT (**C. odontorhiza**) **flowers later**; usually smaller, seldom over 8 in. tall; ovaries often already enlarged at flowering, dominating the **tiny (to 0.16 in), barely open flowers**. In a wide range of woodland habitats, dry to moist but rarely wet, in most of the central and eastern U.S. Scattered throughout TN. Frequent. August–October.

NOTES: The species name *wisteriana* honors Charles Wister (1782–1865), an American botanist who first discovered **Spring Coralroot** in PA. • Spring Coralroot is a saprophyte that obtains nutrients indirectly from decaying organic material in the soil. Studies show that it has a mutualistic relationship with mycorrhizal fungi found among the rhizomes. Individual plants do not flower every year, and lengthy periods may pass between flowerings. An abundance of flowers may be found one year, whereas the next year there may be only a few flower stalks. The rhizomes survive in a semi-dormant state during non-flowering years.

DAVID KOCHER

Pink Lady's Slipper • *Cypripedium acaule*

GENERAL: Perennial herb with scapes (leafless flowering stalks) 6–18 in. tall. **LEAVES:** Basal, **2**, **opposite**, elliptic, 4–10 in. long, dark green, densely hairy, **deeply pleated**. **FLOWERS:** Solitary; 3 **sepals** (lower 2 fused into 1) and 2 **lateral petals yellowish green to purplish brown; lower petal (lip) a showy pouch, pink**, 1.5–2.5 in. long, with rose veins, lip opening a vertical front division with edges folded inward. April–May. **FRUITS:** Ellipsoid capsules, 1.0–1.75 in. long. **WHERE FOUND:** A variety of habitats, but mainly in acidic, mixed coniferous, and hardwood forests and woodlands recovering from fire or logging, from northern AL to northern MN, eastward. In TN, in the Eastern Highland Rim, eastward, also Hickman County in the Western Highland Rim. Occasional.

NOTES: The genus name *Cypripedium* is derived from the Greek *Kypris*, "Venus," and *pedilon*, "a shoe" or "little foot," in reference to the shape of the flower. Lady's slippers are also referred to as "moccasin flowers." This species is also called American Valerian because, like European Valerian (*Valerian officinalis*), it was used as a sedative to treat nervous conditions and depression.

Southern Lady's Slipper
Cypripedium kentuckiense

GENERAL: Perennial herb to 36 in. tall, with a hairy stem. **LEAVES:** Alternate, mostly sheathing, oval to lance-ovate, 5–8 in. long and ½ as wide, **strongly pleated. FLOWERS:** 2 long, **purplish brown, twisted lateral petals** and 3 wavy-edged sepals (lower 2 fused into 1); **lower petal (lip) a showy pouch, cream to dark yellow,** often dimpled, 2.5 in. long; **lip opening large,** tip slopes sharply downward; borne at the top of a leafy stem. May–June. **FRUITS:** Ellipsoid capsules, 1.25–2.0 in. long, 0.3–0.5 in. wide. **WHERE FOUND:** Rich, alluvial floodplains, from VA, KY, and AL, west to OK and TX. In TN, in Decatur, Franklin, and Scott counties. Rare.

NOTES: Though large and beautiful, **Southern Lady's Slipper** surprisingly remained unknown until recently, having previously been classified as a robust southern form of **Large Yellow Lady's Slipper** (p. 452). However, the later flowering time, alluvial habitat, and broad, open pouch separate these 2 species. • The attractive flowers of yellow lady's slippers resemble bright yellow slippers (lower lip) tied with greenish yellow to purplish brown ribbons (twisted upper petals and sepals). The size, shape, coloration, fragrance, and habitat of the yellow-flowered lady's slippers vary tremendously, giving rise to the naming of a number of species and varieties by various authors.

ED HONICKER

Small Yellow Lady's Slipper
Cypripedium parviflorum

GENERAL: Perennial herb, 6–20 in. tall, with a hairy stem. **LEAVES:** Alternate, usually 3, mostly sheathing, pleated, hairy, oval to lance-ovate, 2–6 in. long and ½ as wide. **FLOWERS:** 2 twisted **lateral petals** and 3 sepals (lower 2 fused into 1) **dark reddish brown; lip petal a yellow pouch, less than 1 in. long; lip opening relatively small,** with a relatively long "toe"; flowers 1–2. April–May. **FRUITS:** Ellipsoid capsules, 1.0–1.5 in. long. **WHERE FOUND:** Shady, moist, upland, deciduous woodlands, swamps and wetlands, rocky slopes. A northern species extending south to AL and GA in the mountains. In TN, from the Cumberland Plateau, eastward, in Johnson, Sullivan, Claiborne, Sevier, Blount, Loudon, Polk, Cumberland, Sequatchie, and Van Buren counties. Infrequent. *C. calceolus* var. *parviflorum*.

NOTES: *Cypripedium* species rarely survive being transplanted and should be left in their natural habitat for others to enjoy. • Pollinators are lured to lady's slippers by bright colors and pleasant fragrance. When a pollinator (usually a bee) enters the pouch, it finds no nectar. Once inside, the insect can escape only by squeezing through one of the 2 small openings at the rear of the pouch, where its back is coated with pollen as it exits.

DENNIS HORN

Large Yellow Lady's Slipper
Cypripedium pubescens

GENERAL: Perennial herb, 8–32 in. tall, with hairy stems. **LEAVES:** Alternate, 3–5, widely spaced on the stem, mostly sheathed, **pleated**, hairy, oval to lance-ovate, 4–8 in. long and ½ as wide. **FLOWERS:** 2 twisted **lateral petals** and 3 **sepals** (lower 2 fused into 1), **greenish brown to brownish yellow; lip petal a yellow pouch, 1 in. long or more; lip opening relatively small**, with a relatively long "toe"; flowers 1–2. April–May. **FRUITS:** Ellipsoid capsules, 1.0–1.5 in. long. **WHERE FOUND:** Open, moist, deciduous woodlands and rocky slopes, in most of the eastern U.S. except the southern Coastal Plain and thinly scattered in the western U.S. Widely distributed throughout TN. Occasional. *C. calceolus* var. *pubescens*, *C. parviflorum* var. *pubescens*.

NOTES: Of the 3 yellow lady's slippers found in TN, **Large Yellow Lady's Slipper** is the species that is most commonly seen and photographed. • *Cypripedium* roots were used medicinally for nervousness as a substitute for valerian. There is no evidence of its effectiveness.

Showy Lady's Slipper, Queen Lady's Slipper • *Cypripedium reginae*

GENERAL: Showy perennial herb, 24–36 in. tall, from a stout rhizome; hairy, robust stem. **LEAVES:** Alternate, 3–5, broad, sheathing, **pleated**, 4–10 in. long and over ½ as wide, densely hairy. **FLOWERS:** 2 **lateral petals**, not twisted, and 3 **sepals** (lower 2 fused into 1) **soft white; lower lip** a broad, horizontal **pouch, magenta to rose pink**, 1–2 in. wide, with shallow, **white vertical furrows**; 1–4 flowers at or near the stem tip, each with a prominent vertical, green bract. May–June. **FRUITS:** Ellipsoid capsules, 1.2–1.75 in. long, 0.6 in. wide. **WHERE FOUND:** Wetlands throughout the northeastern and north-central U.S. and adjacent Canada, extending southward to a very few seepy calcareous slopes and streambanks in northeastern TN. Exceedingly rare in TN, being at the very southern edge of its range.

NOTES: This spectacular wetland species is the state flower of MN, the only state flower that is an orchid. It is also the provincial emblem of Prince Edward Island, Canada. • This and other lady's slipper species may cause contact dermatitis in sensitive individuals.

Showy Orchis
Galearis spectabilis

GENERAL: Showy, smooth perennial herb, 3–10 in. tall, from a short, fleshy root; flowering stalks thick, relatively short, sharply ridged. **LEAVES:** Basal, 2, **nearly opposite,** thick, **glossy,** dark green, widely elliptic, 4–8 in. long. **FLOWERS:** 2 lateral petals and 3 sepals **pink to lavender,** converging to form a hood; **lip usually white;** flowers 1 in. long, borne in a raceme. April–May. **FRUITS:** Ellipsoid capsules, 0.7–1.0 in. long. **WHERE FOUND:** Rich, hardwood forests, especially near streams or at the base of slopes, from southeastern Canada and most of the eastern U.S., south to GA and MS. In TN, from the Eastern Highland Rim, eastward, also Davidson, Cheatham, Montgomery, and Chester counties. Occasional. ***Orchis spectabilis***.

DICK DOUB

NOTES: Orchids are experts at tricking insects into their corollas, which lack nectar. Instead, they have packets of pollen, called pollinia, that cannot be used as food by insects. Orchids attract their pollinators with elaborate deceptions, including distended hairs and papillae on the lips and complicated fragrance lures. In search of food, an insect is tricked into visiting flower after flower, depositing and receiving pollen as it goes.

Downy Rattlesnake Plantain
Goodyera pubescens

GENERAL: Perennial herb, 6–20 in. tall; stout, hairy, vertical scape emerges from a leafy rosette in early summer. **LEAVES:** In a **basal rosette, evergreen,** ovate, 1.5–3.5 in. long, bluish green with a **network of white veins** and a **broad, white stripe** down the center. **FLOWERS:** White, hairy, rounded, about 0.25 in. long, **sac-like lower lip;** in a dense cylindric raceme on the upper ¼ of the scape. July–August. **FRUITS:** Small, erect, ovoid capsules. **WHERE FOUND:** Dry woodlands from Québec to MN, south to FL and AR. In TN, from the Western Highland Rim, eastward, also Henry County in West TN. Frequent.

Notes: The individual tiny flowers are quite attractive when viewed through a 10x lens. • The common name comes from the unusual markings on the leaves, said to resemble those on the skin of a rattlesnake, and also the medicinal use of the root for treating snakebites. The basal rosette of leaves gives the plant its similarity to plantains. • Herbal folklore says that Native American women believed that rubbing this plant on their bodies would make their husbands love them more. The leaves were made into a tea to improve appetite and to treat colds and kidney ailments.

JERRY DROWN

Lesser Rattlesnake Plantain
Goodyera repens

GENERAL: Perennial herb, typically 4–8 in. tall. **LEAVES:** In a **basal rosette**, 3–7, green, ovate, 0.5–1.8 in. long, relatively faint, white veins, **without broad, white stripe**. **FLOWERS:** White, about 0.15 in. long, conspicuously hairy, **V-shaped lip**; in a **1-sided raceme** of (usually) up to 20 flowers. July. **FRUITS:** Erect, ovoid capsules. **WHERE FOUND:** Cool, moist, mountainous forests usually in the proximity of conifers, from NY to MN and AK, south in the Rocky Mountains to AZ and NM, and in the Appalachian Mountains to TN and NC. In Sevier, Cocke, Greene, Unicoi, Washington, Carter, and Johnson counties in East TN. Infrequent.

NOTES: This species is smaller than **Downy Rattlesnake Plantain** (p. 453). It is also called **Creeping Rattlesnake Plantain** because it spreads from slender rhizomes. • *Goodyera* is one of several orchid genera known as "jewel orchids" because of their colorful and richly patterned foliage.

DENNIS HORN

Crested Coralroot
Hexalectris spicata

GENERAL: Saprophytic perennial herb, 6–32 in. tall, without chlorophyll, not parasitic. **LEAVES:** Essentially leafless except for a few sheathing scales and triangular bracts, 0.2–0.3 in. long. **FLOWERS:** 2 lateral petals and 3 sepals, yellowish brown with brownish purple striations, spreading, about 0.8 in. long, reflexed at the tips; lip petal yellowish white with bright purple, fleshy ridges; colorful flowers in a loose terminal raceme. July–August. **FRUITS:** Ellipsoid capsules, strongly 3-ribbed, hanging, about 1 in. long. **WHERE FOUND:** Neutral or calcareous soils of rocky woodlands and forested streambanks. Thinly scattered in most of the southern U.S., north to OH, IL, and KS. In East TN, also Grundy, Putnam, Rutherford, and Davidson counties in Middle TN. Occasional.

NOTES: This saprophytic plant is devoid of chlorophyll, obtaining nutrients indirectly from decaying organic material in the soil. • The genus name *Hexalectris* is Greek for "six cock," referring to the purple fleshy ridges on the lip, somewhat resembling a rooster's crest (cockscomb). Interestingly, there are usually 7 rather than 6 purple ridges on the lip. The species name *spicata* means "spiked."

KURT EMMANUELE

Small Whorled Pogonia · *Isotria medeoloides*

GENERAL: Smooth, stout-stemmed perennial herb, 4–10 in. tall, predominantly **pale greenish throughout**. **LEAVES:** In a **whorl of usually 5**, elliptic, up to 3 in. long, at the top of the stem below the flower, fully expanded (even if still drooping) before the flowers mature. **FLOWERS:** 2 greenish lateral petals cover all but the tip of the lip; **lip petal whitish**, 0.6 in. long; 3 **spreading, greenish sepals**, not much longer than the lip; usually solitary, terminal, on a pedicel 0.4–0.6 in. long. May. **FRUITS:** Erect, cylindric capsules. **WHERE FOUND:** Well-drained, recovering deciduous woodlands. Possibly the rarest orchid east of the Mississippi River, with isolated populations from southern Ontario and ME, south to MO, TN, and GA. Known only from Hamilton and Washington counties in East TN. Rare.

NOTES: This plant is very similar to **Large Whorled Pogonia** (see below). • The species name *medeoloides* is derived from the resemblance of the vegetative parts to **Indian Cucumber Root** (p. 419), of the genus *Medeola*. • Part of the reason for this orchid's rarity is the propensity of individual plants to remain dormant for very long periods of time.

DENNIS HORN

Large Whorled Pogonia · *Isotria verticillata*

GENERAL: Smooth, stout, **purplish-stemmed** perennial herb, 4–12 in. tall. **LEAVES:** In a **whorl of usually 5**, oblanceolate, to 3.5 in. long, near the top of the stem below the flower; begin to expand when the flower is fully developed and continue to enlarge after fertilization. **FLOWERS:** 3 long, thin, tapering, **purplish sepals**, up to 2 in. long, radiating outward; 2 lateral **greenish yellow petals**, covering all but the end of the lip; **lip petal** with 2 **purplish side lobes**, an expansive, downcurved, **yellowish white middle lobe**, and a fleshy green central ridge; usually solitary, terminal, on a pedicel 0.8–2.2 in. long. April–May. **FRUITS:** Erect, ellipsoid capsules, 1.0–1.25 in. long. **WHERE FOUND:** Various acidic soil habitats, including moist woodlands, in most of the eastern U.S. Sporadic across TN, but may be locally abundant. Occasional.

KURT EMMANUELE

NOTES: This species may be confused with **Small Whorled Pogonia** (see above) and **Indian Cucumber Root** (p. 419) in the Lily Family. **Large Whorled Pogonia** is recognizable by its reddish purple stem and sepals, and the fruit stalk that is longer than the fruit capsule. In contrast, Small Whorled Pogonia has a pale greenish appearance with a waxy, whitish coating covering the leaves, stem, and flower, and the fruit stalk is slightly shorter than the fruit capsule. The whorled leaves of both of these orchids resemble those of Indian Cucumber Root, however Indian Cucumber Root has a thin, wiry, and somewhat white cobwebby or cottony stem, compared to the stout, hollow, and smooth stems of the Large and Small Whorled Pogonias (Patrick *et. al.*, 1995).

Lilyleaf Twayblade
Liparis liliifolia

GENERAL: Smooth perennial herb, 3–10 in. tall. **LEAVES: Opposite,** 2, spreading, **basal, glossy, green,** elliptic, 2–6 in. long, clasping the stem. **FLOWERS:** Delicate, 0.6–1.0 in. wide; **3 pale green, narrow, spreading sepals,** 2 hidden behind the lip; **2 lateral petals purple, thread-like,** curved backward; lip petal **translucent purplish to brownish,** broadly obovate; up to 25; prominent flowers in a loose, angled raceme; flowers open from bottom to top. May–June. **FRUITS:** Ellipsoid capsules, 0.6 in. long. **WHERE FOUND:** Moist forest slopes and streambanks, from NH to MN, south to GA, MS, and OK. Middle and East TN, also Madison and Chester counties in West TN. Occasional.

NOTES: Twayblade, meaning "two blade," refers to the pair of leaves that clasp the stem. The genus name *Liparis* is from the Greek *liparos*, "fat" or "shining," referring to the smooth, lustrous leaves. The species name *liliifolia* means "lily-leaf," indicating the resemblance of the leaves to those of some members of the Lily Family. This plant is also known as Mauve Sleekwort.

Loesel's Twayblade
Liparis loeselii

GENERAL: Smooth perennial herb, 3–10 in. tall. **LEAVES: Basal,** 2, **elliptic,** 2–6 in. long, **usually light to whitish green,** more vertical than spreading, sheathing the base of the stem. **FLOWERS:** Opaque, **light green to yellowish,** 0.5 in. wide or less; 3 narrow sepals; **2 hair-like lateral petals;** lip petal curved downward at the tip and upward at the sides; up to 12 flowers in a raceme. May–June. **FRUITS:** Ellipsoid capsules, 0.5 in. long. **WHERE FOUND:** Favors moist to wet places in cool ravines, seepage slopes, and swamps. A mainly northern species that extends south to AR and AL. Thinly scattered in Middle and East TN, in Carter, Coffee, DeKalb, Grundy, Humphreys, Lewis, Roane, Stewart, Unicoi, and Warren counties. Infrequent.

NOTES: The species was named in honor of Johann Loesel (1607–55), a German botanist and author of Prussian flora. Only 2 *Liparis* species are found in TN. • In 1980, P.M. Catling documented that **Loesel's Twayblade** makes use of raindrops for pollination ("rain-assisted autogamy"). Raindrops hit and dislodge the pollen onto the stigma, apparently assisted by the upturned lip, which deflects the raindrops toward the anther.

Southern Twayblade
Listera australis

DICK SOOY

GENERAL: Perennial herb, generally 3–8 in. tall. **LEAVES: Opposite, 2,** about midway on the slender stem, **dark green**, ovate, 0.4–1.4 in. long, abruptly pointed. **FLOWERS: Maroon,** 0.5 in. long or less; 3 sepals and 2 lateral petals inconspicuous; **lip petal deeply cleft** into **2 slender prongs**; up to 25 flowers in a loose terminal raceme. March–April. **FRUITS:** Small, slender capsules, on distinct stalks. **WHERE FOUND:** Low, moist woods with rich humus and a shady overstory. A Coastal Plain species with disjunct populations inland to KY and AR. In TN, known from only Fayette and Coffee counties. Rare. **SIMILAR SPECIES:** KIDNEYLEAF TWAYBLADE (*L. smallii*), also called APPALACHIAN TWAYBLADE, has flowers with a **wide lip divided into 2 broad, divergent lobes**, their hues a range of **greenish brown pastels**. Moist mountain woods, frequently under hemlock or rhododendron, from northern GA to KY and PA in the Appalachian Mountains. In TN, in Carter, Cocke, Greene, Johnson, Monroe, Sevier, and Unicoi counties. Infrequent. June–July.

NOTES: • The *Listera* genus is named for Martin Lister (1638–1711), an English naturalist. The species name *australis* means "southern," indicating the usual range of **Southern Twayblade**. • Southern Twayblade is the earliest orchid to bloom in TN. Its entire vegetative span from emergence to maturity is short, generally no more than 1 month.

Green Adder's Mouth • *Malaxis unifolia*

DENNIS HORN

GENERAL: Small, **smooth** perennial herb, 3–10 in. tall, **completely green**. **LEAVES: Solitary**, smooth, oval to elliptic, 1.5–3.0 in. long, attached about halfway up the stem and wrapped fully around it. **FLOWERS: Numerous, 0.12 in. wide or less**, pale green; inflorescence a terminal raceme, curiously forming a flat-topped cluster of buds above the open flowers until all the flowers in the raceme are mature. May–August. **FRUITS:** Obliquely ovoid capsules, 0.25 in. long, 0.1 in. wide. **WHERE FOUND:** Damp woods and bogs from southern Canada, south to FL and TX, and in all of the eastern U.S. Scattered throughout TN in rich humus soils of dry to moist woods and hillsides of mixed forests, less often in open areas. Occasional.

NOTES: The genus name *Malaxis* is Greek for "soft," referring to the texture of the leaves. The species name *unifolia* is Latin for "one leaf." • The small size of this plant makes it easy to overlook in the field. However, once found, it is easy to identify by its unique, completely green appearance. • Although this is the only *Malaxis* species in TN, 12 other species are found in the U.S. and Canada.

Yellow Fringed Orchid
Platanthera ciliaris

GENERAL: Erect, smooth, leafy perennial herb, 12–36 in. tall, from fleshy tuberous roots. **LEAVES:** Alternate, glossy green, **keeled, lanceolate,** 2–8 in. long, sheathing the lower stem, reduced to bracts above. **FLOWERS:** **Bright orange** to yellow, 0.5 in. wide, 1.5 in. long; 3 petal-like, spreading, broadly oval sepals; 2 linear lateral petals; **lip petal** with long, deep **fringes, longer than the lip is wide;** prominent spur longer than the flower or even the ovary with pedicel; in a many-flowered raceme. July–August. **FRUITS:** Ellipsoid capsules, 0.25–0.5 in. long. **WHERE FOUND:** A variety of habitats, either moist or dry sites in sandy, acidic soils, near springs, in pinelands or open woods, and occasionally on rocky slopes, in most of the eastern U.S. East and Middle TN. Frequent. *Habenaria ciliaris*.

NOTES: The flowers of this strikingly beautiful orchid are often closer to bright orange than yellow. • This species is considered a "butterfly specialist" because it attracts and is pollinated by butterflies. • Folklore says that the Cherokee used the flowers as bait on their hooks when fishing. Native Americans used the roots to make a tea to treat headaches and "flux" (diarrhea).

Small Green Woodland Orchid
Platanthera clavellata

GENERAL: Sparsely leaved perennial herb, 6–16 in. tall, with a spindly appearance. **LEAVES:** Usually **1 major leaf,** low on the stem (but not basal), clasping, keeled, **oblanceolate,** 2–6 in. long. **FLOWERS:** Small, **pale yellowish green;** 3 petal-like, broadly oval, spreading sepals; 2 short, broad lateral petals; **lip petal short, blunt,** almost rectangular, **tipped with 3 rounded lobes;** thin spur, about 0.5 in. long, usually enlarged asymmetrically at the end to **resemble a club** (clavellate); inflorescence a lax terminal cluster. July–August. **FRUITS:** Small, ellipsoid capsules. **WHERE FOUND:** Wet woodlands and adjacent to forested streambeds throughout the eastern U.S. and TN. Frequent. *Habenaria clavellata*.

NOTES: Until the 1970s, most botanical manuals included the fringed or rein orchids within the *Habenaria* genus. The genus name *Platanthera* is Greek for "broad anther," referring to the almost fang-like anthers, and is one of several characteristics used to distinguish this genus from *Habenaria*. The species name, *clavellata*, is Latin for "club-shaped," in reference to the clubbed spur of this species.

DENNIS HORN

Yellow Crested Orchid · *Platanthera cristata*

GENERAL: Erect, leafy perennial herb, 8–32 in. tall, from fleshy, tuberous roots. **LEAVES:** Alternate, shiny green, **lanceolate, keeled,** 2–6 in. long, sheathing the lower stem, reduced to bracts above. **FLOWERS: Orange-yellow,** about 0.33 in. wide; 3 petal-like, broadly oval, spreading sepals; 2 lateral petals, curved upward, short-fringed at the tips; **lip petal** about 0.25 in. long, margins fringed, fringes **shorter than the solid width of the lip; small spur, shorter than the lip,** about ½ the length of the ovary; inflorescence a densely flowered, cylindric raceme. July–August. **FRUITS:** Cylindric-ellipsoid capsules, 0.3–0.5 in. long. **WHERE FOUND:** Mainly a species of the southeastern U.S., but extending north along the Atlantic Coast to NH. In TN, confined mainly to swampy areas and moist, sandy sites of the Cumberland Plateau and Eastern Highland Rim, in Fentress, Cumberland, Putnam, White, Van Buren, Coffee, Grundy, Franklin, and Moore counties. Infrequent. *Habenaria cristata*.

DENNIS HORN

NOTES: The species name *cristata,* "crested," refers to the fringed lip. • This species is also known as **Orange Crested Orchid** and **Crested Fringed Orchid.** It resembles a small version of **Yellow Fringed Orchid** (p. 458).

Southern Tubercled Orchid
Platanthera flava var. *flava*

GENERAL: Erect, leafy perennial herb, 6–20 in. tall, often forming dense colonies. **LEAVES:** Alternate, lanceolate, 2–8 in. long, 2–3 on the lower stem, reduced upward to **short bracts that do not protrude past the flowers. FLOWERS:** Yellowish green; 3 petal-like, broadly oval, spreading sepals; 2 short lateral petals, curved upward; **lip petal short, stubby, recurved,** about 0.2 in. long and **nearly as wide,** with 2 small lateral lobes and a pronounced central tubercle near the base; in a loose terminal spike of 10–40 flowers. July–August. **FRUITS:** Obliquely ellipsoid capsules, 0.7 in. long. **WHERE FOUND:** Wet forests and floodplains, from VA and southern MO, southward. Middle and West TN. Occasional. *Habenaria flava* var. *flava*. **SIMILAR SPECIES:** NORTHERN TUBERCLED ORCHID (*P. flava* var. *herbiola*) has **floral bracts longer than the flowers** and **lip is much longer than wide.** Wet ground, ditches, and flood-plains. A northern variety, found from southeastern Canada and ME to MN, south to NC and MO. In TN, found in only a few mountain counties in East TN. Rare. June–August. *H. flava* var. *herbiola*.

MARY MARTIN SCHAFFNER

NOTES: The species name *flava* means "yellow," and the variety name *herbiola* means "grass-green," referring to the predominate colors **Northern Tubercled Orchid.** • Rein or fringed orchids (*Platanthera* spp.) are technically defined by a separate sticky pad (viscidium) attached to each pollen mass (pollinium), exposed in varying degrees, and stigmatic lobes that do not obscure the entrance to the nectary. They are also characterized by erect, smooth stems and a terminal raceme or spike. Keeled alternate stem leaves are sheathed below and rapidly reduced to bracts above. The flower lip opens to a relatively long spur behind it. • *Platanthera* is the largest genus of our native orchids. Twelve species are found in TN.

PAUL SOMERS

Large Purple Fringed Orchid
Platanthera grandiflora

GENERAL: Smooth, leafy, robust perennial herb, 12–48 in. tall, from fleshy, elongated roots. **LEAVES:** Alternate, **lanceolate, keeled**, to 8 in. long, sheathing the lower stem, reduced to bracts above. **FLOWERS:** Rose purple, showy; 3 petal-like, oval sepals, 2 lateral sepals swept back at an angle; 2 short, lateral petals, curved upward; **lip petal**, to 0.7 in. wide and 1 in. long, deeply divided into 3 flared, distinct **lobes, deeply fringed (1/3 or more the length of the lobe)**, with a **squarish to roundish** (never dumbbell-shaped) **opening** at the base, leading to the spur and nectary; inflorescence a dense, cylindric terminal raceme. June–August. **FRUITS:** Ellipsoid capsules, 0.5–0.7 in. long. **WHERE FOUND:** Along streams or in moist open meadows, mainly in the northeastern U.S. and southeastern Canada, extending south in the mountains to GA and NC. In TN, in the Blue Ridge Mountains in Carter, Greene, Johnson, and Sullivan counties. Rare. *Habenaria grandiflora*.

NOTES: The species name *grandiflora* means "large flower." • This species and **Small Purple Fringed Orchid** (p. 463) are quite similar. The easiest method of telling them apart is to look at the opening to the nectary at the base of the lip. In **Large Purple Fringed Orchid**, the opening is round to squarish, whereas Small Purple Fringed Orchid has a constriction in the middle of the opening to the nectar spur, giving the opening a sort of figure 8 or dumbbell shape.

KURT EMMANUELE

Yellow Fringeless Orchid
Platanthera integra

GENERAL: Slender, erect, leafy perennial herb, 12–24 in. tall, with fleshy, tuberous roots. **LEAVES:** Alternate, 1–2 (2nd leaf much smaller), narrow, **lance-linear**, 2–8 in. long, **folded**, recurved, reduced to bracts above. **FLOWERS:** Bright orange-yellow; 3 spreading, petal-like sepals; 2 small lateral petals, curved upward; **lip petal with tiny, rounded teeth (not fringed)**; inflorescence a small, dense, cylindric or conical raceme, 1.5 in. wide. August. **FRUITS:** Ellipsoid capsules about 0.4 in. long. **WHERE FOUND:** Open, acidic swamps and moist meadows on the Coastal Plain from NJ to TX with disjunct populations in Middle TN, in Coffee, Warren, Van Buren, and Bledsoe counties. Rare. *Habenaria integra*.

NOTES: The species name *integra* refers to the undivided or unfringed (integral) lip. • The individual flowers in the inflorescence open from the bottom up. Thus, the raceme is at first conical, but soon becomes cylindric, full of tightly clustered, rich orange-yellow flowers.

Monkey-Face Orchid
Platanthera integrilabia

GENERAL: Beautiful perennial herb, to 36 in. tall.
LEAVES: Alternate, 2–3, green, **lanceolate**, up to 8 in.
long, sheathing the lower stem, reduced to bracts
above. **FLOWERS: Luminescent white, fragrant;** 2 narrow, lateral petals, curved upward; **lip petal** long, thin,
finely serrated (not fringed); 3 sepals, 2 lateral sepals
swept back to clasp the ovary, giving the flower a
narrow frontward appearance; downward-curved
spur, 1.6–2.0 in. long, **more than 2x the length of the
flower;** 6–15 flowers in a loose raceme. Early to
mid-August. **FRUITS:** Ellipsoid capsules, about 0.5 in.
long. **WHERE FOUND:** Moist, sandy meadows and
swamps, and along forested creeks and bogs.
Restricted to the Cumberland Plateau and southwestern foothills of the Appalachian Mountains
from VA and KY, south to AL and GA. In TN, in the
Cumberland Plateau and a few counties in southeastern TN. Occasional. *Habenaria blephariglottis*
var. *integrilabia*.

NOTES: Monkey-Face Orchid was considered a
regional variety of the **White Fringed Orchid**
(*P. blephariglottis*) until Carlyle Luer elevated it to full species status in 1975. It is an
infrequent but welcome sight in TN. • Research shows that another *Platanthera* species
(not found in TN), Blunt-Leaf Orchid (*P. obtusata*), with smaller flowers, is actually pollinated by mosquitoes. Most *Platanthera* species are pollinated by butterflies.

Ragged Fringed Orchid
Platanthera lacera

GENERAL: Smooth, erect, leafy perennial herb, usually
10–30 in. tall, **greenish overall. LEAVES:** Alternate, 2–5,
lanceolate to oval, to 1.6 in. wide and 6 in. long, much
reduced upward. **FLOWERS: Creamy green;** 3 spreading,
petal-like, oval sepals; 2 slender lateral petals, curved
upward; **lip petal,** to 0.8 in. long and wide, **deeply
cleft into 3 lobes,** with tips deeply and **irregularly
lacerated, appearing tattered;** 20–40 flowers in an
elongated raceme. May–July. **FRUITS:** Erect, ellipsoid
capsules, 0.6 in. long. **WHERE FOUND:** Wet, open, or
thin woods, moist slopes, meadows, and roadside
ditches from Newfoundland to southeastern Manitoba,
south to GA and TX. Sporadic in Middle and East TN,
also Henderson County in West TN. Occasional.
Habenaria lacera.

NOTES: The species name *lacera* means "torn" or
"lacerated," referring to the deeply cut or fringed
lip of the flower. This species readily hybridizes
with other fringed orchids to form attractive but
confusing intermediates. Studies have shown that
noctuid moths and hawkmoths (*Sphinx* spp.)
pollinate this plant.

DENNIS HORN

Snowy Orchid
Platanthera nivea

GENERAL: Erect, leafy perennial herb, 8–24 in. tall, from fleshy, tuberous roots. **LEAVES:** Alternate, 2–3, green, **lanceolate, keeled**, 2–10 in. long, sheathing the lower stem, reduced to bracts above. **FLOWERS:** **Ultra-white**, relatively wide and flat, about 0.5 in. across, appear to be upside down; **unfringed lip uppermost, bent backward**; yellow column (united filaments and style); 3 petal-like, spreading sepals, **2 lateral sepals slightly twisted**, partially exposing the back surface; long, horizontal spur is curved upward at the end; numerous flowers in a slender, cylindric, raceme with a conical tip. July–August. **FRUITS:** Cylindric capsules, 0.3–0.5 in. long, strongly ribbed. **WHERE FOUND:** Open, wet barrens, and acidic bogs, on the Coastal Plain from NJ to TX and inland to AR and TN. In TN, a disjunct population is found only in Coffee County in Middle TN. Rare. *Habenaria nivea*.

Notes: The species name *nivea*, meaning "snowy," and the common name both refer to the truly "snow white" flowers. This plant is also known as Bog Torch, as it lights up the bogs where it often grows.

KURT EMMANUELE

Padleaf Rein Orchid • *Platanthera orbiculata*

GENERAL: Erect, smooth perennial herb, 10–20 in. tall, from several long, fleshy roots. **LEAVES:** Basal, **2, opposite**, broadly rounded, **spreading flat on the ground**, about 4 in. long and wide, deep lustrous green above, silvery beneath. **FLOWERS:** Greenish white, fragrant; 3 spreading petals, 2 lateral petals curved upward; **lip petal thin, pendant**, about 0.7 in. long; 3 petal-like, widely spreading sepals, 2 lateral sepals reflexed; column (united filaments and style) with a prominent projection on each side; **spur is longer than the lip** and incurved toward the tip; inflorescence a loose, vertical, cylindric raceme. June–August. **FRUITS:** Erect, obovoid-ellipsoid capsules, slightly curved, 0.4–0.6 in. long. **WHERE FOUND:** Moist coniferous or hardwood forests. Widespread in Canada, extending south into the northeastern U.S. and in the mountains to NC and TN. In TN, in Claiborne, Carter, Sullivan, Johnson, Unicoi, and Grundy counties. Infrequent. *Habenaria orbiculata.*

NOTES: The species name *orbiculata* means "circular" or "round," in reference to the large, rounded leaves of this species. • This species tends to flower infrequently, most likely because of the amount of energy required for flowering and the restricted light that is available in the shady habitats where this plant grows.

Purple Fringeless Orchid
Platanthera peramoena

GENERAL: Erect, smooth, leafy perennial herb, 14–42 in. tall. **LEAVES:** Alternate, 2–5, green, **keeled, lanceolate,** up to 5 in. long, sheathing the lower stem, reduced to bracts above. **FLOWERS:** Rose purple; 2 lateral petals relatively small, curved upward; **lip petal,** about 0.75 in. wide, **deeply divided into 3 widely spreading lobes, margins serrated (not fringed),** middle lobe of the lip sometimes deeply notched; 3 petal-like, broadly oval sepals; inflorescence a terminal raceme. July–August. **FRUITS:** Ellipsoid capsules, 0.6 in. long. **WHERE FOUND:** Moist woods, streambanks, and damp meadows, in the Ohio and lower Mississippi River Valleys, extending east to central NC and MD. Throughout TN, but more prevalent in West TN and the Western Highland Rim, thinly scattered elsewhere. Occasional. *Habenaria peramoena*.

Notes: The species name *peramoena* means "very beautiful," referring to the flowers of this strikingly attractive orchid. • This orchid may occur in large numbers at a given location one year and then disappear almost completely the next. This appearance and disappearance is highly dependent on rainfall amounts in a given year, with the plant becoming dormant or not flowering when conditions become too dry.

OTTO R. HIRSCH

Small Purple Fringed Orchid
Platanthera psycodes

GENERAL: Showy, erect, perennial herb, 8–48 in. tall, with a fluted, leafy stem. **LEAVES:** Alternate, 2–5, dark green, **lanceolate, keeled,** up to 8 in. long, sheathing the lower stem, reduced to bracts above. **FLOWERS:** Rose purple, often pleasantly fragrant; 3 petal-like, spreading, oval sepals, 2 lateral sepals swept back at an angle; 2 lateral petals finely toothed, curved upward; lip petal, to 0.5 in. wide and 0.6 in. long, deeply divided into 3 distinctive, flared **lobes, fringed less than 1/3 the length of the lobe;** base of the lip has a **dumbbell- or bowtie-shaped** (never squarish or roundish) **opening to the spur and nectary;** inflorescence a rounded cylindrical raceme. June–July. **FRUITS:** Ellipsoid capsules, about 0.6 in. long. **WHERE FOUND:** Moist, thin, or open woods, along streams, or in wet roadside ditches of upper elevations. Most of southeastern Canada, the northeastern U.S., and south in the mountains to GA. In TN, confined to the eastern mountainous areas, specifically Polk, Monroe, Sevier, Greene, Unicoi, Carter, and Johnson counties. Infrequent. *Habenaria psycodes*.

NOTES: This is an exquisite and showy orchid. The species name *psycodes* means "butterfly-like," presumably referring to the flower shape. • This species is remarkably similar to **Large Purple Fringed Orchid** (p. 460).

JERRY DROWN

MARY MARTIN SCHAFFNER

Rose Pogonia
Pogonia ophioglossoides

GENERAL: Slender, erect perennial herb, 4–28 in. tall, with a smooth, round stem, green above, purplish below. **LEAVES: Solitary,** halfway up the stem, ascending, **elliptic,** succulent, to 4 in. long. **FLOWERS: Pink,** 1 in. across; 3 spreading, lanceolate, petal-like sepals; 2 lateral petals curved upward and inward; **lip petal spoon-shaped, with magenta fringes** at the tip and edges and **yellowish bristles** in the center; terminal, usually solitary in the axil of a floral bract. May–June. **FRUITS:** Narrowly ellipsoid capsules, 0.3–0.5 in. long. **WHERE FOUND:** Favors permanently wet places, particularly marshes, seepy slopes, often in sphagnum moss. Most of the eastern U.S. except the central Mississippi River Valley. In Middle and East TN, in Coffee, Warren, Van Buren, Sequatchie, White, Cumberland, Fentress, Blount, and Johnson counties. Infrequent.

NOTES: The genus name *Pogonia* comes from the Greek *pogonias,* "bearded," referring to the crest on the lip of most species. The species name *ophioglossoides* literally means "resembling a snake's mouth," but actually refers to the plant's resemblance to Adder's Tongue Fern (*Ophioglossum* spp.) with its solitary leaf.

DENNIS HORN

Shadow Witch
Ponthieva racemosa

GENERAL: Perennial herb, 5–24 in. tall, from numerous, stout, fleshy roots. **LEAVES:** In a **flat, leafy basal rosette,** 3–8, smooth, thin, **elliptic,** 1.5–5.0 in. long, **bright green above,** silvery beneath. **FLOWERS: Whitish,** predominantly **flat, horizontal,** about 0.5 in. long; pronounced **green veins on triangular lateral petals and ovate sepals; lip petal uppermost,** with a **pointed tip** and a green, pouch-like center; inflorescence a loose, cylindric, terminal raceme. September. **FRUITS:** Ellipsoid capsules, 0.5 in. long. **WHERE FOUND:** Shady, calcareous seeps or streambanks, moist ravines, floodplains, and shady edges of ponds, mainly in the Atlantic Coastal Plain from southeastern VA to FL and TX. Disjunct populations in TN in Franklin and Warren counties. Rare.

NOTES: This plant is also known as **Hairy Shadow Witch** and Mrs. Britton's Shadow Witch. • The *Ponthieva* genus was named in honor of Henri de Ponthieu, a French West Indies merchant who sent collections of new plants back to Europe in 1778. The species name *racemosa* refers to the inflorescence, a raceme.

Nodding Ladies' Tresses · *Spiranthes cernua*

GENERAL: Perennial herb, 8–18 in. tall, often in large colonies; stems have **knob-tipped hairs**. **LEAVES:** Alternate, green, **narrowly oblanceolate**, 2–8 in. long, pliable, reduced to bracts above, **persistent** (present at flowering). **FLOWERS:** White, tubular, 0.3–0.6 in. long, **usually fragrant**; 3 petal-like sepals and 2 lateral petals project forward; **lip petal often light yellowish green**; flowers arranged in 3–4 gently twisted columns, in a **cylindric spike** without much tapering at the top. September–October. **FRUITS:** Ellipsoid capsules, 0.3 in. long. **WHERE FOUND:** Moist, relatively open, acidic places in most of the eastern U.S., from central KS eastward. Throughout TN. Frequent. **SIMILAR SPECIES:** YELLOW LADIES' TRESSES (**S. ochroleuca**) is **slightly larger**, to 20 in. tall, and **leafier**, with **larger bracts** above the base; **flowers are yellowish** inside; **spike appears pointed**. Well-drained and sometimes shady locations, in the northeastern U.S., south to TN and NC. In TN, in Dickson, Cumberland, Sumner, and Sevier counties. Rare. October. FRAGRANT LADIES' TRESSES (**S. odorata**) is **taller** (12–36 in.) and **leafier**; flowers are **strongly fragrant**; **lip is white** with a **yellowish center**; **stoloniferous**, forming clumps or colonies. Wet places, even standing water, mainly in the southeastern U.S. Coastal Plain, inland to KY and AR. In TN, in Knox, Humphreys, and Sumner counties. Rare. October.

NOTES: The species name *cernua* means "nodding," in reference to the flowers. • **Nodding Ladies' Tresses** was first described in 1753 by the Swedish naturalist, Carl von Linné (Linnaeus), who is often referred to as the "father of taxonomy". • Nodding Ladies' Tresses was used medicinally by Native Americans as a tea to treat urinary disorders and venereal disease, and as a wash to strengthen weak infants.

DENNIS HORN

Green-Lipped Ladies' Tresses, Slender Ladies' Tresses · *Spiranthes lacera* var. *gracilis*

GENERAL: Smooth perennial herb, 4–16 in. tall, from fleshy roots. **LEAVES:** In a **basal rosette**, 3–5, **ovate**, short-petioled, 1–2 in. long, normally **wither before flowering**. **FLOWERS:** Whitish, tubular, 0.15–0.25 in. long, **bright green inside the lip**; narrow sepals and lateral petals project forward; usually arranged in a single loose or compact spiral. August–September. **FRUITS:** Ellipsoid capsules, 0.25 in. long. **WHERE FOUND:** Open woods and grassy areas, in most of the eastern U.S. from the Great Lakes to the Gulf Coast. In TN, from the Western Highland Rim eastward. Frequent. *S. gracilis*. **SIMILAR SPECIES:** PEARL TWIST (**S. tuberosa**), also called LITTLE LADIES' TRESSES, is 6–12 in. tall, with **pure white flowers**, 0.1–0.2 in. long, arranged in a single long spiral; basal rosette of 2–3 small, oval leaves normally withers prior to flowering. Relatively dry, open places, in most of the eastern U.S. from NY to MI and KS, southward. Throughout TN. Frequent. July–September.

NOTES: Green-Lipped Ladies' Tresses is often visited by the Little Glasswing butterfly. • The genus name *Spiranthes* means "coil flower." The common name refers to the resemblance of the coiled or spiraled floral arrangement (along the spike) to curled or braided hair. The degree of spiraling ranges from none, forming essentially a 1-sided column, to being twisted so tightly that the flowers appear to be borne in 3–4 vertical columns. The leaves are mostly basal, surrounding the vertical flower stalk, and the flowers are mainly whitish and tubular in shape. Species of ladies' tresses are so similar that identification is often difficult even for an experienced botanist. Eight species are found in TN.

DENNIS HORN

DENNIS HORN

Shining Ladies' Tresses, Wideleaf Ladies' Tresses • *Spiranthes lucida*

GENERAL: Smooth perennial herb, 4–12 in. tall, with a somewhat hairy spike. **LEAVES:** Basal, 3–4, broad, **glossy**, **elliptic**, 2–5 in. long, clasping on the lower stem. **FLOWERS:** White, tubular, 0.25–0.5 in. long, **upper surface of lip bright yellow**, interrupted by thin, dark green stripes; in a spike of tightly clustered flowers, usually arranged in 3 spiral columns. May–June. **FRUITS:** Ellipsoid capsules. **WHERE FOUND:** Sunny, moist places adjacent to waterways (streambanks, lakeshores, marshes). A mainly north-eastern U.S. species that extends south to AL. In TN, in Claiborne, Carter, Franklin, Johnson, Roane, Overton, White, and Lewis counties. Infrequent.

NOTES: The species name *lucida* means "shining," in reference to the glossy leaves. • The bright yellow marking on the lip and the wide, shiny leaves are distinctive characteristics of this species. It is also the earliest *Spiranthes* species to flower in TN. • Unique among North American *Spiranthes*, **Shining Ladies' Tresses** is designed to place pollen on the "chin" of its pollinators, which approach the flowers upside-down, whereas other ladies' tresses place the pollen on the "forehead," near the eyes of the pollinator.

DICK SOOY

Oval Ladies' Tresses, Lesser Ladies' Tresses • *Spiranthes ovalis*

GENERAL: Perennial herb, 8–16 in. tall, stem with **knob-tipped hairs**. **LEAVES:** Basal and alternate, 2–3, **narrowly oblanceolate**, the lowest to 5 in. long, **arch** outward **away from the stem**, **present** on the lower stem **at flowering time**. **FLOWERS:** Pure white, tubular, usually 0.2–0.25 in. long; in a spiraled **spike tapered at both the top** (new buds) **and bottom** (wilting older flowers) to form an oval. September–October. **FRUITS:** Ellipsoid capsules, 0.2 in. long. **WHERE FOUND:** Moist and shady woodlands in most of the southeastern U.S., from PA to IL, southward. Scattered locations throughout TN. Occasional.

NOTES: The species name *ovalis* is Latin for "egg-shaped" or "oval," in reference to the shape of the inflorescence. • Thirty to forty years ago this plant was considered quite rare in TN. Increased awareness has led to many recent discoveries and **Oval Ladies' Tresses** is now known from over 20 counties in the state. • The spiraling flower arrangement of ladies' tresses is a result of uneven cell growth, which results in the twisting of the flower stems.

Spring Ladies' Tresses · *Spiranthes vernalis*

GENERAL: Often robust perennial herb, 8–48 in. tall, with copiously **pointed hairs** on the upper stem. **LEAVES:** Basal and alternate, 3–5, **stiff, linear-lanceolate**, 2–10 in. long, reduced to bract-like sheaths upward on the stem, present at flowering time. **FLOWERS:** White to cream, fragrant, tubular, 0.25–0.3 in. long, **pale yellow to greenish yellow inside lip**; inflorescence a spike of 1 long spiral of flowers. July–September. **FRUITS:** Ellipsoid capsules, 0.25 in. long. **WHERE FOUND:** Open, often grassy areas, from central KS to IL to MA, southward. Scattered throughout TN. Occasional.

NOTES: Under a strong lens, the hairs on the stem and inflorescence are seen to be sharply pointed, rather than with an enlarged spherical tip as in other *Spiranthes* species. • The species name *vernalis* means "of spring," even though, in TN, this species doesn't flower before July. In the north, it flowers even later in the year. This plant is also known as **Grass-Leaved Ladies' Tresses** and Upland Ladies' Tresses. • Native Americans and herbalists have used ladies' tresses to treat skin infections and eye problems. According to folklore, a European species of ladies' tresses was used as an aphrodisiac.

HUGH & CAROL NOURSE

Cranefly Orchid · *Tipularia discolor*

GENERAL: Erect perennial herb, with a slender scape (right photo), 8–26 in. tall, arising in midsummer after the leaf has withered. **LEAVES:** Single, basal, **elliptic**, 3–4 in. long, **pleated, dull green** blotched with purple above, rich satiny **purple beneath** (left photo), unfurls in autumn and persists throughout the winter, withering in late spring. **FLOWERS:** Watery-translucent, purplish green (or bronze or yellowish), **asymmetric (lopsided)**, 0.6–0.75 in. wide; 3 sepals and 2 lateral petals narrow, similar; lip petal 3-lobed, middle lobe elongated; slender, tubular spur extends backward from the lip; numerous flowers in a terminal raceme. July–August. **FRUITS:** Hanging, ellipsoid capsules, 0.5 in. long. **WHERE FOUND:** Upland or rich, damp, acidic woodlands, in the eastern U.S. from the Ohio River Valley, southward. Throughout TN. Common.

DENNIS HORN

NOTES: The flowers of this species are asymmetric (lopsided), with one petal overlapping the dorsal sepal, somewhat resembling a cranefly and giving the plant its common name. It can be very difficult to spot in the shady forest understory of midsummer after the leaf has disappeared as the flowers blend into the background of leaf litter on the forest floor.

JERRY DROWN

DICK SODY

Three-Birds Orchid · *Triphora trianthophora*

GENERAL: Small perennial herb, 3–10 in. tall, appearing delicate and fragile; **flowering stems purplish green. LEAVES:** Alternate, **oval, clasping, bract-like**, to 0.5 in. long. **FLOWERS:** Pinkish white; 3 sepals and 2 lateral petals similar, oblonceolate; **lip petal white**, about 0.5 in. long, 3-lobed, with 3 parallel **green ridges in the center**; 1–several (commonly 3) flowers arise singly on pedicels from the upper leaf axils, often nodding. August–September. **FRUITS:** Ellipsoid capsules, 0.3–0.4 in. long. **WHERE FOUND:** Rich, damp woodland humus, throughout the eastern U.S. from ME to WI and NE, southward (except along the southeastern Atlantic Coast). Thinly but widely distributed in TN. Occasional.

NOTES: Sometimes the pedicels are not rigid enough to support the flowers firmly, resulting in a nodding effect. • Individual flowers last only about 1 day, but many plants in a colony (even many colonies within a sizable area) may have 1 or more flowers open simultaneously, apparently triggered synchronously by the drop in normal nighttime temperature, or other factors.

Glossary

Page numbers indicate where a term is illustrated.

acaulescent: without an upright, leafy stem; the stem usually subterranean

achene: small, dry, single-chambered, one-seeded fruit that does not split open when mature, with the seed coat and ovary wall separate (p. 478)

actinomorphic: radially symmetric (p. 476)

acuminate: a tip with sides that are variously concave and tapering to a point (p. 472)

acute: sharply ending in a point with straight or slightly convex margins (p. 472)

adnate: the fusion or growing together of unlike parts

aerial: any plant parts that occur above the ground or, in aquatic plants, above the water

alkaloid: any of numerous nitrogen-containing plant compounds, some of which are poisonous (e.g., strychnine) and others with medicinal uses (e.g., morphine, codeine)

alternate: situated singly at each joint or node (e.g., as leaves on a stem) or regularly between other organs (e.g., as stamens alternate with petals)

annual: a plant that completes its life cycle in one growing season

anther: the pollen-bearing portion of the stamen (p. 475)

apex: tip

appressed: lying flat or pressed against the surface

aquatic: growing in the water, either entirely or partially submerged

aril: an appendage or outer covering of a seed

ascending: growing upward at an angle (obliquely)

attenuate: with a long, gradual taper; narrower than acute (p. 472)

auricle: an ear-shaped lobe or appendage at the base of a leaf or other organ

awn: a slender bristle or hair, usually at the tip of a structure

axil: the angle between a side organ (e.g., a leaf) and the part to which it is attached (e.g., a stem)

axillary: arising from an axil

barb: a stiff, hooked hair

barbellate: having small barbs

basal: located at the base or arising from it (e.g., leaves at the base of a stem)

beak: a firm, prolonged, slender tip

beard: a tuft or clump of hairs

berry: pulpy or juicy, many-seeded, indehiscent fruit (p. 478)

biennial: a plant that completes its life cycle in two growing seasons

bifurcate: twice forked

bilabiate: bilaterally symmetric and distinctly divided into two "lips" (p. 475)

bipinnate: twice pinnate

biternate: twice ternate; a ternate leaf with each branch divided again into three parts

blade: the broad, flat part of a leaf or petal

bract: a reduced leaf at the base of a flower or an inflorescence (p. 475)

bracteate: having bracts

branch: a division of a stem or other organ

palmately trifoliolate

pinnately trifoliolate

pinnately compound

palmately compound

bipinnately compound

ternately decompound

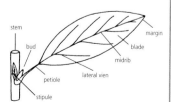

simple leaf

Leaf shapes

filiform   *subulate*

linear   *elliptic*

lanceolate   *falcate*

oblong   *spatulate*

orbicular

deltoid

bristle: a hair-like projection

bulb: a fleshy, underground food storage organ made up of overlapping, swollen scales or leaf bases

bulbil: a small, bulb-like structure, often located in a leaf axil or in place of a flower

bulblet: a small bulb, usually borne on a stem or in an inflorescence

calcareous: chalky, alkaline soil rich in calcium carbonate (lime)

calyx: the outermost whorl (sepals) of the perianth, usually green or sometimes colored (p. 475)

calyx tube: the basal or tubular portion of a fused calyx; the sepals may be fused wholly or in part

campanulate: bell-shaped (p. 476)

capsule: a dry fruit that splits open when mature and is made up of two or more carpels (p. 478)

cardiac glycoside: a two-parted compound, made up of a sugar (glycone) and an aglycone, that acts as a powerful heart stimulant; has therapeutic uses but is potentially toxic; found in foxglove (*Digitalis*) and lily-of-the-valley (*Convallaria*)

carpel: the ovule-bearing structure of a flower; a simple pistil or one member of a compound pistil

cathartic: a strong laxative substance that stimulates bowel movement; purgative

caudex: the woody base of a perennial plant

caulescent: having an aboveground stem

cauline: on or along the stem, as opposed to being basal

chaff: thin, dry scales or bracts; often used for the bracts in the flower head of Asteraceae

chambered: having inner cavities or compartments

chlorophyll: the green-colored substance produced by photosynthetic plants

ciliate: with hairs on the margin, especially on leaves and bracts (p. 472)

clasping: embracing or surrounding, usually in reference to a leaf base around a stem (p. 473)

clavate: club-shaped

claw: the narrow, petiole-like base of a petal or sepal

cleft: divided into segments to near the middle

cleistogamous: bearing self-pollinating flowers that do not open, as in the violets (Violaceae) and gentians (Gentianaceae)

compound: of two or more similar parts

compound leaf: a leaf with two or more leaflets (p. 469)

conical: cone-shaped

connate: the fusion or joining of similar structures

constricted: abruptly narrowed

cordate: heart-shaped, notched at the base (p. 471)

corm: a solid, more or less round, underground stem

corolla: a collective term for the petals or the whorl(s) of the floral envelope between the sepals and stamens (p. 475)

corona: a crown or series of petal-like structures; situated between the petals and stamens in *Passiflora* or on the petals of *Hymenocallis*

corymb: a broad, flat-topped indeterminate inflorescence in which the pedicels are of various lengths and with the outermost flowers opening first (p. 477)

corymbose: resembling a corymb

creeping: growing along (or beneath) the surface of the ground and producing roots at intervals (usually at joints)

crenate: margins with shallow, round, or blunt teeth (p. 472)

crenulate: diminutive of crenate

crisped: with irregularly curled, wavy edges, usually in reference to leaf margins

cross: a hybrid

cross-pollination: the transfer of pollen from one flower to the stigma of another

cuneate: wedge-shaped, usually in reference to leaf bases (p. 472)

cyanthium: the reduced, cymose, cup-like inflorescence of *Euphorbia*, in which the entire multiflowered structure mimics a single, perfect flower

cylindric: elongated and round in cross-section

cyme: a determinate inflorescence, often broad and flattened, in which the central flower opens first (p. 476)

cymose: resembling a cyme

deciduous: falling after completion of its normal function, often at the approach of a dormant season

decompound: more than once compound

decumbent: reclining or lying on the ground, but with the tip turned upright

decurrent: with the leaf bases extending downward and attached to the petiole or stem (p. 473)

dehiscent: opening at maturity by means of slits, lids, pores, or teeth (e.g., a seed capsule)

deltoid: triangular (p. 470)

dentate: with coarse, sharp teeth that point outward (p. 472)

dermatitis: inflammation of the skin characterized by redness, itching, and/or lesions

dichotomous: forked into two equal branches

dicotyledon (dicot): one of the two major subdivisions of flowering plants (angiosperms), with two seed leaves (cotyledons); includes most flowering plants

dioecious: having male (staminate) and female (pistillate) flowers on separate plants

discoid: disk-shaped

disk: the central portion of the flowering head that bears the disk flowers of many Asteraceae

disk flower: a flower with a tubular corolla (Aster Family, Asteraceae); p. 477

dissected: divided into slender segments

distal: found at or near the tip of an organ

disjunct: disconnected; usually referring to populations of the same species that are separated by great distances

distinct: separate, not united; more generally meaning evident or obvious

diuretic: a substance that stimulates kidney function and increases urine production

divergent: broadly spreading from a common point of center

divided: compound, cut into separate parts

Doctrine of Signatures: an ancient belief, popularized in the 17th century, that each plant displays a sign or "signature" that indicates how it should be used, correlating plant features to human organs or ailments (e.g., a plant with liver-shaped leaves would be used to treat liver disease)

dorsal: on the upper (outer) side, the side away from the stem; opposite of ventral

drooping: inclining or hanging downward; nodding

drupe: a fleshy, pulpy, one-seeded fruit in which the seed has a protective stony covering (p. 478)

drupelet: a small drupe

ellipsoid: an elliptic solid

elliptic: oval; broadest near the middle and tapering to both ends (p. 470)

emergent: growing above the surface of soil or water

emetic: a substance used to induce vomiting

endemic: growing only in a particular region

entire: a leaf margin without teeth, hairs, or spines (p. 472)

Leaf shapes (cont'd)

trullate

rhombic

ovate

hastate

sagittate

cordate

reniform

Leaf apices | Leaf margins

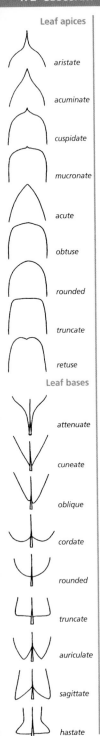

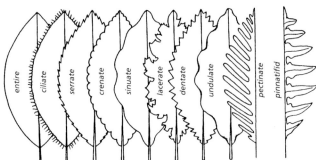

escape: a cultivated plant found growing in the wild

ethnobotany: the study of the relationships of humans with plants, especially with regard to a particular community or culture

even-pinnate: a compound leaf with an even number of leaflets, the terminal leaflet absent

evergreen: having foliage that remains green year round

exserted: extending outward and beyond, as in stamens from the corolla throat or tube

falcate: sickle-shaped (p. 470)

farinose: covered with white, mealy powder

fascicle: a small bundle or dense, close cluster

fertile: capable of reproductive function

filament: the stalk of a stamen; the filament supports the anther (p. 475)

filiform: thread-like (p. 470)

fleshy: plump, firm, and pulpy; succulent

flower: the structure responsible for reproduction

flux: watery diarrhea

follicle: a dry, single-chambered pod-like fruit, splitting open along a single line on one side at maturity (p. 478)

fringed: edged with a row of hairs

fruit: the mature, ripened ovary, together with any other structures that ripen with it as a unit

funnelform: shaped like a funnel (p. 475)

fusiform: thickened in the middle and tapered to both ends

gastroenteritis: an inflammation of the stomach and intestines

genus: a group of related plants or animals constituting a category of biological classification below family and above species; the first word of a scientific name indicates the genus

gibbous: swollen on one side, usually at the base

glabrous: not hairy; smooth

gland: in plants, a surface depression, bump, or appendage that produces a thick, sticky, or greasy fluid

glandular: having glands (p. 474)

glandular-hairy: having both glands and hairs

glaucous: covered with a whitish, waxy powder

globose, globular: round, spherical

glochid: a barbed spine or bristle found on members of the Cactus Family (Cactaceae)

glomerule: a dense or compact cluster of flowers

glume: one of the two sterile bracts at the base of a grass spikelet

glycoside: a two-parted compound made up of a sugar (glycone) and an aglycone, usually becoming poisonous when the sugar is separated from the aglycone during digestion

habit: a plant's characteristic appearance, especially its shape and growth pattern

habitat: the environment in which a plant normally grows

hastate: leaves with the general shape of an arrowhead, but with pointed basal lobes turned outward at right angles; halberd-shaped (p. 471)

head: a dense cluster of sessile flowers (p. 477)

herb: a plant without woody aboveground parts that dies back to the ground in winter

herbaceous: herb-like

hip: the fleshy receptacle of roses (Rosaceae), enclosing the achenes

hispid: having long, bristly hairs (p. 474)

hispidulous: minutely hispid

hoary: covered with whitish hairs

hood: a concave or strongly arching flower part

horn: a beak-like accessory flower structure found in milkweeds (Asclepiadaceae)

host: a plant that nourishes a parasite

hyaline: transparent

hypanthium: a nearly flat or cup-shaped structure produced from the fusion of sepals, petals, and stamens; it may be free from or attached to the ovary (p. 475)

included: contained within a structure (e.g., stamens within a corolla); not projecting

incurved: curved inward

indehiscent: not opening at maturity; generally applies to fruits such as achenes, berries, and drupes

indeterminate: an inflorescence of potentially unlimited growth; the terminal flower maturing last and thereby not arresting elongation

inferior ovary: the ovary position in which the perianth and stamens are inserted above the ovary, so that the ovary is embedded within the hypanthium or receptacle (p. 475)

inflorescence: the arrangement of flowers (pp. 476–77)

internode: the portion of the stem between two nodes or points of leaf insertion

introduced: brought in from another region (e.g., from Europe), not native

involucre: one or more series of bracts immediately surrounding a flower cluster

irregular flower: a flower with petals that are dissimilar in form or orientation; asymmetric

jointed: articulated; having distinct nodes or joints

keel: the two anterior united petals of certain members of the Bean or Pea Family (Fabaceae); a prominent longitudinal ridge

labiate: having a lip or lips

lacerate: torn or irregularly cut or divided (p. 472)

lanceolate: lance-shaped; narrow; broadest near the base and tapering to the tip (p. 470)

lateral: on the side of

latex: milky plant juice

leaf: a primary appendage of most plants, borne on a shoot or stem

leaflet: a single segment of a compound leaf

legume: a dry fruit from a simple pistil that opens along two lines or sutures (e.g., of the Bean or Pea Family, Fabaceae); p. 478

lenticular: lens-shaped; biconvex

ligulate: strap-shaped; having ligules

ligule: the strap-shaped part of the ray flowers of asters (Asteraceae); the appendage at the juncture of the leaf sheath and blade of grasses (Poaceae)

linear: long and narrow with parallel sides throughout most of the length (p. 470)

lip: a projection or expansion of a structure, such as the specialized petal of an orchid

Leaf attachments

sessile

clasping

decurrent

perfoliate

connate-perfoliate

peltate

Surface features

hispid   *villous*

strigose   *lanate*

stellate   *tomentose*

sericeous   *glandular*

lepidote   *hirsute*

puberulent   *pilose*

lobe: a rounded or strap-shaped division of a leaf, petal, or other structure

locule: a compartment, cavity, or cell of an ovary, fruit, or anther

loment: a type of legume fruit with constrictions between the seeds (p. 478)

margin: the edge of a flat structure, usually a leaf

mericarp: an individual carpel that separates in a compound fruit

mesic: a habitat that is moderately moist, but not wet

midvein: the central vein of a leaf

monocotyledon (monocot): one of the two major subclasses of flowering plants (angiosperms), with one seed leaf (cotyledon); includes lilies, orchids, trilliums, and grasses

monoecious: having male (staminate) and female (pistillate) flowers on the same plant

mucilage: a sticky, slimy, gelatinous plant substance

mycorrhiza: the mutually beneficial (symbiotic) association of certain fungi with the roots of certain plants (e.g., orchids)

native: originating in a particular place; indigenous

naturalized: an introduced plant that has adapted to the local environment, where it grows wild

nectary: a nectar-secreting gland or area

nerved: having prominent longitudinal lines or veins

net-veined: having a branched network of veins

nodding: reclining or hanging downward; drooping

node: the area of a stem where one or more leaves are attached

nutlet: a small, hard, dry, one-seeded fruit or part of a fruit that does not split open when mature

oblanceolate: lanceolate with the broadest part above the middle

oblate: spherical, but slightly flattened at the top and bottom

oblong: longer than broad with more or less parallel sides (p. 470)

obovate: essentially ovate, but narrowed at the base and rounded above

obovoid: essentially ovoid, but wider above the middle

obtuse: blunt or rounded at the tip (p. 472)

ocrea: a tubular, nodal sheath formed by the fusion of two stipules of many smartweeds (Polygonaceae)

odd-pinnate: a compound leaf with an odd number of leaflets, the terminal leaflet present

opposite: paired; situated across from each other at the same joint (not alternate or whorled)

orbicular: round (p. 470)

ovary: the structure at the base of a pistil that contains the young, undeveloped seeds (ovules); p. 475

ovate: broadly rounded at the base and narrowed above (p. 471)

ovoid: egg-shaped

ovule: the structures within the ovary that, after fertilization, become the seeds (p. 475)

palate: a raised portion of the lower lip of a corolla

palmate: divided into three or more lobes or leaflets diverging from one point, like fingers on a hand (p. 469)

panicle: an indeterminate branching raceme; the branches of the primary axis are raceme-like and the flowers are on pedicels (p. 477)

paniculate: resembling a panicle

papillose: having small bumps or wart-like protuberances

pappus: the highly modified outer perianth series (hairs, bristles, or scales) of asters (Asteraceae), located at the tip of the achene

parasite: an organism that gets its nourishment chiefly from a live organism to which it is attached

pedicel: the stalk of a single flower of an inflorescence

pedicellate: having a pedicel

peduncle: the stalk supporting an inflorescence or the flower stalk of species with solitary flowers

peltate: attached away from the margin (p. 473)

pepo: a fleshy fruit with a tough rind, for example, cucumber (Cucurbitaceae)

perennial: a plant that lives for three or more years, usually flowering and fruiting for several years

perfect: bisexual; a flower with both stamen(s) and pistil(s)

perfoliate: having leaf bases that completely surround the stem, the stem appearing to pass through the leaf (p. 473)

perianth: a collective term for the calyx and corolla (when present); see below

pericarp: the mature ovary wall

perigynium: (perigynia) the inflated sac enclosing the achene in sedges (Cyperaceae)

persistent: remaining attached long after normal function has been completed

petal: one segment of the corolla, often white or brightly colored (see below)

petiolate: having a petiole

petiole: a leaf stalk (p. 469)

pinnate: with parts (usually leaflets) arranged on both sides of a central stalk or vein, like bristles on a feather; feather-like (p. 469)

pinnatifid: deeply cut or divided in a pinnate fashion (p. 472)

pistil: the female organ of a flower, bearing the ovule and usually consisting of an ovary, style, and stigma (see below)

pistillate: a female flower; bearing pistil(s) but no functioning stamens

pith: the spongy center of a plant's supporting stem

plicate: folded; fan-like

plumose: resembling a feather; a central axis with fine hairs or side branches

pod: a dry fruit that splits open to release its seeds

pollen: the powdery contents of an anther, each grain containing the male cells

pollinate: to transfer pollen from an anther to a stigma

pollination: the process of pollinating

pollinium: (pollinia) a mass of waxy pollen, as in orchids

poultice: an herbal preparation spread on a cloth and applied externally to the body

proboscis: a beak

Ovary position

superior

hypanthium
superior

half-inferior

inferior

Corolla shapes & symmetry

bilabiate (2-lipped)

salverform (trumpet-shaped)

funnelform (funnel-shaped)

urceolate (urn-shaped)

Flower parts

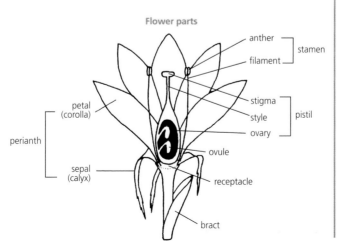

**Corolla shapes &
symmetry (cont'd)**

rotate (wheel-shaped)

*campanulate
(bell-shaped)*

*actinomorphic
(radially symmetric)*

*zygomorphic
(bilaterally symmetric)*

Inflorescence types

solitary

raceme   *spike*

spathe

spadix

*helicoid
cyme*

simple cyme

prostrate: lying on the ground but not rooting

puberulent: minutely hairy (p. 474)

pubescent: covered with soft hairs

pulp: the fleshy, juicy tissue of a fruit

punctate: with translucent or colored dots, depressions, or pits

purgative: a strong laxative substance that stimulates bowel movement; cathartic

quadrangular: four-angled

raceme: an elongate, unbranched, indeterminate inflorescence with pedicellate flowers (p. 476)

racemose: resembling a raceme

rachis: the main axis of an inflorescence or a compound leaf (p. 469)

radially symmetrical: developing uniformly on all sides, like spokes on a wheel

radiate: spreading outward from the center

ray flower: a flower with a strap-like (ligulate) corolla (Aster Family, Asteraceae); p. 477

receptacle: the end of the stem to which flower parts (or, in Asteraceae, the flowers) are attached (p. 475)

reclining: leaning or bending down

recurved: curved under, especially in reference to leaf margins

reflexed: abruptly bent or turned back or down

regular: a flower in which the members of each circle of parts (or at least the petals and sepals) are similar in size, shape, and orientation; radially symmetric

reniform: kidney-shaped (p. 471)

reticulate: resembling a net

retrorse: turned backward or away from the tip

retuse: notched at the tip (p. 472)

revolute: leaf margins rolled toward the lower side

rheumatism: inflammation of the joints, tendons, or muscles

rhizomatous: having a rhizome

rhizome: an underground stem with nodes, buds, and roots

rhombic: diamond-shaped; with the outline of an equilateral oblique-angled figure (p. 471)

root: the part of a plant that anchors it and absorbs nutrients from the soil

rootstock: a rhizome

rosette: a circular cluster of leaves at or near ground level

rotate: wheel-shaped; flat and circular (p. 476)

runner: a slender stolon

saccate: bag- or pouch-shaped

sagittate: arrowhead-shaped; with basal lobes pointed downward (p. 471)

salverform: having a slender corolla tube that flares abruptly (p. 475)

sap: the juice of a plant

saponin: any of a group of glycosides that forms a soapy lather when agitated in water; used in detergents and emulsifiers; some are toxic, but others have medicinal properties

saprophyte: an organism that lives on dead organic matter

scabrous: rough to the touch

scale: small leaves or bracts; any small, thin, or flat structure; a pappus type in asters (Asteraceae)

scape: an erect, leafless stalk that bears the inflorescence or flower; may have bracts or scales

schizocarp: a fruit that splits into several parts (carpels)

secund: an inflorescence in which the flowers appear to be borne on only one side of the peduncle

seed: a fertilized, mature ovule

sepal: one of the segments of the calyx; part of the outer floral envelope (p. 475)

serrate: saw-toothed; having sharp, forward-pointing teeth (p. 472)

sessile: attached directly, without a petiole or pedicel (p. 473)

sheath: a tubular structure surrounding a stem or other organ (e.g., the lower part of a leaf that surrounds the stem)

shoot: a young branch, twig, or stem

shrub: a woody plant, usually with multiple stems

silicle: a pod-like fruit much like a silique, but shorter, less than twice as long as wide

silique: a pod-like fruit of certain members of the Mustard Family (Brassicaceae), splitting longitudinally, leaving a center partition with seeds

simple leaf: a leaf not divided into distinct leaflets; the margin may be entire or variously divided (p. 469)

solitary: borne singly (p. 476)

spadix: a thick, fleshy spike (p. 476)

spathe: a leafy bract that subtends and often partially surrounds an inflorescence (p. 476)

spatulate: spoon- or spatula-shaped, rounded above and narrowed to the base (p. 470)

spicate: resembling a spike

spike: a elongate, unbranched, indeterminate inflorescence with sessile flowers (p. 476)

spreading: extending outward horizontally

spur: a slender, often nectar-bearing, tubular or sac-like extension of some perianth part(s); a hollow appendage on a petal or sepal

squarrose: recurved at the tip

stalk: the stem-like support of a structure (e.g., a petiole or peduncle)

stamen: the male, pollen-bearing organ of a flower (p. 475)

staminate: a male flower; bearing stamen(s) but no functioning pistil(s)

standard: the uppermost, usually broad petal of a flower of the Bean or Pea Family (Fabaceae)

stellate: star-like; hairs with radiating branches (p. 474)

stem: the main axis of a plant

sterile: not producing viable seed; infertile

stigma: the uppermost, pollen-receiving portion of the pistil (p. 475)

stipule: an appendage, usually paired, at the base of a leaf petiole (p. 469)

stolon: a horizontally spreading stem or runner on the ground, usually rooting at nodes or tips

stoloniferous: having stolons

stoma: a tiny opening in the epidermis of plants, bounded by a pair of guard cells that can close off the opening by changing shape

striate: having distinct longitudinal lines or ridges

style: the usually slender portion of the pistil between the stigma and the ovary (p. 475)

subsessile: with a minute or partial stalk; nearly sessile

subtend: to be directly below and close to

succulent: a plant having thick, juicy stems and/or leaves

superior ovary: an ovary inserted above and free from the perianth and stamens (p. 475)

suture: the point of union or separation of organs

taproot: a primary descending root

tendril: a modified leaf or stem by which a plant climbs or supports itself

Inflorescence types (cont'd)

corymb

panicle

thyrse

compound umbel

verticil

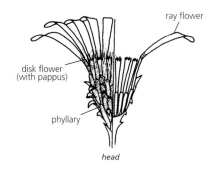

ray flower

disk flower (with pappus)

phyllary

head

Fruit types

drupe

berry

pome

aggregate

follicle

utricle

loment

legume

capsule

achene

tepal: a segment of a perianth that is not clearly differentiated (except by point of insertion) into calyx and corolla

terete: cylindric; round in cross-section

terminal: at the end, or top, of

ternate: occurring in threes (p. 469)

terrestrial: living or growing in the soil; a land plant

tetragonal: four-angled; quadrangular

thyrse: a compact cylindrical or ovoid panicle in which the main axis is indeterminate and the lateral branches are determinate (p. 477)

tomentose: having dense, woolly hairs (p. 474)

trailing: flat on the ground but not rooting

trichome: a bristle or hair-like projection

trifoliate: three-leaved

trifoliolate: a compound leaf with three leaflets (p. 469)

tripinnate: three times pinnate, with leaflets twice divided again

truncate: with a nearly straight tip or base, as if cut cleanly across (p. 472)

tuber: a thick, underground storage stem

tubercle: a small, wart-like projection

tuberculate: having tubercles

turgid: swollen, but filled within

umbel: a flat-topped or somewhat rounded, indeterminate inflorescence in which the flower stalks arise from a common point, much like the stays of an umbrella (p. 477)

umbellate: having umbels

umbellet: one of the umbel clusters in a branched (compound) umbel

urceolate: urn-shaped; wide at the bottom and constricted at the tip (p. 475)

utricle: a small, indehiscent, thin-walled, one-seeded, inflated fruit (p. 478)

valve: one of the pieces into which a pod or capsule splits

vein: a strand of connecting tubes (vascular bundle), especially if visible externally

ventral: on the lower (inner) side closest to the stem; opposite of dorsal

vermifuge: a substance used to expel worms from the body; anthelmintic

vernal: of spring

verticil: a whorl, usually of flowers or leaves at a node (p. 477)

vesicle: a small bladder or air cavity

villous: with long, soft, but not matted hairs (p. 474)

whorl: three or more structures, usually leaves, at a node

wing: a thin, flat extension or projection from the side or tip; one of the two side petals in a flower of the Bean or Pea Family (Fabaceae)

zygomorphic: bilaterally symmetric (p. 476)

Illustrations and text from *Guide to the Vascular Plants of the Blue Ridge* by B. Eugene Wofford. Copyright 1989 by the University of Georgia Press. Reprinted by permission of the University of Georgia Press.

With further adaptations from *Plants of the Rocky Mountains* by Linda Kershaw, Andy MacKinnon, and Jim Pojar. Edmonton: Lone Pine Publishing, 1998.

References

Adams, K. and M. Casstevens. 1996. *Wildflowers of the Southern Appalachians.* John F. Blair, Winston-Salem, NC.

Adkins, L.M. 1999. *Wildflowers of the Appalachian Trail.* Menasha Ridge Press, Birmingham, AL, and Appalachian Trail Conference, Harper's Ferry, WV.

Ajilvsgi, G. 1984. *Wildflowers of Texas.* Shearer Publishing, Fredericksburg, TX.

Barnard, S.E. and S. Fass Yates. 1998. *Wildflowers.* North American Wildlife Series. Reader 's Digest Association, Pleasantville, NY.

Barnes, T.G. and S.W. Francis. 2004. *Wildflowers and Ferns of Kentucky.* University Press of Kentucky, Lexington, KY.

Barth, G.F. 1991. *Insects and Flowers: The Biology of a Partnership.* Princeton University Press, Princeton, NJ.

Barton, B.S. 1798. *Collections for an Essay towards a Materia medica of the United States, Parts 1 and 2.* Reprint, 1804, 1900. Bulletin of the Lloyd Library, Cincinnati.

Bartram, W. 1791. *Travels through North & South Carolina, Georgia, East & West Florida.* Reprinted as *Travels of William Bartram*, 1955. Edited by Mark Van Doren. Dover, New York.

Baskin, C.C. and J.M. Baskin. 1975. Additions to the Herbaceous Flora of the Middle Tennessee Cedar Glades. *Journal of the Tennessee Academy of Science* 50:25–26.

Baskin, J.M., E. Quarterman, and C. Caudle. 1968. Preliminary Checklist of the Herbaceous Vascular Plants of Cedar Glades. *Journal of the Tennessee Academy of Science* 43:65–71.

Baskin, J.M. and C.C. Baskin. 1984. Cedar glade endemics in Tennessee, and a review of their autecology. *Journal of the Tennessee Academy of Science* 64:63–74.

Batson, W.T. 1987. *Wildflowers in the Carolinas.* University Press of South Carolina, Columbia, SC.

Bechtel, H., P. Cribb, and E. Launert. 1981. *The Manual of Cultivated Orchid Species.* MIT Press, Cambridge, MA.

Bolyard, J.L. 1981. *Medicinal Plants and Home Remedies of Appalachia.* Charles C. Thomas, Springfield, IL.

Borror, D.J. 1971. *Dictionary of Word Roots and Combining Forms.* Mayfield Publishing, Palo Alto, CA.

Bowen, B. 1995. Purple loosestrife: An exotic invader of Tennessee's wetlands. *Tennessee Conservationist* 61:28–30.

Braun, E.L. 1950. *Deciduous Forests of Eastern North America.* Hafner, New York.

Brill, S.B., and E. Dean. 1994. *Identifying and Harvesting Edible and Medicinal Plants in Wild (and Not So Wild) Places.* Harper-Collins, New York.

Britton, N.L. and A. Brown. 1970. *An Illustrated Flora of the Northern United States and Canada.* 3 vols. Dover, New York.

Brown, L. 1979. *Grasses: An Identification Guide.* Houghton Mifflin, Boston.

Campbell, C.C., R.W. Hutson, W.F. Hutson, and A.J. Sharp. 1995. *Great Smoky Mountain Wildflowers*, 5th ed. Windy Pines Publishing, Northbrook, IL.

Case, F.W. and R.B. Case. 1997. *Trilliums.* Timber Press, Portland, OR.

Catling, P.M. 1980. Rain-assisted autogamy in *Liparis loeselii* (L.) L.C. Rich. (Orchidaceae). *Bulletin of the Torrey Botanical Club* 107:525–529.

Chester, E.W., ed. 1989. The Vegetation and Flora of Tennessee. Proceedings of a symposium sponsored by the Austin Peay State University Center for Field Biology. *Journal of the Tennessee Academy of Science* 64:3.

Chester, E.W. and W.H. Ellis. 1989. Plant Communities of Northwestern Middle Tennessee. *Journal of the Tennessee Academy of Science* 64:75–78.

Chester, E.W. and W.H. Ellis. 1995. *Wildflowers of the Land Between the Lakes Region, Kentucky and Tennessee.* Austin Peay State University, Clarksville, TN.

Chester, E.W., B.E. Wofford, R. Kral, H.R. DeSelm, and A.M. Evans. 1993. *Atlas of Tennessee Vascular Plants, Vol. 1. Pteridophytes, Gymnosperms, Angiosperms: Monocots.* Austin Peay State University, Clarksville, TN.

Chester, E.W., B.E. Wofford, and R. Kral. 1997. *Atlas of Tennessee Vascular Plants, Vol. 2. Angiosperms: Dicots.* Austin Peay State University, Clarksville, TN.

Clebsch, E.E.C. 1989. Vegetation of the Appalachian Mountains of Tennessee East of the Great Valley. *Journal of the Tennessee Academy of Science* 64:79–84.

Coffey, T. 1993. *The History and Folklore of North American Wildflowers.* Houghton Mifflin, New York.

Coombes, A.J. 1994. *Dictionary of Plant Names.* Timber Press. Portland, OR.

Couplan, F. 1998. *The Encyclopedia of Edible Plants of North America.* Keats Publishing, New Canaan, CT.

Darlington, W. 1849. *In Memorial of John Bartram and Humphry Marshall.* Reprint, 1967. Hafner, New York.

Dean, B.E., A. Mason, and J.L. Thomas. 1973. *Wildflowers of Alabama and Adjoining States.* University of Alabama Press, Tuscaloosa, AL.

Denison, E. 1998. *Missouri Wildflowers.* Missouri Dept. of Conservation, Jefferson City, MO.

DeSelm, H.R. 1989. The Barrens of Tennessee. *Journal of the Tennessee Academy of Science* 64:89–96.

DeSelm, H.R., B.E. Wofford, R. Kral, and E.W. Chester. 1994. An Annotated List of Grasses (Poaceae, Gramineae) of Tennessee. *Castanea* 59:338–353.

Dioscorides. 512. *The Greek Herbal of Dioscorides: Illustrated by a Byzantine.* English translation by John Goodyer, 1655. Robert T. Gunther, ed., 1934. Reprint, 1968. Hafner, New York.

Duke, J.A. 1997. *The Green Pharmacy.* Rodale Press, Emmaus, PA.

Duncan, W.H. and M.B. Duncan. 1999. *Wildflowers of the Eastern United States.* University of Georgia Press, Athens, GA.

Duncan, W.H. and L.E. Foote. 1975. *Wildflowers of the Southeastern United States.* University of Georgia Press, Athens, GA.

Eastman, J. 1992. *Forest and Thicket.* Stackpole Books, Mechanicsburg, PA.

Ellis, W.H. and E.W. Chester. 1989. Upland swamps of the Highland Rim of Tennessee. *Journal of the Tennessee Academy of Science* 64:97–102

Elpel, T.J. 1998. *Botany in a Day*. Hops Press, Pong, MT.

Fernald, M.L. 1950. *Gray's Manual of Botany*, 8th ed. Corrected printing, 1970. Van Nostrand Reinhold, New York.

Foster, S. and J.A. Duke. 2000. *A Field Guide to Medicinal Plants and Herbs, Eastern and Central North America*. Houghton Mifflin, Boston.

Foster, S. and R. Caras. 1994. *Venomous Animals and Poisonous Plants*. Houghton Mifflin, Boston.

Fralish, J.S. and F.B. Crooks. 1989. Forest Composition, Environment and Dynamics at Land Between the Lakes in Northwest Middle Tennessee. *Journal of the Tennessee Academy of Science* 64:107–112.

Gattinger, A. 1901. *The Flora of Tennessee and a Philosophy of Botany*. Gospel Advocate, Nashville, TN.

Gleason, H.A. 1963. *New Britton and Brown Illustrated Flora of the Northeastern United States and Adjacent Canada*, 3rd ed. 3 vols. New York Botanical Garden, Bronx, New York.

Gleason, H.A. and A. Cronquist. 1991. *Manual of Vascular Plants of Northeastern United States and Adjacent Canada*. New York Botanical Garden, Bronx, New York.

Gupton, O.W. and F.C. Swope. 1986. *Wild Orchids of the Middle Atlantic States*. University of Tennessee Press, Knoxville, TN.

Gupton, O.W. and F.C. Swope. 1989. *Fall Wildflowers of the Blue Ridge and Great Smoky Mountains*. University Press of Virginia, Charlottesville, VA.

Guthrie, M. 1989. A Floristic and Vegetational Overview of Reelfoot Lake. *Journal of the Tennessee Academy of Science* 64:113–116.

Hamel, P. 1993. *Tennessee Wildlife Viewing Guide*. Falcon Press, Helena, MT.

Heineke, T.E. 1989. Plant Communities and Flora of West Tennessee between the Loess Hills and the Tennessee River. *Journal of the Tennessee Academy of Science* 64:117–120.

Hemmerly, T.E. 1990. *Wildflowers of the Central South*. Vanderbilt University Press, Nashville, TN.

Hemmerly, T.E. 2000. *Appalachian Wildflowers*. University of Georgia Press, Athens, GA.

Hemmerly, T.E. 2002. *Ozark Wildflowers*. University of Georgia Press, Athens, GA.

Hinkle, C.R. 1989. Forest Communities of the Cumberland Plateau of Tennessee. *Journal of the Tennessee Academy of Science* 64:123–130.

Houk, R. 1993. *A Natural History Guide: Great Smoky Mountains National Park*. University of Tennessee Press, Knoxville, TN.

Hunter, C.G. 1988. *Wildflowers of Arkansas*. 2nd ed. Ozark Society Foundation, Little Rock, AR.

Hunter, C.G. 1989. *Trees, Shrubs, & Vines of Arkansas*. Ozark Society Foundation, Little Rock, AR.

Jones, R.L. 1989. A Floristic Study of Wetlands of the Cumberland Plateau of Tennessee. *Journal of the Tennessee Academy of Science* 64:131–134.

Justice, W.S. and C.R. Bell. 1968. *Wildflowers of North Carolina*. University of North Carolina Press, Chapel Hill, NC.

Kershaw, L., A. MacKinnon, and J. Pojar. 1998. *Plants of the Rocky Mountains*. Lone Pine Publishing, Edmonton, AB.

Klimas, J.E. and J.A. Cunningham. 1974. *Wildflowers of Eastern America*. Alfred A. Knopf, New York.

Knutson, Roger M. 1974. Heat Production and Temperature Regulation in Eastern Skunk Cabbage. *Science* 186:746–747.

Kurz, D. 1999. *Ozark Wildflowers*. Falcon Press, Helena, MT.

Ladd, D. 1995. *Tallgrass Prairie Wildflowers*. Falcon Press, Helena, MT.

Lewis, W.H. and M.P.F. Elvin-Lewis. 1977. *Medical Botany*. John Wiley and Sons, New York.

Lowe, J. 2001. *Tennessee Gardener's Guide*. Cool Springs Press, Nashville, TN.

Luer, C.A. 1975. *The Native Orchids of the United States and Canada excluding Florida*. New York Botanical Garden, Bronx, New York.

Luther, E.T. 1977. *Our Restless Earth: Geological Regions of Tennessee*. University of Tennessee Press, Knoxville, TN.

Martin, L.C. 1984. *Wildflower Folklore*. East Woods Press, Charlotte, NC.

Martin, L.C. 1989. *Southern Wildflowers*. Longstreet Press, Atlanta, GA.

Martin, W.H. 1989. Forest Patterns in the Great Valley of Tennessee. *Journal of the Tennessee Academy of Science* 64:137–144.

McKinney, L.E. 1989. Vegetation of the Eastern Highland Rim of Tennessee. *Journal of the Tennessee Academy of Science* 64:145–148.

McKinney, L.E. 1992. *A Taxonomic Revision of the Acaulescent Blue Violets (Viola) of North America*. Botanical Research Institute of Texas, Fort Worth, TX.

Midgley, J.W. 1999. *All About Tennessee Wildflowers*. Sweetwater Press, Birmingham, AL.

Midgley, J.W. 1999. *Southeastern Wildflowers*. Crane Hill, Birmingham, AL.

Miller, N.A. and J. Neiswender. 1989. A Plant Community Study of the Third Chickasaw Bluff, Shelby County, Tennessee. *Journal of the Tennessee Academy of Science* 64:149–154.

Moerman, D.E. 1998. *Native American Ethnobotany*. Timber Press, Portland, OR.

Mohlenbrock, R.H. 1986. *Guide to the Vascular Flora of Illinois, Revised and Enlarged Edition*. Southern Illinois University Press, Carbondale and Edwardsville, IL.

Moore, H.L. 1994. *A Geologic Trip Across Tennessee by Interstate 40*. University of Tennessee Press, Knoxville, TN.

Neal, B. 1992. *Gardener's Latin*. Algonquin Books, Chapel Hill, NC.

Newcomb, L. 1977. *Newcomb's Wildflower Guide*. Little, Brown and Company, Boston.

Nilsson, K.B. 1994. *A Wild Flower by Any Other Name: Sketches of Pioneer Naturalists Who Named Our Western Plants*. Yosemite Association, Yosemite National Park, CA.

Peterson, L. 1978. *A Field Guide to Edible Wild Plants*. Houghton Mifflin, Boston.

Peterson, R.T. and M. McKenny. 1968. *A Field Guide to Wildflowers of Northeastern and North-central North America*. Houghton Mifflin, Boston.

Petrides, G.A. 1998. *A Field Guide to Eastern Trees*. Houghton Mifflin, Boston.

Pohl, R. W. 1978. *How to Know the Grasses.* Wm. C. Brown, Dubuque, IA.

Pojar, J. and A. MacKinnon. 1994. *Plants of the Pacific Northwest Coast.* Lone Pine Publishing, Edmonton, AB.

Pridgeon, A. 1992. *The Illustrated Encyclopedia of Orchids.* Timber Press, Portland, OR.

Priestley, M.P. and J. Benson. 2004. *Go Take a Hike! A Guide to Hiking on the Domain of Sewanee: the University of the South.* University of the South, Sewanee, TN.

Pritchard, M. S. 1977. Exploring Savage Gulf: A Last Chance for Wilderness. *Tennessee Conservationist* 43:8–11.

Quarterman, E. 1975. A Piece of Prairie. *Tennessee Conservationist* 40:10, 35.

Quarterman, E. 1989. Structures and Dynamics of Limestone Cedar Glade Communities in Tennessee. *Journal of the Tennessee Academy of Science* 64:155–158.

Quarterman, E., B.H. Turner, and T.E. Hemmerly. 1972. Analysis of Virgin Mixed Mesophytic Forests in Savage Gulf, Tennessee. *Bulletin of the Torrey Botanical Club* 99:228–232.

Radford, A.E., H.E. Ahles, and C.R. Bell. 1968. *Manual of the Vascular Flora of the Carolinas.* The University of North Carolina Press, Chapel Hill, NC.

Ramseur, G.S. Some Changes in the Vegetation of the Great Smoky Mountains. *Journal of the Tennessee Academy of Science* 64:159–160

Rickett, H.W. 1966. *Wildflowers of the United States, Volume Two: The Southeastern States, Parts One and Two.* New York Botanical Garden, Bronx, New York.

Robbers, J.E. and V.E. Tyler. 1999. *Tyler's Herbs of Choice, the Therapeutic Use of Phytomedicinals.* Haworth Press, New York.

Sandburg, F. and D. Corrigan. 2001. *Natural Remedies, their Origins and Uses.* Taylor and Frances, New York.

Schmalzer, P.A. 1989. Vegetation and Flora of the Obed River Gorge System, Cumberland Plateau, Tennessee. *Journal of the Tennessee Academy of Science* 64:161–168.

Small, J.K. 1933. *Manual of the Southeastern Flora.* University of North Carolina Press, Chapel Hill, NC.

Smith, A.I. 1979. *A Guide to Wildflowers of the Mid-South.* Memphis State University Press, Memphis, TN.

Smith, AW. 1963. *A Gardener's Book of Plant Names.* Harper & Row, New York, Evanston, Illinois, and London.

Smith, R.M. 1998. *Wildflowers of the Southern Mountains.* University of Tennessee Press, Knoxville, TN.

Somers, P., ed. 1986. Symposium: Biota, Ecology, and Ecological History of Cedar Glades, *Association of Southeastern Biologists Bulletin* Vol. 33, No. 4.

Somers, P. 1989. Revised List of the Rare Plants of Tennessee. *Journal of the Tennessee Academy of Science* 64:179–184.

Stokes, D. and L. 1984. *A Guide to Enjoying Wildflowers.* Little, Brown & Co., Boston.

Stupka, A. 1964. *Trees, Shrubs, and Woody Vines of Great Smoky National Park.* University of Tennessee Press, Knoxville, TN.

Steyermark, J.A. 1963. *Flora of Missouri.* Iowa State University Press, Ames, IA.

Thien, L.B. and B.G. Marcks. 1972. The Floral Biology of *Arethusa bulbosa, Calopogon tuberosus* and *Pogonia ophioglossoides. Canadian Journal of Botany* 50:2319–2325.

Thomas, R.D. 1989. The Vegetation of Chilhowee Mountain, Tennessee. *Journal of the Tennessee Academy of Science* 64:185–188.

Timme, S.L. 1989. *Wildflowers of Mississippi.* University Press of Mississippi, Jackson, MS.

Turner, N.J. and A.F. Szczawinski. 1991. *Common Poisonous Plants and Mushrooms of North America.* Timber Press, Portland, OR.

Vogel, V. 1970. *American Indian Medicines.* University of Oklahoma, Norman, OK.

Wells, D. 1997. *100 Flowers and How They Got Their Names.* Algonquin Books of Chapel Hill, Chapel Hill, NC.

Wharton, M.E. and R.W. Barbour. 1971. *The Wildflowers and Ferns of Kentucky.* University Press of Kentucky, Lexington, KY.

Wharton, M.E. and R.W. Barbour. 1973. *Trees and Shrubs of Kentucky.* University Press of Kentucky, Lexington, KY.

Williams, J.G. and A.E. Williams. 1983. *Field Guide to Orchids of North America.* Universe Books, New York.

Wofford, B.E. 1989. Floristic Elements of the Tennessee Blue Ridge. *Journal of the Tennessee Academy of Science* 64:205–207.

Wofford, B.E. 1989. *Guide to the Vascular Plants of the Blue Ridge.* University of Georgia Press, Athens, GA.

Wofford, B.E. and E.W. Chester. 2002. *Guide to the Trees, Shrubs, and Woody Vines of Tennessee.* University of Tennessee Press, Knoxville, TN.

Wofford, B.E. and R. Kral. 1993. *Checklist of the Vascular Plants of Tennessee.* Botanical Research Institute of Texas, Fort Worth, TX.

Yatskievych, G. 1999. *Steyermark's Flora of Missouri, Vol. 1.* Missouri Botanical Garden, St. Louis, MO.

Web Sites

Haughton, C. Purple Sage. http://www.purplesage.org.uk/.

Integrated Taxonomic Information System. http://www.itis.usda.gov/.

National Park Service. Green Medicine. http://www.nps.gov/.

Nearctica. http://www.nearctica.com/.

Reed, D. Wildflowers of the Southeastern United States. http://www.2bnthewild.com/.

United States Department of Agriculture Plants National Database. http://plants.usda.gov/.

United States Fish & Wildlife Service. The Endangered Species Program. http://endangered.fws.gov/.

University of Tennessee Herbarium. http://tenn.bio.utk.edu/.

World Health Organization. http://www.who.int/en/.

Index

Names in **bold** typeface indicate primary species.

Editors

Dennis Horn is an engineer, naturalist, amateur botanist, and wildflower photographer. A charter member of the Tennessee Native Plant Society, he is currently the TNPS vice-president and a member of the Scientific Advisory Committee for Rare Plants in Tennessee. For over 40 years, Dennis has traveled from the Mississippi River to the Blue Ridge Mountains studying and photographing Tennessee wildflowers, and he has presented numerous wildflower slide programs for garden clubs, civic groups, and plant conferences. Dennis was awarded a Certificate of Merit by the State of Tennessee in 2003 for his conservation efforts. He lives in Tullahoma with his wife, Sherry, and son, Brandon.

An interpretive naturalist and writer, **Tavia Cathcart** brings extensive knowledge of ethnobotany, folklore, and mythology of plants to this book. A native of Middle Tennessee and an active member of the TNPS, her search for plants and their stories has taken her from the highest peaks of the Sierra Nevada Mountains to rarely visited coves in the Smoky Mountains. She has run her own award-winning consulting and writing business for nearly two decades, specializing in teaching and environmental projects. Her writings have been published in national and regional journals, anthologies, and conservation magazines.

Thomas E. Hemmerly is professor of biology at Middle Tennessee State University, Murfreesboro, where he teaches courses in medical botany and economic botany. He holds a Ph.D. in plant ecology from Vanderbilt University and has authored more than 50 articles in scientific journals. Among his books are *Appalachian Wildflowers* and *Ozark Wildflowers*, both published by University of Georgia Press.

David Duhl is a native of New Jersey who has made Nashville his home since 1980. His work has been widely published in books, magazines, and calendars, and has been used in corporate proposals and commercial projects. David teaches the art of nature photography at Nashville State Community College and at the Great Smoky Mountains Institute at Tremont, and leads photo tours for groups of interested photographers.